THE MODERN LIBRARY
of the World's Best Books

INTELLIGENCE IN THE MODERN WORLD
JOHN DEWEY'S PHILOSOPHY

>>>

The publishers will be pleased to send, upon request, an illustrated folder setting forth the purpose and scope of THE MODERN LIBRARY, *and listing each volume in the series. Every reader of books will find titles he has been looking for, handsomely printed, in unabridged editions, and at an unusually low price.*

>>>

INTELLIGENCE
IN THE MODERN WORLD
JOHN DEWEY'S PHILOSOPHY

EDITED, AND WITH AN INTRODUCTION BY
JOSEPH RATNER

THE MODERN LIBRARY
NEW YORK

THE MODERN LIBRARY

IS PUBLISHED BY

RANDOM HOUSE, INC.

BENNETT A. CERF · DONALD S. KLOPFER · ROBERT K. HAAS

Manufactured in the United States of America
Printed by Parkway Printing Company   *Bound by H. Wolff*

Let us admit the case of the conservative: if we once start thinking no one can guarantee where we shall come out, except that many objects, ends and institutions are doomed. Every thinker puts some portion of an apparently stable world in peril and no one can wholly predict what will emerge in its place.

—*John Dewey*

ACKNOWLEDGMENTS

ORDINARILY, this would not be called a coöperative volume. But in a very real sense it is such, for without the generous coöperation of the publishers of John Dewey's works, this volume would have been impossible. It is a great pleasure to record that they enthusiastically responded, not merely in theory but in practice, to the idea of this book and by their permissions contributed whatever they could to its fullest realization.

Especially deserving of gratitude—from the reader as well as Editor—are Henry Holt and Company, Minton, Balch and Company, and Dr. Alfred L. Hall-Quest, Editor of the *Kappa Delta Pi* Lecture Series. Henry Holt and Company, in addition to granting permission to reprint from works they have published in the past, also granted permission to print selections from the manuscript of Mr. Dewey's *Logic: The Theory of Inquiry* which they are to publish in the near future. To my knowledge, this is an act of magnanimity unprecedented in the history of publishing.* Minton, Balch and Company were only less unprecedented in their liberality and generosity, contributing more selections than any other one publisher. Dr. Hall-Quest gave permission to reprint selections from *Experience and Education,* first published as recently as February, 1938. The exceptional coöperation of the above-mentioned enabled the Editor both to make this volume comprehensive in its range and to bring it up to date.

* When this was written, in July, 1938, we had planned to issue this volume before Henry Holt and Company had published Mr. Dewey's *Logic,* on October 20, 1938.

The complete list of publishers of John Dewey's books to whom acknowledgments and thanks are due for permission to reprint follows:

D. C. Heath and Co.:
How We Think (revised edition, 1933)*

Henry Holt and Company, Inc.:
Human Nature and Conduct (1922)
Logic: The Theory of Inquiry (1938)
Reconstruction in Philosophy (1920)
The Public and Its Problems (1927)
Ethics (Dewey and Tufts, revised edition, 1932)
Characters and Events (a collection of essays in social and political philosophy edited by Joseph Ratner, 2 vols., 1929)

Houghton Mifflin Company:
Interest and Effort in Education (1913)

Dr. Alfred L. Hall-Quest, Editor *Kappa Delta Pi* Lecture Series:
The Sources of a Science of Education (1929, published by Horace Liveright and Company)
Experience and Education (1938, published by the Macmillan Company)

The Macmillan Company:
Democracy and Education (1916)

Minton, Balch and Company:
Art as Experience (1935)
Individualism Old and New (1930)
Liberalism and Social Action (1935)
The Quest for Certainty (1929)
Philosophy and Civilization (1931)

* The year of publication is included for the interest such information may have for the reader.

The Open Court Publishing Company:
  Experience and Nature (first edition, 1925, second
    edition, 1929)

The University of Chicago Press:
  Essays in Experimental Logic (1917)

Yale University Press:
  A Common Faith (1934)

For permission to reprint articles and selections from
articles by John Dewey, acknowledgments and thanks
are due to the editors of the following publications:

  The Bulletin of The New York Academy of Medicine
  The Educational Forum
  The Journal of the Barnes Foundation
  The International Journal of Ethics
  The New Republic
  The Social Frontier
  Harvard Tercentenary Publications
  The School and Society

For analogous permission thanks are due to the following
    foundations:
  National Education Association of the United States
  Foreign Policy Association
  The League for Industrial Democracy

The editor has some acknowledgments of his own to
make. For permission to use quotations in his *Introduction*
and *Editor's Note,* he is indebted to the following:

Harcourt, Brace and Company:
  War as an Instrument of National Policy, by James T.
    Shotwell

Sir Norman Angell:
  The Defence of the Empire

The Macmillan Company:

Adventures of Ideas

Science and the Modern World

Process and Reality, by Alfred North Whitehead

Encyclopedia of the Social Sciences

Finally, it should be recorded here that of the Editor's contributions to this volume, Mr. Dewey, because of a variety of circumstances, was able to read only the first seven sections of the Introduction before publication. I am greatly indebted to him for several valuable criticisms and suggestions.

J. R.

New York City

CONTENTS

INTRODUCTION TO
JOHN DEWEY'S PHILOSOPHY
By JOSEPH RATNER

INTRODUCTION TO JOHN DEWEY'S PHILOSOPHY

By Joseph Ratner

I

FOR THOSE who believe it is the philosopher's task to juggle the universe on the point of an argument, Dewey is a complete disappointment. The world he starts out with and also ends with is the common world we all live in and experience every day of our lives. To start out with the familiar world of common experience is not altogether a philosophic novelty. Some philosophers have consciously done that before and the others, despite their more exalted intentions, have had to do the same thing to some extent; for they too are human beings and to hoist themselves into another world by their intellectual bootstraps, they must first at least take hold of those common things. But for a philosophy which encompasses every important intellec-tual and cultural activity to end, as well as begin, with the world of everyday life is altogether novel, an achievement unique in the history of thought.

There are, of course, arguments in Dewey's philosophy. It could not be otherwise, for philosophy is just one long argument. But the world Dewey argues about is not a world his arguments have created. His arguments rest on, refer to and are controlled by experience of the common world. Control of philosophic arguments about the world by experience of the world is what Dewey fundamentally means by empiricism in philosophy, by scientific or ex-perimental method. There are arguments in science and

3

plenty of them. But the last word in science always rests not with the arguments, but with the facts, with the observations and experiments, with the laboratory experience of the scientist, be that laboratory one which he has artificially constructed for himself, or be it the laboratory into which he has converted the natural world of stones and stars. This relationship between arguments and experience is so firmly established, so integral a part of scientific technique and practice, that it is now taken as a matter of course and no scientist, no matter how mathematical or theoretical he may be, would even dream of disputing it. A scientist who refused to submit his arguments or theory to the test of observation and experiment on the ground that theory was higher than practice, or on any other ground he could imaginably concoct, would be laughed out of scientific court. And the same attitude would be taken toward such an imaginary scientist by every philosopher today.

But there are many philosophers still extant who, with regard to their own arguments or theories, disdain to recognize similar obligation. Certainly, scientific theories must submit to the test of practical experience, but philosophic theories, ah! they are different! In the realm of philosophy, theory is superior to practice, theory is completely independent of practice, theory is entirely separated from practice, theory has its own infallible ways and means of establishing its own irrefutable Truth, and practice and experience have, with respect to these philosophic ways and means and this philosophic Truth, no authority whatsoever. They are immaterial, incompetent and irrelevant.

Now Dewey's basic position, his basic argument about philosophic method, is that theory in philosophy is no more privileged than theory in science. If theory in science must submit to the test of practice and experience, theory in philosophy must do likewise. Philosophers are the same breed of men as scientists, the brains of both are alike, the product of the same earthly evolution. For philosophers to believe they are endowed with unique powers giving them access to special realms of Being and revealing to them knowledge of special Truths is a gross piece of self-delusion. Philosophers are gifted with no supernal powers of insight denied other mortals. There are no exclusive regions of Being or Reality into which a philosopher alone can enter because he carries a philosophic passport—made out by himself. The only genuine passport, the only passport commanding entrance into Being, Reality, Nature or whatever else you care to call it, by capital letter or small, is the passport that is filled out, signed, countersigned, stamped and sealed by public experience. And until philosophers recognize this, until they accept their common humanity with good grace and without mental reservations, they cannot hope to perform any intelligent function and make philosophy a living thing, a progressive force in our common human life.

That it should still be necessary to argue for experimentalism in philosophy is anomalous, as Dewey has tirelessly driven home. In science, the practical issue over experimentalism was fought in the sixteenth and seventeenth centuries and to the practical victory of experimentalism in science all the marvelous scientific achievements of the past two hundred and fifty years are to be ascribed. That this issue should still be of primary debate in philosophy is as bad a case of cultural lag as one could ever hope to come across, especially when one takes into account the fact that it has been the boast of philosophy that she is by history and by nature the intellectual leader, the one that is always found at the very head of the line of march.

What is the reason for the backwardness of philosophy?

Why do philosophers continue to oppose the demand that their theories be based on experimental grounds and undergo experimental tests? Such opposition smacks of antediluvian kicking against the pricks, true enough, but it would be silly to think it is due merely to unregenerate antediluvianism. Nor can the opposition with any show of justice be chalked up as a result of obtuseness, natural or acquired, or as the result of ignorance of scientific history. The reasons, as Dewey has shown with voluminous clarity, are not ascribable to any personal shortcomings of philosophers as a class, but lie embedded in the heart of our culture, in the traditional forces operative in the social, political, religious, educational, philosophic and even scientific spheres.

Modern culture stems from heterogeneous roots. It is more a cultural compendium than a cultural complex. There is everywhere a medley of forces at work and the scene, wherever one looks, is full of strife. In some very few and very restricted areas, there has already been achieved some measure of outer harmony and integration, but it is outer, superficial and not thorough. The conflict between modern methods, understanding and ideals, and traditional attitudes, beliefs and objectives where it has disappeared from the surface has disappeared only to persist below. The least probing discloses intensified discord and widened division. And this is true whether one considers together and in relation two or more areas of modern culture or considers each area separately and alone. The spectacular conflicts rage across the open fields, while confusions smoulder and agitate underground. The backwardness of philosophy is an expression and reflection of the widespread and varying cultural lags. It is both a symptom and a symbol of the outer clashes and inner confusions, of the essentially discordant, unintegrated character of modern culture. Philosophy, aspiring to a secret vision of eternal existence, has fallen heir to the social ills of mortal experience.

The general state of modern culture explains the situation in philosophy but, for Dewey, explanation is not excuse. Explanation of any trouble is, for him, the starting point for intelligent and thorough re-examination; it defines the problem to be faced and the task to be done. Philosophy is omnipotent and philosophers exercise absolute sway only in their Platonic dreams—dreams that have never beguiled Dewey. However, it cannot be significantly denied by any one that philosophy has had and still has some social power and whatever the measure of that power may be, that is also, for Dewey, the measure of philosophy's social responsibility for the future of human culture as well as for the present and past. To what precise extent philosophy has helped bring about the existing divisions, the multifarious splits in modern cultural life is a question that can never be accurately answered. It will also forever be impossible to estimate to what precise extent the discords and confusions have been perpetuated by the theoretical sanctions they have received from the great systems of modern philosophy. But quantitatively exact answers to these questions are not at all necessary for reaching the sound conclusion that philosophy is in fact and in honor bound to shoulder some of the blame in both instances. Answers of quantitative exactitude are even less necessary, if that is possible, for reaching an intelligent judgment as to what should be the function and purpose of philosophy in the present juncture in our social life.

In so far as philosophy has wielded social influence it is responsible for the existing state of affairs; and in so far as it does and will continue to wield such influence its real task in the present cultural epoch is mapped out by the indisputable nature of the epoch itself. It is not to help perpetuate and justify the existing state and disorder of things, but, to the reach of its ability, to help find a way into a better order, an order in which there will be social unity of mind as a consequence of achieving civilized integration of intelligent life. This is, for Dewey, the supremely important task confronting philosophy, its all-comprehensive task, the only one that genuinely brings philosophy into commerce with the universal. If it can be justly said of philosophy that it is uniquely equipped to undertake any task, then it is this one. And yet this is just the task modern philosophy has either approached obliquely or else outrightly shirked on the pretext that philosophy had more vital concerns, more universal objectives to attain, that its elected destiny was to circumnavigate the great ocean of Being.

Philosophic pretensions to superhuman universality inevitably generate theories that degrade human life and experience to subhuman estate. While pretending jurisdiction over all time and existence, such theories actually function to support and justify the practices of intolerance and the barbarities of fanaticism. To rid philosophy of pretentiousness—the prolific mother of evil—is the all-controlling, all-permeating purpose of Dewey's lifework. By the example of his own work, a work eloquent with the fire of his conviction that philosophy has a real and useful, a vitalizing and humanizing function to perform, modest though it may be, Dewey has, for close on half a century, continued to call upon his fellow philosophers to have done with their building of sandpiles on the shores of human life and to come inland and help build habitations fit for men.

II

Properly to understand Dewey's conception of the relation between philosophy and culture, it is essential to keep focused in mind that Dewey conceives philosophy to be one part of culture, interacting with all other parts with varying degrees of sensitivity and effectiveness. Put strictly, Dewey always thinks of philosophy *in* culture, not of philosophy *and* culture. That he does not always write as he thinks, on this matter as on others, is not something for which he is solely to blame. Dewey, after all, did not inherit his own mature philosophy, nor was he taught it in school, college or university. His mind, like the mind of everyone, was first informed with the issues, ideas and language produced before his time. And, like every original thinker, it was only by working with the material he acquired that he was able to work through it. That there should be signs and evidences in his writings of the uphill intellectual road he has travelled is a natural consequence, and something every intelligent person not only does find but expects to find in the work of every creative thinker, no matter of what period or place. Faultless lucidity and articulation in writing, like faultless execution in painting, are possible only for those who are superficial in treating their subjects, or superficial in accepting what is current, or superficial in both.

Because philosophy is *in* culture, one part interacting with other parts, it is basically to falsify matters to interpret philosophy's cultural role as being either all cause or all effect. In any interacting system there is inevitable a cross-weaving or intersection of cause and effect. In fact, such cross-weaving or intersection is precisely what interaction means.

Only by doing intellectual violence to the actual con-

dition and state of affairs can philosophy be torn out of
its cultural environment and be set up as something isolated and apart. The violence of this act is not mitigated
but compounded when it is made for and followed up by
bringing philosophy into relation again with the remainder
of culture in a way that makes philosophy exclusively
either the cause or the effect of that remainder. The net
amount of logical falsity and empirical distortion stands
unaltered whether the act of violence and its sequel are
done in the name of a theological, idealistic, materialistic or dialectic theory or any combination and permuta-
tion of these.

Of course it would also be false to assert that philosophy
has maintained equally effective interactive relations with
all the cultural forces constituting its environment, that
its interactive integration with its environment has been
complete and perfect. The actual history of philosophy—
like the actual history of all affairs human and divine—
is a mixed record of failures and successes.

In so far as modern philosophy has been in interactive
relations with the social, political, economic and scientific
forces and movements, it has developed in fruitful and
distinctive ways so that modern philosophy is actually
and recognizably different from the philosophy of any
other epoch in human history. And by virtue of the same
interactive relations, and in the measure that they have
been effectively sustained, modern philosophy has undoubtedly contributed to the distinctive and fruitful development of other members in the cultural system. But
none of the areas of modern culture has been in full interaction with any other area, let alone with all the others.
This is true, with especial emphasis, of philosophy. In
consequence, it has also been stagnant and uniform, rep-
etitious of its modern self and its pre-modern history.

To be sure, modern philosophy has successfully escaped being outwardly marked by stagnation, uniformity and repetition. It presents a continually changing face and seems to be always going in at least ascending and widening spirals. This pleasing, even flattering outer appearance is, however, mostly deceptive, for it is maintained by the momentum derived from modern philosophy's few genuine interactive relations and which could not be entirely wiped out.* Inwardly, and for the most part, modern philosophy has been going in narrowing and flattening circles.

III

It can be argued—as many have actually argued—that since there is internal division in every area of modern culture and loosejointedness and conflict between all, modern philosophy, by exhibiting like features, shows it is really in the modern step and that it would be badly out of step if it exhibited contrary features. There is virtue in this argument, but it is the virtue of its content of fact, not of argument. True enough, only a fanciful philosophy can be fully integrated in a culture which is mostly otherwise. Those modern systems wherein all things are neatly disposed of and settled down in permanent wedlock, as in Hegel, or in a dual state of permanent marriage and irremediable divorce, as in Kant, are intellectual fantasias

* In a pioneering essay, *"The Significance of the Problem of Knowledge,"* Dewey traced in illuminating outline the interactive relations between, on the one hand, the leading social, economic, political and scientific movements of modern times, and on the other, the development of the two dominant issues in modern philosophy—the sensationalist-empiricist and the rationalist. This essay, reprinted in *The Influence of Darwin on Philosophy* (1910) was first published in 1897 and so antedates by some years the socio-economico-politico-culturo-historical wave of interpretation which has recently swept over many current writers and swept away so many more.

rather than philosophies. In the one case as in the other they do not fulfill but betray the cause of intelligence which is the supreme cause of philosophy—the cause philosophy cannot forsake without losing her mind and soul. This is the virtue of fact in the argument.

But the argument, if it is an argument at all, implies more than the facts. All arguments worthy of the name carry the mind forward by presenting possibilities that lead to the discovery and help in the making of further fact. Thus understood, how stands it with the argument in question? What possibilities does it present? What conception of philosophy does it imply or assume? How does it see and define the function of philosophy in the changing course of cultural history and development? The answers to these questions are not difficult to find. Clearly, the argument fundamentally implies or assumes that philosophy is inherently merely an effect produced by the remainder of the cultural forces which are alone really operative as cause. And in necessary line with this basic principle or assumption, the only possibility it presents is that philosophy must forever continue in this ineffectual role. This point of view was advanced by the Hegelian argument, though it runs counter to Hegel's cardinal tenet that Mind is the one and absolute cause and philosophy (in fact, his own philosophy) is the highest realization of Mind in the empirical world. The Marxian argument advances the same doctrine and also with the self-same contradictoriness, though its contradiction runs in the opposite direction. It is consistent with the ground-plan of the materialist interpretation of past cultural history and inconsistent with the revolutionary program for realizing future cultural history. This is but one instance of the net identity in logical falsity of idealist and materialist theories pointed to before.

Determinism is a magical word and, when supplemented by the adjective "rigid," its magical effectiveness is beyond all hindrance and recall. In the mouth of Idealism, rigid determinism—called by the more pleasant sounding names Destiny, Divine Will, etc.—instantaneously converts the confused and conglomerate history of man into the inevitable unrolling of the perlucid Divine Idea; in the mouth of Materialism it performs a no less magical act of conversion, but instead of the unrolling being the fulfillment of an all-necessitating Idea, designedly leading us by the nose, the unrolling becomes the fulfillment of an all-necessitating congress of material forces pushing us blindly from behind. If choice were absolutely restricted to either one or the other of these two the latter is, beyond doubt, on human and practical not cosmic and theoretical grounds preferable.* For it keeps us unremittingly conscious of the fact that we have behinds, something those who are led by the nose will only rarely and hesitantly admit. However, and fortunately, our choice is not restricted to the either-or of these two. Actually, as is empirically verified and verifiable, our anatomy faces both ways and there is nothing inherent in the nature of the mind, no constitutional, ineradicable defect which forever prevents it from displaying a like virtuosity.

On the contrary! To look before and after and think of what is not but may become through our efforts controlled and directed by what we see before and after is the very essence of mind and what it naturally does when not blocked in the exercise of its function. This, too, is the essence and function of philosophy as a phase of cultural mind or intelligence.

* As cosmic doctrines, there are no intelligible, let alone intelligent reasons for preferring one over the other. In this respect they are more than alike: they are identical.

The development of philosophy can be aided or hindered by the cultural forces with which it contemporaneously interacts. About this there can be no sensible question. But the aid or hindrance is in every such case partial, not total. God helps those who help themselves because nothing exists which cannot in some way help itself. And what is capable of self-help is capable also of self-hindrance. The blockage philosophy may suffer or the freedom it may derive from the operation upon it of other forces is never an automatic effect of a one-way operating cause or series of causes; it is always the consequence of interaction. The order and connection of ideas in philosophy are not the same as the order and connection of events in society. If there were this one-to-one correspondence or parallelism, philosophy would always be exactly abreast of its times. It could never possibly fall behind or get ahead. Actually, however, as history empirically verifies, philosophy has done both. Therefore, whenever philosophy is frustrated or liberated, the causes for that must also be partly ingredient in philosophy itself, in its own complement of ideas, in its history and development up to the time under examination. For philosophy does not merely interact with contemporaneous social forces and events; more than any other human intellectual enterprise it interacts with its own past. In this case, "interact" is too generous a word because, as is the great burden of one of Dewey's arguments, philosophy rather carries its own past along with it too often and too much as a dead and deadening weight. However this may be, (it is an issue to be discussed later), certain it is that the historical development of philosophy contributes to the determination of philosophy's selectivity and sensitivity of response in interactive relations. And its selectivity and sensitivity, as of any one time, contribute to the determination of the influences it undergoes, how it accepts them or rejects them, to what extent in each case and to what frustrating or liberating end.

Hence the philosophic reason for and import of Dewey's constant excursions into historical analysis and evaluation. In his recent writings, analysis and criticism of classic Greek theories of nature, knowledge and mind figure ever more prominently. Forty and thirty years ago the Hegelian and Kantian philosophies and their derivatives were the main objects of his critical attention; thirty and twenty years ago, it was the then contemporary realisms of all varieties, American and English. But with *Experience and Nature* (1925), a great, though not unheralded, change took place: the foregoing receded into the background while into the focus of critical examination were placed the philosophies of Plato and Aristotle; and this interchange of position between modern and ancient philosophies has become more and not less marked with each succeeding volume.

The reasons for these two major changes in critical orientation are different. The earlier one occurred because of a change in the philosophic scene. For a number of causes, not the least of which was Dewey's own work, the Idealisms, in the first decade of this century, were fast disappearing from effective life and continued examination of them would have been socially as well as philosophically useless. The philosophies then in need of critical attention were the flock of Realisms, for with all the lustiness of the newly born they were disputing with experimentalism its claim to win the rising generation of philosophers.

The later change (1925) occurred for a far different reason. It was the result of a deepened insight on Dewey's part into the nature and sources of the basic ideas controlling the major movements of modern, and the newest movements of contemporary, philosophy. Dewey then saw that as long as these causative ideas continued to work in the bowels of the western mind, there would be no end to the forthcoming of new editions of the old unexamined assumptions. To struggle with each fresh variation on the ancient theme was an endless and hopeless task. It was like trying to conquer Antaeus by bouncing him on the ground.*

The validity of any thesis about the past must be established, in the first instance, by demonstrating its explanatory force for that past. And there is only one way of doing this when that past is the history of ideas, namely, by logical analysis and theoretical appraisal. This necessity weighs with equal force upon all philosophical investigators, be they experimentalists or not. But what distinguishes experimentalists from all others is their recognition that this is only in the first instance. If the analysis and appraisal are sound they must, in the second instance, be capable of experimental verification in the present and to be accepted must successfully pass this test.

For the past is not blocked off from the present by an impassable abyss; if it were, the abyss would also be impassable for us since, as abysses go in the empirical world, they cut off both sides and we would never be able to get over to the past to investigate it by any means, theoretical or otherwise. In fact, we would never know there was a past, and talk about being influenced by it would be impossible even as sheer hallucination. In some transcendental philosophies and also in some philosophies which claim to be realistic, for reasons only known to their au-

---

* Since this volume presents the philosophy of Dewey and not the history of his development, selections of detailed historical criticism have been limited to those dealing with the Greeks.

thors, abysses, to be sure, do not operate in this pedestrian, empirical way. They cut off only one side, wiping out all routes from the past to the present while leaving always intact at least one route from the present to the past—a route through the transcendental air. Needless to say, Dewey has no such inspired conception of things, real or possible. No one has ever defended the cause of possibilities more vigorously and consistently than he. He has championed possibilities in season and out, along with others and alone. But to win his support they must be possibilities that can actually be realized. And this goes for abysses too. The fact that the only kind that can be introduced into Nature and experience are abysses that, in the very act of introducing them, must also be rendered congenitally incapable of operating with equa' effectiveness on both sides of their job, is conclusive evid-ence for Dewey—and should be for any one—that the enterprise envisions not a real possibility but a chimera. Real possibilities are limited by the continuities in experience and Nature.

The validity of Dewey's thesis that in the elements of Greek thought carried along in the modern mind are to be found the generating causes both of the problems that have clogged and stultified modern philosophic intelligence and of the solutions which have repeatedly been proposed, often in sheer intellectual desperation—this thesis is experimentally proved to the hilt by the current revival of Idealism.* And further experimental verification, if such be needed, is supplied by the latest exhumation of medievalism.

* This revival, initiated chiefly by scientists—Eddington, Jeans, and others—began a few years after Dewey's first complete statement of his thesis in *Experience and Nature* (1925). Dewey's complete *development* of his thesis is in *The Quest for Certainty* (1929), which at one point specifically takes up for reply the work of Eddington.

IV

The theory of knowledge is pivotal in modern philosophy. All other issues have revolved around it and all problems peculiarly modern have been generated by it. It began, in Locke, as the universal solvent; it became, in Hume, the universal corrosive; and in Kantian and post-Kantian philosophies it ended up as the source of universal confusion. Judged by empirical standards of performance, there is nothing in the record of the theory of knowledge, or epistemology, to justify keeping it in its position of hegemony. On the contrary. Everything in its record necessitates, let alone justifies, that it be removed from its position if not, indeed, thrown out entirely.

The whole modern epistemological industry is principally supported and kept going by one fundamental assumption concerning the nature of mind and what it does when it knows. To be sure there are almost as many different kinds of elaborations and refined involvements of theory as there are philosophers, but when these secondary and tertiary outgrowths are cut away, what is left, as Dewey has shown, is an unmistakable identity. And this identity in conception of mind and its mode of operation has, in all essentials, been carried over without critical examination and often without even knowing it, from Greek speculation.

The Greek conception of mind and its mode of knowing, Dewey has aptly and accurately called "the spectator theory." The physical eye, according to the Greeks, is a positive source of emission of light and hence there inescapably takes place some sort of interaction between the eye seeing and the thing seen. Both being parts of the physical world which is in constant process of change, both are also necessarily involved in producing change. Although by a familiar figure, as familiar to Plato and Aristotle as to us, we speak of the mind "seeing" and even of the "mind's eye," the mind is, for them, distinguished from the eye in this basic and all-important respect: it does not, in knowing, interact with the object known. Plato and Aristotle, it is true, did not hold that the mind is like a slate which passively accepts what is written on it and has no activity at all. The mind, to know, has to act, has to envisage its object, to grasp it. But—and this "but" is crucial—the mind's activity is a "pure activity," that is, one which does not produce any change whatever in the object it acts upon. It is an actionless action— like the action of a spectator on the benches following the scene being played on the stage above or below.

The Greek philosophers did not arrive at their spectator theory by looking into the mind and thus finding out how it works. The method of introspection has been tried in the modern world for hundreds of years and with what uncertain, universally unestablishable results every one knows. The ancients made very little pretense of examining the mind by itself, whether by introspection or any other method. What they wanted were results absolute and certain and there was only one way, they knew, of getting them, namely, by logical reasoning, ratiocination, theoretical argument. They were all the more inclined, in this case, to find the answers to their questions by a process of inferential reasoning because the mind and knowing were for them of secondary, not primary, philosophic interest and concern. They came upon them in their search for something else.

The main objective controlling all Greek inquiry, scientific as well as philosophic, was what Dewey has again illuminatingly and accurately called "the quest for certainty." All human beings are implicated in the hazards and uncertainties of existence. And all human beings have been at least sufficiently practical, sufficiently motivated by mundane desire to want to eliminate hazard and uncertainty from life and to enjoy a state that is safe and sure. Since this objective can never be attained with absolute perfection in this world, the royal road that has time and again been sought by all peoples is the road of imagining another world wherein none of the hardships and at least all of the delights of this world are to be found and perpetually to be enjoyed. In these all-human respects, the Greeks were, of course, the same as others. What distinguishes them from all their forerunners and contemporaries is the epochal, world-revolutionary discovery made by their mathematicians and philosophers. Rivaling the poets and prophets (whom we now insignificantly call mythologists) the Greek mathematicians and philosophers discovered a new royal road to the heart's fondest and deepest desire—to the realm of eternal and immutable Being, replete with all that is good, true and beautiful and providentially devoid of everything else.

Now it takes no great wit to see that when the mind knows the eternal and immutable, it does not change what it knows in the act of knowing it. And it requires no greater wit to see that the eternal and immutable must have existed before the mind gained knowledge of it and that the mind, in knowing it, has no hand whatsoever in creating its Being. Take, then, as starting point, that Being, eternal and immutable, is the object of knowledge and by a line of inference as easy and compelling as the line demonstrating that the angles of an equilateral triangle are equal, you reach the Greek conclusion concerning the nature of the mind and its mode of knowing. To some, perhaps, this line of inference may seem far too simple, at any rate for philosophers to have really taken it. But Greek philosophers, unlike too many moderns, made a virtue of simplicity. They were quite thoroughly *en rapport* and in sympathy with their culture, and simplicity very profoundly characterizes it throughout—in sculpture and morals, architecture and politics, literature and religion, music and mathematics.

In fact, Greek philosophers were simple enough in their reasoning to be consistent along the main line. The natural world in which we live and act is a world of change, and from this position they never backed down. Knowledge of what constantly changes—the distinguishing trait of Becoming—can, obviously, never be eternal, absolute and certain; and from this position too they never backed down. Therefore knowledge of Becoming, of the world which practical action deals with, is not really knowledge but a bastard species of it which they called opinion. Real knowledge is of Being and only of Being. The realm of Being is eternal and unchanging and hence presents an object which once known is known forever and which when known at all is known with absolute certainty. That there is such a realm and also that we have knowledge of it they had proof in mathematics—new and absolutely certain proof, superseding the old and wavering proof of oracles and seers. Mathematics did not of course exhaust the contents of the realm of Being. It was, for the philosophers, rather a sign and symbol, an evangel of the happy tidings that a new road had been opened up which would take them where they always wanted to go and which made certain they would find what they always wanted to find. The new royal road was infinitely superior, in safety and comfort, to the one formerly used. And for philosophers, it was hardly a drawback that they alone could travel over it. Indeed, possession of exclusive right-of-way caused them none too secret pleasure and exultation. Plato, certainly, lost no time in giving public and peremptory notice to the poets and all other rivals that their day was over.

Now the Greek theory of eternal and immutable Being and its antiphonal spectator theory of mind entered into the bloodstream of modern thought at its very inception. They entered not only by way of philosophy and religion, in which fields they had luxuriantly flourished under the fervid care of medieval logicians and theologians; more importantly, they entered by way of science—more importantly because totally unsuspected and unacknowledged there. And since that time the attractive, ever-entrancing forms of Greek philosophy have circulated in every area, place and part of modern mentality and they create, wherever they are, an iridescent intellectual mirage.

The founders of modern science made a great show of being pure and uncontaminated philosophically. With one accord they attacked philosophy which meant, for them, medievalized Aristotelian logic and its stifling progeny. To free thought from the theological stranglehold, enforced in the temporal realm by the Church, was, they all recognized, the precondition of intellectual and scientific advance. In their march against the powers of darkness they were guided by the lamp of Euclid which they held aloft. But, alas, Euclid's mathematics and Aristotle's logic both involve the same basic presuppositions; they both rest on the same fundamental conceptions of knowledge, nature and mind; they are both results of the same type of metaphysical thinking and scientific method.

It was of undoubted advantage to fight the medievalized Aristotle with the unmedievalized Euclid, but as far as essentials are concerned it was tantamount to using a genuine form and product of Greek thinking as a weapon against a form that had been perverted. Aristotle's logic had been used by the medievalists to discourage and choke off all independent and original observation of nature; how much of a perversion this is and how serious can easily be appreciated when it is remembered that his logic was a presentation of the formal principles underlying the conduct of his own manifold and intensive naturalistic observations and was intended (and was so used by the Greeks) as a guide to further such.

The fathers of modern science, in addition to reclaiming mathematics and gaining unrestricted rights to observe nature—both strictly within the scientific limits of the genuine Greek tradition—also introduced, it is true, a new and non-Greek method of experimentation. This methodological novelty was destined to become all-important in the progress of scientific knowledge and the development of scientific ideas but, at the time of its introduction, it had only a supplementary intellectual value. It would be an exaggeration to say that it was first chiefly prized, not for its scientific but for its polemical power in the liberation movement. But the exaggeration would be nearer the truth than would be any contrary statement. Even in Newton's work, the most self-consciously "experimental" of all, the supreme right-of-way was given to mathematics and not to experimental findings whenever the two came in conflict and blocked each other's path. In other words, the supreme right-of-way in the foundations of modern science was given to Greek ideas of method and science.

The anti-philosophical front presented by the fathers of modern science has been faithfully kept up by the vast and the most influential majority of their descendants. The latter are never so zealous as when they are warding off the sporadic advances of modern philosophy and never so firm and consistent as when rejecting its more formal proposals. This attitude of theirs has naturally been a continual source of irritation to philosophers and the ground for extensive, bitter and recurrent complaint. Only occasionally has the situation been relieved by off-stage laughter. But, forsooth, the whole business—if we may ignore for the moment its tragic consequences—has all along been really a huge joke and the proper subject for unrestrained hilarity. For the philosophy modern scientists took from the Greeks they handed back to modern philosophers as science; and the latter, instead of at once spotting the intellectual sleight-of-hand and calling the game, were taken in by it to a man. Certainly there is some excuse for philosophers being thus easily deceived during the intellectually tumultuous years opening our epoch. But there is hardly excuse for philosophers who insist on staying deceived even now. Not that vulgar and childish delight in mystification entices and holds contemporaries in ludicrous trance. It is something more mature and for that reason more profoundly disturbing. As long as the deception is kept up, the staple and routine occupations of philosophers are not threatened; their intellectual habits, now easy, familiar and dear through long usage, can go on unreflectively grinding out philosophical reflections forever. And the by now standardized relation of philosophy to science—an unstable and explosive compound of envy and condescension—can be perpetuated, though not unperturbed.

One basic feature initially characterized all modern liberation movements: they advanced against the social and intellectual tyranny of Church and State, their oppressive authoritarianism, by appealing to the superior integrity, nature, authority and power of the individual.* In religion, this appeal took the form of Protestantism;

---

* This feature, of course, continued to dominate until well into the nineteenth century.

in law and revolution the form of inalienable natural rights; in economics the form of *laissez faire;* in social ethics the form of the greatest good for the greatest number; in progressive politics the form of universal suffrage and representative, parliamentary government. In science and philosophy, the two predominantly theoretical areas of culture, the direction of the appeal was also essentially the same: the rationalist scientists and philosophers appealed to the natural light of reason brightly burning in the individual mind, while the empiricists appealed no less surely to the inextinguishable light and all-conquering power of individual experience. Although the differences between rationalists and empiricists developed to serious proportions later on, at the outset, especially as far as concerns their common opposition to the manifold medievalisms and oppressions, the differences were tactical rather than strategic.*

It is possible, I think, to prove with reasonable surety that against oppression hardened in institutions and enforced by socially guarded and perpetuated dogmas only the assault of individualism, under whatever form it may be, has revolutionary power and effect. But whether or not this can be established as a principle, certain it is as a fact that modern culture started, and for nearly three hundred years won, all its greatest battles under this standard. Because of this prevailing cultural fact, to call it no more, it was inevitable that in taking over Greek ideas, the spectator theory of mind should assume first and dominating place, acknowledged and unacknowledged, in the thinking of the period. Wherever it went, the spectator theory of mind necessarily brought along with it the

* Dewey did not see this important point at the time of writing *"The Significance of the Problem of Knowledge"*; it is the one serious shortcoming in that great essay. It may also be pointed out that many still fail to see it.

theory of eternal and immutable Being, for they are an inseparable pair and play only together. But in modern thought, the original relation obtaining between them in Greek speculation was consistently reversed; their positions relative to each other were permanently exchanged. This didn't matter very much in the sixteenth and seventeenth centuries, for their music, though badly off key, was sweet and melodious to any ear that, perforce, had hitherto heard only the harsh and grating, dull and offensive noise of medievalism. But by the eighteenth and nineteenth centuries, the consequences of the reversal or exchange had worked themselves through, far and wide; the simple tune for two had been amplified on orchestral scale and that it now mattered very much indeed was plain to every ear that could distinguish loud discord from quiet harmony, and to every eye that was not permanently shut and could see the difference between playing every which way and playing in unison.

V

When we look back over the histories of modern science and philosophy, from the vantage-point of the present time, one fact stands out clearly and boldly like the sphinx in the desert, and like the sphinx it too presents an enigmatical face. Although science and philosophy started out in community of effort, and with a common set of fundamental ideas, the courses they have run are not the same. They are not even parallel. They are divergent, so that the nearer we approach our own time the further apart they are. Now you may lightly say that there is really nothing strange about this, and certainly nothing enigmatical. For two activities to start from a common center and from that point onward to diverge in ever-widening degree is the sort of thing that happens every day and moreover the only kind of thing that can or should happen when their destinations lie in different directions. But this answer, true enough in what it says, does not at all meet the case in hand. The paths of philosophy and science have been progressively divergent not because their avowed, respective destinations lie in different quarters and each is intent on the shortest route. Just the contrary is the case. They are divergent *precisely because* they both have vowed to reach the *same* ultimate destination and by the quickest way. And this, surely, is an enigma.

But like all enigmas, the real explanation of it is not to be found in something more enigmatic and mysterious still —be it in the puniness of the finite reason strangely wrestling with the Infinitude of the Universe and being constantly thrown back; or in the inwardly palpitating Secret of Philosophy which cannot be exposed and live in the light of day because it is fetched from depths beyond all reckoning—in contrast to the dead contents of science which can be written in open script for any eye plainly to read because they are scraped off the surface of things; or vice versa, and so on. The real explanation, as Dewey has shown, is to be found in something really quite simple and historically to our human hand.

What is the common, ultimate destination of modern science and philosophy? To say it is the Truth is too vague to lead us anywhere. But to say it is the eternal and immutable Reality leads us straight home, into the theoretical heart of modern science and philosophy—and back to the bosom of the Greeks.

The first success of science in its quest for certainty was wonderfully great, so wonderful that nearly three hundred years elapsed before science matured sufficiently to have serious doubts of its own as to whether or not it had exclusively and permanently captured eternal and immutable Reality first crack out of the box. It must, however, be said immediately on behalf of most scientists today that they have not allowed themselves to become too discouraged by these doubts. Recent revelations have set them back somewhat and shaken their early confidence, but most of them still hope to succeed in finally and exclusively cornering Reality in the next try, or in the try after that, and they steadfastly aim that way.

Nothing attracts like success. Why, then, were philosophers repelled and driven off at an obtuse angle by the first great victory of science? The answer is found in the field on which victory was won. Science discovered the eternal and immutable Reality in material masses and motion and the laws governing masses in motion. It was not, of course, just the fact that they were material masses and physical motion that assured scientists they had found what they were looking for. It was the eternal, indestructible nature of the constituent particles of the masses, and the eternal, unchangeable nature of the laws of motion that proved to them, with the inerrant simplicity and unshakable certainty of mathematics, that their conviction of success was true and not the fanciful product of their dream.

Now philosophers, like common men, have eyes and the eyes see colors—but colors, said the new science, are not ultimately real; philosophers have ears and ears hear sounds—but sounds, said the new science, are not ultimately real; philosophers have noses and noses smell smells—but smells, said the new science, are not ultimately real; philosophers have hands and hands feel surfaces, temperatures, and textures, rough and smooth, hot and cold, wet and dry, soft and hard—but soft and hot, wet and dry, cold and smooth and rough, said the new science, are not ultimately real; philosophers have tongues and tongues taste things bitter and sweet—but bitter and sweet, said the new science, are not ultimately real. All these, the new science said, are only words. And all the rest of them, and all like them, are also only words, or as Galileo formulated it, they "are not anything else than names." The only genuinely, ultimately real things are the atoms and their qualities of shape, size, hardness, motion, number, mass, inertia.* Really, in the last analysis, it is the tongue which is wholly at fault, the real obstruction blocking our path to the ultimately real! If it did not keep on foolishly uttering these words or names, misleading us, all would immediately accept with joyous heart and unquestioning mind the words of golden truth spoken by scientists!

Without exception the fathers of modern science had nothing to say destructive of the medievalized soul-substance or mind and its complement of ideas and sentiments, desires, purposes and plans. To have denied the ultimate reality of the mind at that early stage would have been intellectually suicidal for scientists, since it was on the power of the mind that they publicly rested their claim to have discovered the ultimately real. It would also have been socially suicidal, what with the powerful backing the soul or mind enjoyed in secular prison and religious stake. As to which of these arguments, the intellectual or the social, was really effective and determined the scientists upon the course they took the reader should experience no great difficulty in deciding for himself. For the scientists without exception, Galileo as well as Newton, had also publicly rested their claim to have discovered the genuinely and ultimately real on the irrefragable nature of sensory evidence. How else, for example, did

* The list of "primary" or ultimately real qualities varies from scientist to scientist. The list above is a Galilean-Newtonian mixture.

Galileo defend against the holy doctors of the Church who for their "scientific" knowledge of Nature relied more insistently on the words of Aristotle than on the words of God—how else did Galileo defend against the holy doctors the reality of the satellites of Jupiter, except on the ground that he saw them with his very own sensory organs, namely, his eyes? How else did Newton prove that hardness, for instance, was an eternal, inalienable characteristic of the indestructible ultimately real atom, except by empirical inference which explicitly asserted that the testimony of the senses was of unimpeachable validity?*

Socially and religiously the senses were, in Galilean-Newtonian days, intrinsically sinful.† For Galileo and Newton, therefore, to turn completely round on their "scientific" axes and put the senses scientifically as well as socially and religiously in bad odor, was gratifying, not reprehensible, to State and Church. The State was pleased because Science by exposing the temporal, this-worldly vanity of the senses was contributing its strength, however much or little it might be, toward the fulfillment of the State's objectives: the restraint and control of the this-worldly desires of the people. And the Church, naturally, in its dual capacity of Temporal and Spiritual Power was doubly pleased because science denounced the senses to be

* Notice that "hardness" is a primary or ultimately real quality; but "softness" is only a "word" or "name" or—secondary quality. This accounts for what may have seemed to the reader an error in the preceding paragraph where the phrase "soft and hard" was used first and then in the repetition of the list only "soft" was included.

† The doctrine of "original sin" with its correlative "the intrinsic moral depravity of the senses" are by no means completely dead yet. At the present time, in fact, new life is being assiduously pumped into these doctrines by the strangest crew that ever manned the "idealistic" pumps in history. And the "pumps" employed are as strange as the assortment of "pumpers"—ranging from bombs and bullets to prayers and papal bulls designed to finish off what the bombs and bullets leave undone.

as palpably false and treacherous means for gaining knowledge of this world, as the Church denounced them to be fatal and perditious means for gaining the knowledge and bliss of the next.

But with respect to the soul-substance or mind, some social-religious compromise was imperative, irrespective of what scientists might or might not think in the privacy of their cabinets. And Descartes hit upon the very neatest compromise, one which may be taken as accurately symbolic of the whole early philosophico-scientific movement.* He sequestered the soul-substance or mind in the pineal body, in the smallest area of the brain he knew of, and central enough to comport with the dignity of its new and exalted occupant. That part of the physical world—the pineal body—Descartes said, in effect, belongs to you, O! defenders and guardians of the soul-substance or mind, and we shall never trespass within its holy bounds! But the rest of the human body—let us be perfectly clear about it—and the rest of the world, belong to us, to the mathematical and physical scientists!

Descartes' compromise obviously could not endure forever, nor indeed for very long. Just as soon as science felt its oats and felt sufficiently secure socially so that it need no longer fear the secular instruments of persecution used by the Church, science naturally and inevitably advanced its claim of divine right to investigate and explore every-

---

* The one exception is Spinoza—and of course a great one. The treatment Spinoza and his works received not merely from the illiterate but from his peers, is among the best evidences proving that *social,* not intellectual, considerations either consciously or unconsciously dictated the "compromise." In Descartes' case, the dictation was thoroughly conscious; he knew what he was doing and why. In Newton's case it was as completely unconscious; he was a "true believer" and his interest in the English translation of the alleged speech of God actually exceeded his interest in the works of creation. For ampler discussion of Spinoza's case, see my Introduction to *The Philosophy of Spinoza* (The Modern Library, 1927).

thing and everywhere. You may think that mathematical physicists would always have the need of upholding the ultimate reality of the mind, if only out of sheer self-interest and self-preservation, else they lose their necessary and primary guarantee that what they discover, mathematically, is actually the ultimately real. But to think so is naïve. For what further need of the mind have they, once Science itself, in all its glittering panoply of power, stands boldly in the field, its feet firmly planted on the eternal foundation-stones of the universe!

Because of Descartes' compromise, and the general socio-scientific situation it symbolizes, philosophers first acutely experienced the need of defending their sensory organs against the deprivations of science. How did it come about that all of us, scientists as well as philosophers and common persons, sensed such qualities as colors and sounds and what status, really, can be given them? Merely to call them names, as Galileo does, may be finally satisfactory for the scientist who is professionally so enraptured by his own work that he has no mind for anything else. But such summary disposal of secondary qualities can hardly be permanently satisfying for the philosopher whose professional interests are of universal scope and for whom there is nothing too small or too insignificant to merit and receive his thoughtful and tender consideration. Not that in the common life and world of man, colors and sounds and all other secondary qualities are a small item, like the hairs on his head or the sparrows in his fields. But compared to the soul or mind and all its longings and belongings, they are; and the soul or mind had been left untouched by science. Indeed, had not science solicitously placed it in an inviolable sanctuary beyond the reach of all molesting and harm from itself or others?

Call it clairvoyance, premonition or what you will. Or say, if you like, it is the fair and just reward that comes to those who take it upon themselves to defend the orphaned and the lowly. When the period of compromise was nearing its end, and the mind was in imminent danger of being imperiously sucked into the whirling stream of atoms forever, it was the secondary qualities that came to the rescue and saved the philosophers from falling into the dark and bottomless pit.

Very rarely are philosophers poets, even though, frequently, they robe their writings with rich and colorful imagery and make them reverberant with sonorous poetical effects. Only very rarely are they even like Wordsworth, hardy men of two senses, let alone like Coleridge and Keats, hardy men of five senses and for whom, without colors and sounds, without tastes and smells and textures, all places would be a blank hell though they be fastly secured in heaven. With few worthy exceptions, modern philosophers, especially since the time of Berkeley, have found secondary qualities of primary value because they can be used as means of argument to gain their own, and not the qualities' ends. Berkeley's great discovery was not that secondary qualities are the glorious garment of Nature and of which she cannot be deprived by any scientific means. What he joyfully discovered was that secondary qualities are the Achilles heel of science and struck there the monster could be slain. Incidentally, it is true, the earth we commonly enjoy would then be regained for man, but what was far more important to the good bishop and the motive forcing his attack, was that man would thus be reclaimed for God.

If science does not adequately account for this world— and the fact that science leaves secondary qualities inexplicably hanging in mid-air establishes this—then, rea soned Berkeley, the conclusion follows that philosophy, as an enterprise independent of and unconstrained by science is necessary. Merely to be necessary is something, of course, but not enough. Philosophy has to prove that it is also competent. And to do this, obviously, philosophy must first demonstrate that it can succeed where science has dismally failed. Philosophy, that is, must give secure and intelligible status to secondary qualities, give to them the reality they were denied by science. And at this point Berkeley was overcome by his most brilliant idea and made straight for a dazzling *coup*. It is not imperative, he saw, that the reality philosophy gives to secondary qualities be identical with the reality claimed by science for its atoms and such of their primary qualities as it could keep from changing into secondary ones. This was the great and egregious mistake Locke had made; because of it he was forced into the ludicrous position of vigorously accepting Newton's science and then feebly complaining about some of its results. Philosophy can escape from the insufferable and insoluble Lockean dilemma, can effectively demonstrate its competence, can firmly establish its complete independence of science and can, moreover, do all these marvelous things at once and in one by the simple expedient of giving to secondary qualities a reality *different* from that of the atoms and primary qualities, but a reality nonetheless securely founded and ultimately real. How can this be done? Very easily. Link secondary qualities not to the senses but to the as-yet-undisputed reality of the mind; the mind (also by still common consent) is linked to God and by divine devolution of power, secondary qualities are established as substantially real. (The atoms and primary qualities were, according to Descartes and Newton, the creation of God and their eternal reality was dependent upon and guaranteed by the

Eternal Will.) Thus science, reasoned Berkeley, is over-turned by its own mistake, confounded by its own dis-tinction. Let science keep its primary qualities—if it can.*
Philosophy has shown who is the true possessor of knowl-edge of this world, who the proud and faithful protector of the reality of God's visible creation.

But surely, you will say, the mind, in throwing its own mantle of reality about secondary qualities, could have been motivated only by a noble altruism. By thus sharing itself with others, how could it have been seeking merely benefits for itself? Surely it is an act unselfishly pure, con-cerned solely with using fairly and justly what science had meanly and despitefully used, with charitably raising up what science had cast down. On the face of it the act does, assuredly, carry these benign features. But, alas, it is only on the face of it. Actually it was a method of using the indisputable natural reality of the secondary qualities to give body to the reality of the mind, a means for resus-citating the mind's fast failing spirit. Once the mind was revived and strengthened by this natural and wholesome food, what did the Idealists do? Did they acknowledge the mind's natural indebtedness and return natural good for natural good received? Not at all. They used the boost in spirit they had thus surreptitiously obtained for the mind to catapult the mind into a transcendental reality and then, with base ingratitude, they turned on the sec-ondary qualities and spitefully made them blind wan-derers in a phenomenal world.

* Berkeley's really significant and permanently valuable contri-bution was in showing that science can *not* keep its primary quali-ties, that is, that all qualities are in the same boat. However, the only proper conclusion this demonstration leads to is precisely the one Berkeley and subsequent philosophy (up to pragmatism and instrumentalism) did not make. To discuss it at this point would therefore be to complicate matters to no good end. It will be taken up later.

Which is in all essential particulars doing to secondary qualities exactly what science had originally done. Instead of the Galilean-Newtonian "scientific" distinction between primary and secondary qualities, you have, with Kant, the "metaphysical" distinction between noumena and phenomena, between the empirical world and trans-cendental Reality, which became in some post-Kantian developments the distinction between what only appears to be real, but really isn't, and what is known by the mind's inner and unaided power to be exclusively and ulti-mately Real and Is. The "metaphysical" distinction un-doubtedly sounds more soul-filling and grandiose than the "scientific," but deflate the artificial grandiosity and the two distinctions, though expanded in different ways and not always in one-to-one correspondence, are, for all intel-ligent purposes, the same.

You will say that this is only what Kant and the Kantians did but that Hegel, sensing the keen wrong, redressed it forthwith. Yes, Hegel did redress the wrong— by giving it another cloak. The mind, Kant thought, could get along entirely on its own in all its categorically im-perative business, business having to do with its own soul's salvation. And for all lesser business, though the mind could not get along on its own entirely, it was suf-ficient if, from its transcendental seat, it occasionally looked down on the empirical world; by occasionally peer-ing into the blind, phenomenal world, its noumenal eyes would see enough for thought. Hegel realized this wasn't so. The mind needed the natural world for all its business, ideal and real, for its own soul's categorical salvation no less than for everything else and that it could not get along without the natural world for a moment; it con-stantly needed it. Occasional contacts with it, occasional peerings down into it were not enough for thought. But did this recognition, on Hegel's part, of the constant need and dependency of the mind show him that the mind must be returned to its natural environment where it could and would naturally feed, and that leaving it where Kant had put it was leaving it, not in a transcendental heaven, but up a tree? Not a bit of it. To satisfy the constant and natural craving of the mind for natural food, Hegel tried, by an act of unnatural violence, to force the mind to swallow the natural world whole! Instead of permanently satisfying the hunger of the mind, this grotesque act of intellectual outrage gave it convulsive indigestion. And the spasmic regurgitations of Absolute Idealism are splattered over all the pages of subsequent cultural history.

VI

Because of the malicious exploitation made of secondary qualities by Idealism, the whole discussion of the theory of knowledge was subsequently narrowed down to a discussion of the theory of perception as the critical point of attack. To dissociate secondary qualities from the mind was the all-important thing to do. For just as soon as this dissociation is effected, the Absolute Mind is deflated and Idealism collapses like a punctured balloon.* This proves negatively what was asserted positively before, namely, that the attempt to give secondary qualities the reality of the mind was not really for the end of saving them but was a means whereby their natural reality could be used to bolster up and secure the vanishing reality of the "substantive" mind, or soul. William James, in a brilliant sentence written in 1904 said: "Those who still cling to 'consciousness' are clinging to a mere echo, the

---

* This is most neatly seen in G. E. Moore's thirty-page *Refutation of Idealism* (1903), which has been the originating and orienting point of practically all British Realism. Bertrand Russell is possibly Moore's very first disciple; he certainly is his foremost one

faint rumor left behind by the disappearing 'soul' upon
the air of philosophy." The echoes of the "soul" would
have completely died out in philosophy long before our
century had not Idealism resorted to necromancy and by
percussion instruments spread the deafening clamor of
ghosts.

Pragmatists, realists and instrumentalists have approached and accomplished the critical task of dissociation in different ways. If the result of evacuating the mind
of its universal pretensions were an isolated or isolable
matter, the differences in methods used by these various
schools would be practically irrelevant. But the consequences of the critical operation are neither isolated nor
isolable. As with the operations performed by a surgeon
on the human body, so with the critical operations performed by philosophers on ideas. Upon the instruments
and skill with which a tumor is removed, the recovery of
the patient depends. And the more malignant the tumor,
the greater the skill and the better and finer the instruments must be. Done unskilfully and with the wrong instruments, it matters not with what nicety and dispatch
the outer parts are sewn up again. The superficial wound
heals, but at the real seat of trouble new and serious complications set in. There is a limit to the cuttings and
removals a human body will undergo. A tumor, no matter
how malignant, cannot grow forever, in new areas or old,
because the body dies. With ideas, however, there is no
limit—at any rate, none that has ever been reached and
of which we with certainty know. And all ideas, malignant or benign, are in this respect alike: they spread from
one area of the cultural body to every other and there is
no stopping them.

If the *fact* of severing secondary qualities from the
mind were of self-sufficient importance and the *method*

of no philosophic consequence, then Dr. Johnson's method would be the very best, for it is so short and every one can use it. He kicked a stone and found it behaved as stones had always behaved and not as an idea.* That, for him, was refutation enough of Berkeley. And considered *sheerly as refutation* enough it is, final and complete, and no philosopher has improved upon it or can because all refinements of philosophical refutation must end up, when they do not begin, in the mode of Dr. Johnson. For his refutation is the *experimental coup de grace.* We all accept without question that a complicated piece of scientific apparatus kicking an electron out of its orbit can thereby, with rightful authority, kick a scientific theory in or out. Well, the human foot is itself not uncomplicated in structure—if you believe only complicated apparatus can perform operations of experimental test, which is, of course, not so. And the human foot too has the ability and rightful authority to kick a philosophic (or scientific) theory in or out. "I would rather," writes Dewey, "take the behavior of the dog of Odysseus upon his master's return as an example of the sort of thing experience is for the philosopher than trust to" philosophers' theorizings about experience.† A dog is a whole animal and the foot is only a part, but the point of reference and the contact are the same. To this extent, Dr. Johnson has certainly not received his proper philosophic due.

* It should perhaps be explicitly stated that Dr. Johnson, as a man of letters, as a person whose profession was handling and dealing with ideas, was as competent an *authority* on the macroscopic behavior of ideas (or their general, overt characters) as, say, a scientist of comparable distinction would be an *authority* on the macroscopic behavior of his subject-matter (electricity or whatnot). That Dr. Johnson was also as *qualified an expert* on the macroscopic behavior of stones as Bishop Berkeley (or any other philosopher or scientist) can, perhaps, be left as too obvious for statement.

† *Experience and Nature,* (first edition), page 6.

However, the *fact* of severance is not everything; it is necessary, it is indispensable, but it is not sufficient. The surgeon must remove the tumor, that is certainly clear; but the *method* he uses, *how* he removes it, is equally important, for the removal and the method of removal cannot be separated; they continually interact and it is the consequences of their interaction that determine the life and health of the patient. When it is so intricately complicated and delicate a matter as the life of the mind that is at stake, the importance of the consequences of the method employed is of course immeasurably increased, not lessened.*

The severance of secondary qualities from the mind reduces the mind to its natural size. It loses its *a priori* bigness and no longer needs a supernatural, transcendental realm to house its unnatural, swollen grandeur. The mind becomes something that *can* be included in the order of Nature, as a part having its natural function and place. The emphasis on *can* cannot be made too strong. For the mind does not automatically find its proper place as a soldier, when called to attention, automatically falls in line. Especially is this so after a bout of fever as wild and fearful as German Idealism. To return the mind to its place in the order of nature, to accustom it in the performance of its natural functions, to teach it to find its inner and highest joy in the fulfillment of its cultural obligations is a long and difficult task for deliberate art. This reconstructive, rehabilitative work, to be completely successful, requires, of course, the coöperative effort of all cultural forces, of all society. But the starting of this tremendously important and complex task, getting it under way, is peculiarly the philosopher's job—at any

* Notice, in the quotation above, that Dewey says "rather." The qualification is important.

rate, as Dewey conceives it. Indeed, it is the one job which, when accepted by philosophy, intelligently legitimates or justifies its claim to universal (*i. e.* cultural) leadership. This peculiarly philosophic part of the greater undertaking no philosophy can adequately perform except it does its critical work properly.

Hence Dewey's insistence on the present need of philosophy to devote itself to criticism and the methods of criticism. For the ideas a philosopher uses in his critical operations necessarily become part of the foundational ideas for his reconstructive and constructive follow-up work. This is true universally, a consequence flowing from the very nature and process of thinking. Wherein philosophers can and do differ from one another is in degree of awareness of this necessity, and in the competency of the critical apparatus they respectively possess. Of course, no philosopher has yet appeared who in his work shows that he is fully conscious of, and at every point alert to, all the implications of his critical work; nor is it possible to develop and construct a critical apparatus that will make any (let alone every) philosopher thus perfect. To be perfect philosophically is to be absolutely infallible—a possibility directly open only to God and indirectly open only to those erstwhile human thinkers who by retroactive edict (promulgated by His proper intermediaries) have been canonically uplifted into the ranks of angels.

On the other hand, it is also impossible for a philosopher to be totally unconscious of and unalert to the implications of such critical apparatus as he may possess, for such a one would not be a philosopher at all, and would not have any critical apparatus in the first place. Like all human works, the works of philosophers are to be found ranging between the extremes of perfection and imperfection and none of them reaching either. In this respect at least, they all exemplify with equal clarity and naturalness the universal cosmic characteristic William James never tired of celebrating: "Ever not quite."

Dewey, more persistently perhaps than any other contemporary, uses his critical apparatus and the results they yield as part of the basis for his constructive philosophy. This has caused a great deal of confusion on the part of many of his readers, whereas it should have enabled them to follow his thought with clear, if not easy, understanding. In saying this I have neither intention nor desire to shift all cause of confusion from Dewey's writings to his readers' minds. In view of what has already been said on this point, such would be ridiculous. But too much stress cannot be put upon the general principle at issue because unless it is firmly grasped, it is practically certain that any reader of Dewey will keep on being confused no matter how often and how studiously he reads him. Failure to understand the fundamental reason for and meaning of Dewey's persistent use of his critical results for constructive purposes has, beyond any doubt, been one of the most prolific sources of unenlightened and unenlightening attacks upon his work.* To the same cause may also be chiefly traced the failure of Dewey's twenty years' controversy with American and English realists, for that controversy was circumstantially concerned with this one basic point. That his fears about the competency of the Realists' critical apparatus were not unwarranted and his prophecies as to their eventual outcome were not without ground are proven conclusively by the way in which neo-Idealism has grown out of and sucked the strength from the Realistic movements.†

* The reader, if he so desires, may also consider the above paragraphs as stating the basic reason for my writing *this* Introduction and not another.

† This does not contradict what was said earlier. Neo-Idealism

VII

"A clash of doctrines," writes Whitehead, "is not a disaster—it is an opportunity." There are some "ifs" involved. It is an opportunity, or perhaps better said, it becomes (or is made) an opportunity *if* the clash stimulates intelligent response and not blind reaction; *if* the clash is taken not merely as a sign that something is wrong but is utilized as the starting point and control of inquiry into causes; *if* the inquiry into causes is not handicapped and stultified by impounding certain issues in a sacrosanct reservation, thus compelling inquiry to stop short at the first arbitrary point where a makeshift solution can be gerrymandered; *if* the inquiry is so conducted that it fearlessly re-examines and reconstructs everything necessary for a stable and fruitful solution, exempting nothing from scrutiny and reconstruction—above all not exempting the doctrinal foundations.

The clash of doctrine between science and philosophy on the all-determining, all-controlling issue considered in the foregoing pages is an excellent example not of an opportunity utilized but of a disaster prolonged. Consciously and unconsciously, philosophers exempted from critical examination and reconstruction certain conceptions both of science and philosophy. If you like to be excessively generous, you can say they inquired into and re-valuated everything—until they reached foundational principles. There they stopped short, with the necessary consequence that their solutions were makeshift and unstable, arbitrary and unfruitful in all but harmful ways.

draws *immediately* from the Realisms, which is the point just made. It can do so because the Realisms carry in them the fundamental errors of Greek philosophy, which is the comprehensive point made before. That neither the older neo-Realisms nor the newer neo-Idealisms are critically conscious of their historical sources and the basic repetitiousness of their views is a fact theoretically responsible for both.

Berkeley is one of the clearest illustrations of this and because of his pivotal influence, also one of the most important. He argumentatively demonstrated that all qualities are in the same boat, that it is impossible to classify qualities into two (or more) orders, distinguished from each other by quality of reality. If any quality is real, then all qualities are real. If any quality is of a modified or suspect reality, then in the same way and to the same degree, the reality of all qualities becomes modified or suspect. This conclusion is indubitably sound. But Berkeley unfortunately arrived at it by way of an argument the objective of which was to prove that all qualities are directly dependent for their very existence upon perception and therefore are creatures of mind. This tie-up was particularly vicious in its consequences because, although in theoretical purity it perhaps need not be so, it was practically inevitable that refutations of Berkeley—an idealism, of which there are legion—should almost automatically result in resuscitating and re-stabilizing (if not illegitimately re-validating) the "scientific" distinction between qualities his argument destroyed. But apart from this particular tie-up in Berkeley's argument, and without wishing in any way to minimize the extent and deleterious character of its historical influence—apart from this tie-up, Berkeley's whole method of approach, which became standard for subsequent philosophy, is vicious: it blinds the philosophic as well as scientific mind to the real issues and problems involved.*

* Berkeley's *method* of approach is of course still standard for Idealistic philosophers, whatever branch of Idealism they profess; but it is also standard for all British Realists, like Moore, Russell and Whitehead; and for all American philosophers who follow the British lead. The attack on Berkeley's *method* and so on all modern philosophy that led into it and all that developed out of it was initiated by C. S. Peirce—the logical father of pragmatism. The new *method* of philosophy, both as critical and constructive instrument, which Peirce began, was developed to some extent by

For when you develop a philosophic theory as ground for the assertion that all qualities are of equal reality, by that intellectual act you are also forced to assert, explicitly or implicitly, that the distinction between reality of qualities as it is made in science is valid within the domain of science. And from this tacit or overt admission only one consequence can follow, namely, what exactly has followed in modern philosophy: Inquiry into the legitimacy of and reason for the distinction as it is made in science is completely sidetracked and as substitute for this intelligent inquiry an unintelligent contest is staged between rival systems of "metaphysics:" in one corner the perennial champion "scientific metaphysics" and in the other the (theoretically) endless succession of "philosophic" contenders for the crown. Dewey's detailed exposure of the tragi-comedy of this whole procedure is one of the great pieces of philosophic analysis.*

All the philosophic criticisms and attacks in the world will not persuade scientists to abandon any principle or distinction as long as they believe, whether rightly or wrongly, that the principle or distinction performs some scientific work. In this respect they are as loyal to their science as the best of philosophers are to philosophy; and the sooner all philosophers realize this and conduct themselves in accordance with such realization the better it will be for all. On the other hand, if scientists can be shown, or in some other way come to see for themselves, that a principle or distinction does not perform any scientific work, either in the form in which it is made or because it is inherently incapable, no matter how formulated, they will,

---

William James and was carried out practically to its full critical and constructive *methodological* limits by Dewey. This method is a new contribution to philosophy and, we may well be proud, a distinctively, even exclusively, American contribution.

* *The Quest for Certainty* is the *locus classicus*.

without further argument, modify it immediately or drop it entirely as the case may be. And in this respect, alas, it must be said, scientists are vastly superior to the majority of philosophers—if one may fairly judge by the howl of protest which arose when James and Dewey made known* and began to develop "the principle of work" as the basic criterion or test for all philosophic ideas.

Einstein, about five years ago, opened a famous lecture by saying: "If you wish to learn from the theoretical physicist anything about the methods he uses, I would give you the following piece of advice: Don't listen to his words, examine his achievements."† This piece of advice loses none of its excellent qualities when it is extended to include the whole field of science; in fact, it considerably gains in excellence when applied to the basic methodology of all modern science. And in the latter sense, Dewey began following it some forty-odd years before it was given.‡ In his analysis of scientific method, of what science is, Dewey has been strictly guided and controlled by his examination of what scientists do. He has not, however, been able entirely to ignore what scientists say since so many influential philosophers have repeated their sayings, and their sayings and the repetitions of them have

* Peirce was first as originator of "the principle of work" (pragmatism) and first in time of publication (1878). Not until James (1898) and Dewey (1897) took up the idea and began developing it, did it begin to claim attention and exert influence. Peirce didn't approve of many of the ways in which James developed "the principle of work" and violently criticized him. Neither did Dewey approve of all James' developments and he also criticized him—but without violence and to much greater effect.

† On the Method of Theoretical Physics, the Herbert Spencer Lecture, delivered at Oxford University, June 10, 1933.

‡ Peirce's essential contribution to the pragmatist movement consists precisely in giving "Einstein's advice" and the underlying reason for it. Einstein, grievous to say, in his capacity not as scientific practitioner but of philosophic interpreter of science has always been critically unable to follow "Einstein's advice."

fostered the all-absorbing philosophic problem of modern times. Furthermore, it may be noticed in passing that even if science had not been a great determining force in modern philosophy, because of science's enormous influence in modern cultural life and the social standing scientists enjoy as examples, if not indeed paragons, of intelligence, it would be for the philosopher of first-rate importance to inquire into and find the answer to the great question: Why do scientists do one thing and say another and contrary thing?

Dewey's historical exposition of Greek philosophy and its modes of entrance into modern thought and his analysis of the theory of knowledge give the root-answer to this question. Starting from different loci in the western intellectual world, they converge toward this double objective, their critical forces uniting in this double point: they show that the distinction between primary and secondary qualities *as it is made in science* has no validity *in science* and performs *no scientific work:* and they show *how* this non-scientific, in fact anti-scientific, distinction, came to be made in the first place and *how* it has been fundamentally supported ever since. Dewey thus cuts under the ground of the whole modern controversy between philosophy and science; and by removing the source whence modern philosophers have drawn self-justifying reasons for setting up rival systems of "metaphysical" reality, he has also thereby removed the source of all modern intellectual jugglery in philosophy—as his own critical and constructive philosophy experimentally shows.

The real proof—and the only proof philosophers should adduce or resort to—that the "scientific" distinction is false in the form in which it is made in science is provided by science itself. Every time science performs an experiment it necessarily abrogates or invalidates the distinction—and if this is not conclusive proof of falsity, then there is no proof of falsity anywhere or anyhow to be found. Science abrogates or invalidates the distinction every time it performs an experiment because every experiment is carried out in the world of common experience and the *final authority*, for validation or invalidation of scientific theory, always rests with events in the "macroscopic" field of sense-perception, to use one of Dewey's analytical terms. For instance, the final verdict as to whether or not there was any ether-drift was rendered by the registration of visual effects on the interferometer employed in the famous Michelson-Morley experiment (1887). What the visual effects—the black-bands —meant, how they were to be interpreted, became a scientific, theoretical problem of the first magnitude. But be it noted—and this alone is of crucial importance here—a scientific theory was not needed to determine whether or not the black-bands, as seen with the eyes, were actually real. That they were real was unequivocally and unhesitatingly accepted by all scientists. Indeed, only because the reality of the black-bands was never in question and beyond all dispute, only because their reality could not be *scientifically* challenged in any way, was a theory necessary to explain—not their existence or occurrence —but their causes, or, what amounts to the same thing, their interconnections with other existences or events.

Because the Relativity Theory, among other things, did this job of explanation it was in so far confirmed. One case of confirmation is rarely enough, especially when the theory is very complex, comes after the facts and is devised to explain those facts. Furthermore, the Relativity Theory required for its explanation of the black-bands a revolutionary change in the fundamental concepts of Newtonian physics. Hence the extraordinary significance of

Einstein's prediction that if adequate visual attention were directed thereto, it would be observed that light rays are bent in passing the sun. This was an experimental test which the Relativity Theory proposed for itself and this is all that "prediction" of this sort scientifically means. The "foretelling" is scientifically nothing: what is everything scientifically is that by foretelling a hitherto unobserved event, the Theory proposes and provides an experimental test for itself wherefrom all possibility of "collusion" or *ex post facto* explanation is clearly and rigorously excluded. When, in 1921, the bending of the light rays was first photographically observed, Einstein's theory received its most exciting and dramatic confirmation. But human excitement and drama aside, this confirmation was in every scientific respect on all fours with the confirmation the theory received from the black-bands of the interferometer or the irregularities of Mercury's orbit *— both of which were known to science long before. If a theory were to come along to-morrow morning that satisfactorily explained all that the Relativity Theory explains and did not "predict" anything new at all, it would nevertheless displace the Relativity Theory if, in one significant way or another, preferably in its mathematics, it was also simpler or more consistent. A number of alternative theories have in fact already been proposed. None has succeeded in gaining acceptance not because none has made "predictions" of hitherto unobserved events, but because none has proved capable of doing all the explaining, or

* The other fairly well-known achievement to the credit of the Relativity Theory: the Law of Gravitation which it yields, unlike Newton's Law accounts for certain irregularities in Mercury's orbit; the irregularities are macroscopic events observed by our senses supplemented by telescopes and other apparatus (which latter are constructed, manipulated and observed by our senses and are also, of course, macroscopic events). It need hardly be stated explicitly that the indubitable and indisputable reality of the irregularities confirms the theory and not the other way about.

all the scientific work, the Relativity Theory does now.

What is true in the foregoing example as to the relation between scientific theory on the one hand and observation of macroscopic events on the other, is true in all cases. The reality or existential quality of what is observed in the experiment proves (or disproves) the validity of the theory; the theory does not and cannot confer reality or existential quality on what is observed. And what scientific theory has no power to confer, it naturally has no power to take away. The methods of scientific experimental practice unequivocally and definitively prove that all qualities are *in science and for science of equal reality*.

If scientific theory has no power to confer reality or existential quality on what is observed, still less—if the concept "less than nothing" be granted feasible for the moment—still less has scientific theory the power to confer reality or existential quality upon what is (presumably) *inferred* from the theory. One example should be sufficient. There was a time, and not so long ago, when all scientists firmly (even unshakably) believed in the existence of the ether *because* they believed its existence was not only a proper but a necessary inference from scientific theory then extant. To follow Whitehead's statement of the case: the wave theory of light, Clerk Maxwell's formulae for stresses in the ether, his equations of the electromagnetic field, his identification of light with electromagnetic waves—these major four conspired to give "concurrent testimony to its [the ether's] existence." Nevertheless, as was subsequently shown, the ether and its existence were not the consequences of weighty and legitimate scientific inference but were, in Whitehead's admirable phrase, "merely the outcome of metaphysical craving." * If the same may not yet be said of the current

* *The Principles of Natural Knowledge,* pp. 20 and 25.

belief in the existence of atoms, in the precise form in which atoms figure in contemporary scientific discourse, at least the same may be reasonably suspected as probably being the case. It is quite proper, therefore, to reserve one's complete agreement with Bridgman for some future, unspecifiable date, when he writes: "It is one of the most fascinating things in physics to trace the accumulation of independent new physical information all pointing to the atom, until now we are as convinced of its physical reality as of our hands and feet."* It may well so happen that the fascination, rather than warranted scientific evidence and reasons, will, in the future, be held accountable for the experience of conviction Bridgman and his peers now enjoy.

How, then, did the false and scientifically untenable distinction between qualities (with respect to their reality) gain entrance into science, and once inside, what has spuriously perpetuated its residence there? Or, if you like, how were scientists made inveterate victims of "metaphysical craving?" The only answer ever proposed that satisfies all the facts to be explained is Dewey's analysis of Greek doctrine and his exposition of the peculiar way in which it has operated in modern times.

The Greek doctrine that scientific knowledge is knowledge of eternal and immutable Reality consistently functioned to make it inconceivable for the Greeks that the world of change could be scientifically studied and known. They wrote out their own prescription for science and their scientific activities were conducted in accordance with the directions they themselves prescribed. Conse-

* *The Logic of Modern Physics,* p. 59. On the same page Bridgman says the atom "is evidently a construct." Hands and feet *may* be "constructs" (whether they are or not Bridgman does not tell), but they are not "evidently" so or if so at least evidently *not* in the same sense.

quently, though their science was restricted in fundamental character, and by our standards was hardly science at all,* they did not get into the muddle of contradictions, confusions and absurdities which has mired modern
thought.

Modern scientists, however, began by taking precisely
the world of change as their subject for scientific study,
and to help them on their way, they introduced the
method of experimentation which is no less and no other
than a method whereby the natural changes going on can
be further increased and complicated in manifold ways
by changes deliberately made. From the Greek point of
view (and in this case, *not* excepting any Greek), this is
confounding confusion, science gone insane. But as events
have fully demonstrated, it is science really come to its
senses, and intelligence come into its own.

Unfortunately, in one crucially important respect modern scientists did not display anywhere near the intelligence the Greeks did. Instead of writing out a new prescription for science, one in accordance with their own
new scientific practice, the moderns carried along the old
Greek formula as self-evidently sacrosanct. To this one
failure, to this original sin against intelligence, can be
traced the generation of all our severest, purely intellectual ills. Since the moderns did not follow the directions
prescribed by the Greek formula either as to which subject-matter could and should be scientifically studied and
which not, or as to the method to be employed in scientific

---

* Einstein and Whitehead for instance, agree with Dewey (independently, of course) that Greek science was hardly science as
we understand it now. Einstein (as far as I know) is more sweeping than Whitehead who at least excepts Aristotle (the biologist)
and Archimedes and an unnamed number of astronomers from his
statement that the work of the Greeks "was excellent; it was genius. . . . But it was not science as we understand it." (*Science
and the Modern World*, p. 10).

investigation, the only way the moderns could possibly use the formula was by applying it *ex post facto,* by giving it a reverse english. The prescription says: only the eternal and immutable Reality (or Being) can be scientifically studied and known. The moderns perforce had to read this backwards so as to make it retroactively mean: whatever we scientifically know is *ipso facto* eternal and immutable Reality. Do we know, scientifically, the shapes and sizes and motions of things? We do. Hence these are constituents of ultimate Reality, eternal and immutable. Do colors and sounds, etc., form part of our body of scientific knowledge? They do not. Hence they are not constituents of ultimate, eternal and immutable Reality. Of course the prescription was not exhausted by this one application. It could be and was re-applied every time science changed, whether by expansion or revision, so that at different periods in the history of modern science different things have been the ultimate constituents of eternal and immutable "scientific" Reality: sizes and shapes and motions and atoms and phlogiston and waves and ether and quanta and rays and—that last infirmity of all eternal and immutable "Scientific Reality"—Eddingtonian pointer-readings on measuring-machines planned by human ingenuity and made by human hands!

The voluminous discussion of Eddington's pointer-readings has obscured rather than revealed his more important representative or symbolic significance. It is too often and too widely taken for granted that contemporary scientists, because they have wave mechanics and relativity theories, therefore must, in their basic theoretical orientation, be a breed far removed from their more simple-minded and scientifically unsophisticated modern classical forbears like Galileo and Newton. Such is far from being the case, and Eddington is unhappily the best proof of the distance. "Our chief reason," writes Russell, "for not regarding a wave as a physical object seems to be that it is not indestructible." Since science simply must have something indestructible, something eternal and immutable, consequently, as Russell goes on to say, "We seem *driven* to the view advocated by Eddington, that there are certain invariants [i.e. "mathematical invariants resulting from our formula for interval"] and that (with some degree of inaccuracy) our senses and our common sense have singled them out *as deserving names.*" * Shades of Plato and Galileo? Yes! But also, alas! for Galileo (though not for Plato). What Eddington and Russell (at that time) consider as deserving *names* are not secondary qualities but such *primary* things of science as (among others) energy and mass! The primacy of "mathematical invariants" originally served Eddington as basis for his Idealism. Later on, pointer-readings partially, but not wholly, superseded mathematical invariants and in consequence his Religious Mysticism partially, but not wholly, superseded his Idealism. This progress—or more accurately said—this progression is in a fairly natural line and as straight as can be expected in the circumstances.† Russell's own "line of progression" which is neither straight nor single will be considered further on.

Philosophers too were all the time in possession of the same Greek formula and were not outdone by the scientists in assiduity and virtuosity in using it. If modern philosophers have frequently lagged behind the scientists it is because they have had to wait until scientists from time to time decided what they were going to include as constituents of ultimate Scientific Reality and what they

* *Analysis of Matter* (1927), pp. 82-83; italics mine.
† For a meticulous and merciless expose of the philosophic pretensions of Eddington, Jeans *et. al.*, see L. S. Stebbing, *Philosophy and the Physicists* (Methuen, 1937).

were going to eject or discard therefrom; for it is out of the changing discards of scientists that philosophers in one way or another have had principally to build up and fill up their systems of Metaphysical Reality. As all-inclusive ideological receptacles of Ultimate Reality, scientists have used in various combinations Space, Time and Matter, and the so-called "materialistic" philosophers have followed them with simple devotion;* while "idealistic" philosophers, for corresponding purposes have, in various combinations, used Sensation, Perception, Consciousness, Idea and Mind. The straddling or half-and-half philosophers—who are in the vast majority—have had one in-

---

* One of the more bizarre of the absurdities now being given wide currency is that Communism is the source of Materialism, if not really identical with it. Whereas of course the illustrious fathers and founders of Materialistic Philosophy are none other than Galileo, Descartes and Newton. As for the differences between the Newtonian and Marxian varieties of Materialism they unquestionably redound to the favor of the latter. For Newtonian materialism, apart from its appalling intellectual poverty, is such a childishly dreary mechanical affair—an unimaginative push-and-pull business. But the Marxian Materialism goes along in ever more novel ways, developing itself and the universe (at the same time) in accordance with the magical antics of the Hegelian Idealistic dialectics secreted in its vitals. Whatever one may think of the philosophical value of Idealistic Magic (even when seemingly covered up with materialistic sober-sense), every fair mind must admit that the Magic does confer on the philosophy appropriating it the semblance if not the substance of organismic character. And almost any organismic philosophy, no matter how bad, is better than any mechanical philosophy no matter how good.

A cognate absurdity, and no less bizarre, sedulously being cultivated by the same people, in the same quarters and for the same ends, is that only Marx (or only a "materialist" like Marx) could believe and teach that "religion is the opium of the masses." This report is the product of nothing but ignorance and superstition, or if not of these two, then of something much worse: malice aforethought. For so high-minded and genuinely "idealistic" a thinker as John Ruskin believed and taught precisely the same thing: "Our national religion," says Ruskin in *Sesame and Lilies,* "is the performance of church ceremonies and preaching of soporific truths (or untruths) to keep the mob quietly at work, while we amuse ourselves."

tellectual foot precariously poised on Matter and the other precariously poised on Mind, their systems precariously swaying over the yawning gulf between.

With the impartiality possible only to theory purely and completely disconnected from actuality, the Greek formula has worked, in all cases and in all respects, for scientists and philosophers alike. When read backwards and applied *ex post facto*, it obligingly confers all highest "scientific" or "metaphysical" blessings if, when and as desired. It works with endless perfection, like a syllogism—indeed like a charm.

VIII

Philosophy, whatever else it may be, is an enterprise of thought. Whether a philosopher's reasons are good or bad, really reasons or only rationalizations is as the case may be—and *what* it may be in any given case is itself discoverable only by using a method or process involving reasoning. To *establish* that it is the one or the other we must establish the *reasons* for *that* determination. Philosophy, James somewhere said, is an obstinate attempt to think clearly. If in the works of philosophers the obstinacy is sometimes more pronounced than the clarity, well, that is just additional evidence (if such be needed) that philosophers are human beings and that philosophy is not a Transcendental unveilment of Preëmbodied Thought, Eternal and Immutable, but is a thoroughly human *enterprise,* an *historical* activity, and like all human historical activities, consequently displays the temporal powers and deficiencies of person, period and place.

Dewey is indefatigable in criticism of ancient classical philosophy. If repeating in one's own works what the ancients wrote in theirs makes one a classicist, then Dewey certainly isn't one. But if *doing* for and with the cultural material of one's own epoch what the classicals *did* for and with theirs makes one a classicist, then of all modern and contemporary philosophers Dewey has the best claim to the title. For what did Plato and Aristotle— considering their work from the fundamental standpoint of philosophic method—what did they *do?* They analyzed and evaluated the science of their time, and in terms of their analyses and evaluations constructed their philosophies, their theories of knowledge, mind and nature. About this there can be no sensible doubt. It is serially written on almost every page of Plato's *Dialogues* and it is the undebatable purpose of Aristotle's logic: the five books of the *Organon* systematically bring together, codify and amplify the series of principles, methods and rules the *Academy* and the *Lyceum* found in and developed out of the Greek sciences. Of course the philosophies of Plato and Aristotle are not the same as the sciences of that period. Philosophy is not identical with science. But the *reasons* and *methods* of reasoning, in Plato and Aristotle, are in part a direct transcription and in part a development and adaptation for the usages of philosophy, of the reasons and the methods of reasoning exemplified in ancient mathematics primarily and ancient medicine very secondarily.

Now Dewey's whole philosophic effort is concerned with doing for our epoch what the classicals did for theirs. Just as they took *their* science as exemplar of what knowledge is, and the *method* of their science as standard of the *method of knowing,* so Dewey takes *modern* science as exemplar of what knowledge is, and the *method* of *modern* science as standard of the *method of knowing.* But of course there is one great difference between Dewey and his classical forbears. They could approach most if not all their philosophic problems and "attack them" to quote

James "as if there were no official answer preoccupying the field." *That* is an advantage no subsequent philosopher has ever been able to enjoy. After more than two millennia, Plato and Aristotle still preoccupy the philosophic field, and never so securely and completely as when unofficially.

Experimentalism is one of the two basic terms Dewey has used to designate his philosophy. The other is *instrumentalism*. The latter designation was the one first used, and though it has never been discarded or disavowed, it has, in recent years, been allowed to recede into secondary place. And that is where it rightfully or logically belongs because the basis of Dewey's constructive philosophy is his analysis and evaluation of experiment. The primary designation of Dewey's whole philosophy *is* experimentalism because its foundation is his *philosophy of the experiment*.

That the method of experimentation is the very essence of the method of modern science is the flesh and blood (not the bone) over which Dewey's whole philosophy contends. Grant that Dewey's analysis of scientific experimentation is in its principal contentions sound and valid and you will have to grant that pretty much everything else fundamental in his philosophy is sound and valid. Deny the general validity of his claim concerning the place and function of experimentation in scientific method and then, no matter how much else of his philosophy you may like and accept, it will be a liking and accepting of thises and thats. Which of course is the thing to do—if you are interested in doing that sort of thing. But to pick an idea up here and another down there and to bundle the disconnected pickings together with heterogeneous pieces of memorial string is *not* understanding a philosophy—whatever else it may be.

I do not of course mean that a philosophy *is* a philoso‧ phy only when everything in it is flawlessly interrelated or hangs perfectly together (and therefore can only be understood when understood this way). Still less do I mean that a philosophy *is* a philosophy only when it has a stated principle or set of principles from which every‧ thing else in it "deductively" comes down with the flow‧ ing inevitability of logical precision. As for the first, no philosophy ever written has been without errors, slips, gaps, obscurities, confusions, vaguenesses, mistakes, con‧ tradictions and other insufficiencies of one logical sort and another. And as for the second, it is seven parts myth and three parts folly to believe there is any system (philo‧ sophic, scientific or mathematical) that has, to‧start with, just so many axioms, so many postulates, so many defi‧ nitions, and has, to end up with, just so many theorems— the latter "deduced" from the former by logical squeeze. What I do mean is this: every philosophy, if it is a phi‧ losophy to be taken seriously at all, has some vital or‧ gans and they, on the contents in the philosopher's system, perform functions very much like those performed on the contents of his body by its vital organs. And, naturally there are all sorts of malcoördinations, imbalances and waste products in both cases.

The fact that every great philosophy has some vital‧ izing and organizing center has of course nothing to do with determining whether the philosophy is *of* the or‧ ganism (an "organismic philosophy") or *of* the mecha‧ nism (a "mechanistic philosophy"). A philosophy of the mechanism can be very vitally organic in the sense we here mean, and a philosophy of the organism can be quite fatally mechanical—just as there can be a living skeletol‧ ogy and a dead sociology.

From one point of view, it must undoubtedly seem that

the issue concerning the place and function of experimentation in modern science is one that could be settled very easily. To determine what Greek scientists did we are reduced to the extremity of laboriously excogitating a few fragmentary records, and about such there can always be endless dispute. But to find out what modern scientists do, why that should be simple, indeed a cinch. There are hundreds, even thousands of scientists contemporaneously about and they do the same sort of scientific thing their modern forbears did—only better. To settle the issue, then, all philosophers need do is make a field trip to scientific laboratories and, if they don't understand anything they see the scientists doing, the scientists are there and if you ask them they will tell. If it were as simple as this, simple indeed would the settlement be. But, alas, it is far from being so simple. For one thing to get philosophers to make the field trips would itself be a difficult and complicated business. If they were willing and ready to do *that,* then perhaps half the battle would be over. And for another thing, even if you got them to go, the chances are too great that they *would* ask the scientists what they didn't know and, forgetting all about Einstein's advice, *would* listen to what they were told.

It is impossible to settle the *philosophic* issue over experimentation simply by visiting the laboratories because philosophers, like other mortals (scientists included), understand what they see as they have been accustomed to see and understand. Philosophers are *acquainted* with the fact that scientists have laboratories and make experiments, as well acquainted with this fact as are the scientists themselves. But acquaintance, like familiarity, breeds contempt rather than understanding. To understand the *meaning* of experimentation it is first of all necessary to get rid of an inherited set of philosophic ideas, to overcome the *set* those ideas have given to philosophic thinking.

The operation of the Greek formula which has dominated the interpretation of modern scientific inquiry has also, and to the same extent, quite naturally dominated the interpretation of the *method* of modern scientific inquiry. It is obvious why and how: a theory which holds that the objects of scientific knowledge are eternal and immutable constituents 'of Ultimate Reality must also hold that no procedure that is itself not conversant with eternality and immutability can possibly be an *integral* part of the *method* of science. A fixed habit of thinking, like any fixed habit of doing, maintains its own procedure by excluding all others. And a system of ideas or method of interpretation that has become traditional *is a social habit* and not a "purely intellectual" system. Wherefore the strange "intellectual" behavior, with respect to experimentation, that marks the great tradition in modern philosophy and also the philosophies of contemporaries—experimentalism excepted.

Whitehead and Russell are the two greatest of Dewey's contemporaries and their philosophies are, in general range, as comprehensive as his. Furthermore, just as Dewey's philosophy is fundamentally derivative from his analysis of scientific method, so their philosophies are derivative from their analyses of the same. There is therefore a genuine basis for comparatively studying these three philosophies. The method of contrast and comparison is particularly valuable in an introductory enterprise. By taking these three philosophies together we shall be able to see more clearly than any other way what are the fundamental issues involved and what are the main methodological consequences that result for philosophy from making practical experimentation an integral part of the procedure of scientific method.

Of course one doesn't have to be Dewey or a Deweyan to recognize that, as a matter of indisputable fact, experimentation has had *something* to do with the advance of modern science. This is one of those "stubborn facts" —to use James' phrase—that cannot be denied, though like everything else it can be minimized or ignored. And contemporary philosophers do persistently minimize and then ignore experimentation in science,* even when, as not too frequently happens, they *seem* intent on doing otherwise. Thus, for instance, Whitehead:

> The reason why we are on a higher imaginative level is not because we have finer imaginations, but because we have better instruments. In science, the most important thing that has happened during the last forty years is the advance in instrumental design. This advance is partly due to a few men of genius such as Michelson and the German opticians. It is also due to the progress of technological processes of manufacture, particularly in the region of metallurgy. The designer has now at his disposal a variety of material of differing physical properties. . . . These instruments have put thought onto a new level. A fresh instrument serves the same purpose as foreign travel; it shows things in unusual combinations. *The gain is more than an addition; it is a transformation.* (*Science and the Modern World* [1925], pp. 166-167; italics mine.)

Coming from a philosopher who is, by reputation and in fact, free of the double taint of experimentalism and instrumentalism, the above tribute is handsome, and taken by itself as tribute, is as handsome as any experimentalist-instrumentalist could pay. But philosophy is not a rhetorical enterprise of paying tributes—as no one knows better than Whitehead. It is a critical and evaluative enterprise

* Science, hereinafter, means "modern science" unless otherwise qualified.

of thought. This being the case, and it also being the case
that recent experimentation has contributed not merely to
the gross technological progress of science but to the development and uplifting of that finest and purest aspect of
science, as of human experience, namely, its "imaginative
thought," should not the analysis and evaluation of experimentation be a proper and significant part of the philosophic task? Are not the *implications* of the statement
quoted as deserving of Whitehead's careful and faithful
exploration as any other of comparable importance—for
surely the uplifting of thought to a higher imaginative
level is *very* important? And these questions are particularly relevant in Whitehead's case for he and not another
wrote four years after the above citation:

> Whatever is found in 'practice' must lie within the
> scope of the metaphysical description. When the de-
> scription fails to include the 'practice', the metaphysics
> is inadequate and requires revision. There can be no
> appeal to practice to supplement metaphysics, so long
> as we remain contented with our metaphysical doc-
> trines. Metaphysics is *nothing but* the description of the
> generalities which *apply to all the details of* practice.
> (*Process and Reality*—An Essay in Cosmology [1929]
> p. 19; italics mine.)

That experimentation *is* the 'practice' of science is certainly not something for which we need argue. Moreover,
since the 'practice' of science at least sometimes exerts a
decisive, transformative influence upon the 'theory' of
science there are *two* reasons (and both mandatory, one
should think) for including experimentation within one's
metaphysical scope. For "in one sense Science and Philosophy are merely different aspects of one great enterprise of the human mind." * But despite his own doctrines
metaphysically general, and his own observations scien-

* *Adventures of Ideas* (1933), p. 179.

tifically particular, Whitehead most definitely believes otherwise—when it is the 'practice' of experimentation that is at issue. His conclusive (and comprehensive) staccato word on the subject is this: "Discussions on the method of science *wander off* onto the topic of experiment. But experiment is *nothing else* than a mode of cooking the facts for the sake of exemplifying the law." * To damn with faint praise is an old established custom, in philosophy and out; but to dismiss, as beneath consideration, *after* making acknowledgments for extraordinary services rendered is rather new—in philosophy at least!

Certainly Michelson's genius and experiments, the work of the German opticians, the perfected processes of metallurgical manufacture, are constituent and contributory bases of the theoretical scientific achievements of the past forty years and more. But to select these instances of contributions made by experiments and instruments to the development of scientific theory, *as if they were*

---

* *Adventures of Ideas* p. 111; italics mine. "Conclusive and comprehensive" not merely because in the last volume of his philosophic 'trilogy.' The *Preface* states that "the three books—*Science and the Modern World, Process and Reality, Adventures of Ideas* —are an endeavor to express a way of understanding things . . . each book can be read separately; but they supplement each other's omissions and compressions." However it may be in other respects, the Indexes to all three books concur in *omitting* the term experiment or any of its linguistic derivatives. This is not due to systematic carelessness but is indicative of Whitehead's estimation of experimentation as of negligible philosophic import. Experiment finds no place in *any* of Whitehead's philosophical books. Neither is the term experiment or any of its derivatives philosophic enough or relevant enough for discussions of the nature of science to find a place in the Indexes of: Russell's *Our Knowledge of the External World* (1914), *The Analysis of Mind* (1921), *Philosophy* (1927), *The Analysis of Matter* (1927); Broad's *Scientific Thought* (1923), Eddington's *The Nature of the Physical World* (1928); and, to come down to the positively logical revelation of the nature of science Carnap's *The Logical Syntax of Language* (1937). These Indexes no more than Whitehead's are systematically careless; they are carefully and selectively philosophical as the reader can find out by reading the books.

unique and isolated cases, is not only to be historically in-accurate but—what is much worse—to be philosophically, logically, metaphysically, cosmologically and scientifically unsound. Without historical antecedents, it will be granted, the existential *occurrence* of the experiments and instruments would be sheerly miraculous. But it is surely also as clear that were the birth of the instruments and experiments never so normal and natural, their contribution to the development of theoretical science—their raising of the level of imaginative thought—would be a sheer case of miraculous *intervention* (levitation, if you can pardon a pun) *unless* they were elements *integrally functioning in the methodology* of science. Miracle for miracle —occurrence or intervention—the one is as bad as, if not worse than, the other.

When Whitehead says: "Michelson's experiment could not have been made earlier than it was. It required the general advance in technology and Michelson's experimental genius," he avoids making the occurrence of the experiment a miraculous event. But he does nothing to relieve the miraculous quality of its consequences or effects. Indeed, he is forced, will-he, nill-he, to leave it as miraculous—forced because he isolates the past forty years' experimentation, because his tribute is nothing more than a tribute, of the character of a ceremonial compliment which, having been paid, he can then pass on to really serious things. That Whitehead does isolate recent experimentation (with respect to its "intervention"), does take it out of historical continuity and technical continuity in the development of the *method* of science is most clearly and briefly revealed in his statement concerning Galileo in the paragraph immediately preceding the last quotation:

Galileo dropped heavy bodies from the top of the leaning Tower of Pisa, and demonstrated that bodies of different weights, if released simultaneously, would reach the earth together. So far as experimental skill, and delicacy of apparatus were concerned, this experiment could have been made at any time within the preceding five thousand years. The *ideas involved merely* concerned weight and speed of travel, ideas which are familiar in ordinary life. The whole set of ideas might have been familiar to the family of King Minos of Crete, as they dropped pebbles into the sea from high battlements rising from the shore.*

Now it is simply not the case that in Galileo's experiment (taking the Pisa experiment to be his), "the ideas involved merely concerned weight and speed of travel which are familiar in ordinary life"—(though what is *merely* about such ideas, even if the experiment was merely about them is surely strange to tell; as strange as it would be to tell what is *merely* about the measurement of the velocity of light, or the *measurement* of anything.) Any more than the apocryphal Newtonian experiment involved ideas *merely* concerned with the falling of an apple on a human head—though the occurrence of falling apples *is* very familiar in ordinary life, something that obviously cannot be said even for the mere existential *occurrence* of light and heavy bodies falling at different rates. Galileo's Pisa experiment involved the fundamental ideas of Aristotelian physics and cosmology, and though familiar at that time to some, they were not of ordinary life. That the earth was the fixed center of the physical universe was then familiarly believed; but that the earth is "the *end* of motion for those things which are heavy,

* *Science and the Modern World,* pp. 167-168; italics mine. Scholarship since Whitehead wrote the above has pretty conclusively determined that Galileo didn't perform the Pisa experiment. But whether he did or not is of purely antiquarian interest. For if he didn't drop weights from the Tower of Pisa, he did roll balls down an inclined plane and did many other experimental things.

and the celestial spheres . . . the *end* of motion for those things whose natures lead them upwards" * are *not* ideas which ordinary life casts up in the routine course of the day. This teleological cosmology—the "rational" basis for the Aristotelian dogma that heavy and light bodies fall at different rates—required for its working out and logical perfecting the whole great line of Greek thinkers which Aristotle closed. And what Galileo's Pisa experiment did was to destroy the Aristotelian cosmology and physics and lay the foundations for the new physics and the new cosmology.†

Russell, who sometimes has more, and sometimes less but at no time any serious philosophic (or logical) use for the topic of experiment, has nevertheless, with his usual clarity, summarized the case for the Pisa experiment:

> Before Galileo, people believed themselves possessed of immense knowledge on all the most interesting questions in physics. He established certain facts as to the way in which bodies fall, *not very interesting on their own account, but of quite immeasurable interest as examples* of real knowledge and of a *new method* whose future fruitfulness he himself divined. But his few facts sufficed to destroy the whole vast system of supposed knowledge handed down from Aristotle, as even the palest morning sun suffices to extinguish the stars. (*Our Knowledge of the External World*, p. 240; italics mine.)

Making an experiment or fashioning an instrument may well be likened to foreign travel. But it is a commonplace

---

* *Ib.*, p. 11; italics mine.

† The falling of the apple is an apocryphal experiment but it popularly (and not too inaccurately) symbolizes Newton's scientific achievement as summed up in his Law of Gravitation. Similarly the Pisa experiment symbolizes Galileo's scientific work. Good scholarship is good, I know, but a good symbol is oftentimes better —of course when it does *not deny but reveals* the *meanings* disclosed by good scholarship.

that foreign travel is not even additive, let alone transformative, but vulgarly agglutinative *unless* the traveler, before his travels, has *learnt how* to make his ordinary, every day, common doings, *experiences* of value. Education, like so much else, if it does not begin at home, does not continue abroad. And the Pisa experiment very accurately symbolizes the period and the process of homely *learning how* modern scientific man had to first go through to make himself ready and to equip himself for the continuation of his education in ever new foreign parts unknown.

The family of King Minos or, for that matter, the families of cliff-dwellers could have dropped pebbles and the like, and most probably did—the cliff-dwellers at any rate. They could also have noted the weights of the pebbles, watched their speed of fall, and observed whether or not they landed together. They had the pebbles and cliffs, the hands to heft and the eyes to see. They had the equipment or apparatus necessary. But whatever ideas these doings could have involved for them, they could *not* have involved the ideas of the Pisa performance. For the Pisa event was not just a dropping or letting things fall. Nor was it just an observing of what took place or happened when they did fall. It was a deliberate, not a casual act; and it was deliberate, furthermore, not in the general sense that Galileo didn't act impulsively, on the spur of the moment, but had "thought about it" first; the act was deliberate in the *scientific* sense of being performed with a view to fulfilling an intellectual end: it was a dropping or letting fall of different weights for the purpose of *testing a set of ideas*. Because the Pisa performance *carried within itself* this scientific end-in-view, the two different weights could, as they fell, carry the Aristotelian physics and cosmology down with them; and could, when they touched ground, cause a new physics and cosmology to arise.

The Pisa performance was even more than *an* experiment: it was the introduction and establishment of the new *method* of experimentation. Pisa, as a symbol in the history of thought, marks the death of Aristotelianized medievalism and celebrates the birth of intelligence in the modern world.

IX

"The work of Galileo was not a development, but a revolution." * Like all revolutions it *started* something which led to further developments. Hence it is true to say, as does Russell, that Galileo's few facts sufficed *to destroy* the whole vast system of Aristotelian knowledge *if* you take the statement, not literally, but proleptically, *and if* you take "the few facts" to mean the new *method* of inquiry Galileo established (of which new method the few facts were the then result). And by taking the statement proleptically, I mean taking it that way *today*: after some three hundred years of continuous use and development, the new method of scientific inquiry has succeeded in finally destroying Aristotelianism in the technical fields of the most important natural sciences; but Aristotelianism (including the Platonism it both supports and is supported by) is very much alive and kicking in our current culture generally and in our social "sciences," philosophies and logics in particular.

Why is it that in the technical fields of science, the revolution in *method* initiated by Galileo has already been substantially completed, has, in our time, carried through its last fundamental reform, whereas in other fields, including fields as intellectual as philosophy and logic, the

* *Infra,* p. 324.

revolution is just about now seriously getting under way?
The easy answer is to invoke a distinction between "natural" sciences and "social" sciences—leaving it up to
philosophy and logic to "crash" into the one class or the
other or stay out on the limb. This answer is easy, if not
very neat; but it is just too easy to make any *explanatory*
sense. The "distinction" simply repeats, as an explanation,
the fact to be explained. It is the "logic of explanation"
of ancient and medieval vintage working over their time:
opium puts to sleep *because* of its dormative power; there
is a difference in the development of scientific investigation of the natural and the social *because* the former is
"natural" and the latter "social."

The backwardness of philosophy, logic and all social
inquiries does not explain the *forwardness* of the natural
sciences. It simply exposes and emphasizes the need for
an explanation. De-socialize the natural sciences as much
as you like, place them, if you will, completely outside the
boundaries of human society in a realm or sphere apart,
above or below, you have not thereby answered the question the contrast raises: you have only stated it; you have
not thereby solved the problem it involves: you have only
posed it. Let it be granted, for the sake of argument, that
the natural sciences are *now* beyond the reach of influence or connection with social institutions, forces and
all that goes with the latter. It is an undeniable fact of
modern history—let alone of all human history—that
they were not *always* there.* Hence the more you conceive
the social to be retarding or inherently inimical to the
development of science, the more must the "natural" sciences have been able to overcome in reaching their present estate. In so far as the "natural" sciences are *now*

* It is also undebatable that they are not *there* always now; witness the transfer of "science" from the laboratories to the chancelleries of Germany and Italy.

distinguished and distinguishable from the "social" sciences it is a *distinction* they have achieved; it is a *result*, not a gift ("something given" or a "datum"); it is a *consequence*, not a cause. The invocation of the "distinction" between "natural" and "social" *subject-matters* to explain the differences between "natural" and "social" *sciences* doesn't even explain the differences away. It just leaves them precisely where and as it *finds* them.*

A philosophy or logic of science cannot, without being foolish, take refuge in a "distinction" in subject-matter to explain the advance of the natural sciences in modern times. And the more the "distinction" is asserted to be *in rerum natura* as a ground for the explanation the greater the folly of the philosophy or logic becomes. The evidence of Aristotelian physics is sufficient to prove this conclusively. The subject-matter (of or *in* Nature) did not change when Galileo appeared. What did change was the *method* of investigating the subject-matter. And the employment and development of that new method resulted in the consequences which we now call the "natural" sciences. If Aristotle were suddenly recalled to life, he would think our "natural" sciences most *un*natural. In fact, it is not necessary to recall Aristotle to life to get this "test." When Eddington "goes Aristotelian" (unbeknownst to himself) we have the same result. And of course Eddington is not the only one who "goes" this way. The sphere or domain of operation of the Greek formula is far more embracive.

A discussion of the obstacles in the way of employing the method initiated by Galileo in the fields of philosophy and the social sciences is not here in point. Obviously, *that*

---

* There is a reverse form of the argument criticized, which starts with the social (or economic) as omnipotent and then the "natural" sciences become a reflection or duplication of the "social." An absurdity stated in reverse is still an absurdity.

question cannot be intelligently examined and discussed until judgment has been reached as to what *is* the method that has made the natural sciences so forward. And herein precisely lies the importance of the analysis of method in the physical sciences for the philosopher—for the philosopher, at any rate, of Dewey's sort. For Dewey, the "natural" (or physical) is not a realm disconnected and set apart from the "social" (or mental). There is not, for him, an abyss between the two. *If* there were an abyss, then the business of the philosopher would be to stay on his side of it—on whichever side he decided a philosopher belonged. And if, defying the impossible, he chose *both* sides and persisted in flitting across the abyss, to and fro, one could of course admire him for his miraculous versatility, but one could not learn anything from him, any time he came across from the "other" side. For though he, being a miraculous philosopher, could flit across the abyss, the abyss being *in Nature,* would absolutely prevent the transportation of goods.

Because Dewey does not believe there is an abyss between the 'natural' and the 'social' the study of the method of investigation employed in the so-called natural sciences is of primary philosophic concern. For *there* the method has been most consistently employed, most carefully and successfully developed, has resulted in the most important body of *tested* knowledge we possess. To study the *method* there is, consequently, the best place to study it. And since there is no abyss between the 'natural' and the 'social' it is not only possible, but certain, that *some* of the goods can be transported. And they need not be transportable bodily—like furniture in a van—to fulfill the necessary conditions of valuable transportation.

When a "distinction" in subject-matter between the "natural" (physical) and "social" (mental) is used as *ground* for explaining the differences between the "natural" (physical) and "social" (mental) sciences, the "distinction," if it does not start out as a variant term for "separation," is forced to grow into an assertion of an abysmal separation in order to maintain itself. And when the so-called natural sciences are separated from the social, are taken out of their context in human history, and out of relation to human activity, then an adequate and satisfactory explanation of the natural sciences themselves becomes impossible.

X

There are certain "gross or macroscopic" features, characteristic of scientific history from Galileo and Newton to Michelson and Einstein about which there is no serious disagreement.

All, for example, agree that science is in constant process of change. When this comprehensive feature is examined more closely or finely it is also universally agreed that the changes are continuous but irregular: that sometimes they succeed each other more rapidly, sometimes more slowly; sometimes they are more pronounced in one scientific area, sometimes in another; sometimes they are fundamental—having to do with the foundations of science—and sometimes they are, not trivial, but concerned with details.

It is agreed also that changes in science, as overtly displayed in its history, are roughly of two general kinds: changes of addition or expansion; and changes of substraction or correction (revision). And it is also agreed that these two kinds are not separate and distinct, having nothing to do with each other, but are related and interactive: sometimes the addition of new scientific knowledge or expansion of scientific inquiry into new areas reacts back into the old, requiring the making of corrections or revisions in the latter; sometimes it is the reverse interaction that takes place—correction or revision of old knowledge initiating or determining expansion into new fields.

It is also agreed that the corrections and expansions in science *to be scientific* must be developments proceeding or issuing from the methods of inquiry and the knowledge gained through inquiry. Any correction or expansion that is made in response to pressures exerted by non- or extra-scientific forces, or that is not submitted to the *tests* that have been developed through employment of the method of inquiry *is not science.* Keep science *in* its context of other human enterprises, and what this means is perfectly clear. It means that certain methods, rules, principles, standards have been developed by human beings and that these *define* science. There is no area or subject-matter that is inherently or "by Nature" non- or extra-scientific. But for any item of knowledge involving any subject-matter or area to be an item of *scientific* knowledge, *that item* must go through the processes and pass the tests that have themselves been tested and established through prior inquiries and that *define* what science is.

The integrity of science is *not* preserved, any more than it is established, by giving it an "autonomy" that separates it and makes it "independent" of human activity. It is not preserved—because science is changing, both in items of knowledge and in details of its methods. The methods are being developed, the tests are made more rigorous, the analyses more precise. If the body of scientific knowledge, or the method of scientific inquiry, is separated from human activity, given a trans-human "autonomy," then it loses, not gains, its integrity. For then how explain the changes? But as a human activity, scientific knowledge and scientific method have the integrity and "autonomy" of any enterprise tested by methods developed in the course of human experience. Baking bread is a method of treating and preparing materials for human consumption developed out of *baking* bread. The first bakers of bread were not as expert as bakers today. Looking backwards, bakers of today may indeed not consider them to have been *really* bakers of bread at all. However that may be, bakers of bread today have their methods, standards and tests. And anything *to be* bread has to pass those tests. In this sense, baking too is "autonomous."

If baking bread is too lowly and mean an "example"— or too far removed from the realm of the scientific—consider the case of geometry. Einstein, in his lyrical moments, can write:

> She [Greece] for the first time created the intellectual miracle of a logical system, the assertions of which followed one from another with such rigor that not one of the demonstrated propositions admitted of the slightest doubt—Euclid's geometry. (*Herbert Spencer Lecture*)

Now in so far as Euclid's geometry was considered thus "miraculous" like all miracles it stopped things, didn't start them, closed the road to better understanding, didn't open it. It took geometers just about two thousand years to get over all the stultifying consequences of *that* miracle. When in the second quarter of the nineteenth century, non-Euclidean geometries began to appear, they were, by the miracle-believing mathematicians, construed as outrageous, perhaps even insane, attacks on the eternal historicity of Euclid's miracle; but as the subsequent events have shown, the non-Euclidean geometries, by exposing the miracle, liberated the geometer, and contributed greatly to further the liberation of the philosopher, logician and physicist. So that the mathematical logician can write concerning the Euclidean geometry, as does Russell:

> The rigid methods employed by modern geometers have deposed Euclid from his pinnacle of correctness. Countless errors are involved in his first eight propositions. That is to say, not only is it doubtful whether his axioms are true, which is a comparatively trivial matter, but it is certain that his propositions do not follow from the axioms which he enunciates . . . it is nothing less than a scandal that he should still be taught to boys in England. (*Mysticism and Logic,* pp. 94-95.)

It undoubtedly is a scandal that "the tedious apparatus of fallacious proofs for obvious truisms which constitutes the beginning of Euclid" (Ib. p. 62) should be taught contemporary learners when a much superior apparatus of geometry has already been developed. But in the history of man's learning geometry and the methods of rigorous mathematical proof, Euclid's geometry played its good, as well as bad part. The methods, standards and tests now employed in geometry were developed by using, among other things, Euclid's geometry as a method to be studied, revised, changed and reconstructed in terms and by means of methods which were the consequences of, or which were developed in the course of, mathematical and allied inquiries. And by the same general process, the methods and tests are being further developed almost daily. Set Euclid's geometry in a realm apart from human activity, and if correct, then its correctness is a miracle. And if not correct, as long as it is a miracle, there is no way of correcting it. Miracles do not submit to correction. For just as soon as they do they cease to be miraculous.

It would complicate matters to no good end if we tried to discuss here the way in which extra- or non-scientific, social, political or economic forces may influence *scientific* research. But one illustration may be helpful to the general point. A politician orders scientists to produce, let us say, synthetic rubber. Here, say some current thinkers, is a case of science receiving its direction (or perhaps I should say its "directive") from "politics." But where did the politician get the idea that there was a possibility of making synthetic rubber? To suppose he got that idea out of his own head is to suppose the miraculous. Also, because the politician issues an order that synthetic rubber should be made—his order does not convert the scientific possibility into a scientific actuality. To believe it does, or to argue in a manner that presupposes it does, is to believe the politician is what he wants others to believe he is— an omnipotent miracle-man. And, certainly, there is no intelligent reason for believing *that*. The *development* of science can not be *directed* by the politician, big businessman, etc., but it can be *exploited by* them—which is a totally different thing. And science can of course also be starved, strangled or killed by the politician and big businessman, by starving, strangling or killing the scientists.

That *corrections,* to be *scientific* (or what is the same thing, to be worthy of intelligent acceptance), must be made by methods developed by inquiry, and in response to needs of *test* growing out of inquiry, is also best seen when science is placed in the social context and when contrasted, for instance, with the "method of correcting" science initiated and enforced by *political* demands.*

* Heisenberg, in a lecture delivered in 1934 in Berlin, said that Michelson's experiments and Einstein's theory of relativity "belonged to the absolutely certain bases of physics." A Dr. Rosskothen (a high school teacher) heard the lecture and wrote in complaint to Reich Director Dr. Alfred Rosenberg, Commissioner appointed by the Fuhrer to supervise the Philosophical Instruction of the National Socialist (Nazi) Movement: "should such a man [Heisenberg] occupy a chair at a German university? In my opinion, he should be given the opportunity to make a thorough study of the theories of the Jews of the Einstein and Michelson type, and no doubt a concentration camp would be an appropriate spot. Also a charge of treason against people and race would not be out of place." To which on November 24, 1934, Dr. Alfred Rosen-

"Nazi science" isn't something new; it is the revival of something, alas, very old. It is as old as religion and in the Western World the Nazi "scientific" model is the Catholic Church. The Catholic Church burnt books in the public place, and since losing secular control over that place, has continued to burn them in the silent fires of the *Index*. The Church also still outrageously falsifies history; witness, for example, its marginal notations to the Old Testament. The Church also coerced scientists into keeping quiet, and sometimes even succeeded in getting them to recant, witness, for example, the case of Galileo. But no scientist (or any person of intelligence) accepts Galileo's *recantation* as science. *That's* the difference.

berg, through his Staff Director, replied: "The Reich Director of the N.S.D.A.P., Commissioner appointed by the Leader to Supervise the Philosophical Instruction of the National Socialist Movement, states in answer to your communication that he shares your opinion in principle. He has taken steps to draw the attention of Professor Heisenberg to the reprehensible passages in his speech, and made clear to him, in the form of a reprimand, that he must refrain from remarks of this nature, which have to be regarded as an insult to the Movement. Unfortunately, in view of foreign opinion, it is not possible to administer a sharper reproof to Professor Heisenberg or, which would certainly be desirable, to dismiss him." (Quoted in *The Yellow Spot,* a collection of facts and documents relating to three years' persecution of German Jews, with an Introduction by The Bishop of Durham. Knight Publications, New York, 1936.) According to Dr. Rosenberg, the unique contributions of the "culture-creating" Nordic blood—of which Nazi blood is the highest culmination—the unique contributions of this blood are "the ideals of honor and spiritual freedom." What these Nazi "ideals" mean with respect to science, Dr. Rust, Reich Minister of Education, made clear on June 30, 1936 when, on the occasion of the 550th anniversary of Heidelberg he proclaimed: "The old idea of science based on the sovereign right of abstract intellectual activity has gone forever" [*sc.* "in Germany"]. And what Dr. Rust meant is completely clarified by *Deutsche Justiz:* publication of the German Ministry of Justice: "A handful of force is better than a sackful of justice." Most appropriately, before the Heidelberg Nazi celebration, the inscription "To the Living Spirit" was replaced by "To the German Spirit"; and the statue of Athena, Goddess of Wisdom, replaced by the German Eagle. The Nazis did what *they* could so that there may not be any Nazi-discordant note—and then some Harvard professors had to go there and accept "honorary degrees"!

XI

To recapitulate the macroscopic features about which there is complete agreement, or at any rate, no serious disagreement among philosophers: Science is in constant process of change; the changes are not hit-and-miss, helter-skelter, sporadic innovations, interruptive and disconnected shifts from one position to another, but are changes consequent upon employing methods of inquiry, and to some extent always issue out of knowledge antecedently achieved and to the rest of the extent are new acquisitions which in turn, and to some extent, lead back into prior knowledge, both of content and method; the changes are determined by needs and established by methods of test developed by and in the process of inquiry; the events or changes of science are not a mere chronological succession but constitute an interconnected series indisputably exemplifying the characteristics of growth or development. In sum: the series of changes in science, from Galileo to Einstein, exhibit the continuity of a self-expanding and self-correcting *history*.

Up to this point agreement. But when you take the next step and assert that a philosophy or logic of science must be competent to explain (or account for) this *history*, must be able to give the reasons for its continuity and direction of development—all except Dewey and Deweyan experimentalists balk. No! they say. The history of science is one thing, and the nature of science is another. Science has a history, but it is not a history. Science is a *system*. And they mean by system a mathematical-logical system: so many axioms, so many postulates, so many definitions, so many theorems, all tied with inevitable deductibility together by so many principles (which latter may or may not also be in the system). Thus, for instance, Russell:

There are three kinds of questions which we may ask concerning physics or, indeed, concerning any science. The first is: What is its logical structure, considered as a deductive system? What ways exist of defining the entities of physics and deducing the propositions from an initial apparatus of entities and propositions? This is a problem in pure mathematics, for which, in its fundamental portions mathematical logic is the proper instrument. (*The Analysis of Matter*, 1927, pp. 1-2.)

Now when you take this to be the first or primary question, the second question is bound to be one you can never answer—unless a series of contradictions be considered an answer. The second question is:

. . . the application of physics to the empirical world. This is, of course, the vital problem: although physics *can be pursued as pure mathematics*, it is not as pure mathematics that physics is important. What is to be said about the logical analysis of physics is therefore only a *necessary preliminary* to our main theme. The laws of physics are believed to be at least approximately true, although they are *not logically necessary;* the *evidence* for them is empirical. All empirical evidence consists, in the last analysis, of *perceptions;* thus the *world of physics must be*, in some sense, *continuous* with the *world of our perceptions*, since it is the latter which *supplies* the *evidence* for the *laws* of physics. (L.c.p.6; italics mine.)

By "application of physics to the empirical world" Russell does not of course mean "application" in the vulgar sense of "applied science"—making machines, telegraphy, radio, airplanes and so on. He means, in what sense, or to what degree can the mathematical-logical system of "physics" be said to be *about* the empirical world. Having *first* pursued physics, as pure mathematics (and the purity of mathematics *is* its *logical, non*-empirical nature) the question as to how physics is *connected* with the empirical world necessarily becomes a *problem*. But if physics *can* be pursued as pure mathematics, then in what sense can it be true that the laws of physics are *not* logically necessary—since pure mathematics *is* pure logic (or vice versa) and the mathematical necessity of the one is the logical necessity of the other (or vice versa)? To say "it is not as pure mathematics that physics is *important*" is to misstate and confuse the case he propounds. For, obviously, it is not as pure mathematics that physics is *physics*—since its laws are not *logically necessary*, but rest on empirical evidence.

The logical systematization of the body of knowledge (known as "physics") results rather inevitably (and understandably) in a "logical" structure or *system;* but if the systematization is of *physics* (and not say, of anthropology, Egyptology, or whatever else), it must be because *physics* is, at the very least, *about* the *physical* (empirical) world—and, at the most, may be of it or *in* it—before ever the logical systematization was undertaken. Russell certainly *knew* when he was writing his *The Analysis of Matter* that he was not writing, say, his analysis of *politics*. One has only to read his *Freedom and Organization,* for example, and compare the two to have conclusive evidential proof. If, as Russell himself goes on to say, if the world of physics *must be,* in some sense, *continuous* with the world of our perceptions (the empirical world) how *can* there *be* a "second question" concerning (in Russell's sense of the term) "the *application* of physics to the empirical world?" To *apply* a world (the world of physics) to a world it is already and *necessarily continuous* with (the empirical world) is a very strange thing to try to do. And when you try to do it, you naturally find it presents a difficult, "mysterious" problem which even the strength of the mathematical-logical instrument is insufficient to solve. Why *raise* such a problem? Or why try to solve *such* if any one else raises it? True enough, Russell provides himself with a *verbal* reason for raising the problem when he says: the world of physics must be, *in some sense,* continuous with the world of our perceptions. But, it is also true, he doesn't provide himself for very long, for he goes right on to say *in what sense it must be continuous,* namely, it must be continuous in a sense *sufficient* to *supply* the *evidence for the laws of physics.* But a law of physics is *scientifically established* when the *evidence for it is supplied.* Surely, then, sufficient unto the laws *must be* the *evidence* thereof—as sufficient unto the *continuity* is the evidence of the *laws.*

Russell's third question, or problem, carries the self-contradiction to its logical conclusion. The third problem is presumably arrived at by combining the first and second problems together, by trying to *fuse* them in some way. But the "third" problem is, in fact, nothing more than a *repetition* of the "second" problem in a different form; the difference being due to the desire to get out of the "second" problem not the outcome for *physics* (i.e. the solution of the "first" problem) but the outcome for *metaphysics* (i.e. the solution of the "second" problem)—or as Russell puts it:

> . . . the outcome for ontology—i.e. [to get the answer to] the question: What are the ultimate existents in terms of which physics is true (assuming that there are such)? And what is their general structure? And what are the relations of space-time, causality, and qualitative series respectively? . . . We shall find, if I am not mistaken, that the objects which are mathematically *primitive in physics,* such as electrons, protons, and points in space-time, are all *logically complex* structures composed of entities which are *metaphysically more primitive,* which may be conveniently called "events." It is a matter for mathematical logic to show *how to construct,* out of these, the objects required by the mathematical

physicist. It belongs also to this part of our subject to inquire whether there is anything in the *known world* that is not part of *this metaphysically primitive material of physics.* Here we derive great assistance from our earlier epistemological inquiries, since these enable us to see *how physics and psychology can be included in one science,* more concrete than the former and more comprehensive than the latter. Physics, *in itself,* is exceedingly abstract, *and reveals only certain mathematical characteristics* of the material with which it deals. It does *not* tell us *anything* as to the *intrinsic character of this material.* Psychology is preferable in this respect . . . by bringing *physics and perception together,* we are able to *include psychical events in the material of physics,* and to give to physics the greater concreteness which *results from our more intimate acquaintance* with the *subject-matter of our own experience.* To show that the traditional separation between physics and psychology, mind and matter, is not metaphysically defensible, will be one of the purposes of this work; but the two will be brought together, *not by subordinating* either to the other, but by *displaying each* as *a logical structure* composed of what, following Dr. H. M. Sheffer, we shall call "neutral stuff." (Ib. pp.9-10; italics mine.)

In saying that Russell, in his "third" problem carried the self-contradiction to its *logical* conclusion, I was, of course, very much in error. By tradition, "metaphysics" (or "ontology") is supposed to deal with the absolutely "first" or "ultimate" things (the "metaphysically *primitive*") and hence, when you use the terms, you cannot help but get the *feeling* that at last you have hit bottom. But to stop increasing the "number" of problems just because you *feel* the thud of finality is to come to a psychological *stoppage,* not to reach a *conclusion* of logic. When you start with a contradiction, as Russell's own mathematical-logic teaches in its Theory of Types, you can go on forever, carrying the contradiction in another "form" (or "formulation") from one "level" (or type) to the next, and never reach a *lógical* conclusion because the hierarchy is without logical end.

And this is demonstrated, or at any rate, exemplified, in Russell's attempts at solving his "third" problem. "To bring physics and psychology together, *not by subordinating* either to the other," is his comprehensive purpose. And it is reasonable to understand that by *"not subordinating* either to the other" is meant that *with respect to each other* they will be given *some coördinate* status, though with respect to the "neutral stuff" anything might happen to them; but whatever does happen to them, because of the activity of the neutral stuff, will happen to both alike. For the "stuff" *is neutral*—and will do to "physics" what it does to "psychology" with an equal mind or will (or whatever else). Or, to put it in another way: it is Russell's explicitly avowed purpose to develop a philosophy which will bring psychology and physics *together* but which will *not allow* "physics" to swallow "psychology," either the one definitively the other, or both definitively in turn.

To go into the details of Russell's arguments is impossible and also unnecessary. The statement of his "three questions" or problems *defines* the course his argument *must* take. Far from its being true that only in mathematical-physics is "prediction" possible it is possible to "predict" in philosophy as well. Given Russell's three problems, the *general* line (not the details—they vary from philosopher to philosopher, and from time to time in the same philosopher) is laid down.*

* This, of course, is what Dewey proved to the hilt in his *Experience and Nature* and *The Quest for Certainty*. Given the "Greek formula" and the rest of philosophic discussion (with endless variations in detail) follows as a matter of inescapable logical course. In Russell's philosophy we have the "Greek formula" working in its latest (or almost latest, for there are the Logical Positivists) mathematical-logical dress.

When Russell is dealing with his "first" problem—the world of physics taken by itself—he is predominantly (if not always) dealing with what the title of one of his books called: "Our knowledge of the external world." If, in dealing with the first problem, Russell cannot always and consistently stay "outside" that is not through lack of trying. But since he is after the mathematical-logical structure or system of "physics" it is inevitable that the sheer operation of his logical symbolism should every now and then drag him "inside."

When (having finished with the problem of the logical structure of "physics" as a "deductive system"), Russell passes on to his second problem we find what one could predict, namely, that the further he gets on with his second problem, the further "inside" he gets. And that he should finally wind up so far "inside" that everything is "inside the head" may appear shocking to some, but is no logical surprise. In the *statement* of his second problem Russell, true enough, tried to protect himself: "the world of physics must be, *in some sense,* continuous with the world of perceptions." But three words offer no real protection. They are no match against the logical force of his whole philosophic method:

We do not know much about the contents of any part of the world except our own heads; our knowledge of other regions, as we have seen, is wholly abstract. But we know our percepts, thoughts and feelings in a more intimate [i.e. "concrete"] fashion. Whoever accepts the causal theory of perception is compelled to conclude that percepts are in our heads, for they come *at the end* of a causal chain of *physical events* leading, *spatially,* from the *object* to the *brain* of the percipient. . . . And with the theory of space-time as a structure of events, which we developed in the last two chapters, there is no sort of reason for *not* regarding a percept as being in the head of the percipient. . . . It follows from this that what the physiologist sees when he examines a brain is *in* the physiologist, not in the brain he is examining. What is in the brain by the time the physiologist examines it if it is dead, I do not profess to know; but while its owner was alive, part, at least, of the *contents* of his brain consisted of his percepts, thoughts and feelings. Since his brain *also* consisted of electrons, we are compelled to conclude that an electron is a grouping of events, and that, if the electron is in a human brain, some of the events composing it are likely to be some of the "mental states" of the man to whom the brain belongs. . . . I do not wish to discuss what is meant by a "mental state"; the main point for us is that the term must include percepts. Thus a percept is an event or a group of events, each of which belongs to one or more of the groups constituting the electrons in the brain. This, I think, is the *most concrete* statement that can be made about electrons; everything else that can be said is more or less abstract and mathematical. (Ib. pp. 319-320; italics mine.)

To ask Russell what he means by the "percept" being at the *end* of a causal chain; what he means by the causal chain leading, *spatially, from* the object *to* the brain; what he means by "physiologist" who "examines" a "brain" of someone else; *how* he came to *know* that when the owner of a brain is dead, what the physiologist sees in it is different from what he sees when the owner is alive (though in both cases *all* the physiologist sees is in *his* head, and *he* is presumably alive both times); what he means by saying the brain "*also* consisted of electrons"— whether he means "electrons" concretely, or only abstractly and mathematically; and if he means that electrons are "concrete" groupings of events *in the same sense* in which he means "percepts, thoughts and feelings" are concretely or "intimately" known then why does the brain *also* consist of electrons? . . . to ask Russell these questions and dozens like them may have value as a "logical exercise" but he can give no answer to them other than the kind of answers he has already given. For the logical operation of his philosophic method will allow for no other sort of answers.

So when Russell comes to his "third" problem, we find him repeating on a more generalized plane, or in terms of more generalized formulations, precisely what his "solution" of the "second" problem would logically lead one to expect (or predict):

> On the question of the *material* out of which the *physical world* is constructed, the views advocated in this volume have, perhaps, more affinity with idealism than with materialism. What are called "mental" events, if we have been right, are *part of the material of the physical world,* and what is in our heads is *the mind* (with additions) *rather than what the physiologist sees through* his microscope[!] It is true that we have not suggested that *all* reality is mental. The positive arguments in favor of such a view, whether Berkeleyan or German, appear to me fallacious. The sceptical argument of the phenomenalists, that, whatever else there may be, we cannot know it, is much more worthy of respect. (Ib. pp. 387-388; italics mine.)
>
> While, on the question of the stuff of the world, the theory of the foregoing pages has certain affinities with idealism . . . the position advocated as regards scientific laws has more affinity with materialism than with idealism. . . . There are psychological laws, physiological laws, and chemical laws, which cannot *yet* be *reduced to* physical laws. (p. 388; italics mine.)
>
> So far as causal laws go, therefore, physics seems to be *supreme among the sciences,* not only as against other sciences of matter, but also as against the sciences that deal with life and mind. There is, however, *one important limitation* to this. We need to know in what *physical circumstances* such-and-such a percept will arise, and we *must not neglect* [!] the more intimate qualitative knowledge which we possess concerning mental events. *There will thus remain a certain sphere which will be*

outside physics. . . . It is obvious that a man who can
see knows things which a blind man cannot know; *but a
blind man can know the whole of physics.* Thus the
knowledge which other men have and he has not is *not
a part of physics.* (p. 389; italics mine.)

Since "there is thus a sphere *excluded from physics"*
(p. 389) the hasty reader, one insufficiently disciplined in
the subtleties of mathematical logic, and insufficiently
hardened by the rigors of fundamentally pure methods of
symbolic-logical proof—such a reader might come to the
conclusion that Russell has, at the end, at any rate, left
some part of "psychology" unsubordinated and unsubor-
dinatable to "physics" (or is it vice versa?); that with
respect to each other there is a real difference betwen the
two; and hence has (to some extent) fulfilled his comprehensive pledge given at the start: to show "how
physics and psychology can be included in one science,
more concrete than the former and more comprehensive
than the latter." Although the last quotation (p. 389) was
taken from *near* the end of the book, the *end* of it is,
I take it, the last sentence, or two. And the penultimate
sentence reads as follows:

As regards the world in general, both physical and
mental, *everything* that we know of its *intrinsic character* is derived from the *mental* side, and *almost* everything that we know of its causal laws is derived from the
physical side. (p. 402; italics mine.)

The "mental side" has the edge so far because Russell (in 1927) is not quite certain but what there may also
be some "causal laws" which are derived from the mental
side—whatever it is that Russell *here* means by "derived."
But the edge which the "mental side" enjoys in the penultimate sentence is very short-lived—as short-lived as the
sentence.

Disregarding "the world in general," the ultimate sen
tence reads:

> But from the standpoint *of philosophy* the distinc-
> tion between physical and mental is *superficial and un-
> real*.*

XII

"The question of whether we should *begin* with the
simple or the complex appears to me the most important
problem in philosophic method *at the present time";*
the *complex* Dewey defines as "the gross, macroscopic,
crude subject-matters in primary experience" and the
simple he defines as "the refined, derived objects of reflection." † Russell's philosophy, of which we have just
had a representative sample, is an illustrious contemporary exemplification of the *consequences* that unavoid-
ably ensue when the method of beginning with refined, derived objects of reflection is followed. Dewey's philosophy is a *consequence* of following the other method. The
contrast between the two philosophies, whatever else it
does, should materially help the reader to understand

---

* Other books of Russell's give variations of the same conclusion,
though sometimes they may *seem* different. Thus in *The Analysis of
Mind* (1921): 1. "One of the main purposes of these lectures is to
give ground for the belief that the distinction between mind and
matter is not so fundamental as is commonly supposed." (p. 108)
2. "I think that what has *permanent* value in the outlook of the
behaviorists is the feeling that *physics* is the most *fundamental science* at present in existence." (Preface) 3. "All our data, both in
physics and psychology, are subject to *psychological* causal laws;
but physical causal laws, strictly speaking, can only be stated in
terms of matter, which is both inferred and constructed, never a
datum. In this respect *psychology is nearer* to what *actually is*."
(P. 308—last sentence of book; italics mine throughout.) In all
Russell's treatments of the subject, the same with limited variations will be found. But enough, if not too much, has already been
quoted here.

† *Infra,* p. 1061; p. 1044; italics mine.

how fundamentally serious for *philosophy* the issue over *scientific* method is. For Dewey and Russell both agree that philosophy, to be significant and intelligent, must be *scientific*, that is, must follow in its inquiries the *method of science*. With respect to these philosophies, the double-issue over method, scientific and philosophic, is squarely and explicitly joined.*

But furthermore, and more generally, the contrast should also help the reader toward understanding that fundamental differences in *philosophies* are *not explained* by the "personality" differences in *philosophers*. Just as the fundamental differences in the physics of Galileo and Aristotle, or of Einstein and Newton, are *consequences* of differences in *methods* of inquiry employed, so with respect to fundamental differences in philosophies. That philosophers have "personality" differences is not hereby denied. Neither is it denied that personality differences are dominant, even predominant, in many (but not all) philosophies. But to make "personality differences" the *ground of explanation* for the predominance of "personality differences" in philosophies, is to repeat as *explanation* of the fact the very fact *to be* explained. It is to convert a *consequence* into a cause; it is to set up a distinction *in subject-matter* as explanation of the *result of methods of inquiry*. For it is the *methods of inquiry* employed by philosophers that make it possible for their

* Those modern and contemporary philosophers who turn their backs in part or in whole on science and scientific method and claim another and totally different method for philosophy (like Berkeley, Hegel, Bergson, and latterly Whitehead, do so *because of* and *in terms of* their conception or *interpretation* of science and scientific method. Also, those who spurn science always claim their philosophy is a "Higher Science" or "Knowledge"). So that actually the fundamental issue in *all* philosophy from the time of Galileo is one and the same—whether frankly and explicitly faced or left implicit and evaded.

"personality" differences to achieve and retain predominance in their philosophies.*

To determine whether inquiry should begin with refined objects of reflection or macroscopic subject-matters in primary experience is the problem *philosophers* are faced with today. In this sense it is a *philosophic* problem. But not in any other. It is the fundamental methodological problem of all inquiry, irrespective of the field in which inquiry goes on. Galileo, for example, was faced with this problem when he undertook to inquire into the physical world and the motions of physical things. Should he begin with the refined objects of reflection which constituted the Aristotelian-medieval "science of physics"? Or should he begin with the macroscopic subject-matter in primary experience? When he decided to follow the latter method and climbed the Tower of Pisa to put his decision into practical effect, *modern* science was launched upon its career and a revolution got under way.

Contrariwise, the medieval scholastics remained medieval because they began with refined objects of reflection and insisted on staying with them.

> Within the sphere of dialectic debate, the Scholastics were supremely critical. They trusted Aristotle because they could derive from him a coherent system of thought. It was a *criticized* trust. *Unfortunately* they *did not reflect* that some of his main ideas depended upon his *direct acquaintance with experienced fact*. They trusted to the *logical* coherence of *the system as a guarantee* of the unrestricted relevance of his primary notions. Thus they accepted his confusion—where there was confusion—of superficial aspects with fundamental principles of widest generality. Their *method for the furtherance* of natural knowledge was endless debate, unrelieved by recurrence *to direct observation*. Un-

* See *supra*, p. 71.

fortunately also their instrument of debate, Aristotelian logic, was a *more superficial weapon* than they deemed it. Automatically it kept in the background some of the *more fundamental topics for thought*. Such topics are the quantitative relations examined in mathematics, and the complex possibilities of multiple relationship within a system. All these topics, and others, were kept in the background by Aristotelian Logic. (Whitehead: *Adventures of Ideas,* pp. 149-150; italics mine.)

As heirs of twentieth century science we can look back to the period before Galileo and confidently speak as Russell does of "the whole vast system of *supposed* knowledge handed down from Aristotle." But *how* did it come about that that knowledge was *rendered* supposititious? As heirs of quantum physics and Relativity Theory of Space-Time we can also look back to the vast system of Newtonian science, with its indestructible, eternal billiard-ball atoms, and its Absolutism of Space and Time, and with equal confidence declare that the latter is a vast system of supposed knowledge. But again the same basic question is relevant: *How* did it come about that the Newtonian system, *in its fundamentals,** was rendered supposititious?

If we search for an answer to either or both of these vital questions (they are really two continuous parts of one question) by pursuing "physics" as "pure logic" or as "pure mathematics" we are doomed to failure. Aristotle's physics, as a logical system, was as coherent as they come; whereas the system of Galileo was very much otherwise. Similarly with the change in science that was realized during the past fifty years. As Russell unambiguously points out: "The physics of Newton, considered

---

* There are of course a vast number of *items* of Newtonian knowledge that are as good today as they ever were; and the same can be said for as *comparatively* large a number of *items* in the Aristotelian corpus of knowledge.

as a deductive system, had a perfection which is absent from the physics of the present day." * But Galileo's badly systematized "few facts," not Aristotle's well-systematized many, are the "examples of *real* knowledge." And the ("purely") *mathematical inferiority* of present-day physics does not stand in the way of its being, for scientists and philosophers (Russell himself included), *scientifically superior knowledge.*

Of course Russell and Whitehead, when they face critical turning-points in the *history* of physical inquiry of the gigantic sort exemplified by the change from Aristotelian physics to Galilean, and from Newtonian to Einsteinian, find it necessary to abandon "pure logic" and "pure mathematics" and they surrender to necessity. They introduce at *such points* references to "direct observation," "new method," "experimental and technological [instrumental] progress," but having done so, they immediately pass back to the consideration of physics as "pure logic" or as "pure mathematics" leaving the intervenient preceding and succeeding *history* of physical inquiry to take care of itself. This method of wandering off and on the topic of experiment not only makes nonsense out of the history of scientific thought; it makes unintelligible the nature of science in particular and the nature of all knowledge in general.

Consider some of the things Whitehead says about the change from the medieval-Aristotelian to the Galilean method of scientific knowledge-getting:

> "Galileo keeps harping on how things happen, whereas his adversaries had a complete theory as to why things happen. . . . It is a great mistake to conceive this historical revolt as an appeal to reason. On the contrary, it was *through and through* an anti-intel-

* *The Analysis of Matter,* p. 13.

lectualist movement. It was the return to *the contemplation of brute fact;* and it was based on a recoil from the *inflexible rationality of medieval thought."* (*Science and the Modern World,* p. 12; italics mine.)

You may well ask what is so inflexibly *rational* about "thought" which uses "endless debate" as "a method for the furtherance of natural knowledge." You may also ask why it is that the Historical Revolt is a return to the *contemplation of brute fact* when the *consequence* of that "anti-rationalism" * is that

> . . . although in the year 1500 Europe knew less than Archimedes who died in the year 212 B.C., yet in the year 1700, Newton's *Principia* had been written and the world was well started on the modern epoch. (*Ib.* p. 8)

Are we to understand that Whitehead *means* that modern *science* really is anti-rational, anti-intellectualist? And if so, why call it *knowledge?* Of course not! When he passes over from his *contemplation* of the "logical perfection" of the "supremely critical dialectic debate" of the scholastics to his *contemplation* of modern science, his contemplation changes during the passage:

> Aristotle by his Logic throws the emphasis on classification. The popularity of Aristotelian Logic retarded the advance of physical science throughout the Middle Ages. If only the schoolmen had *measured instead of classifying,* how much they might have learnt!
> Classification is a halfway house between the immediate concreteness of the individual thing and the complete abstraction of mathematical notions . . . in the *procedure* of relating mathematical notions to the facts of nature, by counting, by measurement, and by geometrical relations, and by types of order, *the rational contemplation is lifted.* . . . Classification is necessary. But *unless* you can progress from classifica-

* *Ib.* p. 74.

tion to mathematics, your *reasoning* will not take you very far. (*Ib.* p. 43; italics mine.)

Did not Galileo and his co-workers of the seventeenth century have something to do with introducing the "procedure of relating mathematical notions to the facts of nature," and so have something to do with *"lifting the rational* contemplation"? Judging by Whitehead's statement that this Historical Revolt was not an appeal to reason but was anti-intellectualist, anti-rationalist, a return to the contemplation of brute fact, one might be tempted to think not; but to yield to the temptation would be irrational, illogical:

> In the seventeenth century the influence of Aristotle was at its lowest, and mathematics recovered the importance of its earlier period [up to Archimedes]. It was an age of great physicists and great philosophers; and the physicists and philosophers were alike mathematicians. . . . In the age of Galileo, Descartes, Spinoza, Newton, and Leibniz, mathematics was an influence of the first magnitude in the formation of philosophic ideas. But the mathematics, which now emerged into prominence, was a very different science from the mathematics of the earlier epoch. It had gained in generality, and had started upon its almost incredible modern career of piling subtlety of generalization upon subtlety of generalization; and of *finding,* with each growth of complexity, *some new application, to physical science,* or to philosophic thought. (*Ib.* p. 44; italics mine.)

That these statements, taken together and in relation, don't make sense is too obvious to need any demonstration. But Whitehead is not an irresponsible thinker; his contradictions and oscillations are not expressions of his "personality." The critical imbalance of his thought (on this topic and others) is a *consequence of his method* of philosophic inquiry which in turn determines and is determined by his conception (better, *pre*-conception) of logic and science (knowledge). A mind less original, less powerful and great than Whitehead's would easily find "rest" at one extreme or the other, or at that most precarious and delusively "restful" place of all—at the half-and-half point between.*

When philosophies of science (knowledge) and scientific method dismiss or neglect to take into central account "the topic of experiment" then are they doomed to wander off and wander about like the arguments of Shades in Purgatory who can look in both directions but can continue in neither.

XIII

If the schoolmen had measured instead of classified they would have learned much more. But they would have learned immeasurably more even with their classifying if only they had relaxed their "inflexible rationality of thought" and renewed "acquaintance with experienced fact." Or, to put it in Deweyan phraseology, the schoolmen would have vastly increased their real knowledge if they had not, by endless dialectic debate, kept themselves revolving in the circle of their refined objects of reflection and had instead turned for guidance and control to the gross, macroscopic, crude subject-matters in experience.

It was not the Aristotelian Logic that made the medievalists go round in dialectic circles. It was the way they *used* that Logic that caused them to do that. Aristotle's Logic is explicitly based upon and explicitly refers to experience of qualitative fact. Given the method of beginning with refined objects of reflection and staying with them, it makes no difference at all fundamentally whether

* All this applies to Russell too.

you use a Logic of Classification or a Mathematics of Measurement. The chances are not only good, they are absolutely perfect, that if the schoolmen had "measured" instead of classified they would have remained schoolmen for all that. This is not a conjecture. It is a demonstrated certainty. For this is precisely what has happened with the "schoolmen" of modern and contemporary times. As Whitehead says: *"the sort of person* who was a scholastic doctor in a medieval university, today is a scientific professor in a modern university." * This is not to praise the scholastic doctor but to damn the scientific professor.†And foremost among such "scientific" professors must of course be placed the "scientific professors of philosophy," —those particularly who seek to make philosophy "scientific" by making it "mathematical-symbolical," "symbolical-formal," "positively logical." It doesn't have to work like a syllogism to be able to work like a charm!

Aristotle's Logic was a "superficial weapon" because Greek science was exclusively concerned with the *superficial* qualities of natural things and their *superficial* relations (hot, cold, wet, dry, light, heavy, up, down, etc.) the qualities and relations, namely, that are displayed on the *superficies,* the qualitative faces and relations of things that can be experienced by direct observation, that we can become acquainted with by simply *looking* at, by

---

* *Adventures of Ideas,* p. 149; italics mine. There was of course *another* "sort of person" too—for example, William of Occam *in* the university, and the far, far greater Roger Bacon *out.*

† The schoolmen "trusted Aristotle" not because he could help them make a coherent system of thought, but because the Church enforced upon them the task of "cohering" *its* doctrines. Wherefore their "criticized trust" involved no reflection on their part concerning the basic dependence of Aristotelian Logic upon experienced matter of fact. The Church has never been overly insistent upon turning to experience for guidance and knowledge. It has a supply of "eternal knowledge" ready-made. There is no insufficiency, among "mathematical schoolmen" today, of mystery-mongering, nor are "mathematical theologians" wanting, either.

beholding as a spectator. There are many qualities, many combinations of qualities (natural things) and a few large relations that can be directly experienced. And with such as these, taken *as is*, as directly or immediately experienced, classification is the only logical thing that can be done. The schoolmen put Aristotle's syllogism to the fore; but it is his classification that is the "weapon" of natural science.* Anyway, whether they classified little of the natural world open to observation and syllogized much, the fundamental point Dewey makes over and over again is alone of commanding importance: no conflict was introduced between the world the Greeks and the schoolmen experienced (for even the schoolmen were alive, had eyes and ears, etc.) and their "science" of that world.†

Aristotle's Logic (even the syllogism alone) doesn't preclude recurrence to observation or to macroscopic subject-matter in primary experience; it encourages and fosters such recurrence. But it does absolutely, definitely *preclude* "quantitative relations." Whitehead is temporarily generous‡ to a great historical fault when he says

* In Aristotle's natural science (physics etc.), *relations* (geometrical and spatial, such as up and down) figure. The syllogism can *relate* but cannot handle *relations*. A "logic of relations" is one of the achievements of modern logic. Aristotle perhaps would be surprised by this novel development. But he would be certainly surprised to learn that his syllogism was taken as the instrument of *investigation* and not what it obviously is (and is only fitted to be) —an *auxiliary* to classification.

† The schoolmen when they were wrong were still wrong about qualities and qualitative behavior, and since what they didn't know couldn't hurt them they never tried to find out whether they were wrong. The Church got terribly hurt when someone told them they were wrong—as Copernicus, Kepler and Galileo began to do. (They still get hurt in the same way and for the same reasons.)

‡ Aristotle's Logic "*entirely* leaves out of account the interconnections between real things. . . . [It] *renders* an interconnected world of real things *unintelligible*. The universe is shivered into a multitude of disconnected substantial things . . . But substantial thing *cannot* call unto substantial thing." (*Adventures of Ideas*, pp. 169-170; italics mine.) But the schoolmen, by following this

Aristotle's logic "kept in the background" the "quantitative relations examined in mathematics." For Aristotle, "quantitative relations" are "accidents," of no metaphysical (cosmological) import, mutable and changeable, not eternal and unchanging. Hence they are not objects of *scientific* knowledge, and a logic of science need make no provision for them—except to "put them in their place" (which is "out").

The change from the method of classifying and syl logizing without observing, to observing and classifying without syllogizing, accounts for the modern progress made by such descriptive sciences of nature as "natural history." But the great change in modern science occurred when the change was made from the method of classifying to the method of quantitatively measuring.

Observation is involved in measuring; to measure the rate of fall, for instance, you have to observe the bodies falling. But observation is not all, and it is not enough. Eye-measurement of rate of fall is at best a rough estimate, not a quantitative measurement of any mathematical exactitude. One method and one method only makes possible the *modern* "procedure of relating mathematical notions to the facts of nature," namely, the *method of experimentation.* To be able to measure quantitative relations of change, it is absolutely essential to be able to *control* the changes, to stop them and start them, to accelerate them and retard them. If it is an accident, then it is a very happily symbolic one that at the outset of modern science of motion, *acceleration* was defined as a change in *direction* or velocity. For in *experimental* control of change, a control exercised for the ob jective of making mathematical, quantitative measure

logic by the method of endless dialectic debate, exhibited "the in flexible rationality of thought"!

ment, the two amount to the same. Otherwise they do not.

"The procedure of *relating* mathematical notions to facts of nature" is Whitehead's phrase. And when you refuse to make *experimentation* an integral, functioning element in scientific procedure, "relating" is the only term you can use. Take experimentation *out of* scientific method and leave mathematics *in,* and the procedure of "relating" mathematics to the facts of nature blossoms into the great "mysterious" problem of modern and contemporary philosophy, the problem, in Russell's phrase "of the *application* of physics to the empirical world." And the piling of "mathematical logic" on top of "mathematical physics" only deepens and darkens the "mystery" and increases and intensifies the *in*solubility of *that* probblem.

By leaving experimentation out of modern scientific method, there is also created a mysterious *historical* problem which deserves far more attention than it has received. It deserves in fact the utmost philosophical attention because even a full recognition of the historical mystery might serve to stimulate universal solution of the modern "scientific" mystery. For "the procedure of *relating* mathematical notions to the facts of nature, by counting, by measurement, and by geometrical relations and by types of order" is an exact description of what *Greek scientists tried to do.* This, precisely, is what Pythagoras started and what the *Academy* under Plato carried forward to the Greek *end.* To say that Aristotle was a biologist "though he was not thereby ignorant of mathematics" * and that Aristotle turned Greek scientific thought away from mathematical measurement and into the classificatory procedure, is to ascribe to Aristotle an

---

* *Science and the Modern World,* p. 43. As a matter of fact, as some scholars are coming to realize, Aristotle was at least as good a mathematician as Plato, and the chances are he was much better.

extraordinary influence and, moreover, of the kind he could not possibly have exercised over his fellow Greeks. "Following the Leader" is *not* a philosophic (or intelligent) game. And Greek scientists *were* philosophers.

The plain historical matter of fact is that the Pythagoreans, the mathematicians, were, with respect to the development of Greek science and philosophy, on the ground floor. They were the most closely-knit Brotherhood of Scientists-Philosophers of the Greek world; Plato's *Academy* was nothing more than their Athenian home, after being driven out of Croton in Sicily and elsewhere. The only comparable society of scientists were the physicians, organized by Hippocrates and they came later. Only superficial reading of history backwards (making Greek philosophers and scientists into sheepish "scholastic doctors" and Aristotle into the Church, the omnipotent shepherd of the sheep) can yield the conclusion that Aristotle deflected the course of Greek scientific thought out of "relating mathematical notions to the facts of nature" into the halfway house of "classifying" those facts. Rather must the case have been that the Greek mathematical development, as a procedure of investigating nature, quickly reached an impasse and Aristotle's Logic was the only way out. And for this there is conclusive proof.

The original Pythagoreans did try to "relate" *quantitative* measurement to natural facts. But they very soon had to change their whole mathematical business. For they discovered early that there was a "number" that wasn't a whole number—namely, the square root of two. *Before* the discovery of the square root of two, Pythagoras could have said as Einstein did in 1933: "Our experience up to date justifies us in feeling sure that in Nature is actualized the ideal of mathematical simplicity. It is my conviction that pure mathematical construction enables us to discover the concepts and the laws connecting them which give us the key to the understanding of the phenomena of Nature." *But after,* Pythagoras and the Pythagoreans (and all Greeks) were considerably shaken in their feeling of conviction. They *had* an ideal of mathematical simplicity and they stuck by that ideal. Whole numbers and the relations between whole numbers were alone *ideally* simple; they alone were Rational, the object of Pure Thought and the object of Pure Thought was alone Ultimate Nature. Hence the square root of two could not *be* an object of Pure Thought, could not *be* an actualization of Nature, could not *be* Rational. It was an inexpressible, an unthinkable, without any *Reason* in it, without any *Measure* in it—incommensurable, in fact. It was "without measure" and hence not Rational, but Irrational. Hence also, it could not possibly be used for "measuring Nature" or any "Ultimate thing" in Nature —for Ultimate Nature was a Logos, a Rationality, and all *real* actualizations in Nature were "wholes," "measurables," "rational numbers."

Though Pythagoreans differed among themselves in details, though Aristotle differed from Plato in details, though Greek biologists and physicians differed from all the mathematicians and logicians in details, *all* Greek scientists and philosophers, physicians, biologists and mathematicians agreed with each other in fundamental principle: the rational, the measurable, the logical, the reasonable (they all mean the same thing) is the "whole." And why did they so agree? *Because* the qualities, combinations of qualities (natural things) and relations between qualities and combinations of qualities which are directly observed in experience, are always "wholes." To be able to "relate" mathematical notions to the "facts of nature," when those facts of nature are *taken as is,* taken as "something given," as we are directly and immediately acquainted with them, as macroscopic subject-matter in primary experience—to be able to "relate" mathematical notions to these facts of nature, the mathematical notions must be *qualitatively like* the facts to which they are to be "related": they also must be *qualitative wholes.*

It is a fact that with the "facts of nature" as directly experienced there is very little that can be done in the way of "relating" mathematical notions to them.* And there is very much less that can be done when you hold to your ideal of mathematical simplicity that Nature *must* actualize. Hence the Greek scientists, mathematical-philosophical, and logically-mathematical, were, in their procedure of relating mathematical notions to the facts of nature, rapidly reduced to the level of *observing* (spectatorially beholding) such shapes and proportional relations of shapes and sizes as they could, and of classifying and systematically analyzing and developing their static and "whole" relationships. (Euclidean geometry and Eudoxian theory of ratio and proportion.) The syllogism is the novelty which Aristotle contributed. But the fundamental procedure of his logic—observation and analytical-synthetic classification—is in essentials precisely what Greek mathematics had come to. Aristotle's Logic, from start to finish, is a logic of "wholes." Everything else is not *in* logic (or science), because nothing else is an eternal and immutable part of the Logos of Ultimate Nature. Everything else is an "accident": not an actualization of *Rational* Nature, but a manifestation of *ir*rational Matter. And among these "accidentals"—manifestations of

* Even now—statistics apart. And to speak of 7 1/8 persons per square mile, etc., would have *horrified* the Greeks. What madness! What insane irrationality! What sacrilegious defiance of the Logos of Nature! In sum, how dreadfully *un*scientific, *un*mathematical.

matter, not realizations of Form—are quantitative relations, naturally.

Now the great historical mystery is this: if Greek science is *not* science as we understand it (Aristotle excepted, according to Whitehead) *how account* for the extraordinary difference between the success of modern science and the failure of Greek science in the procedure of relating mathematical notions to the facts of nature?

> Why did the pace suddenly quicken in the sixteenth and seventeenth centuries? . . . Invention stimulated thought, thought quickened physical speculation, Greek manuscripts disclosed what the ancients had discovered. (*Science and the Modern World*, p. 8)

If it is true, as Whitehead avers, that Greek science is *not* science as we understand it, then, surely, the discovery of Greek manuscripts could not have exercised a *positive* determining influence in *creating* the beginnings of modern science. Rather must the case have been that by the time of Galileo, the *practice* of modern science had gotten so well on its way that no *theory* of science, not even of the Greeks, could throw it off its *practical course.* (Though it could throw the *theory* of modern scientific practice off its natural theoretical course. Which it did.) When Whitehead writes further on:

> The history of the seventeenth century science reads as though it were some vivid dream of Plato or Pythagoras. In this characteristic the seventeenth century was only the forerunner of its successors (*Ib*. p. 48.)

it is historically and scientifically impossible to agree with him. Since Pythagoras and Plato, while living, devoted all their energy to finding ways and means of circumventing, of stopping, precisely the sort of mathematical development (with respect to the facts of Nature and with respect to mathematics itself) that took place in the seventeenth century, had they read the science of that century and its successors it would have seemed to them, if the truth must be told, like some vivid nightmare. They would be much more inclined to agree with Whitehead's other statement about the seventeenth century: that it was a return to the contemplation of brute fact. Except that they would want to add: it was *not contemplation* and *not of fact*. "Facts" of Nature for the Greeks are rational, and when "contemplated" are seen to be such. Seventeenth century science, for them, would be a brutish distortion and mutilation of facts of nature. It would be a travesty and outrage of "mathematical contemplation of nature." And hence for precisely the *opposite* reason—because of its mathematical aspects—they would agree with Whitehead in saying the Historical Revolt was anti-intellectualist, anti-rationalism.*

XIV

The double mystery—of the impotence of Greek mathematical science of Nature and the omnipotence of modern mathematical science of Nature—is solved at one and the same time when "the topic of experiment" is introduced into the theory of scientific method. Greek mathematics had a very brief and not very glorious career as an instrument of investigation of Nature, because Greek mathematical scientists tried to "relate" mathematical notions to the facts of nature, taking those facts as di-

---

* "It follows from the Deism [of seventeenth century scientists like Newton] which is part of the whole conception, that the Laws of Nature will be exactly obeyed. Certainly, what God meant he did. When he said, Let there be light, there was *light* and not a mere imitation or a statistical average." (*Adventures of Ideas,* p. 145.) Without Deism, the Greeks believed light is *light* and not an imitation or statistical average. But for *scientific* knowledge of light, light *is* a "number of vibrations," a quantitative formula, whether statistical or not. Hence the nightmare.

rectly experienced, *as is*. Modern mathematics, on the other hand, has had a glorious and ever more wonderfully fruitful career as an instrument of investigating nature, precisely *in so far as* modern scientists abandoned the objective of "relating mathematical notions to the facts of nature" (taken as is) and began experimentally changing, controlling as-given facts of nature for the sole objective of instituting mathematical relations *between* the facts that were the resultants or consequences of their experimentation. And in pursuit of this dominant objective of establishing quantitative relations between facts, modern science has *in practice* more and more abandoned all pretense of holding to an "ideal of mathematical simplicity" and has less and less observed scruples in experimentally tearing apart the "given" (directly experienced) facts of nature and in experimentally bringing them into experimentally new relations. To the extent that science from Galileo onward *integrated* mathematics in experimental procedure, brought it under the control of experimentation and used it for instituting and formulating *relations between experimental findings,* it was successful and fruitful, and, to the extent that it did not, it blocked, retarded, distorted, obstructed the advance of scientific knowledge. The progress of physics from Galileo and Newton to Michelson and Einstein is the progress of effecting a more complete integration of experimental findings and mathematical formulations, bringing the latter under control of the former.

It was a consistent practice with Newton whenever there was a conflict between the then known experimental findings and the theoretical demands of the then known mathematics, always to enforce the latter. Because Newton did not summarily expropriate the basic rights of experimentation all at once, by a single comprehensive decree, but invariably cautiously argued them away as each specific occasion arose by means of the theory of mathematical priority and superiority, Newton has, perhaps not inappropriately, been held up as the paragon of purest British intelligence. However, it was the omnipresence of the "Greek formula" in modern scientific mentality, rather than the force of Newton's arguments, that established his "method of compromise" as the canonical procedure for mathematical-physicists everywhere.*

Newton's "method of compromise" and the "scientific world" of eternal billiard-ball atoms, Absolute and separated Space and Time, and immutable (invariant) mathematical laws of Nature he set up by means of his method, endured for approximately two and a half centuries. That the method was not disavowed sooner is not a tribute to its probity; it is a tribute to the overwhelming force of the Greek philosophic formula. That the "scientific world" stood up for as long as it did is not a tribute to its strength: it was kept going, at enormous intellectual and social price by the almost infinite ingenuity of modern scientific minds. And when new mathematical formulations enforced by new experimental findings could no longer be brought within the Newtonian system with any consistency at all, ingenuity lapsed into ingenuousness:

> In time, most physicists came to disbelieve in absolute space and time, while retaining the Newtonian technique, which assumed their existence. In Clerk Maxwell's *Matter and Motion,* absolute motion is asserted in one passage and denied in another, with hardly any attempt to reconcile these two opinions. (*The Analysis of Matter,* pp. 14-15.)

* "Except the blind forces of Nature nothing moves in this world, which is not Greek in its origin." Sir Henry Sumner Maine's *words,* but representative of practically universal nineteenth century scientific and philosophic belief.

That the Newtonian reign should ever come to an end was simply inconceivable to Newtonians. The basic structure of the Newtonian system was eternal and immutable. If the alleged empirical certainty of indestructible Newtonian atoms ("the imperishable foundation-stones of the universe" according to Clerk Maxwell) had, by radioactivity and Rutherford's experimental bombardment of the atoms, become slightly less than absolute, then all the more reason for gradually shifting the eternality and immutability of the system back onto the original ground of the transempirical absolute certainty of Mathematics (the "invariant laws"). As a "deductive system" after all, the Newtonian had a high degree of perfection. But instead of solving the problems presented by experimental findings, the Newtonian method kept piling them up ever higher. And it is the last straw that breaks the camel's back. In this case, the black-bands in Michelson's interferometer.

What happened to the "eternal basic structure" of Newtonianism, to its immutable cosmological framework reputedly riveted "scientifically" to the three absolute pillars of Space, Time and Matter by eternally true and eternally enduring, non-corrodible struts and bolts of pure mathematics, every one knows. By reversing the Newtonian policy of giving to mathematics absolute authority to determine the meaning and to control the theoretical development of experimental findings, that is, by establishing the forthright and uncompromising procedure of giving to experimental findings first the authority to determine the meanings of mathematical-physical concepts and then the final authority to control their development and formulation in all respects relevant to the science of nature, Einstein accomplished in *scientific practice* the full enstatement of *experimentalism*. The verified

success of Einstein's reversal of the Newtonian policy
has demonstrated beyond all doubt and with a precision
science alone is capable of, that for three hundred years
Newtonianism had been driven from one extremity to
another, and had latterly been forced to live ever more
precariously from experimental hand to theoretical mouth
because of one basic methodological fault: it had literally
upset the true relation between experimental findings and
theoretical (mathematical) formulations. It had been
living methodologically upside down.

Physics can be pursued as "pure mathematics" but it
is not as pure mathematics that physicists have pursued
it. If Nature actualizes the ideal of *mathematical* simplicity, and the pursuit of this ideal is the historic pursuit of modern physics, then physicists have gone about
their pursuit in ever wilder and stranger ways. To discover the ideal of *mathematical* simplicity we should
study mathematics, symbolic logic, perhaps even Logical
Positivism, so that we may be able to settle upon that
ideal, for it reveals itself only within a system of (mathematical) symbols. But to discover the simplest mathematical formulation of the complexities experimentally produced, though we must still study mathematics, our
problem is significantly different. The ideal of mathematical simplicity in modern physics is the ideal of the
simpl*est* formulation—no matter how complex from the
standpoint of the ideal of mathematical simplicity—the
actualities of Nature as experimentally discovered will allow. The ideal of the simplest is not the ideal of simplicity.

From the standpoint of pure mathematics neither
the continuity nor the *direction* of change of modern
physics can be accounted for. In multifarious ways, the
system of modern physics has expanded, and from
Newton's time onward physicists have certainly tried to

preserve its theoretical systematic face. But the expansions, even within the limits of the theoretical system, were not in response to demands made by theoretical principles of the system. The expansions and revisions were necessitated by the need for bringing into the system new experimental findings as they were mathematically formulated. When it is forced to, mathematical physics keeps its theoretical face by adding supplementary laws, and even exceptions. In common-sense practice, we keep adding new exceptions to the old rule and think nothing of it. But in science, exceptions are scandalous, and the practice observed is that of reformulating old rules so that the exceptions will be included, and cease to be exceptions. The ideal of having one system in which all laws and rules belong is very powerfully operative with theoreticians. Just as Euclid took Greek mathematics, as is, and systematized it in accordance with certain principles of codification, so the science of physics, as it at any one time is, or any body of knowledge, can be taken as is, and formally arranged, systematized and codified according to certain rules, principles, methods and standards of pure mathematics or mathematical logic. That such efforts are important and valuable cannot be doubted; and that they involve dangers also cannot be doubted— witness Euclid's miracle. The practical emphasis on theoretical system in present day physics is a consequence of the fact that it is in many fundamental respects absent. Which is as good a demonstration as any that the *direction* of scientific change in physics is not due to considerations of "pure system."

The progress of physics from Galileo and Newton to Michelson and Einstein is the progress of effecting the complete integration of experimental findings and mathematical formulations, by bringing the latter under control of the former. The laboratory physicist does the experimenting; the theoretical does the theorizing. This is a social division of labor, not a separation of the one activity from the other. Michelson's experiment required the work of prior theoretical physicists just as much as it required the general advance in technological design and manufacture. Without theoretical developments and mathematical formulations, the interferometer experiment could neither be nor be conceived. Similarly with Einstein's theoretical formulation: without the prior experimental developments of physics, it could neither be nor be conceived. The *problems* of the theoretician are determined by the results obtained in the laboratory; and the solutions of the theoreticians have to solve *those* problems. Einstein had to develop scientific ideas or meanings that would satisfactorily or successfully solve the problem which the results of Michelson's experimental apparatus raised.*

In all theoretical physics, there is a certain admixture of facts and calculations; so long as the combination is such as to give results which observation confirms, I cannot see that we can have any *a priori* objection [to the "heterogeneity of space-time in Einstein's system]. Dr. Whitehead's view [which objects to the "heterogeneity"] seems to rest upon the assumption that the principles of scientific inference ought to be in some sense 'reasonable.' Perhaps we all make this assumption in one form or another. But for my part I should prefer to infer 'reasonableness' from success, rather than set up in advance a standard of what can be regarded as credible." (Russell: *The Analysis of Matter,* pp. 78-79.)

To attempt to assess the contribution of laboratory ex-

* As Whitehead excellently remarks: "On the whole, it is better to concentrate attention on Michelson's interferometer, and to leave Michelson's body and Michelson's mind out of the picture." (*Science and the Modern World,* p. 173.)

perimentation, taken by itself and of mathematical formulation and systematization, taken by itself, is to attempt the impossible. For the fruitfulness of modern
scientific method is dependent upon the interactive union
of the two. Now one, now the other, may be temporarily
dominant in a specific case. But what gives continuity to
modern scientific activity is their continuous interactivity;
and what gives the direction to the continuity is the exercise of control by experimentation as the final authority
for testing theory and pronouncing upon the validity of
the mathematical formulations.

Aristotle and Plato die hard. The work of the experimental physicist and theoretical physicist, though inter-
locked and interwoven, can be for certain purposes distinguished. But the Greek Formula is not satisfied with
making them distinguishable; it must make them separated and separable. "It is obvious," writes Russell, "that
a man who can see *knows* things which a blind man can
not know; but a blind man can *know* the *whole of physics*." The whole of physics! Experimentation and all that
laboratory experimentation involves has nothing to do
with the "science of physics" and is not necessary for
the knowledge thereof! For a blind man can "know" the
abstract, mathematical propositions of "physics," its formulas and numbers, and that is *all* that *scientific* knowledge of the physical world is! Could a race of blind men
create modern and contemporary physics? Could they
come to know? Could they even find out which abstractions and which mathematical formulations and which entities and propositions they should select from the mathematical heaven as makings for their "deductive system of
physics"? But why ask the Greek Formula *these* questions. *How* we come to know is a matter of trivial *history*
and has nothing to do with the *nature* of the case. Knowl-

edge has nothing to do with knowledge-getting; knowing has nothing to do with the process of coming to know. Knowing is the contemplation of the object of knowledge. And contemplation is all the knowledge thereof.

In the actual conduct of scientific inquiry, the full and unhampered interactivity of mathematical thinking and experimental doing is now an accomplished fact. Leave out the element of experimental doing, and no matter what other elements you bring in, and from where and how many, the creation and development of modern science become an inexplicable mystery, an old-fashioned miracle in fact. Especially mysterious and miraculous does modern science become when the element of mathematics is made the determining one in its history and nature. Not that mathematics can or should be left out of modern account. Any more than the writer of *Hamlet* can or should leave out Ophelia. To compare the role of mathematics in the history of thought (and also in the history of science) to the part of Ophelia "is singularly exact. For Ophelia is quite essential to the play, she is very charming—and a little mad." * But without Hamlet there is no modern play at all. Though Hamlet may sometimes make Ophelia desperate, without him she goes completely insane. The madness of mathematics is not an inherent characteristic; it is a consequence that results from failure of union with experiment. And the "divinity" of that madness—is just Plato's story. Mathematics is no more mad and no more divine than any other instrument of investigation and communication, than any other system of ideas; and when brought under the control and direction of experimental doing mathematics is as sensible in experience as the rest. And without the direction and control of experimental doing, when disunited and sepa-

* *Science and the Modern World*, p. 31.

rated from practice, all ideas become mad. As the great Greek physician said: "All things are alike human or alike divine—it makes no difference how you call them."

The method of modern scientific inquiry is the method of experimentation: the functional integration of theory and practice. Separate and divorce theory from practice and you make the history of thought unintelligible and the progress and nature of modern scientific knowledge one unending and ever-increasing irrationality. But unite the two in your theory of scientific method as they are now completely united in the conduct of scientific inquiry and the unintelligibility disappears, and the nature and course of modern science become clear. We then see that the work of Galileo was not a development but a revolution; and the work of Einstein is not a revolution but a development. For the abiding significance of the work of Einstein is that it scientifically clarifies and fully enstates the meaning of the work of Galileo: that experiment is a method for developing theories and establishing evidences for theories, for bringing the findings of practice and the formulations of theory into continuous interactive relation the consequences of the interaction being scientific knowledge. For in this way experimental evidence continuously controls the formulation of the law and prevents it from ever cooking the facts.

By freeing the experimental method from the arbitrary and distorting limitations of "pure theory"—by freeing it from the operations of the Greek Formula—Einstein has made possible the full realization and actualization of the method of intelligence in the technical scientific domain. But the spirit of the Greek Formula is still actively abroad in the philosophic and cultural land, shackling the freedom of intelligence in the modern world.

XV

Galileo's method of breaking through the self-enclosed circle of refined objects of reflection was not a *specific*. It was not a remedy capable only of breaking the magical spell of the Aristotelian-medieval dialectic "system of natural science." What Galileo discovered was a *general* method, available and adaptable for use by all, and when used proves a competent remedy against the circular charm of any dialectic-logicalism, any self-involved system of refined objects of reflection, no matter what the area or field of the system, no matter what the enclosure may be and by what name it is called—physics, chemistry, biology, psychology, economics, sociology, ethics, esthetics, religion, theology, philosophy, logic. Galileo's method is thus universally competent, not because it is itself a piece of counter-magic, an omnipotent *word* or *saying*, but because it is a quite thoroughly natural *deed* or *doing*.

The method of *beginning* with gross, macroscopic, crude subject-matter in primary experience performs in the conduct of philosophic inquiry qualitatively the same function as is performed in the conduct of scientific inquiry by the method of beginning with the subject-matter revealed in the laboratory experiment.*

The emphasis falls on *beginning* and cannot fall too hard. Dewey, who begins with the gross and macroscopic,

---

* The Tower of Pisa is as much a piece of laboratory apparatus as a micrometer—cruder but qualitatively or functionally the same. Galileo's telescopic lens was comparatively as crude when compared with the lenses (photographic-telescopic) used by astronomers at Sobral. Nevertheless Galileo's telescopic observation in 1610 was as humanly dramatic and scientifically as significant and conclusive as the observations in 1921. Galileo's astronomical observation took one part of the Copernican theory out of the realm of theoretical speculation, and the observational expedition to Sobral could do no more for the Einstein theory.

does not *stop* there. That's where he *starts*. *From* there he goes *into* the realm of the refined, derived objects of reflection, and while in that realm, he is as analytical, dialectical, argumentative, ratiocinative, technically logical, logically synthetical, abstruse and abstract—*i.e.* to sum it up—as "purely theoretical" as the veriest philosophers of the opposite methodological school. But there is this enormous difference between Dewey and philosophers of the opposite method* even in the respect in which they most closely approach or cross each other: for Dewey, his dialectical, ratiocinative or formal-logical work is an *interval* or phase of his complete philosophic undertaking. Just as he does not begin, so he does not stay with the refined objects of reflection. Whatever subject-matter in primary experience he started from, he started *from* that subject-matter *because* that subject-matter raised a *problem*. The *objective* of his technical-philosophic excursion, or his formal-logical work, is to solve that problem. Hence, to be *through,* he must get back where he started from; to be through with that *philosophic* job the refined objects of reflection he has on hand after doing all the formal-logical work, *must lead back into* the subject-matter of primary experience, the gross and macroscopic subject-matter which constituted the starting point, the point of origin, of the inquiry. When they do so lead back into the gross and macroscopic subject-matter, then and only then does *Dewey* know that *that* philosophic task is done, for that leading back into the macroscopic subject-matter is the final or ultimate experimental test of the validity of the philosophic solution which *he,* in his professional capacity as philosopher, can give.

* The fact that the up-to-the-minute practitioners of the opposite method use the symbolisms of mathematical logic or logical positivism and Dewey does not is a *technological* difference and not a difference in *fundamental* methods of philosophy.

The emphases, in the last sentence, on "Dewey" and "he", are made not to call attention to the emergence of differences between experimentalism in philosophy and experimentalism in science, but to sharpen perception of the *identities* that obtain.

It is too obvious, I take it, to need any argument that the philospher *qua* philosopher—or in his strictly professional capacity—in aiming to become scientific (experimentalist) can aim to become so in a manner comparable to the scientific (experimentalist) *theoretician,* not the scientific (experimentalist) laboratorian. It is absolutely essential, therefore, in examining and evaluating any method or any element in a method that claims it can make philosophy *scientific*—in the sense of science as we understand it now—it is absolutely essential to keep constantly and centrally in mind that the philosopher, under this conception of science and scientific inquiry, can do only *half* of the total work of philosophic inquiry, and the more strictly only half, the more fully or completely scientific philosophic inquiry is. Failure to keep this central in mind, is partly responsible for the argument over "scientific method in philosophy" going on forever in circles of wilder and wilder amaze. Failure to keep this in mind is to be guilty of using, under guise of examining the validity of a method for making philosophy scientific, a conception of science that violates the fundamental nature of science *as we understand it now*. And hence violates also the fundamental nature of any philosophy that could possibly be scientific. It is to be guilty of using the Greek Formula again, uncritically and without acknowledgment, but this time in the form of the *absolute standard* that can automatically measure any method and infallibly determine whether or not it is capable of making *philosophy* scientific.

It is also too obvious, I take it, to need any argument to prove that the scientific theoretician—for example, the theoretical physicist—checks and rechecks every argument in his theory before *he* makes it public. After it is published, it has to undergo (and is thoroughly subjected to) public examination. And to be acceptable and accepted by the scientific public, theoreticians and laboratorians both, it has first successfully to pass a series of laboratory tests which the theoretician, as theoretician, couldn't possibly make.

However, there is always one kind of *practical test* that the theoretician not only can perform, but must perform and constantly does perform. Einstein, for example, *knew*, before ever he started, that his line of reasoning, his mathematical calculations, his formulations of refined objects of scientific reflection had to lead back into the black-bands of the Michelson interferometer.* He knew that any theory had to pass *that* experimental test. He knew that his theoretical-physics job was not done unless and until his theory did that. Any system of refined mathematical-physical objects of reflection that did not lead back into the black-bands but led away from them— that led to the conclusion, say, that the bands were not black nor bands—Einstein knew beforehand would not be worth the paper it was written on, no matter how infinitesimally small the piece. When his theory led him back into the black-bands, *Einstein* knew, as far as *he,* as theoretician could know, that *his* theoretical job was done.†

Einstein—as any theoretical scientist—knew *beforehand* that his theory must terminate in the consequences

* This is not all it had to lead back into, but it is enough for the purposes here.
† See footnote above.

of the experiment as experienced in the laboratory, because the control of theoretical solution by laboratory consequences is established in the conduct of scientific inquiry. (Completely established, as we have seen, by Einstein's own work). The course of theoretical elaboration and solution in scientific inquiry is *controlled by* the subject-matter as experienced in the experiment. If philosophic inquiry is to become scientific, it too must be controlled in qualitatively identical way. In proposing any methods to make philosophy scientific, or in reaching a judgment with respect to any methods proposed with this end-in-view, it is necessary to establish whether the method under evaluation, or undergoing judgment, does or does not enable the philosopher to be controlled in his inquiry in a way *qualitatively or functionally comparable* to the way in which the theoretician in science is controlled in his inquiry. The method of beginning with the gross and macroscopic subject-matter in primary experience performs this function. It is the beginning of experimentalism in philosophy, the beginning not everything. But it is the necessary beginning, and because necessary, is sufficient to disqualify as unscientific or anti-scientific any method of philosophic inquiry that begins, or pretends to begin, otherwise.

XVI

Scientific inquiry is "controlled inquiry." * To control, it is necessary to be controlled; to exercise *control over*, it is necessary to be *controlled by*.* *Controlling* without *being controlled* is possible only to creatures who are impotently omnipotent; being controlled without controlling is possible only to creatures who are omnipotently impotent. Both such kinds of creatures or beings are febrile

* Dewey, *infra*, p. 885, p. 930.

figments of diseased imaginations, the one rationally indistinguishable from the other, except in the respect that each imagines the absurdity or impossibility of the other in reverse.* In the activities of Nature, as in the activities of human nature, *controlling* and being *controlled by* are each indispensable for the other, are interdependent or continuously interactive.

When science is taken in the gross and macroscopic, the general consequences of the interactivity of *controlling* and being *controlled by*, as that interactivity goes on between the theoretical and laboratory functions within inquiry, can be readily enough seen and in their generality easily enough denoted. This Whitehead does when he points out that "Every scientific memoir in its record of the 'facts' is shot through and through with interpretation." † And Russell does the same when he points out that "In all theoretical physics, there is a certain admixture of facts and calculations." ‡ Each of these statements in its own way unambiguously denotes (points to) the *consequences* of interactivity, within inquiry, between laboratory fact and theoretical interpretation. The two statements quoted, separately and together, point to the general fact that within scientific inquiry the laboratorian is controlled by the theoretician and the theoretician is controlled by the laboratorian. And of course, in the respect

---

* The best theologians of the Church—following Aristotle and Plato—have realized that God cannot be so omnipotent that He is never *controlled by* anything. "What God *meant* He did." His doing was therefore *controlled by* His meaning. Since His meaning is Eternal and Immutable, it is *His* complete undoing when He is made to undo anything he has done. Miracles destroy God's nature without saving the world. For further discussion of this problem in terms of theological "miracles," see my Introduction to *The Philosophy of Spinoza* previously referred to. The discussion of the same topic, in terms of scientific law and continuity in Nature, comes into the argument further on.

† *Process and Reality*, p. 22.

‡ *The Analysis of Matter*, p. 79; see fuller quotation, *ante*.

that the one is *controlled by* the other, the other is, in that same respect, and from *his* standpoint, *controlling* the one. The *controlling* and *controlled by* do not take turn and turn about. They operate criss-crosswise and interweave.

The theoretician and laboratorian, although they are each controlled by the other's results—and in this respect may be said to be similar—are *controlled* by them in radically different ways, or to radically different ends—and in this respect they are basically dissimilar or functionally unlike.

The theoretician in searching for the solution of a problem taken from the laboratory is *controlled by* the facts the laboratorian obtained; that is, he is controlled by the consequences of the interactions which were set going in and through the organization of the physical-experimental apparatus in the experiment. And the laboratorian, in searching for an experiment that will put to the test the solution of a problem taken from the theoretician is *controlled by* the solution in constructing his apparatus and organizing the experiment. Obviously, and in both cases: the theoretician must solve *that* problem; and the laboratorian must test *that* solution. Precisely upon this interchange or cross-weaving of control (controlling and being controlled by) depends the existence and maintenance of the interactivity between the theoretical and laboratory functions in scientific inquiry. And the more precisely this interchange or cross-weaving of control, the greater and finer the precision in the results of scientific knowledge.

So much for the general similarity. Now for the specific and radical difference. The theoretician must *solve* that problem *as taken;* his solution must explain the facts *as they were found* in the laboratory—whence they were "taken" by him for solution or whence he received them as a "gift" ("something given" a *datum*). There are no limitations placed beforehand upon the theoretician* as to *how* he explains or solves the problem. He can make his solution simple or complex, new or old; but no matter how simple or how complex, how old or how new, one thing is absolute and final; his solution *must terminate* in those facts *as given or taken;* the *outcome* of his solution must leave those facts as found. If there are any methodological ultimates in scientific inquiry, then this is one of them.

The laboratorian is under a radically different obligation with respect to the solution "taken" or "given." He is under obligation to *put it to the test* and *not* to prove it right (or wrong). The *outcome* of the laboratory experiment is not something the laboratorian is under scientific obligation to contrive. Very much the opposite: his contrivances (apparatus) must be such that the *outcome* for the solution (as to whether it is right or wrong, correct or incorrect, true or false, acceptable or in acceptable scientifically) will be settled or determined by the *consequences* of the experiment. Michelson's interferometer put the ether-theory to the test; it did not prove it right. Michelson, in constructing the interferometer and in organizing the experiment had to be (and was) *controlled by* the ether-theory; otherwise his experiment would have been irrelevant, or beside the point. But it would have been infinitely worse than an irrelevant experiment, it would have been a fraud, if Michelson had devised an instrument and organized an experiment so that the *outcome,* the *consequences* of it would be predetermined one way or the other. If Michelson had cooked an experiment for the sake of producing facts that would invalidate the ether-law (theory, solution), the outcome of his ex-

---

*I am speaking of the *current* practice in science. It was not always so nor do all contemporary philosophers of science think it should be so even now. See *ante,* p. 111.

periment would not have constituted a theoretical problem for scientists to solve; the problem scientists would then have been faced with would have been the very practical one of publicly disqualifying Michelson. Then, Michelson's body and Michelson's mind would have been the whole pseudo-scientific picture, and Michelson's interferometer would have made no scientific picture at all.

The *outcome* of the laboratory test does not have to prove the theory (solution) right; and it does not have to prove it wrong; the outcome may be such as to prove that the theory cannot as yet be put to decisive laboratory test. In which latter case, the issue as to the validity of the theory (solution) continues unsettled and undetermined, making further tests or further organizations of experiments necessary; and to accomplish such further laboratory experiments further elaboration and reformulation of the theory (solution) may be needed.

Experimentalism in science does not mean that every theory (solution) has to be such that it can be put to the decisive laboratory test immediately, or in its first formulation. The ether-theory (the solution of many scientific problems) had been kicking around in modern science for two hundred years or more before it was brought to the laboratory test. The amount of theoretical formulation and re-formulation that went into its development was simply enormous. Only because of the general advance in science during this historical period, advance in theoretical formulation and practical methods of laboratory experimentation, was Michelson (his genius thrown in) able to devise an instrument and organize an experiment that put the ether-solution to critical test. The only requirement fundamental in experimentalism, whether in philosophy or science, is that any solution to be acceptable as a *solution*, as a piece of scientific *knowledge*, must first pass the laboratory test. Only when at last it does or does not pass a decisive test, is it to be accepted as a *known* solution or rejected because *known not* to solve.

If there are any methodological ultimates in scientific inquiry, then this is one of them: the outcome of the laboratory test is *not* determined by the apparatus as organized in the experiment *taken by itself*. When the outcome is thus determined, you have either the honest manufacturing of contrivances or machines—which is not a case of *inquiry;* or else you have the dishonest manufacturing, or faking of evidences. Which is also not inquiry—though frequently called so—and now ever more frequently in certain parts not unknown. The outcome of the laboratory test, when the test is part of inquiry, is determined by the *consequences* of the natural subject-matter working in and through the organization of the experiment. This methodological ultimate of laboratory procedure is of course the *original* or the basis of the methodological ultimate in theoretical scientific procedure. Hence the primacy and ultimacy of laboratory experience in determining the *total* course and controlling the direction of inquiry.

NOTE. The interactivity of *controlling* and *controlled by* within the process of scientific or "controlled inquiry" is fundamental in Dewey's analysis of the logic of inquiry. Inquiry originates in a problem or difficulty and terminates in a test. We are *controlled by* the problem at the beginning of any case of inquiry and by the test at the ending. The phases through which the process of inquiry passes are phases of passing from one interactivity of *controlling-controlled by*, to another, the achievement or consequences of one phase being carried along into the next, giving any case of inquiry its self-corrective and self-expansive character. The complete *controlling*, with respect to *that* case, is the final issue or consequence of the complete process when the inquiry is successful. When the problem is solved, then we do control *that* problem and are no longer *controlled by* it. That is what solving means. We have *done* and so *know* how and what to do.

However, because the factor of *controlling* is the critical turning point in the history of scientific inquiry, and the determining issue in the philosophic controversy or debate, in the course of Dewey's specific discussions the factor of *controlled by* is often pushed into the background. Because it is in the background, it does not follow that it is not working *in* Dewey's discussion. It is just working in the shade. The reader should always bear this in mind. For with a few very rare exceptions Dewey always does. And where he does *not*, all the more reason why the reader *should*.

There are rare cases, portions of discussions, where *controlled by* gets pushed so far into the background that the consequences of its working are hardly appreciable, they have practically vanished. There is one passage included in this book in which, as far as I can find out, it has to all intents and purposes vanished altogether. And as far as I know it is the only passage in all Dewey's writings.* It's a *rara avis* which it would be a shame not to let the reader catch for himself. However, even this rare bird is only in passage, not in stoppage. And therefore having caught the bird, the reader should not stop but go on.

The term "controlled inquiry," like all terms, carries its

---

* I don't vouch that it is the only one. I go by the fact that it took me so by surprise, was so novel an experience to me. After that novel experience, I didn't go back and make a statistical research through all Dewey's writings. If the reader finds more than one in the text of this book, the keener he or she.

dangers within it. Concentrate on and magnify the dangers, and the dangers can easily be converted into seeds of its own destruction. Since all terms carry dangers within them, by this ferocious method of conversion, the process of intelligent inquiry and rational life can be made into a passage from one destruction to another. If the reader likes to live that sort of "heroic life," he is welcome to do so. And if he further wants to call *that* "intelligent" (of a superhuman variety of course), there is no way of stopping him from doing so, nor would it be worth the effort to stop him. But it is *not scientific* intelligence.

I do not, of course, in any sense wish to imply that Dewey's lapses in the course of discussion are *solely caused* by any one term or combination of terms. Terms are themselves consequences, not aboriginal or "metaphysically primitive" causes. Terms also have their further consequences when used in further discussion or inquiry. They are therefore not entirely without blame. But to put all responsibility for error on terms is nonsensical. The reasons for Dewey's lapses are complex and many. Dewey, like all human thinkers, is quite human. And like all human beings, in the course of a specific argument he is sometimes carried along too far in that course.

XVII

That the theoretician and laboratorian may be one person is of course to be understood all along. It usually happens that the laboratory genius is not the same person as the theoretical genius, just as the great musical composer is seldom the great performer. But this is as it may be. To speak of the theoretician and laboratorian (in physics or any other field) is a handy way of speaking of the theoretical and laboratory *activities* functioning in scientific inquiry. And it is also in part necessary, and in part eminently advisable to speak in this way because scientific inquiry is a human activity, undertaken and carried through by human beings. Whether the laboratorian and theoretician are, in any given case of inquiry, one person or two or many is another consideration. Because of the historical continuity of scientific inquiry—the involvement of problem in problem and solution in solution—they are always many, very many, neither one nor two. However, the fundamentally important point concerning the logical analysis of inquiry is that whether they be one, two or many, the laboratorian must, to some extent, be a theoretician and the theoretician must, to some extent, be a laboratorian because in the function of each, the activity of the other is internally involved.

Within inquiry, the theoretical and laboratory activities are constantly undergoing integration. When, with respect to any one case or problem inquired into, the integration is finished or completed, then in *that* respect inquiry reaches its *logical conclusion* and an item of tested, grounded, verified knowledge is added to the scientific store. But the macroscopic fact that scientific inquiry is still going strong, and going stronger today than at any other period, is all the evidence needed to prove that inquiry is in historical process, that the method of controlled inquiry does not deliver a once-and-for-all system wherein theoretical and laboratory activities are with finality integrated, wherein they are with respect to each other "under control" in the sense in which the military speak. The method of controlled inquiry is a method of controlling, a method of integrating, and as the method is pursued it systematically effects further integration between the two, progressively moving as each progresses.

Controlled inquiry—the method of experimentation—extends from the laboratory to the theoretical study and *includes* them both. The one without the other is not scientific inquiry as we understand it now. Experimentalism in science is impossible without the laboratorian and it is also impossible without the theoretician. Both are experimentalists, each performing, within the total process of experimental or controlled inquiry, a distinctive and distinguishable, but not separated and separable share of the work.

To some readers, perhaps, it may still seem that the last statement begs the whole issue. Such readers may think that if you start by putting the scientific theoretical and laboratory activities within scientific inquiry, it is not too amazing that you should find them each performing a distinctive but not separated, a distinguishable but not separable share of the work of scientific inquiry. It would be really too amazing only if you found them doing otherwise. This criticism would be valid and conclusively destructive *if* it were the case that *the statement puts* the theoretical and laboratory activities within inquiry, and *if* it were also the case that the statement, having first put them there, then offers itself as an *explanation* or accounting of their presence there.

If the statement were these two things, then, perhaps, it would be a "logical positivistic" statement on the order of Carnap's Logical Positivism.* But whether or not the latter, it would with certainty be a statement exemplifying the old dialectic whereby it is *explained* that opium puts to sleep *because* of its sleep-inducing powers. But the statement is neither of these two things.

As for the first, the statement does not *put* the scientific theoretical and laboratory activities any place. It *points*

---

* "Perhaps" because I take Carnap's *The Logical Syntax of Language* as defining his Logical Positivism. And this book is quite old, dating way back to 1937.

to where they are found. The statement is not a "definition" of what the term "scientific inquiry" is going to be
used as meaning. It is a *report* of what scientific inquiry
is existentially found to be. The statement is fundamentally denotative in logical function. That Dewey may possibly be a biased reporter, and his report be a product of
his bias, is not at all too sinful a thought to harbor against
any philosopher. Hence the great value of the reports
handed in by such competent philosophers as Whitehead
and Russell, who, though not without bias either, are certainly not biased in favor of Dewey's logic. "Every scientific memoir in its record of the 'facts' is shot through and
through with interpretation." "In all theoretical physics,
there is a certain admixture of facts and calculations."
These two reports of eminently competent individual
philosophers, of a competence within the technical fields
of science and mathematical physics far superior to Dewey's, corroborate Dewey's report to the hilt. The "interpretation" that shoots through the memoirs of facts is
existential evidence, gross and macroscopic, that *within*
the results of the scientific laboratorian, the consequences
of the work of the scientific theoretician are *found.* The
"admixture" of facts in the calculations of all theoretical
physics is *existential evidence,* gross and macroscopic, that
within the results of the scientific theoretician the consequences of the work of the scientific laboratorian are
found.

Of course, Whitehead and Russell are not the only other
philosophers who report the same findings as Dewey. But
the multiplication of reports is of no philosophic value.
As far as the particular report under discussion is concerned, all philosophers report the same. If they didn't
there wouldn't be any philosophic controversy such as the
modern and contemporary world displays. That's what all

the shooting is precisely about.* The report is general.

As for the second point—whether Dewey's report is an explanation or offers itself as an explanation of what it reports. The statement "within inquiry, theoretical and laboratory activities each perform a share of the total work of inquiry" no more *explains* that state of affairs than do the statements of Whitehead and Russell *explain* what they respectively state. Our Deweyan statement is logically distinguishable from the two statements of Whitehead and Russell in that it comprehends them both. What their statements say separately, our statement says together. There is a logical gain, in explicitness and comprehension of statement, but not an *explanatory* gain. All three statements are logically of the same order—descriptive or denotative.

Without going into elaborate details, a descriptive statement is a description of what is found. If you want to rest on your description you may do so. But the description is not an explanation. It is a denotation of what is *to be* explained. If it is a description of the explanation, a denotation of what is found at the end of an explanatory inquiry, then it is customary to call that the conclusion. The statement that opium puts to sleep is a description. To present that description as an explanation is to convert an effect directly into a cause which is equivalent to taking the same thing twice over, once as "effect" and once as "cause," which is no gain at all except in confusion.

A description denotes *how* things are found. If *within* the *results* of the laboratorian and theoretician, taking their results separately, the consequences of the work of the other are found, then, in searching for an *explanation*

---

* There is a great difference, of course, between "all the shooting being precisely about this," and "all the shooting about this being precise."

of the one case or the other or both we must be *controlled by* this fact. Unless we believe in miraculous or supernatural intervention, or in some strange, inexplicable principle of transmigration, the gross and macroscopic subject-matter in this primary experience, the irreducible and stubborn fact that the *results* of laboratorian and theoretician are what they are, must be the consequence of some natural process of interactivity and must be evidence of some natural relation of continuity going on between the laboratory and theoretical functions. The disclosure of the nature of that interactivity and continuity is the disclosure of the explanation.

There is of course a vast difference between an explanation of *how* things as a matter of fact are, and an explanation of how they *should be* in order to meet certain desirable or desired specifications. But again, unless we believe in miracles (in which case we need believe in nothing else and have no *reason* for any inquiry into anything), the knowledge of the specifications desirable and the knowledge *how* to change things so they will fulfill the specifications are both consequences of learning first of all *how things are*.

By learning how things are in Euclid, geometers gradually learnt how things in geometry should be, and through knowledge of how they are and guided by the specifications of how they should be, geometry was reconstructed and is still on the advance. So in every case. If this were not so in every case of scientific advance, the method of scientific inquiry would not be self-corrective and self-expansive. That it is so is also a *report* of the existential facts of scientific history, not an explanation of those facts.

The *how* and the *should*, within any intelligent undertaking, mark a difference, a distinction, not a separation. You can know that things should be different only as a consequence of knowing how they are. You can know how to transform them into what they should be, only by first knowing how they are made as they are. It is a commonplace that modern science began when inquiry into *how* things are was undertaken. In any sense in which "Why?" is intelligent, then it is "How?" read backwards. In any sense in which "should be" is intelligent then it is "how they are" read forwards. In any sense in which "must" is intelligent then it is when "how things are" and "how they should be" are one and the same. Any other sense of "must" consists in taking the *de facto* "how" and converting it blindly into a *de facto* "should be." Because the latter is then called *de jure* doesn't make its mode or method of acquisition of that character any the less *de facto*.

Now with respect to the specific case in hand, namely, how things are now in science, both Whitehead and Russell agree with Dewey in believing that that is the way they should be—from point of view, that is, of general methodology or way of scientific procedure.*

Whitehead does not believe that the "interpretation" *should* be taken out of the record of the facts, nor does Russell believe that the "facts" *should* be taken out of the calculations of theoretical physics. If you do the first, the record of the facts becomes not even a "contemplation of brute facts," not even a brutish contemplation of brute fact. It becomes no *record* at all. If you do the second— if you evacuate the calculations of theoretical physics of all facts—you may have the calculations left, but they are miserable, misshapen and bereft, meaningfully belonging nowhere, nowhere finding meaningful place no matter

* As for detailed procedures, and detailed results of procedures, there is always room for improvement, and on this point, too, our three philosophers fully agree.

how they are then pursued: they cannot be *physics* any more—because the facts have all been evacuated; they cannot be "pure mathematics" any more—because the calculations were made in connection with the facts, and in that connection inevitably and irretrievably lost their purity.

Whitehead and Russell, that is, do not say: "It is true, within the record of scientific fact there are interpretations to be found; and within the record of scientific theories there are facts to be found, *but* this is only the way things are now and they *should* be different and our philosophies of science and scientific method—our logics —are dedicated to the task of bringing about this difference." Whitehead and Russell say, "*How* things are now inquired into by scientific method, is the way they *should* be inquired into; *how* scientific inquiry is now conducted is the way it *should* be conducted." They say, in short, how we (now scientifically) think is the way in which scientific thinking should be carried on.*

When Dewey says that theory and practice function within scientific inquiry, or that the theoretical and laboratory functions are interactive within inquiry, he is making a report, in his own terms, of the macroscopic fact upon which all reports agree. When he goes on further and says that all logics of scientific method or scientific inquiry *should be controlled by* this fact, and that the *outcome* of all logical calculations concerning scientific method *should terminate* in that fact—he is going beyond the reportorial to the scientific-philosophic function. He is laying down a *rule of method* that logicians of scientific

---

* The title of Dewey's early book on logic, *How We Think,* has been a great stumbling block to "logicians." That it has been is a sufficient indication of how seriously they believed that the method and objective of science are to find out the *how.*

method should follow. He is laying down the rule that all our logical analyses and theoretical calculations concerning scientific method must be *controlled by* our findings as to *how* scientific inquiry is done. To say that Dewey is "laying down this rule of method" is of course only a manner of speaking. What he is doing is saying that we *must* carry over into our method of logical inquiry the method of inquiry discovered in science *if* our logical inquiry is to be scientific. Since *how* the method of science is now, is the way scientific method *should be,* the "must" is an intelligent conversion of the *de facto* how things are into a *de jure* state of affairs.

When the whole course of our logical calculations is controlled by the gross and macroscopic findings in primary experience of scientific inquiry, it is of course not amazing that the outcome of that course of logical reflection should terminate in those findings—that our explanation should end by explaining the findings we started out to explain. This is not amazing, but then the objective of philosophy—of scientific philosophy—is not to be amazing. And when our course of logical reflection is *not* controlled by the findings we started out to explain, it is also not amazing that we should *lose control over* the course of our logical calculations and that the outcome of that course should be any which irrelevant way—that the explanation should end by not explaining what we started out to explain but should end up by being an explanation that needs to be itself explained by an endless series of explanations. Although *this* endless outcome is not "in itself" amazing, but what one would naturally expect to result from the uncontrollable method pursued, the outcome is *how* amazing when it is presented not "as it is in itself" but "as in the logic of scientific method."

XVIII

Controlled inquiry involves exercise of control over, *controlling* as well as being *controlled by*. The theoretical experimentalist and laboratory experimentalist—who divide between them the total process of experimental (or controlled) inquiry—exercise *control over,* each in his own way. Each has his own distinctive means and methods, relevant and competent to handle his respective share of the total work, the means and methods of each being developed in the course of fulfilling or realizing the partial function, within inquiry, that each performs.

The laboratory experimentalist—to consider him first "by himself" for a spell—exercises *control over* by means of his laboratory apparatus and the methods of handling the apparatus that he progressively and cumulatively develops in and through the process of laboratory experimentation. "A technical description of the uses of the microscope in biology is not part of the philosophy of the sciences."* Nor of the philosophy or logic of scientific method. And what applies to the technological technicalities of the usages of the microscope applies equally to the technological technicalities of all laboratory equipment and methods. So nothing more need be said on *this* topic, else we would be in imminent danger of wandering off, and not staying on, the topic of experiment.

The laboratorian primarily exercises *control over* his instruments. That he can control them is neither accidental nor providential: he's constructed them that way. Taking an instrument by itself, control over it is pretty nearly absolute, in the sense that, taking a clock by itself, you can turn the hands at will. But a clock—in the laboratory at any rate—is not constructed as a plaything for passing the time of day, but as an instrument for telling

---

* Whitehead, *The Concept of Nature,* p. 1.

the passage of time. The laboratorian never constructs a piece of apparatus so he can control *that*. He is not concerned with constructing apparatus for the pure and beautiful sake of constructing apparatus. He is not a toy-manufacturer or a manufacturer of any sort, not even of automobiles. The laboratorian wants to control something else; and it is with the purpose or end-in-view of controlling that something else that he turns to the making of instruments that will give him that control. That something else is his "material"—whatever it may be, physical, chemical, biological, psychological, social.

Primarily, the laboratorian has control over his instruments, and through them, secondarily, control over his material. But his primary *objective, with respect to control,* is control over the latter and not over the former. With respect to control, control over the material is his *end;* control over his instruments, his *means* to that end.

The control the laboratorian exercises over his material by means of his instruments is a *secondary* control in another very important respect: taking one or more instruments by themselves, his control over them is pretty nearly absolute—in the sense explained above. But when the instruments are used for exercising control over the material being inquired into, the degree of control drops, the extent of the drop varying from case to case. This drop in control is also neither accidental nor providential. It is a *consequence* of the way in which the laboratorian *organized* his instruments into an experiment. For his inclusive or final end-in-view—inclusive or final because including the whole experiment and determining the end for which the experiment is organized—is not the perpetuating of his control over what he already has under control or (which is the same thing) the reproducing of what he can already produce. If the latter were his inclusive or final end-in-view he would not be setting up an *experiment,* he would be in a totally different business, the business of quantity manufacturing of one sort or another. The inclusive or final end of the laboratorian with respect to any experiment he organizes is *discovery,* the discovery, namely, of what the *consequences* will be of the *interactivities* set going *in* that experiment. Every experiment is a new experiment, a *new* organization, instituting new interactivities within that organization, and what the consequences of new interactivities will be one must perforce wait upon the issue to tell.

Experiments that methodically *repeat* experiments already performed are also experiments and have the function in scientific inquiry of testing or corroborating results previously obtained. If the *result* of a "repeater" were a predetermined or foregone conclusion, it would have no scientific corroborating power, and would not be an experiment at all. Although an experiment performed for corroboratory test is from point of view of methodical set-up —the organization of material and instruments—a "repeater" it is from the logical standpoint, which embraces its function in inquiry, a *new* experiment. For the consequences, the results of the methodical repetition are still problematic, have still—to use James's phrase—to be "cashed in."

The *partial end,* the control over the material is the "end" *within* the process of inquiry. The final or inclusive end is the end-in-view of which the whole inquiry is undertaken and for which *that* experiment is set up. Taking any experiment, it is of the utmost importance to distinguish between these two "ends." They are distinct, not separate. But they are functionally distinct. The end *within* any case of inquiry functions as one of the means in the conduct of that inquiry; the *end* which is the final consequence—the ending of that inquiry—is the attainment of the knowledge gained through that inquiry. The final consequence of any experiment, with respect to *that* experiment, is never a means but only an end. If it were not for the rampant confusion over means and ends, this point would be too commonplace even to whisper about. For obviously, what comes at the ending of any historical process cannot possibly be a *means* in that same historical process. Effects are effects and not their own causes. And conclusions, endings of inquiry are effects. That a conclusion of one inquiry can be used as a means in another inquiry should also be too obvious to mention. If it couldn't, there would be no inquiry at all but a spasmic jolting from thing to thing, like the actions of grasshoppers or fleas.

The material the laboratorian is inquiring into, and the instruments by means of which he conducts his experimental inquiry are distinguishable from one another, but are *not* separated and disconnected. The laboratorian hasn't got "material" in one hand and "instruments" in the other, each unrelated and unbeknown to the other; and he doesn't "apply" the instruments "to" the material (or vice versa) the way, for example, the one hand "applies" soap "to" the other when the left hand doesn't know what the right hand is doing. The instruments are themselves organizations of the material, and the material is *in* the organization of the instruments constituting the experiment. The material is *in,* not metaphorically, but actually, that is, interactively. The whole business of laboratory experimentation is not to organize an experiment to show that the same causes produce the same effects,* but to find out what are the *consequences* when new *interactivities* are caused.

* This *is* the business of corroborating experiments, "repeaters."

For the experimental laboratorian, the sky is the limit. Anything goes. According to Aristotelian logic (still widely used) the "nature" or "essence" of glass may be glass, wood wood, metal metal and so on pretty nearly forever; but for the laboratorian all things whatsoever are alike in only one fundamental respect: they are things to be brought together in new ways so that new interactivities may be set going and new consequences may ensue. And the consequences of the interactivities *are* the *natures* of things in and for science. As the laboratorian advances with the general advance in scientific knowledge, technological and theoretical, his instruments become more numerous, more precise, more powerful, and his organizations of the instruments into experiments become more elaborate, more delicate and more productive of new consequences because of the increased variety, in kind and degree, of the interactivities instituted in the material through and by means of the experiment. And so the laboratorian discovers that the same old "stuff" has ever more and ever different natures, or "essences."

The sky is the limit for the laboratorian. But where that limit is the laboratorian does not know. It is seriously to confuse matters therefore to say that the laboratorian is *controlled by* his *material*. In setting up any experiment, the laboratorian is controlled by his *knowledge of* the material as gained through prior experiments. He knows what the limits of the material are, as those limits were revealed in the consequences of prior experiments. But *those* limits are not *the* limits. Hence the new experiment. In passing from one experiment to the next, the laboratorian is *controlled by* his knowledge gained antecedently; and the consequences of any experiment that is the "next" are *limited by* the organization of interactivities which constitutes *that* experiment. Every experiment has its lim

itations; but what the limits of the material and instruments are (as interactive within that organization) the
laboratorian does not know until the *consequences* of *that*
experiment tell him. Since you cannot be *controlled by*
anything you don't know—in any sense of "control" involved in "controlled inquiry" or intelligent method*—it
is much better to speak of the laboratorian being *limited
by* his material.

It is well known that we can't count up to the last possible number. In the case of counting numbers, we know
pretty well that the next one will be one more than the
one antecedent, and so there is no intelligent point in trying to count them even as far as we can go. But in the case
of laboratory experiments, we do not know that the consequences of the next one will be just something more on
the same line and to be added to the consequences of the
antecedent experiment. Every experiment is a new experiment; it sets up a question or poses a problem; and what
the answer will be is problematic until the consequences
have been "cashed in." The consequences of the *next* experiment may not be in the same line at all; they may not
be additive but transformative of knowledge; they may
not add to the sum antecedently amassed but upset the
whole previous account. The result will be an *increase* in
our knowledge true enough, but it will be an increase not
by way of addition and accretion but by way of subtract-

---

* Being pushed and pulled around by the law of gravitation,
etc., is not being "controlled by" the law; it is being *limited by* the
law. Human beings are *limited* to going around with the earth in
its orbit; even when we fly we don't really fly away. The same
thing applies to "human nature and conduct." When we "act" in
terms of our "instincts," "intuitions," "inspirations," coming we
know not whence and going we know not where, we are not "controlled by" them; we are pushed and pulled around by them; we
are then animated *machines*, limited corporations; not intelligent,
controlling, human beings.

ing and overturning. In simpler language, the *next* consequence may not be reformatory but revolutionary.

XIX

There is no special virtue or power, philosophic or scientific, internally resident in the *word* "interactivity." As far as words go, "interaction" is just as good; by usage they could be made identical. That precisely is the great danger. In the intellectual as in other worlds, possession is practically the whole of the law, and an idea or meaning long inhabitating the field will prevent any new idea from getting in or will swallow it up if and when perchance it does. Especially will this happen if the new idea comes clothed in an old word or a close derivative of it.

When a new idea comes clothed in old raiment, it practically invites its own annihilation. But new clothes, though they may slow up the pace of destruction, do not automatically function to prevent unwarranted demise. There is no royal road to enduring life, and no known method of insuring the life of a new idea. Some have an extraordinary gift for coining strange new words, like Whitehead and Peirce. But the philosophic procedure by coinage has its many drawbacks as well as advantages. There is also the great method of terminological coinage which goes by the name of symbolic logic. That the newest symbols may be just a disguise of the oldest ideas—a disguise which may deceive the symbolists more often than the non-symbolic—the history of the self-same symbolic logic is right there to tell.

The usage to which "interaction" has been put, the meaning it has become encrusted with during centuries of working in a Newtonian intellectual world, is all that is the matter with it. Newton's Third Law of Motion states that "An action is always opposed by an equal reaction; or, the mutual actions of two bodies are always equal and act in opposite directions." The phrase "action and reaction are equal and opposite" has come to be the dominant definition of the meaning of "interaction."

If "action" and "reaction" were equal and opposite, there could be neither the one nor the other. For just as soon as any "action" started, supposing it to start somehow, it would be immediately estopped by the "reaction." It would always be an irresistible force meeting an immovable object. When such is the case, they might just as well not meet, but each stay at home. Meeting can do nothing for or to either, since they cannot *interact* when they meet. Their meeting in other words can only be purely formal, never real.

Newton claimed that his laws of motion were "derived from phenomena." He tells us that "the main business of natural philosophy [science] is to argue from phenomena without feigning hypotheses and to deduce causes from effects." Letting the term "deduce" pass for the time being, this procedure if followed would be equivalent to what Dewey calls the method of beginning with the gross and macroscopic subject-matter in experience. For effects are what we primarily experience, not the causes we "deduce." Newton also recognized that the "causes" we deduce should not be the "effects" over again. "To tell us that every species of things is endowed with an occult specific quality by which it acts and produces manifest effects, is to tell us nothing." The cause should be *equal to producing* the effect—but it should not be the same as the effect, if it is to tell us anything. However, as Newton goes on to say, "to derive two or three general principles of motion *from phenomena* and afterwards to tell us how the properties and actions of *all corporeal things follow* from those manifest principles, would be a very great step in philosophy [science]."* Such derived principles Newton considered his laws of motion to be.

Newton gives us the "experimental" phenomena whence he "derived" his Third Law.

> "Whatever presses or pulls something else, is pressed or pulled by it in the same degree. If a man presses a stone with his finger, his finger is also pressed by the stone. If a horse *draws* a stone tied to a rope, the horse *will be* (so to speak) *drawn back equally* towards the stone: for the rope being stretched at both ends will by the same attempt to relax itself urge the horse towards the stone and the stone towards the horse; and *will impede the progress of one as much as it promotes the progress of the other.* (*Principia*, [Evans and Hain editions] 1871, Axioms, or Laws of Motion. Italics mine.)

Obviously, if it were true that the stretched rope impeded the progress of the horse *as much as* it promoted the progress of the stone, the horse and stone would neither of them be moving and the stretched rope, like Buridan's Ass, would be transfixed by its own immobility.

Of course it can be said that Newton meant his "experiment" to be taken this way; that he was not considering the motion of the rope relative to the earth, but was taking horse, stone and stretched rope "in isolation." The three constitute the experimental situation and he is concerned only with what goes on *within* that system. If this is so, then it is still a fundamental error on his part to say that the rope, within the system, "will impede the progress of the one as much as it promotes the progress of the other." If the system is stationary, is self-enclosed, then the rope, to maintain the "dynamic equilibrium," will have to *impede* the progress of the one as much as it *impedes*

---

* From Newton's *Opticks,* quoted in Burtt, *The Metaphysical Foundations of Modern Science,* pp. 219, 258; italics mine.

the progress of the other. But let us consider this fundamental error as a temporary slip and pass it by too, for the time being.

Suppose we take it as a system in "dynamic equilibrium," the horse pulling, but not moving the stone with the rope stretched between. The rope is stretched because the pulls are equal and opposite. Now if we call the pull of the horse "action" and the pull of the stone "reaction," do we not get Newton's result? Does it not follow that throughout the length of the rope, action and reaction are equal and opposite? If at any point along the rope they were not, would not the rope, at that point sag and the whole stretch be gone?

But if we call the pull of the horse "action" and the pull of the stone "reaction," what are we going to call the rope? What *is* the rope? Action and reaction embrace within their "conjunctive union" the total world of motion. But within that world of motion the rope is not included. The rope is neither "action" nor "reaction." And *how* are we going to *cut* this mysterious rope that binds two physical pulls or "forces" together and is itself nothing physical? How are we going to cut it to find the "equality and opposition" of action and reaction which is supposed to be resident throughout its length? Action and reaction can never meet face to face within this mysterious rope. If they ever met head-on within the rope, they would stop each other dead in their tracks, and what would happen to the rope then? *Within* this rope, action and reaction must pass each other by. There is no use, therefore, in taking any one "point" along the rope unless we can *split* that point. Since splitting "points" is no occupation for anyone, let us say the rope is a "union" of two unsplittable lines and that action and reaction stream through these lines, each one in its own line and in the opposite direction. Within the rope,

these two equal and opposite streams will be exactly opposite to each other along their routes only in the sense that
two parallel lines are opposite each other. And any part of
one stream will also be exactly opposite any part of the
other stream, if "action" and "reaction" travel through
their respective "lines" like two beams of light traveling *in
vacuo* in an Einsteinian universe.

Newton, of course, was not thinking of an Einsteinian
universe in which the velocity of light traveling *in vacuo*
is "absolute." He started with an "absolute equality" instead of ending with one. For even if Newton's stone is a
stone, and his horse a horse, his rope is not a rope. It is
neither "action" nor "reaction." It does not participate in
the goings on. It is absolutely neutral between the two. To
be able to keep "action" and "reaction" equal and opposite, the rope must have two transmission lines, and both
lines must be vacuous media of transmission. There is only
one "rope" that is equipped to do this job with the mathematical perfection required in the Newtonian "world of
physics.": the two lines of an equality sign in a mathematical equation. The left side of an equation is equal and opposite to the right side. And transmission from one side to
the other in either direction is done with mathematical
simultaneity.

XX

When in the natural course of walking through a field
we come across a horse, stone and stretched rope between,
that organization of objects is not the gross and macroscopic subject-matter in our primary experience. In primary experience that organization is experienced as included within the field within which we are walking and
within which we also are included. The field is not a uniform mathematical abstraction. It is a field full of other

contents, and if our gross and macroscopic primary experience did not include the field and these other contents—
if they also did not appear in our primary experience—we
neither would nor could macroscopically discriminate the
horse, stone and stretched rope between as a particular
organization of objects *within* that field. The "field" would
be a uniform mist, and when there are no differences in
distribution within the mist, not even the mystical shapes
of things come out. The total "field" would, in fact, be like
Newton's rope. And without the horse and stone how
would Newton have found that rope between?

Within the wider natural field—the environment—the
organization of horse, stone and stretched rope is a "state
of affairs," as Dewey sometimes calls it. As macroscopically experienced, it is a consequence, an effect, a result.
It is, in his technical, logical language, a *situation*. As a
consequence, an effect, a state of affairs, it is a phase of a
history, having continuities with the past and moving into
the future. There is something doing. The horse is pulling,
the rope is stretching, and the stone is not going in the direction of the horse's pull because it is being pulled in
another direction and is going in that.

Horse, rope and stone are organized together and are
interacting with one another. The subject-matter in our
primary experience of that situation is a consequence of
the interactions going on, an effect, not the cause. Horse,
stone and rope have not swallowed each other up and if
unhitched they would not, because of that, vanish each
into nothingness. They are interacting with each other and
also with other things. Each thing in the interactive system constituting that situation is an individual thing
within its own distinguishable boundaries because of multitudes of interactivities going on within it. But it is a thing
at all, and not a figment, because the boundaries within

which its own individual interactivities are going on are not boundaries that shut it off from interactivity with other things within the greater environment. On the contrary. It would not be a natural thing at all, individualized or non-individualized, if it were not for the multiple interactivities it sustains and is sustained by with things beyond its own boundaries. If it were in interactive relations with more things within a greater environment, it would be more fully individualized, not less. The extent of individualization of a thing is not determined by its boundaries, for every stone has its boundaries, and though stones are individualized, their extent of individualization is not notably great. The extent of individualization of a thing is determined by the range and qualitative kinds of interactive relations it enters into with other things.

The horse is distinguishable from the stone and the rope from both because each is a different organization of interactivities within its own boundaries. But the latter in turn are not primeval, aboriginal causes but consequences of prior interactivities and modes of interactivity which are maintained in the enduring present.

Taking any individual object, we may call it, within its own boundaries, an interactive continuum. But it is always a continuum, so to speak, partial not complete. For no continuum of interactions of an individual thing is self-sustaining. It can sustain itself only by interacting with other interactive continua. Modes and patterns of organization of interactions differ from one another, distinguishing kinds of things, and individuals or individual variations within each kind. But each kind and each individual within each kind interacts with other kinds of interactive continua. When the continuum of interactions constituting a horse interacts with the interactive continua constituting blades of grass, the pattern or organization of the horse is further maintained. When a horse interacts with the interactive continuum constituting a bolt of lightning, his pattern or organization of interactions is destroyed. Every individual thing, to paraphrase Dewey, is a qualitative whole of qualities in interactive qualitative relations. The pattern or organization within the individual is the qualitative consequence of qualitative interactions.

The consequences, effects, results are not dematerialized effluvia which the "causes" cast up and then recede to do something likewise on another occasion. The "causes" are always where the effects are; the causes of any situation or thing—as an interactive continuum (in the sense defined) —are *within* that situation or thing. But not *all* the causes. Only some. Those causes namely constituting the interactions going on within that interactive continuum, within the boundaries of that situation or thing.*

Since the boundaries of one thing do not cut it off from other things but each thing is embedded in its own interactive locality, we can *use* one thing, which is an effect, as a means for finding out the causes of another thing, by bringing the two into interactive relations. We can organize them, that is, into an experiment.

The horse-stone-and-rope is as good an organization of an experiment as any other. But *to be* an experiment, we cannot start by taking it as Newton did. That was the end of the experiment, the consequence. That was the phase of the "sequential order of events" constituting the experiment which *closed* the sequence of events. An experiment is in the experimenting; there has to be a sequence of events; a longitudinal section of a history; it must have beginning and middle period as well as an ending. If we take the "ending" alone, we can only contemplate it as a

---

* Cause is an old name for a system of interactivities going on, and effect an old name for the qualitative consequences of the interactions.

brute fact, or enjoy or suffer it as an event in our emotional or esthetic experiencing.

An experiment is an organization of interactions. It is an organization of "doings-undergoings" to use Dewey's homespun phrase. The resultant of the doings-undergoings is what is *done*. To get that done is the purpose or idea of the experimenting. Or, to put it more generally, to observe what the "done" will be. Before the rope is stretched there is a stretching; before the horse pulls, he is doing-undergoing something else; before the rope is tied around the stone, it is a stone without the rope tied around it. At what phase of the inclusive history we begin our experimenting is as the case may be, depending upon what we are experimenting for, what our idea is, our plan. But there must be *some* beginning of every experiment which leads into but is not the same as the ending.

Within the organization of the experiment, horse, stone and rope are all constitutive interactive members. If the objective, the end-in-view of the experiment, of organizing that system of interactions, is to find out how much pull-ing the rope will stand, then the rope is the material being inquired into, and the stone and horse are the instruments. If the objective is to move the stone, then the horse and rope are instruments and the stone is the material. If the objective is to determine how much the horse can pull, then the stone and rope are instruments and the horse the material. Within every experiment there are instruments and material, something used as the means of inquiry and something inquired into. The consequences in the material of the interactions set going within the experiment con-stitute the objects of the closing, final, experimental ob-servation. They are the "effects" and when written up in scientific memoirs are the "final facts of the case." The consequences are the "reactions" of the interactions.

Of course, there are consequences in all the constitutive members of the interactive experimental system. If there weren't, it would not be an interactive system. Apart from this logical argument, which may appear circular, there is the existential, macroscopic evidence that objects which function as material in one experimental situation function as instruments in another. There is no reason to suppose that they undergo miraculous transformations in passing from one situation to the next. If there were any non-interacting member in any experimental situation, no inquiry would be possible and that situation would not be experimental. Witness the case with Newton's rope.

It takes two actions to make one interaction. And the consequence of an interaction is a new action. This is in logical formulation, not in existential fact. In Nature there are no actions which are stripped to the bare state of homogeneous oneness. All actions are themselves consequences of systems of interactions of various complexities of organization. However, for formal logical analysis, we may consider instrument and material as unitaries (however complex they may be) and the organization of instrument and material in an interactive system as constituting an experiment.

Every experiment is a doing-undergoing. Not metaphorically, but formal-logically speaking, the instrument is the "doing" and the material the "undergoing." For the instrument is an instrument to the extent that it is that by means of which we exercise *control over;* the material is what we are *limited by*—it is the undergoing.

No instrument is all compact with "doing" and no material we can in *any* way handle is all compact with "undergoing." Within experimental inquiry, instrument and material enter into interactive relations, and so they are interdependently doing-undergoing. The degree to which we are *controlling* the experiment going on, is the definition of the instrument functioning in *that* inquiry. It is always a degree, never an "absolute."

We are *doing* the inquiry by means of the instrument. The material is *undergoing* inquiry. The *consequence* of the interactivity of the doing-undergoing within the experimental situation is the *ending* of that inquiry. The consequence, as the ending of a controlled history, of events, is what is *known*.* It is the effect, and effects are gross and macroscopic subject-matter in primary experience. The effect brings us back to primary experience. But the *effect* now in our primary experience is not a brute fact we can only stare at in dumb "contemplation" or in animal amazement. The *effect* is a state of affairs, a situation that is achieved through controlling a history. It is the terminal phase of a sequential order of events within which sequence we have had a guiding hand. As such an effect it carries the meanings of its history within it. It is a *conclusion,* and hence we can always look at it with understanding—and sometimes even with delight.

XXI

"By the nature of the case, causality, however it be defined, consists in the sequential order itself, and not in the last term which as such is irrelevant to causality, although it may, of course, be, in addition, an initial term in another sequential order." * The nature of the case Dewey here speaks about is the case of Nature. However we define causes and effects they are both within Nature and constitute the same historical series. To discriminate causes in Nature from effects in Nature is to introduce distinc-

---

* In terms of the Aristotelian logic, the *doing* is the predicate, the *undergoing,* the subject and the copula is the interaction of the doing-undergoing that results in the conclusion. The conclusion is what is *known* and constitutes the *judgment.* See, *infra,* pp. 902f.

tions within a continuously moving history. It is not to cut Nature into two halves, the first half the causes, the second half the effects and nothing but the cut in between. Still less is it to isolate one event, and set it up as the aboriginal beginning or the ultimate ending, as the "metaphysically primitive" mechanical or teleological "cause" of all. "The view held—or implied—by some mechanists, which treats an initial term as if it had an inherent generative force which it somehow emits and bestows upon its successors, is all of a piece with the view held by teleologists which implies that an end brings about its own antecedents. Both isolate an event from the history in which it belongs and in which it has its character. Both make a factitiously isolated position in a temporal order a mark of true reality, one theory selecting initial place and the other final place. But in fact causality is another name for the sequential order itself; and since this is an order of a history having a beginning and end, there is nothing more absurd than setting causality over against either initiation or finality."*

Nature is an inclusive history of multitudinous ongoing histories, the comprehensive interactive continuum consequent upon the interactivities of an infinite number of interactive continua of an indefinite number of general kinds. When the second law of thermodynamics will have brought about the heat-death of the universe, this will not be the case. The sequential order of Nature will have then reached a term that is irrelevant to all subsequent terms because no subsequent terms will ensue. Interactivity will then have ceased and continuity in Nature might just as well be a mathematical line. Passage from one end of Nature to the other will be an uneventful event, no undergoing at all, because every locality will be exactly like every other locality and nothing doing in any of them. To

Infra, p. 1055.

distinguish and interconnect within such a universe would be a waste of time—supposing there were any time left to waste. But there will then be no making of distinctions, for all differences will have been annihilated in the absolute uniformity and for the same reason there will be no making of interconnections; interactivity will have ceased and the selfsame absolute uniformity will be the only connection left. When that Nature eventuates, it will be the end of all events and as irrelevant to all its antecedents as to its non-eventuating succeedents. For it will be carrying none of its antecedents within it. When such a time will come to the universe is not the point here. What is in point is that we are able prospectively to write the history of that dead, indistinguishable and non-existential event because it has not yet arrived. We are able to include that non-historical event in the history of the universe because there is a contemporaneous, ongoing history within which to include it.

The Nature within which we live is an ongoing history of ongoing histories. When an event is connected with another event as cause-effect, that connection is the exemplification of the continuity between them. But that connection of continuity is the funded history of interactions and the effect is the funded consequence, the terminal phase of the inclusive history of cause-effect. "The two principles of continuity and interaction are not separate from each other. They intercept and unite. They are, so to speak, the longitudinal and lateral aspects" * of every history, of every situation, of every sequential order, of every connection of cause-effect.

The union and interception of continuity and interaction can be very simply illustrated. Half a dozen ivory billiard balls placed in line will transmit to each other the impulse the first ball receives from the cue. The impulse is not

* *Infra,* p. 669-670.

transmitted in a one-way linear series of pushes from next to next, starting with the first ball and going down the line, this one-way linear series being followed by a similar one-way linear series of pushes traveling in the reverse direction. The billiard balls are made of ivory; they are not Newtonian atoms. The cue is made of wood and is not external to the world within which the billiard balls are. Each ivory ball is "alive," as billiard experts rightly say. And so is the cue. When the cue hits the first ball, the ball hits right back. The consequence of that unequal contest is the reaction of the first ball and it crashes into the next, and so on with every ball down the line. At no point do you have cause following effect and effect following cause; at every point you have a cross-weaving or interweaving of actions, that is, interactions, and each interaction is an interweaving of cause-effect.

Wherever there is interaction there also is continuity. The interaction is the continuity taken laterally or cross-sectionally; the continuity is the interaction taken longitudinally or historically. The maintenance of the interception and union of continuity and interaction constitute or create an interactive continuum.

The billiard balls illustrate also how it is that interactivity is the creative matrix of individuality. Assume to start with that the billiard balls are all alike in every character of their composition. Just as soon as they are placed in line and the interactivity is set going by the interaction between the cue and the first ball, the balls become differentiated from each other by the variations in their actions and interactions. Initially, these differentiations or variations are solely due (by hypothesis) to their respective positions in the lineup, their nearness to or remoteness from the starting interaction. But suppose that the interactivity continues for an appreciable length of time.

What happens as a consequence? The differentiations result in internal changes in the balls themselves. At the very least, they wear out at different rates (for they are in different positions in the lineup) and hence lose or gain resiliency at different rates. Two billiard balls differing in resiliency are no longer exactly alike in every character of their composition. They have become, in so far forth, individualized.

No two actual billiard balls are, of course, actually identical to start with. For theoretical purposes of illustration, their differences may be ignored, though for the practical purposes of playing billiards their differences may not be ignored—as any expert billiardist will tell.

Every actual billiard ball is an amazingly complex organization of interactivities within its own boundaries. Its "pervasive qualitative unity," to use Dewey's phrase, is a *consequence* of interactions, and is as stable as the stability of organization of interactions of which it is the consequence. We may, following Whitehead, call the billiard ball a "society" instead of an interactive continuum, and the stable organization of interactions within the billiard ball, the "personal order" of that society or billiard ball. This "personal order" may also be called the "causal law" of that society.*

When the interactivities of the six billiard balls are kept going for a sufficiently long period of time, the consequence is the creation of a new qualitative whole, a new interactive continuum, a new society. In the process of creation of the new society, the members are changed, both as to their own individual boundaries and the "personal order" of each. The boundaries of the new society, or the new interactive continuum are vastly different from the boundaries of each of the separate members before the new

* *Process and Reality,* p. 137-139ff.

society was created. They are also vastly different from the boundaries of the members as constituent and interactive within the new society. The new society taking it as a totality has its "personal order," its "causal law" its pervasive qualitative unity.

If the reader finds this consequence of the interactivity of six billiard balls too strange and difficult to accept, let such reader substitute six astronomical bodies that begin to interact with one another and after an appreciable length of astronomical time settle down in a planetary system. Or if astronomical stretches of time are repugnant, for whatever personal reason it may be, any other substitution will serve as well, as long as the items substituted are actual things within Nature, that is, things capable of *interacting*.

The personal order, causal law, pervasive qualitative unity of any new society is not the arithmetical sum of the orders, laws or qualitative unities of the constitutive interactive members as they are *within* that society nor, of course, as they were before the emergence of the new society. Every interactive continuum or individual thing is a qualitative whole of qualitative interactions. There are quantities of qualities in Nature but nothing in Nature has the quality of a sheer quantity. The consequence of interactivity of two qualitative unities is a qualitative transformation. If qualitative transformation is not the consequence, then no interaction has taken place.

The constitutive interactive members within a society are never without their own individual orders, causal laws, or qualitative unities. If within a "society" there are no individual differences within the constitutive, interactive members, then you have no members and no society at all. You have a Newtonian "atom." That the latter is a pure figment of mathematical imagination fortunately no

argument is at this date needed to prove. Within nature
there are no "individual things" that are not members of a
society and discriminable as members within that society
because of natural differences. When theoretical physicists
push their analytical reductions of experimental findings to
the limit, they still have left on their hands an electron and
proton within an atom, electron and proton differing from
each other, and the "atom" within which they are, differing
from both.

As Whitehead states it:

> A society is, for each of its members, an environment
> with some element of order in it, persisting by reason of
> the *genetic* relations between its own members. Such an
> element of order is the order prevalent in the society.
> (*Process and Reality,* p. 138; italics mine.)

When two interactive continua, two societies, each with
its own stable organization of interactions, its personal
order, causal law, or pervasive qualitative unity begin to
interact, they in that new interaction begin to suffer "disorder." The process of reaching a new stable organization
of interactions is the process of creating a new order, or a
new society. However, no more than effect *follows* cause
does a new stable organization of interactions, a new order
follow upon disorder. Cause-effect are interwoven; interaction and continuity intercept and unite. Likewise with
"disorder-order." The new order, which is an ordering or
organization of interactivities, is not an effluvium, a residue cast up, or supernatural excrescence which "supervenes" (to use Santayana's esthetic term) *after* the disordering is all over. The new ordering is constantly and
continuously in the making throughout the period of so-
called "disorder." Such periods are "transitional" only in
the sense that the disordering-ordering process is in transit, is taking place. Isolate the beginning of the history,

when the "disorder" (or interaction) began, and then isolate the ending of that same history when the new stable organization of interactivities has been established, and compare your two "isolated events" and the period in between becomes a "pure transition," a period when all is chaos, and wherein no "law and order" can be found.

When a new stable organization of interactions is achieved, that new order or causal law is the funded consequence of the total history. The new pervasive qualitative unity is the definite and emphatic emergence, in primary experience, of the consequence of internal stabilization of interactivities reached. Taking the whole period, from beginning to ending, longitudinally or historically there is a continuity of disordering-ordering interactivity, the new ordering emerging continuously through the genetic process. The "genetic process" is of course not something in addition to the history of interactions of disordering-ordering but just another name for that process. Any cross-section or lateral segment of the period will exhibit the disordering-ordering interactivity with the qualitative characters or consequences emergent in that segment. For at no lateral section will there be sheer interactivity, without a qualitative consequence or product of that interactivity. To suppose the former is to suppose the absurd or miraculous—that is, that there is a period of interaction that is purely non-qualitative and then there "supervenes" a qualitative character. It is to suppose there are "causes" without "effects." Whether at any section we take we can discern the qualitative consequence emergent in that section is another matter. It is also another matter, or the same matter, whether we can discern the interactivity going on irrespective of the size of the segment we take.

When two interactive continua or two orders are beginning to interact, the new situation created by that initiation of interaction is a situation of conflict, disturbance, unsettlement—to use Dewey's terms. The *issue,* the consequence, is the outcome of the interactivity and what it will be, in any genuine experimental situation, is problematic. Whether the outcome will be progressive or regressive, whether the funded consequence will be an increase or decrease with respect to the original "investment" that went into the interactive situation is as the case may be. The history of change is "progressive or evolutionary" even when it runs down hill. It is one of the great misfortunes of the term "evolution" or "evolutionary" that it became identified with an "upward and onward" unidirectional meaning. Evolutionary development is evolutionary development irrespective of the direction in which it is heading. The idea of an automatic upward trend was one of the supreme "scientific" absurdities of the nineteenth century, still persisting in the twentieth century. It was natural history with a shot of ancient theology in the arm. No idea is more fatal to human progress in the upward direction than the belief that the necessary and hence automatic functioning of "evolutionary processes" will take human beings up to the next step. Dewey's whole critical philosophy may be considered as one extensive exposé of the fallacy and the danger of letting Providence—in the modern scientific era variously nicknamed the "laws of Nature," the "laws of evolution," the "laws of dialectical materialism"—shape and take care of the destiny of human ends.

Of course no organization of interactions, no order or causal law of a society is so stable that it suffers no change. The stability is always a case of degree, never an absolute and eternal kind. Every system of ordered interactions is to some extent a disordered system. The element of order, as Whitehead says, is the order prevalent in that society.

It is prevalent, not omnipotent. "A thing may endure *secula seculorum* and yet not be everlasting; it will crumble before the gnawing tooth of time, as it exceeds a certain measure. Every existence is an event." * What Dewey here calls the gnawing tooth of time is the disordering factor involved in any interaction. It's not the tooth but the gnawing of the tooth that counts.

We have so far been considering societies or interactive continua as within themselves, leaving the "environment" in the shadowy background. Analytically, inhabitant and habitat can be distinguished from one another, but it has sufficiently well been demonstrated that they are symbiotically related. Moreover, as is clear in the quotation from Whitehead above, the society constitutes the immediate environment of its members.

But every society is included within a larger environment. To quote Whitehead further on this point:

There is no society in isolation. Every society must be considered with its background of a wider environment . . . the given contributions of the environment must at least be permissive of the self-sustenance of the society. Also, in proportion to its importance, this background must contribute those general characters which the more special character of the society presupposes for its members. But this means that the environment, together with the society in question, must form a larger society in respect to some more general characters than those defining the society from which we started. Thus we arrive at the principle that every society requires a social background, of which it is itself a part. In reference to any given society the world of actual entities [interactive continua, situations, occasions, individual societies] is to be conceived as forming a background in layers of social order, the defining characteristics becoming wider and more general as we widen the background. Of course the remote actualities of the back-

* Infra, p. 1051-1052.

ground have their own specific characteristics of various types of social order. But such specific characteristics have become irrelevant for the society in question by reason of the inhibitions and attenuations introduced by discordance, that is to say, disorder. (*Process and Reality,* p. 138.)

The outline of fundamental, general agreement between Dewey and Whitehead is the reason for this quotation just now. So we need not stop to consider the points in the passage which are indicative of specific differences in the two philosophies. They will emerge in the course of the subsequent argument—in case they have not emerged as yet.

An ivory billiard ball placidly resting on a billiard table in the Union Club in New York City is within the same Nature as an electron dancing around near the center of the sun. Billiard ball and electron are both included within the larger environment which includes the sun and New York City. However, by virtue of the "inhibitions and attenuations" introduced between the localities of the electron and billiard ball, the historical careers of these two are significantly irrelevant to each other. Within the locality where the electron is dancing, the dancing of the electron is productive of some consequences. Although it may be hard to believe it, yet it is true that within the locality where the ivory ball is placidly resting, it also is productive of consequences. Irrelevance with respect to each other of two restricted histories, by virtue of attenuation of interactivity between the localities within which these histories transpire, is not evidence of "discontinuity" or of breaks in nature, in the sense of abysses between. It is evidence of attenuation, of diminution of interactivity to the point where no appreciable consequences are the result. However, even the billiard ball and the electron can be made significantly relevant to each other by including

them in an environment that is sufficiently wide, and by
making the interactive functions within that embracive society sufficiently *narrow*. By the conjoint process of widening the environment and narrowing the range of interactivity, it might even be possible to make the billiard ball
relevant in the political history of the United States. However, whether or not this can be done, it is by this double
process of widening the environment and narrowing the
range of interactivity that, scientifically, our solar system
and Betelgeuse for example become connected minor histories within a larger history. And so on, illustrations without end.

XXII

Inquiry proceeds by making distinctions and every distinction is also a connection. If there were no natural differences in Nature and no natural interactions going on,
inquiry could not proceed. The nature of Nature makes
inquiry possible and not the other way about. Within the
history of Nature, inquiry is one of the emergent histories,
it is a proceeding included within the larger procession. It
does not follow the whole procession after it has gone by,
nor does it come into existence before the whole procession
has started. It is neither trailing the rear nor leading at the
point just above the head.

The existence of inquiry is an exemplification of one
of the existential differences matured within Nature. As an
existential difference within differences, inquiry can and
does make further existential differences. This is saying the
same thing said just before in another way. If the procedure of inquiry did not make differences within Nature, it
would not be one of the goings on in Nature. It would be
completely outside Nature. And if by some miraculous

sleight-of-word we put it "inside," then our miracle—like all miracles—does nothing to alter the situation, except to make it worse if, while "inside" inquiry it is a non-interacting member, neither changing nor being changed nor making changes. The nature of the case before the miracle is the same as after, only now we have a miracle on our hands to "explain." Whatever cannot participate in the goings on, is completely outside even when you call it in. If the miracle makes inquiry interactive, the consequence of changes and productive of other changes, it is again a useless encumbrance. The goings on within Nature can take better care of that. On this point, too, Whitehead is in general agreement with Dewey:" The very possibility of knowledge should not be an accident of God's goodness; *it should depend on the interwoven natures of things.* After all, God's knowledge has equally to be explained." *

For inquiry to make existential differences within Nature, it is not of course necessary for inquiry to be competent to change everything in Nature, to make the whole procession different. To be competent to do this it would have to be outside the procession. Although both Archimedes and common experience have proved this with sufficient conclusiveness to satisfy ordinary intelligences, some idealistic philosophers (and scientists too) are still holding out against the proof. It is also not necessary for Dewey's fundamental proposition, that inquiry be able to make existential changes in the major divisions of the natural procession. The procedures of human inquiry are incompetent to change the monotonous rounds the earth makes about the sun. Because the planets go round in circles is, however, no reason why human beings should. Inquiry makes changes within the localities where inquiry

* *Process and Reality,* p. 289; italics mine.

goes on, and the extent and range of these localities is not determinable philosophically and is not fixed but is determined by and in the advance of inquiry itself.

When the philosophic or logical analysis of inquiry is controlled by the experimental procedure of inquiry as that appears in gross and macroscopic experience of inquiries, there is no difficulty at all in establishing the naturalness and validity of the foregoing. It becomes almost too obviously natural to bear mentioning. Newton to the contrary notwithstanding, experimental inquiry cannot come *after* the goings on in the experiment have ended nor, of course, can the inquiry start or finish *before* the process has begun. Experimental inquiry is a procedure that works within and while the processes inquired into are going on.

Furthermore, when laboratory activity is made an integral functioning element within inquiry, the validity of the proposition that inquiry is an existential procedure the consequence of which is the production of existential changes, is also quite naturally established. In the laboratory existential changes are made. No one questions that. Finally, when theoretical activity is also made an integral functioning element within inquiry, and hence interactive with the laboratory activity—the consequence of their interactivity constituting scientific or controlled inquiry—there is similar natural ease experienced in establishing the validity of the proposition that theoretical activity within inquiry is instrumental in the production of existential changes.

The difficulties come into philosophy and logic only when theoretical activity is separated from practical activity. And when that separation is made, and the sublime exaltation of theory maintained as a primitive metaphysical gift—and like all gifts, to be accepted without asking any questions and to be purely enjoyed—difficulties do not attach themselves merely to the proposition or propositions just enunciated: they simply swarm over every topic and every part of every topic modern and contemporary philosophers inquire into. With a vengeful justice that may or may not be actually divine, the difficulties especially congregate thick and fast about the topic of theoretical activity, and are unceasingly harassing. The "purity" of theoretical activity which is originally invoked "to explain" the nature and progress of scientific inquiry has in turn to be "explained" by a still purer and hierarchically higher pure theoretical activity. The first pure theoretical activity being called "scientific," the second naturally becomes "metaphysical." That the hierarchical series ends abruptly with the latter is again a matter of pyschological stoppage and not of logical conclusion. The term "metaphysics" is as wonderfully effective psychologically when the pure theoretical pursuit is hierarchically pursued in the line of ascent as when it is pursued in the line of descent: when it is introduced it just as effectively gives the feeling of having hit the ultimate ceiling as of having hit the ultimate floor.

The latter "metaphysical case" is exemplified in the philosophy of Russell, the former in the philosophy of Whitehead.

XXIII

"The concept of an ideally isolated system," writes Whitehead, "is essential to scientific theory." As an instance of such a system he cites Newton's First Law of Motion. In explanation of what he means by the concept of an ideally isolated system, Whitehead goes on to say:

This conception embodies a fundamental character of things, without which science, or indeed any knowledge on the part of finite intellects, would be impossible. The "isolated" system is not a solipsist system, apart from which there would be non-entity. It is isolated as *within* the universe. This means that there are truths respecting *this* system which require *reference* only to the remainder of things by way of a uniform systematic scheme of relationships. Thus the conception of an isolated system is not the conception of substantial independence from the remainder of things, *but of freedom from casual contingent dependence* upon detailed items within the rest of the universe. Further, this freedom from casual dependence is required only in respect to certain abstract characteristics which attach to the isolated system, and not in respect to the system in its full concreteness. (*Science and the Modern World*, p. 68; italics mine.)

It is hardly necessary to point out, after what has already been said, that there is no difference between Dewey and Whitehead as to the *general* issue that when we "isolate" a system within Nature we do not substantially tear it out of Nature. The continuity within Nature effectively prevents that. We have to isolate because scientific inquiry can get on only by attacking Nature piecemeal. But Nature is not in pieces.

There is also hardly any need for pointing out that there is no difference between Dewey and Whitehead as to the *general* issue whether or not this "conception"—without which, truly enough, no knowledge whatsoever could be acquired—"embodies a fundamental character of things." Things are isol*able* within Nature because things within Nature are different. And they are theoretically isolable, but not substantially separable, because they are connected within Nature. The conception of an ideally isolated system, isolated as within Nature, is, therefore, an exemplification of fundamental characters in Nature. It exemplifies at the same time both the existence of differences and the existence of continuity.

So far so good and general agreement so far. But the agreement is general. Just as soon as we probe deeper all the *specific* differences between Dewey's philosophy and logic and Whitehead's begin to crop out, one after another. And they are all consequences of the one comprehensive fundamental difference between Dewey and Whitehead, namely, that Dewey does not substantially tear out experimental practice from scientific inquiry, whereas Whitehead does precisely this thing. This is *the* difference between these two philosophers, and the consequences of this difference appear and reappear in every specific context of their respective philosophies. Because of this fundamental difference the more closely these philosophies approach each other, the more clearly, emphatically and irreconcilably do they stand apart.

The theory of scientific theory is the formal meeting-place of all philosophic differences. Here some differences have their formal-logical point of origin whence they issue to work their way through the macroscopic domains of philosophic inquiry, growing to ever larger macroscopic size as they proceed; here differences originally developed in the macroscopic fields are reduced to the microscopic size of derived, refined objects of logical reflection. All differences are gathered together, systematically or otherwise, in this central sheepfold of philosophy. That this should be so is of course natural. Philosophy itself is a professional theoretical activity and if it didn't do this sort of thing it could never pull itself together.

The main issue of difference between Dewey and Whitehead is also the main issue in the whole of Western philosophy. The only specific differences relevant for examination here are such as will help to lead the reader up to, if not into, the significance of Dewey's philosophy.

XXIV

In what sense does Whitehead mean that the concept of
an ideally isolated system is *essential* to scientific theory?
In the passage quoted his meaning is ambiguously implicit; in another passage he makes it quite explicit. "All
scientific progress *depends* upon *first* framing a formula
giving a general description of observed fact." That he
means "first" in the sense that would make scientific
theory *dependent* on the *prior* existence or operation of a
metaphysical theory, he also in the same place makes quite
explicit; in fact, his whole metaphysical construction is an
elaborate exemplification and justification of this sense.
". . . speculative extension beyond direct observation
spells some trust in metaphysics . . ." "Apart from metaphysical *presuppositions* there can be no civilization"—
and science is of course a major ingredient in civilization.
"Metaphysical *understanding guides* imagination and
justifies purpose" *—in science as out.

Since the framing of the formula, according to Whitehead, is a generalization of observed fact, the observation
of fact is of course "antecedent" to the theoretical formulation. But it is "antecedent" not in any logical sense, but
in a brute existential sense; it existentially comes before, it
is merely precedent, purely ancillary. That observation of
fact can be thus brutally existential, without any logical
significance, and without requiring some "metaphysical"
precondition, presupposition or precursive cause is itself
not due to any logical theory but to the simple fact that
Whitehead accepts observation as a *de facto* existential occurrence. This accords accurately with Whitehead's account of Galileo's contribution to scientific method—I
mean with that one of his two accounts which described

* *Adventures of Ideas,* pp. 163-164; italics mine.

the Historical Revolt, of which Galileo was the scientific leader—as anti-rationalist, anti-intellectual, as a return to the "contemplation of brute fact."

That Whitehead was not able to keep consistently to that macroscopic description of the macroscopic *history* of modern scientific method we have already seen. And the vacillations, oscillations and contradictions there macroscopically manifested are repeated microscopically when he concerns himself with the *nature* of scientific method, taking the latter analytically, in terms of derived, refined objects of philosophic reflection.

Observation of fact comes first, merely first, in the ancillary sense indicated above:

> Without the shadow of a doubt, all science bases itself upon this procedure. It is the first rule of scientific method—Enunciate observed correlations of observed fact. This is the great Baconian doctrine, namely, Observe and observe, until finally you detect a regularity of sequence. (*Adventures of Ideas*, p. 149.)

Hence the only trouble with the scholastics was that they trusted to the inflexible rationality of their metaphysical dialectic without renewing periodically their acquaintance with observable fact. By establishing the habit of brute contemplation of brute fact, by starting the anti-rationalist, anti-intellectual Revolt, Galileo, if he did not put modern science on its feet, at any rate put it under the necessary "restraint."

Science begins for Whitehead when theory begins, but to get scientific theory beginning, to get it on its feet and keep it going, "metaphysics" is necessary. It is "metaphysical *understanding* that *guides* imagination and *justifies* purpose." To go *beyond* the direct observation of fact is of course an act of imagination, and to frame a formula which is a generalization of observed fact is of course the fulfillment of scientific purpose. This purpose needs justification therefore in "metaphysical understanding" because it can find no justification in the facts directly observed. The latter are just brute facts and "observation" of them is apparently as brutish as the facts observed. But if this is so, what possible virtue can there be in the great Baconian doctrine? What profit to observe and observe until you finally detect a regularity of sequence? What is this regularity of sequence? When the enunciation is made of "the observed correlations of observed facts" is *that* the formula framed, or is the formula something else and beyond?

To accept "observation of fact" as a *de facto,* brute existential occurrence is one thing. But to accept the framing of a formula as an existential occurrence is however quite another. For a formula is a theory and a theory is a going beyond existence and cannot be "derived" from existence. The scientific formula cannot find justification in the facts because the latter are merely precedent to it; and of course it cannot find justification in itself. The Great Metaphysical Tradition is dead set against it. Otherwise how can it be that a "metaphysical understanding" justifies a scientific formula, but that metaphysical understanding does not require a super-metaphysical understanding to justify *it?* If the metaphysical understanding must be accepted on its *de facto* face, what reason is there for not accepting the scientific understanding on *its de facto* face? If metaphysics were introduced to explain something *further,* a complication or development which scientific understanding does not explain—then there might be some reason for the metaphysical extension. But that is not what Whitehead introduces metaphysical understanding for. He introduces it to *explain* the formulation of the observed correlations of observed fact. But the regularity of sequence, the observed correlations of observed fact, is presumably explained by the great Baconian doctrine: Observe and observe. The formula *is* the enunciation of the regularity observed. Do we need a metaphysical understanding to be able to "enunciate"? The metaphysical understanding is introduced to explain the explanation. And when so introduced, like the miracle discussed before, it does nothing to alter the situation except to make it worse: we have now a metaphysical understanding to explain.

If Whitehead were able to forget about the observation of fact, and the scientific necessity of renewing periodically the observation of fact, his philosophy would be able to exhibit the inflexible rationality of scholastic logic. His dialectic circle of scientific formula and metaphysical presupposition of scientific formula would be self-enclosed. But no philosopher of the logic of modern science can do this. "In all theoretical physics, there is a certain admixture of facts and calculations." "Every scientific memoir in its record of the 'facts' is shot through and through with interpretation." Even if a metaphysical philosopher desired to keep the interpretation and let the "facts" go, he could not do this as long as he has any regard for science. That Whitehead has a fundamental regard for science goes without saying. By "speculation" he does not mean irresponsible reverie that with so many passes as "deep metaphysical" thought. Nor does he mean the acrobatic juggling with metaphysical "categories" characteristic of German philosophy and carried to supreme heights of absurdity by Hegel. As Whitehead brilliantly remarks, Hegel's "procedure is [such] that when in his discussion he arrives at a contradiction, he construes it as a crisis in the universe." For Whitehead "speculative boldness must be balanced by *complete humility before logic and before fact.*" * And

* *Process and Reality*, p. 25; italics mine.

hence Whitehead repudiates the "belief that logical inconsistencies can indicate anything else than some antecedent
errors." *

Complete humility before logic and before fact is a wise
provision of restraint for speculative boldness. But this
provision of restraint unfortunately only functions to intensify the problem as to how metaphysical understanding
can "guide and justify" scientific theory. Humility before
what logic? Restraint by *which* fact? "Every memoir in its
record of the 'facts' is shot through and through with interpretation." Are we to be completely humble before *such*
facts? Obviously not. Whitehead puts such "facts" in sus-
picion-engendering quotation marks. If we must *trust*
metaphysical understanding to get beyond any direct observation of fact, whence issues the "logic" by which "speculative boldness" is to be restrained? Whitehead does not
get self-enclosed in a dialectic circle only because he consistently involves himself in logical inconsistencies. The
latter cannot indicate anything else than some antecedent
errors—but they can indicate *that*.

And Whitehead's antecedent error is his dismissal of laboratory experimentation as irrelevant for the philosophic
understanding of the topic of scientific method. Scientific
method then falls apart into two disconnected halves: direct observation of fact on the one hand and framing of
formulas on the other.

The direct observation of fact *precedes* scientific theoretical formulation, but does not follow through. The framing of the formula *succeeds* the direct observation of fact,
but does not follow from. It is impossible to leave the two
in final and irrevocable unrelatedness not because the historic philosophic mission is to find some unity and this

* *Process and Reality,* p. viii. This is number ix and the last in
the "list of prevalent habits of thought, which are repudiated" by
Whitehead It is also in some respects the most important.

great purpose cannot be gainsaid—although in Whitehead this purpose is extraordinarily active. It is impossible to leave the unrelatedness final and irrevocable because of the indubitable macroscopic subject-matter in primary experience of modern science: the interprenetration of fact and theory. The natural tie between fact and theory being discarded at the outset, there is only one other way known to philosophy of establishing a tie: the introduction of a "metaphysical understanding" which serves like the stretched rope between Newton's horse and stone.

XXV

In Dewey's philosophy interaction and continuity intercept and unite. To give any special precedence or dominance to the one or the other *within* his philosophy would be to distort his philosophy and rob it of its unique strength. But within the history of philosophy, ancient, modern and contemporary, the weight of novelty and importance of contribution falls upon *interaction*. For there are a variety of "continuities" and various systems of philosophy have been developed in celebration of the varieties. To go no further afield than our two principal contrasting philosophies—those of Russell and Whitehead—they also are devoted to the end of establishing continuity. Some of Russell's strangest and most contradictory conclusions, in fact, are due to his efforts in search of "continuity" and the kind of "continuity" he uses. He manages to get everything "inside the head" because "causal continuity" makes that necessary, the causal continuity alleged to be firmly established by "physics." To get any other result, says Russell, we would have to suppose a "preposterous kind of discontinuity." (*Philosophy*, [1927] p. 140.) And rather than do that, a preposterous conclusion is apparently preferable from the standpoint of "logic" and "philosophy."

In Whitehead's philosophy also "continuity" is the dominant theme. And, despite the fact that in some domains of philosophic inquiry Whitehead has developed "continuities" with a wealth of detail and fineness of analytic precision superior to Dewey, Whitehead lands in the strangest and most contradictory conclusions—also because of the kind of conception of "continuity" he employs. Whitehead, unlike Russell, is not restrained by the kind of "causal continuity" alleged to be established by "physics"; as a creator of the "philosophy of the organism" the biological sciences carry great weight with him. However, in the philosophies of neither Whitehead nor Russell can it be said that "interaction" plays any significant role. At the risk of possible exaggeration, I would say that in the philosophies of neither do you find any interaction at all.* And at the same risk, I would say that you will not find any interaction in any contemporary philosophy of equal rank— any philosophy that has not itself been produced under the influence of Dewey.

And where there are no interactions there are no consequences—both in the Deweyan sense explained, in the sense macroscopically experienced by everyone, in the sense that is emphatically evident in the performance of laboratory experiments. The failure of philosophers "to wander off on the topic of experiment" when dealing with the topic of scientific method and all other topics of philosophy is the root source of the failures of those philosophers. A contradiction or logical inconsistency in a philosophy is not evidence of a crisis in the universe. It is evidence of antecedent error in that philosophy. But a contradiction is also evidence of something more: a contradic-

---

* If their philosophies exhibited fundamental consistency, there would be no risk attached to making this statement. For obviously, there can be no *interaction* where practice is extruded *ab initio* as irrelevant.

tion is evidence of discontinuity, of a break, or an irreconcilable conflict in the system. A philosophy that cannot proceed in its establishment of "continuity" except by going from one contradiction to another is not fulfilling its avowed purpose, is not realizing its acknowledged objective.

That Newton's "world of physics" should ever have been taken as the ultimate revelation of the reality of the physical world or of Nature was due, as we have seen, to the operation of the Greek Formula. But philosophers, who are living and thinking beings, could never rest satisfied with that acceptance. Instead of getting rid of the superstition, inherited from Plato, that any "theoretical science" is *ipso facto* the ultimate reality of the subject-matter it is alleged to be about, philosophers began constructing rival systems, aided in their efforts in the nineteenth and twentieth centuries by the new sciences of biology, psychology and latterly Einsteinian physics.

The fundamental constituents of Newton's "world of physics" were the atoms—mathematical points shot through and through with physical interpretation. The atom was a thing without internal differences, eternal and unchangeable. About the nature of the Newtonian atom no inquiry could therefore be made and nothing said. It had to be accepted as an ultimate and very brutish "fact." One atom could be distinguished from another by the purely external means of the something "between" them. But no atom ever got inside any "between" and no "between" ever got inside an atom. Like the stretched rope between horse and stone, all "relations" in the Newtonian world "tied things apart."

The "mechanics" of the Newtonian world of physics were mathematically perfect. The ultimate atoms could be put through all the known mathematical paces without ever an *interaction* taking place to disturb the perfect mathematical balance. Every now and then the physical world would seem to intrude and upset the calculations, but the ultimate metaphysical, mathematical balance of the system for several hundred years went along quite unperturbed. Of the general features of the Newtonian "world of physics" Whitehead well writes:

> . . . space and time, with all their current mathematical properties are ready-made for the material masses; the material masses are ready-made for the "forces" which constitute their action and reaction; and space, and time, and material masses, and forces are alike ready-made for the initial motions which the Deity impresses throughout the universe. (*Process and Reality*, p. 143-144.)

Newton had everything perfectly "related" in his "world of physics" but everything "related" was external to the relation between. "Is there, in the end," Bradley asked, "such a thing as a relation which is merely *between* terms? Or, on the other hand, does not a relation imply an underlying unity and an inclusive whole?"* Whitehead agrees with Bradley and so does Dewey—but for fundamentally different reasons and in different ways. Both Bradley and Whitehead ask whether *in the end* there can be such a relation. Dewey asks whether there can be such *in the beginning*. Bradley and Whitehead ask whether *in the end* all things are not *interrelated;* Dewey asks whether *in the beginning* all things are not *interactive*.

If you start out as Bradley did, by taking "external relations" exemplified in the Newtonian "world of physics" as the nature of relations in the physical world or empirical Nature, you will naturally "in the end" reach a philosophy wherein the situation is reversed. Instead of

* Quoted in Whitehead, *Adventures of Ideas*, p. 296; italics in original.

saying that the Newtonian "world of physics" was only a mathematicized "appearance" of the reality of the empirical world (and a very poor and distorted appearance at that), Bradley, as all other Idealistic philosophers, identified the "world of physics" with the physical world and then made the latter an "appearance" of a Supernatural Absolute Reality.

Russell escapes from Bradley's ending only because he abandons his project of "continuity" in the end. Whitehead does not abandon his project and though he is "in sharp disagreement with Bradley, the final outcome is after all not so greatly different."* And the reason for the approximate identity of outcome is rather simple. *In the beginning* they start with "relations," whereas "relations" are arrived at *in the ending* of philosophic as of scientific inquiry. *In the beginning,* in the gross and macroscopic subject-matter in primary experience, there are *interactions*.

"Once with internal relations, always with internal relations" says Whitehead (*Science and the Modern World*, p. 230). On behalf of Newton, if not of all mathematical physicists, it might be said "once with external relations, always with external relations." And on behalf of Dewey it can be said "once with interactions, always with interactions," *but* the relations between systems of interactions or interactive continua (societies, situations or local histories) may be "external" or "internal" *depending* upon the extent and quality of the *interactivity* between the systems of interactions or interactive continua involved. When by virtue of the "inhibitions and attenuations" the interactivity has decreased so that there are no appreciable *consequences* of the interactivity in the members in that interactive system, then the members *are* in so far *external* to each other. The billiard ball on the billiard table in

* *Process and Reality,* p. vii.

New York City and the electron dancing round the center of the sun are, when judged by the *interactivity between them,* externally related. When we unite the billiard ball and electron by some system of relations, then *within that system* they are internally related and *that relation* is not merely between them but implies an inclusive whole and an underlying unity. That inclusive whole or underlying unity is precisely what the *system* provides.

For a philosophy not to be able to maintain distinctions between natural differences is as vicious and disastrous as not to be able to maintain connections between things that are interconnected. Every interaction is the interception and union of continuity and difference. The actions within any interaction are different—otherwise there would be no interaction. That actions within an interaction are internally related is obvious. That is what an interaction is. And the consequences of any interaction are internally related to the interaction of which they are the consequences. Things that are interactive are internally related. Things that are not interactive with respect to each other are externally related. Without "inhibitions and attenuations" of interactivity in some respect there could not be systems or organizations of interactivities in other respects. Without external relations there could be no differences. Without internal relations there could be no continuity. Interaction and continuity intercept as well as unite. Without the interception and union, there would be no world and no inquiry in that world. When we are controlled by our gross and macroscopic experience of doings-undergoings, of interactions and consequences, the doctrine of internal relations ceases to be "one of the dubieties of metaphysics"* and the doctrine of external relations ceases to be one of the absolute and self-sufficient certainties of

* *Adventures of Ideas,* p. 147.

mathematical science. Control of philosophic thought by
the gross and macroscopic subject-matter in primary experience saves us from Hobson's nightmarish choice:
either the suffocation of internal relations and nothing but
internal relations; *or,* the vacuous extinction of external
relations and nothing but external relations. In Nature
there are lungs to breathe and air to be breathed. There is
no *reason* why there shouldn't be the same in philosophy.

XXVI

In the beginning, in the laboratory experiment, in the
experience of living beings, in the doings-undergoings of
all things within Nature, there are *interactions and consequences.* In the ending, in the theoretical systems of derived, refined objects of reflection, whether scientific or
philosophic, there are *relations and implications.*

In philosophies and sciences where there are no *interactions,* where the latter are never referred to, where they
are never the objects of denotative reference, of pointing
out, there are no *consequences.*

The corruption of the meaning of "interaction" which
resulted from the workings of Newton's Third Law was
bound to pass over into and corrupt the meaning of the
term "consequences." One illustration of the use of "consequences" in the Newtonianesque sense is of special illuminating value. Whitehead writes:

Mathematics can tell you the *consequences* of your beliefs. For example, if your apple is composed of a finite
number of atoms, mathematics will tell you that the
number is even or odd. But you must not ask mathematics to provide you with the apple, the atoms, and
the finiteness of their number. There is no valid inference from mere possibility to matter of fact, or, in other
words, from mere mathematics to concrete nature. (*Adventures of Ideas,* p. 161; italics mine.)

In no sense, no matter how you take the *belief*, does mathematics tell you a *consequence* of your belief when it tells you, under the conditions given, that the finite number of atoms is "even or odd."

Let us first consider a case which Whitehead clearly does not intend. Let us suppose you make an actual count of the number of atoms in your apple and reach a finite number. That number is the *consequence* of your counting (doing-undergoing) and that number is the content of your belief. The consequence of your counting is that you *know* the finite number you reached and you know that it is even or you know that it is odd. You know which one.

By the process of counting you reached say the finite number 100. The *consequence* of your belief, says mathematics, is that your number is "even or odd." Suppose you take this "consequence" (as you should if it really is a consequence) as a questioning of the result reached and so you go back and count again. As a consequence of your second counting you reach say the number 101. The consequence of your belief, says mathematics, is that your number is "even or odd." After a time you might catch on, and after a further time still you might even get tired of that game. It's just like the game "true or false."

Now let us consider the case Whitehead clearly intends —when you have not made an actual count. Does mathematics in such case tell you a *consequence* of your belief when you provide it with a finite number of atoms and it tells you the number is "even or odd"? If you do not provide mathematics with a definite finite number, what can you provide it with? What can the *content* of your *belief* be? Why, it can only be that selfsame formula: a finite number "even or odd." The fact that you are providing mathematics with a finite number of *atoms* is only a joker in the case. For it is presupposed or assumed that atoms are always wholes, that they do not split, and hence any number of atoms will always be a finite whole number. You will never get 100 1/3 atoms, which is a number that is not "even or odd." A finite number of whole numbers (atoms) *is* a number that is "even or odd" when the number is not definitely specified. That is what a finite number of whole numbers mathematically means. Bring to mathematics a *belief* the content of which is "even or odd" and mathematics will tell you the "consequence" of your belief is "even or odd." We have the same thing taken twice over, once as "belief" and once as "mathematics." (Just as Newton took the same thing twice over, once as the Third Law of Motion and once as the horse, stone and stretched rope between.)

There is another possibility of interpretation to be briefly explored. Suppose you don't know anything about mathematics. Suppose you have, like some pre-literates, counted up only to four. Mathematics, that is, mathematicians who have gone beyond your limited researches in the divine art, can tell you what *consequences they have reached as a result of their inquiries.* In this sense, mathematics told Descartes Euclidean geometry and algebra— and then Descartes turned round and told mathematics what it didn't know before—analytical geometry. In this sense mathematics told Newton and Leibnitz what previous mathematicians had discovered as a *consequence of their inquiries* and then they turned round and told mathematics what it didn't know before—Fluxions or Calculus In this sense, mathematics can tell you what mathematicians have learnt up to the time of the telling. But mathematics cannot tell you anything that has not yet been found out, any *consequence* of mathematical inquiry that has not yet been reached.

But even when thus pedagogically interpreted, mathematics is not telling you a consequence of your *belief*—if you take the belief psychologically. Mathematics is the last inquiry on earth that can tell you what the consequences of any belief are—even when the content of the belief is mathematical. Witness the illustrious case of Pythagoras. He held the belief that numbers are "even or odd." When mathematics told him that there is a number that is neither even nor odd but both (the square root of 2) the *consequence of his belief* in "even or odd" was that he wouldn't believe what his own mathematical researches told him: he wouldn't believe that the square root of 2 was really a number at all, an object of rational mathematical thought and true mathematical belief. Pythagoras wasn't the first mathematician nor the last philosopher whose mathematical beliefs had consequences of this order. Whitehead himself is by far the greatest contemporary mathematical-philosopher whose mathematical beliefs have in this respect quite thoroughly Pythagorean consequences. Whitehead objects to the "casual" heterogeneity of space-time in Einstein's system because it is "inherent in my [Whitehead's] theory to maintain the old division between physics and geometry."* The details in the case between Whitehead and Einstein are much more complicated than in the case Pythagoras confronted. But the two cases are in principle identical. It was inherent in Pythagoras' theory to maintain the old division between even and odd. When a number came along that exhibited a casual heterogeneity of even-and-odd, Pythagoras would have nothing to do with it. And all good Greek mathematicians and philosophers followed his lead.

Mathematics can tell no one any consequence of any belief. And mathematics, pure mathematics, can tell no

---

* Quoted from Whitehead's *The Principle of Relativity* in *Analysis of Matter*, p. 77.

consequences of anything—probability theories notwithstanding. There is no valid inference from mere mathematics to concrete nature. And consequences are in concrete nature. Mathematics is the *consequence* of inquiry, and the consequences of mathematical inquiry *when used* have further consequences.

The practically inseparable complementary of the intellectual habit of calling "consequences" what are plainly not consequences, is the intellectual habit of not calling consequences what are plainly consequences. One illustration from Whitehead will amply exemplify the latter.

Whitehead is critical of "the Positivist doctrine concerning Law, namely, that a Law of Nature is *merely an observed* persistence of pattern in the *observed succession* of natural things: Law is then merely description."[*] In analytical description of this doctrine, Whitehead has the following essential things to say:

It [Positivism] presupposes that we have direct acquaintance with a succession of things. This acquaintance is analysable into a succession of things observed. But our direct acquaintance consists not only in distinct observations of the distinct things in succession, but also it includes a comparative knowledge of the successive observations. Acquaintance is thus cumulative and comparative. The laws of nature are nothing else than the observed identities of pattern persisting throughout the series of comparative observations. Thus a law of nature says something about things observed and nothing more.

The preoccupation of science is the search for simple statements which in their joint effect will express everything of interest concerning the observed occurrences. This is the whole tale of science, *that* and nothing more. It is the great Positivist doctrine, largely developed in the first half of the nineteenth century, and ever since

* *Adventures of Ideas,* p. 147; italics mine.

growing in influence. It tells us to keep to things observed, and to describe them as simply as we can. That
is all we can know. Laws are statements of observed
facts. This doctrine dates back to Epicurus, and embodies his appeal to the plain man, away from metaphysics and mathematics. The observed facts of clear
experience are understandable, and nothing else. Also
"understanding" means "simplicity of description."
(*Adventures of Ideas*, pp. 147-148; italics in original.)

The above account is an accurate description of the fundamentals of "the great Positivist doctrine" of which the
current school of Logical Positivism is one of the hybrid
offshoots. Although Whitehead is critical of Positivism, he
is roundly critical—he turns right around and adopts their
position. Thus on the heels of the above, he goes on to say:

> *Without doubt this* Positivist doctrine contains a
> *fundamental truth about scientific methodology.* For ex-
> ample, consider the greatest of all scientific generaliza-
> tions, Newton's Law of Gravitation:—Two particles of
> matter attract each other with a force directly propor-
> tional to the square of their distance. The notion of
> "force" refers to the notion of the addition of a com-
> ponent to the vector acceleration of either particle. It
> also refers to the notion of the masses of the particles.
> Again the notion of mass is also explicitly referred to in
> the statement. Thus the mutual spatial relations of the
> particles, and their individual masses, are required for
> the Law. *To this extent* the Law is an expression of the
> *presumed characters* of the particles concerned. *But the
> form of the Law,* namely the product of the masses and
> the inverse square of the distance, *is purely based upon
> description of observed fact.* A large part of Newton's
> *Principia* is devoted to a *mathematical investigation
> proving that the description is adequate for his pur-
> poses;* it collects many details under one principle.
> *Newton himself insisted* upon this very point. *He was
> not speculating; he was not explaining.* Whatever your
> cosmological doctrines may be, the motions of the
> planets and the fall of the stones, so far as they have

been directly measured, conform to his Law. *He is enunciating a formula which expresses observed correlations of observed facts.**

We have previously quoted in part the paragraph that immediately succeeds the above. For the benefit of completing the context of discussion, the paragraph is cited here entire:

> *Without the shadow of a doubt, all science* bases itself upon *this* procedure. It is the first rule of scientific method—Enunciate observed correlations of observed fact. This is the great Baconian doctrine, namely, Observe and observe, until finally you detect a regularity of sequence. The scholastics had trusted to metaphysical dialectic giving them secure knowledge about the nature of things, including the physical world, the spiritual world, and the existence of God. *Thence they deduced* the various laws, immanent and imposed, which reigned supreme throughout Nature. (*Adventure of Ideas,* p. 149; italics mine.)

Whitehead's grievance against "the great Positivist school of thought [which] at the present time reigns supreme in the domain of science" is that its

> aim . . . is to confine itself to fact, with a discard of all speculation. Unfortunately, among all the variant schools of opinion, it is the one which can least bear confrontation with the facts. It has never been acted on. It can never be acted on, for it gives no foothold for any forecast of the future around which purpose can weave itself. (L. c. p. 159.)

The great Positivist doctrine—and the Logical Positivist doctrine—cannot bear confrontation with the facts. But the facts it cannot bear confrontation with are the facts of scientific methodology. However, if you accept the Positivist doctrine as a true account of scientific methodology, if you accept, with them, the *consequences* of a long and

* *Adventures of Ideas,* p. 148; italics mine.

complicated procedure of inquiry as the enunciation of direct observation of observed correlations of observed fact, the belated introduction of a "metaphysical understanding" of "speculative boldness" to guide imagination and justify purpose *in the future* does not help matters any. The future grows out of the present and the great trouble with Positivism is that it doesn't take care of the present. Just as the term "metaphysics" has the psychological effect of giving the user thereof the feeling of having hit the bottom of the bottom floor or the top of the top ceiling, so "Positivism" has the psychological effect of giving the user thereof the feeling of standing on the level.

"As long as man was unable by means of the arts of practice to direct the course of events, it was natural for him to seek an emotional substitute; in the absence of actual certainty in the midst of a precarious and hazardous world, men cultivated all sorts of things that would give them the *feeling* of certainty. And it is possible that, when not carried to an illusory point, the cultivation of the feeling gave man courage and confidence and enabled him to carry the burdens of life more successfully. But one could hardly seriously contend that this fact, if it be such, is one upon which to found a reasoned philosophy." *

Philosophic reasonings, like all reasonings, generate feelings of certainty. And no individual philosopher can ever escape from having those feelings engendered in him. A philosopher is at least as human as a scientist and usually he is more so. When a philosopher introduces a second explanation to explain what the first was introduced to explain and then introduces a third explanation to explain the second, we have gross and macroscopic evidence that something is seriously wrong with the first explanation and that the philosopher in question is aware

* *Infra*, p. 297-298; italics in original.

that this is the case. When the philosopher stops with his third explanation because of the feeling of certainty engendered in the process, that may be a satisfactory way of enabling that philosopher to carry the burdens of his philosophy. But no subsequent philosopher ever feels under obligation to carry the burdens of his predecessors in the same old way. He wouldn't be a philosopher if he did. However, if he follows the same method of pyramiding explanations he will soon discover that he can escape the burdens of his predecessors only by adding new burdens. And they usually turn out to be reconstructed complications of the old.

The histories of Whitehead and Russell exemplify this to unfortunate perfection. They began by making a clean sweep and then started out from symbolic-logical scratch. But what they failed to sweep out was the traditional method of philosophy. And that brought all that was so industriously swept out back in again.

As long as the old method prevails in philosophy—no matter what the symbolic disguise—the same forlorn history will be repeated. No burden will ever be removed and philosophy, instead of becoming lighter and clearer in its historical passage, will become weightier and weightier, a denser and denser mass of fiercely entangled "eternal problems."

XXVII

A formula is a formulation. In itself it is a finished and completed thing. Any given "ideally isolated system" such as the First Law of Motion is a formula. As such it is the final term of a sequential history of inquiry. Instead of all scientific progress depending upon *first* framing a formula, just the opposite is true: the framing of a formula is the fulfillment, the realization, the *consequence*

of scientific progress made. As the last term of that sequential order of inquiry, it is irrelevant to scientific
progress, although it may, of course, be, in addition, an
initial term in another sequential order of inquiry. And
when it is made such an initial term in another inquiry,
then of course it does become relevant to *further* scientific
progress. The Third Law of Motion, for example, is another of Newton's "ideally isolated systems," the final
term, the consequence of another order of inquiry. And in
reaching that conclusion, there can be no doubt Newton
was helped by using the notion of the First Law. So, too,
on a vastly more complicated scale, with the formula
which constitutes the Law of Gravitation. It is the net
consequence, the terminal result, of an elaborate history
of inquiry involving the use of all the "notions" Whitehead
specified—and many more besides.

When scientific theoretical inquiry is as highly developed as it is in modern times, the use of ideally isolated
theoretical systems—formulae—is a matter of course. And
to continue theoretical inquiry on the same high level, and
to further the development of that high level the continued use of ideally isolated theoretical systems becomes
a matter of necessity. *In this sense,* the concept of "ideally
isolated systems" is *essential* to scientific theory.

However, there is a fundamental difference between the
concept of *an* ideally isolated system, and the concept of
"ideally isolated systems." The former is the concept of a
specific system which is the consequence of inquiry undertaken and completed. The "truths" it contains are the
truths attained. The latter is the general concept of a
method of procedure. It contains no "truths" at all but
is part of the *method* of attaining truths. And like every
method of procedure, it is itself the *consequence* of pro-

ceeding. It is developed in the course of using that method of procedure.

Every specific isolation is the *consequence* of an activity involving the use of the method of isolating. When, a while back, we were considering the laboratory experimentalist "by himself," we *had* him "by himself" as a consequence of having performed an act of isolation. It was an achievement, a consequence of inquiry, not a datum or gift to inquiry. We are now so expert, so habituated to using the method of isolating—in some cases—we take the consequences for granted, as if they were naturally coming to us and we did not have to go out and get them.

Because laboratory and theoretical activities are interactive *within* inquiry, the consequence of performing the initial act of isolating did not separate the laboratory activity from the theoretical, but isolated it as *within* inquiry. If we had stopped after achieving that initial consequence, *that* consequence would have been the total content of our "ideally isolated system." The "truth" contained in *that* "ideally isolated system" would have been the sole "truth" that laboratory experimentation can be isolated as within inquiry. That would be a "truth" of that system because that system was the consequence of inquiry undertaken and carried to that completion. The enunciation of the proposition "laboratory experimentation can be isolated within inquiry" would be the formulation of the consequences achieved, of the scientific progress made.

However, we didn't stop there but continued with our inquiry. As a consequence of that continuance we acquired further "truths." The content of our initially ideally isolated system was increased. Some of the further consequences, some of the further truths, were, for example, that laboratory experimentation involves the use of instruments and materials; that an experiment is an organization of instruments and materials in accordance with a plan; that an experiment is performed with an end-in-view.

Now "plan" and "end-in-view" are theoretical elements, consequences of theoretical activity. Without going over the whole ground again, suffice to say that the *general* consequence of our inquiry into the conduct of laboratory activity was that the *consequences* of theoretical activity are internally involved at every point; that the continuity and interaction of the two intercept and unite.

If laboratory experimentation can be isolated within scientific inquiry, naturally, the same can be done with scientific theoretical experimentation. In fact, the consequence of isolating either one is that the other is also thereby isolated, since the two comprise the totality of scientific inquiry.

When we were analyzing the conduct of laboratory activity, we were constantly compelled to take into account the consequences of theoretical activity. Had we based our analytical inquiry on the antecedent presupposition that laboratory experimentation is "practice" and separated from "theory," the consequence of that presupposition would have been that no analysis would have been possible. Such an antecedent condition would have been a cause sufficient to have the effect of extruding laboratory activity from inquiry into scientific method.

When, having achieved the initial isolation of the scientific theoretical activity, we proceed to inquire further into it, we are likewise compelled to take into account the laboratory activity. In the one case as in the other, the compulsion is essentially inevadable because of the functional interactivity of theoretical and practical activities.

The compulsion is inevadable. But like all compulsions

working in theoretical enterprise—of which philosophy is one—it is postponable. In fact, if it couldn't be postponed, there would be no theoretical activity of any sort. For all thinking or deliberation consists precisely in postponing what has to be done. In technical psychological terms, thinking, deliberation is consequent upon practical responses being delayed. Only by metonymy, however, is thinking itself a "delayed response." When thinking goes on, it delays the overt response further. But thinking is a *consequence* of a mode of socio-biologic organization of interactivity, not a metaphysically primitive condition or cause. There has to be a response delayed before thinking can come into existence and delay a response.

In the "purest" theoretical activities—in symbolist poetry, symbolic logic, pure mathematics, and some metaphysical philosophies—the compulsion of taking into account the consequences of practical activity can be indefinitely postponed. Just as soon as it seems imminent that the next turn will lead back into practice, all that it is necessary to do is to write another symbolist poem, develop another symbolic-logical distinction, inquire further into pure mathematics, excogitate some more metaphysical philosophy.

Such theoretical activities, or at least some of them, have a special fascination for the philosopher. A philosopher is occupationally, if not constitutionally, prone to dismiss the technological uses of the microscope in biology as irrelevant for a philosophy of the sciences or the logic of scientific method. And having dismissed the microscope at the very outset of his inquiry into scientific method, he thinks no more of it. Being a theoretician himself, he knows *he* is not going to use a microscope in the conduct of *his* inquiry. However, when he comes to the technological uses of the calculus in physics, he does not dismiss *that* as irrelevant for a philosophy of the sciences or the logic of scientific method—especially if the calculus is not the old one of Newton but the new tensor calculus of Einstein. And having started out by following the lead of his own bent, the philosopher can go on and on, indefinitely postponing taking into the account of his theoretical analysis the consequences of practical activity. He may even reach the point Russell early reached, of making the "philosophy of mathematics" the *whole* of the "philosophy of scientific method."

However, the ideally isolated systems Whitehead asserted to be essential to scientific theory were not of the "pure" theoretical sort. As an instance of the kind of system he meant, he cited Newton's First Law of Motion: "Every body continues in its state of rest, or of uniform motion in a straight line, except so far as it may be compelled by force to change that state." He did not, as an instance of the kind of system he meant, cite a formula like A is A or $a+b=b+a$. For Whitehead, as we have already seen, there is no valid inference from mere mathematics to concrete nature. The systems essential for scientific theory are such as are ideally isolated *within* concrete Nature. Hence Whitehead's concern to make clear that such systems are not substantially torn *out* of Nature.

Newton's Third Law of Motion is as much an instance of an ideally isolated system as his First Law. Formally considered, it is in fact much better because it has explicitly formulated two terms and a relation between, which is the barest minimum for any ideal system. Since we have had some dealings with the Third Law, we may as well continue with it. It is legitimate to make this substitution, for what Whitehead says has application to all ideally isolated systems. He is enunciating a general character of the conception. Also we may legitimately

substitute the Third Law for the Law of Gravitation—as
far as any general argument is concerned. If the form of
the Law of Gravitation is "purely based upon description
of observed fact," why, so is the Third Law of Motion.
Newton himself insisted on this very point, as we have
already seen. According to Newton, the Third Law—like
all his Laws—is "derived from phenomena." He was not
explaining, he was not speculating, he was simply enunciating a formula which expressed the observed correlations of observed facts. And like the Law of Gravitation, the Third Law "collects many details under one
principle."

XXVIII

When we take a horse out of one field we can do so
only by taking that horse, in the same process, into
another field. We can take one thing in nature out of one
sequential order of events, only by bringing that thing into
another sequential order of events. In homely language,
we can go *from* one place in nature only by going *into*
another place in nature. That we can, as a matter of
practical reality, take a number of things in nature from
different places and bring them together in one place, is
not a consequence of any theory about nature but an
exemplification of one of the ways in which nature goes on

Now when as experimental laboratorians we take a horse
out of one field, a rope out of another, and a stone out of a
third, and bring them all together into the laboratory we
have, to quote Whitehead, "freed" those three things
"from casual contingent dependence upon detailed items
within the *rest* of the universe." That is, we have brought
them into casual contingent dependence upon detailed
items within the laboratory. For so far, we have only
brought them *into* the laboratory—which, like every other

place, is just another place in Nature. It is only by a futuristic figure of speech that we can say we have already "scientifically isolated" the horse, stone and rope. We have only gathered them together—as people gather together in a theater before the show begins.

The items within the laboratory (including the laboratory itself) are like all items within the universe. Within the laboratory there are items that are "casual" as far as the inquiry to be conducted is concerned; but there are also other items which are not casual, but *causal,* with the respect to the experiment to be performed.* The scale, pulley, meter or other piece of apparatus *when organized with the three objects into an experiment* is a necessary causal factor, and not a casual contingent one because we have it under control and know how it will behave when made an interactive member of the interactive system which the experiment constitutes.

If we had no experimental apparatus within the laboratory, things which we can exercise control over, bringing the objects into the laboratory would be of no scientific consequence. Horses can be looked at, contemplated, in the fields where they roam as well as in the laboratory—if not better.

A scale is a scientifically isolated physical system. A perfect scale is a perfect, ideally isolated physical system. Since there are no perfect scales, we may say that *in so far* as it is an instrument whose behavior we have standardized and regulated *to that extent* is it an *ideally* isolated physical system. And having made this qualification once, we need not make it again. It is taken for granted throughout the sequel.

* "From the standpoint of control and utilization, the tendency to assign superior reality to causes is explicable. A 'cause' is not merely an antecedent; it is that antecedent which if manipulated regulates the occurrence of the consequent." Infra, p. 1055.

The scale as an instrument of inquiry is the consequence of a long series of practical-theoretical investigations carried to completion. As a thing, within its own boundaries, the physical scale is no different from the stone within its boundaries. Within Nature both are interactive continua, neither superior to the other in this respect. When the stone is on the floor of the laboratory, scale and stone are as casually related, as externally related, as contingently related as the stone and the tree nearby the stone in the field out of doors.

When, however, we put the stone on the scale, the situation is radically changed. With respect to the progress of inquiry, the stone and scale are, within the experimental situation thus created, fundamentally different. The scale becomes an instrument of investigation, and the stone the material to be investigated.

The scale, let us say, is in perfect condition. It has been perfectly standardized as a consequence of a series of interactions. Although standardized, it is not standardized at one fixed point. The pointer of the scale is not fixed at the marking o or 100. The scale is so constructed that it can *interact* with things put on it, and the consequences of the interactions are different as the interactive things put on it differ.

Before the stone is placed on the scale, the scale is a settled, completed, finished thing. It rests in the bosom of the laboratory the way a stone rests in the bosom of the pasture and both rest in the bosom of Nature. When we put the stone on the scale, when we organize the two into an interactive system, the settled system of the scale is unsettled, and the final consequence of the new unsettlement is that a new dynamic equilibrium is achieved. When the pointer comes to rest, the interactions, the doings-undergoings within the experimental situation in

clusive of the scale and stone have come to their conclusion. Stone and scale now constitute one interactive
continuum, contained within the new boundaries which
their interactivity has created. They have united their
forces and face the world with a common or united front.

If the scale were so constructed that it entered into
the interactivity completely, so that it put its whole soul
and being into the doings-undergoings within the experimental situation, we would be no better off, with respect
to inquiry *into the stone*, than we were before. Isolated
hydrogen and isolated oxygen when made to interact with
each other in the chemical laboratory do put everything
they are and have into the doings-undergoings. Both are
consumed in the interactivity and the consequence is something new. We know as result of that experiment that when
hydrogen and oxygen interact completely, neither preserving a thought of saving itself, that *water* is the consequence. But what we know is equally divided between the
two. Both went into the doings-undergoings and neither
of them came out. We have learnt something about both,
but nothing about either one of them alone through the
instrumentality of the other.

The scale is constructed so that it won't do that sort of
thing. It will enter into interactions but not so completely
as to lose itself. It will let the stone upset its balance, but
it keeps its head. The scale, in other words, is within two
situations simultaneously, within the experimental situation and within its own situation within the universe.
Hence the scale weighs the stone.

When the scale and stone have reached their conclusive
adjustment and have settled down together, we look at the
pointer of the scale and make the reading. We *know* how
much the stone weighs, not because we "contemplate" the
pointer on the face of the scale, but because the scale is

a construction, an instrument, the net accumulated consequence of a history of inquiry, of doings-undergoings,
practical and theoretical. Furthermore, the place where
the pointer is at rest is a *new* consequence, the stable
effect of the stable organization of interactivities the scale
and stone have reached. If the pointer always stayed at the
same place of rest it would give no reading. Whenever it
gives a reading, it is because there has been a passage of
the pointer from one place into another, the mode of
passage controlled or regulated by the organization of the
vital organs of the scale. The reading is the concluding
phase of that passage, and that concluding phase includes
within itself the historical sequence of events of which it
is the net effect. The reading is a *fact* shot through and
through with meaning. It is a refined object all ready for
subsequent scientific reflection.

When we "ideally isolate" the pointer where it comes to
rest from the historical passage through which it went
before it reached that point of rest; and when we go
further and "ideally isolate" the total scale from the
history of inquiry of which it is the end-result, when we
do these things* we get the Eddingtonian consequence.
Eddington gratuitously condemns himself to the vacuous
dizziness of going round from one meter to the next and
finding nothing but numbers at every place he stops. And
Eddington's fate is not unlike that of the gas-meter man
who, having taken down meaningless numbers the livelong
day, escapes, at the fall of darkness, into another world.

XXIX

Let us now consider the Third Law. It is an "ideally
isolated system" isolated as within Nature. "All scientific

---

* They are really one thing done twice over: once microscopically, and once macroscopically.

progress depends upon first framing a formula." The Third
Law is our formula. It is already framed and now we
want to progress. As an ideal formula, it should be an
ideal instrument of inquiry into things. That is its whole
virtue, the reason for its exaltation. It tells us the way of
the land. So let us consider the Third Law as an instrument, in the sense that a scale is, something with which
we can take the measure of things and find something out
about them with respect to their doings-undergoings, their
actions and reactions.

Not unduly to prejudice the case, let us not take the Law
to the horse, stone and stretched rope between, whence
Newton "derived it" but to a contemporary horse, stone
and stretched rope between. And what do we find? We find
that when we take the Law purely theoretically, we always
get "action and reaction are equal and opposite." No
matter how we *theoretically* "apply" that Law "to" our
contemporary state of affairs—applying it to the whole of
it or any part of it, longitudinally or laterally—it cuts the
same way. The horses are different, the ropes are different,
the stones are different but the Third Law remains the
same. The horse may be pulling and relaxing, the rope may
be stretching and sagging, the stone may be moving and
resting but the Third Law will tell us none of these things.
As long as we listen to the Third Law we will hear it
repeating "action and reaction are equal and opposite."
As far as advancing our scientific knowledge is concerned,
our application no more advanced our knowledge than
Newton advanced his scientific knowledge when he brought
the Third Law to his horse, stone and stretched rope between. He started with the Third Law and ended with
the same.

With respect to Newton's experimental situation as with
respect to ours, the Third Law, when theoretically applied,

was as casual, as contingent an item within the universe
as any blade of grass waving in the breeze at the antipodes.

The Third Law, like any ideally constructed refined
object of reflection, is standardized to give one reading
only; and when taken by itself gives only one reading—
like a yardstick, which always says "one yard." But there
is this great difference between a physical yardstick and
a Law. If you apply a yardstick end-on, and proceed in an
ongoing line, you get one yardstick, two yardsticks, three
yardsticks. You get ahead. You count up. But when you
count three applications of the Third Law, no matter how
you proceed in your theoretical process of application, you
get "action and reaction are equal and opposite" once,
twice, thrice. You can count, but cannot count up. Since
after three applications you get thrice, not three, once is
enough.

The "application" of the yardstick is only by an unfortunate habit of language an "application to;" actually,
it is an experimental doing-undergoing within Nature. The
yardstick, as it moves through place into place, is interacting—as the scale interacts. Hence, unlike the Third
Law when theoretically applied, it gives the measure of
the land and not the measure of itself. Sometimes part of
the interactive organization of the yardstick happens to
be a human being. But mileage-meters, and meters of
whatever sort, are experimental demonstrations that the
human being is not needed for that kind of instrumental
operation.

Any formula, any refined object of reflection, is the
consequence of inquiry. Take it by itself, in "isolation,"
and it is a finished, completed thing. When you theoretically apply it to a situation you are still taking it by itself.
And hence it will always give the reading of itself and not
of the situation to which it is applied. The Third Law,

or any other formula, is in this respect precisely like the formula "even or odd." Provide the mathematical formula "even or odd" with any number and it will always say "even or odd." Whether that number is even or is odd is something that you will never discover by means of theoretically applying the formula. To discover what that number is, you have to undertake the requisite inquiry.

A formula is the consequence of scientific progress made. Stop there, and that is where your science stops. The formula can become an esthetic object, a headache, a bore, a means of earning a livelihood by pedagogically putting it into the heads of others, and a possible variety of other things. But it does not become an instrument of scientific progress until something further is done with the formula in the course of another inquiry. In its solitary confinement, in its ideal isolation, the formula, if we may trust Aristotle, becomes either a god or a brute. For living experience, there is no genuine difference between the alternatives. The inevitable consequence of deification is the brutalization of human life.

XXX

There is only one way of finding out whether in an actual existential situation "action and reaction are equal and opposite," and that is by making an experimental laboratory test. For such a test, laboratory instruments are necessary, ideally isolated physical systems in the sense explained. Newton was no laboratorian and his test of the Third Law was no experimental test. The immortal achievement of Einstein fundamentally consists in making scientists realize the difference between theoretical scientific construction and experimental laboratory testing of the constructions theoretically reached. The experimental laboratory testing of conclusions reached by scientific theoreticians is now made by laboratorians competent and instrumentally equipped to do that part of the total scientific work. Einstein completed the revolution Galileo started.

The instruments of the theoretical physicist today are all of a mathematical quality because the *material* the theoretician receives from the laboratorian is already mathematicized. The material of the theoretical physicist is constituted by the refined objects of scientific-physical reflection which are consequences of laboratory experimentation and which he finds in the "memoirs." The records of the facts come from the laboratory and they come shot through and through with mathematical meaning. But obviously there must be something in the facts besides the mathematical interpretation, otherwise there would be no distinguishing between the two. This is what James called the "irreducible and stubborn facts" and what we have called, slightly modifying Dewey's phrase, the subject-matter in the primary laboratory experience.

Like the material and instruments of the laboratory physicist, so with the material and instruments of the theoretical physicist: they are distinguishable from one another but not separated and disconnected. Pure mathematics is separated and disconnected from the refined objects of scientific-physical reflection received from the laboratory. But pure mathematics is not the *instrument* the theoretical physicist uses. The mathematics already *in* the scientific-physical refined objects he receives from the laboratorian, is *de-purified* and the theoretical physicist in pursuing his inquiry into those objects and searching for a solution to the problem they raise, must constantly de-purify the mathematics he uses to be able to continue in his pursuit. "The mathematics in which the physicist is interested was developed for the *explicit* purpose of describing the behavior of the external world, so that it is certainly no accident that there is a correspondence between mathematics and nature."* This is not altogether so. The contemporary physicist is interested in the non-Euclidean geometries and they were not developed for the explicit purpose of describing the behavior of the external world. There is also the celebrated case of conic sections which for some eighteen hundred years was of no interest to the physicist. The physicist today is, generally speaking, interested in all pure mathematical systems and in the construction of more and more of them. Also, since physics became mathematical, the production of pure mathematics has vastly increased. In the world of intelligent activity, where there is a demand or need, there is concerted effort made to supply.

But the pure mathematical systems are, for the physicist, his instrumental *sources*. They are not his instrumental *resources* until by *using* them in his inquiry into refined scientific-physical objects—the facts or *data* he has received from the laboratorian—he has converted them into such. Pure mathematics may be as pure as the angelic hordes, but for the physicist, they are only half-raw material that must be further fashioned, by use, before they become finished instruments.† "In all theoretical physics there is a certain admixture of facts and calculations" *because* the whole process of physical theorizing consists in continuously "admixing" the two in a certain way.

* Bridgman, *The Logic of Modern Physics,* pp. 60-61; italics mine.

† The theoretical physicist is not peculiar in having others supply *sources* of material for his instrumental uses. The laboratorian also has as *sources* the productions of industrial and fine arts— and for him too, the products, however finished and final whence they are taken, are only half-raw materials which become *resources* for laboratory experimentation only as they are used and changed in laboratory practice.

XXXI

Every instrument in the laboratory is the physical embodiment of the consequences of histories of interactivity of theoretical and laboratory functions in inquiry. The current microscope, for example, unites within itself the end-results cumulatively attained in the historical course of progressively integrating the consequences, corrective and expansive, of theory and practice. Every laboratory instrument is a (relatively) ideal physical system of interactions (or an interactive continuum) isolated within Nature. The more ideally organized, the more completely "isolated" within itself, the more carefully standardized, then the more adequate the instrument for further and furthering inquiry. The measure of our control in laboratory experimentation is measured by the range and quality and number of our ideally isolated physical systems—by our instrumental equipment.

The microscope today is constructed in accordance with the specifications of a formula. The formula of the microscope, *qua* formula, in its strictly professional capacity, is theoretical. But the formula is itself a product, the cumulative end-result of the same inclusive histories of inquiry of which the microscope is the physical product or end-result. The practical history of making glass, polishing, silvering, and so on, is as much *internally involved* in the finished product which constitutes the formula, as the theoretical history of *formulating the consequences* of polishing, silvering and so on, is *internally involved* in the finished product which constitutes the microscope.

The formula of the microscope is an ideally isolated theoretical-physical system, isolated as within Nature. The extent of our control in theoretical scientific experimentation is measured by the range and quality and number of our formulae (as just defined)—by our theoretical instrumental equipment.

The distinction between "material" and "instruments" is functional. There are no "materials in themselves" on the one hand and "instruments in themselves" on the other. The material is that which, within the history of inquiry going on, is under investigation, is being inquired into; the instruments are, within that same history, the means used in making the investigation, in making the inquiry. Both material and instruments are therefore within inquiry, the distinction between them existing only while the process of inquiry is going on. The distinction itself is a consequence of inquiry, not an antecedent, or a "cause" making inquiry possible. Outside of the process of inquiry, all things relapse into the "state of nature." A microscope, outside of use in inquiry, is no more an instrument than a boulder on the side of the Himalayas. A formula outside of use in inquiry is no more an instrument of scientific progress than the other side of the moon. We can "contemplate" both—and derive esthetic enjoyment from doing so, each enjoyment differing with the object enjoyed.

If there were things that were aboriginally and ineluctably just "material" and other things that were likewise just "instruments," that state of affairs would not *cause* inquiry, but stop it. The only thing then possible would be the footless process of externally "applying" the instruments "to" the material, and even that would be impossible if you had done a real job of separation, and had not left an ambiguous umbilical attachment somehow dangling between the two.

Within inclusive inquiry—including laboratory and theoretical functions—there is the distinction between material and means. Within each half of inquiry, there is the same distinction prevailing. Because within each half of inquiry there are both material and means (instruments), each half of inquiry can proceed in *partial* independence of the other. The theoretical experimentalist and laboratory experimentalist, taking each one by himself, has his own distinctive ways of exercising control over his material; each is controlled by the consequences of the activity of the other; and each is limited by the limitations of his instruments. There are morphological similarities and identities in the two activities because of the inevitable interactivity of the two.* They interweave and cross-weave, intercept and unite, each working *in* the territory of the other.

The laboratory and theoretical activities, taking them each in their own partial histories, are never exactly abreast. They are always shooting ahead or falling behind each other. The laboratorian, in performing a test or making a new experiment, often creates a new problem, and that is something for the theoretician. The theoretician in solving one problem often broaches another and that is something for the laboratorian.

When we take the macroscopic history of any modern science, the most obvious characteristic is the interweaving and cross-weaving, the interception and union, of new problem and old solution and new solution with old prob-

* The morphological similarities and identities are not here detailed, because it would involve a repetition of Sections XVIII and XX, substituting "theoretical" instruments and means for laboratory or practical instruments or means.

Because the consequences or products of theoretical activity are always *means* for guiding, regulating, practical activity—particularly so in scientific inquiry—Dewey calls all consequences of theoretical activity, *when taken by themselves, means,* and hence makes the distinction, within the theoretical activity of "material means and procedural means." (*Infra,* p. 912.) This is one way of emphasizing his fundamental doctrine. However, the same distinction between material means and procedural means can be made within the laboratory activity.

lem in an indefinite variety of ways and extents. It is this interdevelopmental process of inquiry that makes modern science progressive and cumulative, ever richer and more fruitful in consequences. When our logic of the nature of inquiry is controlled by the gross and macroscopic subject-matter presented in primary experience by the history of inquiry, the need for introducing, as Whitehead does, "metaphysical understanding" and "speculative boldness" to explain the *further* progress of science disappears.

In illustrating concretely the need for "metaphysics," Whitehead details Percy Lowell's calculations which led to the discovery of the new planet Uranus. Whitehead describes the complex calculations involved in the approved style of the Positivists. Then he goes on to say that the Positivists woud claim that "we have only to look in the sky, towards Percy Lowell's moving point, and we shall see a new planet." And in reply to this Whitehead says:

> Certainly we shall not. All that any person has seen is a few faint dots on photographic plates, involving the intervention of photography, excellent telescopes, elaborate apparatus, long exposures and favourable nights. The new explanation is now involved in the *speculative* extension of a welter of physical laws, concerning telescopes, light, and photography, laws which *merely claim to register observed facts.*

However, continues Whitehead:

> This narrative, framed according to the strictest requirements of the Positivist theory, is a travesty of the plain facts. The civilized world has been interested at the thought of the newly discovered planet, *solitary and remote,* for endless ages circling the sun and *adding its faint influence* to the tide of affairs. *At last it is discovered by human reason, penetrating into the nature of things* and laying bare the necessities of their interconnection. The *speculative* extension of laws, *baseless*

on the Positivist theory, are the obvious issue of *speculative, metaphysical trust* in the *material permanences such as telescopes, observatories, mountains, planets,* which are behaving towards each other according to the necessities of the universe, including theories of their own natures. The point is, that speculative extension *beyond direct observation* spells some trust in metaphysics, however vaguely these metaphysical notions may be entertained in explicit thought. . . . Metaphysical understanding guides imagination and justifies purpose. Apart from metaphysical presupposition there can be no civilization.

There is a moral to be drawn as to the method of science. All scientific progress depends on first framing a formula giving a general description of observed fact. . . . At one stage, the method of all discovery conforms to the Positivist doctrine. There can be no doubt that, with this restriction of meaning, the Positivist doctrine is correct." (*Adventures of Ideas,* pp. 163-164; italics mine.)

Whitehead's account of the "real" nature of the method of discovery of Uranus is as much a "travesty of the plain facts" he himself recites as is the Positivist account. The Positivist theory is, true enough, baseless; but it is baseless throughout. At *no* stage does the method of *discovery* conform to the Positivist doctrine. It is only when the baseless Positivist theory is taken as point of departure that it becomes necessary to invoke "metaphysical extensions."

Whitehead is too great a mind to be satisfied with any easy solution, too great to accept any standardized scheme handed down. Hence his contradictions and oscillations. When he has the formula dominantly in mind, as the object of Rational Thought, the object discovered by "human reason penetrating into the nature of things" then it is the "facts" that are shot through and through with interpretation. The "facts" are then merely antecedent to the framing of the formula. When he follows the Positivist doctrine and has the facts dominantly in mind, then the formulas become replicas of the facts, enunciations of the observed correlations of observed facts, and as direct, as immediate, and as locally bound and restricted as the facts and the observation of the facts are assumed to be. In such case, obviously, the formula becomes as merely antecedent, as purely ancillary as the "facts" were in the first case. Antecedent to what? Antecedent, of course, to the Rationalists' future. Hence, just as the facts when they were purely antecedent had to be given a shot of interpretation, so now, the formula has to be given a shot of "metaphysical understanding." But the "metaphysical understanding"—which must be humble before both logic and fact—turns out to be, on examination, none other than the formula in a faint futuristic disguise. Speculative boldness empowers the formula, when thus transformed, to reach back and collar itself so that it may enact its own purpose. All purposes being proleptic in nature, the self-captured formula is thus enabled to lead itself into its own future.

But when we keep our footing in the natural world and are controlled in our philosophic reflections by the gross and macroscopic doings-undergoings in primary experience, the whole scheme of metaphysical apparatus becomes a useless, when not vicious, encumbrance. We can pass from situation to situation, with the passage of Nature, carrying along the consequences of our intelligent labor as we move from one task to the next, using the consequences already attained as means for further progress.

Our theories do not make knowledge possible. "The very possibility of knowledge . . . should depend on the interwoven nature of things." Not only should our knowledge so depend—it does. The historic development of scientific knowledge is not the consequence of Scientific, Philosophic or Logical Theory *furnishing* Nature with continuity—furnishing Nature therewith by assertive metaphysical fiat because continuities are indispensable for knowledge and "The Theory of Knowledge" wants knowledge to go on. Without there being natural existential continuities in Nature, there would be no knowledge at all— not even the knowledge that to have knowledge continuities are necessary.

But the continuities are not all. The interwoven nature of things is not interwoven in a system of eternal bonds, immutable and transcendent. The interweaving is the consequence of interactivity, and the interweaving changes as the interactivities change. Knowledge is an exemplification of both continuity and interaction in Nature and without either knowledge would perish, for Nature would stop.

The future grows out of the present activity and the present grows out of the past. When we are controlled by our gross and macroscopic primary experience we are able to bring under control our derived, refined objects of reflection—no matter how bold they are in their criticism The bolder the better. When our philosophic and scientific understanding is controlled by experience, imaginative purpose has its natural roots and a natural mentor— no matter how far it leaps into the future. The further the better. Our purpose, being the consequence of controlled inquiry, does not weave around us in a beckoning haze, but leads through our history, carrying within itself the justification that that history can give. And as we act further upon our purpose, it gains or loses justification in the process of acting upon it because our acting is under our intelligent control. In science as out, guidance comes through undergoing, and justification is a consequence of doing.

XXXII

When Whitehead and Russell use, as they constantly do, such phrases as "mathematics tells" or "physics tells," they are not engaged in "personifying" mathematics or physics. The phrases, however, are not just "semantic" modes of speech, verbal or linguistic "conventions" of the English or philosophic language: they are indicative or revelatory of the fundamental logic or rationale of the traditional philosophic method they follow. That method consists in treating the *consequences* of inquiry—mathematical, physical, psychological or whatever—as if they were directly *given*, as if they were primitive gifts or data. This method of substituting derived, refined objects of reflection for the gross and macroscopic subject-matter in primary experience does not result in any "personification" in the vulgar sense of the term—because Plato succeeded in taking all the vulgarity out of it. However, it is the refined philosophical or logical equivalent of personification, namely, the depersonalized personification that is technically known by the not too unambiguous term "hypostatization."

Plato put his refined objects of reflection *in rerum Supernatura*. Aristotle, except for his Moveless Mover, thought that was going a bit too far, and so he put his refined objects of reflection *in rerum Natura*. Dewey, in his criticism of Greek philosophy, has always been unduly partial toward Plato and unnecessarily harsh toward Aristotle on the ground that Plato, by putting his Ideas in a Transcendental Realm, at least left Nature alone, whereas Aristotle by putting his remodelled Platonic Ideas (species and genera) within Nature, immobilized the natural process of change within a fixed routine. This argument of Dewey's is far from well taken. It is making Aristotle shoulder the blame for the benighted centuries that succeeded the downfall of Greece. By putting his refined objects of reflection *in rerum Natura,* Aristotle put them where they could be empirically got at and tested. That they were not empirically tested before Darwin is no fault of Aristotle's. But it is to his credit—as against Plato—that he did put them where Darwin could empirically find them to be or not to be. Darwin was thus enabled empirically to explode Aristotelianism in natural history and do it once for all.

The natural inclination of every modern scientist is to be an Aristotelian—in the general sense that he puts his Laws, Formulae or whatever *in* Nature. It is the natural inclination, because every modern scientist is, when behaving normally, a naturalist. He wants, as Newton put it, to "deduce" causes from effects, to "derive from phenomena" all his knowledge. Newton put his Laws and Atoms *in* Nature and because he put them there, they were eventually dislodged from there, not by an "experiment" of the sort Newton performed, but by the consequences of actual laboratory experimentation.

Now in this general sense, Dewey is also an Aristotelian. His doctrine that knowledge is an exemplification of one of the ways of Nature; his doctrine that all knowledge must have passed experimental test before it can be considered knowledge—are sufficient proofs of this general statement. "Experience is *of* as well as *in* Nature."* And knowledge is one of the consequences of modes of experience. In this general sense, every naturalist, philosophic or scientific, is an Aristotelian. Not because he follows Aristotle, but because, in this general sense, Aristotle followed Nature. But Aristotle also followed Plato—and therein lies the difference.

Dewey's logic and philosophy are comprehensively di-

* Infra, p. 1041.

rected against the fallacy of substituting refined, derived objects of reflection for the gross and macroscopic subject-matter in primary experience. And as far as this fundamental argument goes, it is a matter of secondary importance in what realm or part of what realm the transplantation is consummated: whether they are put deep down in the interior of natural things where only the penetrating eye of "human reason" can find them; or whether they are sprinkled on the surface of things where the great Positivist or the Logical Positivist can pick them up as he runs; or whether they are placed in a Supernatural Superstratosphere whereto only the "vision of contemplation" can, by gazing and gazing, ascend, and there in its loftiest moment of transfixion momentarily behold, as through a glass very darkly, the faint Forms esthetically transfixed.

As far as concerns Dewey's theoretical doctrine, it is a matter of secondary importance in which of these three localities the substitution is allegedly effected. The substitution is always invalid. From the practical standpoint, however, the invocation of the Transcendental or Supernatural Realm has the most serious consequences of the three. And the Transcendental Platonic Realm—variously modernized and anaesthetized—is still the last, when not the first, refuge most frequently sought by philosophers in unnatural distress.

XXXIII

THE method of beginning with the gross and macroscopic subject-matter in primary experience is a *method* of beginning. Hence, like all methods, it works throughout the whole undertaking. Inquiry is not like a race and the beginning of inquiry is not the line that is left behind at the pop of the gun. With every step taken in

the course of inquiry there is a new beginning issuing from
a new ending; but beginning and ending do not follow
upon each other—they intercept and unite. In walking
along, the right foot does not follow upon the left—
both are working through the whole stride. What is an
ending or what a beginning depends upon the functional
position as determined within that moment of inquiry.
But every beginning is an ending and every ending is a
beginning because both are always *in medias res.*

When Dewey says that the most important problem
of philosophic method today is that of determining
whether or not philosophers should begin with the gross
and macroscopic or the derived and refined, he is not
entirely correct. His statement is made within the context
of philosophical discussion and is consequently already
somewhat "refined" itself. As a matter of fact, all philosophers must start with the gross and macroscopic, and
do. The gross and macroscopic *problem* is therefore that
of getting philosophers to realize how they do as a matter of fact start and getting them to be controlled by their
realization. Only when they are controlled by such realization can they exercise control over their philosophic
reflections and proceed in their inquiry with understanding and intelligence.

It is obvious from the whole preceding discussion that
the gross and macroscopic subject-matter changes as we
pass from one area of inquiry to another within the
same field and changes still more when we pass from one
field of inquiry into another. It is also obvious that the
gross and macroscopic subject-matter within any case of
inquiry is not merely a penumbral field but is working
within that activity of inquiry. When a laboratorian is
weighing a stone, the gross and macroscopic subject-matter in that primary laboratory experience includes the

scale as well as the stone and much more besides. Laboratorians take scales for granted, but in that grant are included as a minimum the whole laboratory and the history of inquiry of which the scale and the methods of using a scale are the consequences. How much of accumulated consequences of prior activities of inquiry is directly working in any specific case of inquiry under way, how much is in the background, how much is irrelevant is as the case may be. And what the case may be is never finally known until that inquiry is completed. Recall, for instance, Whitehead's impressive sketch of the consequences of prior activities of inquiry involved in the laboratory testing of Percy Lowell's new planet. And Whitehead was giving just a general sketch—he did not go into the enumeration of details. Recall, also, his sketch of the consequences of prior activities of inquiry involved in the formulation of Newton's Law of Gravitation. And in this case too he was just giving a general sketch, he was by no means giving an exhaustive account.

The practice of substituting refined objects of reflection for the gross and macroscopic subject-matter in primary experience is also a *method,* that is, it is a procedure which involves making the substitutions at every point where a refined object of reflection previously obtained comes into the inquiry and at every point where a refined object of reflection is the consequence of the inquiry under way. A wholesale substitution can be made after the whole inquiry is over, but during inquiry substitutions must be continuously made throughout the process.

In the quotations from Russell the continuity of the process of substitution is well displayed.

At one moment Russell means by "physics" the empirical world, and at another moment, in the same argument, he means by "physics" the "logical constructs of

the science of physics." When Russell descends from the
generalized statements of his "problem" to specific cases,
the situation doesn't improve but if anything becomes
worse. Thus, for example, when he tries to bring together
"physics" and "perception"—which unification is the
objective of his whole undertaking—Russell suddenly begins talking, in the most "unrefined" fashion imaginable,
about such crude, macroscopic, gross subject-matters as
"brain" and "physiologist" and "microscope" and so on.
However, Russell also keeps in mind that Science has
discovered that it takes light from the Sun some eight
minutes to travel the distance of 82,000,000 miles between
the Sun and the Earth. Because of this fact, and others of
similar nature, the "causal continuity" in "physics" makes
it absolutely impossible to escape from the conclusion that
"What the physiologist sees when he is examining a brain
[by means of a microscope] is in the physiologist, not in
the brain he is examining." Where the "physiologist" and
where the "microscope" and where the "brain" are is a
matter of some doubt. For by virtue of his same doctrine
of "continuity" Russell also reaches the conclusion, "We
do not know much about the contents of *any* part of the
world except our *own* heads; our knowledge of other regions is *wholly abstract.*" From the last statement it
follows that the "brain" and "physiologist" and "microscope"—in so far as Russell knows anything about them
—are wholly abstract.* And so they are. At one moment

---

* It also follows that the distance between Sun and Earth and
the time it takes light to travel are also wholly abstract. When
this consequence of Russell's *conclusion* is given its full legitimate
value, the scientific *ground* for his conclusion is completely destroyed. The *ground* of a conclusion is the *reason* of and for
that conclusion. There can therefore be nothing more illogical or
irrational than a "conclusion" which can be maintained only by
destroying the "ground" upon which it is based or from which it
is allegedly derived.

of his argument they are abstractions perched on the mathematical point of Transcendental Peak. And so also they are not. For at the next moment of his argument, they are hurtling down the side of the Transcendental Mountain into the very depths of the "metaphysically primitive events" at the bottom of all. And so finally they are neither. For all during his argument, the brain, physiologist and microscope are also the gross and macroscopic objects that ordinary experience is familiar with. It is only by virtue of their being always the latter that Russell can keep up his "logical" argument at all.

In the course of a discussion of Berkeley's doctrine, Russell makes clearer than usual what his "logic" is:

In spite of the logical merits of this [Berkeley's] view, I cannot bring myself to accept it, though I am not sure that my reasons for disliking it are any better than Dr. Johnson's. I find myself constitutionally incapable of believing that the sun would not exist on a day when he was everywhere hidden by clouds, or that the meat in a pie springs into existence at the moment when the pie is opened. I know the logical answer to such objections, and *qua logician* I think the answer a good one. The logical argument, however, does not even tend to show that there are *not* non-mental events; it only tends to show that we have no right to feel sure of their existence. For my part, I find myself in fact believing in them in spite of all that can be said to persuade me that I ought to feel doubtful.

There is an argument, of a sort, against the view we are considering. I have been assuming that we admit the existence of other people and their perceptions, but question only the inference from perceptions to events of a different kind. Now there is no good reason why we should not carry our logical caution a step further. I cannot verify a theory by means of another man's perceptions, but only by means of my own. Therefore the laws of physics can only be verified by me in so far as they lead to predictions of *my* percepts. If then, I refuse to admit non-mental events because they are not verifiable, I ought to refuse to admit mental events in every one except myself, on the same ground. Thus I am reduced to what is called "solipsism", i.e. the theory that I alone exist. This is a view which it is hard to refute, but still harder to believe. I once received a letter from a philosopher who professed to be a solipsist, but was surprised that there were no others! Yet this philosopher was by way of believing that no one else existed. This shows that solipsism is not really believed even by those who think they are convinced of its truth. (*Philosophy* [1927], pp. 290-291; italics in original).

It is obvious that the solipsist made an enormous blunder writing to Russell. *Qua logician,* the solipsist had a very good case. "It is hard to refute." But then the solipsist went ahead and wrote a letter to another philosopher—and lo! he showed that he really did not believe, deep down in his solipsist heart, the strength of his "solipsist logic." Now the only important point about this episode is that Russell does not take the letter as constituting in any way an experimental, scientific invalidation of the "logic." For Russell himself, *qua logician,* the solipsist argument is still a hard one to refute—even after he received the letter. And, pray, what sort of letter was it? Where was it? Was it in Russell's head or in the head of the solipsist who sent it? Was it wholly abstract? No more than the solipsist "believed" his "hard-to-refute-logic" does Russell "believe" in his substitutions of refined objects of reflection—logical constructs—for the gross and macroscopic subject-matter in primary experience. *Qua logician,* Russell can, with an easy mind, go through the intellectual, mathematical-symbolic jugglery; but *qua* a human being he cannot believe it. Moreover, it is only by bringing into his "logical" exercise the allegedly non-logical, what he believes but seems to have no rational argument for; it is only by constantly bringing this "extra-logical" within the operations of his dialectics that his dialectics can exhibit the semblance of moving along. Otherwise, Russell would be going around in a very narrow and self-enclosed circle. In sum, logic, for Russell, is precisely what logic was for the scholastics. His "inflexible rationality of thought" is of exactly the same order. The fundamental fact about Russell's "logic" is that experimental *test* has no place in it at all, has no *logical* standing whatsoever.

Whitehead, in his procedure of substituting refined objects of reflection for the gross and macroscopic subject-matter in primary experience, follows a different route and ends up at the opposite pole. Russell, as the reader remembers, finally reached the point where all distinctions between physics and perception, between mind and matter, were superficial and unreal. Since Russell's whole philosophic undertaking was devoted to the end of bringing the two together, without subordinating either to the other, his final conclusion (in *The Analysis of Matter*, of course) throws at least a glare of superficiality and unreality over his whole undertaking. In general terms, Russell's logical progress consists in making distinctions and then throwing them away so that at the end he is left with nothing at all. Whitehead proceeds in the reverse direction. He proceeds by making distinctions, and then internally involving them in each other so that at the end he has everything in everything else—which consequence also obliterates distinctions.

Thus, for instance, he starts:

"Actual entities—also termed 'actual occasions'—are the final real things of which the world is made up. There is no going behind actual entities to find anything more real. They differ among themselves: God is an actual entity, and so is the most trivial puff of ex-

istence in far-off empty space. But, though there are
gradations of importance, and diversities of function,
yet in the principles which actuality exemplifies all are
on the same level. The final facts are, all alike, actual
entities; and these actual entities are drops of experience, complex and interdependent." " . . . actual entities are the only *reasons*; so that to search for a *reason*
is to search for one or more actual entities." (*Process
and Reality* pp. 27-28 and 37; italics in original).

Now this statement—leaving out the actual entity
"God"—is on all fours with Dewey's fundamental position. It is another way of stating that the gross and
macroscopic subject-matters in primary experience—the
puffs of smoke and the stellar systems—are, with respect
to existential quality, all on exactly the same level. This
is also the fundamental doctrine as actually operative in
the conduct of scientific inquiry. The black-bands in the
interferometer are just as real as the super-galactic system. Since there is no going behind actual entities to find
anything more real, the *ultimate* or metaphysically real
is, precisely those actual entities themselves. And this too
is thoroughly in accordance both with Dewey's doctrine
of logic and the practice of science. Since the ultimate
test of the validity of any theory is made by the laboratory experiment, the subject-matter as experienced in the
laboratory experiment is the ultimately real, scientifically.
Finally, since the actual entities or occasions are ultimately real, their differences, their gradations in importance, their qualitative characters, their existential extents must also be ultimate and real.

However, although Whitehead avers that speculative
boldness must be humble before "logic" and "fact," the
operation of his dialecticism carries him progressively
away from both. Whitehead ends up by saying: "Each
actual entity is a throb of experience *including the actual*

world within its scope." (Ib. p. 290; italics mine.)
"No two actualities can be torn apart; each is all in all.
Thus each temporal occasion embodies God, and is em-
bodied in God." (Ib. p. 529)

A contradiction in a system of philosophy is evidence
of some antecedent error. A fundamental contradiction
is evidence of a fundamental error. It is obvious that
Whitehead's final conclusion contradicts his basic doctrine as fundamentally as Russell's final conclusion contradicts his initial basic statement of doctrine (in *The
Analysis of Matter*). And both conclusions are rather fantastic. It is fantastic to say that the most trivial puff of
existence in far-off empty space *includes the actual world
within its scope*. And the statement itself, in addition to
its fantasticality, is self-contradictory. If each actual
entity includes the actual world within its scope, there
is no puff of existence, and there is no far-off empty
space. Everything is in everything else: each is all in all.
Whitehead does not get everything "inside the head" as
Russell sometimes does, but as far as this aspect of his
final doctrine is concerned he might just as well.

There is a world of difference between the final conclusions of Whitehead and Russell, taking the content of
the conclusions by themselves. But they reach their dia-
metrically opposed conclusions by using a "logic" or
"method of philosophy" that is fundamentally the same.
By using the same "logic" the doctrine of the one can
be converted into the doctrine of the other by a simple
dialectical twist. Russell, *qua logician,* is well aware of
this, as we have seen. We have also seen that Russell is
never always of the same mind as to which way the dialectical twist should be turned. Although Russell and
Whitehead both humbly bow down before "logic" and
are in the vanguard of those who uphold the "inflexible

rationality of thought" when it comes to any critical juncture, when, in the course of their allegedly "rational" philosophic inquiry a showdown can no longer be post-poned, it is always their "logic" that gives way and bows down to their "feeling" or their "metaphysical trust" or whatever.

A "logic" which makes it necessary constantly to resort to heroic, last-minute, extra-logical measures in order to keep the "logical" argument going and the philosophy afloat, is a "logic" that is not without its strong emotional appeal. It makes "philosophy" very exciting, quite a romantic adventure. But such a "logic," whatever its extra-logical merits may be, is *not* a scientific logic, for it does not display any of the fundamental characteristics of the logic of controlled inquiry.

XXXIV

THE refined objects of reflection—of whatever sort they may be—are consequences of inquiry. They are products not originals. They are the end-results that have come through the mill. Dewey's favorite metaphor for the "mill of inquiry" is that of a "refinery." Whence his technical term "refined." Our discussion of the "meth- od of isolation" is an amplification of Dewey's doctrine of the "method of refining."

When you refine gold ore, for instance, the pure gold that is the end-result of the refining process was in the crude, raw materials. The refining process removed the dross or all extraneous matter and got the pure gold to-gether. But the final product is qualitatively the same as the original. Now this metaphor adequately covers those cases of refined objects of reflection which go under the various names of primary and secondary qualities, per-cepts, sensations, and all natural qualitative objects.

That is, it covers those refined objects of reflection which were the "elements" of Greek "scientific thought" and which appear in every descriptive and classificatory natural science. It is fundamental to Realist doctrine, and also Positivist, that these "elements" are "directly observed" that they appear in thought precisely as they are *in rerum Natura,* that they are not consequences of inquiry, but are the "given" or the data which a providential Nature hands out to inquiry. At one time, some Realists were fond of saying that the mind was like a searchlight. As it flashed around, it immediately saw what was there and as immediately knew what it saw. When it happened to light upon an "ultimate simple" it had a case of "infallible knowledge" as Whitehead used to say. This flashlight theory of the mind is of course the Greek Formula disguised as a modern implement.

The metaphor of the "refinery" is adequate for illustrating the process whereby are obtained the refined, derived objects of reflection of the sort just mentioned, but it is no good at all when extended to the case of refined objects of modern *scientific* reflection. The mill of modern scientific inquiry—if a metaphor must be used—is like a chemical mill where alloys are made. In making an alloy, there is a double process involved: first, there is the process of "refining" or "isolating" the natural elements, and second, there is the process of bringing them into interactive relations, the consequence of the interactivity being a new object, qualitatively unlike either of the originals.

Dewey's use of the same metaphor for both cases is unfortunate. But he does not confuse the two kinds of results obtained; in fact, his whole argument is devoted to showing how fundamentally different these two kinds of refined objects of reflection are.

Newton's Third Law of Motion is a good example of a modern scientific object of reflection. The Third Law may be considered as a miniature "world of physics" and the horse, stone and stretched rope between as a miniature empirical world, as the gross and macroscopic subject-matter in primary experience. One form of Russell's problem of the "application of physics to the empirical world" is the problem of the application of the Third Law to the horse, stone and rope. The High Rationalist Tradition in modern and contemporary philosophy, working with the Greek Formula up its sleeve, substitutes the Third Law for the horse, stone and rope and claims that the substituted article is the Ultimate Reality. Whitehead and Russell both follow this tradition but reluctantly; they cannot persuade themselves to follow it all the way. For Whitehead the horse, stone and rope are merely a cooking of the facts for the sake of exemplifying the Law. That Newton did cook the facts, there can be no doubt. But when Newton's cooking is all over, and he presents Whitehead with a complete "ready-made" world, Whitehead doesn't like it.

Of Newton's "ready-made world" Whitehead says that it cannot "survive a comparison with the facts." Neither can the Third Law survive a comparison with the facts. However, Whitehead goes on to say that "Biology is reduced to a mystery; and physics itself has now reached a stage of *experimental* knowledge inexplicable in terms of the categories of the *Scholium*." * Newton's world of physics, when substituted for the empirical world does, true enough, make a mystery of biology, but it makes a mystery of pretty much everything else. The trouble with Newton's "physics" is not that it reduces everything to the explanatory level of mechanical

* *Process and Reality,* p. 144, italics mine.

action. The great trouble with it is that it cannot even explain without involving itself in fundamental contradiction such an elementary mechanical action as the horse actually pulling the rope. It took close to two and a half centuries to prove to theoretical physicists that the standard and defining case of the nature of Nature is not the case where a stretched rope· is transfixed between an immovable stone and immobile horse. Of course there are times when a horse cannot pull a stone along the surface of the earth, but even at such times the horse, if he is a horse at all, can move over the face of the earth himself. The Third Law of Motion apart from being symbolically a miniature "world of physics" is actually the standard, defining and ultimately controlling Law in Newton's complete "world of physics." The change from the Newtonian to the Einsteinian physics is the change that results from taking as the standard and defining case, the case where the horse is pulling the stone and moving along the face of the earth. If you take your position on that moving rope and begin to plot its mathematical formulation you fall head first into Einsteinian mathematics.

It is of course something to be thankful for that physicists now realize that the world is in motion, really and not just fictitiously. Unfortunately, they have come to that realization by way of such an incredibly circuitous route, they are still dazed by their journey and are afraid to believe it is true. And in their loftiest moments of "inspiration" they of course still desire to substitute Einstein's final equation for the real world, just as they formerly substituted Newton's initial equation for the real world.*

* Purely formally speaking, the Einsteinian development consists in throwing the Third Law out at the "basis" of physics and

Now Dewey's philosophy is about a world that is actually in motion, that is really moving and not just playing at moving. And Dewey's logic is controlled by the fundamental fact that the horse is pulling the rope and horse, stone and stretched rope between are moving along the face of the earth. This fundamental fact is the fact Dewey's whole philosophy is controlled by. Dewey sometimes calls this fact "the practical character of reality." *

The application of the Third Law of Motion to the horse, stone and rope is one form of Russell's problem of the "application of physics to the empirical world." The other form of his problem is hidden away in his statement that "the world of physics must be, in some sense, continuous with the world of our perceptions." I say "hidden away" because what the "world of physics" is, in this case, depends entirely upon the course of the argument. Sometimes it is the empirical world, sometimes it is the "laws of physics," sometimes it is the electrons, protons, and whatnot which are identifiable with neither. However, if we take the summing up of his position on this form of his problem, it is fairly evident what it involves. "It is obvious that a man who can see knows things which a blind man cannot know; but a blind man can know the whole of physics. Thus the knowledge which other men have and he has not is not a part of physics." A blind man who can know the whole of physics is, obviously, a person of great intelligence. There are millions of persons who are not blind who would experience the great-

bringing it back in at the "top." All the moving platforms, trains, etc., used in accounts of the Einstein Theory are really no better than the horse, stone and stretched rope between moving along the face of the earth.

* This is the title of an essay in *Philosophy and Civilization* (1931), originally written in 1908.

est difficult in understanding any of physics. On the score
of intelligence, there is no difference then between Russell's blind man and a seeing man who also can know
the whole of physics. I suppose it is also fair to assume
that the blind man in question has his other senses intact, that he can hear, touch, taste and smell. The *only*
difference between the two men therefore is that the
seeing man can see "secondary qualities," namely, those
secondary qualities that require unimpaired vision. And
it is on *this* difference that Russell rests his penultimate
conclusion that "there is thus a sphere excluded from
physics." (*The Analysis of Matter,* p. 389.)

We began by considering the problem of "secondary
qualities" and this brings us back to the beginning. The
genuineness of this problem is not the point here. Nor
is it relevant to the point that Russell in the course of
his discussion of the problem introduces many other differences and in the last three pages of his book temporarily reintroduces them again. What is in point here is
that the second form of Russell's problem—the problem
of secondary qualities (in an excessively simplified form,
this time) continues to be the imperishable foundation-
stone of the philosophic discussion.

The inextricable mixing up of the two forms of the
problem—the shifting from one kind of refined object
of reflection to a totally different kind—keeps the philosophic discussion alive, gives it an ever-changing and
ever more complicated face. Russell's discussion of the
same problem in *Our Knowledge of the External World*
(1914) follows exactly the same general lines as his discussion in 1927. But it was vastly simpler, internally.
At that time (1914) the Einsteinian "world of physics,"
with its manifold mathematical complications, and Space-
Time had not yet come into its own. Hence, in that ear-

lier volume, Russell could start off by dismissing Time
as irrelevant for physics and therefore irrelevant for philosophy. The "temporal", then was *merely* temporal. The
case with Time now is rather different. Just as in 1914
Russell took the Newtonian "world of physics" as something "given," so in 1927 Russell takes the Einsteinian
"world of physics" as something "given." This method
of procedure is not peculiar to Russell. It is part of the
inherent methodology of the "rationalist" tradition in
philosophy; it is the "logical" method that exhibits "inflexible rationality of thought."

It is fundamental in Dewey's analysis of the problem
to maintain the distinction between the two general
kinds of refined objects of reflection noted above. His
extension of the metaphor of "refining" to cover both
kinds of refined objects is unfortunate. But in view of the
nature of philosophic discussion and controversy this extension is understandable. Furthermore, the standardized
consequences of inquiry that persist as the stable foundations of the controversy are the "ultimate simples" that
are obtained from the gross and macroscopic subject-matter in primary experience by the process of "refining."
Hence Dewey's emphasis on this process is not only understandable but also justifiable within the context of the
great debate.

XXXV

"PHILOSOPHY" writes Whitehead "destroys its usefulness when it indulges in brilliant feats of explaining
away. . . . Its ultimate appeal is to the *general consciousness of what in practice we experience*. Whatever
thread of presupposition characterizes social expression
throughout the various epochs of *rational* society must
find its place in philosophic theory. Speculative boldness

must be balanced by complete humility before logic, and before fact. It is a disease of philosophy when it is neither bold nor humble, but merely a reflection of the temperamental presuppositions of exceptional person-alities.

"Analogously, we do not trust any recasting of scientific theory depending upon a *single performance of an aber-rant experiment,* unrepeated. The ultimate test is always widespread, recurrent experience; and the more general the rationalistic scheme, the more important this final appeal." *

Dewey's statement on the same general topic is as follows: "A first-rate test of the value of any philosophy which is offered us is this: Does it end in conclusions which, when they are referred back to *ordinary* life-ex-periences and their predicaments, render them more sig-nificant, more luminous to us, and make our *dealings* with them more fruitful? Or does it terminate in rendering the things of *ordinary* experience more opaque than they were before, and in depriving them of having in 'reality' even the significance they had previously seemed to have? Does it yield the enrichment and increase of power of ordi-nary things which the results of physical science afford when applied in every-day affairs? Or does it become a mystery that these ordinary things should be what they are, or indeed that they should be at all, while philosophic concepts are left to dwell in separation in some technical realm of their own? It is the fact that so many philos-ophies terminate in conclusions that make it necessary to disparage and condemn primary experience, leading those who hold them to measure the sublimity of their 'realities' as philosophically defined by remoteness from

* *Process and Reality,* p. 25; italics mine.

the concerns of daily life, which leads cultivated common sense to look askance at philosophy." *

These two statements very closely approach each other, and yet, as in cases already considered, the more closely they come together the further apart they are. And in this instance, as in all others, for one and the same reason: Whitehead never actually reaches the point where he is ready to consider "practice" as a functioning, integral factor in inquiry. Whitehead, as Russell, will on occasion recognize that an appeal must be made to "experiment" or "practice" and that such appeal is "ultimate" but he will never "wander off on the topic of experiment" to the extent of effecting an integrative, interactive union of theory and practice.

Dewey says that the test of a philosophy is whether or not the conclusions when referred back to *ordinary* life-experiences make the latter more significant and our *dealings* with them more fruitful. Whitehead says that the ultimate appeal or test is to "the general consciousness of what in practice we experience." This test is altogether different from Dewey's. For "the *general consciousness* of what in practice we experience" is more likely than not to turn out to be, not actual, practical, or experimental behavior, but simply a "philosophy of practice" over again. So that Whitehead's "test" will really be of the kind Newton performed when he "tested experimentally" his Third Law, by "relating" it to the horse, stone and stretched rope between. And that this is so is evident in Whitehead's next sentence, that philosophic theory must include or find a place for all the threads of presupposition that are found in the various epochs of "rational society." "Rational society" consists

* *Infra*, p. 1046; italics mine.

of the various systems of ideas, philosophic, cultural, and scientific that are found to be rational. Although White-head does not believe that Newton's "ready-made world of physics" can survive a comparison with the facts, he also believes that *that* "world of physics" must never-theless be included in any cosmology, or philosophy of Nature. Now there can be no doubt that Newton's "world of physics" merits some sort of inclusion in a compre-hensive philosophy. But no theory of philosophy can be *tested* by reference to that "world of physics" any more than that "world of physics" can be *tested* by a theory of philosophy. The *test* of any theory scientific or philosophic is experimental in the practical sense, in the sense of do-ing-undergoing.

Whitehead gives another statement of his conception of the method of philosophy which more sharply points up the fundamental difference we have been consider-ing:

" . . . the true method of philosophical construction is to frame a scheme of ideas, the best that one can, and unflinchingly to explore the interpretation of experience in terms of that scheme." (Ib. p. x)

By following this method, it is obvious that "experience" will always turn out to be a replica of the "scheme of ideas" in terms of which "experience is unflinchingly ex-plored." Newton constructed his scheme of ideas contained in his Third Law and then unflinchingly explored the interpretation of "experience" in terms of that scheme. And he found that "experience" and the Third Law agreed with one another, that they were in one-to-one correspondency, that the harmony between them was perfect. When you take the same thing twice over once as "experience" and once as "scheme of ideas" you will always get Newton's perfect results. And this taking of the same thing twice over is what Realists staunchly hold to be the fundamental method of discovering Truth!

Any scheme of ideas is already the interpretation of "experience"—of the experience of which that scheme of ideas is the formulated consequence. When that scheme of ideas is the unflinching formulation of the consequences of *that* experience, then that genuine occasion for being unflinching is over. The *next* occasion for being unflinching is when we *test* that scheme of ideas by practical, experimental doings-undergoings whether the practical experimentation be in the laboratory or in ordinary life-experiences, in our daily *dealings* with things. It is necessary to be unflinching on *this* next occasion because the scheme of ideas which is thus undergoing genuine test, may not survive the trial.

It cannot be denied of course that it also requires a high degree of "unflinchingness" to follow the "method" that Whitehead prescribes for philosophers. The "inflexible rationality of thought" he advocates is not easily acquired. When we use any given scheme of ideas for the interpretation of experience in terms of that scheme, there are bound to arise many occasions—when we adventure abroad and our "explorations" are wide enough—that may well cause the stoutest philosophic heart to quail. I doubt whether there is, in the world today, a philosopher of stouter heart than Russell. And yet Russell "flinched" when it came to accepting some of the "answers" which he *qua logician* (or *qua* schematizer of ideas) believed were "good logical answers." However, it must be said on behalf of Russell, that his "flinchings" were not final, but only temporary twinges. When, in *The Analysis of Matter,* he reached the very last sentence, Russell had to make his final interpretation of experience in terms of his scheme of ideas. And then, on the very pin-point standpoint of philosophy, Russell unflinchingly made his last stand (in that book, of course). Likewise with Whitehead. During the course of his philosophic "interpretations" of experience in terms of his scheme of ideas, there are many occasions when he "flinches." But when the last stand has to be made, he unflinchingly makes the last stand.

One of Whitehead's great contributions to philosophy is his discovery of an oft-repeated and widespread fallacy in modern thought which he calls "the fallacy of misplaced concreteness." But a far greater philosophic fallacy, and in its consequences infinitely more destructive of what Dewey calls intelligence, is "the fallacy of misplaced unflinchingness."

XXXVI

THE mathematics in which the physicist is interested was developed for the explicit purpose of describing the behavior of the external world, so that it is certainly no accident that there is a correspondence between mathematics and nature." This statement of Bridgman's is correct only when it is interpreted to mean that there is a "correspondence" between the mathematics used in describing nature and *the nature that is the consequence of using that mathematics*. Thus it is no accident certainly that there is a "correspondence" between Newton's Third Law and Newton's horse, stone and stretched rope between. In any other sense than this, there is no "correspondence" at all.

It is also no accident that there is a "correspondence" between a microscope constructed in accordance with the specifications of a formula and the formula in accordance with which the microscope is constructed.

If you take the microscope in one hand and the formula

of the microscope in the other and examine them alternately you will find, as Spinoza would say, that the order and connection of ideas in the formula are the same as the order and connection of things in the microscope. Now the formula of the microscope is what Whitehead calls an "ideally isolated system." And, says Whitehead, "This means that there are truths respecting *this* system which require *reference* only to the remainder of things by way of a uniform systematic scheme of relationships." If you develop a systematic scheme of relationships with the consistency and perfection exhibited by Spinoza, you will get Spinoza's result. The "correspondency" of microscope and formula of the microscope, when extended or referred to the remainder of things within the universe becomes the doctrine that there are two orders, one the order of ideas (Mind, Formulae) and the other the order of things (Matter, Bodies) the two orders running in parallel lines or in one-to-one correspondency.

Of course, Spinoza did not leave the two orders each alone by itself. Just as soon as you bring on the one hand and on the other in juxtaposition, you are philosophically bound to "unite" them. And so Spinoza included them in one comprehensive order of Nature. But if there are two such orders in Nature, and they parallel each other, they parallel each other. That's that, and that is all there is to it. It is an "irreducible and stubborn fact." Comprehending them in one inclusive embrace doesn't make their parallelism more parallel, and leaving them without the embrace doesn't make their parallelism any less parallel. Precisely the same holds true, for example, of Newton's Absolute Space and Absolute Time. They also were two "orders" and they "paralleled" or "corresponded" in one-to-three-and-three-to-one mathematical formal perfection and including them in One Sys tem of Nature didn't change their Newtonian relations one bit. It also didn't help matters very much as far as the progress of scientific theory is concerned.

When you take two end-results, like the microscope and the formula of the microscope, two consequences which are the products of the self-same historical process of inquiry, they are each bound to contain characteristics which "exemplify" or "parallel" or "correspond" to the characteristics of the other. The interactivity of which they are the joint product has taken care of that. It could not be otherwise. When you take two such products, and "compare" them with one another you will always find, says Dewey, that they will be in one-to-one harmony. Then the "existence" of the one will reflect the "essence" of the other; the "mind" of the one will portray the "matter" of the other; the "form" of the one will reveal the "body of the other"; the "law" of the one will express the "conduct" of the other; the "fact" of the one will exemplify the "proposition" of the other; the "refined object of reflection" of the one will mirror the "subject-matter in experience" of the other; and so on in every field and in every case. And of course also in every case vice versa if not also versa vice. For as Leibniz put it, the "harmony is pre-established."

Although the harmony between a microscope and the formula of the microscope is entrancingly perfect when "pre-established," the differences between the two are enormous. And it is only by neglecting the differences in the first place, that the one-to-one correspondency can be obtained. When, after having made the correspondency, an appeal to "experience" is inadvertently made, all the "eternal problems" of philosophy begin to crop out again. And as long as the same "method of philosophy" is pursued, these problems will never be solved.

XXXVII

"WE do not trust," writes Whitehead, "any recasting of scientific theory depending upon a single, aberrant experiment, unrepeated. The ultimate test is always widespread, recurrent experience; and the more general the rationalistic scheme, the more important is this final test." But if a single experiment is aberrant, we would not trust any recasting of scientific theory depending upon it, no matter how widespread and recurrent that experiment had become through sheer repetition. Newton's "experiment" with the Third Law was, for example, an aberrant experiment if ever there was one. Repetition of that experiment would perpetuate, not test, the aberration.

And this particular Newtonian aberration has been "tested" by making it widespread and recurrent. Newton has been the model "experimental" scientist and his system the model of all scientific systems. Theoreticians in all fields, possessed of a "modern classical" cast of "scientific" mind have, with studied envy and anxiety, followed the lead of Newton. By carrying his "method" into their fields of inquiry, they were certain that their results would be truly scientific. And following Newton's method has meant starting with a formulation patterned after the Third Law.

And so we have, for example, in "classical, scientific economics" the fundamental Law that "supply equals demand"—equal and opposite. Supply follows demand and demand follows supply and this "iron law" of economic nature—like the rope between horse and stone—holds the economic world perfectly together—providing you only let it alone, let it go and let it pass. And in "classical psychology" we have a similar exemplification of the same "iron law." Idea equals sensation or idea follows sensation and sensation follows idea and this keeps Mind and Body together—providing again that you only let it alone, let it go and let it pass.

For such a psychology, it was of course an inestimable boon when the neurological system was discovered. For the neurological system was, obviously, the very conduit needed. Like Newton's rope, it could be the vacuous go-between. When, under the inspiration of greater scientific exactitude, the shift was made to the terms "stimulus" and "response" the same fundamental Law prevailed; stimulus equals response, equal and opposite.

Of course, no scientific theory is ever dependent upon a single experiment. It may conceivably happen that a scientific theory has to be changed because of the consequences of one experiment. But the scientific theory, both before and after the change, is not dependent upon that one experiment alone—any more than the laboratory experiment is self-dependent. As Whitehead himself so clearly described, every scientific theory (or formula) is an organization of accumulated consequences of prior activities of inquiry. And likewise with every laboratory experiment.

When philosophic theory of scientific method is controlled by the indubitable, gross and macroscopic fact that theories and laboratory experiments are the funded consequences of histories of inquiry, the significance of the appeal to widespread and recurrent experience is radically clarified. For then it is seen that an appeal to a single laboratory experiment is, by the very nature of the case, a concentrated appeal to widespread and recurrent experience. A single experiment no matter how extensive and internally complex it may be is, to be sure, a limited experiment. It does not encompass the

totality of the universe within its scope. There is, therefore, need for recurring to further experimental laboratory tests as new formulations are reached or as old
formulations are carried into new fields. The need is a
constant and progressive one. In scientific inquiry it is
not the case that the more general the rationalistic
scheme (or the more comprehensive the theory) the more
important is the final or experimental test. The process of
experimental testing is continuous throughout the development of scientific theory; it occurs at every stage. One
can make a distinction of "importance" such as Whitehead makes, only at the expense of violating the basic
continuity and interactivity of the developmental process
of scientific or controlled inquiry.

Every practical or theoretical instrument—from the
crudest practical tool to the most highly refined mathematical symbol—is inherently a *social* product. Every
case of experimental testing is an appeal to "widespread
and recurrent experience." According to some philosophic
theories of experience, human experience is a private, convulsive, peristaltic movement occurring inside an aboriginally individualized psyche or soul; according to
others, it is the automatic registration of private effects
on a private brain inside a private head. Whether such
extremely diseased modes of human experience are possible or not, we need not stop to inquire. But such modes
of experience—supposing, for the argument, that they
may occur—do not define the *rational* mode, the standard mode of experience which constitutes the ultimate
test of theory. Rational experience is experience as organized and realized in the performance of an experiment. Dewey's philosophy of the experiment is his philosophy of experience. The method of experimentation defines the nature of the method of socialized intelligence.

Dewey's recasting of philosophic theory depends upon his theory of the experiment. Originally, Dewey's philosophy acquired the designation "instrumentalism." Although by usage the term "instrumentalism" could be made equivalent in meaning to the term "experimentalism" in the current intellectual epoch it is practically impossible to do so. By commonsense standards of thinking and judging, an "instrument" necessarily implies something for which it is an "instrument"; an "instrumental theory of knowledge" would therefore by the same standards imply that knowledge was instrumental, not to "instrumental knowledge" (which is an absurdity) but to consummatory modes of experience, which are non-instrumental.

But the absurd interpretation of "instrumentalism" as the "philosophy or logic of the instrument" was inevitable. For the "logics of the instrument" are the dominant unending varieties of "rationalistic logics." The inflexible rationality of scholastic thought was, precisely, an inflexible idolatry of the "logical" instrument then available to their hand. The most popular idolatry of the instrument now current is that exhibited in the Logical Positivist movement. Carnap's Logical Positivism very closely nears the ultimate philosophic apotheosis of Esperantism.

When the term instrumentalism is made secondary to experimentalism there remains no terminological ground for confusing Dewey's philosophy with any "philosophy of the instrument."

XXXVIII

IF the problems of philosophy were inherently, and not just formally, technical, their "eternal" perpetuation would not matter so very much. But the "eternal" problems of philosophy are the social problems *par excellence*.

In the process of technical formulation they have lost all the obvious features and characteristics of the social. It is not true that nothing can rise higher than its source; witness every case of development. But it is true that nothing can rise so high above its source that it becomes entirely disconnected therefrom and after its disconnection first begins to live a real and flourishing life off its own transcendental vitals. Technical terms, linguistic forms, symbolic devices, can make a problem look like nothing else on earth. They can do wonders in facial transformation. But even the most potent of these devices and instrumentalities cannot perform miracles.

Contemporary philosophers are of course distinguishable in many ways from medieval scholastics. But in so far as contemporaries accept standardized problems and seek for their solution by dialectically arranging standardized parts, they are every whit as medieval as the veriest scholastics of ten centuries ago. And from point of view of fundamental method of philosophy it matters very little by what names such philosophers designate their philosophies, nor whence nor how they obtain their standardized equipment.

There can be no intelligent objection to standardizing instrumental equipment, theoretical and practical. Standardization is necessary for efficiency and precision in control. But there is fundamental cause for intelligent objection when control over the standardized equipment is substituted for control in the solution of an actual problem which the use of the standardized equipment can give. When such substitution is made, the use of the equipment, instead of enriching experience and helping its growth, stunts and distorts it.

The multiplication of theoretical instrumentalities widens the mental horizon and increases the possibilities that can be entertained in thought. The multiplication of practical instrumentalities increases power for trying out possibilities, for changing and reconstructing existential events. When practical and theoretical instruments are developed in interactive relation with each other, we have the cumulative and progressive advance exhibited in the history of modern science. When the practical and theoretical activities are separated from each other, we have the kind of "advance" exhibited in the tragic history of modern society.

Some form and degree of separation of theory from practice is to be found in every field of modern thought and in every area of social life. Theoretical solutions of the problems generated by the separation of theory from practice in the fields of thought do not, of course, automatically function to solve the problems that are everywhere to be found in contemporary society. The actual solution of actual social problems can be accomplished only by employment of actual social instrumentalities.* The philosopher, in his professional capacity, is a theoretician, not a laboration. This does not relieve him of social responsibility, but defines the kind of responsibility he can be legitimately expected professionally to assume.

The fundamental problem in philosophy is the problem of scientific method. With respect to some specific problems, alternative solutions are possible, but with respect to the basic problem of scientific method there is no valid alternative to Dewey's solution. If this Introduction has any one comprehensive purpose, then it is to indicate the reasons why this is so.

---

* In the Editor's Note, Chapter Nine, which is devoted to a discussion of the Outlawry of War, some of the difficulties and problems involved in using social instrumentalities for the solution of an actual social problem are concretely considered. Nothing more is therefore said on this topic here.

Of course I do not mean that the whole world—not even the whole world of philosophy—is to be found in Dewey's works. Nor do I mean that whatever is in his works is perfect, that every solution he offers is the right solution and every analysis he makes is the final and correct analysis. Such is far from being the case. Some criticisms of Dewey have been explicitly made in the foregoing pages and others are implicit. And many needful criticisms of Dewey the reader can undoubtedly make for himself; and the foregoing may possibly help the reader in this direction.

But the all-important problem, social as well as philosophic, is the problem of method. There is nothing inherent in the nature of things that makes it possible for the method of experimentation—or of controlled inquiry—to be employed in certain fields and nowhere else. From the fact that Dewey's analysis of controlled inquiry is fundamentally the correct analysis and no valid alternative is possible—from this fact it does not follow that the body of knowledge in Dewey's philosophy (or in any one else's) is crystallized and fixated as "eternal and immutable." Just the opposite follows. Galileo started a revolution in method which has proved its singular validity, not by immobilizing a body of knowledge, but by making it possible for that body to change and grow. The employment of controlled inquiry—or the method of intelligence—in the fields of philosophy and the social sciences, and all human affairs, can prove its validity only in the same way.

INTELLIGENCE IN THE MODERN WORLD
JOHN DEWEY'S PHILOSOPHY

CHAPTER ONE

THE MEANINGS OF PHILOSOPHY

I · Philosophy and Culture*

VOLUMES have been written about each term of our theme. What *is* civilization? history? philosophy? Yet time passes, and as ambiguities and complexities cannot be eliminated by definition, we can only circumvent them by begging questions. But as to one of the terms at least, namely, philosophy, we shall frankly make what is begged explicit. A statement of the relations of philosophy to the history of civilization will, after all, only expound, in some indirect manner, the view of philosophy to which one is already committed. Unless this fact is faced, we shall not only beg the issue, but we shall deceive ourselves into thinking that we are setting forth the conclusions of an original inquiry, undertaken and executed independently of our own philosophical conceptions.

As for myself, then, the discussion is approached with the antecedent idea that philosophy, like politics, literature, and the plastic arts, is itself a phenomenon of human culture. Its connection with social history, with civilization, is intrinsic. There is current among those who philosophize the conviction that, while past thinkers have reflected in their systems the conditions and perplexities of their own day, present-day philosophy in general, and one's own philosophy in particular, is emancipated from

* From *Philosophy and Civilization,* pp. 3-12.

the influence of that complex of institutions which forms culture. Bacon, Descartes, Kant, each thought with fervor that he was founding philosophy anew because he was placing it securely upon an exclusive intellectual basis, exclusive, that is, of everything but intellect. The movement of time has revealed the illusion; it exhibits as the work of philosophy the old and ever new undertaking of adjusting that body of traditions which constitute the actual mind of man to scientific tendencies and political aspirations which are novel and incompatible with received authorities. Philosophers are parts of history, caught in its movement; creators perhaps in some measure of its future, but also assuredly creatures of its past.

Those who assert in the abstract definition of philosophy that it deals with eternal truth or reality, untouched by local time and place, are forced to admit that philosophy as a concrete existence is historical, having temporal passage and a diversity of local habitations. Open your histories of philosophies, and you find written throughout them the same periods of time and the same geographical distributions which provide the intellectual scheme of histories of politics, industry, or the fine arts. I cannot imagine a history of philosophy which did not partition its material between the Occident and the Orient; which did not find the former falling into ancient, medieval, and modern epochs; which in setting forth Greek thought did not specify Asiatic and Italian colonies and Athens. On the other hand, those who express contempt for the enterprise of philosophy as a sterile and monotonous preoccupation with unsolvable or unreal problems, cannot, without convicting themselves of Philistinism, deny that, however it may stand with philosophy as a revelation of eternal truths, it is tremendously significant as a revelation of the predicaments, protests, and aspirations of humanity.

The two views of the history of thought are usually proffered as unreconcilable opposites. According to one, it is
the record of the most profound dealings of the reason with
ultimate being; according to the other, it is a scene of pre-
tentious claims and ridiculous failures. Nevertheless, there
is a point of view from which there is something common
to the two notions, and this common denominator is more
significant than the oppositions. Meaning is wider in scope
as well as more precious in value than is truth, and philosophy is occupied with meaning rather than with truth.
Making such a statement is dangerous; it is easily misconceived to signify that truth is of no great importance under
any circumstances; while the fact is that truth is so infinitely important when it is important at all, namely, in records of events and descriptions of existences, that we extend its claims to regions where it has no jurisdiction. But
even as respects truths, meaning is the wider category;
truths are but one class of meanings, namely, those in
which a claim to verifiability by their consequences is an
intrinsic part of their meaning. Beyond this island of
meanings which in their own nature are true or false lies
the ocean of meanings to which truth and falsity are irrelevant. We do not inquire whether Greek civilization was
true or false, but we are immensely concerned to penetrate
its meaning. We may indeed ask for the truth of Shakespeare's Hamlet or Shelley's *Skylark*, but by truth we now
signify something quite different from that of scientific
statement and historical record.

In philosophy we are dealing with something comparable
to the meaning of Athenian civilization or of drama or a
lyric. Significant history is lived in the imagination of man,
and philosophy is a further excursion of the imagination
into its own prior achievement. All that is distinctive of
man, marking him off from the clay he walks upon or the

potatoes he eats, occurs in his thought and emotions, in what we have agreed to call consciousness. To know the structure of sticks and stones, an enterprise in which, of course, truth is essential, apart from whatever added control it may yield, marks in the end but an enrichment of consciousness, of the area of meanings. Were significance identical with existence, were values the same as events, idealism would be the only possible philosophy. Thus scientific thought itself is finally but a function of the imagination in enriching life with the significance of things; it is of its peculiar essence that it must also submit to certain tests of application and control.

It is commonplace that physically and existentially man can but make a superficial and transient scratch upon the outermost rind of the world. It has become a cheap intellectual pastime to contrast the infinitesimal pettiness of man with the vastnesses of the stellar universes. Yet all such comparisons are illicit. We cannot compare existence and meaning; they are disparate. The characteristic life of man is itself the meaning of vast stretches of existences, and without it the latter have no value or significance. There is no measure of physical existence and conscious experience because the latter is the only measure there is for the former. The significance of being, though not its existence, is the emotion it stirs, the thought it sustains.

It follows that there is no specifiable difference between philosophy and its role in the history of civilization. Discover and define some characteristic, some unique function in civilization, and you have defined philosophy itself. To try to define philosophy in any other way is to search for a will-o'-the-wisp; the conceptions which result are of purely private interpretation, for they only exemplify the particular philosophies of their authorship and interpretation. Take the history of philosophy from whatever angle and in whatever cross-section you please, Indian, Chinese, Athenian, the Europe of the twelfth or the twentieth century, and you find a load of traditions proceeding from an immemorial past. You find certain preoccupying interests that appear hypnotic in their rigid hold upon imagination and you also find certain resistances, certain dawning rebellions, in struggle to escape and to express some fresh value of life. The preoccupations may be political and artistic as in Athens; they may be economic and scientific as today. But in any case, there is a certain intellectual work to be done; the dominant interest working throughout the minds of masses of men has to be clarified, a result which can be accomplished only by selection, elimination, reduction, and formulation; it has to be intellectually forced, exaggerated, in order to be focused, to be, that is, intellectually, in consciousness, since all clear consciousness by its very nature marks a wrenching of something from its subordinate place to confer upon it a centrality which is existentially absurd. Where there is sufficient depth and range of meanings for consciousness to arise at all, there is a function of adjustment, of logical reconciliation of the ruling interest of the period with preoccupations which had a different origin and an irrelevant meaning. Consider, for example, the uneasy, restless effort of Plato to adapt his new mathematical insights and his political aspirations to the traditional habits of Athens; the almost humorously complacent union of Christian supernaturalism in the Middle Ages with the naturalism of pagan Greece; the still fermenting effort of the recent age to unite the new science of nature with inherited classic and medieval institutions. The life of all thought is to effect a junction at some point of the new and the old, of deep-sunk customs and unconscious dispositions, brought to the light of attention by some conflict with newly emerging directions of activity. Philosophies which emerge at distinctive periods define the larger patterns of continuity which are woven in effecting the longer enduring junctions of a stubborn past and an insistent future.

Philosophy thus sustains the closest connection with the history of culture, with the succession of changes in civilization. It is fed by the streams of tradition, traced at critical moments to their sources in order that the current may receive a new direction; it is fertilized by the ferment of new inventions in industry, new exploration of the globe, new discoveries in science. But philosophy is not just a passive reflex of civilization that persists through changes, and that changes while persisting. It is itself a change; the patterns formed in this junction of the new and the old are prophecies rather than records; they are policies, attempts to forestall subsequent developments. The intellectual registrations which constitute a philosophy are generative just because they are selecting and eliminating exaggerations. While purporting to say that such and such is and always has been the purport of the record of nature, in effect they proclaim that such and such *should* be the significant value to which mankind should loyally attach itself. Without evidence adduced in its behalf such a statement may seem groundless. But I invite you to examine for yourselves any philosophical idea which has had for any long period a significant career and find therein your own evidence. Take, for example, the Platonic patterns of cosmic design and harmony; the Aristotelian perpetually recurrent ends and grooved potentialities; the Kantian fixed forms of intellectual synthesis; the conception of nature itself as it figured in seventeenth and eighteenth century thought. Discuss them as revelations of eternal truth, and something almost childlike or something beyond possibility enters in; discuss them as selections from the existing culture by which to articulate forces which the author believed should and would dominate the future, and they become preciously significant aspects of human history.

Thus philosophy marks a change of culture. In forming patterns to be conformed to in future thought and action, it is additive and transforming in its role in the history of civilization. Man states anything at his peril; once stated, it occupies a place in a new perspective; it attains a permanence which does not belong to its existence; it enters provokingly into wont and use; it points in a troubling way to need of new endeavors. I do not mean that the creative element in the role of philosophy is necessarily the dominant one; obviously its formulations have been often chiefly conservative, justificatory of selected elements of traditions and received institutions. But even these preservative systems have had transforming if not exactly a creative effect; they have lent the factors which were selected a power over later human imagination and sentiment which they would otherwise have lacked. And there are other periods, such as those of the seventeenth and eighteenth centuries in Europe, when philosophy is overtly revolutionary in attitude. To themselves, the turn was just from complete error to complete truth; to later generations looking back, the alteration in strictly factual content does not compare with that in desire and tend, ency of effort.

Of the many objections which may be brought against the conception that philosophy not only *has* a role, but that it *is* a specifiable role in the development of human culture, there are two misconceptions which I wish to touch upon. What has been said, taken without qualifying additions, might suggest a picture of a dominant system of philosophy at each historic period. In fact there are diverse currents and aspirations in almost every historic epoch; the divergence of philosophic systems instead of being a reproach (as of course it is from the standpoint of philosophy as a revelation of truth) is evidence of sincerity and vitality. If the ruling and the oppressed elements in a population, those who wished to maintain the *status quo* and those concerned to make changes, had, when they became articulate, the same philosophy, one might well be skeptical of its intellectual integrity. The other point is much more important. In making a distinction between meaning and truth and asserting that the latter is but one type of meaning, important under definite conditions, I have expressed the idea as if there might be in the processes of human life meanings which are wholly cut off from the actual course of events. Such is not the intent; meanings are generated and in some degree sustained by existence. Hence they cannot be wholly irrelevant to the world of existence; they all have revelatory office which should be apprehended as correctly as possible. This is true of politics, religion, and art as well as of philosophy. They all tell something of the realm of existence. But in all of them there are an exuberance and fertility of meanings and values in comparison with which correctness of telling is a secondary affair, while in the function termed science the accuracy of telling is the chief matter.

In the historic role of philosophy, the scientific factor, the element of correctness, of verifiable applicability, has a place, but it is a negative one. The meanings delivered by confirmed observation, experimentation, and calculation, scientific facts and principles, in other words, serve as tests of the values which tradition transmits and for those which emotion suggests. Whatever is not compatible with them must be eliminated in any sincere philosophizing.

This fact confers upon scientific knowledge an incalculably important office in philosophy. But the criterion is negative; the exclusion of the inconsistent is far from being identical with a positive test which demands that only what has been scientifically verifiable supply the entire content of philosophy. It is the difference between imagination that acknowledges responsibility to logical compatibility with demands of ascertained facts, and a complete abdication of all imagination in behalf of a prosy literalism.

Finally, it results from what has been said that the presence and absence of native-born philosophies is a severe test of the depth of unconscious tradition and rooted institution among any people, and of the productive force of their culture. For sake of brevity, I may be allowed to take our own case, the case of civilization in the United States. Philosophy, we have been saying, is a conversion of such culture as exists into consciousness, into imagination which is logically coherent and is not incompatible with what is factually known. But this conversion is itself a further movement of civilization itself; it is not something performed upon the body of habits and tendencies from without, that is, miraculously. If American civilization does not eventuate in an imaginative formulation of itself, if it merely re-arranges the figures already named and placed, in playing an inherited European game, that fact is itself the measure of the culture which we have achieved. A deliberate striving for an American Philosophy as such would be only another evidence of the same emptiness and impotency. There are energy and activity among us, enough and to spare. Not an inconsiderable part of the vigor that once went into industrial accomplishment now finds its way into science; our scientific "plant" is coming in its way to rival our industrial plants.

Especially in psychology and the social sciences an amount of effort is putting forth which is hardly equaled in the rest of the world. He would be a shameless braggart who claimed that the result is as yet adequate to the activity. What is the matter? It lies, I think, with our lack of imagination in generating leading ideas. Because we are afraid of speculative ideas, we do, and do over and over again, an immense amount of dead, specialized work in the region of "facts." We forget that facts are only data; that is, are only fragmentary, uncompleted meanings, and unless they are rounded out into complete ideas —a work which can only be done by hypotheses, by a free imagination of intellectual possibilities—they are as helpless as are all maimed things and as repellent as are needlessly thwarted events.

Please do not imagine that this is a plea in disguise for any particular type of philosophizing. On the contrary, any philosophy which is a sincere outgrowth and expression of our own civilization is better than none, provided it utters the authentic idiom of an enduring and dominating corporate experience. If we are really, for instance, a materialistic people, we are at least materialistic in a new fashion and on a new scale. I should welcome then a consistent materialistic philosophy, if only it were sufficiently bold, and, in spite of any attendant aesthetic repulsiveness, in the degree in which it marked the coming to consciousness of a group of ideas, it would formulate a coming to self-consciousness of our civilization. Thereby it would furnish ideas, supply an intellectual polity, direct further observations and experiments and organize their results on a grand scale. As long as we worship science and are afraid of philosophy we shall have no great science; we shall have a lagging and halting continuation of what is thought and said elsewhere. As far as any plea is implicit in what has been said, it is, then, a plea for the casting off of that intellectual timidity which hampers the wings of imagination, a plea for speculative audacity, for more faith in ideas sloughing off a cowardly reliance upon those partial ideas to which we are wont to give the name of facts. I have given to philosophy a more humble function than that which is often assigned it. But modesty as to its final place is not incompatible with boldness in the maintenance of that function, humble as it may be. A combination of such modesty and courage affords the only way I know of in which the philosopher can look his fellow man in the face with frankness and with humanity.

II · Philosophy and the Education of Man*

Philosophy has generally been defined in ways which imply a certain totality, generality, and ultimateness of both subject matter and method. With respect to subject matter, philosophy is an attempt to *comprehend*—that is, to gather together the varied details of the world and of life into a single inclusive whole, which shall either be a unity, or, as in the dualistic systems, shall reduce the plural details to a small number of ultimate principles. On the side of the attitude of the philosopher and of those who accept his conclusions, there is the endeavor to attain as unified, consistent, and complete an outlook upon experience as is possible. This aspect is expressed in the word "philosophy"—love of wisdom. Whenever philosophy has been taken seriously, it has always been assumed that it signified achieving a wisdom which would influence the conduct of life. Witness the fact that almost all ancient

* From *Democracy and Education,* pp. 378-386. By permission of The Macmillan Company, publishers.

schools of philosophy were also organized ways of living, those who accepted their tenets being committed to certain distinctive modes of conduct; witness the intimate connection of philosophy with the theology of the Roman church in the middle ages, its frequent association with religious interests, and, at national crises, its association with political struggles.

This direct and intimate connection of philosophy with an outlook upon life obviously differentiates philosophy from science. Particular facts and laws of science evidently influence conduct. They suggest things to do and not do, and provide means of execution. When science denotes not simply a report of the particular facts discovered about the world but a *general attitude* toward it—as distinct from special things to do—it merges into philosophy. For an underlying disposition represents an attitude not to this and that thing nor even to the aggregate of known things, but to the considerations which govern conduct.

Hence philosophy cannot be defined simply from the side of subject-matter. For this reason, the definition of such conceptions as generality, totality, and ultimateness is most readily reached from the side of the disposition toward the world which they connote. In any literal and quantitative sense, these terms do not apply to the subject-matter of knowledge, for completeness and finality are out of the question. The very nature of experience as an ongoing, changing process forbids. In a less rigid sense, they apply to *science* rather than to philosophy. For obviously it is to mathematics, physics, chemistry, biology, anthropology, history, etc. that we must go, not to philosophy, to find out the facts of the world. It is for the sciences to say what generalizations are tenable about the world and what they specifically are. But when we ask what *sort* of permanent disposition of action toward the world the scientific disclosures exact of us we are raising a philosophic question.

From this point of view, "totality" does not mean the hopeless task of a quantitative summation. It means rather *consistency* of mode of response in reference to the plurality of events which occur. Consistency does not mean literal identity; for since the same thing does not happen twice, an exact repetition of a reaction involves some maladjustment. Totality means continuity—the carrying on of a former habit of action with the readaptation necessary to keep it alive and growing. Instead of signifying a ready-made complete scheme of action, it means keeping the balance in a multitude of diverse actions, so that each borrows and gives significance to every other. Any person who is open-minded and sensitive to new perceptions, and who has concentration and responsibility in connecting them has, in so far, a philosophic disposition. One of the popular senses of philosophy is calm and endurance in the face of difficulty and loss; it is even supposed to be a power to bear pain without complaint. This meaning is a tribute to the influence of the Stoic philosophy rather than an attribute of philosophy in general. But in so far as it suggests that the wholeness characteristic of philosophy is a power to learn, or to extract meaning, from even the unpleasant vicissitudes of experience and to embody what is learned in an ability to go on learning, it is justified in any scheme. An analogous interpretation applies to the generality and ultimateness of philosophy. Taken literally, they are absurd pretensions; they indicate insanity. Finality does not mean, however, that experience is ended and exhausted, but means the disposition to penetrate to deeper levels of meaning—to go below the surface and find out the connections of any event or object, and to keep at it. In like manner the philosophic attitude is general in the sense that it is averse to taking anything as isolated; it tries to place an act in its context—which constitutes its significance.

More specifically, the demand for a "total" attitude arises because there is the need of integration in action of the conflicting various interests in life. Where interests are so superficial that they glide readily into one another, or where they are not sufficiently organized to come into conflict with one another, the need for philosophy is not perceptible. But when the scientific interest conflicts with, say, the religious, or the economic with the scientific or esthetic, or when the conservative concern for order is at odds with the progressive interest in freedom, or when institutionalism clashes with individuality, there is a stimulus to discover some more comprehensive point of view from which the divergencies may be brought together, and consistency or continuity of experience recovered. Often these clashes may be settled by an individual for himself; the area of the struggle of aims is limited and a person works out his own rough accommodations. Such homespun philosophies are genuine and often adequate. But they do not result in systems of philosophy. These arise when the discrepant claims of different ideals of conduct affect the community as a whole, and the need for readjustment is general.

The fact that philosophic problems arise because of widespread and widely felt difficulties in social practice is disguised because philosophers become a specialized class which uses a technical language, unlike the vocabulary in which the direct difficulties are stated. But where a system becomes influential, its connection with a conflict of interests calling for some program of social adjustment may always be discovered. At this point, the intimate connection between philosophy and education appears. In fact, education offers a vantage ground from which to penetrate to the human, as distinct from the technical, significance of philosophic discussions. The student of philosophy "in itself" is always in danger of taking it as so much nimble or severe intellectual exercise—as something said by philosophers and concerning them alone. But when philosophic issues are approached from the side of the kind of mental disposition to which they correspond, the life-situations which they formulate can never be far from view. If a theory makes no difference in educational endeavor, it must be artificial. The educational point of view enables one to envisage the philosophic problems where they arise and thrive, where they are at home, and where acceptance or rejection makes a difference in practice.

If we are willing to conceive education as the process of forming fundamental dispositions, intellectual and emotional, toward nature and fellow men, philosophy may even be defined *as the general theory of education.* Unless a philosophy is to remain symbolic—or verbal—or a sentimental indulgence for a few, or else mere arbitrary dogma, its auditing of past experience and its program of values must take effect in conduct. Public agitation, propaganda, legislative and administrative action are effective in producing the change of disposition which a philosophy indicates as desirable, but only in the degree in which they are educative—that is to say, in the degree in which they modify mental and moral attitudes. And at the best, such methods are compromised by the fact they are used with those whose habits are already largely set, while education of youth has a fairer and freer field of operation. On the other side, the business of schooling tends to become a routine empirical affair unless its aims and methods are animated by such a broad and sympathetic survey of its place in contemporary life as it is the business of philosophy to provide.

The reconstruction of philosophy, of education, and of social ideals and methods thus go hand in hand. If there is especial need of educational reconstruction at the present time, if this need makes urgent a reconsideration of the basic ideas of traditional philosophic systems, it is because of the thoroughgoing change in social life accompanying the advance of science, the industrial revolution, and the development of democracy. Such practical changes cannot take place without demanding an educational re-formation to meet them, and without leading men to ask what ideas and ideals are implicit in these social changes, and what revisions they require of the ideas and ideals which are inherited from older and unlike cultures.

III · The Critical Function of Philosophy*

Philosophy is inherently criticism, having its distinctive position among various modes of criticism in its generality; a criticism of criticisms, as it were. Criticism is discriminating judgment, careful appraisal, and judgment is appropriately termed criticism wherever the subject-matter of discrimination concerns goods or values. Possession and enjoyment of goods passes insensibly and inevitably into appraisal. First and immature experience is content simply to enjoy. But a brief course in experience enforces reflection; it requires but brief time to teach that some things sweet in the having are bitter in after-taste and in what they lead to. Primitive innocence does not last. Enjoyment ceases to be a datum and becomes a problem. As

* From *Experience and Nature*, pp. 398-437; *Art As Experience*, pp. 298-310; *Essays in Experimental Logic*, pp. 98-102.

a problem, it implies intelligent inquiry into the conditions and consequences of a value-object; that is, criticism. If values were as plentiful as huckleberries, and if the huckleberry-patch were always at hand, the passage of appreciation into criticism would be a senseless procedure. If one thing tired or bored us, we should have only to turn to another. But values are as unstable as the forms of clouds. The things that possess them are exposed to all the contingencies of existence, and they are indifferent to our likings and tastes.

When criticism and the critical attitude are legitimately distinguished from appreciation and taste, we are in the presence of one case of the constant rhythm of "perchings and flights" (to borrow James' terms), characteristic of alternate emphasis upon the immediate and mediate, the consummatory and instrumental, phases of all conscious experience. If we are misled into ignoring the omnipresence in all observations and ideas of this rhythm, it is largely because, under the influence of formal theories, we attach too elaborate and too remote a signification to "appreciation" and "criticism." Values of some sort or other are not traits of rare and festal occasions; they occur whenever any object is welcomed and lingered over; whenever it arouses aversion and protest; even though the lingering be but momentary and the aversion a passing glance toward something else.

Similarly, criticism is not a matter of formal treatises, published articles, or taking up important matters for consideration in a serious way. It occurs whenever a moment is devoted to looking to see what sort of value is present; whenever instead of accepting a value-object wholeheartedly, being rapt by it, we raise even a shadow of a question about its worth, or modify our sense of it by even a passing estimate of its probable future. It is well upon the whole that we use the terms "appreciation" and "criticism" honorifically, to designate conspicuous instances. But it is fatal to any understanding of them to fail to note that formally emphatic instances are of exactly the same nature as rhythmic alternation between slight agreeable acceptances, annoyed rejections and passing questionings and estimates, which make up the entire course of our waking experience, whether in revery, in controlled inquiry or in deliberate management of affairs.

ii

Criticism is judgment, ideally as well as etymologically. Understanding of judgment is therefore the first condition for theory about the nature of criticism. Perceptions supply judgment with its material, whether the judgments pertain to physical nature, to politics or biography. The subject-matter of perception is the only thing that makes the difference in the judgments which ensue. Control of the subject-matter of perception for ensuring proper data for judgment is the key to the enormous distinction between the judgments the savage passes on natural events and that of a Newton or an Einstein.

It cannot be safely assumed at the outset that judgment is an act of intelligence performed upon the matter of direct perception in the interest of a more adequate perception. For judgment has also a legalistic meaning and import, as in Shakespeare's phrase, "a critic, nay, a night watchman." Following the signification supplied by the practice of the law, a judge, a critic, is one who pronounces an authoritative sentence.

The judge—in the judicial sense—occupies a seat of social authority. His sentence determines the fate of an individual, perhaps of a cause, and upon occasion it settles the legitimacy of future courses of action. Desire for authority (and desire to be looked up to) animates the human breast. Much of our existence is keyed to the note of praise and blame, exculpation and disapproval. Hence there has emerged in theory, reflecting a widespread tendency in practice, a disposition to erect criticism into something "judicial." One cannot read widely in the outgivings of this school of criticism without seeing that much of it is of the compensatory type—the fact which has given rise to the gibe that critics are those who have failed in creation. Much criticism of the legalistic sort proceeds from subconscious self-distrust and a consequent appeal to authority for protection. Perception is obstructed and cut short by memory of an influential rule, and by the substitution of precedent and prestige for direct experience. Desire for authoritative standing leads the critic to speak as if he were the attorney for established principles having unquestionable sovereignty.

Unfortunately such activities have infected the very conception of criticism. Judgment that is final, that settles a matter, is more congenial to unregenerate human nature than is the judgment that is a development in thought of a deeply realized perception. The original adequate experience is not easy to attain; its achievement is a test of native sensitiveness and of experience matured through wide contacts. A judgment as an act of controlled inquiry demands a rich background and a disciplined insight. It is much easier to "tell" people what they should believe than to discriminate and unify. And an audience that is itself habituated to being told, rather than schooled in thoughtful inquiry, likes to be told.

Judicial decision can be made only on the basis of general rules supposed to be applicable to all cases. The harm done by particular instances of judicial sentence, as particular, is much less serious than the net result in developing the notion that antecedent authoritative standards and precedents are at hand by which to judge.

The very meaning of an important new movement in any phase of life is that it expresses something new in human experience, some new mode of interaction of the live creature with his surroundings, and hence the release of powers previously cramped or inert. The manifestations of the movement therefore cannot be judged but only misjudged unless the critic is sensitive first of all to "meaning and life." He is otherwise helpless in the presence of the emergence of experience that has a distinctively new character. Every professional person is subject to the influence of custom and inertia, and has to protect himself from its influences by a deliberate openness to life itself. The judicial critic erects the very things that are the dangers of his calling into a principle and norm.

The blundering ineptness of much that calls itself judicial criticism has called out a reaction to the opposite extreme. The protest takes the form of "impressionist" criticism. It is in effect, if not in words, a denial that criticism in the sense of judgment is possible, and an assertion that judgment should be replaced by statement of the responses of feeling and imagery the object of value evokes. In theory, though not always in practice, such criticism reacts from the standardized "objectivity" of ready-made rules and precedents to the chaos of a subjectivity that lacks objective control, and would, if logically followed out, result in a medley of irrelevancies—and sometimes does.

Were it not for the blunders made by the judicial critic, blunders that proceed from the theory he holds, the reaction of the impressionist theory would hardly have been called forth. Because the former set up false notions of objective values and objective standards, it was made easy for the impressionist critic to deny there are objective values at all. Because the former has virtually adopted a conception of standards that is of an external nature, derived from use of standards developed for practical ends, and legally defined, the latter has assumed there are no criteria of any sort. In its precise signification, a "standard" is unambiguous. It is a quantitative measure. The yard as a standard of length, the gallon as a standard of liquid capacity, are as precise as legal definitions can make them. The standard of liquid measure for Great Britain was defined, for example, by an act of Parliament in 1825. It is a container holding ten pounds avoirdupois of distilled water, weighed in air with the barometer at thirty inches and the Fahrenheit thermometer at sixty-two degrees.

There are three characteristics of a standard. It is a particular physical thing existing under specified physical conditions; it is *not* a value. The yard is a yard-stick, and the meter is a bar deposited in Paris. In the second place, standards are measures of definite things, of lengths, weights, capacities. The things measured are not values, although it is of great social value to be able to measure them, since the properties of things in the way of size, volume, weight, are important for commercial exchange. Finally, as standards of measure, standards define things with respect to *quantity*. To be able to measure quantities is a great aid to further judgments, but it is not itself a mode of judgment. The standard, being an external and public thing, is applied *physically*. The yard-stick is physically laid down upon the things measured to determine their length.

When, therefore, the word "standard" is used with respect to judgment of value objects, nothing but confusion results, unless the radical difference in the meaning now given standard from that of standards of measurement is noted. The critic is really judging, not measuring physical fact. He is concerned with something individual, not comparative—as is all measurement. His subject-matter is qualitative, not quantitative. There is no external and public thing, defined by law to be the same for all transactions, that can be physically applied. The child who can use a yard-stick can measure as well as the most experienced and mature person, if he can handle the stick, since measuring is not judgment but is a physical operation performed for the sake of determining value in exchange or in behalf of some further physical operation—as a carpenter measures the boards with which he builds. The same cannot be said of judgment of the value of an idea or the value of any objects.

Yet it does not follow because of absence of a uniform and publicly determined external object, that objective criticism of value-objects is impossible. What follows is that criticism is judgment; that like every judgment it involves a venture, a hypothetical element; that it is directed to qualities which are nevertheless qualities of an *object*; and that it is concerned with an individual object, not with making comparisons by means of an external preëstablished rule between different things. The critic, because of the element of venture, reveals himself in his criticisms. He wanders into another field and confuses values when he departs from the object he is judging. Nowhere are comparisons so odious as in fine art.

Criticism is judgment. The material out of which judgment grows is the work, the object, but it is this object as it enters into the experience of the critic by interaction with his own sensitivity and his knowledge and funded store from past experiences. As to their content, therefore, judgments will vary with the concrete material that evokes them and that must sustain them if criticism is pertinent and valid. Nevertheless, judgments have a common form because they all have certain functions to perform. These functions are discrimination and unification. Judgment has to evoke a clearer consciousness of constituent parts and to discover how consistently these parts are related to form a whole. Theory gives the names of analysis and synthesis to the execution of these functions.

They cannot be separated from each other, because analysis is disclosure of part as parts of a whole; of details and particulars as belonging to total situation, a universe of discourse. This operation is the opposite of picking to pieces or of dissection, even when something of the latter sort is required in order to make judgment possible. No rules can be laid for the performance of so delicate an act as determination of the significant parts of a whole, and of their respective places and weights in the whole. This is the reason, perhaps, why scholarly dissertations upon literature are so often merely scholastic enumerations of minutiae, and so-called criticisms of paintings are of the order of analyses of handwriting by experts.

Analytic judgment is a test of the mind of the critic, since mind, as organization into perceptions of meanings derived from past intercourse with objects, is the organ of discrimination. Hence the safeguard of the critic is a consuming informed interest. I say "consuming" because without natural sensitivity connected with an intense liking for certain subject-matters, a critic, having even a wide range of learning, will be so cold that he will remain on the outside. Yet, unless affection is informed with the insight that is the product of a rich and full experience, judgment will be one-sided or will not rise above the level of gushy sentimentalism. Learning must be the fuel of warmth of interest.

iii

The difference between genuine, valid good and a counterfeit, specious good is unreal, or it is a difference consequent upon reflection, or criticism, and the significant point is that this difference is equivalent to that made by discovery of relationships, of conditions and consequences. With this conclusion are bound up two other propositions: Of immediate values as such, values which occur and which are possessed and enjoyed, there is no theory at all; they just occur, are enjoyed, possessed; and that is all. The moment we begin to discourse about these values, to define and generalize, to make distinctions in kinds, we are passing beyond value-objects themselves; we are entering, even if only blindly, upon an inquiry into causal antecedents and causative consequents, with a view to appraising the "real," that is the eventual, goodness of the thing in question. We are criticizing, not for its own sake, but for the sake of instituting and perpetuating more enduring and extensive values.

The other proposition is that philosophy is and can be nothing but this critical operation and function become aware of itself and its implications, pursued deliberately and systematically. It starts from actual situations of belief, conduct and appreciative perception which are characterized by immediate qualities of good and bad, and from the modes of critical judgment current at any given time in all the regions of value; these are its data, its subject-matter. These values, criticisms, and critical methods it subjects to further criticism as comprehensive and consistent as possible. The function is to regulate the further appreciation of goods and bads; to give greater freedom and security in those acts of direct selection, appropriation, identification and of rejection, elimination, destruction which enstate and which exclude objects of belief, conduct and contemplation.

Philosophic discourse partakes both of scientific and literary discourse. Like literature, it is a comment on nature and life in the interest of a more intense and just appreciation of the meanings present in experience. Its business is reportorial and transcriptive only in the sense in which the drama and poetry have that office. Its primary concern is to clarify, liberate and extend the goods which inhere in the naturally generated functions of experience. It has no call to create a world of "reality" *de novo*, nor to delve into secrets of Being hidden from common-sense and science. It has no stock of information or body of knowledge peculiarly its own; if it does not always become ridiculous when it sets up as a rival of science, it is only because a particular philosopher happens to be also, as a human being, a prophetic man of science. Its business is to accept and to utilize for a purpose the best available knowledge of its own time and place. And this purpose is criticism of beliefs, institutions, customs, policies with respect to their bearing upon good. This does not mean their bearing upon *the* good, as something itself attained and formulated in philosophy. For as philosophy has no private source of knowledge or of methods for attaining truth, so it has no private access to good. As it accepts knowledge of facts and principles from those competent in inquiry and discovery, so it accepts the goods that are diffused in human experience. It has no Mosaic nor Pauline authority of revelation entrusted to it. But it has the authority of intelligence, of criticism of these common and natural goods.

At this point, it departs from the arts of literary discourse. They have a freer office to perform—to perpetuate, enhance and vivify in imagination the natural goods; all things are forgiven to him who succeeds. But philosophic criticism has a stricter task, with a greater measure of responsibility to what lies outside its own products. It has to appraise values by taking cognizance of their causes and consequences; only by this straight and narrow path may it contribute to expansion and emancipation of values. For this reason the conclusions of science about matter-of-fact efficiencies of nature are its indispensable instruments. If its eventual concern is to render goods more coherent, more secure and more significant in appreciation, its road is the subject-matter of natural existence as science discovers and depicts it.

Philosophy, defined as a logic, makes no pretense to be an account of a closed and finished universe. Its business is not to secure or guarantee any particular reality or value. *Per contra,* it gets the significance of a method. The right relationship and adjustment of the various typical phases of experience to one another is a problem felt in every department of life. Intellectual rectification and control of these adjustments cannot fail to reflect itself in an added clearness and security on the practical side. It may be that general logic cannot become an instrument in the immediate direction of the activities of science or art or industry; but it is of value in criticizing and organizing tools of immediate research. It also has direct significance in the valuation for social or life-purposes of results achieved in particular branches. Much of the immediate business of life is badly done because we do not know the genesis and outcome of the work that occupies us. The manner and degree of appropriation of the goods achieved in various departments of social interest and vocation are partial and faulty because we are not clear as to the due rights and responsibilities of one function of experience in reference to others.

The value of research for social progress; the bearing
of psychology upon educational procedure; the mutual relations of fine and industrial art; the question of the extent and nature of specialization in science in comparison
with the claims of applied science; the adjustment of religious aspirations to scientific statements; the justification
of a refined culture for a few in face of economic insufficiency for the mass, the relation of organization to individuality—such are a few of the many social questions
whose answer depends upon the possession and use of a
general logic of experience as a method of inquiry and interpretation. I do not say that headway cannot be made
in such questions apart from the method indicated: a logic
of experience. But unless we have a critical and assured
view of the juncture in which and with reference to which
a given attitude or interest arises, unless we know the
service it is thereby called upon to perform, and hence the
organs or methods by which it best functions in that service, our progress is impeded and irregular.

We take a part for a whole, a means for an end; or we
attack wholesale some interest because it interferes with
the deified sway of the one we have selected as ultimate.
A clear and comprehensive consensus of social conviction
and a consequent concentrated and economical direction of
effort are assured only as there is some way of locating the
position and rôle of each typical interest and occupation.
The domain of opinion is one of conflict; its rule is arbitrary and costly. Only intellectual method affords a substitute for opinion. A general logic of experience alone can do
for social qualities and aims what the natural sciences
after centuries of struggle are doing for activity in the
physical realm.

This does not mean that systems of philosophy which
have attempted to state the nature of thought and of real-

ity at large, apart from limits of particular situations in the movement of experience, have been worthless—though it does mean that their industry has been somewhat misapplied. The unfolding of metaphysical theory has made large contributions to positive evaluations of the typical situations and relationships of experience—even when its conscious intention has been quite otherwise. Every system of philosophy is itself a mode of reflection; consequently (if our main contention be true), it too has been evoked out of specific social antecedents, and has had its use as a response to them. It has effected something in modifying the situation within which it found its origin. It may not have solved the problem which it consciously put itself; in many cases we may freely admit that the question put has been found afterward to be so wrongly put as to be insoluble. Yet exactly the same thing is true, in precisely the same sense, in the history of science. For this reason, if for no other, it is impossible for the scientific man to cast the first stone at the philosopher.

The progress of science in any branch continually brings with it a realization that problems in their previous form of statement are insoluble because put in terms of unreal conditions; because the real conditions have been mixed up with mental artifacts or misconstructions. Every science is continually learning that its supposed solutions are only apparent because the "solution" solves, not the actual problem, but one which has been made up. But the very putting of the question, the very giving of the wrong answer, induces modification of existing intellectual habits, standpoints, and aims. Wrestling with the problem, there is evolution of new technique to control inquiry, there is search for new facts, institution of new types of experimentation; there is gain in the methodic control of experience.

And all this is progress. It is only the worn-out cynic, the devitalized sensualist, and the fanatical dogmatist who interpret the continuous change of science as proving that, since each successive statement is wrong, the whole record is error and folly; and that the present truth is only the error not yet found out. Such draw the moral of caring naught for all these things, or of flying to some external authority which will deliver once for all the fixed and unchangeable truth. But historic philosophy even in its aberrant forms has proved a factor in the valuation of experience; it has brought problems to light, it has provoked intellectual conflicts without which values are only nominal; even through its would-be absolutistic isolations it has secured recognition of mutual dependencies and reciprocal reinforcements. Yet if it can define its work more clearly, it can concentrate its energy upon its own characteristic problem: the genesis and functioning in experience of various typical interests and occupations with reference to one another.

Because intelligence is critical method applied to goods of belief, appreciation and conduct, so as to construct freer and more secure goods, turning assent and assertion into free communication of shareable meanings, turning feeling into ordered and liberal sense, turning reaction into response, it is the reasonable object of our deepest faith and loyalty, the stay and support of all reasonable hopes. To utter such a statement is not to indulge in romantic idealization. It is not to assert that intelligence will ever dominate the course of events; it is not even to imply that it will save from ruin and destruction. The issue is one of choice, and choice is always a question of alternatives.

What the method of intelligence, thoughtful valuation will accomplish, if once it be tried, is for the result of trial to determine. Since it is relative to the intersection in existence of hazard and rule, of contingency and order, faith in a wholesale and final triumph is fantastic. But some procedure has to be tried; for life is itself a sequence of trials. Carelessness and routine, Olympian aloofness, secluded contemplation are themselves choices. To claim that intelligence is a better method than its alternatives, authority, imitation, caprice and ignorance, prejudice and passion, is hardly an excessive claim. These procedures have been tried and have worked their will. The result is not such as to make it clear that the method of intelligence, the use of science in criticizing and recreating the casual goods of nature into intentional and conclusive goods of art, the union of knowledge and values in production, is not worth trying. There may be those to whom it is treason to think of philosophy as the critical method of developing methods of criticism. But this conception of philosophy also waits to be tried, and the trial which shall approve or condemn lies in the eventual issue. The import of such knowledge as we have acquired and such experience as has been quickened by thought is to evoke and justify the trial.

CHAPTER TWO

THE GREAT PHILOSOPHIC SEPARATION

I · The Quest for Certainty*

MAN who lives in a world of hazards is compelled to seek for security. He has sought to attain it in two ways. One of them began with an attempt to propitiate the powers which environ him and determine his destiny. It expressed itself in supplication, sacrifice, ceremonial rite and magical cult. In time these crude methods were largely displaced. The sacrifice of a contrite heart was esteemed more pleasing than that of bulls and oxen; the inner attitude of reverence and devotion more desirable than external ceremonies. If man could not conquer destiny he could willingly ally himself with it; putting his will, even in sore affliction, on the side of the powers which dispense fortune, he could escape defeat and might triumph in the midst of destruction.

The other course is to invent arts and by their means turn the powers of nature to account; man constructs a fortress out of the very conditions and forces which threaten him. He builds shelters, weaves garments, makes flame his friend instead of his enemy, and grows into the complicated arts of associated living. This is the method of changing the world through action, as the other is the method of changing the self in emotion and idea. It is a commentary on the slight control man has obtained over

* From *The Quest for Certainty*, pp. 3-20.

himself by means of control over nature, that the method of action has been felt to manifest dangerous pride, even defiance of the powers which be. People of old wavered between thinking arts to be the gift of the gods and to be an invasion of their prerogatives. Both versions testify to the sense of something extraordinary in the arts, something either superhuman or unnatural. The souls who have predicted that by means of the arts man might establish a kingdom of order, justice and beauty through mastery of nature's energies and laws have been few and little heeded.

Men have been glad enough to enjoy the fruits of such arts as they possess, and in recent centuries have increasingly devoted themselves to their multiplication. But this effort has been conjoined with a profound distrust of the arts as a method of dealing with the serious perils of life. Doubt as to the truth of this statement will be dispelled if one considers the disesteem in which the idea of practice has been held. Philosophers have celebrated the method of change in personal ideas, and religious teachers that of change in the affections of the heart. These conversions have been prized on their own account, and only incidentally because of a change in action which would ensue. The latter has been esteemed as an evidence of the change in thought and sentiment, not as a method of transforming the scene of life. The places in which the use of the arts has effected actual objective transformation have been regarded as inferior, if not base, and the activities connected with them as menial. The disparagement attending the idea of the material has seized upon them. The honorable quality associated with the idea of the "spiritual" has been reserved for change in inner attitudes.

The depreciation of action, of doing and making, has been cultivated by philosophers. But while philosophers have perpetuated the derogation by formulating and justifying it, they did not originate it. They glorified their own office without doubt in placing theory so much above practice. But independently of their attitude, many things conspired to the same effect. Work has been onerous, toilsome, associated with a primeval curse. It has been done under compulsion and the pressure of necessity, while intellectual activity is associated with leisure. On account of the unpleasantness of practical activity, as much of it as possible has been put upon slaves and serfs. Thus the social dishonor in which this class was held was extended to the work they do. There is also the age-long association of knowing and thinking with immaterial and spiritual principles, and of the arts, of all practical activity in doing and making, with matter. For work is done with the body, by means of mechanical appliances and is directed upon material things. The disrepute which has attended the thought of material things in comparison with immaterial thought has been transferred to everything associated with practice.

One might continue in this strain. The natural history of conceptions about work and the arts if it were traced through a succession of peoples and cultures would be instructive. But all that is needed for our purpose is to raise the question: Why this invidious discrimination? A very little reflection shows that the suggestions which have been offered by way of explanation themselves need to be explained. Ideas derived from social castes and emotional revulsions are hardly reasons to be offered in justification of a belief, although they may have a bearing on its causation. Contempt for matter and bodies and glorification of the immaterial are affairs which are not self-explanatory.

The questions suggested have far-reaching issues. What

is the cause and the import of the sharp division between theory and practice? Why should the latter be disesteemed along with matter and the body? What has been the effect upon the various modes in which action is manifested: industry, politics, the fine arts, and upon morals conceived of as overt activity having consequences, instead of as mere inner personal attitude? How has the separation of intellect from action affected the theory of knowledge? What has been in particular the effect upon the conception and course of philosophy? What forces are at work to break down the division? What would the effect be if the divorce were annulled, and knowing and doing were brought into intrinsic connection with one another? What revisions of the traditional theory of mind, thought and knowing would be required, and what change in the idea of the office of philosophy would be demanded? What modifications would ensue in the disciplines which are concerned with the various phases of human activity?

The distinctive characteristic of practical activity, one which is so inherent that it cannot be eliminated, is the uncertainty which attends it. Of it we are compelled to say: Act, but act at your peril. Judgment and belief regarding actions to be performed can never attain more than a precarious probability. Through thought, however, it has seemed that men might escape from the perils of uncertainty. The exaltation of pure intellect and its activity above practical affairs is fundamentally connected with the quest for a certainty which shall be absolute and unshakeable.

Practical activity deals with individualized and unique situations which are never exactly duplicable and about which, accordingly, no complete assurance is possible. All activity, moreover, involves change. The intellect, however, according to the traditional doctrine, may grasp universal Being, and Being which is universal is fixed and immutable. Wherever there is practical activity we human beings are involved as partakers in the issue. All the fear, disesteem and lack of confidence which gather about the thought of ourselves, cluster also about the thought of the actions in which we are partners. Man's distrust of himself has caused him to desire to get beyond and above himself; in pure knowledge he has thought he could attain this self-transcendence.

There is no need to expatiate upon the risk which attends overt action. The burden of proverbs and wise saws is that the best laid plans of men as of mice gang agley. Fortune rather than our own intent and act determines eventual success and failure. The pathos of unfulfilled expectation, the tragedy of defeated purpose and ideals, the catastrophes of accident, are the commonplaces of all comment on the human scene. We survey conditions, make the wisest choice we can; we act, and we must trust the rest to fate, fortune or providence. Moralists tell us to look to the end when we act and then inform us that the end is always uncertain. Judging, planning, choice, no matter how thoroughly conducted, and action no matter how prudently executed, never are the sole determinants of any outcome. Alien and indifferent natural forces, unforeseeable conditions enter in and have a decisive voice. The more important the issue, the greater is their say as to the ulterior event.

Hence men have longed to find a realm in which there is an activity which is not overt and which has no external consequences. "Safety first" has played a large rôle in effecting a preference for knowing over doing and making. With those to whom the process of pure thinking is congenial and who have the leisure and the aptitude to pursue their preference, the happiness attending knowing is unalloyed; it is not entangled in the risks which overt action cannot escape. Thought has been alleged to be a purely inner activity, intrinsic to mind alone; and according to traditional classic doctrine, "mind" is complete and self-sufficient in itself. Overt action may follow upon its operations but in an external way, a way not intrinsic to its completion. Since rational activity is complete within itself it needs no external manifestation. Failure and frustration are attributed to the accidents of an alien, intractable and inferior realm of existence. The outer lot of thought is cast in a world external to it, but one which in no way injures the supremacy and completeness of thought and knowledge in their intrinsic natures.

Thus the arts by which man attains such practical security as is possible of achievement are looked down upon. The security they provide is relative, ever incomplete, at the risk of untoward circumstance. The multiplication of arts may even be bemoaned as a source of new dangers. Each of them demands its own measures of protection. Each one in its operation brings with it new and unexpected consequences having perils for which we are not prepared. The quest for certainty is a quest for a peace which is assured, an object which is unqualified by risk and the shadow of fear which action casts. For it is not uncertainty *per se* which men dislike, but the fact that uncertainty involves us in peril of evils. Uncertainty that affected only the detail of consequences to be experienced provided they had a warrant of being enjoyable would have no sting. It would bring the zest of adventure and the spice of variety. Quest for complete certainty can be fulfilled in pure knowing alone. Such is the verdict of our most enduring philosophic tradition.

Primitive men had none of the elaborate arts of protection and use which we now enjoy and no confidence in his own powers when they were reinforced by appliances of art. He lived under conditions in which he was extraordinarily exposed to peril, and at the same time he was without the means of defense which are today matters of course. Most of our simplest tools and utensils did not exist; there was no accurate foresight; men faced the forces of nature in a state of nakedness which was more than physical; save under unusually benign conditions he was beset with dangers that knew no remission. In consequence, mystery attended experiences of good and evil; they could not be traced to their natural causes and they seemed to be the dispensations, the gifts and the inflictions, of powers beyond possibility of control. The precarious crises of birth, puberty, illness, death, war, famine, plague, the uncertainties of the hunt, the vicissitudes of climate and the great seasonal changes, kept imagination occupied with the uncertain. Any scene or object that was implicated in any conspicuous tragedy or triumph, in no matter how accidental a way, got a peculiar significance. It was seized upon as a harbinger of good or as an omen of evil. Accordingly, some things were cherished as means of encompassing safety just as a good artisan today looks after his tools; others were feared and shunned because of their potencies for harm.

As a drowning man is said to grasp at a straw, so men who lacked the instruments and skills developed in later days, snatched at whatever, by any stretch of imagination, could be regarded as a source of help in time of trouble. The attention, interest and care which now go to acquiring skill in the use of appliances and to the invention of means for better service of ends, were devoted to noting omens, making irrelevant prognostications, performing ritualistic ceremonies and manipulating objects possessed of magical power over natural events. In such an atmosphere primitive religion was born and fostered. Rather this atmosphere *was* the religious disposition.

Search for alliance with means which might promote prosperity and which would afford defense against hostile powers was constant. While this attitude was most marked in connection with the recurrent crises of life, yet the boundary line between these crucial affairs with their extraordinary risks and everyday acts was shadowy. The acts that related to commonplace things and everyday occupations were usually accompanied, for good measure of security, by ritual acts. The making of a weapon, the molding of a bowl, the weaving of a mat, the sowing of seed, the reaping of a harvest, required acts different in kind from the technical skills employed. These other acts had a special solemnity and were thought necessary in order to ensure the success of the practical operations used.

While it is difficult to avoid the use of the word supernatural, we must avoid the meaning the word has for us. As long as there was no defined area of the *natural*, that which is over and beyond the natural can have no significance. The distinction, as anthropological students have pointed out, was between ordinary and extraordinary; between the prosaic, usual run of events and the crucial incident or irruption which determined the direction which the average and expected course of events took. But the two realms were in no way sharply demarcated from each other. There was a no-man's land, a vague territory, in which they overlapped. At any moment the extraordinary might invade the commonplace and either wreck it or clothe it with some surprising glory. The use of ordinary things under critical conditions was fraught with inexplicable potentialities of good and evil.

The two dominant conceptions, cultural categories one might call them, which grew and flourished under such circumstances were those of the holy and the fortunate, with their opposites, the profane and the unlucky. As with the idea of the supernatural, meanings are not to be assigned on the basis of present usage. Everything which was charged with some extraordinary potency for benefit or injury was holy; holiness meant necessity for being approached with ceremonial scruples. The holy thing, whether place, object, person or ritual appliance, has its sinister face; "to be handled with care" is written upon it. From it there issues the command: *Noli me tangere*. Tabus, a whole set of prohibitions and injunctions, gather about it. It is capable of transmitting its mysterious potency to other things. To secure the favor of the holy is to be on the road to success, while any conspicuous success is proof of the favor of some overshadowing power—a fact which politicians of all ages have known how to utilize. Because of its surcharge of power, ambivalent in quality, the holy has to be approached not only with scruples but in an attitude of subjection. There are rites of purification, humiliation, fasting and prayer which are preconditions of securing its favor.

The holy is the bearer of blessing or fortune. But a difference early developed between the ideas of the holy and the lucky, because of the different dispositions in which each was to be approached. A lucky object is something to be used. It is to be manipulated rather than approached with awe. It calls for incantations, spells, divinations rather than for supplication and humiliation. Moreover, the lucky thing tends to be a concrete and tangible object, while the holy one is not usually definitely localized; it is the more potent in the degree in which its habitation and form are vague. The lucky object is subject to pressure, at a pinch to coercion, to scolding and punishment. It might be discarded if it failed to bring luck. There developed a certain element of mastery in its use, in distinction from the dependence and subjection which remained the proper attitude toward the holy. Thus there was a kind of rhythm of domination and submission, of imprecation and supplication, of utilization and communion.

Such statements give, of course, a one-sided picture. Men at all times have gone about many things in a matter-of-fact way and have had their daily enjoyments. Even in the ceremonies of which we have spoken there entered the ordinary love of the dramatic as well as the desire for repetition, once routine is established. Primitive man early developed some tools and some modes of skill. With them went prosaic knowledge of the properties of ordinary things. But these beliefs were surrounded by others of an imaginative and emotional type, and were more or less submerged in the latter. Moreover, prestige attached to the latter. Just because some beliefs were matter-of-fact they did not have the weight and authority that belong to those about the extraordinary and unaccountable. We find the same phenomenon repeated today wherever religious beliefs have marked vitality.

Prosaic beliefs about verifiable facts, beliefs backed up by evidence of the senses and by useful fruits, had little glamour and prestige compared with the vogue of objects of rite and ceremony. Hence the things forming their subject-matter were felt to be lower in rank. Familiarity breeds a sense of equality if not of contempt. We deem ourselves on a par with things we daily administer. It is a truism to say that objects regarded with awe have perforce a superior status. Herein is the source of the fundamental dualism of human attention and regard. The distinction between the two attitudes of everyday control and dependence on something superior was finally generalized intellectually. It took effect in the conception of two distinct realms. The inferior was that in which man could foresee and in which he had instruments and arts by which he might expect a reasonable degree of control. The superior was that of occurrences so uncontrollable that they testified to the presence and operation of powers beyond the scope of everyday and mundane things.

The philosophical tradition regarding knowledge and practice, the immaterial or spiritual and the material, was not original and primitive. It had for its background the state of culture which has been sketched. It developed in a social atmosphere in which the division of the ordinary and extraordinary was domesticated. Philosophy reflected upon it and gave it a rational formulation and justification. The bodies of information that corresponded to the everyday arts, the store of matter-of-fact knowledge, were things men knew because of what they did. They were products and promises of utilities. They shared in the relatively low esteem belonging to such things in comparison with the extraordinary and divine. Philosophy inherited the realm with which religion had been concerned. Its mode of knowing was different from that accompanying the empirical arts, just because it dealt with a realm of higher Being. It breathed an air purer than that in which exist the making and doing that relate to livelihood, just as the activities which took the form of rites and ceremonies were nobler and nearer the divine than those spent in toil.

The change from religion to philosophy was so great in form that their identity as to content is easily lost from view. The form ceases to be that of the story told in imaginative and emotional style, and becomes that of rational discourse observing the canons of logic. It is well

known that that portion of Aristotle's system which later
generations have called metaphysics he called First Philosophy. It is possible to quote from him sentences descriptive of First Philosophy which make it seem that
the philosophic enterprise is a coldly rational one, objective and analytic. Thus he says it is the most comprehensive of all branches of knowledge because it has for its
subject-matter definition of the traits which belong to all
forms of Being whatsoever, however much they may differ
from one another in detail.

But when these passages are placed in the context they
had in Aristotle's own mind, it is clear that the comprehensiveness and universality of "First" Philosophy are not
of a strictly analytic sort. They mark a distinction with respect to grade of value and title to reverence. For he explicitly identifies his "First" Philosophy—or metaphysics
—with theology; he says it is higher than other sciences.
For these deal with generation and production, while its
subject-matter permits of demonstrative, that is necessary,
truth; and its objects are divine and such as are meet for
God to occupy himself with. Again, he says that the objects of philosophy are such as are the causes of as much
of the divine as is manifest to us, and that if the divine
is anywhere present, it is present in things of the sort
with which philosophy deals. The supremacy of worth
and dignity of these objects are also made clear in the
statement that the Being with which philosophy is occupied is primary, eternal and self-sufficient, because its nature is the Good, so that the Good is among the first principles which are philosophy's subject-matter:—yet not, it
must be understood, the good in the sense in which it has
meaning and standing in human life but the inherently
and eternally perfect, that which is complete and self-
sufficient.

Aristotle tells us that from remote antiquity tradition has handed down the idea, in story form, that the heavenly bodies are gods, and that the divine encompasses the entire natural world. This core of truth, he goes on to say in effect, was embroidered with myths for the benefit of the masses, for reasons of expediency, namely, the preservation of social institutions. The negative work of philosophy was then to strip away these imaginative accretions. From the standpoint of popular belief this was its chief work, and it was a destructive one. The masses only felt that their religion was attacked. But the enduring contribution was positive. The belief that the divine encompasses the world was detached from its mythical context and made the basis of philosophy, and it became also the foundation of physical science—as is suggested by the remark that the heavenly bodies are gods. Telling the story of the universe in the form of rational discourse instead of emotionalized imagination signified the discovery of logic as a rational science. Conformity on the part of supreme reality to the requirements of logic conferred upon its constitutive objects necessary and immutable characteristics. Pure contemplation of these forms was man's highest and most divine bliss, a communion with unchangeable truth.

If one looks at the foundations of the philosophies of Plato and Aristotle as an anthropologist looks at his material, that is, as cultural subject-matter, it is clear that these philosophies were systematizations in rational form of the content of Greek religious and artistic beliefs. The systematization involved a purification. Logic provided the patterns to which ultimately real objects had to conform, while physical science was possible in the degree in which the natural world, even in its mutabilities, exhibited exemplification of ultimate immutable rational objects. Thus,

along with the elimination of myths and grosser superstitions, there were set up the ideals of science and of a life
of reason. Ends which could justify themselves to reason
were to take the place of custom as the guide of conduct.
These two ideals form a permanent contribution to western civilization.

But with all our gratitude for these enduring gifts, we
cannot forget the conditions which attended them. For
they brought with them the idea of a higher realm of fixed
reality of which alone true science is possible and of an
inferior world of changing things with which experience
and practical matters are concerned. They glorified the
invariant at the expense of change, it being evident that
all practical activity falls within the realm of change. It
bequeathed the notion, which has ruled philosophy ever
since the time of the Greeks, that the office of knowledge
is to uncover the antecedently real, rather than, as is the
case with our practical judgments, to gain the kind of understanding which is necessary to deal with problems as
they arise.

In fixing this conception of knowledge it established
also, as far as philosophies of the classic type are concerned, the special task of philosophic inquiry. As a form
of knowledge it is concerned with the disclosure of the
Real in itself, of Being in and of itself. It is differentiated
from other modes of knowing by its preoccupation with a
higher and more ultimate form of Being than that with
which the sciences of nature are concerned. As far as it
occupied itself at all with human conduct, it was to su-
perimpose upon acts ends said to flow from the nature of
reason. It thus diverted thought from inquiring into the
purposes which experience of actual conditions suggests
and from concrete means of their actualization. It translated into a rational form the doctrine of escape from the

vicissitudes of existence by means of measures which do not demand an active coping with conditions. For deliverance by means of rites and cults, it substituted deliverance through reason. This deliverance was an intellectual, a theoretical affair, constituted by a knowledge to be attained apart from practical activity.

The realms of knowledge and action were each divided into two regions. It is not to be inferred that Greek philosophy separated activity from knowing. It connected them. But it distinguished activity from action—that is, from making and doing. Rational and necessary knowledge was treated, as in the celebrations of it by Aristotle, as an ultimate, self-sufficient and self-enclosed form of self-originated and self-conducted activity. It was ideal and eternal, independent of change and hence of the world in which men act and live, the world we experience perceptibly and practically. "Pure activity" was sharply marked off from practical action. The latter, whether in the industrial or the fine arts, in morals or in politics, was concerned with an inferior region of Being in which change rules, and which accordingly has Being only by courtesy, for it manifests deficiency of sure footing in Being by the very fact of change. It is infected with *non*-being.

On the side of knowledge, the division carried with it a difference between knowledge, in its full sense, and belief. The former is demonstrative, necessary—that is, sure. Belief on the contrary is only opinion; in its uncertainty and mere probability, it relates to the world of change as knowledge corresponds to the realm of true reality. That man has two modes, two dimensions, of belief, cannot be doubted. He has beliefs about actual existences and the course of events, and he has beliefs about ends to be striven for, policies to be adopted, goods to be attained and evils to be averted. The most urgent of all practical problems concerns the connection the subject-matter of these two kinds of beliefs sustain to each other. How shall our most authentic and dependable cognitive beliefs be used to regulate our practical beliefs? How shall the latter serve to organize and integrate our intellectual beliefs?

There is a genuine possibility that the true problem of philosophy is connected with precisely this type of question. Man has beliefs which scientific inquiry vouchsafes, beliefs about the actual structure and processes of things; and he also has beliefs about the values which should regulate his conduct. The question of how these two ways of believing may most effectively and fruitfully interact with one another is the most general and significant of all the problems which life presents to us. Some reasoned discipline, one obviously other than any science, should deal with this issue. Thus there is supplied one way of conceiving of the function of philosophy. But from this mode of defining philosophy we are estopped by the chief philosophical tradition. For according to it the realms of knowledge and of practical action have no inherent connection with each other.

Thus the depreciation of practice was given a philosophic, an ontological, justification. Practical action, as distinct from self-revolving rational self-activity, belongs in the realm of generation and decay, a realm inferior in value as in Being. In form, the quest for absolute certainty has reached its goal. Because ultimate Being or reality is fixed, permanent, admitting of no change or variation, it may be grasped by rational intuition and set forth in rational, that is, universal and necessary, demonstration. I do not doubt that there was a feeling before the rise of philosophy that the unalterably fixed and the absolutely certain are one, or that change is the source from which comes all our uncertainties and woes. But in philosophy this inchoate feeling was definitely formulated. It was asserted on grounds held to be as demonstrably necessary as are the conclusions of geometry and logic. Thus the predisposition of philosophy toward the universal, invariant and eternal was fixed. It remains the common possession of the entire classic philosophic tradition.

II · The Historic Mission of Philosophy*

Greek thinkers saw clearly—and logically—that experience cannot furnish us, as respects cognition of existence, with anything more than contingent probability. Experience cannot deliver to us necessary truths; truths completely demonstrated by reason. Its conclusions are particular, not universal. Not being "exact" they come short of "science." Thus there arose the distinction between rational truths or, in modern terminology, truths relating to the relation of ideas, and "truths" about matters of existence, empirically ascertained. Thus not merely the arts of practice, industrial and social, were stamped matters of belief rather than of knowledge, but also all those sciences which are matters of inductive inference from observation.

One might indulge in the reflection that they are none the worse for all that, especially since the natural sciences have developed a technique for achieving a high degree of probability and for measuring, within assignable limits, the amount of probability which attaches in particular cases to conclusions. But historically the matter is not so simple as to permit of this retort. For empirical or observational sciences were placed in invidious contrast to rational sciences which dealt with eternal and universal objects and which therefore were possessed of necessary truth. Consequently all observational sciences as far as their material could not be subsumed under forms and principles sup-

* From *The Quest for Certainty*, pp. 26-36, 67-69.

plied by rational science shared in the depreciatory view held about practical affairs. They are relatively low, secular and profane compared with the perfect realities of rational science.

And here is a justification for going back to something as remote in time as Greek philosophy. The whole classic tradition down to our day has continued to hold a slighting view of experience as such, and to hold up as the proper goal and ideal of true knowledge realities which even if they are located in empirical things cannot be known by experimental methods. The logical consequence for philosophy itself is evident. Upon the side of method, it has been compelled to claim for itself the possession of a method issuing from reason itself, and having the warrant of reason, independently of experience. As long as the view obtained that nature itself is truly known by the same rational method, the consequences—at least those which were evident—were not serious. There was no break between philosophy and genuine science—or what was conceived to be such. In fact, there was not even a distinction; there were simply various branches of philosophy, metaphysical, logical, natural, moral, etc., in a descending scale of demonstrative certainty. Since, according to the theory, the subject-matter of the lower sciences was inherently of a different character from that of true knowledge, there was no ground for rational dissatisfaction with the lower degree of knowledge called belief. Inferior knowledge or belief corresponded to the inferior state of subject-matter.

The scientific revolution of the seventeenth century effected a great modification. Science itself through the aid of mathematics carried the scheme of demonstrative knowledge over to natural objects. The "laws" of the natural world had that fixed character which in the older scheme had belonged only to rational and ideal forms. A mathematical science of nature couched in mechanistic terms claimed to be the only sound natural philosophy. Hence the older philosophies lost alliance with natural knowledge and the support that had been given to philosophy by them. Philosophy in maintaining its claim to be a superior form of knowledge was compelled to take an invidious and so to say malicious attitude toward the conclusions of natural science. The framework of the old tradition had in the meantime become embedded in Christian theology, and through religious teaching was made a part of the inherited culture of those innocent of any technical philosophy. Consequently, the rivalry between philosophy and the new science, with respect to the claim to know reality, was converted in effect into a rivalry between the spiritual values guaranteed by the older philosophic tradition and the conclusions of natural knowledge. The more science advanced the more it seemed to encroach upon the special province of the territory over which philosophy had claimed jurisdiction. Thus philosophy in its classic form became a species of apologetic justification for belief in an ultimate reality in which the values which should regulate life and control conduct are securely enstated.

There are undoubted disadvantages in the historic manner of approach to the problem which has been followed. It may readily be thought either that the Greek formulation which has been emphasized has no especial pertinency with respect to modern thought and especially to contemporary philosophy; or that no philosophical statement is of any great importance for the mass of non-philosophic persons. Those interested in philosophy may object that the criticisms passed are directed if not at a man of straw at least to positions that have long since lost their actuality. Those not friendly to any form of philosophy may inquire what import they have for any except professed philosophers.

At the point in the discussion now reached, it suffices to point out that, in spite of great changes in detail, the notion of a separation between knowledge and action, theory and practice, has been perpetuated, and that the beliefs connected with action are taken to be uncertain and inferior in value compared with those inherently connected with objects of knowledge, so that the former are securely established only as they derived from the latter. Not the specific content of Greek thought is pertinent to present problems, but its insistence that security is measured by certainty of knowledge, while the latter is measured by adhesion to fixed and immutable objects, which therefore are independent of what men do in practical activity.

The other objection is of a different sort. It comes from those who feel that not merely Greek philosophy but philosophy in any form is remote from all significant human concern. It is willing to admit or rather assert that it is presumptuous for philosophy to lay claim to knowledge of a higher order than that given by natural science, but it also holds that this is no great matter in any case except for professional philosophers.

There would be force in this latter objection were it not that those who make it hold for the most part the same philosophy of certainty and its proper object that is held by philosophers, save in an inchoate form. They are not interested in the notion that philosophic thought is a special means of attaining this object and the certainty it affords, but they are far from holding, either explicitly or implicitly, that the arts of intelligently directed action are the means by which security of values is to be attained. With respect to certain ends and goods they accept this

idea. But in thinking of these ends and values as material, as related to health, wealth, control of conditions for
the sake of an inferior order of consequences, they retain
the same division between a higher reality and a lower
that is formulated in classic philosophy. They may be innocent of the vocabulary that speaks of reason, necessary
truth, the universal, things in themselves and appearances.
But they incline to believe that there is some other road
than that of action, directed by knowledge, to achieve ultimate security of higher ideals and purposes. They think
of practical action as necessary for practical utilities, but
they mark off practical utilities from spiritual and ideal
values. Philosophy did not originate the underlying division. It only gave intellectual formulation and justification
to ideas that were operative in men's minds generally.
And the elements of these ideas are as active in present
culture as they ever were in the past. Indeed, through the
diffusion of religious doctrines, the idea that ultimate values are a matter of special revelation and are to be embodied in life by special means radically different from
the arts of action that deal with lower and lesser ends has
been accentuated in the popular mind.

Here is the point which is of general human import instead of concern merely to professional philosophers.
What about the security of values, of the things which are
admirable, honorable, to be approved of and striven for?
It is probably in consequence of the derogatory view held
of practice that the question of the secure place of values
in human experience is so seldom raised in connection
with the problem of the relation of knowledge and practice. But upon any view concerning the status of action,
the scope of the latter cannot be restricted to self-seeking
acts, nor to those of a prudential aspect, nor in general to
things of expediency and what are often termed "utilita-

rian" affairs. The maintenance and diffusion of intellectual values, of moral excellencies, the esthetically admirable, as well as the maintenance of order and decorum in human relations are dependent upon what men do.

Whether because of the emphasis of traditional religion upon salvation of the personal soul or for some other reason, there is a tendency to restrict the ultimate scope of morals to the reflex effect of conduct on one's self. Even utilitarianism, with all its seeming independence of traditional theology and its emphasis upon the general good as the criterion for judging conduct, insisted in its hedonistic psychology upon private pleasure as the motive for action. The idea that the stable and expanding institution of all things that make life worth while throughout all human relationships is the real object of *all* intelligent conduct is depressed from view by the current conception of morals as a special kind of action chiefly concerned with either the virtues or the enjoyments of individuals in their personal capacities. In changed form, we still retain the notion of a division of activity into two kinds having very different worths. The result is the depreciated meaning that has come to be attached to the very meaning of the "practical" and the useful. Instead of being extended to cover all forms of action by means of which all the values of life are extended and rendered more secure, including the diffusion of the fine arts and the cultivation of taste, the processes of education and all activities which are concerned with rendering human relationships more significant and worthy, the meaning of "practical" is limited to matters of ease, comfort, riches, bodily security and police order, possibly health, etc., things which in their isolation from other goods can only lay claim to restricted and narrow value. In consequence, these subjects are handed over to technical sciences and arts; they are no concern of "higher" interests which feel that no matter what happens to inferior goods in the vicissitudes of natural existence, the highest values are immutable characters of the ultimately real.

Our depreciatory attitude toward "practice" would be modified if we habitually thought of it in its most liberal sense, and if we surrendered our customary dualism between two separate kinds of value, one intrinsically higher and one inherently lower. We should regard practice as the only means (other than accident) by which whatever is judged to be honorable, admirable, approvable can be kept in concrete experienceable existence. In this connection the entire import of "morals" would be transformed. How much of the tendency to ignore permanent objective consequences in differences made in natural and social relations; and how much of the emphasis upon personal and internal motives and dispositions irrespective of what they objectively produce and sustain are products of the habitual depreciation of the worth of action in comparison with forms of mental processes, of thought and sentiment, which make no objective difference in things themselves?

It would be possible to argue (and, I think, with much justice) that failure to make action central in the search for such security as is humanly possible is a survival of the impotency of man in those stages of civilization when he had few means of regulating and utilizing the conditions upon which the occurrence of consequences depends. As long as man was unable by means of the arts of practice to direct the course of events, it was natural for him to seek an emotional substitute; in the absence of actual certainty in the midst of a precarious and hazardous world, men cultivated all sorts of things that would give them the *feeling* of certainty. And it is possible that, when not carried to an illusory point, the cultivation of the feeling gave man courage and confidence and enabled him to carry the burdens of life more successfully. But one could hardly seriously contend that this fact, if it be such, is one upon which to found a reasoned philosophy.

It is to the conception of philosophy that we come back. No mode of action can, as we have insisted, give anything approaching absolute certitude; it provides insurance but no assurance. Doing is always subject to peril, to the danger of frustration. When men began to reflect philosophically it seemed to them altogether too risky to leave the place of values at the mercy of acts the results of which are never sure. This precariousness might hold as far as empirical existence, existence in the sensible and phenomenal world, is concerned; but this very uncertainty seemed to render it the more needful that ideal goods should be shown to have, by means of knowledge of the most assured type, an indefeasible and inexpugnable position in the realm of the ultimately real. So at least we may imagine men to have reasoned. And today many persons find a peculiar consolation in the face of the unstable and dubious presence of values in actual experience by projecting a perfect form of good into a realm of essence, if not into a heaven beyond the earthly skies, wherein their authority, if not their existence, is wholly unshakeable.

Instead of asking how far this process is of that compensatory kind with which recent psychology has made us familiar, we are inquiring into the effect upon philosophy. It will not be denied, I suppose, that the chief aim of those philosophies which I have called classical, has been to show that the realities which are the objects of the highest and most necessary knowledge are also endowed with the values which correspond to our best aspirations, admirations and approvals. That, one may say, is the very heart of all traditional philosophic idealisms. There is a pathos, having its own nobility, in philosophies which think it their proper office to give an intellectual or cognitive certification to the ontological reality of the highest values. It is difficult for men to see desire and choice set earnestly upon the good and yet being frustrated, without their imagining a realm in which the good has come completely to its own, and is identified with a Reality in which resides all ultimate power. The failure and frustration of actual life are then attributed to the fact that this world is finite and phenomenal, sensible rather than real, or to the weakness of our finite apprehension, which cannot see that the discrepancy between existence and value is merely seeming, and that a fuller vision would behold partial evil an element in complete good. Thus the office of philosophy is to project by dialectic, resting supposedly upon self-evident premises, a realm in which the object of completest cognitive certitude is also one with the object of the heart's best aspiration. The fusion of the good and the true with unity and plenitude of Being thus becomes the goal of classic philosophy.

The situation would strike us as a curious one were it not so familiar. Practical activity is dismissed to a world of low-grade reality. Desire is found only where something is lacking and hence its existence is a sign of imperfection of Being. Hence one must go to passionless reason to find perfect reality and complete certitude. But nevertheless the chief philosophic interest is to prove that the essential properties of the reality that is the object of pure knowledge are precisely those characteristics which have meaning in connection with affection, desire and choice. After degrading practical affairs in order to exalt knowledge, the chief task of knowledge turns out to be to demonstrate the absolutely assured and permanent reality of the values with which practical activity is concerned!

Can we fail to see the irony in a situation wherein desire and emotion are relegated to a position inferior in every way to that of knowledge, while at the same time the chief problem of that which is termed the highest and most perfect knowledge is taken to be the existence of evil—that is, of desires errant and frustrated?

The contradiction involved, however, is much more than a purely intellectual one—which if purely theoretical would be innocuously lacking in practical consequences. The thing which concerns all of us as human beings is precisely the greatest attainable security of values in concrete existence. The thought that the values which are unstable and wavering in the world in which we live are eternally secure in a higher realm (which reason demonstrates but which we cannot experience), that all the goods which are defeated here are triumphant there, may give consolation to the depressed. But it does not change the existential situation in the least. The separation that has been instituted between theory and practice, with its consequent substitution of cognitive quest for absolute assurance for practical endeavor to make the existence of good more secure in experience, has had the effect of distracting attention and diverting energy from a task whose performance would yield definite results.

The chief consideration in achieving concrete security of values lies in the perfecting of *methods* of action. More activity, blind striving, gets nothing forward. Regulation of conditions upon which results depend is possible only by doing, yet only by doing which has intelligent direction, which takes cognizance of conditions, observes relations of sequence, and which plans and executes in the light of this knowledge. The notion that thought, apart from action, can warrant complete certitude as to the status of supreme good, makes no contribution to the central problem of development of intelligent methods of regulation. It rather depresses and deadens effort in that direction. That is the chief indictment to be brought against the classic philosophic tradition. Its import raises the question of the relation which action sustains to knowledge in fact, and whether the quest for certainty by other means than those of intelligent action does not mark a baneful diversion of thought from its proper office. It raises the question whether mankind has not now achieved a sufficient degree of control of methods of knowing and of the arts of practical action so that a radical change in our conceptions of knowledge and practice is rendered both possible and necessary.

There is a fatal ambiguity in the conception of philosophy as a purely theoretical or intellectual subject. The ambiguity lies in the fact that the conception is used to cover both the attitude of the inquirer, the thinker, and the character of the subject-matter dealt with. The engineer, the physician, the moralist deal with a subject-matter which is practical; one, that is, which concerns things to be done and the way of doing them. But as far as personal disposition and purpose is concerned, their inquiries are intellectual and cognitive. These men set out to find out certain things; in order to find them out, there has to be a purgation of personal desire and preference, and a willingness to subordinate them to the lead of the subject-matter inquired into. The mind must be purified as far as is humanly possible of bias and of that favoritism for one kind of conclusion rather than another which distorts observation and introduces an extraneous factor into reflection.

Except, then, on the premise that the subject-matter of philosophy is fixed properties of antecedent Being, the fact that it is an intellectual pursuit signifies nothing be-

yond the fact that those who engage in it should respect
the canons of fairness, impartiality, of internal consistency
and external evidence. It carries no implication with it—
except on the basis of a prior assumption—save that of intellectual honesty. Only upon the obverse of the adage
that whoso drives fat oxen must himself be fat, can it be
urged that logical austerity of personal attitude and procedure demands that the subject-matter dealt with must
be made lean by stripping it of all that is human concern.
To say that the object of philosophy is truth is to make a
moral statement which applies to every inquiry. It implies
nothing as to the kind of truth which is to be ascertained,
whether it be of a purely theoretical nature, of a practical
character, or whether it concerns the bearing of one upon
the other. To assert that contemplation of truth for its
own sake is the highest ideal is to make a judgment concerning authoritative value. To employ this judgment as a
means of determining the office of philosophy is to violate
the canon that inquiry should follow the lead of subject-
matter.

It is fair, then, to conclude that the question of the
relations of theory and practice to each other, and of philosophy to both of them, has often been compromised by
failure to maintain the distinction between the theoretical
interest which is another name for intellectual candor
and the theoretical interest which defines the nature of
subject-matter. Over and above this fact, there is reason
to suppose that much of the impatience with the suggestion
of the practical in connection with philosophy is due to
the habit of associating "practical" with affairs of narrow
personal concern. The significance of the idea cannot be
thus sheared down without an elimination of intellectual
regard for the values which are to have authority over our

desires and purposes and thus over our entire conduct. It would seem as if only the cynical sceptic would willingly take such a stand.

CHAPTER THREE

PHILOSOPHY AND SCIENCE

I · The Modern Crisis*

IT is more or less of a commonplace to speak of the crisis which has been caused by the progress of the natural sciences in the past few centuries. The crisis is due, it is asserted, to the incompatibility between the conclusions of natural science about the world in which we live and the realm of higher values, of ideal and spiritual qualities, which get no support from natural science. The new science, it is said, has stripped the world of the qualities which made it beautiful and congenial to men; has deprived nature of all aspiration toward ends, all preference for accomplishing the good, and presented nature to us as a scene of indifferent physical particles acting according to mathematical and mechanical laws.

This effect of modern science has, it is notorious, set the main problems for modern philosophy. How is science to be accepted and yet the realm of values to be conserved? This question forms the philosophic version of the popular conflict of science and religion. Instead of being troubled about the inconsistency of astronomy with the older religious beliefs about heaven and the ascension of Christ, or the differences between the geological record and the account of creation in *Genesis*, philosophers have been troubled by the gap in kind which exists between the

* From *The Quest for Certainty,* pp. 40-46.

fundamental principles of the natural world and the reality of the values according to which mankind is to regulate its life.

Philosophers, therefore, set to work to mediate, to find some harmony behind the apparent discord. Everybody knows that the trend of modern philosophy has been to arrive at theories regarding the nature of the universe by means of theories regarding the nature of knowledge—a procedure which reverses the apparently more judicious method of the ancients in basing their conclusions about knowledge on the nature of the universe in which knowledge occurs. The "crisis" of which we have just been speaking accounts for the reversal.

Since science has made the trouble, the cure ought to be found in an examination of the nature of knowledge, of the conditions which make science possible. If the conditions of the possibility of knowledge can be shown to be of an ideal and rational character, then, so it has been thought, the loss of an idealistic cosmology in physics can be readily borne. The physical world can be surrendered to matter and mechanism, since we are assured that matter and mechanism have their foundation in immaterial mind. Such has been the characteristic course of modern spiritualistic philosophies since the time of Kant; indeed, since that of Descartes, who first felt the poignancy of the problem involved in reconciling the conclusions of science with traditional religious and moral beliefs.

It would presumably be taken as a sign of extreme naïveté, if not of callous insensitiveness, if one were to ask why all this ardor to reconcile the findings of natural science with the validity of values? Why should any increase of knowledge seem like a threat to what we prize, admire and approve? Why should we not proceed to employ our gains in science to improve our judgments about values,

and to regulate our actions so as to make values more secure and more widely shared in existence?

I am willing to run the risk of charge of naïveté for the
sake of making manifest the difference upon which we
have been dwelling. If men had associated their ideas
about values with practical activity instead of with cognition of antecedent Being, they would *not* have been
troubled by the findings of science. They would have welcomed the latter. For anything ascertained about the
structure of actually existing conditions would be a definite aid in making judgments about things to be prized
and striven for more adequate, and would instruct us as
to the means to be employed in realizing them. But according to the religious and philosophic tradition of Europe, the valid status of all the highest values, the good,
true and beautiful, was bound up with their being properties of ultimate and supreme Being, namely, God. All
went well as long as what passed for natural science gave
no offence to this conception. Trouble began when science
ceased to disclose in the objects of knowledge the possession of any such properties. Then some roundabout
method had to be devised for substantiating them.

The point of the seemingly crass question which was
asked is thus to elicit the radical difference made when
the problem of values is seen to be connected with the
problem of intelligent action. If the validity of beliefs and
judgments about values is dependent upon the consequences of action undertaken in their behalf, if the assumed association of values with knowledge capable of
being demonstrated apart from activity, is abandoned,
then the problem of the intrinsic relation of science to
value is wholly artificial. It is replaced by a group of
practical problems: How shall we employ what we know
to direct the formation of our beliefs about value and how

shall we direct our practical behavior so as to test these beliefs and make possible better ones? The question is seen to be just what it has always been empirically: What shall we *do* to make objects having value more secure in existence? And we approach the answer to the problem with all the advantages given us by increase of knowledge of the conditions and relations under which this doing must proceed.

But for over two thousand years the weight of the most influential and authoritatively orthodox tradition of thought has been thrown into the opposite scale. It has been devoted to the problem of a purely cognitive certification (perhaps by revelation, perhaps by intuition, perhaps by reason) of the antecedent immutable reality of truth, beauty and goodness. As against such a doctrine, the conclusions of natural science constitute the materials of a serious problem. The appeal has been made to the Court of Knowledge and the verdict has been adverse. There are two rival systems that must have their respective claims adjusted. The crisis in contemporary culture, the confusions and conflicts in it, arise from a division of authority. Scientific inquiry seems to tell one thing, and traditional beliefs about ends and ideals that have authority over conduct tell us something quite different. The problem of reconciliation arises and persists for one reason only. As long as the notions persist that knowledge is a disclosure of reality, of reality prior to and independent of knowing, and that knowing is independent of a purpose to control the quality of experienced objects, the failure of natural science to disclose significant values in its objects will come as a shock. Those seriously concerned with the validity and authority of value will have a problem on their hands. As long as the notion persists that values are authentic and valid only on condition that they are prop-

erties of Being independent of human action, as long as it
is supposed that their right to regulate action is dependent
upon their being independent of action, so long there will
be needed schemes to prove that values are, in spite of the
findings of science, genuine and known qualifications of
reality in itself. For men will not easily surrender all regulative guidance in action. If they are forbidden to find
standards in the course of experience they will seek them
somewhere else, if not in revelation, then in the deliverance of a reason that is above experience.

This then is the fundamental issue for present philosophy. Is the doctrine justified that knowledge is valid in
the degree in which it is a revelation of antecedent existences or Being? Is the doctrine justified that regulative
ends and purposes have validity only when they can be
shown to be properties belonging to things, whether as existences or as essences, apart from human action? It is
proposed to make another start. Desires, affections, preferences, needs and interests at least exist in human experience; they are characteristics of it. Knowledge about nature also exists. What does this knowledge imply and en-
tail with respect to the guidance of our emotional and volitional life? How shall the latter lay hold of what is
known in order to make it of service?

These latter questions do not seem to many thinkers to
have the dignity that is attached to the traditional problems of philosophy. They are proximate questions, not
ultimate. They do not concern Being and Knowledge "in
themselves" and at large, but the state of existence at
specified times and places and the state of affection, plans
and purposes under concrete circumstances. They are not
concerned with framing a general theory of reality, knowledge and value once for all, but with finding how authentic beliefs about existence as they currently exist can

operate fruitfully and efficaciously in connection with the practical problems that are urgent in actual life.

In restricted and technical fields, men now proceed unhesitatingly along these lines. In technology and the arts of engineering and medicine, men do not think of operating in any other way. Increased knowledge of nature and its conditions does not raise the problem of validity of the value of health or of communication in general, although it may well make dubious the validity of certain conceptions men in the past have entertained about the nature of health and communication and the best ways of attaining these goods in fact.

In such matters, science has placed in our hands the means by which we can better judge our wants, and has aided in forming the instruments and operations by which to satisfy them. That the same sort of thing has not happened in the moral and distinctly humane arts is evident. Here is a problem which might well trouble philosophers.

Why have not the arts which deal with the wider, more generous, more distinctly humane values enjoyed the release and expansion which have accrued to the technical arts? Can it be seriously urged that it is because natural science has disclosed to us the kind of world which it has disclosed? It is easy to see that these disclosures are hostile to some beliefs about values which have been widely accepted, which have prestige, which have become deeply impregnated with sentiment, and which authoritative institutions as well as the emotion and inertia of men are slow to surrender. But this admission, which practically enforces itself, is far from excluding the formation of new beliefs about things to be honored and prized by men in their supreme loyalties of action. The difficulty in the road is a practical one, a social one, connected with institutions and the methods and aims of education, not with science nor with value. Under such circumstances the first problem for philosophy would seem to be to clear itself of further responsibility for the doctrine that the supreme issue is whether values have antecedent Being, while its further office is to make clear the revisions and reconstructions that have to be made in traditional judgments about values. Having done this, it would be in a position to undertake the more positive task of projecting ideas about values which might be the basis of a new integration of human conduct.

II · Ancient and Modern Science Contrasted*

There was a time when "art" and "science" were virtually equivalent terms. There is a reminiscence of this period in university organization in the phrase "faculty of arts and sciences." A distinction was drawn between the "mechanical" and the "liberal" arts. In part, this distinction was between industrial arts and social arts, those concerned with things and those concerned directly with persons. Grammar and rhetoric, for example, in dealing with speech, the interpretation of literature and the arts of persuasion, were higher than blacksmithing and carpentry. The mechanical arts dealt with things which were merely means; the liberal arts dealt with affairs that were ends, things having a final and intrinsic worth. The obviousness of the distinction was reënforced by social causes. Mechanics were concerned with mechanical arts; they were lower in the social scale. The school in which their arts were learned was the school of practice: apprenticeship to those who had already mastered the craft and mystery. Apprentices literally "learned by doing," and "doing" was routine repetition and imitation of the acts of others, until personal skill was acquired. The liberal arts were studied

* From *The Quest for Certainty,* pp. 74-97.

by those who were to be in some position of authority, occupied with some exercise of social rule. Such persons had
the material means that afforded leisure, and were to engage in callings that had especial honor and prestige.
Moreover, they learned not by mechanical repetition and
bodily practice in manipulation of materials and tools, but
"intellectually," through a kind of study which involved
mind, not body.

The situation is not recalled as if it had a merely historical significance. It describes in large measure a state
of affairs that exists today. The distinction between
"learned professions" and the occupations of the shop and
factory, with corresponding differences of social status, of
educational preparation, of concern chiefly with material
things or with persons and social relations, is too familiar
to call for recourse to past history. The chief difference in
the present situation is due to the rise of technological industry and of a pecuniary economy, at the expense of the
inherited status of the "gentleman," the owner of large
estates in land. So our allusion is pertinent not to history,
but to still existing conditions that are influential in creating and maintaining the division between theory and
practice, mind and body, ends and instrumentalities.

In addition to this distinction between higher and lower
arts, there always hovered in the background a distinction
between all arts and "science" in the true and ultimate
sense of the words. The liberal arts involved much more
of knowledge and of theoretical study, of use of "mind,"
than did the mechanical. But in their ultimate import
they were still connected with art, with doing, although
with a mode of practice held in higher esteem. They remained within the limits of experience, although of an experience having a kind of value not found in the baser
arts. The philosophic tradition, as for example it is form-

ulated by Aristotle, ranked social arts lower than pure intellectual inquiry, than knowledge as something not to be
put to any use, even a social and moral one. It is conceivable that historically this point of view might have remained a mere laudation of its own calling on the part of
a small intellectual class. But, in the expansion of the
Church as a dominant power in Europe, religion affiliated
this philosophic conception to itself. Theology was regarded as "science" in a peculiar, a unique, sense, for it
alone was knowledge of supreme and ultimate Being. And
the Church had a direct influence over the hearts and
conduct, the beliefs and judgments, of men that a secluded
intellectual class could never win. As the guardians and
dispensers of the truths and sacraments that determined
the eternal destiny, the eternal happiness or misery of the
soul, they effected the embodiment of ideas originating in
philosophy in the culture of Christendom.

"Experience" once meant the results accumulated in
memory of a variety of past doings and undergoings that
were had without control by insight, when the net accumulation was found to be practically available in dealing
with present situations. Both the original perceptions and
uses and the application of their outcome in present doings were accidental—that is, neither was determined by
an understanding of the relations of cause and effect, of
means and consequences, involved. In that sense they
were non-rational, non-scientific. A typical illustration is a
bridge builder who constructs simply on the basis of what
has been done and what happened in the past, without
reference to knowledge of strains and stresses, or in general of physical relationships actually involved; or the art
of medicine, as far as it rests simply upon the accidents of
remedial measures used in the past without knowledge of
why some worked and others did not. A measure of skill

results, but it is the fruit of cut and dried methods, of trial and error—in short it is "empirical."

The disparaging notion of experience framed under such conditions is an honest report of actual conditions; philosophers in setting experience down as inherently inferior to rational science were truthful. What they added was another matter. It was a statement that this inferiority was inherently connected with the body, with the senses, with material things, with the uncertainly changing as over against the certain because immutable. Unfortunately their theories in explanation of the defects of experience persisted and became classic after experience itself, in some of its forms, had become experimental in the sense of being directed by understanding of conditions and their consequences. Two points are especially significant with reference to the split thus produced between the traditional theory of experience and that which results from noting its experimental character.

In the traditional theory, which still is the prevailing one, there were alleged to exist inherent defects in perception and observation as means of knowledge, in reference to the subject-matter they furnish. This material, in the older notion, is inherently so particular, so contingent and variable, that by no possible means can it contribute to *knowledge;* it can result only in opinion, mere belief. But in modern science, there are only *practical* defects in the senses, certain limitations of vision, for example, that have to be corrected and supplemented by various devices, such as the use of the lens. Every insufficiency of observation is an instigation to invent some new instrument which will make good the defect, or it is a stimulus to devising indirect means, such as mathematical calculations, by which the limitations of sense will be circumvented. The counterpart of this change is one in the conception of thought and its relation to knowing. It was earlier assumed that higher knowledge must be supplied by pure thought; pure because apart from experience, since the latter involves the senses. Now, it is taken for granted that thought, while indispensable to knowledge of natural existence, can never in itself provide that knowledge. Observation is indispensable both to provide authentic materials to work upon and to test and verify the conclusions reached by theoretical considerations. A specified kind of experience is indispensable to science instead of all experience setting a limit to the possibility of true science.

There is an objective counterpart of this shift. In the older theory, sense and experience were barriers to true science because they are implicated in natural change. Their appropriate and inevitable subject-matter was variable and changing things. Knowledge in its full and valid sense is possible only of the immutable, the fixed; that alone answers the quest for certainty. With regard to changing things, only surmise and opinion are possible, just as practically these are the source of peril. To a scientific man, in terms of what he does in inquiry, the notion of a natural science which should turn its back upon the changes of things, upon events, is simply incomprehensible. What he is interested in knowing, in understanding, are precisely the changes that go on; they set his problems, and problems are solved when changes are interconnected with one another. Constants and relative invariants figure, but they are relations between changes, not the constituents of a higher realm of Being. With this modification with respect to the object comes one in the structure and content of "experience." Instead of there being a fixed difference between it and something higher—rational thought—there is a difference between two kinds of experience; one which is occupied with uncontrolled change and one concerned with directed and regulated change. And this difference, while fundamentally important, does not mark a fixed division. Changes of the first type are something *to be brought under control* by means of action directed by understanding of relationships.

In the old scheme, knowledge, as science, signified precisely and exclusively turning away from change to the changeless. In the new experimental science, knowledge is obtained in exactly the opposite way, namely, through deliberate institution of a definite and specified course of change. *The* method of physical inquiry is to introduce some change in order to see what other change ensues; the correlation between these changes, when measured by a series of operations, constitutes the definite and desired object of knowledge. There are two degrees of control of change which differ practically but are alike in principle. In astronomy, for example, we cannot introduce variation into remote heavenly bodies. But we can deliberately alter the conditions under which we observe them, which is the same thing in principle of logical procedure. By special instruments, the use of lens and prism, by telescopes, spectroscopes, interferometers, etc., we modify observed data. Observations are taken from widely different points in space and at successive times. By such means interconnected variations are observed. In physical and chemical matters closer at hand and capable of more direct manipulation, changes introduced affect the things under inquiry. Appliances and re-agents for bringing about variations in the things studied are employed. The progress of inquiry is identical with advance in the invention and construction of physical instrumentalities for producing, registering and measuring changes.

Moreover, there is no difference in logical principle between the method of science and the method pursued in technologies. The difference is practical; in the scale of operations conducted; in the lesser degree of control through isolation of conditions operative, and especially in the purpose for the sake of which regulated control of modifications of natural existences and energies is undertaken; especially, since the dominant motive of large-scale regulation of the course of change is material comfort or pecuniary gain. But the technique of modern industry, in commerce, communication, transportation and all the appliances of light, heat and electricity, is the fruit of the modern application of science. And this so-called "application" signifies that the same kind of intentional introduction and management of changes which takes place in the laboratory is induced in the factory, the railway and the power house.

The central and outstanding fact is that the change in the method of knowing, due to the scientific revolution begun in the sixteenth and seventeenth centuries, has been accompanied by a revolution in the attitude of man toward natural occurrences and their interactions. This transformation means, as was intimated earlier, a complete reversal in the traditional relationship of knowledge and action. Science advances by adopting the instruments and doings of directed practice, and the knowledge thus gained becomes a means of the development of arts which bring nature still further into actual and potential service of human purposes and valuations. The astonishing thing is that in the face of this change wrought in civilization, there still persist the notions about mind and its organs of knowing, together with the inferiority of practice to intellect, which developed in antiquity as the report of a totally different situation.

The hold which older conceptions have gained over the minds of thinkers, the sway of inertia in habits of philo-

sophic thought, can be most readily judged by turning to
books on epistemology and to discussions of problems connected with the theory of knowledge published in the
philosophical periodicals. Articles on logical method will
be found which reflect the procedures of actual knowing,
that is, of the practice of scientific inquiry. But logic is
then usually treated as "mere" methodology, having little
(probably nothing would be nearer the mark) to do with
the theory of knowledge. The latter is discussed in terms
of conceptions about mind and its organs; these conceptions are supposed to be capable of adequate formation
apart from observation of what goes on when men engage
in successful inquiry. Of late, the main problem in such
discussions is to frame a theory of "consciousness" which
shall explain knowing, as if consciousness were either a
fact whose meaning is self-evident, or something less obscure in content and more observable than are the objective and public procedures of scientific investigation. This
type of discussion persists; it is, in current conception,
the theory of knowledge, the natural and inevitable way
in which to discuss its basic problems! Volumes could not
say more for the persistence of traditional ideas. The import of even a rudimentary discussion of actual experimental method can hardly be gathered, then, without
bearing in mind its significance as a contrast effect.

While the traits of experimental inquiry are familiar, so
little use has been made of them in formulating a theory of
knowledge and of mind in relation to nature that a somewhat explicit statement of well-known facts is excusable.
They exhibit three outstanding characteristics. The first is
the obvious one that all experimentation involves *overt*
doing, the making of definite changes in the environment
or in our relation to it. The second is that experiment is
not a random activity but is directed by ideas which have

to meet the conditions set by the need of the problem inducing the active inquiry. The third and concluding feature, in which the other two receive their full measure of meaning, is that the outcome of the directed activity is the construction of a new empirical situation in which objects are differently related to one another, and such that the *consequences* of directed operations form the objects that have the property of being *known*.

The rudimentary prototype of experimental doing for the sake of knowing is found in ordinary procedures. When we are trying to make out the nature of a confused and unfamiliar object, we perform various acts with a view to establishing a new relationship to it, such as will bring to light qualities which will aid in understanding it. We turn it over, bring it into a better light, rattle and shake it, thump, push and press it, and so on. The object as it is experienced prior to the introduction of these changes baffles us; the intent of these acts is to make changes which will elicit some previously unperceived qualities, and by varying conditions of perception shake loose some property which as it stands blinds or misleads us.

While such experimentations, together with a kind of experimental playing with things just to see what will happen, are the chief source of the everyday non-scientific store of information about things around us, forming the bulk of "common-sense" knowledge, the limitations of the mode of procedure are so evident as to require no exposition. The important thing in the history of modern knowing is the reinforcement of these active doings by means of instruments, appliances and apparatus devised for the purposes of disclosing relations not otherwise apparent, together with, as far as overt action is concerned, the development of elaborate techniques for the introduction of a much greater range of variations—that is, a systematic variation of conditions so as to produce a corresponding series of changes in the thing under investigation. Among these operations should be included, of course, those which give a permanent register of what is observed and the instrumentalities of exact measurement by means of which changes are correlated with one another.

These matters are so familiar that their full import for the theory of knowing readily escapes notice. Hence the need of comparing this kind of knowledge of natural existences with that obtaining before the rise of the experimental method. The striking difference is, of course, the dependence placed upon doing, doing of a physical and overt sort. Ancient science, that is, what passed as science, would have thought it a kind of treason to reason as the organ of knowing to subordinate it to bodily activity on material things, helped out with tools which are also material. It would have seemed like admitting the superiority of matter to rational mind, an admission which from its standpoint was contradictory to the possibility of knowledge.

With this fundamental change goes another, that in the attitude taken toward the material of direct sense-perception. No notion could be further away from the fact than the somewhat sedulously cultivated idea that the difference between ancient and modern science is that the former had no respect for perception and relied exclusively upon speculation. In fact, the Greeks were keenly sensitive to natural objects and were keen observers. The trouble lay not in substitution of theorizing from the outset for the material of perception, but in that they took the latter "as is"; they made no attempt to modify it radically before undertaking thinking and theorizing about it. As far as observation unaided by artificial appliances and means for deliberate variation of observed material went, the Greeks went far.

Their disrespect for sensibly observed material concerned only its form. For it had to be brought under logical forms supplied by rational thought. The fact that the material was not exclusively logical, or such as to satisfy the requirements of rational form, made the resulting knowledge less scientific than that of pure mathematics, logic and metaphysics occupied with eternal Being. But as far as science extended, it dealt with the material of sense-perception as it directly offered itself to a keen and alert observer. In consequence, the material of Greek natural science is much closer to "common-sense" material than are the results of contemporary science. One can read the surviving statements of it without any more technical preparation than say a knowledge of Euclidean geometry, while no one can follow understandingly the reports of most modern investigations in physics without a highly technical preparatory education. One reason the atomic theory propounded in antiquity made so little headway is that it did not agree with the results of ordinary observation. For this presented objects clothed with rich qualities and falling into kinds or species that were themselves marked by qualitative, rather than by merely quantitative and spatial, differences. In antiquity it was the atomic theory which was purely speculative and "deductive" in character.

These statements would be misunderstood if they were taken to imply an allegation that in ancient science sense gives knowledge, while modern science excludes the material of sense; such an idea inverts the facts. But ancient science accepted the *material* of sense-material on its face, and then organized it, as it naturally and originally stood, by operations of logical definition, classification into species and syllogistic subsumption. Men either had no instruments and appliances for modifying the ordinary objects of observation, for analyzing them into their elements and giving them new forms and arrangements, or they failed to use those which they had. Thus in *content*, or subject-matter, the conclusions of Greek science (which persisted till the scientific revolution of the seventeenth century), were much closer to the objects of everyday experience than are the objects of present scientific thought. It is not meant that the Greeks had more respect for the *function* of perception through the senses than has modern science, but that, judged from present practice, they had altogether too much respect for the *material* of direct, unanalyzed sense-perception.

They were aware of its defects from the standpoint of knowledge. But they supposed that they could correct these defects and supplement their lack by purely logical or "rational" means. They supposed that thought could take the material supplied by ordinary perception, eliminate varying and hence contingent qualities, and thus finally reach the fixed and immutable form which makes particulars have the character they have; define this form as the essence or true reality of the particular things in question, and then gather a group of perceived objects into a species which is as eternal as its particular exemplifications are perishable. The passage from ordinary perception to scientific knowledge did not therefore demand the introduction of actual, overt and observed changes into the *material* of sense-perception. Modern science, with its changes in the subject-matter of direct perception effected by the use of apparatus, gets away not from observed material as such, but from the qualitative characteristics of things as they are originally and "naturally" observed.

It may thus be fairly asserted that the "categories" of

Greek description and explanation of natural phenomena were esthetic in character; for perception of the esthetic sort is interested in things in their immediate qualitative traits. The logical features they depended upon to confer scientific form upon the material of observation were harmony, proportion or measure, symmetry: these constitute the "logos" that renders phenomena capable of report in rational discourse. In virtue of these properties superimposed upon phenomena but thought to be elicited from them, natural objects are knowable. Thus the Greeks employed thinking not as a means of changing given objects of observation so as to get at the conditions and effects of their occurrence, but to impose upon them certain static properties not found in them in their changeable occurrence. The essence of the static properties conferred upon them was harmony of form and pattern. Craftsmen, architects, sculptors, gymnasts, poets had taken raw material and converted it into finished forms marked by symmetry and proportion; they accomplished this task without the prior disintegrative reduction which characterizes modern making in the factory. Greek thinkers performed a like task for nature as a whole. Instead, however, of employing the material tools of the crafts, they depended upon thought alone. They borrowed the *form* provided them in Greek art in abstraction from its material appliances. They aimed at constructing out of nature, as observed, an artistic whole for the eye of the soul to behold. Thus for science nature was a cosmos. It was composed, but it was not a composite of elements. That is, it was a qualitative whole, a whole as is a drama, a statue or a temple, in virtue of a pervading and dominant qualitative unity; it was not an aggregate of homogenous units externally arranged in different modes. Design was the form and pattern intrinsically characteristic of things in their fixed kinds, not something first formed in a designing mind and then imposed from without.

There was no conflict with ideas about values because the qualities belonging to objects of science *are* values; they are the things we enjoy and prize. Throughout nature as a qualitative whole there is a hierarchy of forms from those of lower value to those of higher. The revolution in science effectively initiated by Galileo consisted precisely in the abolition of qualities as traits of scientific objects *as such*. From this elimination proceeded just that conflict and need of reconciliation between the scientific properties of the real and those which give moral authority. Therefore to apprehend what the new astronomy and physics did for human beliefs, we have to place it in its contrast with the older natural science in which the qualities possessed by objects of scientific knowledge were precisely the same as those possessed by works of art, the properties which are one with beauty and with all that is admirable.

The work of Galileo was not a development, but a revolution. It marked a change from the qualitative to the quantitative or metric; from the heterogeneous to the homogeneous; from intrinsic form to relations; from esthetic harmonies to mathematical formulae; from contemplative enjoyment to active manipulation and control; from rest to change; from eternal objects to temporal sequence. The revolution opened the way to description and explanation of natural phenomena on the basis of homogeneous space, time, mass and motion. Heavenly bodies and movements were brought under the same laws as are found in terrestrial phenomena. The idea of the difference in kind between phenomena in different parts of space was abolished. All that counted for science became mechanical properties formulated in mathematical terms: the significance of mathematical formulation marking the possibility of complete equivalence or homogeneity of translation of different phenomena into one another's terms.

The idea of a two-realm scheme persisted for moral and religious purposes; it vanished for purposes of natural science. The higher realm which had been the object of true science became the exclusive habitat of objects connected with values that in their relation to man furnish the norm and end of human destiny. The lower realm of change which had been the subject of opinion and practice became the sole and only object of natural science. The realm in which opinion held sway was no longer a genuine although inferior portion of objective being. It was a strictly human product, due to ignorance and error. Such was the philosophy which, because of the new science, replaced the old metaphysics. But—and this "but" is of fundamental importance—in spite of the revolution, the old conceptions of knowledge as related to an antecedent reality and of moral regulation as derived from properties of this reality, persisted.

III · Philosophic Implications of Modern Science*

Just what did the new experimental method do to the qualitative objects of ordinary experience? Forget the conclusions of Greek philosophy, put out of the mind all theories about knowledge and about reality. Take the simple, direct facts: Here are the colored, resounding, fragrant, lovable, attractive, beautiful things of nature which we enjoy, and which we suffer when they are hateful, ugly, disgusting. Just what is the effect upon them wrought by physical science?

* From *The Quest for Certainty*, pp. 98-104; 125-139.

If we consent for the time being to denude the mind of philosophical and metaphysical presuppositions, and take the matter in the most simple and naïve way possible, I think our answer, stated in technical terms, will be that it *substitutes data for objects*. (It is not meant that this outcome is the whole effect of the experimental method; that as we saw at the outset is complex; but that the first effect as far as stripping away qualities is concerned is of this nature.) That Greek science operated with *objects* in the sense of the stars, rocks, trees, rain, warm and cold days of ordinary experience is evident enough. What is signified by saying that the first effect of experimentation was to reduce these things from the status of objects to that of data may not be so clear.* By data is signified subject-matter for *further* interpretation; something to be thought about. *Objects* are finalities; they are complete, finished; they call for thought only in the way of definition, classification, logical arrangement, subsumption in syllogisms, etc. But data signify "material to serve"; they are indications, evidence, signs, clues to and of something still to be reached; they are intermediate, not ultimate; means, not finalities.

In a less technical way the matter may be stated as follows: The subject-matter which had been taken as satisfying the demands of knowledge, as the material with which to frame solutions, became something which set *problems*. Hot and cold, wet and dry, light and heavy, instead of being self-evident matters with which to explain phenomena, were things to be investigated; they were "effects," not causal principles; they set question marks instead of supplying answers. The differences between the

* For this shift from objects to data see G. H. Mead's essay in the volume entitled *Creative Intelligence*. (Henry Holt and Company, New York, 1917.)

earth, the region of the planets, and the heavenly ether, instead of supplying ultimate principles which could be used to mark off and classify things, were something to be explained and to bring under identical principles. Greek and medieval science formed an art of accepting things as they are enjoyed and suffered. Modern experimental science is an art of control.

The remarkable difference between the attitude which accepts the objects of ordinary perception, use and enjoyment as final, as culminations of natural processes and that which takes them as starting points for reflection and investigation, is one which reaches far beyond the technicalities of science. It marks a revolution in the whole spirit of life, in the entire attitude taken toward whatever is found in existence. When the things which exist around us, which we touch, see, hear and taste are regarded as interrogations for which an answer must be sought (and must be sought by means of deliberate introduction of changes till they are reshaped into something different), nature as it already exists ceases to be something which must be accepted and submitted to, endured or enjoyed, just as it is. It is now something to be modified, to be intentionally controlled. It is material to act upon so as to transform it into new objects which better answer our needs. Nature as it exists at any particular time is a challenge, rather than a completion; it provides possible starting points and opportunities rather than final ends.

In short, there is a change from knowing as an esthetic enjoyment of the properties of nature regarded as a work of divine art, to knowing as a means of secular control— that is, a method of purposefully introducing changes which will alter the direction of the course of events. Nature as it exists at a given time is material for arts to be brought to bear upon it to reshape it, rather than already a finished work of art. Thus the changed attitude toward change to which reference was made has a much wider meaning than that which the new science offered as a technical pursuit. When correlations of changes are made the goal of knowledge, the fulfillment of its aim in discovery of these correlations, is equivalent to placing in our hands an instrument of control. When one change is given, and we know with measured accuracy its connection with another change, we have the potential means of producing or averting that other event. The esthetic attitude is of necessity directed to what is already there; to what is finished, complete. The attitude of control looks to the future, to production.

The same point is stated in another way in saying that the reduction of given objects to data for a knowing or an investigation still to be undertaken liberates man from subjection to the past. The scientific attitude, as an attitude of interest in change instead of interest in isolated and complete fixities, is necessarily alert for problems; every new question is an opportunity for further experimental inquiries—for effecting more directed change. There is nothing which a scientific mind would more regret than reaching a condition in which there were no more problems. That state would be the death of science, not its perfected life. We have only to contrast this disposition with that which prevails in morals and politics to realize the difference which has already been made, as well as to appreciate how limited its development still is. For in higher practical matters we still live in dread of change and of problems. Like men of olden time—with respect to natural phenomena—we prefer to accept and endure or to enjoy— as the case may happen to be—what is, what we find in possession of the field, and at most, to arrange it under concepts, and thus give it the form of rationality.

Before the rise of experimental method, change was simply an inevitable evil; the world of phenomenal exist- ence, that is, of change, while an inferior realm compared with the changeless, was nevertheless there and had to be accepted practically as it happened to occur. The wise man if he were sufficiently endowed by fortune would have as little to do with such things as possible, turning away from them to the rational realm. Qualitative forms and complete ends determined by nature are not amenable to human control. They are grateful when they happen to be enjoyed, but for human purposes nature means fortune, and fortune is the contrary of art. A good that happens is welcome. Goods, however, can be made secure in existence only through regulation of processes of change, a regula- tion dependent upon knowledge of their relations. While the abolition of fixed tendencies toward definite ends has been mourned by many as if it involved a despiritualiza- tion of nature, it is in fact a precondition of the projection of new ends and of the possibility of realizing them through intentional activity. Objects which are not fixed goals of nature and which have no inherent defining forms become candidates for receiving new qualities; means for serving new purposes. Until natural objects were denuded of determinate ends which were regarded as the proper outcome of the intrinsic tendency of nature's own opera- tions, nature could not become a plastic material of hu- man desires and purposes.

Such considerations as these are implicit in that changed attitude which by experimental analysis reduces objects to data: the aim of science becomes discovery of constant relations among changes in place of definition of objects immutable beyond the possibility of alteration. It is interested in the mechanism of occurrences instead of in final causes. In dealing with the proximate instead of with the ultimate, knowledge deals with the world in which we live, the world which is experienced, instead of attempting through the intellect to escape to a higher realm. Experimental knowledge is a mode of doing, and like all doing takes place at a time, in a place, and under specifiable conditions in connection with a definite problem.

Scientific inquiry always starts from things of the environment experienced in our everyday life, with things we see, handle, use, enjoy and suffer from. This is the ordinary qualitative world. But instead of accepting the qualities and values—the ends and forms—of this world as providing the objects of knowledge, subject to their being given a certain logical arrangement, experimental inquiry treats them as offering a challenge to thought. They are the materials of problems not of solutions. They are *to be* known, rather than objects of knowledge. The first step in knowing is to locate the problems which need solution. This step is performed by altering obvious and given qualities. These are effects; they are things *to be* understood, and they are understood in terms of their generation. The search for "efficient causes" instead of for final causes, for extrinsic relations instead of intrinsic forms, constitutes the aim of science. But the search does not signify a quest for reality in contrast with experience of the unreal and phenomenal. It signifies a search for those relations upon which the *occurrence* of real qualities and values depends, by means of which we can regulate their occurrence. To call existences as they are directly and qualitatively experienced "phenomena" is not to assign to them a metaphysical status. It is to indicate that they set the problem of ascertaining the relations of interaction upon which their occurrence depends.

It is unnecessary that knowledge should be concerned with existence as it is directly experienced in its concrete qualities. Direct experiencing itself takes care of that matter. What science is concerned with is the *happening* of these experienced things. For its purpose, therefore, they *are* happenings, events. Its aim is to discover the conditions and consequences of their happening. And this discovery can take place only by modifying the given qualities in such ways that *relations* become manifest. These relations constitute the proper objects of science as such. The elimination of the qualities of experienced existence is merely an intermediate step necessary to the discovery of relations, and when it is accomplished the scientific object becomes the means of control of occurrence of experienced things having a richer and more secure equipment of values and qualities.

There is one common character of all scientific operations which it is necessary to note. *They are such as disclose relationships.* A simple case is the operation by which length is defined by one object placed end upon end upon another object so many times. This type of operation, repeated under conditions themselves defined by specified operations, not merely fixes the relation of two things to each other called *their* length, but defines a generalized concept of length. This conception in connection with other operations, such as those which define mass and time, become instruments by means of which a multitude of relations between bodies can be established. Thus the conceptions which define units of measurement of space, time and motion become the intellectual instrumentalities by which all sorts of things with no qualitative similarity with one another can be compared and brought within the same system. To the original gross experience of things there is superadded another type of experience, the product of deliberate art, of which *relations* rather than qualities are the significant subject-matter. These connections are as much experienced as are the qualitatively diverse and irreducible objects of original natural experiences.

Qualities present themselves as just what they are, statically demarcated from one another. Moreover, they rarely change, when left to themselves, in such ways as to indicate the interactions or relations upon which their occurrence depends. No one ever observed the production of the thing having the properties of water, nor the mode of generation of a flash of lightning. In sensory perception the qualities are either too static or too abruptly discrete to manifest the specific connections that are involved in their coming into existence. Intentional variation of conditions gives an idea of these connections. Through thought of them the things are understood or truly known. Only slowly, however, did there dawn the full import of the scientific method. For a long time the definitions were supposed to be made not in terms of relations but through certain properties of antecedent things. The space, time and motion of physics were treated as inherent properties of Being, instead of as abstracted relations. In fact, two phases of inquiry accompany each other and correspond to each other. In one of these phases, everything in qualitative objects except their happening is ignored, attention being paid to qualities only as signs of the nature of the particular happening in question: that is, objects are treated as *events*. In the other phase, the aim of inquiry is to correlate events with one another. Scientific conceptions of space, time and motion constitute the generalized system of these correlations of events. Thus they are doubly dependent upon operations of experimental art: upon those which treat qualitative objects as events, and upon those which connect events thus determined with one another.

The central question thus arises: What determines the

selection of operations to be performed? There is but one answer: the nature of the problem to be dealt with—an answer which links the phase of experiment now under discussion with that considered in the last chapter. The first effect of experimental analysis is, as we saw, to reduce objects directly experienced to data. This resolution is required because the objects in their first mode of experience are perplexing, obscure, fragmentary; in some way they fail to answer a need. Given data which locate the nature of the problem, there is evoked a thought of an operation which if put into execution may eventuate in a situation in which the trouble or doubt which evoked inquiry will be resolved. If one were to trace the history of science far enough, one would reach a time in which the acts which dealt with a troublesome situation would be organic responses of a structural type together with a few acquired habits. The most elaborate technique of present inquiry in the laboratory is an extension and refinement of these simple original operations. Its development has for the most part depended upon the utilization of physical instruments, which when inquiry was developed to a certain point were purposely invented. In principle, the history of the construction of suitable operations in the scientific field is not different from that of their evolution in industry. Something needed to be done to accomplish an end; various devices and methods of operation were tried. Experiences of success and failure gradually improved the means used. More economical and effective ways of acting were found—that is, operations which gave the desired kind of result with greater ease, less irrelevancy and less ambiguity, greater security. Each forward step was attended with making better tools. Often the invention of a tool suggested operations not in mind when it was invented and thus carried the perfecting of operations still further. There is thus no *a priori* test or rule for the determination of the operations which define ideas. They are themselves experimentally developed in the course of actual inquiries. They originated in what men naturally do and are tested and improved in the course of doing.

This is as far as the answer to the query can be carried in a formal way. Consequences that successfully solve the problems set by the conditions which give rise to the need of action supply the basis by means of which acts, originally "naturally" performed, become the operations of the art of scientific experimentation. In content, a much more detailed answer can be given. For this answer, one would turn to the historical development of science, in which is recorded what kind of operations have definitely been found to effect the transformation of the obscure and perplexing situations of experience into clear and resolved situations. To go into this matter would be to expound the character of the concepts actually employed in the best developed branches of reflection or inquiry.

Neither the scientific nor the philosophic change came at once, even after experimental inquiry was initiated. In fact as we shall see later, philosophy proceeded conservatively by compromise and accommodation, and was read into the new science, so that not till our own generation did science free itself from some basic factors of the older conception of nature. Scientific conceptions were interpreted in the light of the old belief that conceptions to be valid must correspond to antecedent intrinsic properties resident in objects dealt with. Certain properties regarded by Newton as inherent in substances and essential to them, in independence of connectivity, were indeed speedily seen to be relations. Nevertheless, until the promulgation of Einstein's restricted theory of relativity, mass, time

and motion were regarded as intrinsic properties of ultimate, fixed and independent substances.

The difference made by the theory of relativity in the
actual content of scientific theory is of course enormous.
Yet it is not so great as the difference made in the logic
of scientific knowledge, nor as in philosophy. With the surrender of unchangeable substances having properties fixed
in isolation and unaffected by interactions, must go the
notion that certainty is attained by attachment to fixed
objects with fixed characters. For not only are no such objects found to exist, but the very nature of experimental
method, namely, definition by operations that are interactions, implies that such things are not capable of being
known. Henceforth the quest for certainty becomes the
search for methods of control; that is, regulation of conditions of change with respect to their consequences.

Theoretical certitude is assimilated to practical certainty; to *security,* trustworthiness of instrumental operations. "Real" things may be as transitory as you please or
as lasting in time as you please; these are specific differences like that between a flash of lightning and the history
of a mountain range. In any case they are for knowledge
"events" not substances. What knowledge is interested in
is the correlation among these changes or events—which
means in effect that the event called the mountain range
must be placed within a system consisting of a vast multitude of included events. When these correlations are discovered, the possibility of control is in our hands. Scientific objects as statements of these inter-relations are instrumentalities of control. They are objects of the *thought*
of reality, not disclosures of immanent properties of real
substances. They are in particular the thought of reality
from a particular point of view: the most highly general-

ized view of nature as a system of interconnected changes.

Certain important conclusions follow. The test of the validity of ideas undergoes a radical transformation. In the Newtonian scheme, as in the classic tradition, this test resided in properties belonging to ultimate real objects in isolation from one another, and hence fixed or unchanging. According to experimental inquiry, the validity of the object of thought depends upon the *consequences* of the operations which define the object of thought. For example, colors are conceived in terms of certain numbers. The conceptions are valid in the degree in which, by means of these numbers, we can predict future events, and can regulate the interactions of colored bodies as signs of changes that take place. The numbers are signs or clues of intensity and direction of changes going on. The only things relevant to the question of their validity is whether they are dependable signs. That heat is a mode of motion does not signify that heat and cold as qualitatively experienced are "unreal," but that the qualitative experience can be treated as an event measured in terms of units of velocity of movement, involving units of position and time, so that it can be connected with other events or changes similarly formulated. The test of the validity of any particular intellectual conception, measurement or enumeration is functional, its use in making possible the institution of interactions which yield results in control of actual experiences of observed objects.

Ability, through a definite or measured correlation of changes, to connect one with another as sign or evidence is the precondition of control. It does not of itself provide direct control; reading the index hand of a barometer as a sign of probable rain does not enable us to stop the coming of the rain. But it does enable us to change our relations to it: to plant a garden, to carry an umbrella on go-

ing out, to direct the course of a vessel at sea, etc. It enables *preparatory* acts to be undertaken which make values less insecure. If it does not enable us to regulate just
what is to take place, it enables us to direct some phase of
it in a way which influences the stability of purposes and
results. In other cases, as in the arts proper, we can not
only modify our own attitude so as to effect useful preparation for what is to happen, but we can modify the happening itself. This use of one change or perceptible occurrence as a sign of others and as a means of preparing ourselves, did not wait for the development of modern science.
It is as old as man himself, being the heart of all intelligence. But accuracy and scope of such judgments, which
are the only means with power to direct the course of
events and to effect the security of values, depends upon
the use of methods such as modern physics has made
available.

Extent of control is dependent, as was suggested a moment ago, upon capacity to find a connected series of correlated change, such that each linked pair leads on to another in the direction of a terminal one which can be
brought about by our own action. It is this latter condition
which is especially fulfilled by the objects of scientific
thought. Physical science disregards the qualitative heterogeneity of experienced objects so as to make them all
members in one comprehensive homogeneous scheme, and
hence capable of translation or conversion one into another. This homogeneity of subject-matter over a broad
range of things which are as disparate from each other in
direct experience as sound and color, heat and light, friction and electricity, is the source of the wide and free control of events found in modern technology. Common-sense
knowledge can connect things as sign and thing indicated
here and there by isolated couples. But it cannot possibly

join them all up together so that we can pass from any one to any other. The homogeneity of scientific objects, through formulation in terms of relations of space, time and motion, is precisely the device which makes this indefinitely broad and flexible scheme of transitions possible. The meaning which one event has is translatable into the meanings which others possess. Ideas of objects, formulated in terms of the relations which changes bear to one another, having common measures, institute broad, smooth highways by means of which we can travel from the thought of one part of nature to that of any other. In ideal at least, we can travel from any meaning—or relation—found anywhere in nature to the meaning to be expected anywhere else.

We have only to compare thinking and judging objects in terms of these measured interactions with the classic scheme of a hierarchy of species and genera to see the great gain that has been effected. It is the very nature of fixed kinds to be as exclusive with respect to those of a different order as it is to be inclusive with respect to those which fall within the class. Instead of a thoroughfare from one order to another, there was a sign: No passage. The work of emancipation which was initiated by experimentation, setting objects free from limitation by old habits and customs, reducing them to a collection of data forming a problem for inquiry, is perfected by the method of conceiving and defining objects through operations which have as their consequence accurate metric statements of changes correlated with changes going on elsewhere.

The resolution of objects and nature as a whole into facts stated exclusively in terms of quantities which may be handled in calculation, such as saying that red *is* such a number of changes while green is another, seems strange and puzzling only when we fail to appreciate what it signifies. In reality, it is a declaration that this is the effective way to *think* things; the effective mode in which to frame ideas of them, to formulate their meanings. The procedure does not vary in principle from that by which it is stated that an article is worth so many dollars and cents. The latter statement does not say that the article is literally or in its ultimate "reality" so many dollars and cents; it says that for purpose of exchange that is the way to *think* of it, to judge it. It has many other meanings and these others are usually more important inherently. But *with respect to trade*, it *is* what it is worth, what it will sell for, and the price value put upon it expresses the relation it bears to other things in exchange. The advantage in stating its worth in terms of an abstract measure of exchange such as money, instead of in terms of the amount of corn, potatoes or some other special thing it will exchange for, is that the latter method is restricted and the former generalized. Development of the systems of units by which to measure sensible objects (or form ideas of them) has come along with discovery of the ways in which the greatest amount of free movement from one conception to another is possible.

The formulation of ideas of experienced objects in terms of measured quantities, as these are established by an intentional art or technique, does not say that this is the way they *must* be thought, the *only* valid way of thinking them. It states that for the purpose of generalized, indefinitely extensive translation from one idea to another, this is the way to think them. The statement is like any other statement about instruments, such as that so-and-so is the best way of sending a number of telegraphic dispatches simultaneously. As far as it is actually the best instrumentality, the statement is correct. It has to be proved by *working* better than any other agency; it is in process of continuous revision and improvement. For purposes except that of general and extensive translation of one conception into another, it does not follow that the "scientific" way is the best way of thinking an affair. The nearer we come to an action that is to have an individualized unique object of experience for its conclusion, the less do we think the things in question in these exclusively metric terms. The physician in practice will not think in terms as general and abstract as those of the physiologist in the laboratory, nor the engineer in the field in those as free from special application as will the physicist in his work-shop. There are many ways of thinking things in relation to one another; they are, as conceptions, instruments. The value of an instrument depends upon what is to be done with it. The fine-scale micrometer which is indispensable in the successful performance of one operation would be a hindrance in some other needed act; and a watch spring is useless to give elasticity to a mattress.

There is something both ridiculous and disconcerting in the way in which men have let themselves be imposed upon, so as to infer that scientific ways of thinking of objects give the inner reality of things, and that they put a mark of spuriousness upon all other ways of thinking of them, and of perceiving and enjoying them. It is ludicrous because these scientific conceptions, like other instruments, are hand-made by man in pursuit of realization of a certain interest—that of the maximum convertibility of every object of thought into any and every other. It is a wonderful ideal; the ingenuity which man has shown in devising means of realizing the interest is even more marvelous. But these ways of thinking are no more rivals of or substitutes for objects as directly perceived and enjoyed than the power-loom, which is a more effective instrument for weaving cloth than was the old hand-loom, is a substitute and rival for cloth. The man who is disappointed and tragic because he cannot wear a loom is in reality no more ridiculous than are the persons who feel troubled because the objects of scientific conception of natural things have not the same uses and values as the things of direct ex, perience.

The disconcerting aspect of the situation resides in the difficulty with which mankind throws off beliefs that have become habitual. The test of ideas, of thinking generally, is found in the consequences of the acts to which the ideas lead, that is in the new arrangements of things which are brought into existence. Such is the unequivocal evidence as to the worth of ideas which is derived from observing their position and role in experimental knowing. But tradition makes the tests of ideas to be their agreement with some *antecedent* state of things. This change of outlook and standard from what precedes to what comes after, from the retrospective to the prospective, from antecedents to consequences, is extremely hard to accomplish. Hence when the physical sciences describe objects and the world as being such and such, it is thought that the description is of reality as it exists in itself. Since all value-traits are lacking in objects as science presents them to us, it is assumed that *Reality* has not such characteristics.

Knowledge which is merely a reduplication in ideas of what exists already in the world may afford us the satisfaction of a photograph, but that is all. To form ideas whose worth is to be judged by what exists independently of them is not a function that (even if the test could be applied, which seems impossible) goes on within nature or makes any difference there. Ideas that are plans of operations to be performed are integral factors in actions which change the face of the world. Idealistic philosophies have not been wrong in attaching vast importance and power to ideas. But in isolating their function and their test from action, they failed to grasp the point and place where ideas have a constructive office. A genuine idealism and one compatible with science will emerge as soon as philosophy accepts the teaching of science that ideas are statements not of what is or has been but of acts to be performed. For then mankind will learn that, intellectually (that is, save for the esthetic enjoyment they afford, which is of course a true value), ideas are worthless except as they pass into actions which rearrange and reconstruct in some way, be it little or large, the world in which we live.

To magnify thought and ideas for their own sake apart from what they do (except, once more, esthetically) is to refuse to learn the lesson of the most authentic kind of knowledge—the experimental—and it is to reject the idealism which involves responsibility. To praise thinking above action because there is so much ill-considered action in the world is to help maintain the kind of world in which action occurs for narrow and transient purposes. To seek after ideas and to cling to them as means of conducting operations, as factors in practical arts, is to participate in creating a world in which the springs of thinking will be clear and ever-flowing.

When we take the instance of scientific experience in its own field, we find that experience when it is experimental does not signify the absence of large and far-reaching ideas and purposes. It is dependent upon them at every point. But it generates them within its own procedures and tests them by its own operations. In so far, we have the earnest of a possibility of human experience, in all its phases, in which ideas and meanings will be prized and will be continuously generated and used. But they will be integral with the course of experience itself, not imported from the external source of a reality beyond.

CHAPTER FOUR

SCIENCE AND THE FUTURE OF SOCIETY *

THE past four centuries have displayed an ever-increasing revolt against authority, first in the forms in which it was manifested and then against the principle itself. None of its important forms has been immune from assault. The assault was first directed against dominant institutions of Church and State. But the control exercised by Church and State in combination had entered into all phases and aspects of life, in belief and conduct alike. Hence attack upon ecclesiastic and political institutions spread to science and art, to standards and ideals of economic and domestic life. For the practical movement of assault, like every other such movement, had to defend itself on intellectual grounds. The best intellectual defense was attack, and so defense grew into systematic justification, and a social philosophy developed that was critical of the very idea of any authoritative control.

The theoretical system spawned watchwords, rallying-cries, slogans, for popular consumption. One of the latter, by constant iteration, has assumed the status of a comprehensive social and political idea. To many persons it seems to be itself the summary of a profound social philosophy. According to the formula, the one great intellectual prob-

* A paper—under title *Authority and Social Change*—read at the Harvard Tercentenary Conference of Arts and Sciences, September, 1936; here reprinted entire from the volume, *Authority and the Individual* (pp. 170-190) of the Harvard Tercentenary Publications.

lem is the demarcation of two separate spheres, one of authority and one of freedom; the other half of the formula is to maintain this theoretical demarcation as a sharp division in practice. The formula has a corollary. The inherent tendency of the "sphere" of authority is to extend itself unduly, to encroach on the "sphere" of freedom, thus enstating oppression, tyranny, and, in the language of today, regimentation. Hence the right of way must belong to the idea and actuality of individual freedom; authority is its enemy, and every manifestation of social authority and control is therefore to be zealously watched, and almost always to be vigorously opposed. However, since the sphere of liberty has its boundaries, when "liberty" begins to degenerate into "license" the operation of authority is properly to be called upon to restore the balance.

The formula, like most slogans that attain popularity, owes its vogue and influence to the fact that it seems to afford a solution of an outstanding problem while in fact it evades the problem; and, by postponing effort at genuine solution, gives temporary support, sometimes to one of the contending forces, sometimes to the other, and always at the expense of both. For even when it is accepted in its own terms at face value, it leaves the fundamental issue of the rightful extent of the two alleged spheres undecided, their rightful metes and bounds a matter of constant dispute.

The genuine problem is the *relation* between authority and freedom. And this problem is masked, and its solution begged, when the idea is introduced that the fields in which they respectively operate are separate. In effect, authority stands for stability of social organization by means of which direction and support are given to individuals; while individual freedom stands for the forces by which change is intentionally brought about. The issue that requires constant attention is the intimate and organic union of the two things: of authority and freedom, of stability and change. The idea of attaining a solution by separation instead of by union misleads and thwarts endeavor whenever it is acted upon. The widespread adoption of this false and misleading idea is a strong contributing factor to the present state of world confusion.

The genuine import of the formula which divides and apportions the total field of human life and action between freedom and authority is to be found, not in its theoretical statement, but in its relation to the historic events of the past few centuries. As a purely theoretical formula, it claims an inherent validity and universal application which I, for one, find absurd. But when the formula is taken to be the record of a historic period, the case is otherwise. The formula then achieves the significance of a symbol of the distinctive crises of western civilization in recent centuries; it becomes representative of a great historic struggle. In its dual character, the formula celebrates, with one hand, the decay of the institutions which had exercised sway over men's minds and conduct; and, with the other hand, it signalizes the rise of the new social and intellectual forces. The old traditions and established social organizations resisted the new forces in human life and society on their emergence, as being dangerous, even mortal, rivals who came to dispute for the power and privileges they had hitherto exclusively enjoyed. The formula, instead of supplying a means of coping with and solving this historic struggle, offers as a solution what is none other than a theoretical transcript of the nature of the conflict itself. As a guide to understanding and action, the formula is, as I said, absurd. But as a symbol of historic events it is deeply revealing.

Unfortunately, when the struggle first got under way,

the newer forces tended to accept the established institutions at their own evaluation, namely, as necessary expressions of the very principle of authority. Finding the existing institutions oppressive, the new movement reacted against authority as such and began to conceive of authority as inherently external to individuality, and inherently hostile to freedom and the social changes that the overt expression and use of freedom would bring to pass. In consequence, while the new movement should have the credit for breaking down a system that had grown rigid and unresponsive, and for releasing capacities of individuals that had been dormant, its virtual denial of the organic importance of *any* embodiment of authority and social control has intellectually fostered the confusion that as a matter of practical fact in any case attends a time of transition. More particularly, as I shall show later, the new movement failed to acknowledge as authoritative the very power to which it owed its own vitality, namely, that of organized intelligence. Such are the propositions I desire to advance.

For, in the first place, I think a survey of history shows that while the individualistic philosophy was wrong in setting authority and freedom, stability and change, in opposition to one another, it was justified in finding the organized institutional embodiments of authority so external to the new wants and purposes that were stirring as to be in fact oppressive. The persons and classes who exercised the power that comes from the possession of authority *were* hostile to the variable and fresh qualities, the qualities of initiative, invention, and enterprise, in which change roots. The power exercised was the more oppressive and obstructive because it was not just physical but had that hold upon imagination, emotions, and purpose which properly belongs to the principle of authority. Underneath, it was not a conflict between social organization and individuals, between authority and freedom, but between conservative factors in the very make-up of individuals—factors that had the strength that is derived from the inertia of customs and traditions engrained by long endurance—and the liberating, the variable and innovating factors in the constitution of individuals. It was a struggle for authoritative power between the old and the new; between forces concerned with conservation of values that the past had produced and forces that made for new beliefs and new modes of human association. It was also a struggle between groups and classes of individuals—between those who were enjoying the advantages that spring from possession of power to which authoritative right accrues, and individuals who found themselves excluded from the powers and enjoyments to which they felt themselves entitled. The necessity of adjusting the old and the new, of harmonizing the stability that comes from conserving the established with the variability that springs from the emergence of new needs and efforts of individuals —this necessity is inherent in, or a part of, the very texture of life. In the last few centuries the necessity of effecting this adjustment has manifested itself on an unparalleled scale in the arena of human culture. The philosophy which transforms this historic and relative struggle into an inherent and fixed conflict between the principle of authority and the principle of freedom tends, when accepted and acted upon, to present authority as purely restrictive power and to leave the exercise of freedom without direction. To a considerable extent these untoward conditions depict our contemporary estate.

Let me explain briefly what is meant by calling the struggle one between forces that belong to individuals and that, in the interest of individuals as such, need to be adjusted to one another. It is folly psychologically and historically to identify the structure of the individual simply with the elements of human nature that make for variation and that mark one person off from another. The force of habit that leads individuals to cling to that which has been established is a genuine part of the constitution of individuals. In the main, it is a stronger and deeper part of human nature than is desire for change. When tradition and social custom are incorporated in the working constitution of an individual, they have authority as a matter of course over his beliefs and his activities. The forces that exert and exercise this authority are so much and so deep a part of individuals that there is no thought or feeling of their being external and oppressive. They cannot be regarded as hostile to individuals as long as they are built into the habitual beliefs and purposes of the individual. They support him and give him direction. They naturally compel his allegiance and arouse his devotion. Attack upon the authoritative institutions in which custom and tradition are embodied is, therefore, as naturally resented by the individual; it is deeply resented as an attack upon what is deepest and truest in himself.

For by far the greater number of millennia man has lived on the earth, man has been, for the most part, content with things as they, from time to time, are. This is true even of social organizations that seem to us arbitrary exhibitions of despotic force. For ages untold, the human disposition has been to attribute divine origin and sanction to whatever claimed for itself the authority of long tradition and custom. Individuals, instead of seeking change, are more generally afraid of it. If we were justified in putting authority and freedom, stability and change, in opposition to one another, we should be compelled to conclude that for the greater period of human history individuals have preferred authority and stability.

This state of affairs has been reflected in theory. Until a very recent time, the accepted doctrine was that authority existed by nature; or else, by that which was beyond nature—the supernatural. In either case, it was held to exist in virtue of the inherent constitution of the universe and of individual man as part of the universe. In philosophy the conception that social authority exists by nature was formulated by Aristotle. In subsequent periods, the underlying idea was restated by the Stoics, in that quasi-idealistic, quasi-materialistic form that has always been— and still is—the means by which ideas obtain their strongest hold on the popular mind. The Christian philosophers of the Middle Ages re-enstated the doctrine of Aristotle— but with a significant revision. Ultimate authority, they said, must be sought in the supernatural Author of Nature and in the Redeemer of man, for in them alone does it reside. This authority had its earthly representative, interpreter, and agent in the divinely instituted and constituted Church.

Even when the rise of secular dynastic states challenged the supremacy of the Church, the basic idea was not even questioned, let alone challenged. The secular state only claimed that it also existed by divine right or authority, and that its authority was therefore supreme in all the affairs of this life, as distinct from those of the soul in the life to come. Even when popular governments began to flourish, they continued the old idea in a weakened form: the voice of God was now the voice of the People.

The new science endeavored to smooth its thorny path by asserting that it was engaged in thinking the thoughts of God after Him. The rise of new economic forces in turn threatened the supreme authority of existing political institutions. But the new economic forces also claimed the right to supreme authority on the ground that they were pure and literal expressions of natural law—in contradistinction to political laws and institutions which, in so far as they did not conform to the play of economic forces, were artificial and man-made. Economic forces, through their representatives, interpreters, and agents—the official economists and industrialists—claimed the divine prerogative to reign supreme over all human terrestrial affairs. The economist and industrialist and financier were the new pretenders to the old divine right of kings.

The conclusion that emerges from this brief historical survey—a conclusion that would be confirmed by any intensive study of the field—is that the identification of the individual with the forces that make freely for variation and change, to the exclusion of those forces in his structure that are habitual and conservative, is something new and recent. Speaking in general terms, the identification is an expression of special and specific historic events. These events may be condensed and summarized. New methods and conclusions in natural science, with their technological application in new modes of industrial production and commercial exchange of goods and services, found themselves checked and limited by the institutional agencies of Church and State which were the possessors of actual social power and the claimants for exclusive and rightful authority in all the variegated fields of human endeavor. In this conflict, the new forces defended and justified themselves by restricting the very idea of authority to the ecclesiastical and political powers that were hostile to their own free expression, and by asserting that they and they alone represented and furthered the interests of the individual and his freedom. The formula mentioned at the outset of this address, the formula of two separate and independent spheres of authority and freedom, in which primacy in case of doubt belongs to the individual and to freedom—this formula is the net product of the historic conflict.

The final result was a social and political philosophy which questioned the validity of authority in *any* form that was not the product of, and that was not sanctioned by, the conscious wants, efforts, and satisfactions of individuals in their private capacity—a philosophy which took the form of *laissez faire* in economics, and individualism in all other social and political affairs. This philosophy claimed for itself the comprehensive title of liberalism.

Two general conclusions, it seems to me, clearly emerge. First, the older forms of organized power that had exercised authority were revealed as external and oppressive with respect to the new forces that operated through the medium of individuals, and as hostile, in consequence, to all important social change. Second, the new philosophy so tended to decry the very principle of authority as to deprive individuals of the direction and support that are universally indispensable both for the organic freedom of individuals and for social stability.

The result is the present scene of confusion, conflict, and uncertainty. While decrying the principle of authority, and asserting the necessity of limiting the exercise of authority to the minimum needed for maintenance of police order, the new philosophy in fact erected the wants and endeavors of private individuals seeking personal gain to the place of supreme authority in social life. In consequence, the new philosophy, in the very act of asserting that it stood completely and loyally for the principle of individual freedom, was really engaged in justifying the activities of a new form of concentrated power—the economic, which new form, to state the matter moderately, has consistently and persistently denied effective freedom to the economically underpowered and underprivileged. While originating as a social force that effected widespread social change in opposition to, indeed in despite of, the powers that had authority when it began to emerge, economic power has now become, in its turn, an organized social institution that resists all further social change that is not in accord with itself, that does not further and support its own interests as at present existing.

It is for such reasons as these that I affirm that the real issue is not that of demarcating separate "spheres" for authority and for freedom, for stability and for change, but that of effecting an interpenetration of the two. We need an authority that, unlike the older forms in which it operated, is capable of directing and utilizing change, and we need a kind of individual freedom unlike that which the unconstrained economic liberty of individuals has produced and justified—we need, that is, a kind of individual freedom that is general and shared and that has the backing and guidance of socially organized authoritative control.

If the history of man in the past be taken to provide conclusive evidence, it would show that the problem of union of freedom and authority is insoluble as well as unsolved. We have had organized social authority that limited the expression of the variable factors in individuals from which orderly and intentional change proceeds. We have had a time of relatively unconstrained and unchecked individualism, and of resultant change going on rapidly on a wide scale. The suppressive and stagnating effect of institutional authority of a political type has been weakened. But security, and coöperative, ordered, and orderly change, are conspicuous by their absence.

It is completely possible, in my opinion, to recognize the need and important social consequences of the individualistic movement and yet also see that in its past mode of operation it has already run its socially justified and justifiable course. It is possible to acknowledge not merely the valuable historic services it has rendered, but also that its assertion, practical and theoretic, of the value of the variable tendencies of human beings—those that mark off one person from another and that are expressed in initiative, invention, and energetic enterprise—is something that should be permanently embodied in any future social order: it is possible, I say, to acknowledge all the admirable traits and products of the individualistic movement and yet hold that the movement as it has operated up to the present has suffered from a great defect, owing to its absolutistic opposition to the principle of organized authority.

It requires little if any argument to prove that the institutional forms in which authority has been embodied in the past are hostile to change. It suffices, perhaps, to recall that those who have labored to change the forms authoritative power had taken were denounced as heretics, as elements subversive of social order. And, I need hardly add, those who are engaged in similar labor today are similarly denounced. The point that does require emphatic attention is that in spite of possession of power, and in spite of persecution of heretics and radicals, no institution has in fact had the power to succeed in preventing great changes from taking place. All that institutions have ever succeeded in doing by their resistance to change has been to dam up social forces until they finally and inevitably manifested themselves in eruptions of great, usually violent and catastrophic, change.

Nor is argument necessary to prove that the individualistic movement has been allied with a period of immense and rapid changes, many of which, taken one by one, have brought positive benefit to society. The facts speak so loudly for themselves, argument is unnecessary. The intimate connection between the new individualism and social change is seen in the watchwords of the movement: Initiative, Invention, Enterprise. For all of these words stand for the variable elements in the constitution of individuals; they point to the *loci* of departure from what has been; they are the signs which denote the sources of innovation. It is just because they are these signs that they can be so effectively used as watchwords, as signals that arouse the individual to effort and action. Indeed, the connection with change is so intimate that the movement produced that glorification of change as sure and necessary progress which marked the heyday of its influence. But I venture the statement that just as the past manifestation of the principle of authority has failed precisely where its claim was most vehement, namely, in the prevention, or at least in the guidance, of change, so the individualistic movement, taken historically and in the large, has failed to secure freedom for individuals on any commensurate scale —and in any assured way—even for its temporary possessors. The individualistic movement has tended to identify the exercise of freedom with absence of any organized control, and in this way it has in fact identified freedom with mere *de facto* possession of economic power. Instead of bringing freedom to those who lacked material possessions, it has imposed upon them further subjection to the owners of the agencies of material production and distribution.

The scene which the world exhibits to the observer at the present time is so obviously one of general instability, insecurity, and increasing conflict—both between nations and within them—that I cannot conceive that any one will deny the *desirability* of effecting and enstating some organic union of freedom and authority. Enormous doubt will well exist, however, as to the possibility of establishing any social system in which the union is practically embodied. This question, it will be justly urged, is *the* issue that emerges even if the substantial validity of the points so far made is admitted. In fact, it may even be justly urged that this question confronts us as the controlling and decisive question just because, or to the degree that, the validity of my argument thus far is granted.

The weight of the evidence of the past is assuredly strongly against the realization of any such possibility. As far as the idea of organized authority is concerned, the pathos of the collective life of mankind on this planet is its exhibition of the dire human need for some authority; while its ever-mounting tragedy is due to the fact that the need has been repeatedly betrayed by the very institutions that claimed to satisfy it. That all is not well, on the other hand, with the principle of individualistic freedom in the form in which it has been influential up to now, is shown by more than one fact in the present scene of discord and insecurity. Above all is this manifested by the recrudescence of the principle of authority in its most extreme and primitive form—the rise of dictatorships.

As if in substantiation of the old idea that nature abhors a vacuum, it might be contended that economic competitive individualism, free from social control, had created a moral and social vacuum which recourse to dictatorships is filling. In many countries, the demand for collective and organized guidance and support has become so urgent that the very idea of individual freedom has gone into the discard and become an ideal, not to be praised, but to be despised. The regime of economic individualistic liberty is attacked by dictatorships from both the right and the left. In countries in which there are no open and acknowledged dictatorships, the conceptions of liberty and individualism seem to be losing their magic force; and security, discipline, order, and solidarity are, by social transfer, acquiring magic power in their stead. The actual concrete conditions that produce resort to dictatorships vary from country to country. But the phenomenon is so widespread it demands a generalized explanation. The most obvious one is the virtual bankruptcy and moribund state of a regime of individual initiative and enterprise conducted for private gain and subject to no control by recognized, collective authority.

Neither the past nor the present affords, then, any ground for expecting that the adjustment of authority and freedom, stability and change, will be achieved by following old paths. The idea that any solution at all can ever be attained may seem to some romantic and utopian. But the most fantastically unrealistic of all notions is the widely prevalent belief that we can attain enduring stable authority by employing or re-exhuming the institutional means tried in the past; equally fantastic is the belief that the assured freedom of individuals can be secured by pitting individuals against one another in a pitiless struggle for material possessions and economic power. The issue, in my judgment, can be narrowed down to this question: Are there resources that have not as yet been tried out in the large field of human relations, resources that are available and that carry with them the potential promise of successful application?

In raising this question I am aware that it is almost inevitable that what I have said about the human necessity for some kind of collective authority to give individuals direction in their relations with one another, and to give them the support that comes from a sense of solidarity, will appear to be a plea for a return to some kind of social control brought about through, and perpetuated by, external institutional means. If my question is so taken, then the criticism I have made of the alliance that has taken place between the principle of individual freedom and private initiative and enterprise in economic matters will necessarily also seem to be merely an argument for social control by means of a collective planned economy— put forward, of course, with some change in vocabulary. However, the argument in fact cuts in both directions. It indicates that while movements in the direction of collective, planned economy may cure evils from which we are now suffering, it will in the end go the way of all past attempts at organization of authoritative power unless some hitherto untried means are utilized on a large and systematic scale for bringing into life the desired and desirable organic coördination. Otherwise we shall finally find ourselves repeating on a different plane the old struggle between social organization and individual freedom, with the oscillation from one principle to the other that has so characteristically marked the past.

The resource that has not yet been tried on any large scale, in the broad field of human, social relationships is the utilization of organized intelligence, the manifold benefits and values of which we have substantial and reliable evidence in the narrower field of science.

Within a limited area, the collective intelligence which is exemplified in the growth and application of scientific method has already become authoritative. It is authoritative in the field of beliefs regarding the structure of nature and relevant to our understanding of physical events. To a considerable extent, the same statement holds true of beliefs about historical personages and historical events—especially with those that are sufficiently remote from the present time. When we turn to the practical side, we see that the same method is supreme in controlling and guiding our active dealings with material things and physical energies. To a large and significant extent, the Baconian prophecy that knowledge is power of control has been realized in this particular, somewhat narrowly circumscribed area. To be sure, it cannot be said that intelligence, operating by the methods that constitute science, has as yet completely won *undisputed* right and authority to control beliefs even in the restricted physical field. But organized intelligence has made an advance that is truly surprising when we consider the short time in which it has functioned and the powerful foes against which it had to make its way: the foes of inertia, of old, long-established traditions and habits—inertia, traditions, and habits all of them entrenched in forms of institutional life that are effulgent with the prestige of time, that are enveloped in the glamor of imaginative appeal, and that are crowned, severally and collectively, with an emotional halo made of the values that men most prize.

The record of the struggle that goes by the name of "conflict between science and religion," or, if you please, "conflict between theology and science," was essentially a conflict of claims to exercise social authority. It was not a conflict just between two sets of theoretical beliefs, but between two alignments of social forces—one which was old and had institutional power that it did not hesitate to use, and one which was new and striving and craving for recognition against gigantic odds.

What is pertinent, what is deeply significant to the theme of the *relation* between collective authority and freedom, is that the progress of intelligence—as exemplified in this summary story of scientific advance—exhibits their organic, effective union. Science has made its way by releasing, not by suppressing, the elements of variation, of invention and innovation, of novel creation in individuals. It is as true of the history of modern science as it is of the history of painting or music that its advances have been initiated by individuals who freed themselves from the bonds of tradition and custom whenever they found the latter hampering their own powers of reflection, observation, and construction.

In spite of science's dependence for its development upon the free initiative, invention, and enterprise of individual inquirers, the authority of science issues from and is based upon collective activity, coöperatively organized. Even when, temporarily, the ideas put forth in science by individuals sharply diverge from received beliefs, the method used is a public and open method which succeeds only as it tends to produce agreement, unity of belief among all who labored in the same field. Every scientific inquirer, even when he deviates most widely from current ideas, depends upon methods and conclusions that are a common possession and not of private ownership, even though all of the methods and conclusions may at some time have been initially the product of private invention. The contribution the scientific inquirer makes is collectively tested and developed and, in the measure that it is coöperatively confirmed, becomes a part of the common fund of the intellectual commonwealth.

One can most easily recognize the difference between the aim and operation of the free individual in the sphere of science and in that of current individualistic economic enterprise by stretching the fancy to the point of imagining a scientific inquirer adopting the standards of the business entrepreneur. Imagine the scientific man who should say that his conclusion was scientific and in so saying maintain that it was also the product of his private wants and efforts goading him on to seek his private advantage.

The mere suggestion of such an absurdity vividly discloses the gap that divides the manifestations of individual freedom in these two areas of human activity. The suggestion brings into bold relief and in typical form the kind of individual freedom that is both supported by collective, organic authority and that in turn changes and is encouraged to change and develop, by its own operations, the authority upon which it depends.

The thesis that the operation of coöperative intelligence as displayed in science is a working model of the union of freedom and authority does not slight the fact that the method has operated up to the present in a limited and relatively technical area. On the contrary, it emphasizes that fact. If the method of intelligence had been employed in any large field in the comprehensive and basic area of the relations of human beings to one another in social life and institutions, there would be no present need for our argument. The contrast between the restricted scope of its use and the possible range of its application to human relations—political, economic, and moral—is outstanding and depressing. It is this very contrast that defines the great problem that still has to be solved.

No consideration of the problem is adequate that does not take into account one fact about the development of the modern individualistic movement in industry and business. There is a suppressed premise in all the claims and reasonings of the individualistic school. All the beneficial changes that have been produced are attributed to the free play of individuals seeking primarily their own profit as isolated individuals. But in fact, the entire modern industrial development is the fruit of the technological applications of science. By and large, the economic changes of recent centuries have been parasitic upon the advances made in natural science. There is not a single process involved in the production and distribution of goods that is not dependent upon the utilization of results which are consequences of the method of collective, organic intelligence working in mathematics, physics, and chemistry. To speak baldly, it is a plain falsehood that the advances which the defenders of the existing regime point to as justification for its continuance are due to mere individualistic initiative and enterprise. Individualistic initiative and enterprise have sequestered and appropriated the fruits of collective coöperative intelligence. This they have done alone. But without the aid and support of organized intelligence they would have been impotent—perhaps even in those activities in which they have shown themselves to be socially most powerful.

In sum, the great weakness of the historic movement that has laid claim to the title of liberalism and that has proclaimed its operating purpose to be that of securing and protecting the freedom of individuals—the great weakness of this movement has been its failure to recognize that the true and final source of change has been, and now is, the corporate intelligence embodied in science. The principle, as I have already said, cuts in two directions. In so far as the attempts that are now being made in the direction of organized social control and planned economy ignore the role of scientific intelligence, in so far as these attempts depend upon and turn for support to external institutional changes effected for the most part by force, just so far are they re-enstating reliance upon the method of external authority that has always broken down in the past. For a time, while in need of security and a sense and feeling of solidarity, men will submit to authority of this kind. But if history shows anything, it shows that the variable factors in individuals cannot be permanently suppressed or completely eradicated. The principle of individual freedom expressed in the modern individualistic movement is deeply rooted in the constitution of human beings. The truth embodied in it cannot die no matter how much force is brought down upon it. The tragedy of the movement is that it misconceived and misplaced the source and seat of this principle of freedom. But the attempt to uproot and eliminate this principle on behalf of the assurance of security and attainment of solidarity by means of external authority is doomed to ultimate defeat no matter what its temporary victories.

There is no need to dwell upon the enormous obstacles that stand in the way of extending from its present limited field to the larger field of human relations the control of organized intelligence, operating through the release of individual powers and capabilities. There is the weight of past history on the side of those who are cynical or pessimistic about the possibility of achieving this humanly desirable and humanly necessary task. I do not predict that the extension will ever be effectively actualized. But I do claim that the problem of the relation of authority and freedom, of stability and change, if it can be solved, will be solved in this way. The failure of other methods and the desperateness of the present situation will be a spur to some to do their best to make the extension actual. They know that to hold in advance of trial that success is impossible is a way of condemning humanity to that futile and destructive oscillation between authoritative power and unregulated individual freedom to which we may justly attribute most of the sorrows and defeats of the past. They are aware of the slow processes of history and of the unmeasured stretch of time that lies ahead of mankind. They do not expect any speedy victory in the execution of the most difficult task human beings ever set their hearts and minds to attempt. They are, however, buoyed by the assurance that no matter how slight the immediate effect of their efforts, they are themselves, in their trials, exemplifying one of the first principles of the method of scientific intelligence. For they are projecting into events a large and comprehensive idea by experimental methods that correct and mature the method and the idea in the very process of trial. The very desperateness of the situation is, for such as these, but a spur to sustained, courageous effort.

CHAPTER FIVE

THE MODES OF SOCIETAL LIFE

I · The Private and the Public*

THERE is no mystery about the fact of association, of an interconnected action which affects the activity of singular elements. There is no sense in asking how individuals come to be associated. They exist and operate in association. If there is any mystery about the matter, it is the mystery that the universe is the kind of universe it is. Such a mystery could not be explained without going outside the universe. And if one should go to an outside source to account for it, some logician, without an excessive draft upon his ingenuity, would rise to remark that the outsider would have to be connected with the universe in order to account for anything in it. We should still be just where we started, with the fact of connection as a fact to be accepted.

There is, however, an intelligible question about human association: Not the question how individuals or singular beings come to be connected, but how they come to be connected in just those ways which give human communities traits so different from those which mark assemblies of electrons, unions of trees in forests, swarms of insects, herds of sheep, and constellations of stars. When we consider the difference we at once come upon the fact that the consequences of conjoint action take on a new value

* From *The Public and Its Problems*, pp. 12-25.

when they are observed. For notice of the effects of connected action forces men to reflect upon the connection itself; it makes it an object of attention and interest. Each acts, in so far as the connection is known, in view of the connection. Individuals still do the thinking, desiring and purposing, but what they think of is the consequences of their behavior upon that of others and that of others upon themselves.

Each human being is born an infant. He is immature, helpless, dependent upon the activities of others. That many of these dependent beings survive is proof that others in some measure look out for them, take care of them. Mature and better equipped beings are aware of the consequences of their acts upon those of the young. They not only act conjointly with them, but they act in that especial kind of association which manifests interest in the consequences of their conduct upon the life and growth of the young.

Continued physiological existence of the young is only one phase of interest in the consequences of association. Adults are equally concerned to act so that the immature learn to think, feel, desire and habitually conduct themselves in certain ways. Not the least of the consequences which are striven for is that the young shall themselves learn to judge, purpose and choose from the standpoint of associated behavior and its consequences. In fact, only too often this interest takes the form of endeavoring to make the young believe and plan just as adults do. This instance alone is enough to show that while singular beings in their singularity think, want and decide, *what* they think and strive for, the content of their beliefs and intentions is a subject-matter provided by association. Thus man is not merely *de facto* associated, but he *becomes* a social animal in the make-up of his ideas, sentiments and deliberate behavior. *What* he believes, hopes for and aims at is the outcome of association and intercourse. The only thing which imports obscurity and mystery into the influence of association upon what individual persons want and act for is the effort to discover alleged, special, original, society-making causal forces, whether instincts, fiats of will, personal, or an immanent, universal, practical reason, or an indwelling, metaphysical, social essence and nature. These things do not explain, for they are more mysterious than are the facts they are evoked to account for. The planets in a constellation would form a community if they were aware of the connections of the activities of each with those of the others and could use this knowledge to direct behavior.

We take then our point of departure from the objective fact that human acts have consequences upon others, that some of these consequences are perceived, and that their perception leads to subsequent effort to control action so as to secure some consequences and avoid others. Following this clew, we are led to remark that the consequences are of two kinds, those which affect the persons directly engaged in a transaction, and those which affect others beyond those immediately concerned. In this distinction we find the germ of the distinction between the private and the public. When indirect consequences are recognized and there is effort to regulate them, something having the traits of a state comes into existence. When the consequences of an action are confined, or are thought to be confined, mainly to the persons directly engaged in it, the transaction is a private one. When A and B carry on a conversation together the action is a trans-action: both are concerned in it; its results pass, as it were, across from one to the other. One or other or both may be helped or harmed thereby. But, presumably, the consequences of advantage and injury do not extend beyond A and B; the activity lies between them; it is private. Yet if it is found that the consequences of conversation extend beyond the two directly concerned, that they affect the welfare of many others, the act acquires a public capacity, whether the conversation be carried on by a king and his prime minister or by Cataline and a fellow conspirator or by merchants planning to monopolize a market.

The distinction between private and public is thus in no sense equivalent to the distinction between individual and social, even if we suppose that the latter distinction has a definite meaning. Many private acts are social; their consequences contribute to the welfare of the community or affect its status and prospects. In the broad sense any transaction deliberately carried on between two or more persons is social in quality. It is a form of associated behavior and its consequences may influence further associations. A man may serve others, even in the community at large, in carrying on a private business. To some extent it is true, as Adam Smith asserted, that our breakfast table is better supplied by the convergent outcome of activities of farmers, grocers and butchers carrying on private affairs with a view to private profit than it would be if we were served on a basis of philanthropy or public spirit. Communities have been supplied with works of art, with scientific discoveries, because of the personal delight found by private persons in engaging in these activities. There are private philanthropists who act so that needy persons or the community as a whole profit by the endowment of libraries, hospitals and educational institutions. In short, private acts may be socially valuable both by indirect consequences and by direct intention.

There is therefore no necessary connection between the private character of an act and its non-social or anti-social character. The public, moreover, cannot be identified with the socially useful. One of the most regular activities of the politically organized community has been waging war. Even the most bellicose of militarists will hardly contend that all wars have been socially helpful, or deny that some have been so destructive of social values that it would have been infinitely better if they had not been waged. The argument for the non-equivalence of the public and the social, in any praiseworthy sense of social, does not rest upon the case of war alone. There is no one, I suppose, so enamored of political action as to hold that it has never been short-sighted, foolish and harmful. There are even those who hold that the presumption is always that social loss will result from agents of the public doing anything which could be done by persons in their private capacity. There are many more who protest that some special public activity, whether prohibition, a protective tariff or the expanded meaning given the Monroe Doctrine, is baleful to society. Indeed every serious political dispute turns upon the question whether a given political act is socially beneficial or harmful.

Just as behavior is not anti-social or non-social because privately undertaken, it is not necessarily socially valuable because carried on in the name of the public by public agents. The argument has not carried us far, but at least it has warned us against identifying the community and its interests with the state or the politically organized community. And the differentiation may dispose us to look with more favor upon the proposition already advanced: namely, that the line between private and public is to be drawn on the basis of the extent and scope of the consequences of acts which are so important as to need control, whether by inhibition or by promotion. We distinguish private and public buildings, private and public schools, private paths and public highways, private assets and public funds, private persons and public officials. It is our thesis that in this distinction we find the key to the nature and office of the state. It is not without significance that etymologically "private" is defined in opposition to "official," a private person being one deprived of public position. The public consists of all those who are affected by the indirect consequences of transactions to such an extent that it is deemed necessary to have those consequences systematically cared for. Officials are those who look out for and take care of the interests thus affected. Since those who are indirectly affected are not direct participants in the transactions in question, it is necessary that certain persons be set apart to represent them, and see to it that their interests are conserved and protected. The buildings, property, funds, and other physical resources involved in the performance of this office are *res publica,* the commonwealth. The public as far as organized by means of officials and material agencies to care for the extensive and enduring indirect consequences of transactions between persons is the *Populus.*

II · Government and State*

We can hardly select a better trait to serve as a mark and sign of the nature of a state than temporal and geographical localization. There are associations which are too narrow and restricted in scope to give rise to a public, just as there are associations too isolated from one another to fall within the same public. Part of the problem of discovery of a public capable of organization into a state is that of drawing lines between the too close and intimate and the too remote and disconnected. Immediate contiguity, face-to-face relationships, have consequences which

* From *The Public and Its Problems,* pp. 39-69.

generate a community of interests, a sharing of values, too direct and vital to occasion a need for political organization. Connections within a family are familiar; they are matters of immediate acquaintance and concern. The so-called blood-tie which has played such a part in demarcation of social units is largely imputed on the basis of sharing immediately in the results of conjoint behavior. What one does in the household affects others directly and the consequences are appreciated at once and in an intimate way. As we say, they "come home." Special organization to care for them is a superfluity. Only when the tie has extended to a union of families in a clan and of clans in a tribe do consequences become so indirect that special measures are called for. The neighborhood is constituted largely on the same pattern of association that is exemplified in the family. Custom and measures improvised to meet special emergencies as they arise suffice for its regulation.

At the other limit there are social groups so separated by rivers, seas and mountains, by strange languages and gods, that what one of them does—save in war—has no appreciable consequences for another. There is therefore no common interest, no public, and no need nor possibility of an inclusive state. The plurality of states is such a universal and notorious phenomenon that it is taken for granted. It does not seem to require explanation. But it sets up, as we have noted, a test difficult for some theories to meet. Except upon the basis of a freakish limitation in the common will and reason which is alleged to be the foundation of the state, the difficulty is insuperable. It is peculiar, to say the least, that universal reason should be unable to cross a mountain range and objective will be balked by a river current. The difficulty is not so great for many other theories. But only the theory which makes recognition of consequences the critical factor can find in the fact of many states a corroborating trait. Whatever is a barrier to the spread of the consequences of associated behavior by that very fact operates to set up political boundaries. The explanation is as commonplace as is the thing to be explained.

Somewhere between associations that are narrow, close and intimate and those which are so remote as to have only infrequent and casual contact lies, then, the province of a state. We do not find and should not expect to find sharp and fast demarcations. Villages and neighborhoods shade imperceptibly into a political public. Different states may pass through federations and alliances into a larger whole which has some of the marks of statehood. This condition, which we should anticipate in virtue of the theory, is confirmed by historical facts. The wavering and shifting line of distinction between a state and other forms of social union is, again, an obstacle in the way of theories of the state which imply as their concrete counterpart something as sharply marked off as is the concept. On the basis of empirical consequences, it is just the sort of thing which should occur. There are empires due to conquest where political rule exists only in forced levies of taxes and soldiers, and in which, though the word state may be used, the characteristic signs of a public are notable for their absence. There are political communities like the city-states of ancient Greece in which the fiction of common descent is a vital factor, in which household gods and worship are replaced by community divinities, shrines, and cults: states in which much of the intimacy of the vivid and prompt personal touch of the family endures, while there has been added the transforming inspiration of a varied, freer, fuller life, whose issues are so momen-

tous that in comparison the life of the neighborhood is
parochial and that of the household dull.

Multiplicity and constant transformation in the forms
which the state assumes are as comprehensible upon the
hypothesis proposed as is the numerical diversity of independent states. The consequences of conjoint behavior differ in kind and in range with changes in "material culture," especially those involved in exchange of raw materials, finished products and above all in technology, in
tools, weapons and utensils. These in turn are immediately
affected by inventions in means of transit, transportation
and intercommunication. A people that lives by tending
flocks of sheep and cattle adapts itself to very different
conditions from those of a people which ranges freely,
mounted on horses. One form of nomadism is usually
peaceful; the other warlike. Roughly speaking, tools and
implements determine occupations, and occupations determine the consequences of associated activity. In determining consequences, they institute publics with different interests, which exact different types of political behavior to care for them.

In spite of the fact that diversity of political forms
rather than uniformity is the rule, belief in *the* state as
an archetypal entity persists in political philosophy and
science. Much dialectical ingenuity has been expended in
construction of an essence or intrinsic nature in virtue of
which any particular association is entitled to have applied to it the concept of statehood. Equal ingenuity has
been expended in explaining away all divergencies from
this morphological type, and (the favored device) in ranking states in a hierarchical order of value as they approach
the defining essence. The idea that there is a model pattern which makes a state a *good* or true state has affected

practice as well as theory. It, more than anything else, is responsible for the effort to form constitutions offhand and impose them ready-made on peoples. Unfortunately, when the falsity of this view was perceived, it was replaced by the idea that states "grow" or develop instead of being made. This "growth" did not mean simply that states alter. Growth signified an evolution through regular stages to a predetermined end because of some intrinsic nisus or principle. This theory discouraged recourse to the only method by which alterations of political forms might be directed: namely, the use of intelligence to judge consequences. Equally with the theory which it displaced, it presumed the existence of a single standard form which defines *the* state as the essential and true article. After a false analogy with physical science, it was asserted that only the assumption of such a uniformity of process renders a "scientific" treatment of society possible. Incidentally, the theory flattered the conceit of those nations which, being politically "advanced," assumed that they were so near the apex of evolution as to wear the crown of statehood.

The hypothesis presented makes possible a consistently empirical or *historical* treatment of the changes in political forms and arrangements, free from any overriding conceptual domination such as is inevitable when a "true" state is postulated, whether that be thought of as deliberately made or as evolving by its own inner law. Intrusions from non-political internal occurrences, industrial and technological, and from external events, borrowings, travel, migrations, exporations, wars, modify the consequences of preëxisting associations to such an extent that new agencies and functions are necessitated. Political forms are also subject to alterations of a more indirect sort. Developments of better methods of thinking bring about observation of consequences which were concealed from a vision which used coarser intellectual tools. Quickened intellectual insight also makes possible invention of new political devices. Science has not indeed played a large role. But intuitions of statesmen and of political theorists have occasionally penetrated into the operations of social forces in such a way that a new turn has been given to legislation and to administration. There is a margin of toleration in the body politic as well as in an organic body. Measures not in any sense inevitable are accommodated to after they have once been taken; and a further diversity is thereby introduced in political manners.

In short, the hypothesis which holds that publics are constituted by recognition of extensive and enduring indirect consequences of acts accounts for the relativity of states, while the theories which define them in terms of specific causal authorship imply an absoluteness which is contradicted by facts. The attempt to find by the "comparative method" structures which are common to antique and modern, to occidental and oriental states, has involved a great waste of industry. The only constant is the function of caring for and regulating the interests which accrue as the result of the complex indirect expansion and radiation of conjoint behavior.

We conclude, then, that temporal and local diversification is a prime mark of political organization, and one which, when it is analyzed, supplies a confirming test of our theory. A second mark and evidence is found in an otherwise inexplicable fact that the quantitative scope of results of conjoint behavior generates a public with need for organization. What are now crimes subject to public cognizance and adjudication were once private ebullitions, having the status now possessed by an insult proffered by one to another. An interesting phase of the transition from the relatively private to the public, at least from a limited public to a larger one, is seen in the development in England of the King's Peace. A measure instigated by desire to increase the power and profit of the royal dynasty became an impersonal public function by bare extension. The same sort of thing has repeatedly occurred when personal prerogatives have passed into normal political processes. Something of the same sort is manifested in contemporary life when modes of private business become "affected with a public interest" because of quantitative expansion.

A third mark of the public organized as a state is that it is concerned with modes of behavior which are old and hence well-established, engrained. Invention is a peculiarly personal act, even when a number of persons combine to make something new. A novel idea is the kind of thing that has to occur to somebody in the singular sense. A new project is something to be undertaken and set agoing by private initiative. The newer an idea or plan, the more it deviates from what is already recognized and established in practice. By the nature of the case an innovation is a departure from the customary. Hence the resistance it is likely to encounter. We, to be sure, live in an era of discoveries and inventions. Speaking generically, innovation itself has become a custom. Imagination is wonted to it; it is expected. When novelties take the form of mechanical appliances, we incline to welcome them. But this is far from always having been the case. The rule has been to look with suspicion and greet with hostility the appearance of anything new, even a tool or utensil. For an innovation *is* a departure, and one which brings in its train some incalculable disturbance of the behavior to which we have grown used and which seems "natural." As a recent writer has clearly shown, inventions have made their way

insidiously; and because of some immediate convenience.
If their effects, their long-run consequences, in altering
habits of behavior had been foreseen, it is safe to say
that most of them would have been destroyed as wicked,
just as many of them were retarded in adoption because
they were felt to be sacrilegious. In any case, we cannot
think of their invention being the work of the state.*

The organized community is still hesitant with reference
to new ideas of a non-technical and non-technological nature. They are felt to be disturbing to social behavior; and
rightly so, as far as old and established behavior is concerned. Most persons object to having their habits unsettled, their habits of belief no less than habits of overt action. A new idea *is* an unsettling of received beliefs; otherwise, it would not be a new idea. This is only to say that
the production of new ideas is peculiarly a private performance. About the most we can ask of the state, judging
from states which have so far existed, is that it put up
with their production by private individuals without undue meddling. A state which will organize to manufacture
and disseminate new ideas and new ways of thinking may
come into existence some time, but such a state is a matter of faith, not sight. When it comes it will arrive because
the beneficial consequences of new ideas have become an
article of common faith and repute. It may, indeed, be
said that even now the state provides those conditions of
security which are necessary if private persons are to engage effectually in discovery and invention. But this service is a by-product; it is foreign to the grounds on which
the conditions in question are maintained by the public.
And it must be offset by noting the extent to which the

---

* The one obvious exception concerns the tools of waging war.
With respect to them, the state has often shown itself as greedy
as it has been reluctant and behindhand with reference to other inventions.

state of affairs upon which the public heart is most set is unfavorable to thinking in other than technical lines. In any case, it is absurd to expect the public, because it is called in no matter how eulogistic a sense the state, to rise above the intellectual level of its average constituents.

When, however, a mode of behavior has become old and familiar, and when an instrumentality has come into use as a matter of course, provided it is a prerequisite of other customary pursuits, it tends to come within the scope of the state. An individual may make his own track in a forest; but highways are usually public concerns. Without roads which one is free to use at will, men might almost as well be castaways on a desert island. Means of transit and communication affect not only those who utilize them but all who are dependent in any way upon what is transported, whether as producers or consumers. The increase of easy and rapid intercommunication means that production takes place more and more for distant markets and it puts a premium upon mass-production. Thus it becomes a disputed question whether railroads as well as highways should not be administered by public officials, and in any case some measure of official regulation is instituted, as they become settled bases of social life.

In conclusion, we shall make explicit what has been implied regarding the relation to one another of public, government and state. There have been two extreme views about this point. On one hand, the state has been identified with government. On the other hand, the state, having a necessary existence of its own, *per se,* is said then to proceed to form and employ certain agencies forming government, much as a man hires servants and assigns them duties. The latter view is appropriate when the causal agency theory is relied upon. Some force, whether a general will or the singular wills of assembled individuals, calls the state into being. Then the latter as a secondary operation chooses certain persons through whom to act. Such a theory helps those who entertain it to retain the idea of the inherent sanctity of the state. Concrete political evils such as history exhibits in abundance can be laid at the door of fallible and corrupt governments, while the state keeps its honor unbesmirched. The identification of the state with government has the advantage of keeping the mind's eye upon concrete and observable facts; but it involves an unaccountable separation between rulers and people. If a government exists by itself and on its own account, why should there be government? Why should there persist the habits of loyalty and obedience which permit it to rule?

The hypothesis which has been advanced frees us from the perplexities which cluster about both of these two notions. The lasting, extensive and serious consequences of associated activity bring into existence a public. In itself it is unorganized and formless. By means of officials and their special powers it becomes a state. A public articulated and operating through representative officers is the state; there is no state without a government, but also there is none without the public. The officers are still singular beings, but they exercise new and special powers. These may be turned to their private account. Then government is corrupt and arbitrary. Quite apart from deliberate graft, from using unusual powers for private glorification and profit, density of mind and pomposity of behavior, adherence to class-interest and its prejudices, are strengthened by position. "Power is poison" was the remark of one of the best, shrewdest and most experienced observers of Washington politicians. On the other hand, occupancy of office may enlarge a man's views and stimulate his social interest so that he exhibits as a statesman traits foreign to his private life.

But since the public forms a state only by and through officials and their acts, and since holding official position does not work a miracle of transubstantiation, there is nothing perplexing nor even discouraging in the spectacle of the stupidities and errors of political behavior. The facts which give rise to the spectacle should, however, protect us from the illusion of expecting extraordinary change to follow from a mere change in political agencies and methods. Such a change sometimes occurs, but when it does, it is because the social conditions, in generating a new public, have prepared the way for it; the state sets a formal seal upon forces already in operation by giving them a defined channel through which to act. Conceptions of "The State" as something per se, something intrinsically manifesting a general will and reason, lend themselves to illusions. They make such a sharp distinction between *the* state and *a* government that, from the standpoint of the theories, a government may be corrupt and injurious and yet The State by the same idea retain its inherent dignity and nobility. Officials may be mean, obstinate, proud and stupid and yet the nature of the state which they serve remain essentially unimpaired. Since, however, a public is organized into a state through its government, the state is as its officials are. Only through constant watchfulness and criticism of public officials by citizens can a state be maintained in integrity and usefulness.

This is a convenient place for making explicit a qualification which has to be understood throughout. The words "government" and "officers" are taken functionally, not in terms of some particular structure which is so familiar to us that it leaps to the eyes when these words are used. Both words in their functional meaning are much wider in application than what is meant when we speak, say, of the government and officers of Great Britain or the United States. In households, for example, there have usually been rulers and "heads"; the parents, for most purposes the father, have been officers of the family interest. The "patriarchal family" presents an emphatic intensification, on account of comparative isolation of the household from other social forms, of what exists in lesser degree in almost all families. The same sort of remark applies to the use of the term "states," in connection with publics. The text is concerned with modern conditions, but the hypothesis propounded is meant to hold good generally. So to the patent objection that the state is a very modern institution, it is replied that while modernity is a property of those *structures* which go by the name of states, yet all history, or almost all, records the exercise of analogous *functions*. The argument concerns these functions and the mode of their operation, no matter what word be used, though for the sake of brevity the word "state," like the words "government" and "officer," has been freely employed.

III · State and Society*

The problem of the relation of individuals to associations—sometimes posed as the relation of *the* individual to society—is a meaningless one. We might as well make a problem out of the relation of the letters of an alphabet to the alphabet. An alphabet *is* letters, and "society" is individuals in their connections with one another. The mode of combination of letters with one another is obviously a matter of importance; letters form words and sentences when combined, and have no point or sense except in

* From *The Public and Its Problems*, pp. 69-74.

some combination. I would not say that the latter statement applies literally to individuals, but it cannot be gainsaid that singular human beings exist and behave in constant and varied association with one another. These modes of conjoint action and their consequences profoundly affect not only the outer habits of singular persons, but their dispositions in emotion, desire, planning and valuing.

"Society," however, is either an abstract or a collective noun. In the concrete, there are societies, associations, groups of an immense number of kinds, having different ties and instituting different interests. They may be gangs, criminal bands; clubs for sport, sociability and eating; scientific and professional organizations; political parties and unions within them; families; religious denominations, business partnerships and corporations; and so on in an endless list. The associations may be local, nation-wide and trans-national. Since there is no one *thing* which may be called society, except their indefinite overlapping, there is no unqualified eulogistic connotation adhering to the term "society." Some societies are in the main to be approved; some to be condemned, on account of their consequences upon the character and conduct of those engaged in them and because of their remoter consequences upon others. All of them, like all things human, are mixed in quality; "society" is something to be approached and judged critically and discriminatingly. "Socialization" of some sort—that is, the reflex modification of wants, beliefs and work because of share in a united action—is inevitable. But it is as marked in the formation of frivolous, dissipated, fanatical, narrow-minded and criminal persons as in that of competent inquirers, learned scholars, creative artists and good neighbors.

Confining our notice to the results which are desirable,

it appears that there is no reason for assigning all the values which are generated and maintained by means of human associations to the work of states. Yet the same unbridled generalizing and fixating tendency of the mind which leads to a monistic fixation of society has extended beyond the hypostatizing of "society" and produced a magnified idealization of The State. All values which result from any kind of association are habitually imputed by one school of social philosophers to the state. Naturally the result is to place the state beyond criticism. Revolt against the state is then thought to be the one unforgivable social sin.

It is quite true that most states, after they have been brought into being, react upon the primary groupings. When a state is a good state, when the officers of the public genuinely serve the public interests, this reflex effect is of great importance. It renders the desirable associations solider and more coherent; indirectly it clarifies their aims and purges their activities. It places a discount upon injurious groupings and renders their tenure of life precarious. In performing these services, it gives the individual members of valued associations greater liberty and security: it relieves them of hampering conditions which if they had to cope with personally would absorb their energies in mere negative struggle against evils. It enables individual members to count with reasonable certainty upon what others will do, and thus facilitates mutually helpful coöperations. It creates respect for others and for one's self. A measure of the goodness of a state is the degree in which it relieves individuals from the waste of negative struggle and needless conflict and confers upon him positive assurance and reënforcement in what he undertakes. This is a great service, and there is no call to be niggardly in acknowledging the transformations of group and personal action which states have historically effected.

But this recognition cannot be legitimately converted into the monopolistic absorption of all associations into The State, nor of all social values into political value. The all-inclusive nature of the state signifies only that officers of the public (including, of course, law-makers) may act so as to fix conditions under which *any* form of association operates; its comprehensive character refers only to the impact of its behavior. A war, like an earthquake, may "include" in its consequences all elements in a given territory, but the inclusion is by way of effects, not by inherent nature or right. A beneficent law, like a condition of general economic prosperity, may favorably affect all interests in a particular region, but it cannot be called a whole of which the elements influenced are parts. Nor can the liberating and confirming results of public action be construed to yield a wholesale idealization of states in contrast with other associations. For state activity is often injurious to the latter. One of the chief occupations of states has been the waging of war and the suppression of dissentient minorities. Moreover, their action, even when benign, presupposes values due to non-political forms of living together which are but extended and reënforced by the public through its agents.

The hypothesis which we have supported has obvious points of contact with what is known as the pluralistic conception of the state. It presents also a marked point of difference. Our doctrine of plural forms is a statement of a fact: that there exist a plurality of social groupings, good, bad and indifferent. It is not a doctrine which prescribes inherent limits to state action. It does not intimate that the function of the state is limited to settling conflicts among other groups, as if each one of them had a fixed scope of action of its own. Were that true, the state would be only an umpire to avert and remedy trespasses of one group upon another. Our hypothesis is neutral as to any general, sweeping implications as to how far state activity may extend. It does not indicate any particular polity of public action. At times, the consequences of the conjoint behavior of some persons may be such that a large public interest is generated which can be fulfilled only by laying down conditions which involve a large measure of reconstruction within that group. There is no more an inherent sanctity in a church, trade-union, business corporation, or family institution than there is in the state. Their value is also to be measured by their consequences. The consequences vary with concrete conditions; hence at one time and place a large measure of state activity may be indicated and at another time a policy of quiescence and *laissez faire*. Just as publics and states vary with conditions of time and place, so do the concrete functions which should be carried on by states. There is no antecedent universal proposition which can be laid down because of which the functions of a state should be limited or should be expanded. Their scope is something to be critically and experimentally determined.

IV · Communication and Communal Living*

Of all affairs, communication is the most wonderful. That things should be able to pass from the plane of external pushing and pulling to that of revealing themselves to man, and thereby to themselves; and that the fruit of communication should be participation, sharing, is a wonder by the side of which transubstantiation pales. When communication occurs, all natural events are subject to reconsideration and revision; they are readapted to meet

* From *Experience and Nature*, pp. 166-167; *The Public and Its Problems*, pp. 151-155; 158-159; 166-171; 176-184.

the requirements of conversation, whether it be public discourse or that preliminary discourse termed thinking. Events turn into objects, things with meaning. They may be referred to when they do not exist, and thus be operative among things distant in space and time, through vicarious presence in a new medium.

Brute efficiencies and inarticulate consummations as soon as they can be spoken of are liberated from local and accidental contexts, and are eager for naturalization in any non-insulated, communicating part of the world. Events when once they are named lead an independent and double life. In addition to their original existence, they are subject to ideal experimentation: their meanings may be infinitely combined and re-arranged in imagination, and the outcome of this inner experimentation— which is thought—may issue forth in interaction with crude or raw events. Meanings having been deflected from the rapid and roaring stream of events into a calm and traversable canal, rejoin the main stream, and color, temper and compose its course. Where communication exists, things in acquiring meaning thereby acquire representatives, surrogates, signs and implicates, which are infinitely more amenable to management, more permanent and accommodating than events in their first estate.

By this fashion, qualitative immediacies cease to be dumbly rapturous, a possession that is obsessive and an incorporation that involves submergence; conditions found in sensations and passions. They become capable of survey, contemplation, and ideal or logical elaboration: when something can be said of qualities they are purveyors of instruction. Learning and teaching come into being, and there is no event which may not yield information. A directly enjoyed thing adds to itself meaning, and enjoyment is thereby idealized. Even the dumb pang of an ache achieves a significant existence when it can be designated and descanted upon: it ceases to be merely oppressive and becomes important; it gains importance because it becomes representative. It has the dignity of an office.

Associated or joint activity is a condition of the creation of a community. But association itself is physical and organic, while communal life is moral, that is emotionally, intellectually, consciously sustained. Human beings combine in behavior as directly and unconsciously as do atoms, stellar masses and cells; as directly and unknowingly as they divide and repel. They do so in virtue of their own structure, as man and woman unite, as the baby seeks the breast and the breast is there to supply its need. They do so from external circumstances, pressure from without, as atoms combine or separate in presence of an electric charge, or as sheep huddle together from the cold. Associated activity needs no explanation; things are made that way. But no amount of aggregated collective action of itself constitutes a community. For beings who observe and think, and whose ideas are absorbed by impulses and become sentiments and interests, "we" is as inevitable as "I." But "we" and "our" exist only when the consequences of combined action are perceived and become an object of desire and effort, just as "I" and "mine" appear on the scene only when a distinctive share in mutual action is consciously asserted or claimed. Human associations may be ever so organic in origin and firm in operation, but they develop into societies in a human sense only as their consequences, being known, are esteemed and sought for. Even if "society" were as much an organism as some writers have held, it would not on that account be society. Interactions, transactions, occur *de facto* and the results of interdependence follow. But participation in activities and sharing in results are additive concerns. They demand *communication* as a prerequisite.

Combined activity happens among human beings; but when nothing else happens it passes as inevitably into some other mode of interconnected activity as does the interplay of iron and the oxygen of water. What takes place is wholly describable in terms of energy, or, as we say in the case of human interactions, of force. Only when there exist *signs* or *symbols* of activities and of their outcome can the flux be viewed as from without, be arrested for consideration and esteem, and be regulated. Lightning strikes and rives a tree or rock, and the resulting fragments take up and continue the process of interaction, and so on and on. But when phases of the process are represented by signs, a new medium is interposed. As symbols are related to one another, the important relations of a course of events are recorded and are preserved as meanings. Recollection and foresight are possible; the new medium facilitates calculation, planning, and a new kind of action which intervenes in what happens to direct its course in the interest of what is foreseen and desired.

Symbols in turn depend upon and promote communication. The results of conjoint experience are considered and transmitted. Events cannot be passed from one to another, but meanings may be shared by means of signs. Wants and impulses are then attached to common meanings. They are thereby transformed into desires and purposes, which, since they implicate a common or mutually understood meaning, present new ties, converting a conjoint activity into a community of interest and endeavor. Thus there is generated what, metaphorically, may be termed a general will and social consciousness: desire and choice on the part of individuals in behalf of activities that, by means of symbols, are communicable and shared by all concerned. A community thus presents an order of energies transmuted into one of meanings which are appreciated and mutually referred by each to every other on the part of those engaged in combined action. "Force" is not eliminated but is transformed in use and direction by ideas and sentiments made possible by means of symbols.

The work of conversion of the physical and organic phase of associated behavior into a community of action saturated and regulated by mutual interest in shared meanings, consequences which are translated into ideas and desired objects by means of symbols, does not occur all at once nor completely. At any given time, it sets a problem rather than marks a settled achievement. We are born organic beings associated with others, but we are not born members of a community. The young have to be brought within the traditions, outlook and interests which characterize a community by means of education: by unremitting instruction and by learning in connection with the phenomena of overt association. Everything which is distinctively human is learned, not native, even though it could not be learned without native structures which mark man off from other animals. To learn in a human way and to human effect is not just to acquire added skill through refinement of original capacities.

To learn to be human is to develop through the give-and-take of communication an effective sense of being an individually distinctive member of a community; one who understands and appreciates its beliefs, desires and methods, and who contributes to a further conversion of organic powers into human resources and values. But this translation is never finished. The old Adam, the unregenerate element in human nature, persists. It shows itself wherever the method obtains of attaining results by use of

force instead of by the method of communication and enlightenment. It manifests itself more subtly, pervasively
and effectually when knowledge and the instrumentalities
of skill which are the product of communal life are employed in the service of wants and impulses which have
not themselves been modified by reference to a shared interest. To the doctrine of "natural" economy which held
that commercial exchange would bring about such an interdependence that harmony would automatically result,
Rousseau gave an adequate answer in advance. He pointed
out that interdependence provides just the situation which
makes it possible and worth while for the stronger and
abler to exploit others for their own ends, to keep others in
a state of subjection where they can be utilized as animated tools. The remedy he suggested, a return to a condition of independence based on isolation, was hardly seriously meant. But its desperateness is evidence of the urgency of the problem. Its negative character was equivalent to surrender of any hope of solution. By contrast it
indicates the nature of the only possible solution: the perfecting of the means and ways of communication of meanings so that genuinely shared interest in the consequences
of interdependent activities may inform desire and effort
and thereby direct action.

Knowledge is a function of association and communication; it depends upon tradition, upon tools and methods
socially transmitted, developed and sanctioned. Faculties
of effectual observation, reflection and desire are habits acquired under the influence of the culture and institutions
of society, not ready-made inherent powers. The fact that
man acts from crudely intelligized emotion and from habit
rather than from rational consideration, is now so familiar
that it is not easy to appreciate that the other idea was
taken seriously as the basis of economic and political phi-

losophy. The measure of truth which it contains was derived from observation of a relatively small group of
shrewd business men who regulated their enterprises by
calculation and accounting, and of citizens of small and
stable local communities who were so intimately acquainted with the persons and affairs of their locality that
they could pass competent judgment upon the bearing of
proposed measures with respect to their own concerns.

The prime condition of a democratically organized public is a kind of knowledge and insight which does not yet
exist. In its absence, it would be the height of absurdity
to try to tell what it would be like if it existed. But some
of the conditions which must be fulfilled if it is to exist
can be indicated. We can borrow that much from the
spirit and method of science even if we are ignorant of it
as a specialized apparatus. An obvious requirement is freedom of social inquiry and of distribution of its conclusions. The notion that men may be free in their thought
even when they are not in its expression and dissemination
has been sedulously propagated. It had its origin in the
idea of a mind complete in itself, apart from action and
from objects. Such a consciousness presents in fact the
spectacle of mind deprived of its normal functioning, because it is baffled by the actualities in connection with
which alone it is truly mind, and is driven back into secluded and impotent revery.

There can be no public without full publicity in respect
to all consequences which concern it. Whatever obstructs
and restricts publicity, limits and distorts public opinion
and checks and distorts thinking on social affairs. Without
freedom of expression, not even methods of social inquiry
can be developed. For tools can be evolved and perfected
only in operation; in application to observing, reporting
and organizing actual subject-matter; and this application

cannot occur save through free and systematic communication.

The belief that thought and its communication are now free simply because legal restrictions which once obtained have been done away with is absurd. Its currency perpetuates the infantile state of social knowledge. For it blurs recognition of our central need to possess conceptions which are used as tools of directed inquiry and which are tested, rectified and caused to grow in actual use. No man and no mind was ever emancipated merely by being left alone. Removal of formal limitations is but a negative condition; positive freedom is not a state but an act which involves methods and instrumentalities for control of conditions. Experience shows that sometimes the sense of external oppression, as by censorship, acts as a challenge and arouses intellectual energy and excites courage. But a belief in intellectual freedom where it does not exist contributes only to complacency in virtual enslavement, to sloppiness, superficiality and recourse to sensations as a substitute for ideas: marked traits of our present estate with respect to social knowledge. On one hand, thinking deprived of its normal course takes refuge in academic specialism, comparable in its way to what is called scholasticism. On the other hand, the physical agencies of publicity which exist in such abundance are utilized in ways which constitute a large part of the present meaning of publicity: advertising, propaganda, invasion of private life, the "featuring" of passing incidents in a way which violates all the moving logic of continuity, and which leaves us with those isolated intrusions and shocks which are the essence of "sensations."

It would be a mistake to identify the conditions which limit free communication and circulation of facts and ideas, and which thereby arrest and pervert social thought or inquiry, merely with overt forces which are obstructive. It is true that those who have ability to manipulate social relations for their own advantage have to be reckoned with. They have an uncanny instinct for detecting whatever intellectual tendencies even remotely threaten to encroach upon their control. They have developed an extraordinary facility in enlisting upon their side the inertia, prejudices and emotional partisanship of the masses by use of a technique which impedes free inquiry and expression. We seem to be approaching a state of government by hired promoters of opinion called publicity agents. But the more serious enemy is deeply concealed in hidden entrenchments.

Emotional habituations and intellectual habitudes on the part of the mass of men create the conditions of which the exploiters of sentiment and opinion only take advantage. Men have got used to an experimental method in physical and technical matters. They are still afraid of it in human concerns. The fear is the more efficacious because like all deep-lying fears it is covered up and disguised by all kinds of rationalizations. One of its commonest forms is a truly religious idealization of, and reverence for, established institutions; for example in our own politics, the Constitution, the Supreme Court, private property, free contract and so on. The words "sacred" and "sanctity" come readily to our lips when such things come under discussion. They testify to the religious aureole which protects the institutions. If "holy" means that which is not to be approached nor touched, save with ceremonial precautions and by specially anointed officials, then such things are holy in contemporary political life. As su pernatural matters have progressively been left high and dry upon a secluded beach, the actuality of religious taboos has more and more gathered about secular institutions, especially those connected with the nationalistic state.* Psychiatrists have discovered that one of the commonest causes of mental disturbance is an underlying fear of which the subject is not aware, but which leads to withdrawal from reality and to unwillingness to think things through. There is a social pathology which works powerfully against effective inquiry into social institutions and conditions. It manifests itself in a thousand ways; in querulousness, in impotent drifting, in uneasy snatching at distractions, in idealization of the long established, in a facile optimism assumed as a cloak, in riotous glorification of things "as they are," in intimidation of all dissenters— ways which depress and dissipate thought all the more effectually because they operate with subtle and unconscious pervasiveness.

Knowledge cooped up in a private consciousness is a myth, and knowledge of social phenomena is peculiarly dependent upon dissemination, for only by distribution can such knowledge be either obtained or tested. A fact of community life which is not spread abroad so as to be a common possession is a contradiction in terms. Dissemination is something other than scattering at large. Seeds are sown, not by virtue of being thrown out at random, but by being so distributed as to take root and have a chance of growth. Communication of the results of social inquiry is the same thing as the formation of public opinion. This marks one of the first ideas framed in the growth of political democracy as it will be one of the last to be fulfilled. For public opinion is judgment which is formed and entertained by those who constitute the public and is about

* The religious character of nationalism has been forcibly brought out by Carleton Hayes, in his "Essays on Nationalism," especially Chap. IV.

public affairs. Each of the two phases imposes for its realization conditions hard to meet.

Opinions and beliefs concerning the public presuppose
effective and organized inquiry. Unless there are methods
for detecting the energies which are at work and tracing
them through an intricate network of interactions to their
consequences, what passes as public opinion will be "opinion" in its derogatory sense rather than truly public, no
matter how widespread the opinion is. The power for harm
is proportional to the number who share error as to fact
and who partake of a false belief. Opinion casually formed
and formed under the direction of those who have something at stake in having a lie believed can be *public* opinion only in name. Calling it by this name, acceptance of
the name as a kind of warrant, magnifies its capacity to
lead action astray. The more who share it, the more injurious its influence. Public opinion, even if it happens to be
correct, is intermittent when it is not the product of methods of investigation and reporting constantly at work. It
appears only in crises. Hence its "rightness" concerns only
an immediate emergency. Its lack of continuity makes it
wrong from the standpoint of the course of events. It is as
if a physician were able to deal for the moment with an
emergency in disease but could not adapt his treatment of
it to the underlying conditions which brought it about. He
may then "cure" the disease—that is, cause its present
alarming symptoms to subside—but he does not modify
its causes; his treatment may even affect them for the
worse. Only continuous inquiry, continuous in the sense
of being connected as well as persistent, can provide the
material of enduring opinion about public matters.

A glance at the situation shows that the physical and
external means of collecting information in regard to what

is happening in the world have far outrun the intellectual phase of inquiry and organization of its results. Telegraph, telephone, and now the radio, cheap and quick mails, the printing press, capable of swift reduplication of material at low cost, have attained a remarkable development. But when we ask what sort of material is recorded and how it is organized, when we ask about the intellectual form in which the material is presented, the tale to be told is very different. "News" signifies something which has just happened, and which is new just because it deviates from the old and regular. But its *meaning* depends upon relation to what it imports, to what its social consequences are. This import cannot be determined unless the new is placed in relation to the old, to what has happened and been integrated into the course of events. Without coördination and consecutiveness, events are not events, but mere occurrences, intrusions; an event implies that out of which a happening proceeds. Hence even if we discount the influence of private interests in procuring suppression, secrecy and misrepresentation, we have here an explanation of the triviality and "sensational" quality of so much of what passes as news. The catastrophic, namely, crime, accident, family rows, personal clashes and conflicts, are the most obvious forms of breaches of continuity; they supply the element of shock which is the strictest meaning of sensation; they are the *new* par excellence, even though only the date of the newspaper could inform us whether they happened last year or this, so completely are they isolated from their connections.

So accustomed are we to this method of collecting, recording and presenting social changes, that it may well sound ridiculous to say that a genuine social science would manifest its reality in the daily press, while learned books and articles supply and polish tools of inquiry. But the in-

quiry which alone can furnish knowledge as a precondition of public judgments must be contemporary and quo-
tidian. Even if social sciences as a specialized apparatus of
inquiry were more advanced than they are, they would be
comparatively impotent in the office of directing opinion
on matters of concern to the public as long as they are remote from application in the daily and unremitting assembly and interpretation of "news." On the other hand, the
tools of social inquiry will be clumsy as long as they are
forged in places and under conditions remote from contemporary events.

What has been said about the formation of ideas and
judgments concerning the public applies as well to the distribution of the knowledge which makes it an effective
possession of the members of the public. Any separation
between the two sides of the problem is artificial. The
discussion of propaganda and propagandism would alone,
however, demand a volume, and could be written only by
one much more experienced than the present writer. Propaganda can accordingly only be mentioned, with the remark that the present situation is one unprecedented in
history. The political forms of democracy and quasi-dem-
ocratic habits of thought on social matters have compelled
a certain amount of public discussion and at least the sim-
ulation of general consultation in arriving at political decisions. Representative government must at least seem to
be founded on public interests as they are revealed to
public belief. The days are past when government can be
carried on without any pretense of ascertaining the wishes
of the governed.* In theory, their assent must be secured.
Under the older forms, there was no need to muddy the
sources of opinion on political matters. No current of energy flowed from them. To-day the judgments popularly

* This was written in 1927.—Ed.

formed on political matters are so important, in spite of all factors to the contrary, that there is an enormous premium upon all methods which affect their formation.

The smoothest road to control of political conduct is by control of opinion. As long as interests of pecuniary profit are powerful, and a public has not located and identified itself, those who have this interest will have an unresisted motive for tampering with the springs of political action in all that affects them. Just as in the conduct of industry and exchange generally the technological factor is obscured, deflected and defeated by "business," so specifically in the management of publicity. The gathering and sale of subject-matter having a public import are part of the existing pecuniary system. Just as industry conducted by engineers on a factual technological basis would be a very different thing from what it actually is, so the assembling and reporting of news would be a very different thing if the genuine interests of reporters were permitted to work freely.

One aspect of the matter concerns particularly the side of dissemination. It is often said, and with a great appearance of truth, that the freeing and perfecting of inquiry would not have any especial effect. For, it is argued, the mass of the reading public is not interested in learning and assimilating the results of accurate investigation. Unless these are read, they cannot seriously affect the thought and action of members of the public; they remain in secluded library alcoves, and are studied and understood only by a few intellectuals. The objection is well taken save as the potency of art is taken into account. A technical high-brow presentation would appeal only to those technically high-brow; it would not be news to the masses. Presentation is fundamentally important, and presentation is a question of art. A newspaper which was only a daily

edition of a quarterly journal of sociology or political science would undoubtedly possess a limited circulation and
a narrow influence. Even at that, however, the mere existence and accessibility of such material would have some
regulative effect. But we can look much further than that.
The material would have such an enormous and widespread human bearing that its bare existence would be an
irresistible invitation to a presentation of it which would
have a direct popular appeal. The freeing of the artist in
literary presentation, in other words, is as much a precondition of the desirable creation of adequate opinion on
public matters as is the freeing of social inquiry. Men's
conscious life of opinion and judgment often proceeds on
a superficial and trivial plane. But their lives reach a
deeper level. The function of art has always been to break
through the crust of conventionalized and routine consciousness. Common things, a flower, a gleam of moon-
light, the song of a bird, not things rare and remote, are
means with which the deeper levels of life are touched so
that they spring up as desire and thought. This process is
art. Poetry, the drama, the novel, are proofs that the
problem of presentation is not insoluble. Artists have always been the real purveyors of news, for it is not the outward happening in itself which is new, but the kindling
by it of emotion, perception and appreciation.

We have but touched lightly and in passing upon the
conditions which must be fulfilled if the Great Society is
to become a Great Community; a society in which the
ever-expanding and intricately ramifying consequences of
associated activities shall be known in the full sense of
that word, so that an organized, articulate Public comes
into being. The highest and most difficult kind of inquiry
and a subtle, delicate, vivid and responsive art of communication must take possession of the physical machin-

ery of transmission and circulation and breathe life into it. When the machine age has thus perfected its machinery it will be a means of life and not its despotic master. Democracy will come into its own, for democracy is a name for a life of free and enriching communion. It had its seer in Walt Whitman. It will have its consummation when free social inquiry is indissolubly wedded to the art of full and moving communication.

V · The Democratic Form*

Democracy is much broader than a special political form, a method of conducting government, of making laws and carrying on governmental administration by means of popular suffrage and elected officers. It is that, of course. But it is something broader and deeper than that. The political and governmental phase of democracy is a means, the best means so far found, for realizing ends that lie in the wide domain of human relationships and the development of human personality. It is, as we often say, though perhaps without appreciating all that is involved in the saying, a way of life, social and individual. The keynote of democracy as a way of life may be expressed, it seems to me, as the necessity for the participation of every mature human being in formation of the values that regulate the living of men together: which is necessary from the standpoint of both the general social welfare and the full development of human beings as individuals.

Universal suffrage, recurring elections, responsibility of those who are in political power to the voters, and the other factors of democratic government are means that have been found expedient for realizing democracy as the

* From *Democracy and Educational Administration*, an address before the National Education Association, Feb. 22, 1937, and published in *School and Society*, April 3, 1937.

truly human way of living. They are not a final end and a final value. They are to be judged on the basis of their contribution to end. It is a form of idolatry to erect means into the end which they serve. Democratic political forms are simply the best means that human wit has devised up to a special time in history. But they rest back upon the idea that no man or limited set of men is wise enough or good enough to rule others without their consent; the positive meaning of this statement is that all those who are affected by social institutions must have a share in producing and managing them. The two facts that each one is influenced in what he does and enjoys and in what he becomes by the institutions under which he lives, and that therefore he shall have, in a democracy, a voice in shaping them, are the passive and active sides of the same fact.

The development of political democracy came about through substitution of the method of mutual consultation and voluntary agreement for the method of subordination of the many to the few enforced from above. Social arrangements which involve fixed subordination are maintained by coercion. The coercion need not be physical. There have existed, for short periods, benevolent despotisms. But coercion of some sort there has been; perhaps economic, certainly psychological and moral. The very fact of exclusion from participation is a subtle form of suppression. It gives individuals no opportunity to reflect and decide upon what is good for them. Others who are supposed to be wiser and who in any case have more power decide the question for them and also decide the methods and means by which subjects may arrive at the enjoyment of what is good for them. This form of coercion and suppression is more subtle and more effective than are overt intimidation and restraint. When it is habitual and embodied in social institutions, it seems the normal and

natural state of affairs. The mass usually become unaware
that they have a claim to a development of their own
powers. Their experience is so restricted that they are not
conscious of restriction. It is part of the democratic conception that they as individuals are not the only sufferers,
but that the whole social body is deprived of the potential resources that should be at its service. The individuals
of the submerged mass may not be very wise. But there is
one thing they are wiser about than anybody else can be,
and that is where the shoe pinches, the troubles they suffer from.

The foundation of democracy is faith in the capacities
of human nature; faith in human intelligence and in the
power of pooled and coöperative experience. It is not belief that these things are complete but that if given a show
they will grow and be able to generate progressively the
knowledge and wisdom needed to guide collective action.
Every autocratic and authoritarian scheme of social action
rests on a belief that the needed intelligence is confined to
a superior few, who because of inherent natural gifts are
endowed with the ability and the right to control the conduct of others; laying down principles and rules and directing the ways in which they are carried out. It would
be foolish to deny that much can be said for this point of
view. It is that which controlled human relations in social
groups for much the greater part of human history. The
democratic faith has emerged very, very recently in the
history of mankind. Even where democracies now exist,
men's minds and feelings are still permeated with ideas
about leadership imposed from above, ideas that developed
in the long early history of mankind. After democratic political institutions were nominally established, beliefs and
ways of looking at life and of acting that originated when
men and women were externally controlled and subjected

to arbitrary power, persisted in the family, the church, business and the school, and experience shows that as long as they persist there, political democracy is not secure.

Belief in equality is an element of the democratic credo. It is not, however, belief in equality of natural endowments. Those who proclaimed the idea of equality did not suppose they were enunciating a psychological doctrine, but a legal and political one. All individuals are entitled to equality of treatment by law and in its administration. Each one is affected equally in quality if not in quantity by the institutions under which he lives and has an equal right to express his judgment, although the weight of his judgment may not be equal in amount when it enters into the pooled result to that of others. In short, each one is equally an individual and entitled to equal opportunity of development of his own capacities, be they large or small in range. Moreover, each has needs of his own, as significant to him as those of others are to them. The very fact of natural and psychological inequality is all the more reason for establishment by law of equality of opportunity, since otherwise the former becomes a means of oppression of the less gifted.

While what we call intelligence may be distributed in unequal amounts, it is the democratic faith that it is sufficiently general so that each individual has something to contribute, and the value of each contribution can be assessed only as it enters into the final pooled intelligence constituted by the contributions of all. Every authoritarian scheme, on the contrary, assumes that its value may be assessed by some *prior* principle, if not of family and birth or race and color or possession of material wealth, then by the position and rank a person occupies in the existing social scheme. The democratic faith in equality is the faith that each individual shall have the chance and opportunity to contribute whatever he is capable of contributing and that the value of his contribution be decided by its place and function in the organized total of similar contributions, not on the basis of prior status of any kind whatever.

I have emphasized in what precedes the importance of the effective release of intelligence in connection with personal experience in the democratic way of living. I have done so purposely because democracy is so often and so naturally associated in our minds with freedom of *action*, forgetting the importance of freed intelligence which is necessary to direct and to warrant freedom of action. Unless freedom of individual action has intelligence and informed conviction back of it, its manifestation is almost sure to result in confusion and disorder. The democratic idea of freedom is not the right of each individual to *do* as he pleases, even if it be qualified by adding "provided he does not interfere with the same freedom on the part of others." While the idea is not always, not often enough, expressed in words, the basic freedom is that of freedom of *mind* and of whatever degree of freedom of action and experience is necessary to produce freedom of intelligence. The modes of freedom guaranteed in the Bill of Rights are all of this nature: Freedom of belief and conscience, of expression of opinion, of assembly for discussion and conference, of the press as an organ of communication. They are guaranteed because without them individuals are not free to develop and society is deprived of what they might contribute.

CHAPTER SIX

THE INDIVIDUAL IN THE NEW SOCIETY

I · The Individual in the Cultural Crisis*

ANTHROPOLOGICALLY speaking, we are living in a money culture. Our materialism, our devotion to money making and to having a good time, are not things by themselves. They are the product of the fact that we live in a money culture; of the fact that our technique and technology are controlled by interest in private profit. There lies the serious and fundamental defect of our civilization, the source of the secondary and induced evils to which so much attention is given. Critics are dealing with symptoms and effects. The evasion of fundamental economic causes by critics both foreign and native seems to me to be an indication of the prevalence of the old European tradition, with its disregard for the body, material things, and practical concerns. The development of the American type, in the sense of the critics, is an expression of the fact that we have retained this tradition and the economic system of private gain on which it is based, while at the same time we have made an independent development of industry and technology that is nothing short of revolutionary. When our critics deal with this issue instead of avoiding it there will be something really doing.

Until the issue is met, the confusion of a civilization di-

* From *Individualism Old and New*. The passages have been selected and arranged from all parts of the book. Ed.

vided against itself will persist. The mass development, which our European critics tell us has submerged individuality, *is* the product of a machine age; in some form it will follow in all countries from the extension of a machine technology. Its immediate effect has been, without doubt, a subjection of certain types of individuality. As far as individuality is associated with aristocracy of the historic type, the extension of the machine age will presumably be hostile to individuality in its traditional sense all over the world.

There are two "solutions" that fail to solve. One of these is the method of avoidance. This course is taken as far as it is assumed that the only valid type of individuality is that which holds over from the ages that anteceded machine technology and the democratic society it creates. The course that is complementary to the method of escape springs from assumption that the present situation is final; that it presents something inherently ultimate and fixed. Only as it is treated as transitive and moving, as material to be dealt with in shaping a later outcome, only, that is, as it is treated as a *problem,* is the idea of any solution genuine and relevant. We may well take the formula advanced by European critics as a means of developing our consciousness of some of the conditions of the problem. So regarded, the problem is seen to be essentially that of creation of a new individualism as significant for modern conditions as the old individualism at its best was for its day and place.

The first step in further definition of this problem is realization of the collective age which we have already entered.

There is no word which adequately expresses what is taking place. "Socialism" has too specific political and economic associations to be appropriate. "Collectivism" is more neutral, but it, too, is a party-word rather than a descriptive term. Perhaps the constantly increasing role of corporations in our economic life gives a clew to a fitting name. The word may be used in a wider sense than is conveyed by its technical legal meaning. We may then say that the United States has steadily moved from an earlier pioneer individualism to a condition of dominant corporateness. The influence business corporations exercise in determining present industrial and economic activities is both a cause and a symbol of the tendency to combination in all phases of life. Associations tightly or loosely organized more and more define the opportunities, the choices and the actions of individuals. The need of the present is to apprehend the fact that, for better or worse, we are living in a corporate age.

It is of the nature of society as of life to contain a balance of opposed forces. Actions and reactions are ultimately equal and counterpart. At present the "socialization" is largely mechanical and quantitative. The system is kept in a kind of precarious balance by the movement toward lawless and reckless overstimulation among individuals. If the chaos and the mechanism are to generate a mind and soul, an integrated personality, it will have to be an intelligence, a sentiment and an individuality of a new type.

Assured and integrated individuality is the product of definite social relationships and publicly acknowledged functions. Judged by this standard, even those who seem to be in control, and to carry the expression of their special individual abilities to a high pitch, are submerged. They may be captains of finance and industry, but until there is some consensus of belief as to the meaning of finance and industry in civilization as a whole, they cannot be captains of their own souls—their beliefs and aims.

They exercise leadership surreptitiously and, as it were, absent-mindedly. They lead, but it is under cover of impersonal and socially undirected economic forces. Their reward is found not in what they do, in their social office and function, but in a deflection of social consequences to private gain. They receive the acclaim and command the envy and admiration of the crowd, but the crowd is also composed of private individuals who are equally lost to a sense of social bearings and uses.

The explanation is found in the fact that while the actions promote corporate and collective results, these results are outside their intent and irrelevant to that reward of satisfaction which comes from a sense of social fulfillment. To themselves and to others, their business is private and its outcome is private profit. No complete satisfaction is possible where such a split exists. Hence the absence of a sense of social value is made up for by an exacerbated acceleration of the activities that increase private advantage and power. One cannot look into the inner consciousness of his fellows; but if there is any general degree of inner contentment on the part of those who form our pecuniary oligarchy, the evidence is sadly lacking. As for the many, they are impelled hither and yon by forces beyond their control.

The unrest, impatience, irritation and hurry that are so marked in American life are inevitable accompaniments of a situation in which individuals do not find support and contentment in the fact that they are sustaining and sustained members of a social whole. They are evidence, psychologically, of abnormality, and it is as idle to seek for their explanation within the deliberate intent of individuals as it is futile to think that they can be got rid of by hortatory moral appeal. Only an acute maladjustment between individuals and the social conditions under which they live can account for such widespread pathological phenomena. Feverish love of anything as long as it is a change which is distracting, impatience, unsettlement, nervous discontentment and desire for excitement, are not native to human nature. They are so abnormal as to demand explanation in some deep-seated cause.

Instances of the flux in which individuals are loosened from the ties that once gave order and support to their lives are glaring. They are indeed so glaring that they blind our eyes to the causes which produce them. Individuals are groping their way through situations which they do not direct and which do not give them direction. The beliefs and ideals that are uppermost in their consciousness are not relevant to the society in which they outwardly act and which constantly reacts upon them. Their conscious ideas and standards are inherited from an age that has passed away; their minds, as far as consciously entertained principles and methods of interpretation are concerned, are at odds with actual conditions. This profound split is the cause of distraction and bewilderment.

Because of the bankruptcy of the older individualism, those who are aware of the breakdown often speak and argue as if individualism were itself done and over with. I do not suppose that those who regard socialism and individualism as antithetical really mean that individuality is going to die out or that it is not something intrinsically precious. But in speaking as if the only individualism were the local episode of the last two centuries, they play into the hands of those who would keep it alive in order to serve their own ends, and they slur over the chief problem—that of remaking society to serve the growth of a new type of individual. There are many who believe that socialism of some form is needed to realize individual initiative and security on a wide scale. They are concerned about the restriction of power and freedom to a few in the present régime, and they think that collective social control is necessary, at least for a time, in order to achieve its advantages for all. But they too often seem to assume that the result will be merely an extension of the earlier individualism to the many.

Such thinking treats individualism as if it were something static, having a uniform content. It ignores the fact that the mental and moral structure of individuals, the pattern of their desires and purposes, change with every great change in social constitution. Individuals who are not bound together in associations, whether domestic, economic, religious, political, artistic or educational, are monstrosities. It is absurd to suppose that the ties which hold them together are merely external and do not react into mentality and character, producing the framework of personal disposition.

The tragedy of the "lost individual" is due to the fact that while individuals are now caught up into a vast complex of associations, there is no harmonious and coherent reflection of the import of these connections into the imaginative and emotional outlook on life. This fact is of course due in turn to the absence of harmony within the state of society. There is an undoubted circle. But it is a vicious circle only as far as men decline to accept—in the intellectual, observing and inquiring spirit—the realities of the social estate, and because of this refusal either surrender to the division or seek to save their individuality by escape or sheer emotional revolt. The habit of opposing the corporate and collective to the individual tends to the persistent continuation of the confusion and uncertainty. It distracts attention from the crucial issue: How shall the individual refind himself in an unprecedentedly new social situation, and what qualities will the new individualism exhibit?

It is not too much to say that the whole significance of the older individualism has now shrunk to a pecuniary scale and measure. The virtues that are supposed to attend rugged individualism may be vocally proclaimed, but it takes no great insight to see that what is cherished is measured by its connection with those activities that make for success in business conducted for personal gain. Hence, the irony of the gospel of "individualism" in business conjoined with suppression of individuality in thought and speech. One cannot imagine a bitterer comment on any professed individualism than that it subordinates the only creative individuality—that of mind—to the maintenance of a regime which gives the few an opportunity for being shrewd in the management of monetary business.

There is at least this much truth in economic determinism. Industry is not outside of human life, but within it. The genteel tradition shuts its eyes to this fact; emotionally and intellectually it pushes industry and its material phase out into a region remote from human values. To stop with mere emotional rejection and moral condemnation of industry and trade as materialistic is to leave them in this inhuman region where they operate as the instruments of those who employ them for private ends. Exclusion of this sort is an accomplice of the forces that keep things in the saddle. There is a subterranean partnership between those who employ the existing economic order for selfish pecuniary gain and those who turn their backs upon it in the interest of personal complacency, private dignity, and irresponsibility.

Every occupation leaves its impress on individual character and modifies the outlook on life of those who carry it on. No one questions this fact as respects wage-earners tied to the machine, or business men who devote themselves to pecuniary manipulations. Callings may have their roots in innate impulses of human nature but their pursuit does not merely "express" these impulses, leaving them unaltered; their pursuit determines intellectual horizons, precipitates knowledge and ideas, shapes desire and interest. This influence operates in the case of those who set up fine art, science, or religion as ends in themselves, isolated from radiation and expansion into other concerns (such radiation being what "application" signifies) as much as in the case of those who engage in industry. The alternatives are lack of application with consequent narrowing and overspecialization, and application with enlargement and increase of liberality. The narrowing in the case of industry pursued apart from social ends is evident to all thoughtful persons. Intellectual and literary folks who conceive themselves devoted to pursuit of pure truth and uncontaminated beauty too readily overlook the fact that a similar narrowing and hardening take place in them. Their goods are more refined, but they are also engaged in acquisition; unless they are concerned with use, with expansive interactions, they too become monopolists of capital. And the monopolization of spiritual capital may in the end be more harmful than that of material capital.

There are, I suppose, those who fancy that the emphasis which I put upon the corporateness of existing society in the United States is in effect, even if not in the writer's conscious intent, a plea for greater conformity than now exists. Nothing could be further from the truth. Identification of society with a level of uniformity, whatever it be, high as well as low, is just another evidence of that distraction because of which the individual is lost. Society is of course but the relations of individuals to one another in this form and that. And all relations are interactions, not fixed molds. The particular interactions that compose a human society include the give and take of participation, of a sharing that increases, that expands and deepens, the capacity and significance of the interacting factors. Conformity is a name for the absence of vital interplay; the arrest and benumbing of communication. It is the artificial substitute used to hold men together in lack of associations that are incorporated into inner dispositions of thought and desire. I often wonder what meaning is given to the term "society" by those who oppose it to the intimacies of personal intercourse, such as those of friendship. Presumably they have in their minds a picture of rigid institutions or some set and external organization. But an institution that is other than the structure of human contact and intercourse is a fossil of some past society; organization, as in any living organism, is the coöperative consensus of multitudes of cells, each living in exchange with others.

We are given to thinking of society in large and vague ways. We should forget "society" and think of law, industry, religion, medicine, politics, art, education, philosophy —and think of them in the plural. For points of contact are not the same for any two persons and hence the questions which the interests and occupations pose are never twice the same. There is no contact so immutable that it will not yield at some point. All these callings and concerns are the avenues through which the world acts upon us and we upon the world. There is no society at large, no business in general. Harmony with conditions is not a single and monotonous uniformity, but a diversified affair requiring individual attack. It is the part of wisdom to note the double meaning of such ideas as "acceptance." There is an acceptance that is of the intellect; it signifies facing facts for what they are. There is another acceptance that is of the emotions and will; that involves commitment of desire and effort. So far are the two from being identical that acceptance in the first sense is the precondition of all intelligent refusal of acceptance in the second sense. There is a prophetic aspect to all observation; we can perceive the meaning of what exists only as we forecast the consequences it entails. When a situation is as confused and divided within itself as is the present social estate, choice is implicated in observation. As one perceives different tendencies and different possible consequences, preference inevitably goes out to one or the other. Because acknowledgment in thought brings with it intelligent discrimination and choice, it is the first step out of confusion, the first step in forming those objects of significant allegiance out of which stable and efficacious individuality may grow. It might even perform the miracle of rendering conservatism relevant and thoughtful. It certainly is the prerequisite of an anchored liberalism.

Individuality is inexpugnable because it is a manner of distinctive sensitivity, selection, choice, response and utilization of conditions. For this reason, if for no other, it is impossible to develop integrated individuality by any all-embracing system or program. No individual can make the determination for anyone else; nor can he make it for himself all at once and forever. A native manner of selection gives direction and continuity, but definite expression is found in changing occasions and varied forms. The selective choice and use of conditions have to be continually made and remade. Since we live in a moving world and change with our interactions in it, every act produces a new perspective that demands a new exercise of preference. If, in the long run, an individual remains lost, it is because he has chosen irresponsibility; and if he remains wholly depressed, it is because he has chosen the course of easy parasitism.

Individuality is at first spontaneous and unshaped; it is a potentiality, a capacity of development. Even so, it is a unique manner of acting in and with a world of objects and persons. It is not something complete in itself, like a closet in a house or a secret drawer in a desk, filled with treasures that are waiting to be bestowed on the world. Since individuality is a distinctive way of feeling the impacts of the world and of showing a preferential bias in response to these impacts, it develops into shape and form only through interaction with actual conditions; it is no more complete in itself than is a painter's tube of paint without relation to a canvas. The work of art is the truly individual thing; and it is the result of the interaction of paint and canvas through the medium of the artist's distinctive vision and power. In its determination, the potential individuality of the artist takes on visible and enduring form. The imposition of individuality as something made in advance always gives evidence of a mannerism, not of a manner. For the latter is something original and creative; something formed in the very process of creation of other things.

The future is always unpredictable. Ideals, including that of a new and effective individuality, must themselves be framed out of the possibilities of existing conditions, even if these be the conditions that constitute a corporate and industrial age. The ideals take shape and gain a content as they operate in remaking conditions. We may, in order to have continuity of direction, plan a program of action in anticipation of occasions as they emerge. But a program of ends and ideals if kept apart from sensitive and flexible method becomes an encumbrance. For its hard and rigid character assumes a fixed world and a static individual; and neither of these things exists. It implies that we can prophesy the future—an attempt which terminates, as someone has said, in prophesying the past or in its reduplication.

II · The Economic Basis of the New Society*

The imminence of the "next world war" has caused the last World War to recede from thought, discussion and imagination except in negative ways. During the progress of the World War positive attitudes and hopes were generated and positive plans and objectives put forward for the creation of a better human society. The fact that these hopes were betrayed and objectives failed to be realized is evidence of our failure to take advantage of the opportunity that was unquestionably there. It is not a condemnation of those hopes and objectives.

The constructive thought of that period centered about two comprehensive objectives: the establishment of a system of international law that would ensure peaceful relations between nations; and the reorganization of the social and economic relations within nations. Passing over the former objective, let us consider the latter.†

I quote the statement I made then concerning the objectives for internal social reorganization then afoot, plans and programs, it may be pointed out, which claimed the attention not only of progressive individuals but of political parties. Unfortunately, I need make no apology for quoting from an article written nearly twenty years ago. The evils existing then still exist now, the things needing to be done then still need to be done now.

"The first of the deficiencies which will have to be

* Written specially for this volume.—Ed.
† "The former objective" is the subject of Chapter Nine.—Ed.

cared for in any effective reorganization which may take place after the war is the failure of our social order in the past to secure to its members steady and useful employment. It would be difficult to bring any more severe indictment against anything that calls itself a civilization, than the fact that it is not able to utilize the energy, physical, intellectual and moral, of the members who are desirous and anxious of rendering some kind of service, of producing some kind of needed and useful commodity; that it has not been able systematically to give all of its members a chance to do something. The evil, and the unnecessary character of the evil of unemployment is, then, the thing which I would put first, because it represents, in anything that professes to be civilization, the most obvious and definite point of weakness.

"Now, this is serious, not merely from the standpoint of the enormous poverty and misery which insecure and precarious employment entails upon a large part of the population, but, if possible, even more serious because of the undermining of morale, of character, which comes with such a situation as this. We all know how demoralizing charity is. Every society of organized charity is teaching and constantly preaching the evils of indiscriminate charity, how it destroys the character of those who become its recipients. Cannot we generalize this lesson and apply it to the whole industrial situation? What is the effect upon the self-respect of the large classes of men and women who periodically, once in so often, find themselves in large numbers thrown out of employment, and find that they have to beg, not for charity, but for even a chance to do work in turning out commodities or in rendering services which society actually needs? The undermining of confidence in oneself, of respect for oneself, the undermining of faith or belief in the world and in others that comes be-

cause of precarious and insecure tenure of employment is
I think impossible to overestimate. When people find that
they cannot do things that they are capable of doing, the
attitude that comes toward the world is either one of impotence and enfeeblement, or else one of bitterness and
hostility. Now, these things are, perhaps, sufficiently obvious. They are not new. There was plenty of discussion
of the problem of unemployment and the remedies for it,
before the war, but the war in its conduct has made the
consciousness of it more acute and more general, and it
has shown that the problem is not inevitable, that it is capable of human administration and handling. It has
proved that it is possible for men, pooling and organizing
their intelligence and experience, and having the authority
of the government behind them, to take hold of the industrial and economic processes and see to it, even in a period of such great stress as during the war, that no man
or woman who is capable of work shall lack useful,
steady, and reasonably remunerative employment.

"The second evil is the degraded and inhuman standard, or scale, of living which is found on the part of so
many of the industrial population—of course, partly as a
consequence of chronic employment or, at least, insecure
employment, but partly because of the low rate of return
for employment. We are accustomed, of course, to connect low wages and lack of work with poverty and suffering, but we too often fail to translate poverty and the
misery that goes with it into terms of the general vitia-
tion, the general deterioration of the scale of life on the
part of a large element of the population. We fail to note
what an unhuman lowering it means of the standard of
physical health—though here again was a point that was
being agitated more and more, even before the war, involving a consideration of the question of the socially un-

necessary deaths, illnesses, accidents and incapacitations that come from the bad economic conditions under which so much of modern industry is carried on. We need only to think of the conditions under which masses of our populations live, not merely in the slums, but wherever there is a congested industrial population, to realize how low, as compared with the attained standards of the well-to-do element of the population their plane of living really is.

"In the third place, the war has revealed the serious weaknesses and defects which exist with respect to efficiency of production and distribution. Now, this is the particular phase of the matter upon which our existing old social order most prided itself. It might have admitted that it had not done so well with the human side of the problem, but it has been contended that, so far as efficiency in the invention, organization and utilization of the machinery of production and distribution is concerned, the present age is almost infinitely in advance of any that has preceded. Of course, in a certain sense, as compared with older civilizations—those that came before the great industrial revolution—this is true enough; for these mechanical inventions are, of course, the product of scientific discovery. They are the product of the release of men's minds in the study of nature and the mystery of natural forces. It is a great mistake to suppose that our mechanical inventions of machines and implements—the steam engine, the telegraph, the telephone, the motor car, and the other agencies of production and distribution—are the actual fruit of the present industrial order. On the contrary, they are the fruit of the discoveries of a comparatively small number of scientific men who have not labored for recognition and who have never got it, very much —at least, in the way of pecuniary recognition. It simply happened that conditions were such that the men of means, men possessed of the financial and pecuniary resources, could utilize these fruits of natural science.

"Furthermore, efficiency is not an absolute thing; but, of course, as every engineer tells us, it is a matter of ratio. Efficiency is a matter of the ratio which the actual output bears to the available resources; and looked at from that standpoint, not in comparison with the output of past ages, but as a matter of ratio which exists now between the present output and the resources now available, we cannot pride ourselves on having attained any great amount of even industrial efficiency in production. I need hardly remind you of the fact that when greater efficiency was required in England and in this country, the government had to take charge of the distributing agencies, the railroads. I need not remind you of the breakdown in the production and distribution of coal, from which we suffered; and however much or however little the blame for that is to be laid at the doors of any particular individuals, the real difficulty, of course, goes much further back. It goes back to the fact that we have had production and distribution organized on a non-social basis—a basis of pecuniary profit. And when they suddenly had to be switched over to the basis of public need and public service, they naturally broke down. The great inefficiency here is, however, the failure to utilize human power. The great advance has, of course, been in the utilizing of natural power—steam and electricity, the machines, implements, and so on; but we have not succeeded in engaging, enlisting and releasing available human energy.

"The first great demand of a better social order, I should say, then, is the guarantee of the right, to every individual who is capable of it, to work—not the mere legal right, but a right which is enforceable so that the individual will always have the opportunity to engage in some form of useful activity; and if the ordinary economic machinery breaks down through a crisis of some sort, then it is the duty of the state to come to the rescue and see that individuals have something to do that is worth while—not breaking stone in a stone yard, or something else to get a soup ticket with, but some kind of productive work which a self-respecting person may engage in with interest and with more than mere pecuniary profit. Whatever may be said about the fortunes of what has technically been called socialism, it would seem to be simply the part of ordinary common sense that society should reorganize itself to make sure that individuals can make a living and be kept going, not by charity, but by having productive work to do.

"In the second place, war has revealed the *possibilities* of intelligent administration—administration which *could* be used to raise and maintain on a higher level the general standard and scale of living. The minimum wage is not one of the visions of the nations that have been longer in the war than we have; it is not, with them, a dream, an uplift notion: it is an accomplished fact. Great Britain is already spending an immense amount of money for the housing of its laborers, and, as we have found out in connection with our shipping program, we cannot do what we have got to do, unless we first see to it that there are decent, comfortable and sanitary housing facilities for the population. One of the demands which has already been made in England, which would help, also, to take care of the unemployment problem after the war, is that this great work of housing, conducted under national social auspices, shall go on until the slums, with their bad sanitary, moral, and bad esthetic influence, have disappeared and every individual has a home to live in and surroundings to live in which observe the ordinary amenities of human life. The movements for insurance against accident, insurance against illness, insurance against the contingencies of old age, which were already active before the war, have also, of course, been given a tremendous acceleration.

"The third phase that I mention is the need of securing greater industrial autonomy, that is to say, greater ability on the part of the workers in any particular trade or occupation to control that industry, instead of working under these conditions of external control where they have no interest, no insight into what they are doing, and no social outlook upon the consequences and meaning of what they are doing. This means an increasing share given to the laborer, to the wage earner, in controlling the conditions of his own activity. It is so common to point out the absurdity of conducting a war for political democracy which leaves industrial and economic autocracy practically untouched, that I think we are absolutely bound to see, after the war, either a period of very great unrest, disorder, drifting, strife—I would not say actual civil war, but all kinds of irregular strife and disorder, or a movement to install the principle of self-government within industries.

"These three things, then, seem to me the essential minimum elements of an intelligent program of social reorganization."

The idea of reconstruction was at the time the foregoing was written something to conjure with. In retrospect, we may come to the conclusion, widely prevalent today, that the whole idea of social reorganization was an illusion bred of the excited state of mind of the war. If that idea seems an illusion today, it is because we failed to *learn* the lesson, which could be truly learned only by carrying it out into practice. If we fail to learn the lessons of the present day—in fundamental respects identical with those of twenty years ago—then we may be sure that twenty years hence our present most ardent hopes and inspired programs will also be dismissed as illusions.

To quote again:

"Now, in such a situation as this, we are not, I think, entitled to unthinking optimism about the certainty of great progress or about the particular direction which social reorganization will take after the war. There is going to be, of course, a very great demand and a very great pressure, especially from the side of labor, but there will also be a very great inertia, very great obstacles and difficulties to contend with. We are not entitled to assume that automatically there is going to be a desirable reorganization and reconstruction after the war. We may, possibly—it is conceivable—go through a long period of social drifting and social unrest. The question is whether society, because of the experience of the war, will learn to utilize the intelligence, the insight and foresight which are available, in order to take hold of the problem and to go at it, step by step, on the basis of an intelligent program —a program which is not too rigid, which is not a program in the sense of having every item definitely scheduled in advance, but which represents an outlook upon the future of the things which most immediately require doing, trusting to the experience which is got in doing them to reveal the next things needed and the next steps to be taken. Now, the one great thing that the war has accomplished, it seems to me, of a permanent sort, is the enforcement of a psychological and educational lesson. Before the war, most persons would have said, who recognized these evils: Well, they are very great. We all recognize them. We deplore them, but the whole situation is so big and so complicated that it is not possible to do any·

thing about it. We have got to wait for the slow process of evolution. We have got to wait for the working out of unconscious, natural law to accomplish anything serious and important in the way of reorganization. Well, I think the war has absolutely put an end to the right to the claim of anybody to say things of that sort. It is proved now that it is possible for human beings to take hold of human affairs and manage them, to see an end which has to be gained, a purpose which must be fulfilled, and deliberately and intelligently to go to work to organize the means, the resources and the methods of accomplishing those results.

"It seems to me that we cannot in any good conscience return, after the war, to the old period of drifting, so-called evolution, as a necessary method of procedure. The real question with us will be one of effectively discerning whether intelligent men of the community really want to bring about a better reorganized social order. If the desire, the will and the purpose are strong enough, it has been demonstrated that, under conditions of very great strain— abnormal strain and pressure—human beings can get together coöperatively and bring their physical resources and their intellectual resources to bear upon the problem of managing society, instead of letting society drift along more or less at the mercy of accident."*

Events after the war in this country seemed to give the lie to the hopes then entertained. "Return to Normalcy" was not only the slogan but the practice—"normalcy" meaning the old social-economic regime. Attempts at radical social change were defeated in Europe in every country save Russia. Italy and Germany moved into Fascist dictatorships and other European and South American

* All quotations from an article entitled "Internal Social Reorganization After the War," first printed in the *Journal of Race Development*, April 1918; reprinted in *Characters and Events*, vol. II pp. 745 ff.

countries in that direction. Social reorganization did take place but in a direction opposite to that of the hopes entertained by liberals and radicals in the earlier period. Nevertheless, the forecast of "serious internal disorder and unrest" has been fulfilled.

After the world depression of 1929, the earlier idea of reconstruction revived, not under that name but, in this country, under the slogan of the New Deal. It has become increasingly evident that the conditions which caused the World War remain in full force, intensified indeed by the growth of exacerbated Nationalism—which is the direction in which "internal social reorganization" has in fact mainly moved. Failure of the world communities to "meet and forestall" needed change with "sympathy and intelligence" has left us with the old problems unsolved and new ones added.

The change is not, however, a matter of mere addition. Re-grouping of forces has crystallized forces which were more or less in solution and has given a new face, theoretically and practically, to the whole set of social problems that is involved. The urgent and central question at the present time is whether the needed economic-social changes (with which legal and political changes are bound up) can be effected in ways which preserve and develop what was fundamental in earlier liberalism, or whether social control is to be instituted by means of coercive governmental control from above in ways which destroy for a time (a time whose length cannot now be measured) all that was best worth conserving in older democratic ideas and ideals: intellectual and moral freedom; freedom of inquiry and expression; freedom of association in work, recreation and for religious purposes; the freedom of intercourse among nations which, always hampered by tariff-walls and fear of war, is now deliberately suppressed in many countries by a multitude of new technical devices.

This new face of the problem is far from being exhibited solely in Fascist nations, although in them the suppression of liberties of thought, expression and teaching; the dissolution of voluntary groupings, such as trade unions; the threat to voluntary association for worship; and the prevention of free intercourse with other nations have their most marked expression. Nor is the problem confined to the one country in which reconstruction in the line of collectivist control during the early period after the World War made the most headway; for, contrary to the earlier belief in the "withering away of the State," governmental restriction of the essential liberties for which democracy stood has reached, through control of thought, expression, propaganda and direct coercion, a point in which there is little difference discernible between the U.S.S.R. and Fascist countries.

The fundamental problem is also acute in the countries that remain democratic in form and that so far have maintained, though with many violations, the ancient democratic liberties of free inquiry, free assembly, and freedom of voluntary association. For in these countries we have to a very large extent a continuation of the older policy of social drifting plus an amount of social tinkering accompanied by social unrest and uncertainty. Experience has proved that this policy is attended by economic collapse and breakdowns of ever increasing severity. As long as the alternatives set before us are rigid governmental control on the one hand, whether of the Fascist or the Russian type, and "democracy" of the drifting type on the other hand, the question to which I referred in the article quoted, "whether society will learn to utilize the intelligence, the insight and foresight which are available to go at the problem" of economic-social readjustment remains and is even more urgent today in this country than it was when the words were first written.

How much progress has been made in the intervening years? How does the situation now stand? We have a recognition which did not exist before of social responsibility for the care of the unemployed whose resources are exhausted in consequence of unemployment. But at best, the method we employ is palliative: it comes after the event. The positive problem of instituting a social-economic order in which all those capable of productive work will do the work for which they are fitted remains practically untouched. As a result, the conduct of relief and charitable care is almost never at what was termed "at the best." The personal deterioration that results from enforced idleness is a coercion which excludes the idle from the factors that contribute most effectively to decent self-respect and to personal development. While the mass of unemployed have met the situation with patience and even dignity, there can be no question that the corroding influence of living without work, upon the charity of others, private and public, is operating. In the long run, it would be difficult to find anything more destructive of the best elements of human nature than a continued prospect of living, at least of subsisting, in more or less parasitical dependence upon charity, even if it is public.

In saying these things, I am expressing no sympathy for those who complain about the growing amount of money spent upon taking care of those thrown out of productive work and the consequent increase in taxation. Much less am I expressing sympathy with the reckless charges brought against the unemployed of loving idleness and wishing to live at the expense of society. Such complaints and charges are the product of refusal to look at the causes which produce the situation and of desire to find an alibi for their refusal to do anything to remove the causes—causes which are inherent in the existing social-economic regime. The problem of establishing social conditions which will make it possible for all who are capable to do socially productive work is not an easy one. I am not engaging in criticism because it has not been solved. I am pointing out that the problem is not even being thought much about, not to speak of being systematically faced. The reason for the great refusal is clear. To face it would involve the problem of remaking a profit system into a system conducted not just, as is sometimes said, in the interest of consumption, important as that is, but also in the interest of positive and enduring opportunity for productive and creative activity and all that that signifies for the development of the potentialities of human nature.

What gain has been made in the matter of establishing conditions that give the mass of workers not only what is called "security" but also constructive interest in the work they do? What gain has been made in giving individuals, the great mass of individuals, an opportunity to find themselves and then to educate themselves for what they can best do in work which is socially useful and such as to give free play in development of themselves? The managers of industries here and there have learned that it pays to have conditions such that those who are employed know enough about what they are doing so as to take an interest in it. Educators here and there are awake to the need of discovering vocational and occupational abilities and to the need of readjusting the school system to build upon what is discovered. But the basic trouble is not the scantiness of efforts in these directions, serious as is their paucity. It is again that the whole existing industrial system tends to nullify in large measure the effects of these efforts even when they are made. The problem of the adjustment of

individual capacities and their development to actual occupations is not a one-sided or unilateral one. It is bilateral and reciprocal. It is a matter of the state of existing
occupations, of the whole set-up of productive work, of
the structure of the industrial system. Even if there were
a much more widespread and searching concern with the
capacities of individuals and much more preparation of
them along the lines of their inherent fitness and needs
than now exists, what assurance is there in the existing
system that there will be opportunity to use their gifts
and the education they have obtained? As far as the mass
is concerned, we are now putting the social cart before the
social horse.

If we take the question of production, what do we find?
I pass by the basic fact that real production is completed
only through distribution and consumption, so that mere
improvement in the mechanical means of mass production
may, and does, intensify the problem instead of solving it.
I pass it over here because recurring crises and depres-
sions, with the paradox of want amid plenty, has forced
the fact upon the attention of every thoughtful person.
The outcome is sufficient proof that the problem of production cannot be solved in isolation from distribution
and consumption. I want here to call attention rather to
the fact that the present method of dealing with the problem is *restriction* of productive capacity. For scarcity of
materials and surplus of those who want to work is the
ideal situation for profit on the part of those situated to
take advantage of it. *Restriction of production* at the very
time when *expansion* of production is most needed has
long been the rule of *industrialists*. Now the Government
is adopting the same policy for agriculturalists. Those
who practice restriction of production in their own businesses cry out loudly when the Government, following

their example, intervenes to kill pigs, plow under cotton, and reduce the crop of cereals, and does it, moreover, when there is the most urgent need for food. Here again, as in the case of public relief, critics prefer to complain about symptoms rather than to face the cause: The inherent exigencies of the existing social-economic system. Anyone can wax eloquent about the high social function of those who farm, mine and quarry, providing the raw materials not only of food, clothing and shelter but also of all later forms of production of both capital and consumer goods. Anyone can wax pathetic over the plight of agriculture. But under present conditions, the former course is to put the burden of carrying society upon the class now least competent to bear it, and the latter course is to engage in idle sentiment.

The ultimate problem of production is the production of human beings. To this end, the production of goods is intermediate and auxiliary. It is by this standard that the present system stands condemned. "Security" is a means, and although an indispensable social means, it is not the end. Machinery and technological improvement are means, but again are not the end. Discovery of individual needs and capacities is a means to the end, but only a means. The means have to be implemented by a social-economic system that establishes and uses the means for the production of free human beings associating with one another on terms of equality. Then and then only will these means be an integral part of the end, not frustrated and self-defeating, bringing new evils and generating new problems.

The problem today remains one of using available intelligence, of employing the immense resources science has put at our disposal: a pooled and coördinated social intelligence, not the mere scattered individualized intelli-

gences of persons here and there, however high their
I.Q.'s may be. Mere individual intellectual capacities are
as ineffective as are mere personal good intentions. The existence of social objective intelligence brings us back to
the point where we started. Social control effected through
organized application of social intelligence is the sole form
of social control that can and will get rid of existing evils
without landing us finally in some form of coercive control
from above and outside.

A great tragedy of the present situation may turn out
to be that those most conscious of present evils and of the
need of thorough-going change in the social-economic system will trust to some short-cut way out, like the method
of civil war and violence. Instead of relying upon the constant application of all socially available resources of
knowledge and continuous inquiry they may rely upon the
frozen intelligence of some past thinker, sect and party
cult: frozen because arrested into a dogma.

That "intelligence," when frozen in dogmatic social
philosophies, themselves the fruit of arrested philosophies
of history, generates a vicious circle of blind oscillation is
tragically exemplified in the present state of the world.
What *claims* to be social planning is now found in Communist and Fascist countries. The *social* consequence is
complete suppression of freedom of inquiry, communication and voluntary association, by means of a combination
of personal violence, culminating in extirpation, and systematic partisan propaganda. The results are such that in
the minds of many persons the very idea of social planning
and of violation of the integrity of the individual are becoming intimately bound together. But an immense difference divides the *planned* society from a *continuously planning* society. The former requires fixed blueprints imposed

from above and therefore involving reliance upon physical and psychological force to secure conformity to them. The latter means the release of intelligence through the widest form of coöperative give-and-take. The attempt to *plan* social organization and association without the freest possible play of intelligence contradicts the very idea in *social* plann*ing*. For the latter is an operative method of activity, not a predetermined set of final "truths."

When social "planning" is predicated on a set of *"final"* truths, the social end is fixed once for all, and the "end" is then used to justify whatever means are deemed necessary to attain it. "Planning" then takes place only with respect to means of the latter sort, not with respect to ends, so that planning with respect to even means is constrained and coercive. The social result is that the means used have quite other consequences than the end originally set up in idea and afterwards progressively reduced to mere words. As the events of the past twenty years have shown, the seizure of political power by force signifies the continued maintenance of power by force with its continued suppression of the most precious freedoms of the individual spirit. Maintenance of power in order to use force becomes the actual end. Means used determine the end actually reached. The end justifies the means only when the means used are such as actually bring about the desired and desirable end.

Only when reflection upon means and choice of ends are free can there be actual social planning. Every arrest of intelligence (and every form of social dogma is an arrest) obstructs and finally suppresses free consideration and choice of means. The method of social intelligence is primarily concerned with free determination of means to be employed. Until that method of social action is adopted we shall remain in a period of drift and unrest whose final outcome is likely to be force and counterforce, with temporary victory to the side possessed of the most machine guns.

CHAPTER SEVEN

INTELLIGENCE IN SOCIAL ACTION

I·Classes, Groups and Masses*

THERE can be no conflict between *the* individual and *the* social. For both of these terms refer to pure abstractions. What do exist are conflicts between *some* individuals and *some* arrangements in social life; between groups and classes of individuals; between nations and races; between old traditions imbedded in institutions and new ways of thinking and acting which spring from those few individuals who depart from and who attack what is socially accepted. There is also a genuine difference of convictions as to the way in which, at any given time, these conflicts should be met and managed. There are reasons for holding that they are best settled by private and voluntary action and also for holding that they are best settled by means of combined organized action. No general theory about the individual and the social can settle conflicts or even point out the way in which they should be resolved.

But conflicts nevertheless do exist; they are not got rid of by asserting, what is perfectly true, that there can be no wholesale opposition between society and individuals. How are they to be explained, and to what general kinds can they be reduced? In the first place, there is no single thing denominated "society"; there are many societies,

* From *Ethics*, Dewey and Tufts (revised edition), pp. 358-363.

many forms of association. These different groups and classes struggle in many ways against one another and have very diverse values. Men associate in friendship and in antagonism; for recreation and for crime; they unite in clubs and fraternities, in cliques and sects, in churches and armies; to promote science and art and to prey upon others; they unite in business partnerships and corporations. Then these social units compete vigorously against one another. They unite in nations and the nations war with one another; workers combine in trade unions and employers in trade associations and association intensifies struggle between opposite interests. Political life is carried on by parties which oppose each other, and within each party there are contending factions or "wings." Struggle within an organization is indeed a common phenomenon; in trade unions the central organization and the local units often pull different ways, just as in politics there is usually a struggle between forces making for centralization and for local autonomy. Economically, individuals form into groups, and the union accentuates struggle between producer, distributor, and consumer. Church has vied with State for supremacy; the scientific group has at times had to contend with both. Different groups try to get hold of the machinery of government. Officials tend to combine to protect their special interests and these interests are contrary to those of private individuals; it is a recurrent phenomenon for rulers to use power to oppress and harass their subjects. Indeed, so common is it that the whole struggle for political liberty has been represented as a struggle of subjects to emancipate themselves from the tyranny of rulers.

There are then a multitude of conflicts not between individuals and society but between groups and other groups, between some individuals and other individuals.

Analysis shows that they tend to fall into classes marked by similar traits, and these traits help explain why there arose the idea that the conflict is between individual and society.

1. There is the struggle between the *dominant* group and the group or groups, occupying, at the time, an *inferior* position of power and economic wealth. The superior group under such circumstances always thinks of itself as representing the social interest, and represents other groups which challenge its power as rebels against constituted authority, as seeking for the satisfaction of their personal appetites against the demands of law and order. A somewhat striking example of this phase of the matter is seen at the present time in the split between those who hold up the political state as the supreme social form, the culminating manifestation of the supreme common moral will, the ultimate source and sole guarantor of all social values, and those who regard the state as simply one of many forms of association, and as one which by undue extension of its claims into virtual monopoly has brought evils in its train. The conflict is not, as was believed earlier, between the state and individual but between the state as the dominant group and other groups seeking greater liberty of action. It is similar in principle, though often opposite in point of material constituents, to the earlier struggle of political groups to get free from the dominant authority of the church.

2. At a certain stage of such conflicts, the inferior but growing group is not organized; it is loosely knit; its members often do not speak for a group which has achieved recognition, much less for social organization as a whole. The dominant group on the other hand is not only well established, but it is *accepted*, acknowledged; it is supported by the bulk of opinion and sentiment of that

time. A government which at a later period is regarded as thoroughly despotic cannot always have been so regarded. In that case it would have been easily overthrown.

To remain in power a dominant class must at least seem to the mass to represent and to sustain interests which they themselves prize. There is thus added to the conflict of the old and established class with the inferior but developing group, the conflict of values that are generally accepted with those which are coming into being. This for a time takes the form of a struggle between a majority *conserving* the old, and a minority interested in the generation of something new, in *progress*. Since it takes time for an idea to gain recognition and for a value to become appreciated and shared, the new and relatively unorganized, although it may represent a genuinely important social value, is felt to be that of dissenting individuals. The values of a past society which are to be conserved are recognized as social, while those of a future society which has yet to be brought into being are taken to be those of individuals only.

In these two instances, the conflict is commonly thought to be between those interested in order and those concerned in progress, where maintenance of order is interpreted as "social" and the initiation of progress as the function of individuals. Even those whose activity in the end establishes a new social order often feel at the time that the enemy is social organization itself. Moreover, every social order has many defects, and these defects are taken to be signs of evils inhering in every kind of social organization. The latter is felt to be nothing but a system of chains holding individuals in bondage. This feeling grows up particularly when old institutions are decaying and corrupt. As in France in the late eighteenth century and Russia in the late nineteenth, they then call out an intense moral individualism like that of Rousseau and that of Tolstoi respectively. When organization needs to be changed all organization is likely to be felt oppressive. The temporary phenomenon is taken as an illustration of an eternal truth, and the needs of a particular situation frozen into a universal principle.

3. There are also cases in which the troubles of the present are associated with the breakdown of a past order, while existing evils are capable of being remedied only by organized social action. Then the alignment of so-called individual and social is altered, indeed, is virtually reversed. Those who profit by the existing regime and who wish to have it retained are now the "individualists," and those who wish to see great changes brought about by combined action are the "collectivists." These latter feel that institutions as they exist are a repressive shell preventing social growth. They find disintegration, instability, inner competition to be so great that existing society is such only in outward appearance, being in reality what Carlyle called the "society" of his day, namely, "anarchy plus the constable." On the other hand stand those who are at a special advantage in the situation. They extol it as the product of individual energy, initiative, industry, and freedom; these precious qualities will be imperiled by adoption of a plan of conjoint collective activity. They represent the social order desired by others to be one of servility which crushes out the incentives to individual effort, and which creates dependence upon an impersonal whole, putting a vicious paternalism in place of self-reliance. "Collectivism" in their mouths is a term of reproach. In short, those who are on the side of keeping the *status quo* intact are now the "individualists," those who want

great social changes are the "collectivists," since the changes desired are on so large a scale that they can be effected only through collective action.

Consideration of definite conflicts, at particular times and places should be substituted for a general opposition between social and individual. Neither "social" nor "individual," in general, has any fixed meaning. All morality (including immorality) is both individual and social: individual in its immediate inception and execution, in the desires, choices, dispositions from which conduct proceeds; social in its occasions, material, and consequences. That which is regarded as anti-social and immoral at one time is hailed later on as the beginning of great and beneficent social reform—as is seen in the fate of those moral prophets who were condemned as criminals only to be honored later as benefactors of the race. Organizations that were punished as conspiracies by despotic governments have been regarded as the authors of a glorious liberty after their work has succeeded. These facts do not signify that there is no enduring criterion for judgment but that this criterion is to be found in consequences, and not in some general conception of individual and social.

The points just made suggest three angles from which a social problem may be analyzed in detail in order to decide upon the moral values involved. First, the struggle between a dominant class and a rising class or group; secondly, between old and new forms and modes of association and organization; thirdly, between accomplishing results by voluntary private effort, and by organized action involving the use of public agencies. In historic terms, there is the struggle between class and mass; between conservative and liberal (or radical); and between the use of private and public agencies, extension or limitation of public action.

II · The Class Struggle*

We hear a great deal in these days about class conflict. The past history of man is held up to us as almost exclusively a record of struggles between classes, ending in the victory of a class that had been oppressed and the transfer of power to it. It is difficult to avoid reading the past in terms of the contemporary scene. Indeed, fundamentally it is impossible to avoid this course. With a certain proviso, it is highly important that we are compelled to follow this path. For the past as past is gone, save for esthetic enjoyment and refreshment, while the present is with us. Knowledge of the past is significant only as it deepens and extends our understanding of the present. Yet there is a proviso. We must grasp the things that are most important in the present when we turn to the past and not allow ourselves to be misled by secondary phenomena no matter how intense and immediately urgent they are. Viewed from this standpoint, the rise of scientific method and of technology based upon it is the genuinely active force in producing the vast complex of changes the world is now undergoing, not the class struggle whose spirit and method are opposed to science. If we lay hold upon the causal force exercised by this embodiment of intelligence we shall know where to turn for the means of directing further change.

When I say that scientific method and technology have been the active force in producing the revolutionary transformations society is undergoing, I do not imply no other forces have been at work to arrest, deflect and corrupt their operation. Rather this fact is positively implied. At this point, indeed, is located the conflict that underlies the confusions and uncertainties of the present scene. The conflict is between institutions and habits originating in the

* From *Liberalism and Social Action*, pp. 74–85.

pre-scientific and pre-technological age and the new forces generated by science and technology. The application of science, to a considerable degree, even its own growth, has been conditioned by the system to which the name of capitalism is given, a rough designation of a complex of political and legal arrangements centering about a particular mode of economic relations.

The argument drawn from past history that radical change must be effected by means of class struggle, culminating in open war, fails to discriminate between the two forces, one active, the other resistant and deflecting, that have produced the social scene in which we live. The active force is, as I have said, scientific method and technological application. The opposite force is that of older institutions and the habits that have grown up around them. Instead of discrimination between forces and distribution of their consequences, we find the two things lumped together. The compound is labeled the capitalistic or the bourgeois class, and to this class as a class is imputed all the important features of present industrialized society—much as the defenders of the regime of economic liberty exercised for private property are accustomed to attribute every improvement made in the past century and a half to the same capitalistic regime. Thus in orthodox communist literature, from the Communist Manifesto of 1848 to the present day, we are told that the bourgeoisie, the name for a distinctive class, has done this and that. It has, so it is said, given a cosmopolitan character to production and consumption; has destroyed the national basis of industry; has agglomerated population in urban centers; has transferred power from the country to the city, in the process of creating colossal productive force, its chief achievement. In addition, it has created crises of ever renewed intensity; has created imperialism of a new type in frantic effort to control raw materials and markets. Finally, it has created a new class, the proletariat, and has created it as a class having a common interest opposed to that of the bourgeoisie, and is giving an irresistible stimulus to its organization, first as a class and then as a political power. According to the economic version of the Hegelian dialectic, the bourgeois class is thus creating its own complete and polar opposite, and this in time will end the old power and rule. The class struggle of veiled civil war will finally burst into open revolution and the result will be either the common ruin of the contending parties or a revolutionary reconstitution of society at large through a transfer of power from one class to another.

The position thus sketched unites vast sweep with great simplicity. I am concerned with it here only as far as it emphasizes the idea of a struggle between classes, culminating in open and violent warfare as being the method for production of radical social change. For, be it noted, the issue is not whether some amount of violence will accompany the effectuation of radical change of institutions. The question is whether force or intelligence is to be the *method* upon which we consistently rely and to whose promotion we devote our energies. Insistence that the use of violent force is *inevitable* limits the use of available intelligence, for wherever the inevitable reigns intelligence cannot be used. Commitment to inevitability is always the fruit of dogma; intelligence does not pretend to *know* save as a result of experimentation, the opposite of preconceived dogma. Moreover, acceptance in advance of the inevitability of violence tends to produce the use of violence in cases where peaceful methods might otherwise avail. The curious fact is that while it is generally admitted that this and that particular social problem, say of the family, or railroads or banking, must be solved, if at all, by the method of intelligence, yet there is supposed to be some one all-inclusive social problem which can be solved only by the use of violence. This fact would be inexplicable were it not a conclusion from dogma as its premise.

It is frequently asserted that the method of experimental intelligence can be applied to physical facts because physical nature does not present conflicts of class interests, while it is inapplicable to society because the latter is so deeply marked by incompatible interests. It is then assumed that the "experimentalist" is one who has chosen to ignore the uncomfortable fact of conflicting interests. Of course, there *are* conflicting interests; otherwise there would be no social problems. The problem under discussion is precisely *how* conflicting claims are to be settled in the interest of the widest possible contribution to the interests of all—or at least of the great majority. The method of democracy—in so far as it is that of organized intelligence—is to bring these conflicts out into the open where their special claims can be seen and appraised, where they can be discussed and judged in the light of more inclusive interests than are represented by either of them separately. There is, for example, a clash of interests between munition manufacturers and most of the rest of the population. The more the respective claims of the two are publicly and scientifically weighed, the more likely it is that the public interest will be disclosed and be made effective. There is an undoubted objective clash of interests between finance-capitalism that controls the means of production and whose profit is served by maintaining relative scarcity, and idle workers and hungry consumers. But what generates violent strife is failure to bring the conflict into the light of intelligence where the conflicting interests can be adjudicated in behalf of the interest of the great majority. Those most committed to the dogma of inevitable force recognize the need for intelligently discovering and expressing the dominant social interest up to a certain point and then draw back. The "experimentalist" is one who would see to it that the method depended upon by all in some degree in every democratic community be followed through to completion.

In spite of the existence of class conflicts, amounting at times to veiled civil war, any one habituated to the use of the method of science will view with considerable suspicion the transformation of actual human beings into fixed entities called classes, having no overlapping interests and so internally unified and externally separated that they are made the protagonists of history—itself hypothetical. Such an idea of classes is a survival of a rigid logic that once prevailed in the sciences of nature, but that no longer has any place there. This conversion of abstractions into entities smells more of a dialectic of concepts than of a realistic examination of facts, even though it makes more of an emotional appeal to many than do the results of the latter. To say that all past historic social progress has been the result of coöperation and not of conflict would be also an exaggeration. But exaggeration against exaggeration, it is the more reasonable of the two. And it is no exaggeration to say that the measure of civilization is the degree in which the method of coöperative intelligence replaces the method of brute conflict.

It is quite true that what is happening socially is the result of the combination of the two factors, one dynamic, the other relatively static. If we choose to call the combination by the name of capitalism, then it is true, or a truism, that capitalism is the "cause" of all the important social changes that have occurred—an argument that the representatives of capitalism are eager to put forward whenever the increase of productivity is in question. But if we want to *understand,* and not just to paste labels, unfavorable or favorable as the case may be, we shall certainly begin and end with discrimination. Colossal increase in productivity, the bringing of men together in cities and large factories, the elimination of distance, the accumulation of capital, fixed and liquid—these things would have come about, at a certain stage, no matter what the established institutional system given the new means of technological production. For they are the consequences of the latter. Certain other things have happened because of inherited institutions and the habits of belief and character that accompany and support them. If we begin at this point, we shall see that the release of productivity is the product of coöperatively organized intelligence, and shall also see that the institutional framework is precisely that which is not subjected as yet, in any considerable measure, to the impact of inventive and constructive intelligence. That coercion and oppression on a large scale exist, no honest person can deny. But these things are not the product of science and technology but of the perpetuation of old institutions and patterns untouched by scientific method. The inference to be drawn is clear.

The argument, drawn from history, that great social changes have been effected only by violent means, needs considerable qualification, in view of the vast scope of changes that are taking place without the use of violence. But even if it be admitted to hold of the past, the conclusion that violence is the *method* now to be depended upon does not follow—unless one is committed to a dogmatic philosophy of history. The radical who insists that the future method of change must be like that of the past has much in common with the hide-bound reactionary who holds to the past as an ultimate fact. Both overlook the *fact that history in being a process of change generates*

change not only in details but also in the method of di-
recting social change. It is true that the social order is
largely conditioned by the use of coercive force, bursting
at times into open violence. But what is also true is that
mankind now has in its possession a new method, that of
coöperative and experimental science which expresses the
method of intelligence. I should be meeting dogmatism
with dogmatism if I asserted that the existence of this historically new factor completely invalidates all arguments
drawn from the effect of force in the past. But it is within
the bounds of reason to assert that the presence of this
social factor demands that the present situation be analyzed on its own terms, and not be rigidly subsumed
under fixed conceptions drawn from the past.

Any frank discussion of the issue must recognize the
extent to which those who decry the use of any violence
are themselves willing to resort to violence and are ready
to put their will into operation. Their fundamental objection is to change in the economic institution that now
exists, and for its maintenance they resort to the use of
the force that is placed in their hands by this very institution. They do not need to advocate the use of force;
their only need is to employ it. Force, rather than intelligence, is built into the procedures of the existing social
system, regularly as coercion, and in times of crisis, as
overt violence. The legal system, conspicuously in its penal
aspect, more subtly in civil practice, rests upon coercion.
Wars are the methods recurrently used in settlement of
disputes between nations.

What we need to realize is that physical force is used, at
least in the form of coercion, in the very set-up of our society. That the competitive system, which was thought of
by early liberals as the means by which the latent abilities
of individuals were to be evoked and directed into socially

useful channels, is now in fact a state of scarcely disguised battle hardly needs to be dwelt upon. That the control of the means of production by the few in legal possession operates as a standing agency of coercion of the many, may need emphasis in statement, but is surely evident to one who is willing to observe and honestly report the existing scene. It is foolish to regard the political state as the only agency now endowed with coercive power. Its exercise of this power is pale in contrast with that exercised by concentrated and organized property interests.

It is not pleasant to face the extent to which, as a matter of fact, coercive and violent force is relied upon in the present social system as a means of social control. It is much more agreeable to evade the fact. But unless the fact is acknowledged as a fact in its full depth and breadth, the meaning of dependence upon intelligence as the alternative method of social direction will not be grasped. Failure in acknowledgment signifies, among other things, failure to realize that those who propagate the dogma of dependence upon force have the sanction of much that is already entrenched in the existing system. They would but turn the use of it to opposite ends. The assumption that the method of intelligence already rules and that those who urge the use of violence are introducing a new element into the social picture may not be hypocritical but it is unintelligently unaware of what is actually involved in intelligence as an alternative method of social action.

The argument for putting chief dependence upon violence as the method of effecting radical change is usually put in a way that proves altogether too much for its own case. It is said that the dominant economic class has all the agencies of power in its hands, directly—the army, militia and police; indirectly—the courts, schools, press and radio. I shall not stop to analyze this statement. But if one admits it to be valid, the conclusion to be drawn is surely the folly of resorting to a use of force against force that is so well intrenched. The positive conclusion that emerges is that conditions that would promise success in the case of use of force are such as to make possible great change without any great recourse to such a method.

The final argument in behalf of the use of intelligence is that as are the means used so are the actual ends achieved —that is, the consequences. I know of no greater fallacy than the claim of those who hold to the dogma of the necessity of brute force that this use will be the method of calling genuine democracy into existence—of which they profess themselves the simon-pure adherents. It requires an unusually credulous faith in the Hegelian dialectic of opposites to think that all of a sudden the use of force by a class will be transmuted into a democratic classless society. Force breeds counterforce; the Newtonian law of action and reaction still holds in physics, and violence is physical. To profess democracy as an ultimate ideal and the suppression of democracy as a means to the ideal may be possible in a country that has never known even rudimentary democracy, but when professed in a country that has anything of a genuine democratic spirit in its traditions, it signifies desire for possession and retention of power by a class, whether that class be called Fascist or Proletarian.

III · The Meaning and Office of Liberalism*

Since the legal institutions and the patterns of mind characteristic of ages of civilization still endure, there exists the conflict that brings confusion into every phase of present life. The problem of bringing into being a new social orientation and organization is, when reduced to

* From *Liberalism and Social Action,* pp. 76; 47-50; 88-90; 62.

its ultimates, the problem of using the new resources of production, made possible by the advance of physical science, for social ends, for what Bentham called the greatest good of the greatest number. Institutional relationships fixed in the pre-scientific age stand in the way of accomplishing this great transformation. Lag in mental and moral patterns provides the bulwark of the older institutions; in expressing the past they still express present beliefs, outlooks and purposes. Here is the place where the problem of liberalism centers today.

Humanly speaking, the crisis in liberalism was a product of particular historical events. Soon after liberal tenets were formulated as eternal truths, it became an instrument of vested interests in opposition to further social change, a ritual of lip-service, or else was shattered by new forces that came in. Nevertheless, the ideas of liberty, of individuality and of freed intelligence have an enduring value, a value never more needed than now. It is the business of liberalism to state these values in ways, intellectual and practical, that are relevant to present needs and forces. If we employ the conception of historic relativity, nothing is clearer than that the conception of liberty is always relative to forces that at a given time and place are increasingly felt to be oppressive. Liberty in the concrete signifies release from the impact of *particular* oppressive forces; emancipation from something once taken as a normal part of human life but now experienced as bondage. At one time, liberty signified liberation from chattel slavery; at another time, release of a class from serfdom. During the late seventeenth and early eighteenth centuries it meant liberation from despotic dynastic rule. A century later it meant release of industrialists from inherited legal customs that hampered the rise of new forces of production. Today, it signifies liberation from material insecurity and from the coercions and repressions that prevent multitudes from participation in the vast cultural resources that are at hand. The direct impact of liberty always has to do with some class or group that is suffering in a special way from some form of constraint exercised by the distribution of powers that exists in contemporary society. Should a classless society ever come into being the formal *concept* of liberty would lose its significance, because the *fact* for which it stands would have become an integral part of the established relations of human beings to one another.

Until such a time arrives liberalism will continue to have a necessary social office to perform. Its task is the mediation of social transitions. This phrase may seem to some to be a virtual admission that liberalism is a colorless "middle of the road" doctrine. Not so, even though liberalism has sometimes taken that form in practice. We are always dependent upon the experience that has accumulated in the past and yet there are always new forces coming in, new needs arising, that demand, if the new forces are to operate and the new needs to be satisfied, a reconstruction of the patterns of old experience. The old and the new have forever to be integrated with each other, so that the values of old experience may become the servants and instruments of new desires and aims. We are always possessed by habits and customs, and this fact signifies that we are always influenced by the inertia and the momentum of forces temporally outgrown but nevertheless still present with us as a part of our being. Human life gets set in patterns, institutional and moral. But change is also with us and demands the constant remaking of old habits and old ways of thinking, desiring and acting. The effective ratio between the old and the stabilizing and the new and disturbing is very different at different times. Sometimes whole communities seem to be dominated by custom, and changes are produced only by irruptions and invasions from outside. Sometimes, as at present, change is so varied and accelerated that customs seem to be dissolving before our very eyes. But be the ratio little or great, there is always an adjustment to be made, and as soon as the need for it becomes conscious, liberalism has a function and a meaning. It is not that liberalism creates the need, but that the necessity for adjustment defines the office of liberalism.

For the only adjustment that does not have to be made over again, and perhaps even under more unfavorable circumstances than when it was first attempted, is that effected through intelligence as a method. In its large sense, this remaking of the old through union with the new is precisely what intelligence is. It is conversion of past experience into knowledge and projection of that knowledge in ideas and purposes that anticipate what may come to be in the future and that indicate how to realize what is desired. Every problem that arises, personal or collective, simple or complex, is solved only by selecting material from the store of knowledge amassed in past experience and by bringing into play habits already formed. But the knowledge and the habits have to be modified to meet the new conditions that have arisen. In collective problems, the habits that are involved are traditions and institutions. The standing danger is either that they will be acted upon implicitly, without reconstruction to meet new conditions, or else that there will be an impatient and blind rush forward, directed only by some dogma rigidly adhered to. The office of intelligence in every problem that either a person or a community meets is to effect a working connection between old habits, customs, institutions, beliefs, and new conditions. What I have called the mediating function of liberalism is all one with the work of intelligence. This fact is the root, whether it be consciously realized or not, of the emphasis placed by liberalism upon the role of freed intelligence as the method of directing social action.

The ultimate place of economic organization in human life is to assure the secure basis for an ordered expression of individual capacity and for the satisfaction of the needs of man in non-economic directions. The effort of mankind in connection with material production belongs among interests and activities that are, relatively speaking, routine in character, "routine" being defined as that which, without absorbing attention and energy, provides a constant basis for liberation of the values of life—intellectual, esthetic and social. Every significant religious and moral teacher and prophet has asserted that the material is instrumental to the good life. Nominally at least, this idea is accepted by every civilized community. The transfer of the burden of material production from human muscles and brain to steam, electricity and chemical processes now makes possible the effective actualization of this ideal. Needs, wants and desires are always the moving force in generating creative action. When these wants are compelled by force of conditions to be directed for the most part, among the mass of mankind, into obtaining the means of subsistence, what should be a means becomes perforce an end in itself. Up to the present the new mechanical forces of production, which are the means of emancipation from this state of affairs, have been employed to intensify and exaggerate the reversal of the true relation between means and ends. Humanly speaking, I do not see how it would have been possible to avoid an epoch having this character. But its perpetuation is the cause of the continually growing social chaos and strife. Its termination cannot be effected by preaching to individuals that they should place spiritual ends above material means. It can be brought about by organized social reconstruction that puts the results of the mechanism of abundance at the free disposal of individuals. The actual corrosive "materialism" of our times does not proceed from science. It springs from the notion, sedulously cultivated by the class in power, that the creative capacities of individuals can be evoked and developed only in a struggle for material possessions and material gain. We either should surrender our professed belief in the supremacy of ideal and spiritual values and accommodate our beliefs to the predominant material orientation, or we should through organized endeavor institute the socialized economy of material security and plenty that will release human energy for pursuit of higher values.

Since liberation of the capacities of individuals for free, self-initiated expression is an essential part of the creed of liberalism, liberalism that is sincere must will the means that condition the achieving of its ends. Regimentation of material and mechanical forces is the only way by which the mass of individuals can be released from regimentation and consequent suppression of their cultural possibilities. The eclipse of liberalism is due to the fact that it has not faced the alternatives and adopted the means upon which realization of its professed aims depends. Liberalism can be true to its ideals only as it takes the course that leads to their attainment. The notion that organized social control of economic forces lies outside the historic path of liberalism shows that liberalism is still impeded by remnants of its earlier *laissez faire* phase, with its opposition of society and the individual. The thing which now dampens liberal ardor and paralyzes its efforts is the conception that liberty and development of individuality as ends exclude the use of organized social effort as means.

Earlier liberalism regarded the separate and competing economic action of individuals as the means to social well-being as the end. We must reverse the perspective and see that socialized economy is the means of free individual development as the end.

In short, liberalism must now become radical, meaning by "radical" perception of the necessity of thoroughgoing changes in the set-up of institutions and corresponding activity to bring the changes to pass. For the gulf between what the actual situation makes possible and the actual state itself is so great that it cannot be bridged by piecemeal policies undertaken *ad hoc*. The process of producing the changes will be, in any case, a gradual one. But "reforms" that deal now with this abuse and now with that without having a social goal based upon an inclusive plan, differ entirely from effort at re-forming, in its literal sense, the institutional scheme of things. The liberals of more than a century ago were denounced in their time as subversive radicals, and only when the new economic order was established did they become apologists for the *status quo* or else content with social patchwork. If radicalism be defined as perception of need for radical change, then today any liberalism which is not also radicalism is irrelevant and doomed.

IV · Socializing Intelligence*

Why is it, apart from our tradition of violence, that liberty of expression is tolerated and even lauded when social affairs seem to be going in a quiet fashion, and yet is

* From *Liberalism and Social Action,* pp. 51-53; 65-69; 91-92 and *Individualism Old and New,* pp. 151-157. There are two different views expressed in this section on the practical issue of organization of intellectual workers (one taken from *Individualism,* 1929, and one from *Liberalism,* 1935); hence the exceptional procedure of indicating in the body of the text the specific sources of the passages.—Ed.

so readily destroyed whenever matters grow critical? The general answer, of course, is that at bottom social institutions have habituated us to the use of force in some veiled form. But a part of the answer is found in our ingrained habit of regarding intelligence as an individual possession and its exercise as an individual right. It is false that freedom of inquiry and of expression are not modes of action. They are exceedingly potent modes of action. The reactionary grasps this fact, in practice if not in express idea, more quickly than the liberal, who is too much given to holding that this freedom is innocent of consequences, as well as being a merely individual right. The result is that this liberty is tolerated as long as it does not seem to menace in any way the *status quo* of society. When it does, every effort is put forth to identify the established order with the public good. When this identification is established, it follows that any merely individual right must yield to the general welfare. As long as freedom of thought and speech is claimed as a merely individual right, it will give way, as do other merely personal claims, when it is, or is successfully represented to be, in opposition to the general welfare.

Liberalism has to assume the responsibility for making it clear that intelligence is a social asset and is clothed with a function as public as is its origin, in the concrete, in social coöperation.

Henry George, speaking of ships that ply the ocean with a velocity of five or six hundred miles a day, remarked, "There is nothing whatever to show that the men who today build and navigate and use such ships are one whit superior in any physical or mental quality to their ancestors, whose best vessel was a coracle of wicker and hide. The enormous improvement which these ships show is not an improvement of human nature; it is an improvement of society—it is due to a wider and fuller union of individual efforts in accomplishment of common ends." This single instance, duly pondered, gives a better idea of the nature of intelligence and its social office than would a volume of abstract dissertation. Consider merely two of the factors that enter in and their social consequences. Consider what is involved in the production of steel, from the first use of fire and then the crude smelting of ore, to the processes that now effect the mass production of steel. Consider also the development of the power of guiding ships across trackless wastes from the day when they hugged the shore, steering by visible sun and stars, to the appliances that now enable a sure course to be taken. It would require a heavy tome to describe the advances in science, in mathematics, astronomy, physics, chemistry, that have made these two things possible. The record would be an account of a vast multitude of coöperative efforts, in which one individual uses the results provided for him by a countless number of other individuals, and uses them so as to add to the common and public store. A survey of such facts brings home the actual social character of intelligence as it actually develops and makes its way. Survey of the consequences upon the ways of living of individuals and upon the terms on which men associate together, due to the new method of transportation would take us to the wheat farmer of the prairies, the cattle raiser of the plains, the cotton grower of the South; into a multitude of mills and factories, and to the counting-room of banks, and what would be seen in this country would be repeated in every country of the globe.

It is to such things as these, rather than to abstract and formal psychology that we must go if we would learn the nature of intelligence: in itself, in its origin and development, and its uses and consequences.*

Most attacks on the mechanistic character of science are caused by the survival of philosophies and religions formed when nature was the grim foe of man. The possibility of the present, and therefore its problem, is that through and by science, nature may become the friend and ally of man. I have rarely seen an attack on science as hostile to humanism which did not rest upon a conception of nature formed long before there was any science. That there is much at any time in environing nature which is indifferent and hostile to human values is obvious to any serious mind. When natural knowledge was hardly existent, control of nature was impossible. Without power of control, there was no recourse save to build places of refuge in which man could live in imagination, although not in fact. There is no need to deny the grace and beauty of some of these constructions. But when their imaginary character is once made apparent, it is futile to suppose that men can go on living and sustaining life by them. When they are appealed to for support, the possibilities of the present are not perceived, and its constructive potentialities remain unutilized.

There are those who welcome science provided it remain "pure"; they see that as a pursuit and contemplated object it is an addition to the enjoyed meaning of life. But they feel that its applications in mechanical inventions are the cause of many of the troubles of modern society. Undoubtedly these applications have brought new modes of unloveliness and suffering. I shall not attempt the impossible task of trying to strike a net balance of ills and enjoyments between the days before and after the practical use of science. The significant point is that ap-

* From *Liberalism*.

plication is still restricted. It touches our dealings with things but not with one another. We use scientific method in directing physical but not human energies. Consideration of the full application of science must accordingly be prophetic rather than a record of what has already taken place. Such prophecy is not however without foundation. Even as things are there is a movement in science which foreshadows, if its inherent promise be carried out, a more humane age. For it looks forward to a time when all individuals may share in the discoveries and thoughts of others, to the liberation and enrichment of their own experience.

No scientific inquirer can keep what he finds to himself or turn it to merely private account without losing his scientific standing. Everything discovered belongs to the community of workers. Every new idea and theory has to be submitted to this community for confirmation and test. There is an expanding community of coöperative effort and of truth. It is true enough that these traits are now limited to small groups having a somewhat technical activity. But the existence of such groups reveals a possibility of the present—one of the many possibilities that are a challenge to expansion, and not a ground for retreat and contraction.

Suppose that what now happens in limited circles were extended and generalized. Would the outcome be oppression or emancipation? Inquiry is a challenge, not a passive conformity; application is a means of growth, not of repression. The general adoption of the scientific attitude in human affairs would mean nothing less than a revolutionary change in morals, religion, politics and industry. The fact that we have limited its use so largely to technical matters is not a reproach to science, but to the human beings who use it for private ends and who strive to defeat its social application for fear of destructive effects upon their power and profit. A vision of a day in which the natural sciences and the technologies that flow from them are used as servants of a humane life constitutes the imagination that is relevant to our own time. A humanism that flees from science as an enemy denies the means by which a liberal humanism might become a reality.

The scientific attitude is experimental as well as intrinsically communicative. If it were generally applied, it would liberate us from the heavy burden imposed by dogmas and external standards. Experimental method is something other than the use of blow-pipes, retorts and reagents. It is the foe of every belief that permits habit and wont to dominate invention and discovery, and ready-made system to override verifiable fact. Constant revision is the work of experimental inquiry. By revision of knowledge and ideas, power to effect transformation is given us. This attitude, once incarnated in the individual mind, would find an operative outlet. If dogmas and institutions tremble when a new idea appears, this shiver is nothing to what would happen if the idea were armed with the means for the continuous discovery of new truth and the criticism of old belief. To "acquiesce" in science is dangerous only for those who would maintain affairs in the existing social order unchanged because of lazy habit or self-interest. For the scientific attitude demands faithfulness to whatever is discovered and steadfastness in adhering to new truth.

I am suspicious of all attempts to erect a hierarchy of values: their results generally prove to be inapplicable and abstract. But there is at every time a hierarchy of problems, for there are some issues which underlie and condition others. No one person is going to evolve a constructive solution for the problem of humanizing industrial civilization, of making it and its technology a servant of human life—a problem which is once more equivalent, for us, to that of creating a genuine culture. But general guidance of serious intellectual endeavor by a consciousness of the problem would enable at least one group of individuals to recover a social function and so refind themselves. And recovery by those with special intellectual gifts and equipment from their enforced social defection is at least a first step in a more general reconstruction that will bring integration out of disorder.

I do not hold, I think, an exaggerated opinion of the influence that is wielded by so-called "intellectuals"—philosophers, professional and otherwise, critics, writers and professional persons in general having interests beyond their immediate callings. But their present position is not a measure of their possibilities. For they are now intellectually dispersed and divided; this fact is one aspect of what I have called "the lost individual." This internal dissolution is necessarily accompanied by a weak social efficacy. The chaos is due, more than to anything else, to mental withdrawal, to the failure to face the realities of industrialized society. Whether the ultimate influence of the distinctively intellectual or reflective groups is to be great or small, an initial move is theirs. A consciously directed critical consideration of the state of present society in its causes and consequences is a pre-condition of projection of constructive ideas. To be effective, the movement must be organized. But this requirement does not demand the creation of a formal organization; it does demand that a sense of the need and opportunity should possess a sufficiently large number of minds. If it does, the results of their inquiries will converge to a common issue.*

This point of view is sometimes represented as a virtual appeal to those primarily engaged in inquiry and reflection

* From *Individualism* (1929).—Ed.

to desert their studies, libraries, and laboratories and engage in works of social reform. That representation is a caricature. It is not the abandonment of thinking and inquiry that is asked for, but more thinking and more significant inquiry. This "more" is equivalent to a conscious direction of thought and inquiry, and direction can be had only by a realization of problems in the rank of their urgency. The "clerk" and secretary once occupied, if we may trust history, places of great influence if not of honor. In a society of military and political leaders who were illiterate, they must have done much of the thinking and negotiating for which the names of the great now receive credit. The intellectuals of the present are their descendants. Outwardly they have been emancipated and have an independent position formerly lacking. Whether their actual efficacy has been correspondingly increased may be doubted. In some degree, they have attained their liberty in direct ratio to their distance from the scenes of action. A more intimate connection would not signify, I repeat, a surrender of the business of thought, even speculative thought, for the sake of getting busy at some so-called practical matter. Rather would it signify a focusing of thought and intensifying of its quality by bringing it into relation with issues of stupendous meaning.

That liberals are divided in outlook and endeavor while reactionaries are held together by community of interests and the ties of custom is well-nigh a commonplace. Organization of standpoint and belief among liberals can be achieved only in and by unity of endeavor. Organized unity of action attended by consensus of beliefs will come about in the degree in which social control of economic forces is made the goal of liberal action. The greatest educational power, the greatest force in shaping the dispositions and attitudes of individuals, is the social medium in which they live. The medium that now lies closest to us is that of unified action for the inclusive end of a socialized economy. The attainment of a state of society in which a basis of material security will release the powers of individuals for cultural expression is not the work of a day. But by concentrating upon the task of securing a socialized economy as the ground and medium for release of the impulses and capacities men agree to call ideal, the now scattered and often conflicting activities of liberals can be brought to effective unity.

It is no part of my task to outline in detail a program for renascent liberalism. But the question of "what is to be done" cannot be ignored. Ideas must be organized, and this organization implies an organization of individuals who hold these ideas and whose faith is ready to translate itself into action.* Translation into action signifies that the general creed of liberalism be formulated as a concrete program of action. It is in organization for action that liberals are weak, and without this organization there is danger that democratic ideals may go by default. Democracy has been a fighting faith. When its ideals are re-enforced by those of scientific method and experimental intelligence, it cannot be that it is incapable of evoking discipline, ardor and organization. To narrow the issue for the future to a struggle between Fascism and Communism is to invite a catastrophe that may carry civilization down in the struggle. Vital and courageous democratic liberalism is the one force that can surely avoid such a disastrous narrowing of the issue. I for one do not believe that Americans living in the tradition of Jefferson and Lincoln will weaken and give up without a whole-hearted effort to make democracy a living reality. This, I repeat, involves organization.

* This was written in 1935.—Ed.

Objections that are brought against liberalism ignore the fact that the only alternatives to dependence upon intelligence are either drift and casual improvisation, or the use of coercive force stimulated by unintelligent emotion and fanatical dogmatism—the latter being intolerant by its very constitution. The objection that the method of intelligence has been tried and failed is wholly aside from the point, since the crux of the present situation is that it has not been tried under such conditions as now exist. It has not been tried at any time with use of all the resources that scientific material and the experimental method now put at our disposal.

It is also said that intelligence is cold and that persons are moved to new ways of acting only by emotion, just as habit makes them adhere to old ways. Of course, intelligence does not generate action except as it is enkindled by feeling. But the notion that there is some inherent opposition between emotion and intelligence is a relic of the notion of mind that grew up before the experimental method of science had emerged. For the latter method signifies the union of ideas with action, a union that is intimate; and action generates and supports emotion.

Ideas that are framed to be put into operation for the sake of guiding action are imbued with all the emotional force that attaches to the ends proposed for action, and are accompanied with all the excitement and inspiration that attend the struggle to realize the ends. Since the ends of liberalism are liberty and the opportunity of individuals to secure full realization of their potentialities, all of the emotional intensity that belongs to these ends gathers about the ideas and acts that are necessary to make them real.

Again, it is said that the average citizen is not endowed with the degree of intelligence that the use of it as a method demands. This objection, supported by alleged scientific findings about heredity and by impressive statistics concerning the intelligence quotients of the average citizen, rests wholly upon the old notion that intelligence is a ready-made possession of individuals. The last stand of oligarchical and anti-social seclusion is perpetuation of this purely individualistic notion of intelligence. The reliance of liberalism is not upon the mere abstraction of a native endowment unaffected by social relationships, but upon the fact that native capacity is sufficient to enable the average individual to respond to and to use the knowledge and the skill that are embodied in the social conditions in which he lives, moves and has his being. There are few individuals who have the native capacity that was required to invent the stationary steam-engine, locomotive, dynamo or telephone. But there are none so mean that they cannot intelligently utilize these embodiments of intelligence once they are a part of the organized means of associated living.

The indictments that are drawn against the intelligence of individuals are in truth indictments of a social order that does not permit the average individual to have access to the rich store of the accumulated wealth of mankind in knowledge, ideas and purposes. There does not now exist the kind of social organization that even permits the average human being to share the potentially available social intelligence. Still less is there a social order that has for one of its chief purposes the establishment of conditions that will move the mass of individuals to appropriate and use what is at hand. Back of the appropriation by the few of the material resources of society lies the appropriation by the few in behalf of their own ends of the cultural, the spiritual, resources that are the product not of the individuals who have taken possession but of the coöperative work of humanity. It is useless to talk about the failure of democracy until the source of its failure has been grasped and steps are taken to bring about that type of social organization that will encourage the socialized extension of intelligence.*

Accordingly, I do not wish my remarks about escape and withdrawal to be interpreted as if they were directed at any special group of persons. The flight of particular individuals is symptomatic of the seclusion of existing science, intelligence and art. The personal gap which, generally speaking, isolates the intellectual worker from the wage earner is symbolic and typical of a deep division of functions. This division is the split between theory and practice in actual operation. The effects of the split are as fatal to culture on one side as on the other. It signifies that what we call our culture will continue to be, and in increased measure, a survival of inherited European traditions, and that it will not be indigenous. And if it is true, as some hold, that with the extension of machine technology and industrialism the whole world is becoming "Americanized," then the creation of an indigenous culture is no disservice to the traditional European springs of our spiritual life. It will signify, not ingratitude, but the effort to repay a debt.†

* From *Liberalism*.
† From *Individualism*.

CHAPTER EIGHT

NATIONALISM AND INTERNATIONALISM

I·Nationalism and Its Fruits*

LIKE most things in this world which are effective, even for evil, Nationalism is a tangled mixture of good and bad. And it is not possible to diagnose its undesirable results, much less to consider ways of counteracting them, unless the desirable traits are fully acknowledged. For they furnish the ammunition and the armor which are utilized as means of offense and defense by sinister interests to make Nationalism a power for evil.

Its beneficent qualities are connected with its historical origin. Nationalism was at least a movement away from obnoxious conditions—parochialism on one hand and dynastic despotism on the other. To be interested in a nation is at least better than to restrict one's horizon to the bounds of a parish and province. Historically, Nationalism is also connected with the decay of personal absolutism and dynastic rule. Loyalty to a nation is surely an advance over loyalty to a hereditary family endued in common belief with divine sanctions and covered with sacrosanct robes. Much of the superstitious awe and foolish sentiment has indeed passed over into Nationalism, but nevertheless the people of a country as a whole are surely a better object of devotion than a ruling family. Except where national spirit has grown up, public spirit is practically non-

---

* From *Characters and Events,* pp. 798-803.

existent. In addition to these two historical changes, Nationalism is associated with the revolt of oppressed peoples against external imperial domination. If one wants to see one of the most potent motive forces in creating Nationalism, one has only to consider the Greece of fifty years ago, the Ireland of yesterday and the China and India of today.

It is not to the present purpose to consider these gains; but it is to the point that without them Nationalism could not be perverted to base ends. The passionate loyalties which have been produced by struggle for liberation from foreign yokes, by the sense of unity with others over a stretch of territory wider than the parish and village, by some degree of participation in the government of one's own country, furnish the material which, upon occasion, make the spirit of a nation aggressive, suspicious, envious, fearful, acutely antagonistic. If a nation did not mean something positively valuable to the mass of its citizens, Nationalism could not be exploited as it is in the interest of economic imperialism and of war, latent and overt. Carlton Hayes has convincingly pointed out that Nationalism has become the religion of multitudes, perhaps the most influential religion of the present epoch. This emotion of supreme loyalty to which other loyalties are unhesitatingly sacrificed in a crisis could hardly have grown to its high pitch of ardor unless men thought they had found in it the blessings for which they have always resorted to religious faith: protection of what is deemed of high value, defense against whatever menaces this value, in short an ever-present refuge in time of trouble.

But institutionalized religion is something more than a personal emotion. To say it is institutionalized is to say that it involves a tough body of customs, ingrained habits of action, organized and authorized standards and methods of procedure. The habits which form institutions are so basal that for the most part they lie far below conscious recognition. But they are always ready to shape conduct, and when they are disturbed a violent emotional eruption ensues. Practices, after they are adopted, have to be accounted for and explained to be reasonable and desirable; they have to be justified. Hence, along with the emotions and habits, there develops a creed, a system of ideas, a theology in order to "rationalize" the activities in which men are engaged. Faith in these ideas, or at least in the catchwords which express them, becomes obligatory, necessary for social salvation; disbelief or indifference is heresy. Thus Nationalism starting as an unquestioned emotional loyalty, so supreme as to be religious in quality, has invaded the whole of life. It denotes organized ways of behavior and a whole system of justificatory beliefs and notions appealed to in order to defend every act labeled "national" from criticism or inquiry. By constant reiteration, by shaming heretics and intimidating dissidents, by glowing admiration if not adoration of the faithful, by all agencies of education and propaganda (now, alas, so hard to distinguish) the phrases in which these defenses and appeals are couched become substitutes for thought. They are axiomatic; only a traitor or an evilly disposed man doubts them. In the end, these rationalizations signify a complete abdication of reason. Bias, prejudice, blind and routine habit reign supreme. But they reign under the guise of idealistic standards and noble sentiments.

Any one who reads the laudations of patriotism which issue from one source and the disparagements which proceed from another group must have been struck by the way in which the same word can cover meanings as far apart as the poles. The word is used to signify public spirit as opposed to narrow selfish interests. When so employed patriotism is a synonym for intense loyalty to the good of the community of which one is a member; for willingness to sacrifice, even to the uttermost, in its behalf. So taken, it surely deserves all the eulogies and reverence bestowed upon it. But because of nationalistic religions and its rationalization, the test and mark of public spirit becomes intolerant disregard of all other nations. Patriotism degenerates into a hateful conviction of intrinsic superiority. Another nation by the mere fact that it is other is suspect; it is a potential if not an actual foe. I doubt whether there is one person in a hundred who does not associate a large measure of exclusiveness with patriotism; and all exclusiveness is latent contempt for everything beyond its range. The rabies that exultantly sent Sacco and Vanzetti to death is proof of how deeply such patriotism may canker. It extends not only to foreign nations as such, but to foreigners in our own country who manifest anything but the most uncritical "loyalty" to our institutions. Thousands upon thousands of the most respectable element in the community believed they were exhibiting patriotism to the nation or to Massachusetts when they urged the death of men who were guilty of the double crime of being aliens and contemners of our form of government.

Were it not for facts in evidence it would be hard to conceive that any sane man could parade the motto: "My country right or wrong." But, alas, one cannot doubt that the slogan conveyed the feeling which generally attaches to patriotism. That public spirit, an active interest in whatever promotes the good of one's country, is debased and prostituted to such a use, is chargeable to Nationalism; and this fact stands first in its indictment.

It is a trait of unreasoning emotion to take things in a mass and thereby to create unities which have no existence outside of passion. Men who pride themselves upon being "practical" and "concrete" would be incensed beyond measure if they were told that the nation to which they yield such unquestioning loyalty is an abstraction, a fiction. I do not mean by this statement that there is no such thing as a nation. In the sense of an enduring historic community of traditions and outlook in which the members of a given territory share, it is a reality. But the nation by which millions swear and for which they demand the sacrifice of all other loyalties is a myth; it has no being outside of emotion and fantasy. The notion of National Honor and the role which it plays is a sign of what is meant. Individual persons may be insulted and may feel their honor to be at stake. But the erection of a national territorial State into a Person who has a touchy and testy Honor to be defended and avenged at the cost of death and destruction is as sheer a case of animism as is found in the records of any savage tribe. Yet he would be a thoughtless optimist who is sure that the United States will not sometime wage a war to protect its National Honor.

As things now stand and as they are likely long to remain there is really such a thing as national interest. It is to the interest of a nation that its citizens be protected from pestilence, from unnecessary infection; that they enjoy a reasonable degree of economic comfort and independence; that they be protected from crime, from external invasion, etc. But Nationalism has created a purely fictitious notion of national interests. If a large gold field were located just over the border of Alaska, thousands of American breasts would swell with pride, as thousands would be depressed if it happened to lie in British territory. They would feel as if somehow they were personal gainers, as if the Nation to which they belong had somehow integrally promoted its interests. The illustration is somewhat trivial. But the spirit which it indicates is responsible for the acquiescence, if not the active approval, with which the new Coolidge version of international law with respect to property rights of American citizens in foreign countries has been received. For the gist of his revolutionary edition of international law (if he says what he means and knows what he means) is that any property right or property interest of any private citizen or any corporation in a foreign country (doubtless with the tacit understanding that it is not one of the Great Powers) is a National Interest to be protected when necessary by national force.

The culmination of Nationalism is the doctrine of national sovereignty. Sovereignty was originally strictly personal or at least dynastic. A monarch held supreme power; the country was his proper domain or property. The doctrine is historically explicable as part of the transition out of feudalism and the weakening of the power of feudal nobles in the growth of a centralized kingdom. The doctrine was also bound up with the struggle of State against Church and the assertion of the political independence of the secular ruler from the authority of ecclesiastics. As historians have clearly shown, the doctrine of the divine right of kings originally meant that secular monarchs had at least the same kind of divine commission as had Pope or Archbishop. But with the rise of modern territorial states the idea and attributes of Sovereignty passed over from the ruler to the politically organized aggregate called the Nation.

In so doing, it retained all the evils that inhered in the notion of absolute and irresponsible personal power (or power responsible only to God and not to any earthly power or tribunal) and took on new potencies for harm

For disguise it as one may, the doctrine of national sovereignty is simply the denial on the part of a political state of either legal or moral responsibility. It is a direct proclamation of the unlimited and unquestionable right of a political state to do what it wants to do in respect to other nations and to do it as and when it pleases. It is a doctrine of international anarchy; and as a rule those who are most energetic in condemning anarchy as a domestic and internal principle are foremost in asserting anarchic irresponsibility in relations between nations. Internationalism is a word to which they attach accursed significance, an idea to which by all the great means at their disposal they attach a sinister and baleful significance, ignoring the fact that it but portends that subjection of relations between nations to responsible law which is taken for granted in relations between citizens. The doctrine is not of course carried to its logical extreme in ordinary times; it is mitigated by all sorts of concessions and compromises. But resort to war as the final arbiter of serious disputes between nations, and the glorification of War through identification with patriotism is proof that irresponsible sovereignty is still the basic notion. Hence I spoke in terms of the popular fallacy when I referred to the "right" of a state to do as it pleases when it pleases. For *right* is here only a polite way of saying power. It was usual during the World War to accuse Germany of acting upon the notion that Might makes Right. But every state that cultivates and acts upon the notion of National Sovereignty is guilty of the same crime. And the case is not improved by the fact that the judges of what National Sovereignty requires are not actually the citizens who compose a nation but a group of diplomats and politicians.

Patriotism, National Honor, National Interests and National Sovereignty are the four foundation stones upon which the structure of the National State is erected. It is no wonder that the windows of such a building are closed to the light of heaven; that its inmates are fear, jealousy, suspicion, and that War issues regularly from its portals.

II · Ethics and International Relations*

The situation that exists among nations in their relations to one another is such that it tempts even those who ordinarily come far short of cynicism to say that there is no connection between ethics and international relations. The title is also a temptation to indulge in a drastic attack upon present international relations as inherently immoral. One might make out a case for the proposition that they are ruled by force, fraud and secret intrigue, and that whenever moral considerations come into conflict with national ambitions and nationalistic ideas they go by the board. Or, identifying the moral with that which ought to be, whether it is or not, one might appeal to some ideal of what ought to be and point out the discrepancies that are found between this ideal of what should be and what actually is. The latter method naturally terminates in exhortation, in appeal to the moral consciousness of mankind.

These considerations are not adduced in order to develop them, but to suggest the extraordinary confusion that is found in current moral ideas as they are reflected in the ethics of international relations. I do not intend, then, to discuss international relations from the moral point of view, but rather to discuss the uncertain estate, the almost chaotic condition, of moral conceptions and beliefs as that condition bears upon the international situation. Why is it that men's morals have so little effect in regulating the attitude of nations to one another? Even the most cynical would hesitate to declare that the habits, to say nothing of the ideals, of the average decent man and

* From *Characters and Events*, pp. 804-814.

woman in their ordinary affairs were adequately embodied
in the existing reign of hatred, suspicion, fear and secrecy
in international politics. The truth seems to be rather that
man's morals are paralyzed when it comes to international
conduct; that they are swept away and rendered impotent
by larger forces that go their own way irrespective of the
morals that are employed in everyday matters.

The problems suggested by this state of affairs may be
approached from two angles. We may ask what are the
actual forces that have grown so powerful that they have
escaped from moral control? What are the factors that
prevent moral habits and ideas from operation? This
opens a large and extremely complex field to be attacked
only by coöperative efforts of historians, publicists, lawyers, and economists. There is open, however, a less pre-
tentious method of approach. One may make the inquiry
from the side of moral conceptions and doctrines, and ask
whether they are intellectually competent to meet the
needs of the situation. Some of the trouble may be due to
the lack of coherent and generally accepted moral ideas;
not of ideas in a vague and abstract sense but of ideas sufficiently concrete to be operative. This intellectual factor
may not be in itself very large or powerful, and yet it may
represent a factor that, although small in itself, is an indispensable condition of straightening out objective political and economic forces that are much more energetic
and active.

In such an appraisal the historic conditions under which
the laws applicable to international relations were formulated furnish a natural starting point. There can be no
doubt that the intellectual work of Grotius and his successors had great practical influence. It was not academic
and professorial, nor was it conceived primarily in the interests of the claims and ambitions of some particular

state. These men were genuinely international, and for a time they had great effect in appeasing international strife and moralizing actual international relations. These basic contributions all sprang from a common moral source. They all expressed the idea of laws of nature which are moral laws of universal validity. The conception of laws of nature that are the fundamental moral laws of all human conduct of every kind and at all times and places was not a new one. Roman moralists had worked out the idea in connection with Roman jurisprudence; it was familiar to every civilian and canonist, and indeed to every educated man. The Catholic church had made the notion fundamental to its whole doctrine of secular ethics, that is of all obligations not springing from divine revelation. And even these obligations only expressed a higher and more ultimate nature of things not accessible to man's unaided reason. The Protestant moralists and theologians equally built upon the conception; at most they only put a greater emphasis upon an inner light in the conscience of individuals which revealed and acknowledged the laws of nature as the supreme standards of human behavior.

There was thus a principle and method of morals which was universally recognized throughout Christendom; there was also general agreement as to the contents of the code of obligations defined by the principle. The great achievement of Grotius and his followers consisted in studying existing international customs and in criticizing and organizing them by the help of the commonly accepted standard of laws of nature. More than one living authority in jurisprudence—like Pollock—has pointed out the service rendered by the conception of laws of nature in the development of various branches of law, private as well as public, and in equity practice. They all agree that its use in formulating the rules governing international conduct was its first and most conspicuous service. Now I do not mean to intimate that without responsive factors in the actual political and economic situation the intellectual application of the concept of natural laws to international relations would have exercised the moderating and humane influence which followed upon the labors of the school of Grotius. But it is meant that the general unquestioning and pervasive acknowledgment of the law of nature as the supreme ethical standard enabled the moral sentiments and ideals of Christendom to be concentrated upon problems of international conduct, so that whatever moral ideas *can* accomplish in practical regulation of human behavior *was* effectually accomplished.

During the nineteenth century, the notion of natural law in morals fell largely into discredit and disuse outside the orthodox moralists of the Catholic church. Of recent years there has been an increasing recognition that in principle all that is meant by a law of nature is a moral law to be applied to the criticism and construction of positive law, legislative and judicial. It has been pointed out that either we must surrender the notion that moral principles have anything to do with positive laws, international and municipal, or else admit the idea of natural law in some shape or form. But there is a wide difference between admitting the general notion of moral laws over against custom and positive law, and imputing to the law of nature the character and content which were attributed to it by seventeenth century moralists. While Grotius asserted that the law of nature would still be binding even if there were no revelation and no God as supreme lawgiver and judge, yet in the popular mind and in his mind the idea still had a theological background and a religious force. The laws of nature still represented the purposes of God and his injunctions concerning the ways in which his purposes as governing the life of man were to be realized. The secular science as well as the secular morals of the period only substituted "secondary" causes and laws for the primary and direct action of God.

But as men's minds gradually got away from the habit of connecting secular things with theological and religious matters, primary or secondary, the enormous force of the religious associations and sanctions of the law of nature gradually ceased. And among Protestants at least, even among those in whom religious ideas retained their old force in morality, most men got out of the habit of associating the religious factor in morals with laws of nature and indeed, to a large extent, with law at all. Divine love and desire for man replaced the concept of divine commands, injunctions and prohibitions. Thus in international relations, as elsewhere, the notion of a definite and universal moral norm in the shape of laws of nature weakened and died out. Even when retained, as in some texts, it was in perfunctory deference to tradition rather than as a living intellectual force. But its decay has not been accompanied by the development of any other moral principle of equal generality and equally wide current acceptance. In its stead we have a multiplicity of moral doctrines, more or less opposed to one another, and none of them held with any great assurance except by a small band of ardent partisans.

Moreover, aside from the question of religious reinforcement, other factors have rendered the old concept of natural law uncongenial. It was always associated with the idea of reason as a force or faculty in things as well as a force and faculty in minds. The laws of nature signified that certain rational principles are actually embodied in the nature of man in his connection with the rest of nature. To obey the law of nature was all one with obeying the dictates of reason. And reason was thought of not just as a psychological possession of the individual mind but as the bond of unity in society. Even the physical laws of nature, since they were universal and "governed" particular empirical phenomena, were rational. Animals had laws of reason embodied in their structure and instincts which they followed without knowing them. The superiority of man is simply that he can be aware of the rational principles which physical things and animals unconsciously obey. It is not possible, I think, for any one today to estimate the power added to the concept of laws of nature by their implicit and unquestioned association with reason and with the common ends and interests that hold men together in society.

It is hardly necessary to note the various influences that undermined this association and, in undermining it, weakened also the working influence of moral ideas on custom and law. Even among those who might give a formal allegiance to similar ideas, if they were presented already formulated, the ideas have little vital power. Modern science has familiarized even the man in the street with a radically different notion about laws of nature. In writing these pages I have felt almost bound to use the term "law of nature" instead of the words "natural law," so different are the familiar connotations of the latter term. Natural law in the popular conception is physical rather than rational; it is associated with energies—heat, light, gravitation, electricity—not with rationality. And it would be difficult today to get even a serious hearing in most circles for the idea that reason is what holds men together in society. Economists, sociologists, historians, psychologists have worked together to displace this idea, to make it seem unreal and faded, even when they disagree radically among themselves as to just what is the nature of the social tie. When we ask what has taken the place of the old law of nature, of reason in nature and society, we are confronted with a scene of contention, confusion and uncertainty. Where is the moral idea capable of exercising the crystallizing, concentrating and directing force upon positive law and custom once exercised by the idea of laws of nature? Few of those who insist that it is necessary to revive the concept in order to have a basis of criticism and constructive effort would revive the idea in its older shape. And they are divided when asked what we should put in its place. This division among intellectuals would not be of any great importance were it not that it reflects division, confusion and uncertainty in the popular mind.

Of course there have been many attempts to fill the void created by the gradual disappearance from the practical scene of the idea of laws of nature, and some of the attempts have been successful in forming not only schools of thought but in exerting considerable practical influence upon affairs. From among these schools we may select the utilitarian and what for convenience may be called the Hegelian for special consideration. The utilitarian school cannot be charged with lack of definiteness and assurance of conviction. And no candid student of English legal, political and social reforms of the last century can assert that it lacked great practical influence. Ignoring technical details that are connected mainly with a psychology of feelings and pleasures and pains which has been largely outgrown by the advance of mental inquiry, we may say that the formula of the greatest good for the greatest number, every individual to count as one and only one in the enumeration, has been translated into the conviction that social welfare is the last and the legitimate moral standard. Regard for the general welfare is the proper source of all moral rules and moral obligations. Instead of considering antecedent ready-made laws, we should search social *consequences* to find principles of criticism of positive laws and current customs and of plans for legislation and new social arrangements.

Great as was the efficacy of this idea in domestic affairs, where shall we look to find traces of its influence upon international morality? Even admitting that it presents to us a sound view of the moral standard and the source of moral laws, has it been applied with any effectiveness to the conduct of international affairs? As a moral standard it puts upon an equal footing the happiness of citizens of foreign lands and of the home land. Where has this principle determined an important branch of international law? What has it done, I will not say to prevent war, but to mitigate its horrors? To most people, I suppose, the idea of its general application to international relations would seem as Utopian as the literal application of the teachings of Jesus. It is sometimes said the utilitarianism supplies us with a low and somewhat sordid moral principle. But in this respect, at least, it would seem to be too high, too far above and beyond present attainment.

More concretely, various attempts to show that war in particular and methods relying upon force and intrigue in general do not pay, may be said to represent examples of the attempt to apply the utilitarian theory in international affairs. The demonstration that war does not pay even the nations that win is probably sufficiently convincing to most persons since the Great War. But the demonstration and the conviction do not appear to have much practical influence. It is too rationalistic; it assumes in too exclusive a way that men are governed by considerations of advantage, of profit and loss. Not only critics of utilitarianism but a great utilitarian, John Stuart Mill, criticized the earlier Benthamite version, on the ground that it leaned too heavily on the material interests of man without enough regard for the motives that may, according to one's bias, be termed sentimental, ideal or spiritual. And it might almost be said that the very existence of war with its willingness to sacrifice life and property for a cause is proof of the soundness of the criticism. War is as stupid as you please but it does not *persist* because of wrong calculations of profit, even though wrong estimates of national advantage may sometimes play a part in the minds of statesmen in starting a war.

The reasons for the practical failure of utilitarianism in international morality can be found within the doctrine itself. It is a theory not only of the moral standard but also of the moral motive, namely, concern for the general happiness. Now the utilitarians themselves recognized that after consideration for the standard has shown what should be done, the question remains of linking up the moral end with the motives that will make it prevail in conduct. They listed the motives that may be relied upon: natural sympathy with others; education into social ways of looking at conduct; mutual advantage through industrial interdependence, division of labor and exchange; and the penal sanction—personal suffering when anti-social motives are given sway.

Now it is obvious that under existing conditions these motives have little chance to operate in international affairs. The extent of sympathy is conditioned in the concrete among the mass of persons by habitual contact and familiar association. It may work strongly where these conditions are found and be very weak when there are barriers of language, custom, and political affiliation. Sympathy with one's immediate fellows is easily turned into antipathy to the outsider and stranger. Education is limited also by range of contract and intercourse, and at present the forces that educate into nationalistic patriotism are powerful and those that educate into equal regard and esteem for aliens are weak. The economic motive works both ways. As already stated, war almost undoubtedly entails loss for a nation as a whole; the risk of loss through defeat is great. But there are also profiteers, those who stand to gain for themselves, and there is no guarantee that they will not occupy places of power and influence. Aside from profiteering, the existence of protective tariffs shows how far men are from believing that free exchange is of necessity a mutual advantage.

As for the legal penal sanction, that is manifestly totally lacking, since there is no common political superior that makes laws with penalties attached for violation. In short, all the conditions that made utilitarianism domestically and internally effective are either absent or much enfeebled in international relations. It will be understood that these remarks are no more an attack upon utilitarianism than they are a defense of it. They are made not for the sake of making any assessment of utilitarianism but because they throw light upon the present lack of a coherent body of moral ideas that may be efficaciously applied in international matters. The evidence is the more striking in the case of utilitarian moral beliefs, because although not universally accepted—in fact although bitterly attacked—they were none the less effective within a nation.

The type of moral doctrine that for convenience in having a single name was called Hegelian is in fact much wider than any one school of philosophy. It goes back in its cruder form to Machiavelli and Hobbes. Both of these writers were attacked in their own day and ever since that day as immoralists rather than moralists. But nevertheless they represent a distinct type of moral ideas. Their underlying principle, when we eliminate idiosyncrasies of personality and surroundings, is that institutions having authority, especially that institution we call the state, are a necessary precondition of the morality of individuals. Hence, the social organization has a privileged, indeed, a unique moral position. Being the condition without which morality in the concrete is impossible, it is also above morals in the ordinary sense, in the sense in which private persons and voluntary communities are required to be moral. The idea came into later German philosophy not from Machiavelli and Hobbes direct but by a revival of Greek (especially Aristotelian) political ethics interpreted by the teaching of Spinoza. The latter, living in a period of almost universal war, external and civil, with all its attendant insecurity of existence, immensely deepened the teaching of Hobbes. He taught expressly that the authority of the state is a necessary pre-condition of stability of social and personal life and of any widespread freedom and rationality of life. Even the most rational of beings cannot put his rationality into effect and achieve freedom except as he has the external support as well as the positive assistance of others. Without political power most men will be governed by their passions, and the wisest of men will be constantly at the mercy of his environment and of appetite and passion.

The political condition of Germany, internal and external, after the Napoleonic wars created a situation favorable to the revival of these ideas. It also furnished a situation in which these ideas were important intellectual weapons in regenerating and unifying under the hegemony of Prussia the separate and particularistic states of Germany. These ideas, first taught in the universities, were so congenial to the needs of political Germany that they soon bore practical fruit. If they were not active forces in bringing about the centralization of previously scattered political authority they at least formulated the end and gave it intellectual justification.

It is not necessary to spend much time showing that this type of ethical thought, a type which insisted upon certainty, unity and stability of institutions, as utilitarians insisted upon the spread of general personal happiness, did not and could not favorably affect international morality. Its whole tendency was toward an intellectual glorification of the national state. Struggle between states was a necessary incident of history; more than this, it operated to strengthen and consolidate the authority of institutions. Success in war was objective evidence of a superior social organization, and hence of superior morality. If a single peaceful international order is ever attainable it is only by means of a *Pax Romana;* some one state must become so powerful as to be able to enforce its will upon all other communities.

I do not mean to intimate that these two types of moral doctrine exhaust the ethical conceptions that have developed in the void left by the subsidence of the theory of natural law. There are others of considerable importance. But the career of the two selected types may serve to illustrate our main thesis: one important factor in the present problem of ethics and international relations is found on the side of ethical beliefs themselves in their confused and contending divergencies. The trouble does not reside wholly on the practical side. It is not my intent to propose any set of moral beliefs which might in my opinion remedy this state of affairs. I content myself with pointing out that since we are still in a very early period of anything which may be called the modern world there is no ground for despair as to the future. Every condition of life as it moves toward coherent organization develops its own *ethos,* its own standards and codes. A unified moral code will grow up when social relations are better adjusted. It is trite to say that we live in a time of immense transitions; we do not sufficiently note that ethical confusion always attends such epochs.

III · Force, Violence and Law*

The empirical perplexities which attend the question of the relationship of force and law are many and genuine. The war brings home to us the question not only of the relation of force to international law, but the place of force in the economy of human life and progress. To what extent is organization of force in the multitude of ways required for the successful conduct of modern war a fair test of the work of a social organization? From another angle, the reform of our criminal law and our penal methods compels us to consider the significance of force. Are the Tolstoians right in holding that the state itself sets the great example of violence and furnishes the proof of the evils which result from violence? Or, from the other side, is not the essence of all law coercion? In the industrial domain, direct actionists lead us to inquire whether manifestation of force, threatened and veiled if not overt, is not, after all, the only efficacious method of bringing about any social change which is of serious import. Do not the usual phenomena attending strikes show us that the ordinary legal forms are just a kind of curtain drawn politely over the conflicts of force which alone are decisive? Are our effective legislative enactments anything more than registrations of results of battles previously fought out on the field of human endurance? In many social fields, reformers are now struggling for an extension of governmental activity by way of supervision and regu-

* From *Characters and Events,* pp. 782-789; 634-641.

lation. Does not such action always amount to an effort to extend the exercise of force on the part of some section of society, with a corresponding restriction of the forces employed by others? In spite of the fact that the political thinking of the seventeenth and eighteenth centuries is out of date, were not the thinkers of that period clearer headed than we are in acknowledging that all political questions are simply questions of the extension and restriction of exercise of power on the part of specific groups in the community? Has the recent introduction of an idealistic terminology about moral and common will, about juridical and moral personalities, done anything but muddle our minds about the hard fact that all our social questions at bottom concern the possession and use of force; and the equally hard fact that our political and legal arrangements are but dispositions of force to make more secure the other forms of its daily use?

In taking up the writings of the theorists it is not easy to persuade oneself that they are marked by much consistency. With a few notable exceptions, the doctrine that the state rests upon or is common will seems to turn out but a piece of phraseology to justify the uses actually made of force. Practices of coercion and constraint which would be intolerable if frankly labeled "Force" seem to become laudable when baptized with the name of "Will," although they otherwise remain the same. Or, if this statement is extreme, there seems to be little doubt that the actual capacity of the state to bring force to bear is what has most impressed theorists, and that what they are after is some theoretical principle which will justify the exercise of force; so that in a great many cases such terms as common will, supreme will, supreme moral or juridical personality, are eulogistic phrases resorted to in behalf of such justification. The one thing that clearly stands out is that the use of force is felt to require explanation and sanction. To make force itself the ultimate principle is felt to be all one with proclaiming anarchy and issuing an invitation to men to settle all their difficulties by recourse to fighting it out to see which is the stronger. And yet what every political student is profoundly convinced of, is, I suppose, that at bottom every political struggle is a struggle for control, for power.

Although I have raised large questions, it is not my ambition to answer them. I have but outlined a large stage upon which to move about some quite minor figures. In the first place, something can be done, I think, by clarifying certain of the ideas which enter into the discussion. We may, I think, profitably discriminate the three conceptions of power or energy, coercive force, and violence. Power or energy is either a neutral or an eulogistic term. It denotes effective means of operation; ability or capacity to execute, to realize ends. Granted an end which is worth while, and power or energy becomes a eulogistic term. It means nothing but the sum of conditions available for bringing the desirable end into existence. Any political or legal theory which will have nothing to do with power on the ground that all power is force and all force brutal and non-moral is obviously condemned to a purely sentimental, dreamy morals. It is force by which we excavate subways and build bridges and travel and manufacture; it is force which is utilized in spoken argument or published book. Not to depend upon and utilize force is simply to be without a foothold in the real world.

Energy becomes violence when it defeats or frustrates purpose instead of executing or realizing it. When the dynamite charge blows up human beings instead of rocks, when its outcome is waste instead of production, destruction instead of construction, we call it not energy or power but violence. Coercive force occupies, we may fairly say, a middle place between power as energy and power as violence. To turn to the right as an incident of locomotion is a case of power: of means deployed in behalf of an end. To run amuck in the street is a case of violence. To use energy to make a man observe the rule of the road is a case of coercive force. Immediately, or with respect to his activities, it is a case of violence; indirectly, when it is exercised to assure the means which are needed for the successful realization of ends, it is a case of constructive use of power. Constraint or coercion, in other words, is an incident of a situation under certain conditions—namely, where the means for the realization of an end are not naturally at hand, so that energy has to be spent in order to make some power into a means for the end in hand.

If we formulate the result, we have something of this kind. Law is a statement of the conditions of the organization of energies which, when unorganized, conflict and result in violence—that is, destruction or waste. We cannot substitute reason for force, but force becomes rational when it is an organized factor in an activity instead of operating in an isolated way or on its own hook. For the sake of brevity, I shall refer to the organization of force hereafter as efficiency, but I beg to remind you that the use of the term always implies an actual or potential conflict and resulting waste in the absence of some scheme for distributing the energies involved.

These generalities are, it will be objected, innocuous and meaningless. So they are in the abstract. Let us take the question of the justification of force in a strike. I do not claim, of course, that what has been said tells us whether the use of force is justified or not. But I hold that it suggests the way of finding out in a given case whether it is justifiable or not. It is, in substance, a question of efficiency (including economy) of means in the accomplishing of ends. If the social ends at stake can be more effectively subserved by the existing legal and economic machinery, resort to physical action of a more direct kind has no standing. If, however, they represent an ineffective organization of means for the ends in question, then recourse to extra-legal means may be indicated; provided it really serves the ends in question—a very large qualification be it noted. A recourse to direct force is a supplementation of existent deficient resources in effective energy under some circumstances.

Such a doctrine is doubtless unwelcome. It is easily interpreted so as to give encouragement to resorting to violence and threats of violence in industrial struggles. But there is a very large "if" involved—the "if" of greater relative economy and efficiency. And when so regarded, it at once occurs to mind that experience in the past has shown that it is not usually efficient for parties to be judges in their own cause: that an impartial umpire is an energy saver. It occurs to mind, also, that the existing legal machinery, whatever its defects, represents a contrivance which has been built up at great cost, and that the tendency to ignore its operation upon special provocation would so reduce the efficiency of the machinery in other situations that the local gain would easily be more than offset by widespread losses in energy available for other ends. In the third place, experience shows that there is general presumption on the side of indirect and refined agencies as against coarse and strikingly obvious methods of utilizing power. The fine mechanism which runs a watch is more efficient than the grosser one which heaves a brick. Thus the bias against any doctrine which seems under any circumstances to sanction resort to personal and primitive methods of using force against the more impersonal juridical contrivances of society turns out to be *prima facie* justified on the principle of efficiency in use of means.

Over and above this bare presumption, it must be admitted that our organized contrivances are still so ineffective that it is a delicate matter to tell how far a standing menace to resort to crude methods may be a necessary stimulus to the better working of the more refined methods. There is a general presumption in politics against doing anything till it is clearly necessary; and indication of potential force operates as a sign of necessity. In other words social reorganization is usually a response to a threatened conflict.

This conclusion that violence means recourse to means which are relatively wasteful may be strengthened by considering penal measures. Upon the whole, the opinion seems to be current that in such matters force is hallowed by the mere fact that it is the State which employs it, or by the fact that it is exercised in the interests of "justice" —retribution in the abstract, or what is politely called "vindicating the law." When the justification of force is sought in some kind of abstract consideration of this sort, no questions are to be raised about the efficiency of the force used, for it is not conceived as a specific means to a specific end. It is the sacrosanct character thus attributed to the State's use of force which gives pungency to the Tolstoian charge that the State is the archcriminal, the person who has recourse to violence on the largest scale. I see no way out except to say that all depends upon the efficient adaptation of means to ends. The serious charge against the State is not that it uses force—nothing was ever accomplished without using force—but that it does not use it wisely or effectively. Our penal measures are still largely upon the level which would convince a man by knocking him down instead of by instructing him.

My treatment is of course very summary. But I hope that it suggests my main point. No ends are accomplished without the use of force. It is consequently no presumption against a measure, political, international, jural, economic, that it involves a use of force. Squeamishness about force is the mark not of idealistic but of moonstruck morals. But antecedent and abstract principles cannot be assigned to justify the use of force. The criterion of value lies in the relative efficiency and economy of the expenditure of force as a means to an end. With advance of knowledge, refined, subtle and indirect use of force is always displacing coarse, obvious and direct methods of applying it. This is the explanation to the ordinary feeling against the use of force. What is thought of as brutal, violent, immoral, is a use of physical agencies which are gross, sensational and evident on their own account, in cases where it is possible to employ with greater economy and less waste means which are comparatively imperceptible and refined.

It follows from what has been said that the so-called problem of "moralizing" force is in reality a problem of *intellectualizing* its use: a problem of employing so to say neural instead of gross muscular force as a means to accomplish ends. An immoral use of force is a stupid use. I sometimes hear apologies for war which proceed by pointing out how largely all social life is a disguised contest of hostile powers. Our economic life, so it is said, is but a struggle for bread where the endurance and even the lives of laborers are pitted against the resources of employers. Only lack of imagination fails to see the economic war, the industrial battlefield with its ammunition trains and human carnage. Let the point be admitted. What still remains true is that the decisive question is the level of efficiency and economy upon which the deploying of forces goes on. Our present economic methods may be so wasteful, so destructive, as compared with others which are humanly possible, as to be barbarous. Yet competitive commercial methods may represent an advance in the utilization of human and natural resources over methods of war. In so far as they involve greater indirection and complexity of means, the presumption is that they are an advance.

No matter what idealists and optimists say, the energy of the world, the number of forces at disposal, is plural, not unified. There are different centers of force and they go their ways independently. They come into conflict; they clash. Energy which would otherwise be used in effecting something is then used up in friction; it goes to waste. Two men may be equally engaged about their respective businesses, and their businesses may be equally reputable and important, and yet there may be no harmony in their expenditures of energy. They are driving opposite ways on the road and their vehicles collide. The subsequent waste in quarreling is as certain as the immediate waste in a smash-up. The rule that each shall turn to the right is a plan for organizing otherwise independent and potentially conflicting energies into a scheme which avoids waste, a scheme allowing a maximum utilization of energy. Such, if I mistake not, is the true purport of all law.

Either I am mistaken, or those persons who are clamoring for the "substitution of law for force" have their language, at least, badly mixed. And a continuous use of mixed language is likely to produce a harmful mixture in ideas. Force is the only thing in the world which effects anything, and literally to substitute law for force would be as intelligent as to try to run an engine on the mathematical formula which states its most efficient running. Doubtless those who use the phrase have their hearts in the right place; they mean some method of regulating the expenditure of force which will avoid the wastes incident to present methods. But too often the phrase is bound up with intellectual confusion. There is a genuine emotional animosity to the very idea of force. The "philosophy of force" is alluded to scornfully or indignantly—which is somewhat as if an engineer should speak deprecatingly of the science of energy.

At various times of my life I have, with other wearied souls, assisted at discussions between those who were Tolstoians and—well, those who weren't. In reply to the agitated protests of the former against war and the police and penal measures, I have listened to the time-honored queries about what you should do when the criminal attacked your friend or child. I have rarely heard it stated that since one cannot even walk the street without using force, the only question which persons can discuss with one another concerns the most effective use of force in gaining ends in specific situations. If one's end is the saving of one's soul immaculate, or maintaining a certain emotion unimpaired, doubtless force should be used to inhibit natural muscular reactions. If the end is something else, a hearty fisticuff may be the means of realizing it. What is intolerable is that men should condemn or eulogize force at large, irrespective of its use as a means of getting results. To be interested in ends and to have contempt for the means which alone secure them is the last stage of intellectual demoralization.

It is hostility to force as force, to force intrinsically, which has rendered the peace movement so largely an anti-movement, with all the weaknesses which appertain to

everything that is primarily anti-anything. Unable to conceive the task of organizing the existing forces so they may
achieve their greatest efficiency, pacifists have had little
recourse save to decry evil emotions and evil-minded men
as the causes of war. Belief that war springs from the emotions of hate, pugnacity and greed rather than from the
objective causes which call these emotions into play reduces the peace movement to the futile plane of hortatory
preaching. The avarice of munition-makers, the love of
some newspapers for exciting news, and the depravity of
the anonymous human heart doubtless play a part in the
generation of war. But they take a hand in bringing on
war only because there are specific defects in the organization of the energies of men in society which give them
occasion and stimulation.

If law or rule is simply a device for securing such a
distribution of forces as keeps them from conflicting with
one another, the discovery of a new social arrangement is
the first step in substituting law for war. The ordinary
pacifist's method is like trying to avoid conflict in the use
of the road by telling men to love one another, instead of
by instituting a rule of the road. Until pacifism puts its
faith in constructive, inventive intelligence instead of in
appeal to emotions and in exhortation, the disparate unorganized forces of the world will continue to develop outbreaks of violence.

The principle cuts, however, two ways. I know of no
word more often deprived of meaning and reduced to a
mere emotional counter than the word "end," of which I
have made free use. Men appeal to ends to justify their
resort to force when they mean by ends only footless desires. An end is something which concerns results rather
than aspirations. We justify the use of force in the name

of justice when dealing with criminals in our infantilely barbaric penal methods. But unless its use is actually an effective and economical means of securing specific results, we are using violence to relieve our immediate impulses and to save ourselves the labor of thought and construction. So men justify war in behalf of words which would be empty were they not charged with emotional force—words like honor, liberty, civilization, divine purpose and destiny—forgetting that a war, like anything else, has specific concrete results on earth. Unless war can be shown to be the most economical method of securing the results which are desirable with a minimum of the undesirable results, it marks waste and loss: it must be adjudged a violence, not a use of force. The terms honor, liberty, future of civilization, justice, become sentimental phantasies of the same order as the catchwords of the professional pacifist. Their emotional force may keep men going, but they throw no light on the goal or on the way traveled.

I would not wish to cast doubt on anything which aims to perceive facts and to act on their light. The conception of an international league to enforce peace, an international police force, has about it a flavor of reality. Nevertheless force is efficient socially not when imposed upon a scene from without, but when it is an organization of the forces *in* the scene. We do not enjoy common interests and amicable intercourse in this country because our fathers instituted a United States and armed it with executive force. The formation of the United States took place because of the community of interests and the amicable intercourse already existent. Doubtless its formation facilitated and accelerated the various forces which it concentrated, but no amount of force possessed by it could have imposed commerce, travel, unity of tradition and outlook

upon the thirteen states. It was their union, their organization. And no league to enforce peace will fare prosper-
ously save as it is the natural accompaniment of a constructive adjustment of the concrete interests which are already at work. Not merely the glorification of either war
or peace for their own sakes, but equally the glorification
of diplomacy, prestige, national standing and power and
international tribunals at large, tends to keep men's
thoughts engaged with emotional abstractions, and turns
them away from the perception of the particular forces
which have to be related. The passage of force under law
occurs only when all the cards are on the table, when the
objective facts which bring conflicts in their train are acknowledged, and when intelligence is used to devise mechanisms which will afford to the forces at work all the satisfaction that conditions permit.

Our traditional evangelical trust is in morals apart from
intelligence, and in ideals apart from executive and engineering force. Our Christianity has become identified with
vague feeling and with an optimism which we think is a
sign of a pious faith in Providence but which in reality is
a trust in luck, a deification of the feeling of success re-
gardless of any intelligent discrimination of the nature of
success.

It may be that the words idealism and ideals will have
to go—that they are hopelessly discredited. It may be that
they will become synonyms for romanticism, for blind sentimentalism, for faith in mere good intentions, or that they
will come to be regarded as decorative verbal screens behind which to conduct sinister plans. But the issue is real,
not verbal. There remains a difference between narrow
and partial ends and full and far-reaching ends; between
the success of the few for the moment and the happiness
of the many for an enduring time; a difference between

identifying happiness with the elements of a meagre and hard life and those of a varied and free life. This is the only difference between materialism and idealism that counts. And until we act persistently upon the fact that the difference depends upon the use of force and that force can be directed only by intelligence, we shall continue to dwell in a world where the difference between materialism and idealism will be thought to be a matter of opinion, argument and personal taste. To go on opposing ideals and force to each other is to perpetuate this regime. The issue is not that of indulging in ideals versus using force in a realistic way. As long as we make this opposition we render our ideals impotent, and we play into the hands of those who conceive force as primarily military. Our idealism will never prosper until it rests upon the organization and resolute use of the greater forces of modern life: industry, commerce, finance, scientific inquiry and discussion and the actualities of human companionship.

CHAPTER NINE

INTERNATIONAL LAW AND THE SECURITY OF NATIONS

I · On International Coöperation*

NO intelligent person, apart from party politics or the exigencies of consistency with some position taken in the past, favors isolation for its own sake, or is cold to the idea of coöperation. But coöperation with whom and for what? Even those whose natural bias is toward the League of Nations are interested in having light shed on this subject. International coöperation is hardly possible unless there is something international with which to coöperate. What is it and where is it? Are we to coöperate with France and her satellites upon the continent? Or are we to side with Great Britain in her differences of opinion, her fundamental conflicts of policy with France? What is to be our attitude on the subject of reductions of reparations? If responsible French statesmen openly charge the English with a desire to break the Treaty of Versailles because the English propose certain modifications in the reparation clauses, will similar proposals from us which might go further promote international goodwill or international bitterness? What is the American people prepared to offer from its side?

Such questions might be multiplied almost indefinitely.

* From *Characters and Events,* vol. II, pp. 622-626 (first published in *The New Republic,* March 7 and March 28, 1923).

Until they have been carefully thought out and some definite guarantees secured in connection with some definite plan, any specific move toward international coöperation on our part will be but a repetition of what happened when we plunged into the war without having first come to an understanding with our associates, only to find in the end our hands tied in the execution of our own policies by conflicting European policies in general, and secret agreements in particular. And somehow "honor," the honor that demands that gambling debts take precedence of everything else, required that the secret understandings should be carried out in violation of our public utterances and promises publicly accepted by our European associates. Why repeat the experiment without even the excuse of wartime excitement, without the warning of an experience of which we were then innocent?

The question of coöperation is not only a question with whom in Europe we are to coöperate and what for, but also of unity and division of opinion at home. Irrespective of conflict and confusion in Europe, there is equally great confusion and conflict in our own opinion as to what should be done in Europe and how it should be done. It is perhaps for this reason that current pro-League propaganda ignores all details, and appeals to the sentiment against war and assures us that as soon as we join the League, Turkish atrocities will be impossible and the sword will be broken. Who can say with assurance what the prevailing sentiment is with respect to the French invasion of the industrial regions of Germany? There are many influential newspapers which defend it; there are others which are noncommittal and ready to approve or condemn as events turn out. The anti-German hatred aroused by the war is still active; perhaps the mass does not care to think beyond the alleged fact that France suffered so much that Germany still deserves whatever it gets. The moment we are entangled in European affairs this difference of sentiment among us ceases to be a sentimental affair and becomes a matter of public policy and of domestic politics. We shall either be doing something which, no matter in what direction, arouses bitter strife among ourselves, or our representatives abroad will commit us to something for which Congress and the people will not stand, and the history of President Wilson at Versailles will be repeated.

Again, the neglect of Russia is incredible. Russia is still the most populous nation of Europe and potentially the most powerful. Whether ten or forty years pass before the position of Russia is restored makes little difference. Before we talk much more about international coöperation with the world at large and offer ourselves as both Moses and Messiah, might it not be well to find out just what our attitude is with respect to Russia and her part in the world's affairs? We might make Russia an objective test of our willingness and our ability to engage in international coöperation.

Whether we look at the situation in Europe or at home, it is hard to find any evidence of readiness to coöperate in any definite and systematic way, much less to tie ourselves up with that League of governments which embodies all the forces which have brought the world to its present pass. Europe does not want and will not tolerate our coöperation except on its own terms, and it is divided against itself as to those terms. The notion that we have only to offer ourselves as universal arbiter—and paymaster—and all will be well is childish in the extreme. But even if it came anywhere near the actual condition in Europe, who are we that we may serve in such a capacity? Every contending group in Europe is found here: pro-English, pro-French, pro-German, pro-Serbian, pro-Greek and pro-Bulgarian—almost everything pro except pro-Turkish, with all the antis involved in these various partisanships. And in addition we are ignorant, inexperienced, governed by emotion rather than by information and insight. The fact that only appeal to emotion can possibly be successful in engaging us to enter the League of Nations is the most conclusive reason possible for our staying out of it.

Piously speaking, the ruling statesmen of Europe, of course, do not wish war. But neither do they wish to avoid it enough to lead them to reduce armaments, balance budgets, straighten out their affairs, and try to create a decently stable and amicable Europe. Under these circumstances, I submit that we should distrust the motives of some of the Europeans who are anxious to have us get into their politics. They want us now for the same reason that they wanted us during the war—to add power to *their* policies. There are others of whom this is not true; they are desperate because they realize the desperate state of Europe. We are entitled, however, to discount their desire until Europe shows some evidence that it is coming to their point of view. In any case they are naturally—and quite properly—looking at the matter from the standpoint of Europe. What happens to us in case our entrance makes things no better is not their affair. But it *is* our affair.

A Europe which is divided against itself on every important issue is not a Europe in which we are likely to reduce appreciably the risk of war, and it is a Europe in which we intervene at our own peril, at the peril of becoming entangled in the old problems of the balance—that is, the preponderance of power. It is perhaps irrelevant to the present writing,* but I think it is time that we told the European propagandists who are lecturing us both on our

* But it obviously is *not* to the present reprinting.—Ed.

morality and our own best interests that they have a more pressing field of labor in both these respects at home.

These considerations would hold good, even if the American people were prepared to assume the responsibilities urged upon us. The dangers of our entrance would still be enormous. But when we are divided in sentiment and sympathy, when we have no worked-out policy shared by any large number of even the more intelligent part of our electorate, when we are ignorant and inexperienced in foreign affairs, it appears to many of us to be more than dangerous: to be gratuitous folly.*

II · On America's Responsibility†

The "practical idealism" of the United States has perhaps assumed a pharisaical tinge due to over-advertising. Like another fine thing and fine word, "service," it has been cheapened by the use to which it has been put by self-seekers and by those who grab at any idealistic phrase which is current in order to advance any cause in which they are interested. Nevertheless there is an immense fund

---

* The basic reason for Mr. Dewey's opposition to America entering into the League of Nations he forcefully summarized in the following statement: "The League [of Nations] is *not* honestly named. It is a League of governments pure and simple." (*The New Republic,* March 28, 1923; italics in original). If the current proposal for "Collective Security" *seems* to be more honest than the League of Nations, it is through no fault of its proponents. It is undoubtedly obvious to everyone that the members of the proposed "League for Collective Security" are to be *governments;* but the propagandists do their best to minimize and obscure this fact and to make it appear as if "Collective Security" is and will be of, for and by the *peoples* (or nations) involved. Mr. Dewey's reasons for opposing America's entry into the League of Nations apply therefore with augmented force against America's participation in any such "League for Collective Security" as is being currently agitated for. In fact, wherever "League of Nations" occurs in the text the reader can substitute "Collective Security," without altering the essential meaning.—Ed.

† From *Characters and Events,* vol. II, pp. 691-695 (first published in *The Christian Century,* Dec. 23, 1926).

of goodwill and desire to be of help to those in need diffused among the American people. This is no especial credit to us; it would be a shame were it otherwise. It was born of pioneer conditions, fostered by the mobility of life and the need of improvising coöperative adjustments to meet new conditions, and is demanded by the amplitude of our resources on account of which so many are raised above the pressure of personal need. Much of the energy which in other countries drives along political channels goes in this country in voluntary unions devoted to the public welfare.

This fund of goodwill, in spite of all appearances to the contrary, still exists with respect to international affairs. There are definite causes for our attitude of aloofness from European struggles and problems. Large portions of our population migrated here in order to escape ills of one sort or another from which they suffered across the sea. They wanted to get away mentally and morally as well as physically; they still want to forget. In a pinch they are for their old country as against some other country, but in general they are anti-European. The diversity of our immigrant population is another factor. There is hardly a national group which has not a tradition of fear, suspicion, hostility toward some other European nation which is its historic enemy. One of the conditions required in order that these different groups may live in amity on this side of the water is that there should be a tacit agreement to put European questions in the background, to leave them alone as far as possible. Otherwise our politics and our social life would have continued and repeated all the historic strifes of Europe.

Physical distance inevitably carries with it a certain amount of psychological isolation. The mass of people occupied with the things which have to be done in their daily life have little leisure and little call to give much thought to affairs going on in remote places. All the forces of self-preservation work automatically against mixing in matters, especially political ones, which are so far away as to be beyond adequate knowledge, not to say beyond control. Minding one's own business is a form of conduct that commends itself even more nationally than domestically. Consider how close the British Isles are to the continent of Europe, and yet how her whole traditional policy up to very recent years has made in the direction of isolation. Isolation is not a high ideal but it denotes a better state of things than one of meddling which involves the meddler in unpleasant complications and does no one else any good in the end. There is something humorous in the rebukes and advice freely handed out to Americans regarding the selfishness and futility of American isolation, in view of the century-old similar policies of Great Britain in spite of her much closer and more numerous contacts.

Even such a cursory summary as these remarks would be woefully incomplete were there not mentioned the disillusionments following the war. The outcome of the war served as an enormous political education; I do not say a complete or adequate one. But the prevalent feeling of having been fooled—prevailing even among those who think we would have to do the same thing over under like circumstances, only in a different spirit—together with the withdrawal which accompanies this feeling, is not a mere emotional gesture due to temporary fatigue and disgust. It is attended with a much greater knowledge than the American people had before of the realities of European racial and economic rivalries, political intrigues and diplomatic methods. Few have taken the trouble to go into the details of the discussion of war guilt. But great masses of people are convinced that the war merely reflected the European state of mind and of politics. They see, in spite of Locarno and one or two other favorable occurrences, no marked sign that the state of the European mind and politics has undergone any change, save such as is due to exhaustion. Fundamentally the attitude of aloofness is due to a determined aversion to mixing in the complications of European strife, intrigue and mutual treacheries. There is a natural aversion to experiencing the troubles incident to getting mixed up with such a situation. But there is more than that. There is a firm belief that the whole American situation and tradition in international matters is radically diverse from the European system.

This need not imply that we think we are morally better. Admission that present Europeans are not to blame for what they have inherited, nor we deserving because of what we have inherited, does not affect the fact. That fact is the important thing, and the fact is that the two systems are different. The notion that we can really be of help to Europe by joining in their affairs on terms that are set by their unhappy international and diplomatic heritage seems to me silly. We shall simply be drawn in, and our system assimilated to theirs.

What has been said may be taken superficially as a justification of a policy of isolation on our part. The intention is wholly different. A few of the causes of the tendency toward isolation have been stated. Even should one regard them all as evil—which they certainly are not —they exist as facts and help determine the situation. Any realistic thinker, one who wishes not just to be idealistic in his private inner consciousness but to see ideals carried out, must take them into account. They stand as a solid block against certain methods which are most urged upon us as methods of coöperating with European recovery and of assisting the cause of world peace. The

efforts in question come from many high-minded and devoted men and women. But they are pathetic. The whole
set and movement of American affairs doom them to disappointment. The fact that the conscious fund of American idealism with respect to international friendship has
gone so largely into such impossible channels is a large
part of the explanation of why the genuine practical
idealism of the American people has remained latent and
ineffective.

Thus we come to the real purpose of the statement regarding the causes of American aloofness. Upon what
terms and along what lines can American sentiment, belief
and action be mobilized in behalf of the supreme cause of
international understanding and goodwill? The attempt to
force them into channels which are opposed to their very
nature results only in increasing aloofness, in promoting
indifference, or even antagonism. The campaign for the
league court, and its fate, should demonstrate this fact to
any persons with open eyes. It is a pity, a tragedy, to see
so much potential energy for good go to waste because of
misdirection, while so much more potential energy, which
might be roused into activity for international peace, remains passive and inert.

I am accordingly addressing an appeal to those who
have been actively and energetically concerned with bringing Europe and the United States together in behalf of
world peace and amity. Why not search for a method and
agency of operation which calls into play all the actual
and latent practical idealism of the country? Why not
seek means which are in accord with American tradition
and outlook, measures whose consequences do not involve
getting implicated in the heritage of European war politics, and which will afford Europe an opportunity to free
herself from that incubus? Is there anything the United

States can do for Europe half as important as to share in emancipating her from the legalized war system? It is not just the results of the last war which weigh down Europe, which reduce her, which threaten her civilization. It is even more the prospects of the next war, and the next. It is the war system. Relieved from that dead weight and overhanging menace, no one believes that Europe has not enough resources—material, intellectual, moral—to recover herself, and become a leader in the friendly rivalry of civilizations. Anything which we do or can do that serves in whatever way, direct or indirect, closely or remotely, to perpetuate the war system, is a disservice to Europe. Let the practical idealism of the United States do for Europe the one thing* that Europe most needs and the one thing which is most in harmony with American tradition and aspirations, and in time all other needed things will be added.

III · Preconditions of the Security of Nations†

Lamentations as to the gulf which divides the working ethical principles of nations from those animating decent individuals are copious. But they express the pious rather than the efficacious wish of those who indulge in them. They overlook the central fact that morals are relative to social organization. Individuals have to be moral because they can be. They can be because they are partakers in modes of associated life which confer powers and impose responsibilities upon them. States are non-moral in their activities just because of the absence of an inclusive society which defines and establishes rights. Hence they are

* This "one thing" was the search for the method and agency embodied in the plan for Outlawry of War. For discussion of which see below.—Ed.

† From *Characters and Events,* vol. II, pp. 645-648 (first published in *The New Republic,* March 23, 1918).

left to their own devices, secret and violent if need is deemed imminent, in judging and asserting their rights and obligations. The distance which separates the code of intrigue and conquest permissible to nations from the code exacted of persons measures the significance for morals of social organization. The nations exist with respect to one another in what the older writers called a state of nature, not in a social or political state.

The not infrequent saying that international law expresses not true but only moral law is a striking indication of the widespread absence of scientific understanding of morals. The actual fact is that until nations are bound together by the law of a social order, there cannot be any truly moral obligations existing among them. The attempt on the part of a particular nation to conceive of its relations with other nations in genuinely moral terms may be a source of weakness. The bald enunciation of any such position as this is, very properly, shocking. The frank acceptance of the double standard of conduct on the part of Germany has seemed to other nations to be an example of that abolition of all morality commonly known as Machiavellianism. But this attitude of abhorrence is effective only in the degree in which it marks an aspiration for the establishment of a social order among nations wherever moral relations may obtain. The moral deadliness of the assertion of a "higher" morality for a nation lies in its cynical contempt for the possibility of a society of nations where moral regulations would exist. Conversely, if the conception of a federated concert of nations obtains more widely and ardently in America than elsewhere, it is not because we are so much more moral than others that we can conceive of a higher social state; it is rather that being more highly socialized we can conceive of a new morality.

"Conscience," that is the aggregate of the moral sentiments and ideas of man, is not the author and judge of social institutions, but the product and reflex of the latter. They are functions of social organization. They reflect criticism of the existing social order as well as approval of it. But in this capacity they are heralds of a changed social order. They are significant only as they become the pivots about which turn active efforts for the reconstruction of the social order. The notion that it is possible to get bodies of men to act in accord with finer moral sentiments while the general scheme of social organization remains the same is not only futile, it is a mark of the subtlest form of conceit, moral egotism.

If only there were a general recognition of the dependence of moral control upon social order, all of the sentiment and well-wishing opinion that is now dissipated would be centered. It would aim at the establishment of a definitely organized federation of nations not merely in order that certain moral obligations might be effectively enforced but in order that a variety of obligations might come into existence. The weakness on the ethical side of previous discussions of international courts and leagues has been that these have so largely assumed that moral considerations are already adequately cared for, and that it remains only to give them, through proper agencies, legal effect. The result was that moral enthusiasm was no sooner aroused than it was chilled by finding only legal technicalities with which to occupy itself, more international laws, treaties, courts, diplomats and lawyers. It wanted machinery to propel a great new idea and it found itself confronting additions to make the old machinery work better, to keep going the old idea of ultimate national sovereignty and irresponsibility. It found itself confronted with negative provisions for making war more difficult to enter upon, but which refrained from dealing in any positively organized way with those defects in social organization from which wars proceed. All proposals short of a league of nations whose object is not the negative one of preventing war but the positive one of looking after economic and social needs which are now at the mercy of chance and the voracity of isolated states, assume that war is the effect of bellicosity—which is exactly on the intellectual level of the famous idea that it is the dormitive power of opium which puts men to sleep.

Warlikeness is not of itself the cause of war; a clash of interests due to absence of organization is its cause. A supernational organization which oversees, obviates and adjusts these clashes, an organization which, as Mr. Levinson* points out, is possible only with coincident outlawing of war itself, will focus moral energies now scattered and make operative moral ideas now futile. It will align the moral code of state behavior with the best which obtains as to personal conduct.

IV · International Law and the War-System†

Our country has been favored above other nations in its geographical position and by its history. Our remoteness from the great warring countries, our size and our resources have for the most part protected us from the entanglements, the jealousies, suspicions and animosities which the long, sad centuries have decreed to Europe. With such conditions it would be a shame indeed if a spirit of goodwill, a spirit of amity to other nations, had

* Salmon O. Levinson, the author of the *Outlawry of War* idea. —Ed.

† From *Characters and Events*, vol. II, pp. 650-665 (first published in *The Christian Century*, Oct. 18, 1923; it was originally delivered as an address in debate with Manly O. Hudson which accounts for some of the forms of expression used.—Ed.)

not grown up among us. We are sinners above other nations when without the excuse of European nations we surrender to pride, exclusiveness, distrust and the spirit of isolation and the other tendencies that make war so easy. This situation is not a privilege to be enjoyed; it is a trust which we have to use for the welfare of the nations of the world. It is an opportunity, and an opportunity that imposes a responsibility.

We have, to be sure, an economic interest in the peace of the world, since peaceful and industrious nations make the best and safest customers. I would not belittle any motive that tends toward peace. But we have an interest in the peace of the world deeper and broader than that which self-interest dictates. We are bound by the history and spirit of our position in the world, and the law of *noblesse oblige*—the law that urges that every human being shall use his advantages and privileges not for his own enjoyment alone, but as well for the aid and service of his neighbors—lies more heavily upon us than it does upon any other nation that has ever existed. If we should be recreant to this trust we prove ourselves unworthy of our past and of our opportunity.

I believe that, upon the whole, our fellow-countrymen have a feeling for this fact. There are blots upon our escutcheon in our international relations. There are blots, unfortunately, still forming, in our dealings with weaker nations, especially to our south. But as yet I am not ready to admit that the American people is lacking in a profound fund of international goodwill or in the desire to make that effective in action. Our American idealism is not dead, it is not even sleeping; but it is confused, distracted, perplexed. The reason is obvious. It was given a channel of expression in which its manifestation was frustrated, and since then it has not known where to turn or what to try out. It has retired, discouraged, into itself. It has found itself blocked in the manifestation of its will to enter into coöperative relations with European nations; that will has been blocked by the hatreds and intrigues of the political order of Europe, embodied in its diplomacies, its foreign offices and its conference of ambassadors. The disorder of European international relations, including treaties and international law, centers about the war system.

We have the word of Lord Robert Cecil for it that the warmongers are still active in Europe; that the standing armies and navies of Europe are larger than they were before the war; that the budgets devoted to war purposes in Europe, the money raised by taxation of the people for the support of armies and navies, is greater today than it was before the late war, in spite of the overwhelming triumph of the allies, the broken power of the prostrate enemies, and the absence of anybody in sight against whom this increase of military and naval power is to be directed. Naturally, under such circumstances American idealism has been discouraged and is waiting for something that will unite its desire to assist in a real reign of international amity and peace. It is waiting for the discovery of a channel through which it can operate, a channel that does not conduct to the political system of Europe which is at bottom bound up at every point with the war system —a system of deceit and intrigue, predacity and violence. Such a proposition has at last been put before the American people. Its short name is the Outlawry of War.

This name denotes more than a sentiment of moral justice. It denotes a general plan consisting of a few simple, understandable principles. War is not merely thought of and denounced as criminal; it is to be made a public crime by international law. It is not outlawed by rhetorical resolutions passed by either peace societies or parliaments. A judicial substitute for wars as a method of settling disputes is to be created in the form of a supreme court of justice of the world, which will be a real supreme court of justice for and of the world and not the kind of thing to which the phraseology of the story of Voltaire is so readily applied that I will not go out of my way to apply it to the so-called permanent court of international justice. A judicial substitute for wars as a method of settling disputes is created in the form of a supreme court of the nations of the world, the court sitting and deciding cases under and by an international law that has made war a crime and the instigators or breeders of war as much criminals as any other kind of murderers that now infest the earth.

The appeal to law and the court seems to many at first sight cold and dry. There is little glamour about it. Its appeal is to judgment rather than to mere feeling. At second sight, however, it seems to many chimerical; good, but too good to be true. After a period of feeling that it does not amount to much of anything, there is likely to come a feeling that it amounts to altogether too much to be practical. But from personal experience I feel that if any one allows the idea to stay in his mind, there will come a *third period* when the notion is understood, and that understanding it is equivalent to its hearty and enthusiastic acceptance—at least its acceptance by all who believe that the war system is the world's present greatest evil.

It is natural, it is inevitable, that disputes, controversies, conflicts of interest and opinion shall arise between nations as between persons. Now to settle disputes *finally*, whether they are between nations or individuals, the experiences and wisdom of the world have found two methods, and only two. One is the way of the law and courts;

the other is the way of violence and lawlessness. In private controversies the former way is now established. In disputes among nations the way of violence is equally established. The word "established" is used advisedly. The evils of particular wars tend to blind us to a particular fact, namely, that the world lives today under a war system; a system entrenched in politics, in diplomacy, in existing international law and in every court that sits under existing international law.

The proposition, then, is not the moral proposition to abolish wars. It is the much more fundamental proposition to abolish the war system as an authorized and legally sanctioned institution. The first idea is either utopian at present or merely sentiment. This other proposition, to abolish the war system as an authorized, established institution sanctioned by law, contemplated by law, is practical. To grant the difference between these two propositions, one simply to do away with wars and the other to eliminate the war system as the reigning system under which international politics, diplomacy and relations are conducted—to understand the difference between these two propositions is fundamental. Recourse to violence is not only *a* legitimate method for settling international disputes at present; under certain circumstances it is the only legitimate method, the ultimate reason of state.

This fact explains the futility of present courts and of serious efforts at disarmament. It expresses also the source of moral contradiction in present life. In all domestic relations resort to violence is a crime. It is practical to treat it as a crime, however, because there is an alternative method, the method of judicial trial and decision. But in international relations resort to violence is authorized, and it is authorized because of the absence of the alternative, the judicial substitute. In this region, and in this re-

gion alone among human relations, law is on the side of
the use of violence. It is on the side of the use of that
which everywhere else law makes a crime. And I invite
you to consider the serious and fundamental nature of this
contradiction between the moral sentiment of the world
and the international law which it is operating under, and
to ask if there is any probability that the future peace efforts of mankind are really going to be more successful in
reducing or preventing war than the efforts of the past
have been until this condition of things is changed. Disputes are bound to arise. If we do not want them settled
by violence we have got to find some other way to settle
them. And as I have said, the experiences of mankind in
the past have discovered but one way, that of law administered through a court. Before any one, then, speaks
lightly of law and court in this direction, he is bound to
remember that when disputes assume a certain kind of intensity we know of but two ultimate ways of settling
them—the one, the way of violence applied by the interested parties; the other, the way of law, applied by parties as disinterested and impartial as human nature permits to exist.

While the center of the proposition, then, lies in the
idea of a real court, everything depends upon what law
is applied by the court. Under what law does it operate?
And recall again that the present law of nations contemplates and authorizes recourse to war. A provision of international law which outlaws recourse to war is therefore
a pre-condition of a court which in a true sense shall be a
true court of international law and justice. The one objection that I have heard is that a revision or the formation
of international law is a laborious and slow process and
that something needs to be done at once. Well, something
does need to be done at once, but something that amounts

to something and something that is more than a blind gesture of combined hope and desperation.

Now this something which needs to be done at once is
simple and reasonably short in execution. It is largely a
matter of eliminating everything from existing law that is
concerned with war as a method of settling disputes. Do
this, provide a court, and the remaining part of the task
of perfecting and further developing the rules of intercourse and peace will naturally be taken up and worked
out *pari passu* with the function of the court itself. And
here, as in other practical measures, we must ask what
the alternatives are. Even supposing it should take time
to develop an international law which does not recognize
war, I ask you, what better use can be made of the time
than to employ it in this way? Or is it to be employed as
Europe has been employing it since the so-called peace at
Versailles, when six armed disputes since the Treaty of
Versailles have shaken the system of Europe; and there
are other disputes as bitter as any of these which have led
to war, that are still unsettled?

I hope no one will take my word for the extent to
which existing international law is bound up with war system. Consult the texts and decide for yourselves. The immortal work of Grotius is entitled *The Laws of Peace and
War*, laws of war. Two of his three books are devoted
exclusively to the discussion of war and that topic spills
over into the remaining book. Its relation and importance
have not improved in modern treatment. Let me recall to
you the situation of the last Hague conference in 1907,
popularly if ironically termed a peace conference. It
adopted fourteen measures, conventions, rules, relating to
international conduct, of which twelve related to the conduct of war and two related to arbitration and peace. Six
to one in favor of war as against the rules of peace is a

fair measure of the relative importance which war and peace have shown in existing international law.

The last war certainly gave us a sufficiently impressive appearance of the farcical if it were not tragic nature of the efforts by rules of war to humanize war. In the doctrine of self-preservation, military necessity and the like, international law leaves plenty of loopholes for any ingenious nation. But the necessity of the case is that the object of a warring nation is to win the war and not to lose it by reason of humanity and politeness.

The public mind in my humble judgment has been much obfuscated by the distinction between legal and non-legal disputes, justiciable and non-justiciable disputes. The effect is obfuscating, for it tends to create the impression that certain disputes are intrinsically and necessarily non-legal. But all that legal and non-legal means is that certain cases are triable and other cases are not triable; and the important thing is, who decides what cases are triable and what cases are not triable. Any kind of case becomes legal, becomes justiciable, the moment the law and the courts operating according to that law declare that that particular kind of case is a kind of case that the courts should hear and decide.

Now at present any nation can decide arbitrarily that an issue is political and therefore non-legal and non-triable. It can decide for itself that it involves national honor or a vital interest, and hence is subject to no other adjudication than that of resort to arms. A prime condition of a permanent court of international peace and justice is, then, that law and the courts, not the arbitrary will of a party, shall decide what kind of cases under what circumstances are triable by the court. Now undoubtedly one of the chief and one of the difficult functions of those who draw up the new body of international law will be to attempt to draw the line in precisely such cases. This is a matter for experts and not for a layman like myself. But I venture the statement that if there is any real will to peace in the world, it is just those cases which are now alleged to be non-legal in nature which will be declared to be the very ones that most demand and exact the attention of the law and the court.

The third point to which I would call your attention is the question of the penalties for non-compliance with the decisions of the court, the so-called sanctions. Here again I quote the words of the resolution introduced shortly before the termination of the last session of the senate, by Senator Borah. The court is to have for the enforcement of its decrees "the same power as our federal supreme court; namely, the respect of all enlightened nations for judgments resting upon open, fair investigations, impartial decisions and the compelling force of an enlightened public opinion." The essence of that statement is that there is no effort to use armed force to enforce the decisions of the court against the recalcitrant party. In other words, the measure is logical—not merely formally logical but substantially logical in its adherence to the idea that war is a crime. It does not provide an exceptional case in which war shall be resorted to. It should not be forgotten that the use of police power against an individual who is recalcitrant is radically different from the use of power against a nation which is recalcitrant. The latter is war, no matter what name you give it. It involves the use of army and navy, of artilleries and high explosives, blockades, starvation, poison gas, submarines and aeroplane bombs. You do not make that thing the less war by giving it the polite name of police force. You cannot coerce an entire nation save by war. To outlaw war and in the same measure to provide for war is to guarantee the perpetuation of the war system.

But I do not need to dwell upon this, for the situation is the same with respect to this proposition that it is with any other proposition before the American public. I quote with much pleasure from the recent address of Secretary Hughes concerning the proposed entrance of the United States into the league court: "The truth is that the decisions of the court will have the most solemn sanction that it is practicable to obtain. When nations agree to submit a dispute to a tribunal and to abide by the decision, its observance is a point of international honor of the highest sort. You can really have no higher sanction than this, and it is one which will be all the more keenly felt when the decision is not merely one of a temporary tribunal but of a permanent court supported by practically all the nations of the world."

The case does not stand very different in the minds of its supporters from the proposition of the league of nations, as stated by Lord Robert Cecil. I shall not try to enter into all the minutiae of the exegesis of the covenant of the league. President Wilson and Justice Clark insist that it does mean the use of force on the one hand, Lord Robert Cecil and his friends that it does not. To make one exception to the outlawry of war is to open the door to any and all war; that is Lord Robert's statement.

This proposition to outlaw war as it has been outlined is positive and constructive. It is not negative. It is not hostile to any other measure having a tendency to secure the freeing of the world from the menace of the war system. I hesitate, therefore, to contrast it even by implication with any other measure. For the forces of peace we need union, not division. Existing divisions among them are among the greatest assets of those people, powerful out of all proportion to their number, who believe in war.

But, after all, a practical responsibility lies on each one of us. Each one has to ask himself whether he is expending his activities in behalf of some plan which is positive and constructive in effort, or which is divisive and so, relatively to what might be accomplished, is negative. There is no inherent rivalry between the plan proposed and the Hague court or the league court. In the passage I quoted the resolution provides that a judicial substitute for war shall be created, or, if existing in part, be adapted and adjusted. This provision opens the way to a consideration of the claims of the Hague tribunal or the league court, either or both.

Secretary Hoover recently endorsed the idea of Senator Borah, but he added in his Des Moines speech that it was a counsel of perfection beyond any present practicability. While I disavow any desire or intention to speak for the influence of anybody but myself, for which I am bound, whether I want to or not to assume a personal responsibility, I do question the right of Secretary Hoover or anybody else to speak for the people of the United States or the world in stating that "While I am in favor of it, the world is not ready for it yet." I do not feel so sure that I am so much better or wiser than the rest of the world to justify me in making any such statement as that.

The question is one for us to decide. Are we really against the war system, or are we against it in feeling? do we desire to make some friendly gesture, to hold out a little finger a little way across the oceans of discord, but not ready to do something positive and soon? Are we ready to salve our conscience with a pious aspiration, some so-called "step," or do we wish to effect a significant and genuine change in international relations? Until this

question has been put up to the American people and
other peoples, I will not admit the insincerity of the will
of the world—I do not speak of the will of the rulers and
politicians of the world, but of the people of the world—
the insincerity of its will against war.

The proposal before us accomplishes one good-sized
step. It puts up to the people of the world—puts up for
the first time in human history—a proposition which is
simple, which is understandable, which is fundamental,
on the basis of which the peoples of the world can record
whether their will is for peace or for the continuance of
the war system. And as I would again remind you, the
question for our immediate and practical decision is not
whether this proposition will put an end to wars, but
whether we believe that it is worth while for us to make
an effort, and to give the peoples of the world an opportunity to force upon the political leaders of the world the
necessity of going upon record on this point. One thing is
perfectly certain: If the peoples do not want war they
will respond to this proposition. If, on the other hand, it
should turn out they do want war, then war will continue
with increasing horror. I for one do not wish to waste any
further time or energy with any of these propositions
which are perfectly futile if war is bound to go on.

Having heard a number of discussions and objections
upon this point, I would like to ask each one of you before he commits himself to objection to the outlawry of
war whether logically the objection does not imply that
the war system is bound to go on? Now maybe it is, I
cannot prove that it is not; but I only say that such an
objection proves altogether too much, because it makes
every effort, it makes every meeting and every discussion
and every proposition such as we have here now or at any
other time perfectly meaningless and footless, significant

at most simply as a temporary relief of our own personal emotion. And meantime this proposition to outlaw war does put it up to the peoples of the world to find out whether they want the war system to continue or do not want it to continue.

I want to say one word in conclusion about a matter that I should prefer to have said nothing about, this matter of steps, steps, steps. How long have we been taking steps to do away with war, and why have they accomplished nothing? Because *the steps have all been taken under the war system*. It is not a step that we need, it is a right-about-face; a facing in another direction. And when we have committed ourselves to facing in another direction we have all future time to take steps in. No advance in human history that was of any great importance was ever made by taking steps along old lines. Think of that proposition. Taking steps along old lines *aids in perfecting principles and methods that are already established,* but they never initiate the great steps in human progress. These always come by finding a new method of attack upon the problem. I believe the fallacy which most paralyzes human effort today is the idea that progress can take place by more steps in the old wrong direction. We can, if we please, take steps to perfect the international law and international courts under the old system, but let us not delude ourselves into thinking that in improving details of this system we are taking a single step toward the elimination of the war system of the world.

If there be somewhere some grinning devil that watches the blundering activities of man, I can imagine nothing that gives him more malicious satisfaction than to see earnest and devoted men and women taking steps, by improving a legal and political system that is committed to war, to do away with war. The proposition to outlaw war is a step from the standpoint of law, because it means that the development of law which has been going on for countless ages is now to be extended to the only realm of human relationship where violence still controls. If we look back to savage times we find a time when every human relationship that gave rise to dispute was settled by private combat. We have now substituted law and the court for every direction but one. From the standpoint of law, then, I say that the proposal to outlaw war is a real and a logical and a culminating step in the evolution of law. But from the standpoint of war it is no step to improve the rules and laws of war. It is a right-about-face to change the whole method.

I have referred several times to the fact that this outlawry of war is a new mode of approach, an attack from a different angle. And in conclusion I wish to refer to it again. We are asked not merely, what is the ultimate method of procedure, but how are we to proceed? Well, this new method of approach applies here, too. Other schemes for peace, excepting the purely educational and moral ones, have relied upon the initiative of rulers, politicians or statesmen, as has been the case, for example, in the constitution of the League of Nations. Here at last is a movement for peace which starts from the peoples themselves, which expresses their will, and demands that the legislators and politicians and the diplomats give effect to the popular will for peace. It has the advantages of the popular educational movement, but unlike the other educational movements for peace it has a definite, simple, practical legislative goal. When we consider the extent to which politicians, left to themselves—I am especially referring to those diplomats who have to deal with foreign offices—the extent to which they are tied up to the political tradition and institution of war, until they think and act almost entirely in its terms, excepting when the dislike of the common people restrains them, it is not necessary to point out the importance of this difference. Just think what a difference it makes whether you begin with the people and end with the politicians, or begin with the politicians and end by putting something over on the people.

V · Editor's Note*

A reader unfamiliar with the detailed program of the Plan to Outlaw War might (and quite understandably) think that the last sentence in the text above is rhetorical. Such is far from being the case. It epitomizes the *method* or *means* whereby the Outlawrists—from 1921 to 1927— proposed to reach their objective or end. S.O.Levinson, as Chairman of the American Committee for the Outlawry of War in 1923 formulated their policy in the following eight points:

1. Declaration of our international policy by the passage by the United States Senate of the pending resolution† to outlaw war; to be followed by similar parliamentary declarations in other countries.

2. When a substantial number of parliaments have so responded, conference of all civilized nations to be called to execute a general treaty for the abolition and outlawing of war.

3 This Conference to call a Convention for the creation and codification of the international laws of peace

---

* This editorial note is included as part of the text with Mr. Dewey's consent (but the editor is alone responsible for it). The function of this note is twofold: a) to supply the background of information necessary to fill the gap between the preceding and following sections of Mr. Dewey's text; b) to relieve the Introduction of the need for dealing with practical aspects of Mr. Dewey's socio-political philosophy. Such practical and specific discussions are best done "in context."—Ed.

† Introduced by Senator W. E. Borah, Dec. 20, 1922.—Ed.

at which all civilized nations shall have adequate representations.

4. After the code has been created, it shall be submitted to a plebiscite or referendum in each civilized
nation, so that the faith of the peoples of all countries
shall be pledged behind the code.

5. The court shall have jurisdiction over all parties
to a dispute upon the petition of any party to the dispute or of any signatory nation.

6. All petitions, answers, and other pleadings, shall
be in writing and accessible to the public, and all hear-
ings by the court shall be open.

7. The court should sit in the hemisphere of the contending nations; and if the disputants live in opposite
hemispheres, then in the hemisphere of the defendant
nation.

8. All nations shall agree to abide and be bound by
and in good faith to carry out the orders, judgments,
decrees, and decisions of such court.*

It can be seen from the above eight points, that
the means proposed for securing the adoption of the Outlawry plan, were also to function as the means for making
the Treaty when signed and the Code of Law and Supreme Court when created, effective and enduring instruments of international peace. The Outlawrists, from 1921,
consistently opposed all "peace" plans that were predicated on the use of "sanctions." Dewey has summarized
the history of this issue in the movement thus:

"In his first article, written while the war was still being waged (March 9, 1918) Levinson advocated that the
organized force of the world be used against a nation
which violated the new provision of international law.

* Quoted from Kellor, *Security Against War* (Macmillan, 1924),
vol. 2 pp. 787-788.

But from 1921 he and the Committee for Outlawry took the position that the sole reliance was the organized moral sentiment of the world and that even if nations should agree to use force against a recalcitrant nation, there would be no assurance save good faith that that compact in turn would be kept." (*Encyclopedia of the Social Sciences*, article *Outlawry of War* [by John Dewey], vol. xi, p.509; published in 1933 but written not later than the first half of 1931.)

The Outlawrists at no time contemplated the silly and indeed chimerical possibility of successfully outlawing war by "fiat" by mere juristic declaration, by, so to say, legal excommunication. Wrote Mr. Levinson:

> The principle underlying the outlawry of war is this: The law should always be on the *moral* side of every question. But the law of nations *has always been on the wrong* side of the war question. International law has continued to recognize, shelter, protect and reenforce the legal status of war until war has become the *most* lawful thing in civilization. For what with laws of conscription, martial laws and espionage acts, everyone who impedes in the slightest degree the operations of war is a criminal.* . . . The law which should condemn and stigmatize evil, actually embraces and nurtures it, and thereby thwarts the *moral will* of civilization. . . . Not until *the will of mankind* throws the irresistible weight of the majesty of the law on the *moral* side, by destroying war's institutional status, by condemning and outlawing it, will this plague of plagues

* It is eminently worth noting that the Borah Resolution contained this provision: ". . . that every nation should be encouraged . . . to bind itself to indict and punish *its own* international war breeders or instigators and war profiteers . . ." This is not of course invoking "sanctions" since the punishment is to be meted out in *each country* to the *individuals* guilty of instigating war The militarists and not the pacifists would be sent (in the U S.) to Leavenworth, etc.

. . . ever be exterminated." (Quoted in *The Outlawry of War,* pp. 93-94, by C. C. Morrison [Willett, Clark & Colby, 1927]; italics mine.)

For the Outlawrists, the juristic procedure, far from being self-sufficient, and effective for the end, was the very last step in the process; a necessary step, but a culminating step of setting up the formal machinery—like the Constitution of the United States and our Code of Laws. It is unwarrantably charitable to say that those who accused the Outlawrists with believing war could be abolished and outlawed by "legal fiat" were simply silly. It was even too charitable to say of them what Dewey said of the same class of critics in a slightly different connection, namely, that they exhibited "the stupidity of habit-bound minds." (*Characters and Events,* vol. 2, p. 704.)

For the Outlawrists (up to 1927 at any rate), to sign a treaty, to create a code of international peace laws, to set up a Supreme Court of the World (modeled after the United States Supreme Court) were, *taken by themselves,* all verbal and ceremonial gestures, idle expenditures of effort—nay, worse, misleading and world-deceiving efforts; for these acts to be significant and not idle acts, they had to *follow* upon the organization of the moral sentiment of the world; that is, adequate provision had *first* to be made for the *enactment* of the legal instrumentalities, for making them effective and functioning instruments competent to regulate the conduct of nations with respect to each other.

For the reader and student of Dewey's philosophy, the Plan to Outlaw War has especial significance, because not just Dewey the man but Dewey's philosophy worked for Outlawry and had an influential hand in shaping its basic formulation.

As can be seen from the foregoing, in the basic
and genuine Outlawry Plan, means and ends are conceived
together as integral parts of one whole and progressive
historical process. Means and ends are qualitatively continuous with one another and functionally interactive with
one another. They are mutually supporting, mutually fulfilling, mutually realizing. The *means necessary* for securing the worldwide adoption of the Plan and the creation
of its legal instrumentalities are also *the means sufficient*
for enacting or making effective those instrumentalities.
The *means* to be used to create the Court (in which the
Plan heads up) are to be the only support of its decisions
—*the ends;* and *the ends* (the decisions) in turn would
(because supported) further strengthen, deepen and
further organize the already (partially) organized moral
sentiment of the world—*the means*. To formulate the relation of means-ends in its most comprehensive form: the
underlying principle of Outlawry, defining *the end* is that
international law *should* be on the *moral* side of the war
question; and *the means* to be employed in realizing that
end—from start to never-ending finish—is to be and only
to be the *moral will* or *moral sentiment* of civilized peoples *as that will or sentiment is progressively enlightened
and organized by understanding of that end itself; and by
the continuous and progressive interactive functioning of
means-in-ends in the decisions of the Court.*

The Outlawry Plan fulfills the basic requirements of
Dewey's philosophy of instrumentalism; it admirably
and completely exemplifies his conception of *the method of
intelligence* in social affairs. Now the Kellogg-Briand Pact
if not the greatest of all failures in the modern world, is,
at any rate, high on the list. The question relevant here
then is this: To what extent—if at all—may the Kellogg-
Briand Pact be properly and justly considered as a case

testing the validity and practicality of Dewey's philosophy of means-ends in the socio-political sphere, or if you like, of his political liberalism in social action? To put the question in another way: If it were the case that the Kellogg-Briand Pact was the first end-result of *the method of intelligence* as laid down in the Outlawry Plan then it would be justifiable to consider the Pact as being, in so far forth and within the sphere of its operation, of the nature of an historical case experimentally testing the practicability of Dewey's socio-political philosophy; and if it were justifiable so to consider the Pact, then would it also be legitimate to conclude that the failure of the Pact is (in part if not in whole) a failure of intelligence in the modern world.

It comes down then to a matter of historical fact: *How* was the Kellogg-Briand Pact arrived at? Of *what method of procedure* was it in fact the conclusion?

Although it would be eminently instructive and valuable—especially for the current day—to go into all the details of the history, space limitations make such impossible. Besides, for the crucial testing of the issue, a consideration of the main historical events will be sufficient.

From 1918 to the spring of 1927 the Outlawrists followed their method as laid down. From 1923 to 1927 they concentrated their efforts—writing, lecturing, debating, circulating literature—on the Borah Resolution. The passage of that resolution was the first programmatic legal step, and for close to five years it was their rallying point.

And then, on April 6, 1927, something happened. On the tenth anniversary of America's entry into the World War, the late M. Briand as Foreign Minister, gave a statement to the press. After saying things everyone would expect him to say on such an occasion, he went on to say what no one expected him to say:

For those whose lives are devoted to securing this liv-ing reality of a policy of peace the United States and France already appear to the world as morally in full agreement. If there were need for those two great de-mocracies to give high testimony to their desire for peace and to furnish to other peoples an example more solemn still, France would be willing to subscribe pub-licly with the United States to any mutual engagement tending to "outlaw war," to use an American expression, as between these two countries.*

So unexpected was this statement of Briand's that no one paid any attention to it until April 25 when, to quote the great diplomatic historian of the Kellogg Pact,

"the New York *Times* published a letter from Dr. Nicholas Murray Butler which was the real starting point, in the United States at least, of what was ultim-ately to become a proposal for a world-wide treaty. . . . The closing paragraphs of Dr. Butler's letter . . . [were] . . . the ringing challenge which brought the offer of France to the mind and conscience of the Amer-ican people." (J. T. Shotwell, *War as an Instrument of National Policy* [Harcourt, Brace, 1929] pp. 42-43.)

Although Prof. Shotwell, in his pamphlet, referred to the Briand proposal as "the extraordinary offer of the Gov-ernment of France" and in his later book persistently used similar language, the proposal was "extraordinary," "im-portant," etc., etc., only from point of view of those who up to that time (like Drs. Butler and Shotwell) had been opponents of Outlawry and advocates of America's entry into the League of Nations. Not that Briand's proposal made them any the more favorably inclined to *the prin-ciples and method* of Outlawry; but it did soon serve as a means for "uniting the peace movements" in America.

* All quotations from diplomatic documents are taken from J. T. Shotwell, *The Pact of Paris,* Text of Treaty and Related Documents, *International Conciliation,* pamphlet no. 243, October 1928.

From point of view of Outlawry, Briand's proposal was, to speak mildly and charitably of the dead, a piece of solemn humbug. To speak as the facts demand it was an astute piece of chicanery. And Prof. Shotwell's book provides the evidence proving the truth of this statement. In *The Pact of Paris,* published October 1928, Prof. Shotwell wrote:

> "it would be misreading history and falsifying our conception of M. Briand's part in it to attribute to him unworthy motives of clever diplomacy in his first offer of a bilateral agreement, as though it were involving the United States in a disguised alliance." (p. 450)

And in his book (Preface dated October 14, 1928, though published in 1929) he writes of "the imaginative foresight and courage and idealism of M. Briand" (p.83) and so on whenever occasion permits. But the truly informative passages in Prof. Shotwell's book concerning the real nature of M. Briand's offer are such as these:

> "It is difficult now to recall the basis of this mixed and somewhat contradictory appreciation of the French proposal. Almost without our noticing it, the attitude towards France in the United States, and elsewhere in the world as well, *has changed chiefly as a result of this very offer,* for it has come with the emphasis of a climax to the long series of acts of pacification which are the outstanding achievements of the foreign policy of M. Briand. *Now, at last, the charge could no longer stand that the France of the Third Republic was a militaristic nation.* But this had been the general impression in the United States from the days of the discussion over the Treaty of Versailles, an impression strengthened if not justified by the policy of M. Poincaré in the invasion of the Ruhr. Those who knew France well enough knew that the charge of militarism was not justified, but they were relatively few; and so firmly had the other impression become fixed in the popular mind that any state-

ment to the contrary was likely to be treated as if it were merely French propaganda. . . . *The proposal of April 6 was the first definite step towards the complete revision of the attitude towards France.* (*War*, etc., p. 45 & p. 46; italics mine.)

There is no reason to doubt the veracity of Prof. Shotwell's report (l.c.p.46) that M. Briand "in conversation, frankly stated that he did not know how to take American public opinion nor what to make of it." But there is every reason to doubt the reliability of M. Briand's modesty, for it was undoubtedly of the "false" variety. The whole history of the diplomatic negotiations from April 1927 to August 1928 conclusively proves that M. Briand knew how to *take* American public opinion plenty!* But of course he did not know how to take it as well as did the late Sir Austen Chamberlain (then Foreign Minister). After all, an English speaking cousin is a "cousin" and the most astute of Frenchmen still remains only a "friend." But, to give credit where credit is due, it must be said of M. Briand that he was the first European Statesman to see the possibility of exploiting "an American expression" for the purposes of perpetuating European political methods and furthering European political objectives. (European for Briand meaning French of course; and European for Sir Austen meaning British of course.) And on the evidence of Prof. Shotwell just quoted (and there is much more) M. Briand reaped a not inconsiderable reward for having had the "foresight and courage and idealism" to step out of the traditional European lineup and extend a momentarily cordial hand to "an American expression"— to a neologism, so to speak, of the American language.

* Fortunately for Americans, it is a characteristic requirement of all German statesmen (except under the Republic) that they be too stupid to take the public opinion of any people (excepting of course, and with qualifications, their own).

But the late Mr. Kellogg, even after Dr. Butler's ringing challenge, was not impressed either by Briand's April statement nor by his draft treaty of June 20, 1927. When Kellogg finally got round to answering Briand on December 28, 1927 he wrote:

> "In view of the traditional friendship between France and the United States—a friendship which happily is not dependent upon the existence of any formal engagement—. . . it has occurred to me that the two Governments, instead of contenting themselves with a bilateral declaration of the nature suggested by M. Briand, might make a more signal contribution to world peace by joining in an effort to obtain the adherence of the principal powers of the world to a declaration renouncing war as an instrument of national policy. Such a declaration . . . could not but be an impressive example to all the other nations of the world."

Briand's draft treaty of June 20, 1927 was appropriately entitled: "Draft of Pact of Perpetual Friendship between France and the United States." For 150 years—during the entire existence of the United States—the two countries had lived together in common law peace. Was M. Briand assailed by an inexplicable wave of Puritanism which made him feel it was time the two countries should have, as Mr. Kellogg put it, a "formal engagement", that their relation should be "legitimized"? If M. Briand was deeply concerned to set "an example for other nations" by a *bilateral* treaty, why pick on the United States, with whom such a treaty could not possibly change a thing in fact? Why not pick on some other country, say, Germany? A bilateral Pact of Perpetual Friendship signed in 1927 with Germany, containing M. Briand's two Articles (which are substantially identical with the two Articles of the Pact of Paris) would perhaps have meant something, as an example or otherwise.

On January 5, 1928, Briand responded to Kellogg. Certainly France would join in on a *multilateral* pact, *but* instead of declaring to renounce all war the parties to the pact "shall renounce all war of aggression." And when on January 11, Kellogg replied saying "I am not informed of the reasons" for the change from renouncing "all war" to renouncing "all war of aggression," M. Briand gave him the answer on January 21. The essence of this answer is incorporated in the new draft treaty Briand sent to the Governments of Great Britain, Germany, Italy, Japan, and the United States on April 20, 1928.

> Article 1. . . . without any intention to infringe upon the exercise of their rights of legitimate self-defense, *within the framework of existing treaties,* particularly when the violation of certain provisions* of such treaties constitutes a hostile act, solemnly declare that they condemn recourse to war and renounce it as an instrument of national policy; that is to say, as an instrument of individual, spontaneous and independent political action taken on their own initiative and not action in respect of which they might become involved through the obligation of a treaty such as the Covenant of the League of Nations or *any other treaty* registered with the League of Nations. They undertake *on these conditions* not to attack or invade one another.
>
> Article 2. The settlement or solution of all disputes or conflicts, of whatever nature or origin, which might arise among the high contracting parties or between any two of them, shall never be sought on either side except by pacific means.

* The "certain provisions" were *never* specified. In his final Note a month before the Kellogg-Briand Pact was signed (Note of June 23, 1928) Kellogg wrote: "The United States is not informed as to the precise treaties which France has in mind and cannot therefore discuss their provisions." And so on August 27, 1928, the United States again entered into multilateral European relations *without knowing* what treaties and what provisions France and also England (as we shall see) continued to hold as *binding* on the signatories of the Pact.

Article 3. In case one of the high contracting parties should contravene this treaty, the other contracting powers would *ipso facto* be released with respect to that party from their obligations under this treaty.

Article 4. The provisions of this treaty *in no wise* affect the rights and obligations of the contracting parties *resulting from prior international agreements to which they are parties* (italics mine throughout).

This French Draft of April 20, 1928 was of course *not* the treaty signed on August 27. It was Mr. Kellogg's treaty which was *signed*. Mr. Kellogg's Suggested Draft Treaty of April 13, 1928 which he sent to the principal powers, contained a finely sounding preamble and just two articles: Article 1 making the general renunciation of war; and Article 2 identical in phraseology with Article 2 of the French Draft (above).

Now Sir Austen Chamberlain, on behalf of His Majesty's Government, replied to Mr. Kellogg on May 19, 1928. After the usual flourishes, he got down to business. "After making a careful study" of Kellogg's draft treaty and Briand's draft treaty (which was sent out a week after Kellogg's and so was really France's diplomatic reply, or alternative) Sir Austen writes that

"His Majesty's Government feel convinced that there is *no serious* divergence between the effect of these two drafts" (!) . . . "The French proposals, . . . have *merely* added an indication of certain exceptional circumstances in which the violation of that principle [renunciation of war] by one party may oblige the others to take action *seeming* at first sight to be inconsistent with the terms of the proposed pact. His Majesty's Government appreciate the scruples which have prompted these suggestions by the French Government. *The exact fulfillment of treaty engagements is a matter which affects the national honor; precision* as to the scope of such engagements is, therefore, of importance. Each of the suggestions made by the French Government [not, please note, the United States Government!] has been carefully considered from this point of view."

". . . The preservation of peace has been the chief concern of His Majesty's Government and the prime object of all their endeavors. It is the reason why they have given *ungrudging* support to the League of Nations and why they have undertaken the *burden* of the guarantee embodied in the Locarno treaty. . . . For the Government of this country *respect* for the *obligations* arising out of the Covenant of the League of Nations and out of the Locarno treaties is *fundamental*. . . . His Majesty's Government could not agree to any new treaty which would weaken or undermine these engagements on which the peace of Europe rests. Indeed, public interest in this country in *the scrupulous* fulfilment of these engagements is so great" that—

To cut the diplomacy short—His Majesty's Government would *prefer* the French treaty, but are ready to sign the Kellogg treaty *if is clearly understood* that, as Chamberlain started out by saying, "there is *no serious divergence* between *the effect* of these two drafts" (italics mine throughout).

And just to prove that His Majesty's Government were more astute than the French Government in exploiting *all* possibilities of the proposed treaty for their own ends, Sir Austen added the famous paragraph 10:

"I should remind your excellency that there are certain regions of the world the welfare and integrity of which constitute a special and vital interest of our peace and safety. His Majesty's Government have been at pains to make it clear in the past that interference with these regions cannot be suffered. Their protection against attack is to the British Empire a measure of self-defence. It must be clearly understood that His Majesty's Government in Great Britain accept the new treaty *upon the distinct understanding* that it does not prejudice their freedom of action in this respect" (italics mine throughout).

Precision, as Sir Austen said, is of importance, because the exact fulfilment of treaty obligations is a matter which affects the national honor. Paragraph 10 which on the occasion of accepting a treaty that was to make a new future and not repeat an old past promulgates for the first time what became known as "the British Monroe Doctrine." This paragraph must therefore be taken as constituting a *precise* statement of what His Majesty's Government meant despite the apparent fact that (a) they left *unspecified* which regions of the world are "the certain regions" of specially vital interest for their peace and safety; (b) they left *unexplained* what they meant by "welfare" and "integrity"; (c) they left likewise in the misty realm of the *unspecified* and *unexplained* what they meant by "interference." The only definite clew to their meaning, and hence what must be taken as controlling and defining their intention, is the innocent looking phrase "in the past." His Majesty's Government eagerly embraced the new opportunity to show their prime concern to preserve peace (by signing Mr. Kellogg's treaty) *providing* it be clearly understood that His Majesty's Government would *not* be constrained by the treaty to act differently from what they have been "at pains" to show is their method of action in the past. His Majesty's Government's sensitive sense of "national honor" and the pressure of His Majesty's people demanding the "scrupulous fulfilment" of their engagements, would naturally not permit them even to think of doing in the future otherwise than they have done in the past.

One sentence from the Belgian Note of acceptance of the Kellogg draft treaty deserves quotation: "It is pleased to note that the proposed pact will maintain unimpaired the rights and obligations arising from the Covenant of the League of Nations and from the Locarno agreements which *constitute* for Belgium *fundamental guarantees of security.*" In sum, for the principal signatories, the new treaty was understood to guarantee nothing! The outlawing and abolition of war—*that* would not guarantee Belgian security! *but* the prior engagements of course would!

But you will say, Mr. Kellogg after all did not allow himself to be "played for a sucker" and it was *his* treaty that was signed by France and England and the rest on the dotted line. Furthermore, he did not change a word or punctuation mark of his two Articles of April 13, 1928. Despite the French and British Notes there those two Articles stood in his final Text of Draft Treaty of June 23. Had then Mr. Kellogg *really* succeeded in bringing England and France over to *his* point of view? Or was it actually the other way round? Well, apart from the fact that Notes preliminary to signing a treaty and made *conditions* for signing, are actually integral parts of the treaty in practical effect—apart from this fact, there is one tell-tale change that Mr. Kellogg did introduce—but in the *Preamble* of the June 23 Text:

> "any signatory power which shall hereafter seek to promote its national interests by resort to war should be denied the benefits furnished by this treaty."

Now of course if the Kellogg-Briand Pact were really a treaty outlawing war, and were ever intended as such, this addition to the Preamble is the sheerest sort of nonsense. The *only* benefit an *Outlawry* treaty can confer on its signatories is the help it gives in maintaining peace. If *that benefit* is gone, there are no others it can confer. What happens when an *Outlawry treaty* is broken is very simple: those who break the treaty return to the "*state of nature*"—and for such return, no provision need be made.

Indeed, the whole principle of Outlawry is predicated on the fact that when war begins (or peace is broken) nations do inevitably return to the state of nature (or barbarism) and all the glossing over by protocols, conventions, rules regulating warfare *cannot hide that hideous fact*. Mr. Kellogg's addition to the Preamble is of course nothing quite as nonsensical as it would be *if* the Pact were conceived and intended as a genuine Outlawry Pact. It is a rephrasing of Article 3 of the French draft of April 20, 1927; and *that* article has a very clear meaning: it means that whenever any one of the signatories to the Kellogg Pact breaks *that* pact, then, *ipso facto, or automatically,* all the *other* treaties (of which Mr. Kellogg *said* he knew precisely nothing) come into force! Not for nothing, has the Pact of Paris become more familiarly known as the Kellogg-*Briand* Pact.

The general validity of the above interpretation of the meaning of European negotiations relative to the Pact is confirmed by no less distinguished and authoritative an official of the League (and one highly regarded in certain American circles as a seer of events) than Sir Arthur Salter. On the occasion of Kellogg's Note of February 27, 1928, Sir Arthur wrote in his notebook, on March 1, 1928:

> "The American Note published today seems to me, on any broad and long view, incomparably the most important fact in the present international position.
>
> "That a country with the actual and potential strength of the United States of America, at the moment when she has the power to embark upon the kind of imperialistic policy with which corresponding power by a single country has always hitherto been accompanied in the past [for example, Great Britain], should take the lead in proposing a general treaty proscribing war as an instrument of national policy, may well mark a real epoch in history."

"There is obviously, however, a real danger of the broader aspects and wider implications of the proposal being lost sight of, or inadequately assessed, because of minor and more technical preoccupations and short-range views.

"A technical point may be quite sound, and may be made quite intelligible to those familiar with European considerations. But there is the greatest danger that it may be so presented as to give *the impression* in America that it is a *pretext* for general opposition.

"Nor do I see that the technical difficulties in relation to the League are insuperable. The main question or adjustment is really met—or may be met—under the phrase 'as an instrument of national policy'; *and I cannot see why we on our side should create difficulties by asking whether this is meant to safeguard* our Covenant obligations. Its *natural meaning* is that it does; and surely *we should presume that it does—leaving to America the onus of insisting on a narrow* [sic] *meaning if she wants to,* which I see no reason to believe."

"If the opportunity is not to be wasted—and perhaps worse than wasted—a collective reply or replies in identical terms from the Great Powers addressed by the United States of America is essential. *And* particularly *as League interests are at the centre of the problem,* it is natural that agreement should be attempted when the representatives meet at Geneva."

"From a League point of view, if we once have as a basis such a treaty as America proposes, *we can rely on the logic of events* to bring her nearer to the *general League position.*

"Surely it is foolish to say 'What is the use of signing a Treaty not to go to war? You can't go to war without arranging a method of settling disputes; therefore let us not sign.'

"The *right policy* is surely: 'Let us sign the Treaty binding ourselves to achieve the end; having done *that,* the obligation will help—and impel—*all of us* to proceed to take all the further measures necessary for the purpose: *that is, America will be brought step by step,* by the *same process* as that which has moved countries which are nearer to the scene of immediate political *troubles, to something like the League system."* (First published in *The United States of Europe,* Reynal and Hitchcock, Inc., New York, 1933. All quotations taken in consecutive order as they appear, from pp. 230-234. Many passages have been omitted, but none rearranged or changed internally in any way. Italics mine throughout.)

The above citations would be eminently significant (because of the eminence of their author) even if they were intended originally only as private memorials of private thought. But the object of Sir Arthur's note-making was, as he tells us in his Preface, "a double one: first, to clear my own mind and make it easier to decide upon such detailed steps as were within my own competence by some conception of wider policy; and secondly, when I had opinions on questions extending beyond my own activities, to influence my colleagues, or others whose views were likely to determine policy." Sir Arthur's note from which the above citations are taken falls entirely in the second class. That it did not succeed in influencing Sir Austen, at any rate, the latter's official Note of May 19 proves. But the difference, in any case, between Sir Arthur and Sir Austen was a rather unimportant one of tactics. Sir Austen believed the British Government could safely rely only on the imprecision of "precise" statements; Sir Arthur believed one could more securely rely on "the logic of events" to bring America (through the operation of the proposed Pact) into the position of constant partner and supporter of Great Britain (and Europe) in their efforts to carry on as "in the past." For Europeans, be it carefully noted, the *objective or purpose* in accepting Kellogg's multilateral proposal was *never in question:* the only question was *how* to handle the pro-

posal so that the eventual issue would be what *they* desired. As Sir Arthur well "noted": "if it is badly received
or *unskilfully handled,* it may have precisely the opposite
effect; and the United States of America may turn towards
a policy which would ultimately prove the greatest of all
disasters to the rest of the world." (L.c., pp. 230-231;
italics mine.)

The "rest of the world" is of course Europe, and the
greatest of all disasters would be for the "European system" to suffer disaster. In their dealings with America,
the sole question for Europeans, then as now, was *how* to
place the "onus," *not where.* The form of Sir Arthur's
presumption—that it should as a matter of course be
taken for granted that the "onus" would be left with
America—is, from one point of view, more characteristically and completely European (and British) than the
form of Sir Austen's presumption. In substance, however,
they must be admitted as identical.*

* Because the difference is one of degree, not kind. That this is
so, is fully established by the sentence with which Sir Austen closed
his Paragraph 10 (enunciating the "British Monroe Doctrine"):
"The Government of the United States have *comparable* interests
any disregard of which by a foreign Power they have declared that
they would regard as an unfriendly act. His Majesty's Government
believe, therefore, that in *defining their* position they are expressing
the *intention and meaning* of the United States Government."
(Italics mine.) There are at least two specific presumptions in Sir
Austen's one sentence: 1. That his assertion of His Majesty's Government's *undefined* interest in *unspecified* regions of the world is
"comparable" to (or even a "defining" of) President Monroe's doctrine which *specified* the regions, *explained* the "interest," and *defined*
the "interference" by a foreign Power that America would have to
consider and take as an "unfriendly act"; 2. That the United States
Government *in 1928* could *of course* have "intended and meant"
by proposing a multilateral Pact for *outlawing war* nothing but
the adoption and establishment on a worldwide scale of its con-
tinental doctrine *of 1825.* Obviously, it never dawned on His
Majesty's Government that the Outlawry Pact and the Monroe
Doctrine are mutually exclusive, that in so far as the Outlawry
Pact operated at all, to the same extent would it make unnecessary
all other defensive pacts—Monroe Doctrines included; and that

What happened to the Outlawrists during this "diplomatic" period? Up to April 6, 1927 they had kept their Plan in the public realm where ideas are discussed, clarified and disseminated among the people. Did they then after April 6 allow their idea to be transferred into the official diplomatic realm where ideas are manipulated, distorted and "made real" in the particular and peculiar sense in which "realistic politicians" always make ideas and things "real"—did they allow this to happen without putting up a fight? Did they not even denounce the blackguardly* exploitation of the "American expression"? Sad to say, The American Committee for Outlawry did not. Mr. Dewey strongly advised against the new and unexpected alliance, but his counsel did not prevail. Senator Borah reintroduced his Resolution on Dec. 12, 1927 but it was not passed. Why? This is Prof. Shotwell's explanation:

> M. Briand quoted ("to outlaw war") as an American expression and then went on to explain what it meant to him . . . when the phrase came home with this foreign accent upon it, there was chance of misunderstanding on both sides. The consequences of this misunderstanding might have been to accentuate still more the differences in point of view across the Atlantic so that

the full operation of the Outlawry Pact would completely nullify them, or render them all obsolete and void of both "intention and meaning." His Majesty's Government could not possibly conceive themselves doing otherwise than "in the past" (how could they when throughout their "past" they have been perfect in virtue, animated, guided, and controlled only by the "spirit of fair play"?); therefore Sir Austen presumed the same was true of the United States Government. But these are mere specifications of the great principle or presumption regulating His Majesty's Government's relations with America; and, after all, it is the principle that counts: the principle, in Sir Arthur's lucid prose, of "leaving to America the onus."

* *Blackguard, n.* The scullions and lower menials of a great household; also, the servants and hangers-on of an army. *Blackguardly, adv.* Webster's New International Dictionary (1937), p. 280.

M. Briand's effort to unite the peace forces of both countries (sic) might have resulted in weakening them instead. It would almost have certainly done so had the American leaders of the movement to outlaw war *held rigidly to a doctrinaire* point of view. Instead of that, they joined with the rest of the peace movement in America in interpreting the French use of their own phrase in *liberal and practical terms,* and thus made possible a joint movement of all the forces working for international peace in the United States; which was a new and unprecedented thing. (*War,* p. 103, italics mine.)

The peace movement "had never adjusted itself to the practical politics of a developing world. . . . Nowhere else had this extremist tendency of idealism shown itself so unpractical as in the United States, where the peace movement spent most of its energy in mutual antagonisms,—like the theologians of old,—instead of concentrating upon the common purpose of war elimination. Now at last the peace movement in America was united. (L.c. pp. 114-115)

It was the leadership of Senator Borah which made possible this double achievement. (L.c. p. 116)

"Senator Borah's chief preoccupation was not the splitting of juristic arguments but the earnest furtherance of international peace itself; and from first to last he sought to find the way to harmonize his plans with those acceptable to other governments so long as the negotiations kept in mind the honest fulfillment of a single underlying purpose. His policy henceforth was as practical as it was sincere, and once the Administration showed its willingness to take up the Briand treaty of the previous June* nothing further was heard during

---

* Prof. Shotwell seems to have made an inadvertent slip here: Borah reintroduced his Resolution on Dec. 12, 1927; the Administration first "showed its willingness" on Dec. 28—a fortnight later. Can it be that Prof. Shotwell intended to say that Borah used his Resolution as a threat or weapon to bestir the Administration, and that done, let it silently die? It is also necessary, in justice to C. C. Morrison, to note this: In his Addendum to *The Outlawry of War* he did write "The importance of . . . (Briand's April offer) can hardly be exaggerated," (p. 283). He also wrote "I see no reason

the course of the negotiations of the Senate Resolution
to outlaw war. Those negotiations owe much to Senator
Borah; just how much the contemporary historian can
hardly say. But when all was over . . M. Claudel . .
singled out Senator Borah as the one who had done
most, and sent him his formal thanks as representative
of the Government of France. (L.c. p. 113)

The reader is entitled to know more specifically what
Dewey did during this period. From April 6, 1927 to
March 7, 1928 he did nothing.* Then he wrote an article
the main point of which was to make clear that
"the proposal to make the United States a party to a
treaty which outlaws "aggression" is simply, from the European point of view, to make it a party to guaranteeing
the results of the war treaties, with all their injustices. I
fear the aspirations of the American group are far removed in their conception of "aggression" from the realities of the European situation, as these are used to define "aggression" by France and her allies." (*Characters
and Events,* vol. II, p. 701)

And he closes with this sentence:

". . . it is just as well to have no treaties which disguise
the real situation and which lull lovers of peace into a

why the motives of France should be questioned." *But* he goes on
to say, "But there is no need of arguing against this cynical interpretation" and no *argument* is necessary *because* as he says in italics
*"The sinister or selfish character of such a treaty would be clearly
revealed by the attitude of both nations toward the negotiation of
similar treaties with other nations,"* (l. c. p. 298). France's attitude
toward negotiating a similar treaty with other nations was revealed
only on Jan. 5, 1928—at least six months *after* Morrison wrote the
above. Mr. Dewey, by the way, wrote an 18 page Foreword to
Morrison's book—but had not a single word to say about M.
Briand's proposal or Morrison's comments on same.

* Nothing publicly, that is. His efforts to influence the policy of
the American Committee for Outlawry (already referred to) were
made privately. And his *Foreword* to Morrison's book stayed with
the general proposition of Outlawry and studiously avoided the
new practical-political situation that had arisen.

wholly delusive notion of the prospects of peace." * (Ib. p.702)

On May 16, 1928, another article appeared entitled *Outlawing Peace By Discussing War.* The nub of this article is contained in the following paragraphs:

"An amusing trait of the discussion is that when the relation of the League through its members to a nation waging a war is under consideration, the argument assumes that all nations bound by a treaty to go to war will keep their word. But when it is a question of a treaty to settle disputes by other methods than war, the chief consideration is the probability that nations—always, of course, the other nations—will not keep their word, even though given in the most comprehensive and most far-reaching international document ever drawn.

"Treaties to make war have, it would seem, an irresistibly attractive and binding force; treaties not to make war are in all probability scraps of paper." (Ib. p.704)

And the closing paragraphs:

. . . "There may be those, whose ideas do not get beyond headlines, who suppose that the signing of a treaty in general terms would end the whole matter. It is hard to believe that any responsible statesman entertains that idea. Certainly every active proponent of the outlawry idea has always held that any such general statement would, and could, be but a preliminary to providing adequate means for reaching pacific adjustments. It could be but a preliminary for further negotiations respecting arbitration, conciliation, conference, revision of international law to comply with its terms, a world court and so on.

* It is worth recording here that on the day the Pact was signed, Mr. Dewey said to me he was convinced the Pact would hinder not help the realization of the Outlawry objective.

The harm that is done in discussing the present status of the negotiations as if they mainly concerned some future war lies just here. The harm and danger are practical. The American public, and possibly some Senators, need to be prepared for subsequent efforts that will have to be made in order to provide the necessary pacific means of adjustment of disputes. Discussion in terms of what would happen in case of war distracts attention from this essential need. *If discussion does not prepare the public mind for the necessity and we are caught unawares,* then when the treaty has been negotiated, *we may well be in for another failure, a failure humiliating to our national self-respect and tragic in its consequences for the world.*" (Ib. ſp.705-706; italics mine.)

This was the last statement Mr. Dewey wrote during this period. Not until March 1932 did he write again on the subject, and then mainly because he was practically badgered into doing so by an incorrigible optimist who believed that the Stimson Doctrine opened the issue afresh, and that perhaps it could be made the starting point of a new (though very belated) effort to put some Outlawry reality into the Pact. Mr. Dewey was very sceptical, very reluctant and finally consented after days of argumentation and persuasion. (I am intimate to all these details because I was the badgersome optimist.) In that article entitled *Peace—by Pact or Covenant?* he started as follows:

"Since I am writing from the standpoint of the Pact of Paris, I may properly preface my remarks by saying that I feared from the start that the Pact was prematurely adopted. For its power lies wholly in the moral force of the peoples behind it, and there was no adequate evidence that the education of the peoples regarding its meaning had been anything like adequately completed when the

Pact was officially signed. The Pact should have been the conclusion of an irresistible public demand; to a considerable extent it was the termination of the maneuvers of diplomats. There has, therefore, always been the danger that official adoption of the outlawry idea would turn out to be an embalming of the idea rather than an embodiment of it."

And further on:

"The only conclusion to be drawn from the facts of the situation, both those indicative of the value of the Pact in an emergency and those unfavorable to its constructive power, is plain. Lovers of peace should concentrate attention upon the Peace Pact; they should deny themselves the use of all methods of agitation and appeal which are contrary to its letter and spirit. If this were done, the work of public education which was interrupted by the more or less premature official adoption of the Pact would be reundertaken and carried on more vigorously than before. In this case, the Far Eastern embroilment will strengthen the force of the Pact instead of weakening or perhaps destroying it. For the point to be kept steadily in mind is the permanent bearing of the Far Eastern conflict upon the peace machinery of the world. This effect is more important than any other phase of the present armed struggle. I would not yield to any one in sympathetic appreciation of the human tragedy enacted in and around Shanghai. But if we get so stirred up by the scene of death and destruction that we lose sight of its basic cause, the war system, we shall in the end only confer added force upon this system."

And he closed with this paragraph:

I plead then for three things: First, that the basic idea

of the Paris Pact be put to the front and be kept there, and that all judgments and policies relating to the Far Eastern situation be based upon it and upon it alone. Second, that the Pact be carried to its logical conclusion in a common statement of all nations signing the Pact that all demands, acquisitions, pretended rights, obtained in violation of it, are null and void. Third, that the force clauses of the League of Nations Covenant be abrogated so as to bring the Covenant into agreement with the Pact which was signed later, in order that the League influence reënforce that of the Peace Pact instead of working against it." (*The New Republic,* March 23, 1932)

The third demand of course aroused the opposition of American advocates of the League just as vigorously (if not more so) in 1932 as in 1921-1928. And so that led to a request that Mr. Dewey defend his position in fuller and more circumstantial terms. Which he did—and which leads the reader right into the next and last Section of this chapter—(and Dewey's last writing on this whole subject):

It is hardly necessary to answer in formal terms the question previously raised. It is obvious that there is no justification for considering the Kellogg-Briand Pact as an end-result of using *the* method of intelligence in socio-political affairs (nor indeed as the end-result of *any* intelligent method). Its failure therefore cannot be with any justice evaluated as a failure of intelligence in the modern world.

The Pact is just another monumental piece of evidence proving what cannot (for our own good) be proved too often, namely, that European politicians (alias statesmen) always stand ready to use even "American [idealistic] expressions"—though they prefer of course their own linguistic resources—as means for publicly dressing up their

habitual blackguardism.* The only thing the history of the
Pact up to date conclusively proves is that "to begin with
the politicians" *is* "to end by putting something over on
the people." Of course we didn't need the evidence of the
Pact to establish this. But though not necessary for proving the general proposition, the evidence of the Pact is
nonetheless of great *specific* value in these current per-
fervid days. For one of the myths more sedulously cultivated now than perhaps ever before is that England hasn't
really got a "policy," that its tradition is simply to "muddle" along and "muddle" through,—by inspired improvisation, so to speak. In current language what this means is
that England hasn't really got an "ideology" and that the
British Governments have never been a party in an "ideological" conflict; the only "ideology" they stand for is
that of having no ideology, or, as it is more familiarly put,
they only stand for fair play *just* "fair play." If the history
of the Pact, before and after signing, does nothing else it
explodes this preposterous myth. His Majesty's Government in Great Britain today are the worthy ideological
successors, really continuators, of His Majesty's Government of 1928. In fact, the truly accurate designation is
neither "successors" nor "continuators" but fulfillers and
realizers. Since 1931 especially have the British Governments been concretely developing and carrying out in
worldwide practice what the British Government of 1928
was largely able only to write out in worldwide theory
(Note of May 19, 1928). Even if it be granted—and in
view of the multitude of secret treaties of the War it is
granting an awful lot—but even if it be granted that there
was some reasonable justification for Americans being de-

* *Blackguardism, n.* The conduct, language, or practices of a
blackguard. Webster's, *loc. cit.* For definition of blackguard, see
note.

ceived in 1928 by Sir Austen Chamberlain's protestations of the British Government's good faith, of their unwearying work for peace, of their sleepless sense of national honor that requires the scrupulous fulfillment of agreements and engagements with other nations, there is, in 1938, no reasonable justification whatsoever for Americans who continue to be deceived by the British Government—unless, indeed, it can be established that inexcusable political ignorance and "the stupidity of habitbound minds" provide adequate grounds of *reasonable* justification. The British Governments have, since 1931, been concretely exhibiting and proving on a worldwide field of action the precise meaning of the "reservations" that on May 19, 1928 they made the *necessary preconditions* of their signing the Kellogg treaty on August 27, 1928.

It would be well if America realized that the first Japanese invasion of China (1931-32) was fairly directly the result of the "peace" efforts of His Britannic Majesty's Government in 1928 which they made preliminary to and conditional for signing Mr. Kellogg's Pact. According to Prof. Shotwell (1928), "Japan has established a record which should win something more than the official confidence of governments; it should have universal recognition of the high ideals and sincerity of its international dealings with the Western world." (*War,* etc. p. 241) And "It is of the utmost importance to note that Japan was silent concerning any special reservations of its own." (L.c. p. 249) Because on August 27, 1928, Japan signed the Pact without a murmur, so to speak, Prof. Shotwell felt it only fitting and just to devote a special chapter to her action, appropriately entitled *Japan's Renunciation* (the other nations of course had engaged to renounce nothing!) But why *should* Japan have made *special* reservations of its own? How indelicate Westerners really are! Great Britain (and France) had made all the reservations conceivable. Was not the Pact a multilateral treaty, affording (as the Preamble clearly implied) *all* the signatories *all* the benefits thereof? Hence Japan could claim the benefits when and as needed—which is clearly more polite than doing otherwise. And so on November 22, 1932, M. Matsuoka, on behalf of His Imperial Majesty's Government, publicly and officially announced at Geneva that Japan was now ready to claim for itself the "benefit" the British Government had reserved in its Note of May 19, 1928, paragraph 10. Japan, too, had "certain [unspecified] regions of the world" in which she could suffer no "interference" from other Powers because "the welfare and integrity" of such unspecified and expanding regions constituted an interest "special and vital to her own peace and safety." Japan, unfortunately, had been unable officially to assume the load (on August 27, 1928) of the "Asiatic Man's Burden"; but now (November 1932) it was able to follow the noble example of the British Government who had officially shouldered the "White Man's Burden" as their preliminary contribution to ensuring the peace of the world through the Pact of Paris.

But this "example for the nations" which the British Government set on May 19, 1928 was by no means the only way in which they rendered Japan assistance in 1931-1932. How much and how consistently they connived and worked to help Japan in its period of trial, both a) by encouraging and leading her (by their advice) to rebuff all efforts the American Government made to restore peace and to make of the Pact of Paris something politically real and by showing Japan the way (by their example) to refuse to honor (among other things) their signature, not to the Kellogg-Briand Pact, but to the

Nine-Power Treaty—all this and much more H. L. Stimson, then Secretary of State has clearly, documentarily and circumstantially proven in his book *The Far Eastern Crisis* (Harpers, 1936). But verily, as Sir Austen so feelingly wrote, for His Majesty's Government, the scrupulous fulfillment of engagements is a matter of national honor. Moreover, even if they didn't think so, the British peoples did. And, as we all learnt in school, British Imperial Statesmen always tell the truth and only the truth to the peoples of the British Isles—if for no other reason than the fact that the British Government (as we also were taught in school) are so responsive and so responsible.

On a matter so delicate, so intimate, so really important as the British Government's sense of national honor, and their observance of that sense, it is only proper for an Englishman to speak. And so I quote from Norman Angell, who was just a few years ago made "Sir" by His Majesty (i.e., by His Government):

> "In his book [*The Far Eastern Crisis*] Mr. Stimson points out that not only was America prepared to cooperate with Britain and other states in resistance to Japan, *but that again and again the United States took the lead* in initiating policies of resistance, going far beyond League proposals. Not only would League States have had nothing to fear from the United States in measures designated to restrain Japan, but could count upon active co-operation." (The Defence of the Empire, p. 105-106; italics mine.)

And here, as some would say, comes the pay-off:

> "Throughout the whole story of this retreat [of Great Britain] the standing argument of British Government apologists has been that it was unable to act *because others refused to act with it*. Indeed, until the publication of Mr. Stimson's book [for five whole

years, 1931-1936] i.e., *the refusal of the American Government* to co-operate *in any* action against Japan and *the fear* that the United States might indeed embarrass such action was the classic explanation of our impotence." (L.c.113-14)

And just to prove that the British Government are never without some resource to fall back on, Sir Norman goes on to say,

"Since then, [Mr. Stimson's book 1936] *the refusal of the French Government* has been the standing excuse." (Even though, as Sir Norman points out, Stimson's book antecedently proved any such excuse to be a lie).

Norman Angell knows his England, but he displays throughout his remarkable book too much optimism about American intelligence. Thus:

"There may be details here or there of Mr. Stimson's story with which the critic and the historian will disagree. But the point about it which matters is that for years it has been customary to explain the failure to organize collective action in resistance to aggression as due very largely to the absence of America, to the fact that if it came to naval action Britain would find herself in conflict with the United States. *Whatever else Mr. Stimson's contribution may do it disposes of that legend*" (l.c. pp. 114-115; italics mine).

Alas for our innocents at home and abroad! One has only to read the editorials of the New York *Times* or *The Nation* and *New Republic* (to go no further afield) for 1937 to the current day—to find out how powerless indeed Mr. Stimson's book is to "dispose of that legend" in its native land!

Many Americans were shocked, almost horrified, when Lord Halifax made his recent trip to Geneva for the purpose of forcing the League of Nations to break the Stimson Doctrine—the only valuable achievement (such as it is) of the Kellogg-Briand Pact, forced through by Secretary Stimson, single-handed, *against* the determined opposition of the British Government. "What a sad day!" Americans exclaimed. "What a fall and degradation to witness!" And our English-speaking cousins, too! But the only difference between Lord Halifax at Geneva in 1938 as official emissary of Prime Minister Chamberlain (but as real emissary of Il Duce) and Sir John Simon at Geneva in 1931-1932 as the official emissary of Prime Minister MacDonald (but as real emissary of the Emperor of Japan)—the only difference is this: In 1938 circumstances forced the British Government out into the open, and their most desperate attempts to cover up were of no avail; whereas in 1931-1932 circumstances were favorable for their habitual kind of activity and they were able to work under cover so completely that not until 1936 (when Stimson's book was published) were their blackguardism* and hypocrisy (partially) exposed.

History may be terrifying to read but only for fools is history bunk. On June 23, 1938, the New York *Post* begins an editorial with these words:

"The time has come when it is no longer possible to look upon Great Britain as the mere dupe of the Fascist Powers in Europe." *Really*. The only reason *that* time was ever here was because it is always still possible for the United States to be the mere dupe of Great Britain.

In 1927 the French proposal, as Professor Shotwell so admirably phrases it, came "with the emphasis of a climax to the long series of acts of pacification which are the outstanding achievements of the foreign policy of M. Briand." The signing of the Pact of Paris may therefore well be considered a superclimax; and M. Briand on the occasion

---

* For definition of, see ante.

of the ceremonial signing wisely gave Sir Austen Chamberlain credit for an assist. In 1938 the word is not "pacification" but "appeasement" and the achievement of a long series of acts thereto is already notched on Mr. Neville Chamberlain's stick. But his climax is not yet; nor of course his superclimax. Before either happens, as current evidence cumulatively shows, the word will most likely be changed back to "pacification" and what is now referred to most frequently as Chamberlain's "realism" will at the same time be transmuted into his "idealism, foresight, courage, integrity" and so forth.* Whether Chamberlain himself will then be around to distribute the "honors" no one can know. But that credit for the assist to Chamberlain will have to be unanimously given to Mussolini and Hitler (jointly, like some Nobel Peace Prizes, or separately in order of naming) has been for some long time indisputably clear. Whether the American people are to participate in Mr. Neville Chamberlain's climax and superclimax—as they did in M. Briand's only less noxious ones—is the great question that now rests, not in the lap of the gods, but in the minds and intelligences of the American people.

The wisdom of Dewey's fear, as expressed in his article of March 7, 1928, is no less wise today; and by "today" I do not merely mean the specific day of this writing (June 24, 1938) but *any day* American eyes will open on in the calculable and forecastable future. In this sense of "today" it is today not less true but infinitely more true that

> "the proposal to make the United States a party to a
> treaty which outlaws 'aggression' is simply, from the
> European point of view, to make it a party to guar-
> anteeing the results of the war treaties, with all their
> injustices. I fear the aspirations of the American

* *See* Addendum.

group are far removed in their conception of 'aggression' from the realities of the European situation, as these are used to define 'aggression' by France and her allies."

It is the sheerest nonsense for Americans even to suppose let alone believe that Britain and France without the aid of America lack the necessary power to promote the interests of peace, of democratic government and civilized life in Europe. What the British and French Governments genuinely lack is the desire and intention to promote these ends. It is of course true that the British Government have for seven years and with increasing acceleration been laying the groundwork for a European climax and superclimax which when they occur will most probably be beyond their unaided power to control for their own advantage. But why should America aid the British Government *then* when the British Government is doing what it is doing *now*—and has been doing substantially and practically the same thing for years and years? The question is not: Why should America help the British Government pull its chestnuts out of the fire? The question is: Why should America help the British Government put the civilization of the world *into* the fire? And *that* is exactly what the British Governments have been doing with their Anglo-German naval agreement; with their Anglo-Italo-German agreement on Spain (more vulgarly known as the Committee for Non-Intervention in Spain); with their Anglo-German coöperation in Austria, Czechoslovakia, and all Balkan States; with their recent Anglo-Italian Agreement; with their Anglo-Japanese coöperation in China and so on for as long a list as you care to make out.

In Dewey's statement requoted above substitute "plan for collective security" (or "quarantining aggressor nations") for "treaty which outlaws 'aggression'"; substitute for "war treaties" the Agreements, Understandings, Coöperations some of which only are enumerated above; and substitute for "France and her allies" "England and her allies Italy and Germany and her not entirely helpless thrall France"—make these substitutions and Dewey's statement reads for today. The specific European items may change from decade to decade, but the fundamental ideological policy—the political ideology of the war-system—remains always the same.

It is hardly necessary to point out—to return to our basic question of method—that we have no evidence from which we could with certainty infer that *if* the Outlawrists had consistently used the method of intelligence they would have been successful. The method of intelligence— as Dewey has consistently driven home—has yet to be tried on the international scale (not to speak of the national scale here). All we can with confidence say about the Outlawrists is this: if they had stuck to their guns (as Dewey advised) or if they had remained "rigidly doc-trinaire" (as Prof. Shotwell put it) in the critical years 1927-1928 at least a great deal of confusion and leading of the world-public around by the nose would have been forestalled. And this much of doctrinairism not only should they have offered: the American public (had it been sufficiently educated) would have *demanded* this much from them. If the Outlawrists had *really* believed in their procedural plan they could not possibly have aban-doned it the way they did. For to abandon it meant that they did *not* really believe that the *means* they proposed to use were *essentially integrated* with (and hence indis-pensable for) the *ends* to be attained. Only when means are considered as incidental to the achievement of ends, is it possible to substitute one set of means for another set of means. Such practice of substitution is the essence of opportunism; and from opportunism to perfidy is never more than a step.

It is evident from Dewey's statement, "Just think what a difference it makes whether you begin with the people and end with the politicians or begin with the politicians and end by putting something over on the people," that he did not believe that the Outlawry Plan of procedure (or the method of intelligence in social affairs) would prove itself to be absolutely perfect, that is, 100% politician-proof. He believed and maintained that the Outlawry Plan—if carried through as planned—would effectively work to abolish war—not the politicians, though the latter abolition was only less desirable than the former. At some point, the politicians must enter in—there is no way of keeping them out. For public business requires public officers (representatives etc.) and public officers are politicians. The virtue of the procedural Outlawry Plan consisted therefore in the fact that it provided a *method* whereby *before* the politicians entered in, the real and permanent groundwork—the educational work—would have already been done among the peoples, and as many safeguards as possible would already have been created against the deprivations of the politicians. Furthermore, the Plan provided means not only for continuing such groundwork and safeguarding work; it provided means for continually increasing and intensifying such work. Only by the employment of such method, which is the method of intelligence operating in social and political affairs (whatever be their character and scale)—are public officials ever made out of politicians. For politicians are born.

No political idea has ever been thought of that is inherently such as to be impervious to the distortions of politicians. No political instrument has ever been devised and signed—from the Magna Charta to the Constitution of the United States—that cannot be twisted and exploited by politicians. No political institution has ever been established—from the lowliest town-meetings to the loftiest courts—that carries within itself the magic wherewith to repel and thwart the nefarious activities of politicians. Not despite these reasons, but because of these reasons are the introduction and employment of the method of intelligence in socio-political affairs so vital and necessary. For there is a difference—and a greatly significant one—between an idea, instrument or institution which is made by and for the politicians, and an idea, instrument or institution which is made by and for the people. The latter instrumentalities, at least, are not designed by and to the politicians' hands; and to capture them and convert them into instruments of private exploitation, some time and effort on the part of the politicians are required. And the more adequately the peoples have. been educated, and the more adequate their education continues to be, the more difficult is it, and the longer time does it take for the politicians to succeed. It is in these precious intervals preceding "capture" and between "capture" and "conversion" that the peoples are enabled to breathe somewhat more freely, are able to renew their strength and their courage for the next stage of the never-ending battle.

ADDENDUM

In this day of lightning change, the "process of transmutation" naturally proceeds at corresponding pace. Here are a few "samples" indicative of the course of the process, and considering the mouths from which the words are taken, no one can question their high, indeed, all-highest representative character.

A. Prime Minister Chamberlain's statements on His Majesty's Government's Foreign Policy to the House of Commons:

1. February 21, 1938: ". . . I endeavor to state once again my own views upon certain aspects of foreign policy—views which

have never altered and which have been shared by all my colleagues. On a former occasion I described that policy as being based upon three principles. First, on protection of British interests and lives of British nationals; secondly, on the maintenance of peace and, *as far as we can impose it,* a settlement of differences by peaceful means and not by force; and thirdly, the promotion of friendly relations with other nations who are willing to reciprocate our friendly feelings and *who will keep those rules of international conduct without which there can be neither security nor stability.*" (N.Y. *Times,* Feb. 22, 1938; italics mine)

2. February 22, 1938: When challenged by Members of the House of Commons (Mr. Eden particularly) as to the "ethics" of his proposed course of "conversations" with Mussolini, Chamberlain replied: "If it be a great principle of international good faith, then, I take it, the conclusion is that conversations should not be held with countries whose record is not, *like our own, completely clean.* I assume that our record is completely clean. That is a position I can understand, but it is not the position of Mr. Eden." (N.Y. *Times,* Feb. 23, 1938; italics mine)

3. March 24, 1938: "I cannot imagine any events in Europe which would change *the fundamental basis* of British foreign policy, which is the maintenance and preservation of peace. However, that does not mean nothing would make us fight." (N.Y. *Times,* March 25, 1938)

4. July 26, 1938: "I cannot imagine any one in any part of the House who would disagree with what we have so frequently declared to be *the main aim* of the government's foreign policy, namely: the establishment and maintenance of peace and the removal, as far as they may be *practicable,* of *all* causes of possible conflict in the grievances of one country or another. Let not any one in this country or elsewhere imagine that if we are seeking peace we are willing to sacrifice, *even for peace,* British honor and *British* vital interests." (N.Y. *Times,* July 26, 1938; italics mine)

B. Prime Minister Chamberlain on His Majesty's Government's Foreign Policy with respect to the League of Nations:

1. February 21, 1938: "I told the Ambassador [Grandi] we were loyal members of the League and if we [Chamberlain and Mussolini] came to an agreement we should desire to obtain approval of the League for it." (Loc. cit.)

2. February 22, 1938: *"I doubt whether the League will ever do its best work as long as its members are nominally bound to impose sanctions or use force in support of its obligations."*

"I believe that if the League would throw off shams and pretenses which every one sees through, if it would come out with a declaration of what it is prepared to do and can do as *a moral force to focus public opinion* throughout the world, it would justify itself and it would be a real thing. It might draw unto itself again *some of those who have lost faith in it in the past* and a future League might be assured for the benefit and salvation of mankind." (N.Y. *Times,* Feb. 23, 1938; italics mine; the "some" Chamberlain referred to as having lost faith in the League, because it tried to do more than it could succeed in doing, and therefore was unreliable in a practical sense, were Japan and Germany.)

3. March 24, 1938: "I do not deny my original belief in the League as an effective instrument for preserving peace has been profoundly shaken. That arises from the present condition of the League itself due to recent events. . . .

"The best thing we could do for the League would be to nurse it back to health. . . ." (N.Y. *Times,* March 25, 1938)

4. As good as his word (and no need, of course, to be better) Prime Minister Chamberlain sent a special emissary to the League Council to "nurse the League back to health." On May 12, 1938, thus spake Chamberlain through the mouth of Lord Halifax: "Those who seek to establish a better world upon the basis of universal acknowledgment of League principles are clearly right to feel a reluctance to countenance action, however desirable on other grounds, whereby these may appear to be infringed. But when, as here, two *ideals* are in conflict—on the one hand the ideal of devotion, unflinching, but unpractical, to some high purpose; on the other hand the ideal of a practical victory for peace—I cannot doubt that the stronger claim is that of peace.

"All life is, indeed, perpetually confronting us with difficulties not dissimilar. . . . how constantly it is necessary to reconcile that which *may be ideally right* with what is *practically possible.* That is in truth one of the hardest laws which operate in a world so strangely composite of good and evil as that in which we live [God, not Chamberlain, is to blame]; and neither he who forgets ideals in pursuit of practical achievement [example?] nor he who, blinded by the bright light of the ideal [like Haile Selassie and his supporters, including the United States Government through its Stimson Doctrine, maintained inviolate to date], loses sight of the possible will ever make his full contribution to the establishment of conditions on *which alone progress* can be made.

"Thus in an imperfect world [again the Creator is to blame, not even the idealists] the indefinite maintenance of a principle, evolved to safeguard international order without regard to the circumstances in which it has to be applied may have the effect of merely increasing international discord and friction and contributing to those very evils which it was designed to prevent.

"That is the position which His Majesty's Government feels *bound* [by the Chamberlain-Mussolini agreement] to adopt in the case of Ethiopia. . . .

". . . for practical purposes Italian control over virtually the whole of Ethiopia has become an established fact. . . .

"Meanwhile, nothing is gained and much may be lost by the refusal to face facts. Great as is the League of Nations, the ends it exists to serve are greater than itself, and the greatest of these ends is peace." (N.Y. *Times,* May 13, 1938; italics mine)

It was with respect to Lord Halifax's more recent nursing activities in Paris that Anne O'Hare McCormick wrote the following tribute to the noble lord for the New York *Times*. But, surely, the tribute was most signally earned at Geneva when the great speech of which we have only quoted a small homily was delivered: "He [Lord Halifax] is the *perfect* intermediary, scrupulous, safe and accurate. . . . He is spoken of in England as "the efficient saint" the latter designation in reference to his profound piety. . . . Such qualities, coupled with disinterestedness and lack of personal ambition, make Lord Halifax the *ideal* Foreign Secretary for a Prime Minister *determined to conduct his own* foreign policy as the pacificator of Europe." (N.Y. *Times,* July 23, 1938; italics mine)

The League did prove to be a "focus of world opinion" on May 12, but perhaps not quite in the sense Prime Minister Chamberlain had wished it to be on February 22, 1938. The League Council, in fact, refused to accept the solicitous nursing of "the efficient saint." A New York *Times* correspondent, C. K. Streit, sacrilegiously wrote as follows: "Ethiopia provided the spectacle of Britain and France trying legally to undo the resolution in which the League pledged itself not to recognize the conquest, and when they found they were unable to get the Council to reverse it, taking the law into their own hands by asserting that this question is, as Lord Halifax put it, 'One for each member of the League to decide for itself in light of its *own situation and its own obligations.*'" (N.Y. *Times,* May 15, 1938; italics mine)

And on May 13, the New York *Times* begins its editorial: "The *honors* of the occasion go to Haile Selassie. . . ." (Not, as on July 23, to "the efficient saint.")

5. Reviewing his six months' efforts for "appeasement," "pacification," "practical idealism," "realistic practicalism," etc., etc., Prime Minister Chamberlain summed up His Majesty's Government's steadfast loyalty to the League and the future that loyalty envisioned, thus: ". . . it must be a matter of regret that we cannot record any effective action or intervention by the League of Nations. *Of course we know well what is the cause* of this ineffectiveness—ineffectiveness which is likely to persist as long as *some of the most powerful nations of the world are outside the League.*

"We regard the present position of the League as temporary, *and even if it is necessary for a time that the League should renounce the idea of the use of force,* there still remains a wide field of usefulness for the League, in pursuing which the League may well be able to build up a fresh position of confidence and approval, with the result that in time we may find that those nations who have left the League because they did not agree with the use of force by the League may come back to it to take part in this other work.

"And who knows what further developments may then take place once the League can be considered more representative of the world as a whole than it is today? *In that view of the future of the League we intend to give it all the support and encouragement in our power.*

"In the meantime, in the critical situation in which we find ourselves, *we have to fall back on ordinary methods of diplomacy. At* the beginning of the year many of us must have felt that it was likely to be a critical one for good or evil in the history of the world." (N.Y. *Times*, July 27, 1938; italics mine)

To comment with adequate propriety on the beauty of the Prime Minister's "idealism" as expressed either by himself or by his "efficient saint" lies far beyond the range of our powers. His "realism," however, is a subject on which we may venture to say a closing word. The Prime Minister's *complete reversal of judgment*—within five months—as to the conditions the League must satisfy if it is to fully realize its "future . . . for the benefit and salvation of mankind" is eminently worth calling particular attention to, not only for its practical significance in the immediate historical juncture, but for its eternal significance as revelatory of His Majesty's Government's theoretical policy (ideology). On February 22, the Prime Minister said: "I doubt whether the League will ever do its best work as long as its members are nominally bound to impose sanctions or use force in support of its obligations." And it is clear from the rest quoted earlier (and from portions of his speech we did not quote) that he contemplated the revision of the League Covenant so as to remove all "sanction clauses." But on July 26, the very same Prime Minister says: "We regard the present position of the League *as temporary*, and *even if it is necessary for a time that the League should renounce the idea of the use of force*, there still remains a wide field of usefulness . . . etc." Why the complete about face from maintaining the position that the *abandonment* of sanctions is the indispensable condition for the League's benefiting and saving mankind, to the position that the *failure to use sanctions impairs the usefulness* of the League for these "high purposes"—a temporary impairment, happily? And be it noted that the Prime Minister on *both* occasions entertained and expressed the hope that the Great Powers that left the League would return. Why the change? Can it be, that because of his five months' efforts at securing peace he foresees the time fast approaching when: a) the contemptible "little nations" (*who refused the solicitous nursing of the "efficient saint"*) may prove useful to His Majesty's Government in time of war—and of course no Government would be so thoroughly entitled to their aid as His Majesty's, whose general record is "completely clean" and whose special League record is completely brilliant with unswerving loyalty; or can it be that he foresees a day when b) Germany and Japan are back in the League (and Italy active too) and some nations now "in" at that time "out" and then they all together—Great Britain in the lead—will be able to apply "sanctions" with a completely clean conscience and with a right good will?

These alternatives, either one or both (for they are not mutually exclusive by any means), may well indeed be in the Prime Minister's noble mind.

The following night, on July 27, 1938, speaking to the noble Lords in their own House, the "efficient saint" gave utterance to the following:

"There is, however, another aspect of events. It is true that the government have had for more than a century important interests in China. The Japanese Government claim that the action they are taking is for defense of their interests in China, and we have every right to expect them to recognize *that if they have certain interests to protect we have the same and are not unmindful of our responsibilities,* which we have every intention of discharging." (N.Y. *Times,* July 28, 1938; italics mine.)

Thus, within the round period of ten years, the socio-political *method* (now called "ideology") of His Britannic Majesty's Government completes one world-wide operation:

1. May 19, 1928: Sir Austen Chamberlain: *If* we sign, *then* we do so on the condition that we reserve and maintain unlimited right to act "as in the past";

2. November 22, 1932: M. Matsuoka: *If* Great Britain has reserved the right to act as in the past, *then* Japan, as signatory of the Pact, has acquired the benefit of acting that way "in the present";

3. July 27, 1938: Mr. Neville Chamberlain (through the mouth of his "efficient saint" Lord Halifax): *If* Japan has interests in China which it has the right to protect as it (Japan, not China) sees fit, *then* so have we . . . and. . . .

His Majesty's Government in Great Britain already finds it more difficult than "in the past" to conceal their habitual imperial blackguardism behind their changing verbal façades. But, beyond any doubt, their resources of hypocrisy are not yet entirely exhausted—nor is the gullibility of Americans fully satiated. We may therefore confidently predict that with the acceleration of contemporary events ever new devices—conscienceless, ruthless, blackguardly—will be produced, as occasion demands, by the noble-hearted and pure-minded Statesmen of Great Britain. And that the people of America will continue to swallow these new devices with ever-astounding relish.

VI · Sanctions and the Security of Nations*

The problem of the use of sanctions to achieve a peaceful international organization involves many questions. But two great principles run through the complexity of details and reduce them to clarity and order. The first of these principles is that the use of sanctions is imprac-

* From *Are Sanctions Necessary to International Organization?—* a discussion between Mr. R. L. Buell and Mr. Dewey, published as a pamphlet by Foreign Policy Association, June 1932. Mr. Dewey's contribution is here published entire. Editorial changes in text (enclosed in brackets) consist in substituting "it is sometimes urged" etc., for "Mr. Buell urges" etc.

ticable, so much so that any attempt in that direction is sure to make international relations worse instead of better. Even the attempt to push it to the front in discussion is ill-advised, for it distracts attention from the measures likely to be of efficacy in improving the relations among nations. The second principle is that even if the use of coercive force by joint agreement were possible it would be undesirable, since resort to force fastens upon us the war system as the ultimate means of settling international controversies. "Enforcement of peace" is a phrase which combines two contradictory ideas.

i

In spite of Articles X and XVI in the Covenant of the League, the latter has consistently refused to invoke the use of sanctions. Its record in this respect is without a flaw.* This fact is of itself evidence that the notion of applying sanctions is utopian. If the idea is capable of practicable application, how is the policy of the League to be accounted for? If the blame is put on the nations outside the League, it only becomes the clearer that nations are still so divided among themselves that the idea of combined joint action is utopian. If the claim is simply that the Council of the League has failed in its duty, this alternative only proves that even those nations which are most united among themselves are incapable of uniting to employ coercive force.

The statement that the failure of the League is due to the non-adherence of the United States deserves, however, particular attention. As I see the matter, the actual case stands almost at the opposite pole. As a matter of fact it is Americans, those advocating that we join the League, who are most active in urging the policy of sanctions. France is

* See note at end of Chapter—Ed.

committed to the use of sanctions under especial conditions connected with maintaining the sanctity of the Versailles treaty, and with the added qualification of either an international force with its own staff, or military and naval guarantees from Great Britain and the United States. Some of the smaller nations that are satisfied with the *status quo* think sanctions would strengthen their security against the imperialistic tendencies of the greater powers. But in general the great powers are so much opposed to the invocation of sanctions that their attitude is represented by the statement of MacDonald that reference to them in Article XVI is "dead wood" and should be cut out of the Covenant.

The evidence of the steadfast refusal of the powers to resort to sanctions is found in the history of the League at every emergency which has arisen. Sober students and historians who believe thoroughly in the League have praised it on the special ground that it has resorted only to publicity, to conciliation, to the building up of harmonious public opinion and sentiment. Strangely enough it is only advocates of the League on this side of the ocean who criticize the League for failing to use coercive measures: —possibly because of their remoteness from the factors which actually control European action in international matters. I can think of nothing more unrealistic than urging the impossible—in spite of the appearance of realism which is said to attend the "implementing" by force of the conduct of the League.

Since I cannot go over the whole history of the League, I shall select one case which to me is typical. In connection with Locarno, Great Britain agreed to guarantee the Franco-German frontier, while refusing to guarantee the Polish-German settlement. It was everywhere admitted that Great Britain's attitude was dictated in part by the realization that in the latter case she could not carry the other members of the British Commonwealth of Nations with her. What then is the prospect of Britain's signing a blank check in favor of forcible guarantees to be applied all over the world?

And of course there are other causes for the abstinence of Great Britain. Europe is not a united happy family. Even the nations which were allies in the World War have opposed interests. It would be impossible for Great Britain to surrender her traditional foreign policy to the extent of actually promoting France's hegemony on the continent, such as would be effected if Great Britain cordially assented to sanctions in order to guarantee the war settlements in Eastern Europe. The rivalries of nationalistic interests, the sore spots, the resentments, suspicions, and jealousies which exist among the great powers make the execution of united coercive measures impossible; to try to use them would only increase existing antagonisms and fan a dormant flame into a blaze.

The particular point which has been mentioned is of course but one aspect of France's unceasing demand for a guaranteed security of the perpetual force of the Versailles treaties. As Walter Lippmann wrote in the *New York World* in 1927: "Substitute the word 'revision' for the word 'aggression' and the words 'maintenance of the Paris Treaties' for the word 'security' and you have the real meaning of this interminable debate." Aside from the question of right and justice, conflict of interests will continue to forbid that effective unanimity which is required for the use of sanctions. So far as Great Britain and France especially are concerned, the situation was well stated by a writer in the *Round Table* for June 1928: "When the English-speaking world uses the word peace it thinks of a state of things in which not only there is no war, but in which the political structure is the result of general acceptance and is not merely acquiesced in because there is *force majeure* behind it. When France talks about *la paix,* she means rather the political situation created by the treaties of peace. It is a legal rather than a moral situation."

Suppose a case, apart from any reference to the peace treaties, in which Great Britain, France or the United States was pronounced in such default in meeting an international obligation as to justify, under the terms of the Covenant, an appeal to sanctions. Does anybody believe that they would be put into operation? And what would be the effect upon public sentiment in this country if an effort were made to set them in motion? Would the effect be favorable to the promotion of international organization for peace? If one will face in his thought the picture of the reaction that would occur here, the inevitable inflammation of nationalistic sentiment, he will appreciate the effect on any other strong nation of the invocation of sanctions against it. And why limit the scope of the nations which might be affected by it? In the minds of American advocates of sanctions there seems to exist always an unexpressed premise as to just what nation is to be the guilty party.

Let us take a less hypothetical case. Suppose that in 1929 Russia in her dispute with China in Manchuria had gone as far as Japan went in the same province in 1931-32. The feeling against Russia was, on grounds quite aside from her supposed action in Manchuria, such that sanctions might possibly have been invoked against her. But would it have been possible to convince Soviet Russia or her sympathizers in the rest of the world that the real ground for action was the alleged one? And how could the sanctions have been executed? How could they have been made effective? Is it not obvious that nothing but an old-fashioned bigger and better war would have served that purpose? And is it not highly probable, practically certain, that there would have been enough domestic opposition in various nations to prevent punitive action? Could labor in Great Britain have been brought to the use of sanctions?

For we are not on speculative grounds in dealing with the case of Russia. There was an economic "quarantine" of Russia attempted at the height of the hostility to and fear of her communism. Russia suffered undoubtedly; many persons were added to the roll of those who starved to death. But in the end it was unsuccessful except in embittering all Russians, independent of their economic philosophy, against the rest of the world. Even nations much weaker than Russia have the power of withdrawing into themselves and enduring until the storm is spent. During the storm, however, old resentments are renewed and the temper which makes for future war is fostered.

I can only conclude that those who mourn and who rebuke the League because it has not chosen to employ the sanction provided for on paper assume a decadence of nationalistic rivalries and ambitions which does not accord with facts. They assume a harmony in the various Chancelleries of the world which is non-existent. If the assumption of the existence of this harmony were acted upon, the action would merely accentuate the disagreements which already exist. There may not be the most elevated diplomacy in Europe which is conceivable. But its foreign offices are at least wise enough to realize the danger attending an appeal to sanctions, and hence agree to allow the clauses relating to it in the Covenant to become a dead letter. I can but believe then that the League has been well advised in putting up with rebuffs rather than to adopt the sensational and striking course of resort to coercive measures. That which is academic in American discussions would be fatal in Europe. Nor is the matter wholly academic here. Appeal to sanctions keeps alive and invigorates all the attitudes and convictions which have caused us to remain outside the League. Worse than that, it stimulates the activities of the extreme isolationists; it provides them with ammunition, and all in a cause which is hopelessly utopian.

ii

In what I have thus far said I have ignored the distinction drawn by [some] between economic and military sanctions, in behalf of the former and against the latter. Is this distinction practicable in fact? Certainly it is not authorized by anything in the Covenant of the League. Article X declares that nations agree not only to respect but to *"preserve"* territorial integrity. There is no limit set to the means to be employed; to "preserve" means to preserve. Article XVI states the means to be used. Section one specifies economic and financial measures. But the impression that this section stands complete in itself so that invocation of economic sanctions may or may *not* be followed up by military measures has no warrant in the document. It is opposed to its express terms. The two following sections are integral with the first. For the second section begins, "It shall be the duty of the Council in *such* case to recommend to the several Governments concerned what *effective military, naval and air forces, etc.,"* while the third section obligates member-states to permit passage of troops. From the standpoint of the Covenant, economic sanctions are not a possible substitute for war; they are one of the instruments of war.

Those who make the distinction between economic and military sanctions may at least have something in com-

mon with the opponents of sanctions: They should strive
to modify radically Articles X and XVI of the Covenant.
Even then the question remains how far the separation is
practicable, and whether the framers of the League were
not sufficiently realistic in combining the two so that if
reference to military sanctions is eliminated, economic
sanctions should go too.

First let me say something about the prevailing use of
the term "boycott" by the adherents of economic sanctions. Its use is not only loose but is actually misleading.
A boycott is a private individual or group affair, non-
political in nature: a refusal to give economic patronage
either to a particular firm or corporation or to business
representatives of a particular nation. Its nature is indicated by the conditions of its origin in Ireland, and by
Indian and Chinese boycotts. Neither the word nor the
idea has any application in international affairs.* *There* we
can have only embargoes and blockades. In the Covenant
there is of course no such loose and irrelevant term as
boycott. There is *"severance* of all trade or financial relations"; *"prohibition"* of intercourse among nationals, and
"prevention" of all intercourse between nationals, financial, commercial and even personal. The terms are sweeping enough to remind one of a medieval interdict. In any
case, severance and prohibition mean embargoes, while
prevention is meaningless without a blockade.

The question then comes up whether economic sanctions can be *successfully* applied without a blockade by
land or sea: a recourse to war measures. I doubt if an
answer can be given applicable to all cases. In the case of
sanctions applied to a weak nation with the practically

* The statement in this sentence is elliptical or truncated; the
succeeding sentences fill it out. Clearly "neither the word nor the
idea [boycott] has any application in international affairs" *as those
affairs are conducted by governments.*—Ed.

unanimous and earnest support of all other nations the threat of them might operate. But it seems to me clear that even with a nation which is weak (the case of Russia has already been mentioned) there is no assurance that the threat would be successful unless followed by war-measures, while it seems quite certain that the effect upon public sentiment would be to create great resentment and to foster militarism. The nation against which sanctions are used would feel that it had yielded not to the claims of justice but to superior force, quite as much as if it had been defeated in war.

In many cases, all the precedents go to show that a purely economic boycott would not be successful even against weak nations. I think of Turkey in its war of liberation with Greece. Turkey had constant clandestine French support against the help given by Great Britain to Greece; both the French and Italians joined in smuggling arms and munitions through even a blockade for the sake of profit. I can think of but few cases in which desire for profit and political rivalries would not go far to render a so-called economic boycott ineffective. Even in the World War, with all the military and naval resources of the Allies, the blockade of Germany, openly an act of war, was not completely successful.

There is a great deal of talk of a rather irresponsible sort, intellectually speaking, about putting "teeth" into the League and into the Paris Pact. Everything goes to show that *merely* economic sanctions would be a set of poorly made, easily broken, crockery teeth. Teeth in international affairs mean *teeth*—blockades and other war measures. The case of Japan is crucial. It is argued that if the League and the United States had made an early demonstration of the intention to apply economic sanctions in case China and Japan did not submit their dispute to some

kind of adjudication, the Mukden incident would probably have been quickly settled and the Shanghai campaign
prevented.* It is of course extremely difficult to deal with
historic cases in which it is alleged that if something had
happened which did not happen, something else would
have or would not have happened. The speculative character of the proposition is not reduced when [it is some-
times] urged that the peaceful settlement would have been
brought about not only by economic sanctions alone, but
that a blockade would not have been necessary for the
successful operation of the economic sanction. All that
was required, according to [this], was legislation prohibit-
ing the clearance of exports to the "aggressor" state and
the entrance of imports from it.

Speculative hypothesis for speculation, mere "prohibition" without "prevention" would not have been successful in deterring Japan from her course, while it would
have created resentments most detrimental to the development of a world order and would have played into the
hands of the military. We can be pretty sure that Japan
would have withdrawn from the League; that, since the
United States is the chief importer of her goods, she would
have laid up a resentment against us highly provocative
of war, ulterior if not immediate, and that the outcome
would have strengthened the powerful party in Japan
which desires Japan definitely "to go Asiatic."

A realistic appraisal of the probable action of Japan
will have to take into account her peculiar position and
traditions. Westerners are likely to forget that Japan is
not only an island separated from America and Europe
but also from Asia, and that for centuries she pursued a
deliberate policy of seclusion and exclusion. It is impossible to exaggerate the effect of these conditions upon

* See Note at end of Chapter—Ed.

Japanese mentality. The late war taught us how comparatively easy it is in any case for a government to control public opinion by propaganda and by shutting out all news and information contrary to its case. The task is immensely easier to accomplish in Japan. Since the Japanese public believed with intensity of ardor that its cause against China was just and a matter of national self-preservation, it is unrealistic to suppose that merely passing laws, without a blockade and other show of force, would have altered the policy of Japan, or that its effect would have been other than to increase resentment and add to the prestige of the military party.*

The belief that this would have been the case is not a mere matter of speculation. One hundred and thirty-five American missionaries on the ground in Japan signed, without trying to excuse the action of Japan, a statement in which the following sentence is included: "Without necessarily renouncing the use of economic pressure by all the nations against an aggressor as provided in the Covenant of the League we believe in the present circumstances that the threat of an embargo against Japan only serves more fully to unify Japanese public opinion in support of the military policies"—a statement whose moderation makes it the more worthy of credence.

The conception that fear of economic loss will deter any nation whose emotions are inflamed from conducting warfare is disproved by all recent history. Japan is probably the only country in the whole world on whom such fear would have the least deterrent effect. The dread of economic sanctions may be expected to have the most force in those countries in which industrial interests are paramount

* A concrete illustration in point is Mussolini's establishment of the day "sanctions" were imposed by the League as a National (Roman) Holiday devoted to glorifying the Invincible Military Spirit and Power of Italy.—Ed.

and in which they have the most weight in civilian government. In Japan the situation is reversed. Prestige lies with the military because of the strength of the feudal tradition, and the military elements are superior to the civilian in the cabinet. All facts go contrary to the belief that a mere legalistic gesture would suffice to swerve the policy of a country where the military have taken the bit in their teeth in a runaway race and have the support of public opinion. To argue for sanctions and "teeth" and then to stop short in their use is as impossible in fact as it is inconsistent in logic.

By retracing what actually did happen in Manchuria one can reconstruct what probably would have happened if there had been the threat by all the powers of economic coercion of Japan—supposing, that is for the moment, that all the powers had had sufficient unanimity of opinion and policy to make the threat. Day after day there were inquiries and protests. Day after day, the civil authorities made explanations, and gave certain conditional assurances about future actions. Day after day the military went ahead with their foreordained plan of campaign, leaving the civilian authorities blandly to explain that the conditions upon which their promises had been based had not been fulfilled. Events moved rapidly. There is no reason to suppose that Japan would not have followed the same course with a threat of economic sanctions impending until she confronted the world with her *fait accompli* in Manchuria. It is not a pleasant spectacle but nothing is gained by concealing from ourselves that this is the kind of world in which we live.

The retort that all this could not happen if the Paris Pact were implemented with force, or if the teeth in the Covenant were used, merely sets before us the original dilemma. Teeth that are not mere false teeth, only paper teeth, signify a blockade and a readiness to go as far as events make necessary in further use of armed force. If successful, it is the kind of "success" which any war brings with it, a success which events have demonstrated is *not* conducive to an organized world order, and which in the case of Japan would have left intense resentment behind and strengthened the supremacy of the military. Without the use of armed force, the show of economic teeth would have produced resentment without any practical effect in Manchuria, and would have left recourse to purely pacific measures in a position more ridiculous than at present. There is one fact that is now assured and not merely speculative. Japan is actually withdrawing her forces from Shanghai, and an official spokesman admits this is done because Japan incurred the "odium" of the rest of the world. Even if she had withdrawn under a threat of coercion (which with a proud nation like Japan is hardly likely), I submit that the after-effect in Japan would have been a much sorer and more bellicose attitude than now exists.

It should be added that if international economic sanctions had been adopted, China could not have held aloof; she would have been compelled by forces within and without, to be a party to them. Japan has claimed that the non-official boycott in China was sufficient justification for her Shanghai adventure. Obviously if China joined in an official boycott, the alleged excuse of Japan would have been greatly reinforced. Her intensified sense of provocation would have been the basis for carrying her campaign against China as far as she wished. In all probability, her campaign would have extended up the Yangtse valley to Hankow; to Tientsin and Peiping, possibly to Amoy and Canton. All that China gained by refraining from a declaration of war would have been lost.

iii

I turn from the point that economic sanctions cannot be severed from military and still be successful, to another point which bears upon their practicability. Before economic sanctions can be put in operation there must be a determination of the state against which they are to be employed. The term "aggressor nation" is currently employed to describe this state, and it is employed as if it had a recognized standing in the Covenant. In fact it does not appear there, the nearest approach being "covenant-breaking state." But whatever the term, the guilty nation must be settled upon. What is the basis upon which it is assumed that Japan could have been held guilty in time to arrest the Manchurian expedition and prevent the one in Shanghai, even if the rest of the argument for the efficacy of economic sanctions be accepted? The investigating commission to determine the facts of the case has only just arrived in Shanghai—in April, 1932. This fact is a sufficient commentary on the assumption that it is a simple and easy matter to determine the nature and residence of the guilt which justifies the use of sanctions. Doubtless the inquiry might have been expedited; that it could have moved as rapidly as the Japanese army moved, I take the liberty of doubting. And it would have been faced at every step by Japan's claim that the Chinese were the real aggressors, and by the claim that since Japan was being attacked she could not postpone positive action.

There is another special feature complicating the determination of the covenant-breaking state. In its exact form it belongs only to the Sino-Japanese situation, but something corresponding would be found in every complicated dispute between important nations. Japan's claim that China was the real "aggressor" is bound up with the Chinese claim that the treaties ensuing upon the Twenty-One

Demands are not valid, because they were secured under duress—and also, as Chinese civilians unanimously believe, by bribery of Chinese officials. Anyway China served notice as soon as she could that she did not regard them as binding. What a fine situation in which to determine which nation is responsible! Imagine the enthusiasm with which France would greet a decision that treaties obtained under duress are invalid! Even as it is, the international commission will, I imagine, skirt this question, contenting itself with scolding China for neglect in observing her treaty duties. What it would have done if the imposition of economic sanctions and the outbreak of a general war had been dependent upon its decision, I will leave the believers in sanctions to pass upon.

iv

It is asserted that the failure to check Japan in her course has strengthened the idea that reliance must be placed on armed force, has weakened the peace movement and the desire for disarmament, and has set back the prospects of world organization. Specifically, it is urged that non-resistance by force has intensified Japan's faith in armed force as an instrument of national policy; has furthered the belief in China that international agencies cannot be depended upon; has aroused fear in Russia which finds outlet in increased dependence upon armed force, and has created unrest and fear of the consequences of disarmament all over the world.

There is sufficient truth in these statements so that I have no desire to deny them. I agree fully with the statement that "had the League and the United States successfully curbed Japanese militarism and secured a peaceful settlement of the difficulties between China and Japan, the international consciousness of the great powers, especially,

would have been immeasurably strengthened, a fact which
would have greatly facilitated the solution of other press·
ing international problems." But what does such a state·
ment signify in and of itself save that *if* peaceful measures
had achieved a peaceful solution, the state of the world
would now be much more pacific than it actually is? So far
as it is implied that appeal to sanctions would have
"curbed" Japanese militarism (even if we go so far as to
hold that the military would have been scared off from
their adventure), or more generally still would have secured a peaceful settlement, the statement is either a *non
sequitur* or a begging of the question at issue.

It is quite true that pacific means have not up to date
been highly successful in restraining Japanese militarism,
—although it is probable that there has been an arrest*
since it is likely that original plans went much further
than Shanghai. But the assumption that threats of coercive force would have really restrained her militarism
sounds to me much like the pleas we gave way to during
the World War, that militaristic opposition to and conquest of German militarism would sound the death knell
of all militarism. Instead we have a world more completely
armed than in 1914. I submit that by this time we ought
to have got beyond the notion that resort to coercive force
is going to weaken the tendency to resort to coercive
force; it only shifts its focus.

Of course the answer which is constantly made to this
point is that there is a great difference between national
and international force, between war as an instrument of
national policy and international war; that what is now
argued for is "international defense and international
sanctions." I do not see that the analogy with the World
War is at all weakened by this retort. Nations from the

* That it was *only* "an arrest" is now evident.—Ed.

five continents outside of Europe were·in arms against the Central powers. That seems to mark a fair approach to international war and international sanctions. In retrospect, however, matters look very much like an old-fashioned alliance for various ends of nationalistic defense and nationalistic aggrandizement. Although there was a "sacred union," the Allied nations do not seem now united even secularly, to say nothing of sacredly. The world has had its lesson as to the power of a union for the exercise of coercive force to create a real harmony of interest and purpose. A coercive combination against Japan might accomplish a decisive victory more quickly than did the combination against the Germanic powers, and with less suffering and destruction. That it would promote genuine world organization for peace seems to me as illusory in one case as in the other.

Since personally I do not think the argument that economic sanctions would cause suffering to the innocent is at all a conclusive argument against employing sanctions (provided there were assurance that they would really be successful in creating an international order of and for peaceful international relations), I shall only make one remark on this. There are plenty of innocent people in the world suffering at the present time. There can be no justification for adding to their number unless it is clear beyond all reasonable doubt that the addition will really be a factor in promoting a genuine harmony of interests among the nations of the world. And that is just the point to be proved and which has not been proved.

There are certain other points [which are sometimes made] which seem to be irrelevant to the main issue, but which I shall touch upon for the sake of completeness. I do not agree with those who urge that resort at present to sanctions is a European idea and opposition to it is an

American idea. As I have already said, it seems to me that at present Europeans are altogether too realistic to believe in invocation of sanctions, while it is American advocates of the League who urge their use and who urge us to join with Europe in imposing them. In this attitude these Americans are faithful to the role of Wilson in insisting that this factor be made a part of the Covenant. But it can be said with truth that American opposition to the idea of sanctions was a chief factor in keeping the United States out of the League, and that opposition on *principle* as well as on grounds of practicability was a decided factor in generating the American idea of outlawry of the institution of war—that is of war as a juridical means of settling international disputes. In so far, opposition is an American idea.

It is argued that it is inconsistent for those who oppose international sanctions to join in a *private* boycott of Japanese goods. On the contrary, except for those extreme pacifists who believe that any overt act which may inflict suffering on any one else is wrong, such a boycott is the only form that economic action against Japan can consistently take. It *is* a boycott, not a blockade. It does not involve even a suggestion of political force. It expresses moral disapproval in a way which it is hoped will arouse attention. The assertion that a private boycott runs on all fours with a political, financial and commercial interdict logically implies that Japan is correct in her contention that a Chinese boycott of Japanese goods is justification for armed retaliation on the part of Japan, and that Gandhi's boycott of British goods justifies armed retaliation on the part of Great Britain—a position which even the British party of coercive force has not taken in defence of its action.

My discussion would not be wholly ingenuous if I

passed in silence over a phase of the argument which holds that as a matter of fact the great nations did not hesitate to send military and naval forces to Japan in defence of their own national interests. Probably there are some who, independently of their views on the topic of sanctions, would deny this statement. I am not among them. Persons who support the intervention of the United States in Latin America have frequently justified our nationalistic action there on the ground that under the Monroe Doctrine we are really acting as a kind of trustee for European powers. There is another possibility: abstinence from *all* armed intervention. The same is true as to China. The sole alternative to conjoint coercive action is *not* individualistic national action; it is cessation of the policy of protecting, by means of armed force, persons and property voluntarily placed within a jurisdiction where they are endangered. If two great European powers were at war, the United States would not regard it as a hostile act if American property were destroyed when it happened to be located on a field of battle. The same principle can be applied in "backward" countries. All nations might suitably have joined in sending ships to evacuate all nationals endangered by local warfare, but such action as that, while appropriate and desirable, has nothing to do with imposition of sanctions; it is not "defensive" war, national *or* international.

V

The main positive contention for the use of sanctions is that the creation of a "successful international organization" is dependent upon assurance that there is a force at the disposal of coöperative action which can bring the peacebreaker to terms, and that nations will not disarm nor trust themselves to the adoption of exclusively peaceful measures unless there is assurance that an international force will undertake their defense. Short of an international force devoted to keeping the peace it is said that nations will rely upon their own force.

The argument appears to surrender the restriction to economic sanctions. But much more important than this fact is that in as far as it is admitted to have weight, it points straight to the French proposal for an international army and navy under the control of a general staff, while it rests upon the French premise that security is the all important thing, and that security can be guaranteed only by force. If security is the main thing, and if an international army will achieve it and if nothing else will, the conclusion seems to be the necessity of an international army. All the arguments which can be brought against the latter weigh against the premises from which it follows. The argument that international order and a coercive force to enforce peace are so nearly synonymous that we cannot have one without the other proves, if it proves anything, the necessity for a superstate with its own army and navy.

But even so, the argument that the use of sanctions under conditions which now exist is a prerequisite for the creation of an international order puts the cart before the horse. *If* there existed a general concert of interests and harmony of purposes, a specific international organization would at least be practicable of attainment, whether or not it were desirable; and its force might be directed against a recalcitrant nation. But to suppose that the use of combined coercive force is a means of promoting the formation of such an organization—to say nothing of it being the best or only means—is like supposing that individuals can be clubbed into loving each other. It reminds one of the statement given out by the Japanese that they were fighting the Chinese at Shanghai in order to promote the friendly relations of the two nations.

In connection with the argument that organization for coercive purposes (that is, the use of sanctions) is a necessary pre-condition of an internal order [it is sometimes] assumed that the opponents of sanctions believe that "good faith" will *suffice* to create such an order. I do not know who these optimists are, and I regret that I cannot share their optimism.

It is well-known that conditions can be indispensable without being sufficient. I do not see how world organization of and for peace can be brought into existence without the growth of harmony of interests and community of values along many different lines. I do not know of any single device which will bring it automatically into being. But I can think of no one thing more hostile to the development of this needed harmony and community than the overhanging menace of coercive force. All who oppose the invocation of sanctions in international affairs believe that reliance on informed public opinion and good faith is a *sine qua non.* They also believe that it is a power favorable to the growth of stable peace, while the use of force is by its very consequences hostile to such a growth. This brings us to the other basic principle: the undesirability of recourse to coercive force in order to accomplish international ends, of peace, even if it were practicable.

vi

While I sympathize heartily with criticisms of the dangerously exaggerated nationalism which afflicts the world today and agree with those who hold that it constitutes a situation close to international anarchy, I get the feeling in reading some proposals for remedying the situation that the attributes and activities of national states have been merely transferred over to some bigger substitute organization. It is extremely difficult to get away from concepts and modes of thinking which are sanctified by long tradition. It is much easier to seek improvement by setting up some rearrangement of them in a new pattern than it is to develop new concepts and to think in terms of them.

So in reading about "international war," "international defense," and an international order equipped with coercive powers I cannot escape the impression that policies are being framed and plans formed on the basis of an imagination still in thrall to nationalism, at least to that aspect of nationalism which enthrones force as the ultimate arbiter. I realize that this feeling or impression is no argument, but I record it for what it is worth. In grandiose plans for the world-state, it is certainly clear that the start is made with the idea of the state as at present organized, which is then magnified till all states are absorbed into one. I cannot think that emancipation from the evils of nationalism will be obtained by any manipulation of the elements which constitute the nationalistic state, but only by development of that sort of interaction between social units and groupings that is exemplified in the intellectual, industrial, commercial relations of the states of the Union with one another. It is these interactions operating to effect reciprocal advantage for all concerned that holds the states together in unity, not any political entity superimposed upon them and exercising coercive force upon them.

I do not claim the analogy is perfect, but I think no reasonable person will hold that the coercive force of the federal government is chiefly or in any large degree that which keeps the various states together; or that it is a factor of any great importance as compared with the bonds of common tradition, habits of mind, beliefs, information, intercommunication, commerce, etc., which tie the people of the states together. Nor can I imagine any sensible person today who, when he looks at rivalries of interest and latent frictions between sections which still exist, would urge as a remedy the strengthening of coercive force exercised from above upon them. (We tried "force bills" after the Civil War.) I cannot imagine such a person proposing anything but means which will positively intensify the bonds of common interest and purpose which exist among sections. If civil war were finally resorted to it certainly would not be as a desirable remedial measure but as an awful evil which had to be endured.

Coming to definite arguments, that in regard to the analogy of international coercive power with domestic police power in the enforcement of law seems to have reached a deadlock; the reasons put forth by each side do not seem to have much effect on the other. I cannot refrain however from summarizing the reasons which actuate those which deny the justice of the analogy, since they bear directly upon the fact that international coercive force is a form of war—something admitted by both sides to be undesirable.

The most obvious, but at the same time the least fundamental, reason why the proposed analogy breaks down is that, with respect to the internal affairs of the state, there already exists a body of laws (common and statute) which determines both the material and the manner of the use of force; which decides, that is, both the objects for which public force shall be employed and the exact ways in which it shall be used. There is no provision that force may be used for any purpose which a court at any particular time thinks desirable. There is a large body of regulations and precedents which determine as narrowly as possible the circumstances in which and the ends for which public authority will employ force for purposes of execution and restraint. Police, sheriffs, and so forth, are so far from being allowed to employ any kind of force which they judge may be effective that they themselves act under laws which prescribe and limit their use of force. All of these precedent conditions are notoriously lacking in the case of the so-called police application of international sanctions.

I remarked that this particular defective analogy was not so fundamental as others. It points, however, to one which is fundamental. The reasons why there are laws regulating both substance and procedure in the use of police force is because, within each state where the laws run, there is substantial agreement as to important social interests and values. In other words, the laws do not exist because there is the possibility of the use of coercion for their enforcement, but force can be used because the "laws" apart from coercion are the customs, the agreed upon modes of life, of the community; or else they are declarations of the recognized will of the community by *methods* which in the main are self-enforcing in the life of the community. Laws that are enforced are enforced because there is a community consensus behind them. The threat of force does not bring about the consensus. So at this point the analogy between the domestic police force and the use of sanctions as an agency for promoting the formation of a stable and peaceful international order breaks down completely.

The considerations just adduced bring us to the third element of difference. How can the employment of police force against individuals or at most small gangs be thought to have any similarity to the use of force against an entire nation? Not only would the domestic criminal, if known, be reprehended by all about him, but he is, if the force against him is successful, only an insignificant fraction of the population. If the population of New York State were practically unanimous in refusing to obey a federal law, it would not be police which would be called out if it were decided to use coercion, but the army and navy. The result would be civil war, not the ordinary processes of courts and sheriffs. There may be circumstances in which civil war is practically unavoidable. But I cannot imagine any one saying that it is intrinsically desirable or that it should be provided for in advance because such provision is a necessary means of promoting a peaceful order.

Although I am compelled to believe that the use of police force in executing decisions of courts and other legal bodies is necessary in every stage of human civilization so far attained, I confess I cannot understand the satisfaction which upholders of sanctions find in seeking justification for international force in the fact of police force. I am not such an extreme non-resistant that I believe we can dispense with coercion in domestic matters. But that the use of coercive force in domestic force does an immense amount of harm, that at times it is doubtful whether it accomplishes enough good to offset the evil it does, seems to me clear. Ex-Justice Holmes is on record, if I recall correctly, in expressing a doubt on this very point. Doubtless there are still some persons who cling to the abstract notion of vindictive justice. But most civilized persons today are convinced that coercive and punitive forces are last resorts; that the necessity for appealing to them is itself proof that something is wrong in normal social processes, and that the social ideal is to find the measures which will change the causes which make the invocation of force necessary in particular cases. It is a strange thing to me that in the very country and at the very time when it is so tragically apparent that reliance upon coercive force in domestic matters is a broken reed, there should be an active agitation for treating appeal to coercion as the important and necessary condition of good international relations.

The arguments against the practicability of using sanctions overlap the question of desirability. To a considerable degree their use is impractical because the best judgment of the world instinctively realizes its undesirability. What was said about the practical impossibility of invoking sanctions against Great Britain or the United States may also be cited as evidence of its undesirability. But we may use another illustration. South American countries have not all of them as yet reached a condition of stability in their relations to one another. Disputes between them are unfortunately relatively frequent. How many persons even among those who theoretically give assent to the principle of sanctions would think it desirable that the United States engage in a boycott in every dispute which threatens peace between nations there? Is it desirable that the people of the United States should be so stirred up about the Chaco treaty that they would be ready to impose a boycott on either Paraguay or Bolivia, having first juridically determined just which one is at fault? Where is the thing going to stop if it is once adopted as a principle? And if it is not a principle, then it is merely a convenient dodge or mask for getting us involved in an old-fashioned alliance or war. I do not for a moment believe that it is intended to be the latter; I am speaking only of the logic of the thing. But I do believe that some of those who are ardent supporters of sanctions are still so much influenced by sympathies which grow out of the last war, that they, like the French, can imagine only one particular nation or set of nations as the "aggressor" and hence have never generalized the operation of their principle.

To the opponents of sanctions the points which have been made seem sun-clear. The upholders of sanctions

claim, on the other hand, that there is such a real like-
ness of police force and international sanctions that the
latter is as necessary as the former and of the same kind.
It is claimed that sanctions and war are radically different.
I believe that, however, the world will act upon the honored logic that if the animal looks like a frog, jumps like a
frog and croaks like a frog, it *is* a frog. The definition of
war is not determined by intellectual pigeon holes nor
legalistic distinctions, but by the test of behavior. That
which involves general interdictions and blockades, backed
with threat of guns and explosives and poison gases, is
none the less war because called by another name.

I believe that it is a tragic illusion to think that a sharp
line of difference can be drawn between "international
war" and other wars. The idea of war itself perpetuates
that interpretation and treatment of international relations in terms of force which is the stronghold of the war-
system. The custom of curing the bite of a mad dog by
swallowing one of his hairs is innocent in comparison with
the idea of getting rid of coercive force by the use of coercive force.

When the talk of sanctions is directed against a particular nation, it necessarily stimulates the war spirit in it and
in the countries which contemplate the use of sanctions.
The case of Japan affords a good illustration. The demands for invoking sanctions against her were, in the
American populace at large, directly proportional to the
animosity aroused against her. In order to have brought
American public opinion to the point where it would have
been willing to resort to sanctions, it would have been necessary to dwell upon the wrongs committed by Japan,
cruelties, reputed atrocities, until a veritable war spirit
had been created. The technique required would have been
not unlike that used to create willingness to go to war

against Germany, the technique which operated in the case of millions of peace-loving Americans. I am confident that there are many of our citizens, who a few weeks ago would have said they were in favor of a boycott, who are now glad the matter went no further than it did. The difference is that their emotional resentments have cooled off. I do not imply that emotion rather than reason operates in the case of those who argue on principle for the use of sanctions. But I do mean that the general population would sanction sanctions against a particular nation only in the case of long-standing animosity, or else an immediate intense emotional outburst, against her. The idea that this state of things would be merely transitory, and that finally a remote impersonal machinery would set sanctions in operation without an emotional flutter in the breasts of citizens of the nations using sanctions does not agree with human nature as I am acquainted with it. One does not set out on a course of coercion to inflict suffering unless one is emotionally excited.

I stated earlier that I had no doubt that the course of Japan had for the time being at least strengthened militaristic influences in the world, although I held that the attempt to coerce Japan into another course would have only made matters worse. There is no inconsistency between admitting the harm done the peace of the world by Japan's course and at the same time holding that in the larger sense Japan's course has not been a striking success. There is probably no case on record in modern times when moral sentiment, public sentiment, has been so nearly unanimous and so spontaneously expressed. The sentiment and its peaceful expression did not cause Japan to desist. But the position of Japan today is not an enviable one, and while a sensible person hesitates to predict the future, there is good ground for thinking that her position in

China for the future has been rendered less tenable than it would have been had coercion been resorted to. Japan is all but completely on the defensive in the court of public opinion. She has experienced a moral defeat. It is hard to believe that she can live it down without a change in her policies. Appeal to coercion would have convinced her that she had justice on her side; it would have solidified her intransigeant attitude. Now she will have the opportunity to stand all the hard consequences of her conduct as the consequences of her own conduct, and not as something forced upon her, in spite of her righteous conduct, by the jealousy and ignorance of a hostile world. And if we go outside Japan, I doubt if any nation on earth has had the desire to strengthen, to imitate the conduct which has brought such general condemnation upon Japan.* As one who would like to see the real power of the League for peace grow, I believe that her failure to invoke sanctions, even if Japan did not desist (which she probably would not have done anyway) is a real contribution to the cause of world peace, since her action did something to solidify and express the moral judgment of the world. The settlement of disputes by peaceful measures, provided for by the Paris Pact, is recent; its significance is still far from having penetrated adequately into the public consciousness. For example, apologists for Japan as regards Manchuria still think to exculpate her from blame by making known the provocations she received from the Chinese. Admit for the moment that the case stands just as these apologists claim, and their argument totally ignores the fact that Japan has been arraigned because of failure to use the peaceful measures provided for in the Nine-Power Pact and the Pact of Paris in order to remedy her wrongs.

* Entertaining this doubt was justified through the years 1932-1935—a rather long period in contemporary world history.—Ed.

In the degree in which attention is centered on this matter and is not dissipated in the consideration of previous rights and wrongs, we have a new situation in the world and one whose efficacy for peace is immeasurable.

vii

We come now to comparison of the value of sanctions with that of other measures which may be used. First, and with respect to the Paris Pact, I want to say a few words about the subject of "defensive" war. I quite agree with those who hold that "defensive" war logically implies "aggressive" warfare, and the need for some criterion for distinguishing between them. The original idea of the outlawry of war was to outlaw the institution of war and not just some special brand of war. It was pointed out that nothing could destroy the right of self-defense—the same right that an individual has, when violently assailed, to protect himself. This latter right does not depend upon making a distinction between offensive and defensive assault and battery; this is completely outlawed. So with war.

Unfortunately, however, there was not an adequate education of the public in the meaning of the idea of outlawry before its official adoption. Still more unfortunately, there were believers in the necessity of military force among the politicians of the world who strove to give the idea an innocuous meaning, and who tried to turn the fact of self-defense, which is neither a product of law nor capable of being abrogated by law, into the concept of the legality of defensive war. Influential statesmen anxious for the speedy adoption of the Pact indulged in ambiguities. Either M. Briand himself never fully grasped the idea or he was interested in mitigating its force.* For in his speech

* This was and is far too generous a concession to M. Briand, —Ed.

of August 27, 1928, he limited the idea of renunciation of war in a way which left room for introducing the idea of two kinds of war, one of which was not outlawed. He said that it was "war as a means of arbitrary and selfish action" which was outlawed. And several times, as if for the sake of emphasis, he limited the significance of the Pact to "selfish and wilful" war, thus giving ground to those persons who claim that even under the Pact there is a place for a kind of war which is noble and disinterested. Moreover, a number of Americans who had previously ridiculed and opposed the idea of outlawry, and who were devoted to the idea of sanctions, seized upon this loophole; and, making it central in their interpretation of the Pact, brought forward the notion of "international" defensive war.

Consequently there is still an ambiguity in the Pact which can be taken advantage of to sustain the contention that the Pact itself demands international sanctions and war, unless the "defensive war" it permits is to become purely nationalistic. However, there is another and better alternative. That is to clarify international law so that the distinction between the right of self-defense and the concept of "defensive war" is made clear. Had this been done before Japan's incursion into Manchuria, every pretence on her part that she was fighting a defensive war and therefore had not broken the Pact would have been swept away.

The argument is made that the refusal of other nations to admit the legality of accessions of territory, or other gains, resulting from violation of the Paris Pact will not be adequate; that it is a half-way sanction, but *only* a half-way one. The argument is supported on the ground that past non-recognitions have not operated to prevent nations from enjoying the fruits of their aggression. The

argument from precedents overlooks one important difference. The cases cited are refusals of recognition by *particular* nations, as of Great Britain's seizure of Egypt by
France, of various undertakings of the United States with
respect to Latin American countries. The refusal which is
contemplated by the "peace-sanction" (originally suggested by Mr. S. O. Levinson, the author of the Outlawry
idea) is one to be exercised by all nations in common, and
one which, through the influence of Secretary Stimson, has
been officially acted upon by the Assembly of the League.
If there is no difference in results to be expected from isolated national action and organized international action,
what becomes of the argument regarding the difference
between national and international defense, national and
international war? The logic of the argument from the
failure of national non-recognition to the necessary failure
of present and future international non-recognition compels us to conclude that the *only* merit of international
sanctions is that it represents a stronger economic and
military coercive force.

The argument that non-recognition of say Japan's position in Manchuria will not lessen the ability of Japan to
establish herself there so solidly that non-recognition will
mean nothing raises hypothetical questions. It ignores to
my mind the slow but effective operation of imponder-
ables. But speculative matters aside, it raises the question:
Upon what shall those who desire a world organized for
peace depend: upon force and the threat of force, or upon
peaceful measures in the development of common interests
and purposes?

"Peace-sanctions" are not "half-way" sanctions because
they are not sanctions at all in the sense of those who argue for economic and military sanctions. For they do not
involve the application of coercive force. They are sanc-

598 THE SECURITY OF NATIONS

tions simply in the sense in which undesirable consequences which flow intrinsically from the performance of
an act are sanctions. If a nation obtains territory by means
which are juridically banned, then juridically those gains
are null and void. To some it will seem unrealistic to put
faith upon strictly moral agencies and influences. But it
would seem as if the history of war, the history of the
consequences of the use of physical and coercive force,
were enough to convince reasonable persons who want
peace of the unrealistic character of any other means.

We do not insist that good faith and moral pressure are
sure to operate, that they are bound to be sufficient. But
we do say that the measures which can be taken in their
name are more promising roads to stable and enduring
peace than is recourse to coercion, actual or veiled. It is
not now necessary to argue that the possibility of using
the latter rests back upon the former, since the pledge to
use coercive force depends for fulfillment upon the good
faith of the national making it. You cannot employ coercion in an endless regress against those who do not observe good faith, Mr. Buell [writes]. "Admittedly all international obligations in the last resort must rest upon good
faith and the force of public opinion."* Since this is fact
and since it must be the fact, we hold that consistent action upon the basis of the fact is the best way to promote
the positive influence of good faith and public opinion,
while the habit of continuing to think and act in terms of
coercion perpetuates the ideas and emotions which sustain
the institution of war. It correspondingly weakens the operation of the good faith and public opinion which are
admitted to be the ultimate reliance.

Any one of us can sympathize with those who are impatient with the present relations of nations and who are

* In Mr. Buell's contribution, printed in the same pamphlet.—Ed.

indignant with those nations that, after professing a love
of peace and promising to forego the use of warlike measures to settle their disputes, fail to live up to their good
word. Their breach of good faith has the psychological effect of causing us to doubt the efficacy of all good faith
and to imagine that the use of coercion is the only thing
which nations will respect. But in spite of a reaction in this
direction that is natural because of desire for speedy results, all history and understanding of human nature tell
us, I believe, that the view is shortsighted and in the end
defeats its own purpose. I am not convinced beyond every
peradventure of a doubt that the Outlawry of War will rid
the world finally of the war system. If nations insist upon
fighting they will do so, just as individuals commit suicide.

But I am sure of two things: First, that if the peoples
of nations *want* to have done with war, the Outlawry idea
is the best method for giving expression to that desire
which has yet been discovered, and secondly, that it is
fatal for those who welcome the Outlawry idea and who
believe in it to play, even in thought, with the idea of sanctions or coercive force. In so doing they, however, unin-
tentionally, reinstate the idea of war and undermine their
own position. Devotion to sanctions comes naturally and
logically only from those who believe that wars are the
inevitable way of settling disputes between nations, and
who do not believe that the traditional policies of balance
of power and alliances can be done away with. For, in effect, the enforcement of sanctions signifies only that at a
given time and for the time being there is an alliance of
nations which thinks itself sufficiently strong to restrain
by coercion some nation from going to war or else to conquer and penalize that nation if it does go to war. Were it
not for the fear that some one would think that I was
recommending the idea, I would say that the conception of

a *Pax Romana* can be realized more readily by a thorough-going alliance, economic, financial, military and naval, of the British Commonwealth of Nations and the United States than by any scheme of "international defense and war" yet devised.

viii

In the long run, the efficacy of the Paris Pact, of the Outlawry idea in general, depends upon the growth of community of interests and purposes among the nations of the world. The Outlawry agreement, like any jural arrangement, is protective of interests that exist; it reinforces them with the power of pledged good faith. But there are definite measures which can be adopted that will add to the efficacy of dependence upon good faith and public opinion as expressed in the Paris Pact. I believe that if the energies of those who want peace were united to promote these measures, immensely more would be accomplished for peace than will be effected by keeping discussion and thought fastened upon the use of coercion.

1. The Covenant of the League, by modification of Articles X, XV and XVI, can be brought into harmony with the Pact of Paris. Unless this is done, opposition to the adherence of the United States will continue. The one thing most certain in our foreign policy is that we shall not assign to any group of foreign powers a disposition of our own decision as to our future course of action in matters involving war and the threat of war. Quite aside from the attitude of the United States, such action will prevent different methods and measures from assuring peace from interfering with each other and virtually encouraging war-like action—an interference which unfortunately took place in the Sino-Japanese embroglio.

2. There can be formally adopted as a part of interna-

tional law the principle that all occupations, privileges, possessions that are effected in violation of the Peace Pact, that is by acts which are not consonant with the pledge to use only peaceful measures in settlement of disputes, shall be juridically null and void. The principle has been endorsed by the Assembly of the League and can and should be officially incorporated into international law.

3. There should be adopted into international law the principle that any dispute or controversy not brought to settlement by the ordinary processes of diplomacy, or by mediation, conciliation, arbitration, etc., shall remain in *status quo*.* Doubtless this idea is implied in the Paris Pact but if it were made explicit and nations were to pledge themselves to it, a given violation of the Pact would stand out more clearly and the response of public opinion would be quicker and more pronounced.

4. The fundamental distinction between the right of self-defense and the concept of defensive war should be established in international law.

5. The United States should adhere promptly to the World Court to which should be referred, with a view to the enlightenment of public opinion and the unification of the moral judgment of the world, any and every case in which there is a claim that the terms of the Pact have been violated, when the question is not settled by the ordinary means of negotiation among nations.

Finally, it should go without saying that these measures are additional to and not substitutes for the increased use of all possible means of consultation, conference, mediation, arbitration, and all other possible agencies of peaceful settlement. Let us throw our energies into strengthen-

---

* This suggestion like the one in the preceding paragraph is due to Mr. S. O. Levinson and was first made public in the *Christian Century* for February 3, 1932. [Author's note in original.]

ing them and not, because they and the Pact have not as yet been completely successful, fall back upon the continued use of coercive force.

Editor's Note. (p. 567 "The League has consistently refused to invoke the use of sanctions.")

In 1935, the League *seemed* to break its record for consistency by voting sanctions against Italy; in *reality*, however, the case was quite otherwise: the only thing the League consistently preserved was its basic policy of *appearing* to be a League of Nations, while *being* and *acting* as a Combination of Great Powers. The Government of Great Britain assumed the role of leader in the League movement to impose sanctions; the actual record of the Government of Great Britain, acting through, with and for the League, is therefore conclusive evidence as to what *really* transpired in 1935:

Norman Angell, in his book *The Defence of the Empire,* goes into the whole matter at some length. For the purposes here, a few quotations will suffice.

"At *Italy's* request we imposed an embargo upon the export of arms to Abyssinia. Thus, at a time when Italy was feverishly pouring armies into Africa for the purpose of conquering Abyssinia, we showed our 'impartiality' by applying an embargo 'to both parties', an embargo which, while it did not even embarrass Italy, made it impossible for Abyssinia to acquire the means of defence.

"The *Italian demand* that we should refuse licences for the export of arms to Abyssinia *happened to be a breach of our obligation* in the 1930 arms traffic treaty with Abyssinia to allow the Abyssinian Emperor to supply himself with the arms he needed in self-defence. Italy manufactures her own munitions and Abyssinia does not possess a single munitions factory. The argument was that by denying Abyssinia arms 'conciliation' was more likely to succeed." (pp. 144-145; italics mine.)

Again: "The spokesmen of the British Government announced with pride that whatever else it did it would take *no course in the matter of sanctions* which might provoke war with Italy. From that moment the conversation might just as well have ceased. Italy had only to say that in the event of any specified sanction being employed she would fight, for that sanction to go into the 'inapplicable' list. An eminent Italian professor has pointed out that from the moment the British Cabinet announced *'it would be no party to a policy involving war'* the *real* chairmanship of the Sanctions Committee passed to Signor Mussolini." (p. 146; italics mine.)

In support of the Italian professor's conclusion, writes Angell, "There is one supreme piece of evidence which settles the last point. In M. Laval's account of his meeting with Sir Samuel Hoare and Mr. Eden on Sept. 10, 1935, occurs this statement: 'We agreed that hostilities were about to begin almost immediately and . . . we found ourselves *instantaneously* in agreement upon ruling out military measures, not adopting any measure of naval blockade, never contemplating the closure of the Suez Canal—*in a word, ruling out everything that might lead to war.'* " (p. 147; italics mine.)

Further: "Mr. Churchill, who has examined the internal evidence as to whether our sanctions policy was 'real or sham,' writes that from first to last the committee charged with devising sanctions 'conformed docilely to the limitations prescribed by the aggressor. They proceeded to the rescue of Abyssinia on the basis that nothing must be done to hamper the invading Italian armies.' (p. 148).

"Mr. Winston Churchill has summarised the position thus: 'First the Prime Minister had declared that sanctions meant war; secondly he was resolved that there must be no war; and thirdly, he decided upon sanctions.' " (p. 146.)

And continuing to quote Mr. Churchill: " 'It is true that included in the sanctions were many measures, *especially financial* measures, which in the long run would have destroyed the Italian financial power to purchase necessities in foreign countries, and that these would have eventually affected their war-making capacity.

" 'But the chief of these, the financial sanctions, *did*

not require Geneva to impose them. The credit of Italy had already fallen, and was bound to fall, so low that the ordinary market factors would have been *as valid as the League decision.'*

" 'Thus the sanctions which we have been pressing with so great a parade were not real sanctions to paralyse the invader, but merely such half-hearted sanctions *as the invader would tolerate, because in fact they stimulated Italian war spirit.'* " (pp. 147-148; italics mine.)

The above are cited from Mr. Angell's book simply for their bearing on the *question of fact* involved in Mr. Dewey's statements in the text to which this is a note. As for their bearing on the *issue* of the use of sanctions, it is only fair to Mr. Angell (who is an advocate of the use of sanctions) to say that he uses these citations and other evidences to prove that sanctions have never *really* been imposed. (Which proof is also not irrelevant to Mr. Dewey's argument.)

To conclude this note: In 1935 the Governments of Great Britain and France happened to use the League of Nations as their stalking-horse. But that they really did not need to do so has since been amply demonstrated. Great Britain's Committee for Non-Intervention in Spain serves their purposes just as effectively, if not better.

CHAPTER TEN

FUNDAMENTALS OF THE EDUCATIONAL PROCESS

I · The Art of Education*

THE art of education is one in which every person is compelled whether he will or not to take an interest, because it so intimately concerns his own conduct. A person may begin with a narrow interest, one that cares only about, say, the education of his own children or of members of his own profession. But he does not go far before he is forced to note that he is building on a sandy foundation because of deficiencies due to earlier education. Professional education has its results limited and twisted because of the general state of education. Surveying that, it appears that its improvement cannot be made secure merely by better training of teachers. Parents, school officials, taxpayers have the last word, and the character of that word is dependent upon their education. They may and do block or deflect the best laid plans. That is the circle in which education moves. Those who received education are those who give it; habits already engendered deeply influence its course. It is as if no one could be educated in the full sense until everyone is developed beyond the reach of prejudice, stupidity and apathy.

There is no possibility of complete escape from this circle. Education returns upon itself in such a multitude

* From "Body and Mind," published in *Bulletin of the N. Y. Academy of Medicine*, vol. IV, pp. 17-19.

of ways as to render out of the question any short cut solution. It is a matter of accelerating momentum in the right direction, and of increasing the effective energy of the factors that make for removing obstacles. Chief among these obstacles are the practices which are associated with the traditional separation of mind and body and the consequent neglect of informed and intelligent action as the aim of all educational development. The division has affected every subject of study, every method of instruction and discipline. More than anything else it explains the separation of theory and practice, of thought and action. The result is a so-called cultural education which tends to be academic and pedantic, in any case aloof from the concerns of life, and an industrial and manual education which at best gives command of tools and means without intelligent grasp of purposes and ends.

The consequences of this divided education are writ large in the state of our civilization. The physician meets them in a wide range of induced disorders, to say nothing of waste and incapacitation. The walls which mark the separation are beginning to crack, although they are far from crumbling. From all sides the artificiality of isolation from one another of mind and body are commencing to be seen. There is at least the beginning of coöperation between those who are traditionally occupied with the concerns of mind and those busy with the affairs of the body.

The planning of any good school building is an illustrative symbol. Architect, engineer, hygienist, teacher and public official may join forces. But there are still many who should have a say, like the psychologist, who are left out, and such coöperation as there is lacks balance. It would be interesting, for example, to know what physicians would say of the wisdom of the herding together of thousands of children in our gigantic buildings with the en-

forced need of dealing with children en masse and the institution of lockstep methods—would say if they were
consulted and if they thought their voice would be heeded.

The growing interest in pre-school education, nursery
schools and parental education, the development of medical inspection, the impact of social hygiene, the institution
of school visitors and the use of schools as social centers
are other evidences that the isolation of schools from life
is beginning to give way because of coöperative action.
But not even the most optimistic would hold that we have
advanced beyond the outer breastworks. The forces are
still powerful that make for centrifugal and divisive education. And the chief of these is, let it be repeated, the
separation of mind and body which is incarnated in religion, morals and business as well as in science and philosophy. The full realization of the integration of mind
and body in action waits upon the reunion of philosophy
and science in art, above all in the supreme art, the art of
education.

II · Learning and Doing*

There is nothing new or striking in the conception of
activity as an important educational principle. In the form
of the idea of "self-activity" in particular, it has long been
a name for the ultimate educational ideal. But activity
has often been interpreted in too formal and too internal
a sense, and hence has remained a barren ideal without influence on practice; sometimes it becomes a mere phrase,
receiving the homage of the lips only.

To make the idea of activity effective, we must take it
broadly enough to cover all the doings that involve growth
of power—especially of power to realize the *meaning* of
what is done. This excludes action done under external

* From *Interest and Effort in Education*, pp. 65-84.

constraint or dictation, for this has no significance for the mind of him who performs it. It excludes also mere random reaction to an excitation that is finished when the momentary act has ceased—which does not, in other words carry the person acting into future broader fields. It also excludes action so habitual that it has become routine or mechanical. Unfortunately action from external constraint, for mere love of excitement and from mechanical force of habit are so common that these exceptions cover much ground. But the ground lying within these excepted fields is the ground where an educative process is *not* going on.

The kinds of activity remaining as true educative interests vary indefinitely with age, with individual native endowments, with prior experience, with social opportunities. It is out of the question to try to catalogue them. But we may discriminate some of their more general aspects. Since one of the main reasons for taking self-activity in a formal sense was ignoring the importance of the body and of bodily instinct, we may well begin with interest in activity in this most direct and literal sense.

1. It is an old story that the human young have to *learn* most of the things that the young of other animals do instinctively or else with a slight amount of trying. Reflection on this fact shows that in learning these things human offspring are brought to the need of learning other things, and also to acquiring a habit of learning—a love of learning. While these considerations are fairly familiar, we often overlook their bearing upon the fact of physical activities. It follows from them at once that in so far as a physical activity has to be *learned*, it is not merely physical, but is mental, intellectual, in quality. The first problem set the human young is learning to use the organs of sense—the eye, ear, touch, etc.—and of movement—the

muscles—in connection with one another. Of course, some of the mastery achieved does not involve much mental experimentation, but is due to the ripening of physiological connections. But nevertheless there is a genuinely intellectual factor when the child learns that one kind of eye-activity means a certain kind of moving of the arm, clasping of the fingers, etc., and that this in turn entails a certain kind of exploring with the fingers, resulting in experience of smoothness, etc. In such cases, there is not simply an acquisition of a new physical capacity; there is also learning in the mental sense; something has been found out. The rapidity of mental development in the first year and a half of infancy, the whole-hearted intentness and absorption of the growing baby in his activities, the joy that accompanies his increase of ability to control his movements—all of these things are object-lessons, writ large, as to the intellectual significance of actions that (externally judged) are physical.

This period of growth occurs, of course, before children go to school; at least before they go to anything called school. But the amount and the mode of learning in this school of action is most significant in revealing the importance of types of occupation within the school involving the exercise of senses and movement. One of the reasons for the slight advance made in putting in practice the doctrine of self-activity (with its recommendation of mental initiative and intellectual self-reliance, and its attacks upon the idea of pouring in and passive absorption) is precisely that it was supposed that self-activity could be secured purely internally, without the coöperation of bodily action through play, construction of objects, and manipulation of materials and tools. Only with children having specialized intellectual abilities is it possible to secure mental activity without participation of the organs of sense and the muscles. Yet how much of elementary schooling has consisted in the imposition of forms of discipline intended to *repress* all activity of the body! Under such a regime it is not surprising that children are found to be naturally averse to learning, or that intellectual activity is found to be so foreign to their nature that they have to be coerced or cunningly coaxed to engage in it! So educators blamed the children or the perverseness of human nature, instead of attacking the conditions which, by divorcing learning from use of the natural organs of action, made learning both difficult and onerous.

2. In this discussion of physical activity I have had in mind for the most part that of the organs of the body, especially the hands, as employed directly with simple materials, or at most such simple appliances as a pencil, a brush, etc. A higher form of activity involving the sensorimotor apparatus of the body is found when the control over external objects is achieved by means of tools of some sort, or by the application of one material to another. The use of a saw, a gimlet, a plane, of modeling-sticks, etc., illustrate the intervention of tools. The use of a thread in sewing, the application of heat and moisture in cooking or other simple experimentations, illustrate the use of one thing (or mode of energy) to bring about a change in another thing. There is, of course, no sharp distinction, either in practice or in principle, between this form of activity and the more direct kind just discussed. The organs of the body—especially the hands—may be regarded as a kind of tools whose use is to be learned by trying and thinking. Tools may be regarded as a sort of extension of the bodily organs. But the growing use of the latter opens a new line of development so important in its consequences that it is worth while to give it distinctive recognition. It is the *discovery and use of extra-organic*

*tools which have made possible, both in the history of the
race and of the individual, complicated activities of a long
duration*—that is, with results that are long postponed.
And it is this prolongation and postponement which requires an increasing use of intelligence. The use of tools
and appliances (in the broad sense) also demands a
greater degree of technical skill than does mastery of the
use of the natural organs—or rather, it involves the problem of a progressively more complicated use of the latter
—and hence stimulates a new line of development.

There seems to be no better name for the acts of using
intermediate means, or appliances, to reach ends than
work. When employed in this way, however, work must be
distinguished from labor and from toil and drudgery.
Labor means a form of work in which the direct result
accomplished is of value only as a means of exchange for
something else. It is an *economic* term, being applied to
that form of work where the product is paid for, and the
money paid is used for objects of more direct values. Toil
implies unusual arduousness in a task, involving fatigue.
Drudgery is an activity which in itself is quite disagreeable, performed under the constraint of some quite extraneous need. Play and work cannot, therefore, be distinguished from one another according to the presence or
absence of direct interest in what is doing. A child engaged in making something with tools, say, a boat, may
be just as immediately interested in what he is doing as if
he were sailing the boat. He is not doing what he does for
the mere sake of an external result—the boat—nor for the
mere sake of sailing it later. The thought of the finished
product and of the use to which it is to be put may come
to his mind, but so as to enhance his immediate activity of
construction. In this case, his interest is free. He has a
play-motive; his activity is essentially artistic in principle.

What differentiates it from more spontaneous play is an *intellectual* quality; a remoter end in time serves to suggest and regulate a series of acts. Not to introduce an element of work *in this sense* when the child is ready for it is simply arbitrarily to arrest his development, and to force his activities to a level of sense-excitation after he is prepared to act upon the basis of an idea. A mode of activity that was quite normal in its own period becomes disintegrating when persisted in after a person is ripe for an activity involving more thought. We must also remember that the change from an activity with an end near by to one with an end farther off does not come all at once, nor at the same time with respect to all things. A child may be ready for occupation with tools like scissors, paint and brush, for setting a table, cooking, etc., while with respect to other activities he is still unable to plan and arrange ahead. Thus there is no ground for the assumption that children of kindergarten age are capable only of make-believe play, while children of the primary grades should be held to all work and no play. Only the false idea about symbolism leads to the former conclusion; and only a false identification of interest and play with trivial amusement leads to the latter conclusion. It has been said that man is man only as he plays; to say this involves some change from the meaning in which play has just been used. But in the broader sense of whole-hearted identification with what one is doing—in the sense of completeness of interest, it is so true that it should be a truism.

Work in the sense in which it has been defined covers all activities involving the use of intervening materials, appliances, and forms of skill consciously used in achieving results. It covers all forms of expression and construction with tools and materials, all forms of artistic and manual activity so far as they involve the conscious or thoughtful

endeavor to achieve an end. They include, that is, painting, drawing, clay modeling, singing so far as there is any
conscious attention to means—to the technique of execution. They comprehend the various forms of manual
training, work with wood, metal, textiles, cooking, sewing, etc., so far as these involve an idea of the result to be
accomplished (instead of working from dictation or an
external model which does away with the need for
thought). They cover also the manual side of scientific
inquiry, the collection of materials for study, the management of apparatus, the sequence of acts required in carrying on and in recording experiments.

3. So far as this latter interest—the interest in discovery
or in finding out what happens under given circumstances
—gains in importance, there develops a third type of interest—the distinctively intellectual interest. Our wording
should be carefully noted. The intellectual interest is not a
new thing, now showing itself for the first time. Our discussion of the development of the so-called physical activities of a baby, and of the constructive work of children,
youth, and adults has been intended to show that intelligence, in the form of clear perception of the result of an
activity and search for and adaptation of means, should
be an integral part of such activities. But it is possible for
this intellectual interest to be subordinate, to be subsidi-
ary, to the accomplishment of a process. But it is also
possible for it to become a dominating interest, so that instead of thinking things out and discovering them for the
sake of the successful achievement of an activity, we institute the activity for the sake of finding out something.
Then the distinctively intellectual, or theoretical, interest
shows itself.

As there is no sharp line of division in theory, so there
is none in practice. Planning ahead, taking notice of what

happens, relating this to what is attempted, are parts of all intelligent or purposive activities. It is the business of educators to see that the conditions of expression of the practical interests are such as to encourage the developing of these intellectual phases of an activity, and thereby evoke a gradual transition to the theoretical type. It is a commonplace that the fundamental principle of science is connected with the relation of cause and effect. Interest in this relation begins on the practical side. Some effect is aimed at, is desired and worked for, and attention is given to the conditions for producing it. At first the interest in the achievement of the end predominates; but in the degree in which this interest is bound up with *thoughtful* effort, interest in the end or effect is of necessity transferred to the interest in the means—the causes—which bring it about. Where work with tools, gardening, cooking, etc., is intelligently carried on, it is comparatively a simple matter to secure a transfer of interest from the practical side to experimentation for the sake of discovery. When any one becomes interested in a problem as a problem and in inquiry and learning for the sake of solving the problem, interest is distinctively intellectual.

III · The Training of Thinking*

Teaching may be compared to selling commodities. No one can sell unless someone buys. We should ridicule a merchant who said that he had sold a great many goods although no one had bought any. But perhaps there are teachers who think that they have done a good day's teaching irrespective of what pupils have learned. There is the same exact equation between teaching and learning that there is between selling and buying. The only way to

* From *How We Think* (revised edition), pp. 35-57. Reprinted by special permission of D. C. Heath and Co.

increase the learning of pupils is to augment the quantity and quality of real teaching. Since learning is something that the pupil has to do himself and for himself, the initiative lies with the learner. The teacher is a guide and director; he steers the boat, but the energy that propels it must come from those who are learning. The more a teacher is aware of the past experiences of students, of their hopes, desires, chief interests, the better will he understand the forces at work that need to be directed and utilized for the formation of reflective habits.

All our sense and motor organs are, when we are awake, acting and being acted upon by something in the environment. With adults many of these contacts have been made; grown-ups permit themselves to become stale; they fall into ruts of experience and are contented with what happens in these ruts. To children the whole world is new; there is something thrilling to the healthy being in every new contact and it is eagerly sought for, not merely passively awaited and endured. There is no single faculty called "curiosity"; every normal organ of sense and of motor activity is on the *qui vive*. It wants a chance to be active, and it needs some object in order to act. The sum total of these outgoing tendencies constitutes curiosity. It is the basic factor in enlargement of experience and therefore a prime ingredient in the germs that are to be developed into reflective thinking.

In the main, for most persons, the primary resource in the development of orderly habits of thought is indirect, not direct. Intellectual organization originates and for a time grows as an accompaniment of the organization of the means required to realize an end, not as the result of a direct appeal to thinking power. The need of thinking to accomplish something beyond thinking is more potent than thinking for its own sake. All people at the outset, and the majority of people probably all their lives, attain to some ordering of thought through ordering of action. Adults normally carry on some occupation, profession, pursuit; and this furnishes the stabilizing axis about which their knowledge, their beliefs, and their habits of reaching and testing conclusions are organized. Observations that have to do with the efficient performance of their calling are extended and rendered precise. Information related to it is not merely amassed and then left in a heap; it is classified and subdivided so as to be available as needed. Inferences are made by most men not from purely speculative motives, but because they are necessary for the efficient performance of the duties involved in their several callings. Thus their inferences are constantly tested by results achieved; futile and scattering methods tend to be discounted; orderly arrangements have a premium put upon them. The event, the issue, stands as a constant check on the thinking that has led up to it; and this discipline by efficiency in action is the chief sanction, in practically all who are not scientific specialists, of orderliness of thought—provided always that action remains intelligent and does not become routine.

Such a resource—the main prop of disciplined thinking in adult life—is not to be despised in training the young in right intellectual habits. From an early age, children have to select acts and objects as means for reaching ends. With selection go arrangement and adaptation. These operations demand *judgment*. Suitable conditions work unconsciously to build up an attitude favorable to reflective operations. There are, however, profound differences between the immature and the adult with respect to the organized character of their activities—differences that must be taken seriously into account in any educational use of activities: (1) the external achievement resulting from activity is a more urgent necessity with the adult, and hence is with him a more effective means of disciplining the mind than with the child; (2) the ends of adult activity are more specialized than those of child activity.

The selection and arrangement of appropriate lines of action are a much more difficult problem with youth than they are in the case of adults. This very difficulty, however, points to the fact that the *opportunity for selecting truly educative activities* is indefinitely greater in child life than in adult. The factor of external pressure is so strong with most adults that the educative value of the pursuit—its reflex influence upon intelligence and character—however genuine, is incidental, and frequently almost accidental. The problem and the opportunity with the young are selection of orderly and continuous modes of occupation, which, while they lead up to and prepare for the indispensable activities of adult life, have their own *sufficient justification in their present reflex influence upon the formation of habits of thought.*

There is no single and uniform power of thought, but a multitude of different ways in which specific things— things observed, remembered, heard of, read about—evoke suggestions or ideas that are pertinent to a problem or question and that carry the mind forward to a justifiable conclusion. Training is that development of curiosity, suggestion, and habits of exploring and testing, which increases sensitiveness to questions and love of inquiry into the puzzling and unknown; which enhances the fitness of suggestions that spring up in the mind, and controls their succession in a developing and cumulative order; which makes more acute the sense of the force, the *proving* power, of every fact observed and suggestion employed. Thinking is not a separate mental process; it is an affair of the *way* in which the vast multitude of objects that are observed and suggested are employed, the way they run together and are *made* to run together, the way they are handled. Consequently any subject, topic, question, is intellectual not *per se* but because of the part it is made to play in directing thought in the life of any particular person.

For these reasons, the problem of *method* in forming habits of reflective thought is the problem of establishing *conditions* that will arouse and guide *curiosity;* of setting up the connections in things experienced that will on later occasions promote the flow of *suggestions,* create problems and purposes that will favor *consecutiveness* in the succession of ideas. An illustration or two drawn from failure to secure proper conditions will indicate more clearly what is meant. Children are hushed up when they ask questions; their exploring and investigating activities are inconvenient and hence they are treated like nuisances; pupils are taught to memorize things so that merely one-track verbal associations are set up instead of varied and flexible connections with things themselves; no plans and projects are provided that compel the student to look ahead and foresee and in the execution of which the accomplishment of one thing sets up new questions and suggests new undertakings. The teacher may devise special exercises intended to train thinking directly, but when these wrong conditions exist, special exercises are doomed to be futile. The training of thought can be attained only by regulating the causes that evoke and guide it.

With respect to the training of habits of thought, the teacher's problem is thus twofold. On the one side, he needs to be a student of individual traits and habits; on the other side, he needs to be a student of the conditions that modify for better or worse the directions in which individual powers habitually express themselves. He needs

to recognize that method covers not only what he intentionally devises and employs for the purpose of mental
training, but also what he does without any conscious reference to it—anything in the atmosphere and conduct of
the school that reacts in any way upon the curiosity, the
responsiveness, and the orderly activity of children. The
teacher who is an intelligent student both of individual
mental operations and of the effects of school conditions
upon those operations can largely be trusted to select for
himself methods of instruction in their narrower and more
technical sense—those best adapted to achieve results in
particular subjects, such as reading, geography, or algebra. In the hands of one who is not intelligently aware of
individual capacities and of the influence unconsciously
exerted upon them by the entire environment, even the
best of technical methods are likely to get an immediate
result at the expense of forming deep-seated and persistent
bad habits.

IV · Individuality and Freedom*

The history of schools not only in art but in all lines
shows a swing of the pendulum between extremes, though
it must be admitted that the simile of the pendulum is not
a good one, for the schools remain most of them, most of
the time, near one extreme, instead of swinging periodically and evenly between the two. Anyway, the two extremes are external imposition and dictation and "free
expression." Revolt from the costly, nerve-taxing and
inadequate results of mechanical control from without
creates an enthusiasm for spontaneity and "development
from within," as it is often phrased. It is found that children at first are then much happier in their work—but
gradually tend to become listless and finally bored, while

* From *Journal of the Barnes Foundation,* vol. II, pp. 1-6.

there is an absence of cumulative, progressive development of power and of actual achievements in results. Then
the pendulum swings back to regulation by the ideas,
rules, and orders of some one else, who being maturer, better informed and more experienced is supposed to know
what should be done and how to do it.

The metaphor of the pendulum is faulty in another respect. It seems to suggest that the solution lies in finding
a mid-point between the two extremes which would be at
rest. But what is really wanted is a change in the direction
of movement. As a general proposition no one would deny
that personal mental growth is furthered in any branch of
human undertaking by contact with the accumulated and
sifted experience of others in that line. No one would seriously propose that all future carpenters should be trained
by actually starting with a clean sheet, wiping out everything that the past has discovered about mechanics, about
tools and their uses and so on. It would not be thought
likely that this knowledge would "cramp their style," limit
their individuality, etc. But neither, on the other hand,
have carpenters been formed by the methods often used in
manual training shops where dinky tasks of a minute and
technical nature are set, wholly independent of really making anything, having only specialized skill as their aim.
As a rule carpenters are educated in their calling by working with others who have experience and skill, sharing in
the simpler portions of the real undertakings, assisting in
ways which enable them to observe methods and to see
what results they are adapted to accomplish.

Such learning is controlled by two great principles: one
is participation in something inherently worth while, or
undertaken on its own account; the other is perception of
the relation of means to consequences. When these two
conditions are met, a third consideration usually follows

as a matter of course. Having had an experience of the meaning of certain technical processes and forms of skill there develops an interest in skill and "technique": the meaning of the result is "transferred" to the means of its attainment. Boys interested in base-ball as a game thus submit themselves voluntarily to continued practice in throwing, catching, batting, the separate elements of the game. Or boys who get interested in the game of marbles will practice to increase their skill in shooting and hitting. Just imagine, however, what would happen if they set these exercises as tasks in school, with no prior activity in the games and with no sense of what they were about or for, and without any such appeal to the social, or participating impulses, as takes place in games!

If we generalize from such a commonplace case as the education of artisans through their work, we may say that the customs, methods and *working* standards of the calling constitute a "tradition," and that initiation into the tradition is the means by which the powers of learners are released and directed. But we should also have to say that the urge or need of an individual to join in an undertaking is a necessary prerequisite of the tradition's being a factor in his personal growth in power and freedom; and also that he has to *see* on his own behalf and in his own way the relations between means and methods employed and results achieved. Nobody else can see for him, and he can't see just by being "told," although the right kind of telling may guide his seeing and thus help him see what he needs to see. And if he has no impelling desire of his own to become a carpenter, if his interest in being one is perfunctory, if it is not an interest in *being* a carpenter at all, but only in getting a pecuniary reward by doing jobs, the tradition will never of course really enter into and integrate with his own powers. It will remain, then, a mere set of mechanical and more or less meaningless rules that he is obliged to follow if he is to hold his job and draw his pay.

Supposing, again, that our imaginary pupil works for and with a master carpenter who believes in only one kind of house with a fixed design, and his aim is not only to teach his apprentice to make just that one kind of house, but to accept it with all his soul, heart and mind as the only kind of house that should ever be built, the very type and standard model of all houses. Then it is easy to see that limitation of personal powers will surely result, not merely, moreover, limitation of technical skill but, what is more important, of his powers of observation, imagination, judgment, and even his emotions, since his appreciations will be warped to conform to the one preferred style. The imaginary case illustrates what often happens when we pass from the education of artisans to that of artists. As a rule a carpenter has to keep more or less open; he is exposed to many demands and must be flexible enough to meet them. He is in no position to set up a final authority about ends and models and standards, no matter how expert he may be in methods and means. But an architect in distinction from a builder is likely to be an "authority"; he can dictate and lay down what is right and wrong, and thus prescribe certain ends and proscribe others. Here is a case where tradition is not enhancing and liberating, but is restrictive and enslaving. If he has pupils, he is a "master" and not an advanced fellow worker; his students are disciples rather than learners. Tradition is no longer tradition but a fixed and absolute convention.

In short, the practical difficulty does not reside in any antagonism of methods and rules and results worked out in past experience to individual desire, capacity and freedom. It lies rather in the hard and narrow and, we may

truly say, uneducated habits and attitudes of teachers who
set up as authorities, as rulers and judges in Israel. As a
matter of course they know that as bare individuals they
are not "authorities" and will not be accepted by others
as such. So they clothe themselves with some tradition as
a mantle, and henceforth it is not just "I" who speaks, but
some Lord speaks through me. The teacher then offers
himself as the organ of the voice of a whole school, of a
finished classic tradition, and arrogates to himself the prestige that comes from what he is the spokesman for. Suppression of the emotional and intellectual integrity of
pupils is the result; their freedom is repressed and the
growth of their own personalities stunted. But it is not because of any opposition between the wisdom and skill of
the past and the individual capacities of learners; the
trouble lies in the habits, standards and ideas of the
teacher. It is analogous to another case. There is no inherent opposition between theory and practice; the former
enlarges, releases and gives significance to the latter; while
practice supplies theory with its materials and with the
test and check which keep it sincere and vital. But there
is a whole lot of opposition between human beings who set
themselves up as practical and those who set themselves
up as theorists, an irresolvable conflict because both have
put themselves into a wrong position.

This suggests that the proponents of freedom are in a
false position as well as the would-be masters and dicta-
tors. There is a present tendency in so-called advanced
schools of educational thought to say, in effect, let us surround pupils with certain materials, tools, appliances, etc.,
and then let pupils respond to these things according to
their own desires. Above all let us not suggest any end or
plan to the students; let us not suggest to them what they
shall do, for that is an unwarranted trespass upon their

sacred intellectual individuality since the essence of such individuality is to set up ends and aims.

Now such a method is really stupid. For it attempts the impossible, which is always stupid; and it misconceives the conditions of independent thinking. There are a multitude of ways of reacting to surrounding conditions, and without some guidance from experience these reactions are almost sure to be casual, sporadic and ultimately fatiguing, accompanied by nervous strain. Since the teacher has presumably a greater background of experience, there is the same presumption of the right of a teacher to make suggestions as to what to do, as there is on the part of the head carpenter to suggest to apprentices something of what they are to do. Moreover, the theory literally carried out would be obliged to banish all artificial materials, tools and appliances. Being the product of the skill, thought and matured experience of others, they would also, by the theory, "interfere" with personal freedom.

Moreover, when the child proposes or suggests what to do, some consequence to be attained, whence is the suggestion supposed to spring from? There is no spontaneous germination in the mental life. If he does not get the suggestion from the teacher, he gets it from somebody or something in the home or the street or from what some more vigorous fellow pupil is doing. Hence the chances are great of its being a passing and superficial suggestion, without much depth and range—in other words, not specially conducive to the developing of freedom. If the teacher is really a teacher, and not just a master or "authority," he should know enough about his pupils, their needs, experiences, degrees of skill and knowledge etc., to be able (not to dictate aims and plans) to share in a discussion regarding what is to be done and be as free to make suggestions as any one else. (The implication that

the teacher is the one and only person who has no "individuality" or "freedom" to "express" would be funny if it
were not often so sad in its outworkings.) And his contribution, given the conditions stated, will presumably do
more to getting something started which will really secure
and increase the development of strictly individual capacities than will suggestions springing from uncontrolled
haphazard sources.

The point is also worth dwelling upon that the method
of leaving the response entirely to pupils, the teacher supplying, in the language of the day, only the "stimuli," misconceives the nature of thinking. Any so-called "end" or
"aim" or "project" which the average immature person
can suggest in advance is likely to be highly vague and unformed, a mere outline sketch, not a suggestion of a definite result or consequence but rather a gesture which
roughly indicates a field within which activities might be
carried on. It hardly represents thought at all: it is a suggestion. The real intellectual shaping of the "end" or purpose comes during and because of the operations subsequently performed. This is as true of the suggestion which
proceeds from the teacher as of those which "spontaneously" spring from the pupils, so that the former does not
restrict thought. The advantage on the side of the teacher
—if he or she has any business to be in that position—is
the greater probability that it will be a suggestion which
will permit and require thought in the subsequent activity
which builds up a clear and organized conception of an
end. There is no more fatal flaw in psychology than that
which takes the original vague fore-feeling of some consequence to be realized as the equivalent of a *thought* of an
end, a true purpose and directive plan. The thought of an
end is strictly correlative to perception of means and
methods. Only when and as the latter becomes clear dur-

ing the serial process of execution do the project and guiding aim and plan become evident and articulated. In the full sense of the word, a person becomes aware of what he wants to do and what he is about only when the work is actually complete.

The adjective "serial" is important in connection with the process of performance or execution. Each step forward, each "means" used, is a partial attainment of an "end." It makes clearer the character of that end, and hence suggests to an observing mind the next step to be taken, or the means and methods to be next employed. Originality and independence of thinking are therefore connected with the intervening process of execution rather than with the source of the initial suggestion. Indeed, genuinely fruitful and original suggestions are themselves usually the results of experience in the carrying out of undertakings. The "end" is not, in other words, an end or finality in the literal sense, but is in turn the starting-point of new desires, aims and plans. By means of the process the mind gets power to make suggestions which are significant. There is now a past experience from which they can spring with an increased probability of their being worthwhile and articulate.

It goes without saying that a teacher may interfere and impose alien standards and methods during the operation. But as we have previously seen, this is not because of bringing to bear the results of previous experience, but because the habits of the teacher are so narrow and fixed, his imagination and sympathies so limited, his own intellectual horizon so bounded, that he brings them to bear in a wrong way. The fuller and richer the experience of the teacher, the more adequate his own knowledge of "traditions" the more likely is he, given the attitude of participator instead of that of master, to use them in a liberating way.

Freedom or individuality, in short, is not an original possession or gift. It is something to be achieved, to be wrought out. Suggestions as to things which may advantageously be taken, as to skill, as to methods of operation, are indispensable conditions of its achievement. These by the nature of the case must come from a sympathetic and discriminating knowledge of what has been done in the past and how it has been done.

V · The Continuity of the Educational Process*

Education is a constant reorganizing or reconstructing of experience. It has all the time an immediate end, and so far as activity is educative, it reaches that end—the direct transformation of the quality of experience. Infancy, youth, adult life—all stand on the same educative level in the sense that what is really *learned* at any and every stage of experience constitutes the value of that experience, and in the sense that it is the chief business of life at every point to make living thus contribute to an enrichment of its own perceptible meaning.†

The educative process is all one with the moral process, since the latter is a continuous passage of experience from worse to better. Education has been traditionally thought of as preparation: as learning, acquiring certain things because they will later be useful. The end is remote, and education is getting ready, is a preliminary to something more important to happen later on. Childhood is only a preparation for adult life, and adult life for another life.

* From *Reconstruction in Philosophy*, pp. 183-186.
† From *Democracy and Education*, p. 89. By permission of The Macmillan Company, publishers.

Always the future, not the present, has been the significant thing in education: acquisition of knowledge and skill for future use and enjoyment; formation of habits required later in life in business, good citizenship and pursuit of science. Education is thought of also as something needed by some human beings merely because of their dependence upon others. We are born ignorant, unversed, unskilled, immature, and consequently in a state of social dependence. Instruction, training, moral discipline are processes by which the mature, the adult, gradually raise the helpless to the point where they can look out for themselves. The business of childhood is to grow into the independence of adulthood by means of the guidance of those who have already attained it. Thus the process of education as the main business of life ends when the young have arrived at emancipation from social dependence.

These two ideas, generally assumed but rarely explicitly reasoned out, contravene the conception that growing, or the continuous reconstruction of experience, is the only end. If at whatever period we choose to take a person, he is still in process of growth, then education is not, save as a by-product, a preparation for something coming later. Getting from the present the degree and kind of growth there is in it is education. This is a constant function, independent of age. The best thing that can be said about any special process of education, like that of the formal school period, is that it renders its subject capable of further education: more sensitive to conditions of growth and more able to take advantage of them. Acquisition of skill, possession of knowledge, attainment of culture are not ends: they are marks of growth and means to its continuing.

The contrast usually assumed between the period of

education as one of social dependence and of maturity as one of social independence does harm. We repeat over and over that man is a social animal, and then confine the significance of this statement to the sphere in which sociality usually seems least evident, politics. The heart of the sociality of man is in education. The idea of education as preparation and of adulthood as a fixed limit of growth are two sides of the same obnoxious untruth. If the moral business of the adult as well as the young is a growing and developing experience, then the instruction that comes from social dependencies and interdependencies is as important for the adult as for the child. Moral independence for the adult means arrest of growth, isolation means induration. We exaggerate the intellectual dependence of childhood so that children are too much kept in leading strings, and then we exaggerate the independence of adult life from intimacy of contacts and communication with others.

When the identity of the moral process with the processes of specific growth is realized, the more conscious and formal education of childhood will be seen to be the most economical and efficient means of social advance and reorganization, and it will also be evident that the test of all the institutions of adult life is their effect in furthering continued education. Government, business, art, religion, all social institutions have a meaning, a purpose. That purpose is to set free and to develop the capacities of human individuals without respect to race, sex, class or economic status. And this is all one with saying that the test of their value is the extent to which they educate every individual into the full stature of his possibility. Democracy has many meanings, but if it has a moral meaning, it is found in resolving that the supreme test of all political institutions and industrial arrangements shall be the contribution they make to the all-around growth of every member of society.

CHAPTER ELEVEN

SCIENCE AND PHILOSOPHY OF EDUCATION

I · Education as a Science*

THE title—*The Sources of a Science of Education*—may suggest to some minds that it begs a prior question: *Is* there a science of education? And still more fundamentally, Can there be a science of education? Are the procedures and aims of education such that it is possible to reduce them to anything properly called a science? Similar questions exist in other fields. The issue is not unknown in history; it is raised in medicine and law. As far as education is concerned, I may confess at once that I have put the question in its apparently question-begging form in order to avoid discussion of questions that are important but that are also full of thorns and attended with controversial divisions.

It is enough for our purposes to note that the word "science" has a wide range.

There are those who would restrict the term to mathematics or to disciplines in which exact results can be determined by rigorous methods of demonstration. Such a conception limits even the claims of physics and chemistry to be sciences, for according to it the only scientific portion of these subjects is the strictly mathematical. The position of what are ordinarily termed the biological sci-

* From *The Sources of a Science of Education*, pp. 7-18; 28-33.

ences is even more dubious, while social subjects and psychology would hardly rank as sciences at all, when measured by this definition. Clearly we must take the idea of science with some latitude. We must take it with sufficient looseness to include all the subjects that are usually regarded as sciences. The important thing is to discover those traits in virtue of which various fields are called scientific. When we raise the question in this way, we are led to put emphasis upon *methods* of dealing with subject-matter rather than to look for uniform objective traits in subject-matter. From this point of view, science signifies, I take it, the existence of systematic methods of inquiry, which, when they are brought to bear on a range of facts, enable us to understand them better and to control them more intelligently, less haphazardly and with less routine.

No one would doubt that our practices in hygiene and medicine are less casual, less results of a mixture of guess work and tradition, than they used to be, nor that this difference has been made by development of methods of investigating and testing. There is an intellectual technique by which discovery and organization of material go on cumulatively, and by means of which one inquirer can repeat the researches of another, confirm or discredit them, and add still more to the capital stock of knowledge. Moreover, the methods when they are used tend to perfect themselves, to suggest new problems, new investigations, which refine old procedures and create new and better ones.

The question as to the sources of a science of education is, then, to be taken in this sense. What are the ways by means of which the function of education in all its branches and phases—selection of material for the curriculum, methods of instruction and discipline, organization and administration of schools—can be conducted

with systematic increase of intelligent control and understanding? What are the materials upon which we may—
and should—draw in order that educational activities may
become in a less degree products of routine, tradition, accident and transitory accidental influences? From what
sources shall we draw so that there shall be steady and
cumulative growth of intelligent, communicable insight
and power of direction?

Here is the answer to those who decry pedagogical study
on the ground that success in teaching and in moral direction of pupils is often not in any direct ratio to knowledge of educational principles. Here is "A" who is much
more successful than "B" in teaching, awakening the enthusiasm of his students for learning, inspiring them
morally by personal example and contact, and yet relatively ignorant of educational history, psychology, approved methods, etc., which "B" possesses in abundant
measure. The facts are admitted. But what is overlooked
by the objector is that the successes of such individuals
tend to be born and to die with them: beneficial consequences extend only to those pupils who have personal
contact with such gifted teachers. No one can measure the
waste and loss that have come from the fact that the contributions of such men and women in the past have been
thus confined, and the only way by which we can prevent
such waste in the future is by methods which enable us
to make an *analysis* of what the gifted teacher does in-
tuitively, so that something accruing from his work can be
communicated to others. Even in the things conventionally
recognized as sciences, the insights of unusual persons
remain important and there is no levelling down to a uniform procedure. But the existence of science gives common efficacy to the experiences of the genius; it makes it
possible for the results of special power to become part of

the working equipment of other inquirers, instead of perishing as they arose.

The individual capacities of the Newtons, Boyles, Joules, Darwins, Lyells, Helmholtzes, are not destroyed because of the existence of science; their differences from others and the impossibility of predicting on the basis of past science what discoveries they would make—that is, the impossibility of regulating their activities by antecedent sciences—persist. But science makes it possible for others to benefit systematically by what they achieved.

The existence of scientific method protects us also from a danger that attends the operations of men of unusual power; dangers of slavish imitation partisanship, and such jealous devotion to them and their work as to get in the way of further progress. Anybody can notice today that the effect of an original and powerful teacher is not all to the good. Those influenced by him often show a one-sided interest; they tend to form schools, and to become impervious to other problems and truths; they incline to swear by the words of their master and to go on repeating his thoughts after him, and often without the spirit and insight that originally made them significant. Observation also shows that these results happen oftenest in those subjects in which scientific method is least developed. Where these methods are of longer standing students adopt methods rather than merely results, and employ them with flexibility rather than in literal reproduction.

This digression seems to be justified not merely because those who object to the idea of a science put personality and its unique gifts in opposition to science, but also because those who recommend science sometimes urge that uniformity of procedure will be its consequence. So it seems worth while to dwell on the fact that in the subjects best developed from the scientific point of view, the opposite is the case. Command of scientific methods and systematized subject-matter liberates individuals; it enables them to see new problems, devise new procedures, and, in general, makes for diversification rather than for set uniformity. But at the same time these diversifications have a cumulative effect in an advance shared by all workers in the field.

That, in concrete operation, education is an art, either a mechanical art or a fine art, is unquestionable. If there were an opposition between science and art, I should be compelled to side with those who assert that education is an art. But there is no opposition, although there is a distinction. We must not be misled by words. Engineering is, in actual practice, an art. But it is an art that progressively incorporates more and more of science into itself, more of mathematics, physics and chemistry. It is the kind of art it is precisely because of a content of scientific subject-matter which guides it as a practical operation. There is room for the original and daring projects of exceptional individuals. But their distinction lies not in the fact that they turn their backs upon science, but in the fact that they make new integrations of scientific material and turn it to new and previously unfamiliar and unforeseen uses. When, in education, the psychologist or observer and experimentalist in any field reduces his findings to a rule which is to be uniformly adopted, then, only, is there a result which is objectionable and destructive of the free play of education as an art.

But this happens not because of scientific method but because of departure from it. It is not the capable engineer who treats scientific findings as imposing upon him a certain course which is to be rigidly adhered to: it is the third- or fourth-rate man who adopts this course. Even more, it is the unskilled day laborer who follows it. For even if the practice adopted is one that follows from science and could 'not have been discovered or employed except for science, when it is converted into a uniform rule of procedure it becomes an empirical rule-of-thumb procedure—just as a person may use a table of logarithms mechanically without knowing anything about mathematics.

The danger is great in the degree in which the attempt to develop scientific method is recent. Nobody would deny that education is still in a condition of transition from an empirical to a scientific status. In its empirical form the chief factors determining education are tradition, imitative reproduction, response to various external pressures where the strongest force wins out, and the gifts, native and acquired, of individual teachers. In this situation there is a strong tendency to identify teaching ability with the use of procedures that yield immediately successful results, success being measured by such things as order in the classroom, correct recitations by pupils in assigned lessons, passing of examinations, promotion of pupils to a higher grade, etc.

For the most part, these are the standards by which a community judges the worth of a teacher. Prospective teachers come to training schools, whether in normal schools or colleges, with such ideas implicit in their minds. They want very largely to find out *how to do* things with the maximum prospect of success. Put baldly, they want recipes. Now, to such persons science is of value because it puts a stamp of final approval upon this and that specific procedure. It is very easy for science to be regarded as a guarantee that goes with the sale of goods rather than as a light to the eyes and a lamp to the feet. It is prized for its prestige value rather than as an organ of personal illumination and liberation. It is prized because it is thought to give unquestionable authenticity and authority to a specific procedure to be carried out in the school room. So conceived, science *is* antagonistic to education as an art.

To be able to get away for the time being from entanglement in the urgencies and needs of immediate practical concerns is a condition of the origin of scientific treatment in any field. Preoccupation with attaining some direct end or practical utility always limits scientific inquiry. For it restricts the field of attention and thought, since we note only those things that are immediately connected with what we want to do or get at the moment. Science signifies that we carry our observations and thinking further afield and become interested in what happens on its own account. Theory is in the end, as has been well said, the most practical of all things, because this widening of the range of attention beyond nearby purpose and desire eventually results in the creation of wider and farther-reaching purposes and enables us to use a much wider and deeper range of conditions and means than were expressed in the observation of primitive practical purposes. For the time being, however, the formation of theories demands a resolute turning aside from the needs of practical operations previously performed.

This detachment is peculiarly hard to secure in the case of those persons who are concerned with building up the scientific content of educational practices and arts. There is a pressure for immediate results, for demonstration of a quick, short-time span of usefulness in school. There is a tendency to convert the results of statistical inquiries and laboratory experiments into directions and rules for the conduct of school administration and instruction. Results tend to be directly grabbed, as it were, and put into operation by teachers. Then there is not the leisure for that slow and gradual independent growth of theories that is a necessary condition of the formation of a true science. This danger is peculiarly imminent in a science of education because its very recentness and novelty arouse scepticism as to its possibility and its value. The human desire to prove that the scientific mode of attack is really of value brings pressure to convert scientific conclusions into *rules* and standards of schoolroom practice.

Laws and facts, even when they are arrived at in genuinely scientific shape, do not yield *rules of practice*. Their value for educational practice—and *all* education is a mode of practice, intelligent or accidental and routine—is indirect; it consists in provision of *intellectual instrumentalities* to be used by the educator. That is, they *direct his attention,* in both observation and reflection, to conditions and relationships which would otherwise escape him. If we retain the word "rule" at all, we must say that scientific results furnish a rule for the conduct of *observations and inquiries,* not a rule for overt action. They function not directly with respect to practice and its results, but indirectly, through the medium of an altered mental attitude.

I knew a teacher in a training school for teachers who used to tell his students, "If you find that what I am telling you, or what another teacher here tells you, gets in the way of your common sense, of your use of your own judgment in an actual school situation, forget what you have learned and rely upon what your own judgment tells you is the best thing to do under the circumstances."

I never understood this saying to mean that the teacher thought that personal common-sense judgments and intuitions were the sole and sufficient guides of the teacher, or that he regarded the principles and facts which were taught to those in training of no practical value. I imagine that what he said was a negative way of stating that the value of the science, the history and philosophy of education acquired in the training school, resides in the enlightenment and guidance it supplies to observation and judgment of actual situations as they arise. If, in any particular case, the students saw no connection between what they had learned and the school situation, instead of trying to derive a rule from what they had learned they should depend upon their judgment as that had been developed by theoretical learnings and as these might operate unconsciously. In short, it was a way of saying that the value of definite instruction with respect to educational matters consists in its effect upon the formation of personal attitudes of observing and judging.

The net conclusion of our discussion is that the final reality of educational science is not found in books, nor in experimental laboratories, nor in the class-rooms where it is taught, but in the minds of those engaged in directing educational activities. Results may be scientific, short of their operative presence in the attitudes and habits of observation, judgment and planning of those engaged in the educative act. But they are not *educational* science short of this point. They are psychology, sociology, statistics, or whatever.

This is the point upon which my whole discussion turns. We must distinguish between the *sources of educational science* and scientific content. We are in constant danger of confusing the two; we tend to suppose that certain results, because they are scientific, are already educational science. Enlightenment, clarity and progress can come about only as we remember that such results are *sources* to be used, through the medium of the minds of educators, to make educational functions more intelligent.

II · Sources of a Science of Education

A. ON THE BORROWING OF TECHNIQUES*

Educational science cannot be constructed simply by borrowing the techniques of experiment and measurement found in physical science. This could happen only if some way had been found by which mental or psychological phenomena are capable of statement in terms of units of space, time, motion, and mass. It is unnecessary to state that this condition has not been fulfilled. Nor have we as yet any *other* general hypotheses in the light of which to know *what* we are measuring and by which we can interpret results, place them in a system and lead on to fruitful indirect measurements. This principle is practically important at the present time. There is a tendency to assume that we are getting the material of a science of education merely because the techniques of older, better established sciences are borrowed and used.

It is no reproach to a would-be science that in early stages it makes experiments and measurements the results of which lack generalized significance. A period of groping is inevitable. But the lack of an intellectually coherent and inclusive system is a positive warning against attributing scientific value to results merely because they are reached by means of recognized techniques borrowed from sciences already established and are capable of being stated in quantitative formulae. Quantity is not even the fundamental idea of mathematics.

B. EDUCATIVE PROCESSES AS A SOURCE†

The first question which comes before us is what are the place and role of educative processes and results in the school, family, etc., when they are viewed as a *source?*

* From *The Sources of a Science of Education*, pp. 26-27.
† From *The Sources of a Science of Education*, pp. 33-36.

The answer is (1) that educational *practices* provide the data, the subject-matter, which form the *problems* of inquiry. They are the sole source of the ultimate problems to be investigated. These educational practices are also (2) the final *test of value* of the conclusion of all researches. To suppose that scientific findings decide the value of educational undertakings is to reverse the real case. Actual activities in *educating* test the worth of the results of scientific results. They may be scientific in some other field, but not in education until they serve educational purposes, and whether they really serve or not can be found out only in practice. The latter comes first and last; it is the beginning and the close: the beginning, because it sets the problems which alone give to investigations educational point and quality; the close, because practice alone can test, verify, modify and develop the conclusions of these investigations. The position of scientific conclusions is intermediate and auxiliary.

Two conclusions as to the sources of educational science are now before us.

First, educational practices furnish the material that sets the problems of such a science, while sciences already developed to a fair state of maturity are the sources from which material is derived to deal intellectually with these problems. There is no more a special independent science of education than there is of bridge making. Second, material drawn from *other* sciences furnishes the content of educational science when it is focused on the problems that arise in education.

C. GENERAL SOURCES *

We may fairly enough call educational practice a kind of social engineering. Giving it that name at once pro-

* From *The Sources of a Science of Education*, pp. 39-42; 46-51.

vokes notice that as an art it is much more backward than branches of physical engineering, like land surveying, bridge-building and construction of railways. The reason is obvious. After all allowance is made for less systematic training for persons who engage in the art of education, the outstanding fact is that the sciences which must be drawn upon to supply scientific content to the work of the practitioner in education are themselves less mature than those which furnish the intellectual content of engineering. The human sciences that are sources of the scientific content of education—biology, psychology and sociology—for example, are relatively backward compared with mathematics and mechanics.

This statement is not an innocuous truism, for important consequences flow from taking it to heart. In the first place, just as the problems arising on the practical side in modern industry, for example, have been an important factor in stimulating researches in heat, electricity and light, so the problems that show themselves in educational practice should furnish agencies to direct the humane sciences into intellectually fruitful channels. It is not practice alone that has suffered from isolation of thinkers in the social and psychological disciplines from the occurrences taking place in schools. Indifference to the latter, a hardly veiled intellectual contempt for them, has undoubtedly strengthened the rule of convention, routine and accidental opinion in the schools. But it has also deprived the sciences in question of problems that would have stimulated significant inquiry and reflection. Much of the barrenness and loose speculation in the humane sciences is directly due to remoteness from the material that would stimulate, direct and test thought. Nothing in our recent situation is more promising for scientific development than the fact that the intellectual distance between university and elementary school, for example, is lessening.

In the second place, frank recognition of the relative backwardness of the sciences that must form the main content of educational science is a protection as well as a stimulus. Recognition that genuine growth in educational science is dependent upon prior advance in other subjects prevents us from entertaining premature and exaggerated expectations. It would, if fully recognized, deter workers in the field from efforts at premature introduction into school practice of materials whose real value lies only in the contribution they may make to the further building up of scientific content; it would militate against exploitation of results that are as yet only half-baked. And it would impress upon workers in the field of educational science the need for thorough equipment in the sciences upon which the science of education must draw.

At this point, the fact that educational practices are a source of the *problems* of educational science rather than of its definite material is especially significant. Adequate recognition that the source of the really scientific content is found in other sciences would compel attempt at mastery of what they have to offer. With respect to statistical theory this lesson has been pretty well learned. Whether it has been with respect to other disciplines, or even with respect to the separate and exclusive application of statistics to the solution of educational problems, is open to doubt.

Finally, recognition of this obvious fact would be a protection against attempting to extract from psychology and sociology definite solutions which it is beyond their present power to give. Such attempts, even when made unconsciously and with laudable intent to render education more scientific, defeat their own purpose and create reactions against the very concept of educational science.

Learning to wait is one of the important things that scientific method teaches, and the extent to which this lesson has been learned is one fair measure of the claim to a hearing on the part of workers in the field of education.

Special conditions are required if the material of school practices is to be presented to others in such shape as to form the data of a problem. It perhaps suffices to refer, in illustration of this point, to the great improvement already brought in the handling of school reports, both administrative and instructional. Since the value of any piece of research is definitely conditioned by the data at command, it is almost impossible to put too much emphasis upon the importance of records and reports, and of the manner in which they are kept, qualitative as well as quantitative.

The value of this material to the investigator in education is almost like that of systematic and cumulative clinical records for medical science. There is an evident circle in this matter. The kind of reports that are asked for and secured depend upon the existing state of the science, upon the scientific interests that dominate at a particular time. They also furnish data for further inquiries and conclusions. Hence the need that they should not be too rapidly mechanized into a standard fixed form. There must be flexible room for change or else scientific arrest will come from a too rigid fixation of the molds in which data are cast.

This factor of reports and records does not exhaust, by any means, the role of practitioners in building up a scientific content in educational activity. A constant flow of less formal reports on special school affairs and results is needed. Of the various possibilities here I select one for discussion. It seems to me that the contributions that might come from *class-room* teachers are a comparatively neglected field; or, to change the metaphor, an almost unworked mine. It is unnecessary to point out the large extent to which superintendents and principals have been drawn into the work of studying special problems and contributing material relative to them. It is to be hoped that the movement will not cease until all active class-room teachers, of whatever grade, are also drawn in.

There are undoubted obstacles in the way. It is often assumed, in effect if not in words, that class-room teachers have not themselves the training which will enable them to give effective intelligent coöperation. The objection proves too much, so much so that it is almost fatal to the idea of a workable scientific content in education. For these teachers are the ones in direct contact with pupils and hence the ones through whom the results of scientific findings finally reach students. They are the channels through which the consequences of educational theory come into the lives of those at school. I suspect that if these teachers are mainly channels of reception and transmission, the conclusions of science will be badly deflected and distorted before they get into the minds of pupils. I am inclined to believe that this state of affairs is a chief cause for the tendency, earlier alluded to, to convert scientific findings into recipes to be followed. The human desire to be an "authority" and to control the activities of others does not, alas, disappear when a man becomes a scientist.

A statistical study of, say, the reports of the N. E. A., would show the actual percentage of contributions to educational discussion made by class-room teachers on that level. It would perhaps raise the query whether some of the incapacity, real or alleged, of this part of the corps of educators, the large mass of teachers, is not attributable to lack of opportunity and stimulus, rather than to inherent disqualifications. As far as schools are concerned, it is certain that the problems which require scientific treatment arise in actual relationships with students. Consequently, it is impossible to see how there can be an adequate flow of subject-matter to set and control the problems investigators deal with, unless there is active participation on the part of those directly engaged in teaching.

If we now turn to the subjects from which are drawn the materials that are to be brought to bear upon educational problems, we are forced to recognize a fact already incidentally noted. There is no subject-matter intrinsically marked off, earmarked so to say, as the content of educational science. Any methods and any facts and principles from any subject whatsoever that enable the problems of administration and instruction to be dealt with in a bettered way are pertinent. Thus, in all that concerns the bearing of physical conditions upon the success of school work—as in the case of ventilation, temperature, etc., already mentioned—physiology and related sciences are sources of scientific content. In other problems, such as making budgets, cost-accountings, etc., economic theory is drawn upon. It may be doubted whether with reference to some aspect or other of education there is any organized body of knowledge that may not need to be drawn upon to become a source of educational science.

This consideration explains many phenomena in the present situation. It accounts for the rapid growth of interest in the development of scientific content for educational practices in so many different lines of activity. We have become only recently alive to the complexity of the educative process and aware of the number and variety of disciplines that must contribute if the process is to go on in an intelligently directed way. In accounting for the manifestation of enthusiastic activity on the part of some, the situation also explains the sceptical indifference of many about the whole matter. Not merely inert conservatives in the general public but many professors in other lines in universities have not been awakened to the complexity of the educational undertaking. Hence, such persons regard the activities of those in departments of education as futile and void of serious meaning.

Failure to perceive that educational science has no content of its own leads, on the other hand, to a segregation of research which tends to render it futile. The assumption, if only tacit, that educational science has its own peculiar subject-matter results in an isolation which makes the latter a "mystery" in the sense in which the higher crafts were once mysteries. A superficial token of this isolation is found in the development of that peculiar terminology that has been called "pedageese." Segregation also accounts for the tendency, already mentioned, to go at educational affairs without a sufficient grounding in the non-educational disciplines that must be drawn upon, and hence to exaggerate minor points in an absurdly one-sided way, and to grasp at some special scientific technique as if its use were a magical guarantee of a scientific product.

Recognition of the variety of sciences that must be focused when solving any educational problem tends to breadth of view and to more serious and prolonged effort at balance of the variety of factors which enter into even the simplest problems of teaching and administration. The uncontrolled succession of waves of one-sided temporarily dominating interests and slogans that have affected educational practice and theory could thus be reduced.

D. SPECIAL SOURCES

(i) Psychology*

In spite of the wide and indeterminate field of sciences that are sources of scientific content in education, there are certain subjects that occupy a privileged position. By common consent, I suppose, psychology and sociology hold such positions. There is general agreement that psychology lies nearer to the question of means and the social sciences nearer to that of ends, or that the first is more closely connected with *how* pupils learn, whether knowledge or skill, and the latter with *what* they are to learn. But such a statement only brings us to the threshold of the problem of the relation between the "how" and the "what," means and ends. If the how and the what, the psychological and the social, method and subject matter, must interact cooperatively in order to secure good results, a hard and fast distinction between them is fraught with danger. We want a method that will select subject-matter that aids psychological development, and we want a subject-matter that will secure the use of methods psychologically correct. We cannot begin by dividing the field between the psychology of individual activity and growth and studies or subject-matters that are socially desirable, and then expect that at the end in practical operation the two things will balance each other.

An unbiased survey of the situation will, I think, show that the danger is not merely theoretical. When we make a sharp distinction between *what* is learned and *how* we learn it, and assign the determination of the process of learning to psychology and of subject-matter to social science, the inevitable outcome is that the reaction of what is studied and learned upon the development of the person

* From *The Sources of a Science of Education,* pp. 51; 61-64.

learning, upon the tastes, interests, and habits that control his future mental attitudes and responses is overlooked. In that degree the psychological account of the process of personal learning and growth is deficient and distorted. It then deals with a short segment of the learning process instead of with its continuities.

Social needs and conditions are said to dictate, for example, the necessity of instruction in reading, writing and numbers at a fairly early age. It is also recognized that these are useful factors in later personal growth, being the means of opening up learning in a variety of subjects. So far the two aspects seem to be in harmony. But suppose the question of how children learn most effectively to master these skills then be taken up in isolation, and methods are devised to promote the ready acquisition of the skills in question. The larger question is what other habits, including tastes and desires, are being collaterally formed.

That a person can learn efficiently to read and yet not form a taste for reading good literature, or without having curiosities aroused that will lead him to apply his ability to read to explore fields outside of what is conventionally termed good reading matter, are sad facts of experience. Learning to read may develop book-worms, children who read omnivorously, but at the expense of development of social and executive abilities and skills. The question of *what* one learns to read is thus inextricably bound up with the question of *how* one learns to read. Unfortunately, experience shows that the methods which most readily and efficiently bring about skill to read (or write, or figure) in its narrower sense of ability to recognize, pronounce and put together words, do not at the same time take care of the formation of attitudes that decide the uses to which the ability is to be put. This is the more important issue.

It will not do for the psychologist to content himself

with saying in effect: "These other things are none of my business; I have shown how the child may most readily and efficiently form the skill. The rest is up to somebody else." It will not do because one skill is acquired, other abilities, preferences and disabilities are also learned, and these fall within the province of the psychological inquirer. This conclusion does not mean that the demonstration of how a particular skill is most readily formed is of no value. But it does mean that educationally speaking the problems of attendant radiations, expansions and contractions, are in the end more important, and that it is dangerous to take the part for the whole. Nor is it satisfactory to say that the part must be mastered before the whole can be attacked. For, by the nature of the case, the whole enters into the part, that is, it is a determining factor in the *way* in which one learns to read. Thus the consideration of how one learns to read in its connection with its effect upon future personal development and interests demands attention to desirable subject-matter. The social question is intertwined with the psychological.

(*ii*) Sociology*

I come now to the contribution of sociology—by which for present purposes I mean all the social disciplines—to the scientific content of education. Fortunately, it is not necessary to insist at this day and date upon the importance of this factor. Like the word "social," the words "socialized education" are in the air. The questions that call for discussion concern how the idea is to be interpreted. Time permits of mention of only two points. One relates to the position of *social tools*. The most obvious example of such tools is skill in language (reading, spelling and writing) and number. But these are only instances. Man-

* From *The Sources of a Science of Education*, pp. 70-73.

ners also form a social tool and so do morals in one of their aspects. A considerable portion of geography and history do so, and also elementary science, as well as some traits of the fine arts. In fact, it would be hard to draw a line at any point in the educational scheme; consider, for example, the necessities of the professional students in medicine and law to master certain skills and bodies of fact as social tools. The only difference among subjects of the curriculum as to social tools seems to be a matter of degree.

In view of this fact, the current habit of speaking only of some skills as social tools suggests the need for thought. The cause for their being selected as *the* social tools becomes evident, I think, when we notice that the things usually called social tools are the most *formal* parts of the curriculum. These subjects and skill in employing them are formal because they are separated from social content; they are social tools prospectively rather than at the time they are learned. Emphasis upon repetition, making their acquisition a frequency function, is proof of this isolation from direct social subject-matter and value.

I am not going to discuss this point. I use it as an illustration of the current division, found in many subjects, between social tools and social consequences. The net effect of this division upon the contribution social subject-matter makes to educational science is serious. The tools that are recognized to be social are not treated socially but are relegated to the mechanics of psychology. In so far as they are not socially controlled, the social use to which they are finally put is accidental. School practices are in this respect, in many modern schools, ahead of theory. Those engaged in the act of teaching know that the social tools are best acquired in a social context and for the sake of some social application falling within a nearby phase of life.

When skill in and with tools is not socially formed, that is, generated for social ends, the latter are separated from the means by which they should be controlled. To take just one instance: The kind of reading-matter that now most abounds socially, as may be gathered from a glance at newsstands, is largely of a socially *undesirable* character. Yet it can be sold only to readers, to those in possession of the so-called social tools. Pages of exposition would not speak more eloquently of what is bound to happen when educational theory separates, in the name of science, the psychological processes that regulate the mere mechanism of acquiring a skill from the social conditions and needs which have to do with the application of that skill.

The other point about the contribution of sociology to educational science concerns the determination of values, of objectives. The shortest cut to get something that looks scientific is to make a statistical study of existing practices and desires, with the supposition that their accurate determination will settle the subject-matter to be taught, thus taking curriculum-forming out of the air, putting it on a solid factual basis. This signifies, in effect and in logic, that the kind of education which the social environment gives unconsciously and in connection with all its defects, perversions and distortions, is the kind of education the schools should give consciously. Such an idea is almost enough to cause one to turn back to the theories of classicists who would confine the important subject-matter of instruction to the best of the products of the past, in disregard of present and prospective social conditions. It is hard to see any cause for such a procedure except a desire to demonstrate the value of "educational science" by showing that it has something immediate and direct to furnish in the guidance of schools.

(iii) Philosophy*

The philosophy of education is a source of the science of education, but one less often recognized as such. We are, I think, habituated to thinking of the sciences as feeders of philosophy rather than of philosophy as a source of science. Philosophy is looked at by those who dignify it as a subject which analyzes critically the premises that are uncritically assumed in the special sciences, or else as a complete intellectual organization of their results. Others take a less respectful and perhaps more popular view of it, and regard it as a constantly vanishing quantity, dealing by way of opinion and speculation with matters that sciences have not got around to dealing with in a positive way. Personally, I think there is truth in both of these views, but that neither one touches the heart of the relationship of philosophy and science. There is in every subject at every time a serial progression from the more specific to the more general. The only distinction we can profitably draw is to say that science lies toward the specific pole and philosophy toward the general, while there is no definite line where one leaves off and the other begins.

It is because of this fact that there is a reciprocal relation between them, each feeding the other as a source. Were this the time and place, it could be shown from the history of the sciences, mathematical, physical and biological, that ideas originating at the philosophic end (general, often vague and speculative, if you please) have been indispensable factors in the generation of science. An examination of history would also show that there is no steady one-way movement; the movement from general to special is not one that has a definite conclusion that stays put. Specialized results recurrently get too set and rigid because of isolation due to the very specialization by which

* From *The Sources of a Science of Education*, pp. 51-53.

they are obtained. Fermentation and fructification then come in from the pole of general ideas and points of view. Specific results are shaken up, loosened and placed in new contexts.

III · Traditional *vs*. Progressive Education*

Mankind likes to think in terms of extreme opposites. It is given to formulating its beliefs in terms of *Either-Ors,* between which it recognizes no intermediate possibilities. When forced to recognize that the extremes cannot be acted upon, it is still inclined to hold that they are all right in theory but that when it comes to practical matters circumstances compel us to compromise. Educational philosophy is no exception. The history of educational theory is marked by opposition between the idea that education is development from within and that it is formation from without; that it is based upon natural endowments and that education is a process of overcoming natural inclination and substituting in its place habits acquired under external pressure.

At present, the opposition, so far as practical affairs of the school are concerned, tends to take the form of contrast between traditional and progressive education. If the underlying ideas of the former are formulated broadly, without the qualifications required for accurate statement, they are found to be about as follows: The subject-matter of education consists of bodies of information and of skills that have been worked out in the past; therefore, the chief business of the school is to transmit them to the new generation. In the past, there have also been developed standards and rules of conduct; moral training consists in forming habits of action in conformity with these rules and standards. Finally, the general pattern of school

* From *Experience and Education*, pp. 1-13; 17-19.

organization (by which I mean the relations of pupils to one another and to the teachers) constitutes the school a kind of institution sharply marked off from other social institutions. Call up in imagination the ordinary school-room, its time-schedules, schemes of classification, of examination and promotion, of rules of order, and I think you will grasp what is meant by "pattern of organization." If then you contrast this scene with what goes on in the family, for example, you will appreciate what is meant by the school being a kind of institution sharply marked off from any other form of social organization.

The three characteristics just mentioned fix the aims and methods of instruction and discipline. The main purpose or objective is to prepare the young for future responsibilities and for success in life, by means of acquisition of the organized bodies of information and prepared forms of skill which comprehend the material of instruction. Since the subject-matter as well as standards of proper conduct are handed down from the past, the attitude of pupils must, upon the whole, be one of docility, receptivity, and obedience. Books, especially textbooks, are the chief representatives of the lore and wisdom of the past, while teachers are the organs through which pupils are brought into effective connection with the material. Teachers are the agents through which knowledge and skills are communicated and rules of conduct enforced.

I have not made this brief summary for the purpose of criticizing the underlying philosophy. The rise of what is called new education and progressive schools is of itself a product of discontent with traditional education. In effect it is a criticism of the latter. When the implied criticism is made explicit it reads somewhat as follows: The traditional scheme is, in essence, one of imposition from above and from outside. It imposes adult standards, subject-matter, and methods upon those who are only growing slowly toward maturity. The gap is so great that the required subject-matter, the methods of learning and of behaving are foreign to the existing capacities of the young. They are beyond the reach of the experience the young learners already possess. Consequently, they must be imposed; even though good teachers will use devices of art to cover up the imposition so as to relieve it of obviously brutal features.

But the gulf between the mature or adult products and the experience and abilities of the young is so wide that the very situation forbids much active participation by pupils in the development of what is taught. Theirs is to do—and learn, as it was the part of the six hundred to do and die. Learning here means acquisition of what already is incorporated in books and in the heads of the elders. Moreover, that which is taught is thought of as essentially static. It is taught as a finished product, with little regard either to the ways in which it was originally built up or to changes that will surely occur in the future. It is to a large extent the cultural product of societies that assumed the future would be much like the past, and yet it is used as educational food in a society where change is the rule, not the exception.

If one attempts to formulate the philosophy of education implicit in the practices of the newer education, we may, I think, discover certain common principles amid the variety of progressive schools now existing. To imposition from above is opposed expression and cultivation of individuality; to external discipline is opposed free activity; to learning from texts and teachers, learning through experience; to acquisition of isolated skills and techniques by drill, is opposed acquisition of them as means of attaining ends which make direct vital appeal; to preparation for a more or less remote future is opposed making the most of the opportunities of present life; to static aims and materials is opposed acquaintance with a changing world.

Now, all principles by themselves are abstract. They become concrete only in the consequences which result from their application. Just because the principles set forth are so fundamental and far-reaching, everything depends upon the interpretation given them as they are put into practice in the school and the home. It is at this point that the reference made earlier to *Either-Or* philosophies becomes peculiarly pertinent. The general philosophy of the new education may be sound, and yet the difference in abstract principles will not decide the way in which the moral and intellectual preference involved shall be worked out in practice. There is always the danger in a new movement that in rejecting the aims and methods of that which it would supplant, it may develop its principles negatively rather than positively and constructively. Then it takes its clew in practice from that which is rejected instead of from the constructive development of its own philosophy.

I take it that the fundamental unity of the newer philosophy is found in the idea that there is an intimate and necessary relation between the processes of actual experience and education. If this be true, then a positive and constructive development of its own basic idea depends upon having a correct idea of experience. Take, for example, the question of organized subject-matter—which will be discussed in some detail later. The problem for progressive education is: What are the place and meaning of subject-matter and of organization *within* experience? How does subject-matter function? Is there anything inherent in experience which tends towards progressive organization of its contents? What results follow when the materials of experience are not progressively organized? A philosophy which proceeds on the basis of rejection, of sheer opposition, will neglect these questions. It will tend to suppose that because the old education was based on ready-made organization, therefore it suffices to reject the principle of organization *in toto,* instead of striving to discover what it means and how it is to be attained on the basis of experience. We might go through all the points of difference between the new and the old education and reach similar conclusions. When external control is rejected, the problem becomes that of finding the factors of control that are inherent within experience. When external authority is rejected, it does not follow that all authority should be rejected, but rather that there is need to search for a more effective source of authority. Because the older education imposed the knowledge, methods, and the rules of conduct of the mature person upon the young, it does not follow, except upon the basis of the extreme *Either-Or* philosophy, that the knowledge and skill of the mature person has no directive value for the experience of the immature. On the contrary, basing education upon personal experience may mean more multiplied and more intimate contacts between the mature and the immature than ever existed in the traditional school, and consequently more, rather than less, guidance by others. The problem, then, is: how these contacts can be established without violating the principle of learning through personal experience. The solution of this problem requires a well thought-out philosophy of the social factors that operate in the constitution of individual experience.

What is indicated in the foregoing remarks is that the general principles of the new education do not of themselves solve any of the problems of the actual or practical conduct and management of progressive schools. Rather, they set new problems which have to be worked out on the basis of a new philosophy of experience. The problems are not even recognized, to say nothing of being solved, when it is assumed that it suffices to reject the ideas and practices of the old education and then go to the opposite extreme. Yet I am sure that you will appreciate what is meant when I say that many of the newer schools tend to make little or nothing of organized subject-matter of study; to proceed as if any form of direction and guidance by adults were an invasion of individual freedom, and as if the idea that education should be concerned with the present and future meant that acquaintance with the past has little or no role to play in education. Without pressing these defects to the point of exaggeration, they at least illustrate what is meant by a theory and practice of education which proceeds negatively or by reaction against what has been current in education rather than by a positive and constructive development of purposes, methods, and subject-matter on the foundation of a theory of experience and its educational potentialities.

It is not too much to say that an educational philosophy which professes to be based on the idea of freedom may become as dogmatic as ever was the traditional education which is reacted against. For any theory and set of practices are dogmatic which are not based upon critical examination of its own underlying principles. Let us say that the new education emphasizes the freedom of the learner. Very well. A problem is now set. What does freedom mean and what are the conditions under which it is capable of realization? Let us say that the kind of external imposition which was so common in the traditional school limited rather than promoted the intellectual and moral development of the young. Again, very well. Recognition of this serious defect sets a problem. Just what is the role of the teacher and of books in promoting the educational development of the immature? Admit that traditional education employed, as the subject-matter for study, facts and ideas so bound up with the past as to give little help in dealing with the issues of the present and future. Very well. Now we have the problem of discovering the connection which actually exists *within* experience between the achievements of the past and the issues of the present. We have the problem of ascertaining how acquaintance with the past may be translated into a potent instrumentality for dealing effectively with the future. We may reject knowledge of the past as the *end* of education and thereby only emphasize its importance as a *means*. When we do that we have a problem that is new in the story of education: How shall the young become acquainted with the past in such a way that the acquaintance is a potent agent in appreciation of the living present?

In short, the point I am making is that rejection of the philosophy and practice of traditional education sets a new type of difficult educational problem for those who believe in the new type of education. We shall operate blindly and in confusion until we recognize this fact; until we thoroughly appreciate that departure from the old solves no problems. What is said in the following pages is, accordingly, intended to indicate some of the main problems with which the newer education is confronted and to suggest the main lines along which their solution is to be sought. I assume that amid all uncertainties there is one permanent frame of reference: namely, the organic connection between education and personal experience; or, that the new philosophy of education is committed to some kind of empirical and experimental philosophy. But experience and experiment are not self-explanatory ideas.

Rather, their meaning is part of the problem to be explored. To know the meaning of empiricism we need to understand what experience is.

A philosophy of education, like any theory, has to be stated in words, in symbols. But so far as it is more than verbal it is a plan for conducting education. Like any plan, it must be framed with reference to what is to be done and how it is to be done. The more definitely and sincerely it is held that education is a development within, by, and for experience, the more important it is that there shall be clear conceptions of what experience is. Unless experience is so conceived that the result is a plan for deciding upon subject-matter, upon methods of instruction and discipline, and upon material equipment and social organization of the school, it is wholly in the air. It is reduced to a form of words which may be emotionally stirring but for which any other set of words might equally well be substituted unless they indicate operations to be initiated and executed. Just because traditional education was a matter of routine in which the plans and programs were handed down from the past, it does not follow that progressive education is a matter of planless improvisation.

The traditional school could get along without any consistently developed philosophy of education. About all it required in that line was a set of abstract words like culture, discipline, our great cultural heritage, etc., actual guidance being derived not from them but from custom and established routines. Just because progressive schools cannot rely upon established traditions and institutional habits, they must either proceed more or less haphazardly or be directed by ideas which, when they are made articulate and coherent, form a philosophy of education. Revolt against the kind of organization characteristic of the traditional school constitutes a demand for a kind of organization based upon ideas. I think that only slight acquaintance with the history of education is needed to prove that educational reformers and innovators alone have felt the need for a philosophy of education. Those who adhered to the established system needed merely a few fine-sounding words to justify existing practices. The real work was done by habits which were so fixed as to be institutional. The lesson for progressive education is that it requires in an urgent degree, a degree more pressing than was incumbent upon former innovators, a philosophy of education based upon a philosophy of experience.

IV · Philosophy of Experience*

If there is any truth in what has been said about the need of forming a theory of experience in order that education may be intelligently conducted upon the basis of experience, it is clear that the next thing in order in this discussion is to present the principles that are most significant in framing this theory.

I have already mentioned what I called the category of continuity, or the experiential continuum. This principle is involved, as I pointed out, in every attempt to discriminate between experiences that are worth while educationally and those that are not. It may seem superfluous to argue that this discrimination is necessary not only in criticizing the traditional type of education but also in initiating and conducting a different type. Nevertheless, it is advisable to pursue for a little while the idea that it is necessary. One may safely assume, I suppose, that one thing which has recommended the progressive movement is that it seems more in accord with the democratic ideal to which our people is committed than do the procedures of the traditional school, since the latter have so much of

* From *Experience and Education*, pp. 23-52.

the autocratic about them. Another thing which has contributed to its favorable reception is that its methods are
humane in comparison with the harshness so often attending the policies of the traditional school.

The question I would raise concerns why we prefer
democratic and humane arrangements to those which are
autocratic and harsh. And by "why," I mean the *reason*
for preferring them, not just the *causes* which lead us to
the preference. One *cause* may be that we have been
taught not only in the schools but by the press, the pulpit,
the platform, and our laws and law-making bodies that
democracy is the best of all social institutions. We may
have so assimilated this idea from our surroundings that
it has become an habitual part of our mental and moral
make-up. But similar causes have led other persons in different surroundings to widely varying conclusions—to prefer fascism, for example. The cause for our preference is
not the same thing as the reason why we *should* prefer it.

It is not my purpose here to go in detail into the reason. But I would ask a single question: Can we find any
reason that does not ultimately come down to the belief
that democratic social arrangements promote a better quality of human experience, one which is more widely accessible and enjoyed, than do non-democratic and anti-demo-
cratic forms of social life? Does not the principle of regard for individual freedom and for decency and kindli-
ness of human relations come back in the end to the conviction that these things are tributary to a higher quality
of experience on the part of a greater number than are
methods of repression and coercion or force? Is it not the
reason for our preference that we believe that mutual consultation and convictions reached through persuasion,
make possible a better quality of experience than can
otherwise be provided on any wide scale?

If the answer to these questions is in the affirmative (and personally I do not see how we can justify our preference for democracy and humanity on any other ground), the ultimate reason for hospitality to progressive education, because of its reliance upon and use of humane methods and its kinship to democracy, goes back to the fact that discrimination is made between the inherent values of different experiences. So I come back to the principle of continuity of experience as a criterion of discrimination.

At bottom, this principle rests upon the fact of habit, when *habit* is interpreted biologically. The basic characteristic of habit is that every experience enacted and undergone modifies the one who acts and undergoes, while this modification affects, whether we wish it or not, the quality of subsequent experiences. For it is a somewhat different person who enters into them. The principle of habit so understood obviously goes deeper than the ordinary conception of *a* habit as a more or less fixed way of doing things, although it includes the latter as one of its special cases. It covers the formation of attitudes, attitudes that are emotional and intellectual; it covers our basic sensitivities and ways of meeting and responding to all the conditions which we meet in living.

So far, however, we have no ground for discrimination among experiences. For the principle is of universal application. There is *some* kind of continuity in every case. It is when we note the different forms in which continuity of experience operates that we get the basis of discriminating among experiences. I may illustrate what is meant by an objection which has been brought against an idea which I once put forth—namely, that the educative process can be identified with growth when that is understood in terms of the active participle, *growing*.

Growth, or growing as developing, not only physically

but intellectually and morally, is one exemplification of the principle of continuity. The objection made is that growth might take many different directions: a man, for example, who starts out on a career of burglary may grow in that direction, and by practice may grow into a highly expert burglar. Hence it is argued that "growth" is not enough; we must also specify the direction in which growth takes place, the end toward which it tends. Before, however, we decide that the objection is conclusive we must analyze the case a little further.

That a man may grow in efficiency as a burglar, as a gangster, or as a corrupt politician, cannot be doubted. But from the standpoint of growth as education and education as growth the question is whether growth in this direction promotes or retards growth in general. Does this form of growth create conditions for further growth, or does it set up conditions that shut off the person who has grown in this particular direction from the occasions, stimuli, and opportunities for continuing growth in new directions? What is the effect of growth in a special direction upon the attitudes and habits which alone open up avenues for development in other lines? I shall leave you to answer these questions, saying simply that when and *only* when development in a particular line conduces to continuing growth does it answer to the criterion of education as growing. For the conception is one that must find universal and not specialized limited application.

I return now to the question of continuity as a criterion by which to discriminate between experiences which are educative and those which are mis-educative. As we have seen, there is some kind of continuity in any case since every experience affects for better or worse the attitudes which help decide the quality of further experiences, by setting up certain preference and aversion, and making it

easier or harder to act for this or that end. Moreover,
every experience influences in some degree the objective
conditions under which further experiences are had.

But, while the principle of continuity applies in some
way in every case, the quality of the present experience
influences the *way* in which the principle applies. We
speak of spoiling a child and of the spoilt child. The effect
of over-indulging a child is a continuing one. It sets up
an attitude which operates as an automatic demand that
persons and objects cater to his desires and caprices in the
future. It makes him seek the kind of situation that will
enable him to do what he feels like doing at the time. It
renders him averse to and comparatively incompetent in
situations which require effort and perseverance in overcoming obstacles. There is no paradox in the fact that the
principle of the continuity of experience may operate so as
to leave a person arrested on a low plane of development,
in a way which limits later capacity for growth.

On the other hand, if an experience arouses curiosity,
strengthens initiative, and sets up desires and purposes
that are sufficiently intense to carry a person over dead
places in the future, continuity works in a very different
way. Every experience is a moving force. Its value can
be judged only on the ground of what it moves toward and
into. The greater maturity of experience which should belong to the adult as educator puts him in a position to
evaluate each experience of the young in a way in which
the one having the less mature experience cannot do. It
is then the business of the educator to see in what direction an experience is heading. There is no point in his being more mature if, instead of using his greater insight to
help organize the conditions of the experience of the immature, he throws away his insight. Failure to take the
moving force of an experience into account so as to judge

and direct it on the ground of what it is moving into means disloyalty to the principle of experience itself.

The disloyalty operates in two directions. The educator is false to the understanding that he should have obtained from his own past experience. He is also unfaithful to the fact that all human experience is ultimately social: that it involves contact and communication. The mature person, to put it in moral terms, has no right to withhold from the young on given occasions whatever capacity for sympathetic understanding his own experience has given him.

But there is another aspect of the matter. Experience does not go on simply inside a person. It does go on there, for it influences the formation of attitudes of desire and purpose. But this is not the whole of the story. Every genuine experience has an active side which changes in some degree the objective conditions under which experiences are had. The difference between civilization and savagery, to take an example on a large scale, is found in the degree in which previous experiences have changed the objective conditions under which subsequent experiences take place.

In a word, we live from birth to death in a world of persons and things which in large measure is what it is because of what has been done and transmitted from previous human activities. When this fact is ignored, experience is treated as if it were something which goes on exclusively inside an individual's body and mind. It ought not to be necessary to say that experience does not occur in a vacuum. There are sources outside an individual which give rise to experience. It is constantly fed from these springs. No one would question that a child in a slum tenement has a different experience from that of a child in a cultured home; that the country lad has a different kind of experience from the city boy, or a boy on the seashore one different from the lad who is brought up on inland prairies. Ordinarily we take such facts for granted as too commonplace to record. But when their educational import is recognized, they indicate the second way in which the educator can direct the experience of the young without engaging in imposition. A primary responsibility of educators is that they not only be aware of the general principle of the shaping of actual experience by environing conditions, but that they also recognize in the concrete what surroundings are conducive to having experiences that lead to growth. Above all, they should know how to utilize the surroundings, physical and social, that exist so as to extract from them all that they have to contribute to building up experiences that are worth while.

Traditional education did not have to face this problem; it could systematically dodge this responsibility. The school environment of desks, blackboards, a small school yard, was supposed to suffice. There was no demand that the teacher should become intimately acquainted with the conditions of the local community, physical, historical, economic, occupational, etc., in order to utilize them as educational resources. A system of education based upon the necessary connection of education with experience must, on the contrary, if faithful to its principle, take these things constantly into account. This tax upon the educator is another reason why progressive education is more difficult to carry on than was ever the traditional system.

The word "interaction" expresses the second chief principle for interpreting an experience in its educational function and force. It assigns equal rights to both factors in experience—objective and internal conditions. Any normal experience is an interplay of these two sets of conditions. Taken together, or in their interaction, they form what we call a *situation*. The trouble with traditional education was not that it emphasized the external conditions that enter into the control of the experiences but that it paid so little attention to the internal factors which also decide what kind of experience is had. It violated the principle of interaction from one side. But this violation is no reason why the new education should violate the principle from the other side—except upon the basis of the extreme *Either-Or* educational philosophy which has been mentioned.

The statement that individuals live in a world means, in the concrete, that they live in a series of situations. And when it is said that they live *in* these situations, the meaning of the word "in" is different from its meaning when it is said that pennies are "in" a pocket or paint is "in" a can. It means, once more, that interaction is going on between an individual and objects and other persons. The conceptions of *situation* and of *interaction* are inseparable from each other. An experience is always what it is because of a transaction taking place between an individual and what, at the time, constitutes his environment, whether the latter consists of persons with whom he is talking about some topic or event, the subject talked about being also a part of the situation; or the toys with which he is playing; the book he is reading (in which his environing conditions at the time may be England or ancient Greece or an imaginary region); or the materials of an experiment he is performing. The environment, in other words, is whatever conditions interact with personal needs, desires, purposes, and capacities to create the experience which is had. Even when a person builds a castle in the air he is interacting with the objects which he constructs in fancy.

The two principles of continuity and interaction are no

separate from each other. They intercept and unite. They are, so to speak, the longitudinal and lateral aspects of experience. Different situations succeed one another. But because of the principle of continuity something is carried over from the earlier to the later ones. As an individual passes from one situation to another, his world, his environment, expands or contracts. He does not find himself living in another world but in a different part or aspect of one and the same world. What he has learned in the way of knowledge and skill in one situation becomes an instrument of understanding and dealing effectively with the situations which follow. The process goes on as long as life and learning continue. Otherwise the course of experience is disorderly, since the individual factor that enters into making an experience is split.

Continuity and interaction in their active union with each other provide the measure of the educative significance and value of an experience. The immediate and direct concern of an educator is then with the situations in which interaction takes place. The individual, who enters as a factor into it, is what he is at a given time. It is the other factor, that of objective conditions, which lies to some extent within the possibility of regulation by the educator. As has already been noted, the phrase "objective conditions" covers a wide range. It includes what is done by the educator and the way in which it is done, not only words spoken but the tone of voice in which they are spoken. It includes equipment, books, apparatus, toys, games played. It includes the materials with which an individual interacts, and, most important of all, the total *social* set-up of the situations in which a person is engaged.

Responsibility for selecting objective conditions carries with it the responsibility for understanding the needs and capacities of the individuals who are learning at a given time. It is not enough that certain materials and methods have proved effective with other individuals at other times. There must be a reason for thinking that they will function in generating an experience that has educative quality with particular individuals at a particular time.

It is no reflection upon the nutritive quality of beefsteak that it is not fed to infants. It is not an invidious reflection upon trigonometry that we do not teach it in the first or fifth grade of school. It is not the subject *per se* that is educative or that is conducive to growth. There is no subject that is in and of itself, or without regard to the stage of growth attained by the learner, such that inherent educational value can be attributed to it. Failure to take into account adaptation to the needs and capacities of individuals was the source of the idea that certain subjects and certain methods are intrinsically cultural or intrinsically good for mental discipline. There is no such thing as educational value in the abstract. The notion that some subjects and methods and that acquaintance with certain facts and truths possess educational value in and of themselves is the reason why traditional education reduced the material of education so largely to a diet of predigested materials.

The principle of interaction makes it clear that failure of adaptation of material to needs and capacities of individuals may cause an experience to be non-educative quite as much as failure of an individual to adapt himself to the material.

The principle of continuity in its educational application means that the future has to be taken into account at every stage of the educational process. This idea is easily misunderstood and is badly distorted in traditional education. Its assumption is, that by acquiring certain skills and by learning certain subjects which would be needed later (perhaps in college or perhaps in adult life) pupils are as a matter of course made ready for the needs and circumstances of the future. Now "preparation" is a treacherous idea. In a certain sense every experience should do something to prepare a person for later experiences of a deeper and more expansive quality. That is the very meaning of growth, continuity, reconstruction of experience. But it is a mistake to suppose that the mere acquisition of a certain amount of arithmetic, geography, history, etc., which is taught and studied because it may be useful at some time in the future, has this effect, and it is a mistake to suppose that acquisition of skills in reading and figuring will automatically constitute preparation for their right and effective use under conditions very unlike those in which they were acquired.

Nor does failure in preparation end at this point. Perhaps the greatest of all pedagogical fallacies is the notion that a person learns only the particular thing he is studying at the time. Collateral learning in the way of formation of enduring attitudes, of likes and dislikes, may be and often is much more important than the spelling lesson or lesson in geography or history that is learned. For these attitudes are fundamentally what count in the future. The most important attitude that can be formed is that of desire to go on learning. If impetus in this direction is weakened instead of being intensified, something much more than mere lack of preparation takes place. The pupil is actually robbed of native capacities which otherwise would enable him to cope with the circumstances that he meets in the course of his life.

What, then, is the true meaning of preparation in the educational scheme? In the first place, it means that a person, young or old, gets out of his present experience all that there is in it for him at the time in which he has it. When preparation is made the controlling end, then the potentialities of the present are sacrificed to a supposititious future. When this happens, the actual preparation for the future is missed or distorted. The ideal of using the present simply to get ready for the future contradicts itself. It omits, and even shuts out, the very conditions by which a person can be prepared for his future. We always live at the time we live and not at some other time, and only by extracting at each present time the full meaning of each present experience are we prepared for doing the same thing in the future. This is the only preparation which in the long run amounts to anything.

All this means that attentive care must be devoted to the conditions which give each present experience a worth-while meaning. Instead of inferring that it doesn't make much difference what the present experience is as long as it is enjoyed, the conclusion is the exact opposite. Here is another matter where it is easy to react from one extreme to the other. Because traditional schools tended to sacrifice the present to a remote and more or less unknown future, therefore it comes to be believed that the educator has little responsibility for the kind of present experiences the young undergo. But the relation of the present and the future is not an *Either-Or* affair. The present affects the future anyway. The persons who should have some idea of the connection between the two are those who have achieved maturity. Accordingly, upon them devolves the responsibility for instituting the conditions for the kind of present experience which has a favorable effect upon the future. Education as growth or maturity should be an ever-present process.

V · The Organization of Study*

One consideration stands out clearly when education is conceived in terms of experience. Anything which can be called a study, whether arithmetic, history, geography, or one of the natural sciences, must be derived from materials which at the outset fall within the scope of ordinary life-experience.

But finding the material for learning within experience is only the first step. The next step is the progressive development of what is already experienced into a fuller and richer and also more organized form, a form that gradually approximates that in which subject-matter is presented to the skilled, mature person. That this change is possible without departing from the organic connection of education with experience is shown by the fact that this change takes place outside of the school and apart from formal education. The infant, for example, begins with an environment of objects that is very restricted in space and time. That environment steadily expands by the momentum inherent in experience itself without aid from scholastic instruction. As the infant learns to reach, creep, walk, and talk, the intrinsic subject-matter of its experience widens and deepens. It comes into connection with new objects and events which call out new powers, while the exercise of these powers refines and enlarges the content of its experience. Life-space and life-durations are expanded. The environment, the world of experience, constantly grows larger and, so to speak, thicker. The educator who receives the child at the end of this period has to find ways for doing consciously and deliberately what "nature" accomplishes in the earlier years.

It is hardly necessary to insist upon the first of the two conditions which have been specified. It is a cardinal pre-

* From *Experience and Education*, pp. 86-112.

cept of the newer school of education that the beginning
of instruction shall be made with the experience learners
already have; that this experience and the capacities that
have been developed during its course provide the starting
point for all further learning. I am not so sure that the
other condition, that of orderly development toward expansion and organization of subject-matter through growth
of experience, receives as much attention. Yet the principle
of continuity of educative experience requires that equal
thought and attention be given to solution of this aspect
of the educational problem. Undoubtedly this phase of the
problem is more difficult than the other.

It is a mistake to suppose that the principle of the leading on of experience to something different is adequately
satisfied simply by giving pupils some new experiences any
more than it is by seeing to it that they have greater skill
and ease in dealing with things with which they are already familiar. It is also essential that the new objects
and events be related intellectually to those of earlier experiences, and this means that there be some advance
made in conscious articulation of facts and ideas. It thus
becomes the office of the educator to select those things
within the range of existing experience that have the promise and potentiality of presenting new problems which by
stimulating new ways of observation and judgment will ex-
pand the area of further experience. He must constantly
regard what is already won not as a fixed possession but
as an agency and instrumentality for opening new fields
which make new demands upon existing powers of observation and of intelligent use of memory. Connectedness in
growth must be his constant watchword.

That up to the present time the weakest point in progressive schools is in the matter of selection and organization of intellectual subject-matter is, I think, inevitable

under the circumstances. It is as inevitable as it is right and proper that they should break loose from the cut and dried material which formed the staple of the old education. In addition, the field of experience is very wide and it varies in its contents from place to place and from time to time. A single course of studies for all progressive schools is out of the question; it would mean abandoning the fundamental principle of connection with life-experiences. Moreover, progressive schools are new. They have had hardly more than a generation in which to develop. A certain amount of uncertainty and of laxity in choice and organization of subject-matter is, therefore, what was to be expected. It is no ground for fundamental criticism or complaint.

It is a ground for legitimate criticism, however, when the ongoing movement of progressive education fails to recognize that the problem of selection and organization of subject-matter for study and learning is fundamental. Improvisation that takes advantage of special occasions prevents teaching and learning from being stereotyped and dead. But the basic material of study cannot be picked up in a cursory manner. Occasions which are not and cannot be foreseen are bound to arise wherever there is intellectual freedom. They should be utilized. But there is a decided difference between using them in the development of a continuing line of activity and trusting to them to provide the chief material of learning.

The underlying ideal is that of progressive organization of knowledge. It is with reference to organization of knowledge that we are likely to find *Either-Or* philosophies most acutely active. In practice, if not in so many words, it is often held that since traditional education rested upon a conception of organization of knowledge that was almost completely contemptuous of living present

experience, therefore education based upon living experience should be contemptuous of the organization of facts
and ideas.

When a moment ago I called this organization an *ideal*,
I meant, on the negative side, that the educator cannot
start with knowledge already organized and proceed to
ladle it out in doses. But as an ideal the active process of
organizing facts and ideas is an ever-present educational
process. No experience is educative that does not tend
both to knowledge of more facts and entertaining of more
ideas and to a better, a more orderly, arrangment of them.
It is not true that organization is a principle foreign to
experience. Otherwise experience would be so dispersive
as to be chaotic. The experience of young children centers
about persons and the home. Disturbance of the normal
order of relationships in the family is now known by psychiatrists to be a fertile source of later mental and emotional troubles—a fact which testifies to the reality of this
kind of organization. One of the great advances in early
school education, in the kindergarten and early grades, is
that it preserves the social and human center of the organization of experience, instead of the older violent shift
of the center of gravity.

But one of the outstanding problems of education, as of
music, is modulation. In the case of education, modulation
means movement from a social and human center toward
a more objective intellectual scheme of organization, always bearing in mind, however, that intellectual organization is not an end in itself but is the means by which social relations, distinctively human ties and bonds, may be
understood and more intelligently ordered.

When education is based in theory and practice upon
experience, it goes without saying that the organized subject-matter of the adult and the specialist cannot provide

the starting point. Nevertheless, it represents the goal toward which education should continuously move.

Nothing can be more absurd educationally than to make a plea for a variety of active occupations in the school while decrying the need for progressive organization of information and ideas. Intelligent activity is distinguished from aimless activity by the fact that it involves selection of means—analysis—out of the variety of conditions that are present, and their arrangement—synthesis—to reach an intended aim or purpose.

Unless the problem of intellectual organization can be worked out on the ground of experience, reaction is sure to occur toward externally imposed methods of organization. There are signs of this reaction already in evidence. We are told that our schools, old and new, are failing in the main task. They do not develop, it is said, the capacity for critical discrimination and the ability to reason. The ability to think is smothered, we are told, by accumulation of miscellaneous ill-digested information, and by the attempt to acquire forms of skill which will be immediately useful in the business and commercial world. We are told that these evils spring from the influence of science and from the magnification of present requirements at the expense of the tested cultural heritage from the past. It is argued that science and its method must be subordinated; that we must return to the logic of ultimate first principles expressed in the logic of Aristotle and St. Thomas, in order that the young may have sure anchorage in their intellectual and moral life, and not be at the mercy of every passing breeze that blows.

If the method of science had ever been consistently and continuously applied throughout the day-by-day work of the school in all subjects, I should be more impressed by this emotional appeal than I am. I see at bottom but two alternatives between which education must choose if it is not to drift aimlessly. One of them is expressed by the attempt to induce educators to return to the intellectual methods and ideals that arose centuries before scientific method was developed. The appeal may be temporarily successful in a period when general insecurity, emotional and intellectual as well as economic, is rife. For under these conditions the desire to lean on fixed authority is active. Nevertheless, it is so out of touch with all the conditions of modern life that I believe it is folly to seek salvation in this direction. The other alternative is systematic utilization of scientific method as the pattern and ideal of intelligent exploration and exploitation of the potentialities inherent in experience.

In the first place, the experimental method of science attaches more importance, not less, to ideas as ideas than do other methods. There is no such thing as experiment in the scientific sense unless action is directed by some leading idea. The fact that the ideas employed are hypotheses, not final truths, is the reason why ideas are more jealously guarded and tested in science than anywhere else. The moment they are taken to be first truths in themselves there ceases to be any reason for scrupulous examination of them. As fixed truths they must be accepted and that is the end of the matter. But as hypotheses, they must be continuously tested and revised, a requirement that demands they be accurately formulated.

In the second place, ideas or hypotheses are tested by the consequences which they produce when they are acted upon. This fact means that the consequences of action must be carefully and discriminatingly observed. Activity that is not checked by observation of what follows from it may be temporarily enjoyed. But intellectually it leads nowhere. It does not provide knowledge about the situations in which action occurs nor does it lead to clarification and expansion of ideas.

In the third place, the method of intelligence manifested in the experimental method demands keeping track of ideas, activities, and observed consequences. Keeping track is a matter of reflective review and summarizing, in which there are both discrimination and record of the significant features of a developing experience. To reflect is to look back over what has been done so as to extract the net meanings which are the capital stock for intelligent dealing with further experiences. It is the heart of intellectual organization and of the disciplined mind.

I am aware that the emphasis I have placed upon scientific method may be misleading, for it may result only in calling up the special technique of laboratory research as that is conducted by specialists. But the meaning of the emphasis placed upon scientific method has little to do with specialized techniques. It means that scientific method is the only authentic means at our command for getting at the significance of our everyday experiences of the world in which we live. It means that scientific method provides a working pattern of the way in which and the conditions under which experiences are used to lead ever onward and outward.

At every level there is an expanding development of experience if experience is educative in effect. Consequently, whatever the level of experience, we have no choice but either to operate in accord with the pattern it provides or else to neglect the place of intelligence in the development and control of a living and moving experience.

VI · Means and End of Education*

In what I have said I have taken for granted the soundness of the principle that education in order to accomplish its ends both for the individual learner and for society must be based upon experience—which is always the actual life-experience of some individual. I have not argued for the acceptance of this principle nor attempted to justify it. Conservatives as well as radicals in education are profoundly discontented with the present educational situation taken as a whole. There is at least this much agreement among intelligent persons of both schools of educational thought. The educational system must move one way or another, either backward to the intellectual and moral standards of a pre-scientific age or forward to ever greater utilization of scientific method in the development of the possibilities of growing, expanding experience. I have but endeavored to point out some of the conditions which must be satisfactorily fulfilled if education takes the latter course.

For I am so confident of the potentialities of education when it is treated as intelligently directed development of the possibilities inherent in ordinary experience that I do not feel it necessary to criticize here the other route nor to advance arguments in favor of taking the route of experience. The only ground for anticipating failure in taking this path resides to my mind in the danger that experience and the experimental method will not be adequately conceived. There is no discipline in the world so severe as the discipline of experience subjected to the tests of intelligent development and direction. Hence the only ground I can see for even a temporary reaction against the stand-

* From *Experience and Education*, pp. 113-116.

ards, aims, and methods of the newer education is the failure of educators who professedly adopt them to be faithful to them in practice. As I have emphasized more than once, the road of the new education is not an easier one to follow than the old road but a more strenuous and difficult one. It will remain so until it has attained its majority and that attainment will require many years of serious coöperative work on the part of its adherents. The greatest danger that attends its future is, I believe, the idea that it is an easy way to follow, so easy that its course may be improvised, if not in an impromptu fashion, at least almost from day to day or from week to week. It is for this reason that instead of extolling its principles, I have confined myself to showing certain conditions which must be fulfilled if it is to have the successful career which by right belongs to it.

I have used frequently in what precedes the words "progressive" and "new" education. I do not wish to close, however, without recording my firm belief that the fundamental issue is not of new versus old education nor of progressive against traditional education but a question of what anything whatever must be to be worthy of the name *education*. I am not, I hope and believe, in favor of any ends or any methods simply because the name progressive may be applied to them. The basic question concerns the nature of education with no qualifying adjectives prefixed. What we want and need is education pure and simple, and we shall make surer and faster progress when we devote ourselves to finding out just what education is and what conditions have to be satisfied in order that education may be a reality and not a name or a slogan. It is for this reason alone that I have emphasized the need for a sound philosophy of experience.

CHAPTER TWELVE

THE SCHOOLS AND THE SOCIAL WELFARE

I · The Schools in the Social Order*

IT is significant that the great movement for tax-supported public education had its strong impetus in the thirties of the nineteenth century, a time of general economic depression. For the fact is not wholly a coincidence. Labor leaders were among the chief backers of the movement. This is not the place for a review of the positive accomplishments of the movement. They are familiar and are often eulogized, and not without just reason. In many of the States of the Union Huxley's ladder from the kindergarten through the university is an established fact. But now, a century later, in the midst of a still greater economic crisis, there is again a period of a new educational demand and unrest. It is a time to take stock and to consider why and how the existing educational system has failed to meet the needs of the present and the imminent future.

Part of the reason is found in the educational tradition itself. Elementary schooling was everywhere in the past devoted to the promotion of literacy. It was identified with acquiring skill in reading, writing and figuring. Our ancestors would have been possessed of uncanny insight and imagination if they had thought of the purpose of the

---

* From *Education and the Social Order*, a pamphlet published by the League for Industrial Democracy.

common school in any other than traditional terms.
Higher education was almost equally controlled by concern for symbols, namely, advanced mathematics and foreign languages.

Moreover, aside from the tradition of the schools, there
were especial reasons for the emphasis put upon elementary literacy in this country. The "Three Rs" are at all
times the tools for introduction into higher studies; they
have to be mastered if further initiation is to occur. And
there were definite industrial and political causes for emphasis upon them in pioneer America. Manhood suffrage
was becoming general. A mass of illiterate voters was an
obvious menace. Industrialization was commencing, and
the shop worker had a greater need for letters than the
agrarian peasant of the old world. Above all the idea of
opportunity was in the social atmosphere. Ambition that
children should have a better chance than their parents
was almost universal. The mastery of letters was the
open sesame. Sparse pioneer communities had few cultural
facilities. Reading matter was scanty and yet was the only
means of access to the world's culture. The legend of
Abraham Lincoln poring over his books by the light of
the hearthfire is an authentic symbol of the general reverence for letters.

The social and intellectual climate inevitably strengthened the old type of school education. For life outside the
school, at least until after the Civil War, provided abundant opportunity for "practical" education. Many industries were still domestic, and the village had its quota of
small shops combining hand work with elementary machine processes. Moreover, unlike the modern big factory,
the processes were open to view as well as simple and
readily understood. The young people as they grew up
"learned by doing." They participated in what was going

on practically, as well as by observation and in imagination. What is now called vocational education took care of itself to a large extent by the force of conditions in the home, farm and shop; this fact operated to reinforce the traditional devotion of the school to letters.

The method and the aim of education corresponded to the conditions. The method was essentially inculcation— stamping in, in its literal sense. The main material of study was foreign and in a sense artificial. Dogberry to the contrary notwithstanding, reading and writing do not come by nature. Symbols are remote and alien, even when the material they convey are as familiar as "the cat on the mat." Imposition, accompanied by penalties for non-compliance and rewards for submission, was upon the whole the acknowledged method. Pioneer life outside the school contained enough stimulus to free movement and personal initiative to confirm the traditional idea that youth was averse to learning. Thus habits bred outside school created conditions inside the school that made recourse to external imposition and enforced receptivity seem necessary. The traditional notion of "discipline" was developed under these circumstances. The little red schoolhouse of our ancestors was a struggle of wits and often of main strength between pupils and teachers.

The motivation, however, among the abler students was distinctly the appeal to getting on in the world, material success. In this respect, school conditions were in harmony with conditions out of school, however much they were unlike in other respects. With a sparse population and seemingly unlimited natural resources, the appeal to personal ambition was almost boundless. There were always new lands awaiting the enterprising, and mechanical invention was constantly opening new opportunities. The social situation produced by the developing process of industrialization was radically different from that of the saturated industrialization we now have.

Nor was the energy thus stimulated wholly selfish. Rugged individualism was not always a myth, nor were enterprise, initiative, sturdiness and personal thrift always such as to depress other members of the community. The country needed capital for its development of natural resources. Individualistic energy rendered real service to the community and the contrast between the lazy and idle, the thrifty and the ne'er-do-well had a genuine moral significance.

But educationally the important point is that the spirit of getting ahead and the idea that personal advancement was the best way to "serve the community" pervaded the school. It furnished the common ideal and operated as the dominant motive. And under the method of indoctrination which prevailed it became the chief article in the moral and economic faith that was inculcated. It would be a great mistake to read back the situation of the last twenty years or so, and suppose that this indoctrination was the deliberate act of a capitalist class bent on securing its own supremacy.

The common faith was the cult of individual success by means of individual effort. Indoctrination is always most successful when it is both unconsciously given and unconsciously received. When indoctrination was the prevailing method in all subjects, the only cause for surprise would be if it had not been resorted to in promoting the gospel of individual salvation, worldly as well as other-worldly. And in this moral field, it fell in line with the influences of everyday life outside the school, instead of going contrary as it did in most other subjects. Pupils were already inoculated by the atmosphere they breathed. The school enabled the germs to flourish and to make the ideal conscious.

Needless to say, I have been speaking of the pioneer phase of the schools—of the period before the industrial expansion that was stimulated by the Civil War and its aftermath, and which acquired a momentum during the nineties of the last century that swept all before it. The last forty years have been a time of constant educational change. Most teachers are honestly bewildered when they are charged with conservatism or reactionary tendencies in their field. They can point in rebuttal to changes in their own school buildings that, compared with the curriculum and methods of a generation ago, seem nothing short of revolutionary.

Relations of teacher and pupils have been humanized to a large extent. Older methods of "discipline" have been abolished or fallen into disuse. Much greater provision for activity within the school has been made in compensation for the curtailments enforced outside the school. Indoctrination in the school subjects has become more skilful and sugar-coated. Above all, new subjects and new courses of study have been introduced with almost startling rapidity. The world has never seen such a growth of school population in secondary and college education as in this country in the past forty years. School expansion in subjects, in courses, open to students and in numbers of students has kept pace with the industrial expansion.

Nevertheless there has been no fundamental change in spirit and motivation. Indeed, as industry and trade have expanded and wealth and the opportunities for enjoyment and power offered have grown, the individualistic philosophy of success and material advancement has also grown. The current psychology of the people has been capitalistic far beyond the confines of the capitalists. It has permeated not only farmers but the working class. Indeed, while some of the more idealistic immigrants have come here because of anticipated blessings of liberty, the great mass came because they identified liberty with an opportunity for material advancement of themselves, their children and children's children.

The persistence of the earlier psychological and moral motivation has given the many sweeping educational changes to which I have referred a rather external character. Apart from change in basic attitudes, no thoroughgoing reorganization is possible. Indeed, the very addition of new subjects, going on as continually as it has done, has itself produced an educational problem.

It is a common complaint that there is multiplication of studies to the point of confusion and congestion, with the result of constant danger of superficiality and miscellaneous scattering, so that students get a smattering of many subjects and a thorough mastery of none. The situation is a reflex of social aimlessness and dispersiveness. A society that is largely held together by the aim of many individuals to get on as individuals is not really held together at all. Changes occur with breathless rapidity, but they have little organization and next to no center and unified tendency. The curriculum of the schools reflects that situation.

The argument, which is that of history itself, indicates the present dilemma, the present choice that must be made, and the present opportunity. There is only one way out of the existing educational confusion and drift. That way is the definite substitution of a social purpose, controlling methods of teaching and discipline and materials of study, for the traditional individualistic aim.

And, in the schools as in society generally, that change will signify more genuine development of individuality for the mass of individuals. For, in the first place, it signifies the substitution of methods of inquiry and mutual consultation and discussion for the methods of imposition and inculcation. I do not wish to imply that this method still exists in all its ancient force. In fact, teachers have worked out the technique already for the method that needs to be substituted.

But the new method is not widely used and is still, even when employed, definitely limited in its range of application, and for two reasons. One of them concerns the emphasis that is put upon getting things under discussion settled, or in the vocabulary of the teacher making sure that pupils get the "right answer." It is impossible, I think, to exaggerate the hold that this attitude has upon teaching in the schools. Problems are brought up but only that they may be solved and put to bed. There is current the opinion that the only alternative to this course is to leave students' minds in a state of confusion. To some extent such is the result, but it is mainly because they have already been imbued through texts and teachers with the notion there is already in existence the "right" answer to every question that is brought up.

The real alternative to settling questions is not mental confusion, but the development of a spirit of curiosity that will keep the student in an attitude of inquiry and of search for new light. If the result is simply to leave the student with the idea that there are two sides to the question and that there is a great deal to be said on both sides, the effect may be only a new version of the right answer affair; there are now two sides instead of just one. But the open mind is a nuisance if it is merely passively open to allow anything to find its way into a vacuous mind behind the opening. It is significant only as it is the mark of an actively searching mind, one on the alert for further knowledge and understanding. The basic trouble with much teaching, which on some grounds is excellent, is that it does not create wants in the mind, wants in the sense of demands that will go on operating on their own initiative.

This fact brings me to the other reason why the method of external imposition is only scotched, not killed. We live in a world that is changing, not settled and fixed. Even the best established of the natural sciences, physics, is full of unsolved questions and charged with rapid change. But the obvious matter is that the social world is in a state of flux, and that we go on teaching as if the Constitution and our forefathers had finally determined all important social and political questions—a method that leaves pupils later in life ready victims of propaganda and publicity agents. Method is relative to subject-matter and not much of the subject-matter of actual economic and social facts and forces finds its way into even the average high school.

In short we teach the doings and impart the skills of the past, and severely leave alone the forces of the present that are creating the future in which the graduates of our school will some day find themselves. We educate for a static social order which does not exist. We educate for the *status quo* and when the students go forth they do not find anything so settled that it can be called anything of a static kind. What I have said about studying the past does not apply alone or even chiefly to history. In general the students are concerned to learn the *achievements* of the past, whether they be in history, geography, arithmetic, science or civics. They do not learn how these achievements were brought about nor do they learn the relation of the present to these achievements.

II · Education and Social Change*

Attention has been continually called of late to the fact that society is in process of change, and that the schools tend to lag behind. We are all familiar with the pleas that are urged to bring education in the schools into closer relation with the forces that are producing social change and with the needs that arise from these changes. Probably no question has received so much attention in educational discussion during the past few years as the problem of integration of the schools with social life. Upon these general matters, I could hardly do more than reiterate what has often been said.

Nevertheless, there is as yet little consensus of opinion as to what the schools can do in relation to the forces of social change and how they should do it. There are those who assert in effect that the schools must simply reflect social changes that have already occurred, as best they may. Some would go so far as to make the work of schools virtually parasitic. Others hold that the schools should take an active part in *directing* social change, and share in the construction of a new social order. Even among the latter there is, however, marked difference of attitude. Some think the schools should assume this directive role by means of indoctrination; others oppose this method. Even if there were more unity of thought than exists, there would still be the practical problem of overcoming institutional inertia so as to realize in fact an agreed-upon program.

There is, accordingly, no need to justify further discussion of the problem of the relation of education to social change. I shall do what I can, then, to indicate the factors that seem to me to enter into the problem, together with some of the reasons that prove that the schools do have a

* From *The Social Frontier*, May 1937.

role—and an important one—in *production* of social change.

One factor inherent in the situation is that schools *do* follow and reflect the social "order" that exists. I do not make this statement as a grudging admission, nor yet in order to argue that they should *not* do so. I make it rather as a statement of a *conditioning* factor which supports the conclusion that the schools thereby do take part in the determination of a future social order; and that, accordingly, the problem is not whether the schools *should* participate in the production of a future society (since they do so anyway) but whether they should do it blindly and irresponsibly or with the maximum possible of courageous intelligence and responsibility.

The grounds that lead me to make this statement are as follows: The existing state of society, which the schools reflect, is not something fixed and uniform. The idea that such is the case is a self-imposed hallucination. Social conditions are not only in process of change, but the changes going on are in different directions, so different as to produce social confusion and conflict. There is no single and clear-cut pattern that pervades and holds together in a unified way the social conditions and forces that operate. It requires a good deal of either ignorance or intellectual naïveté to suppose that these changes have all been tending to one coherent social outcome. The plaint of the conservative about the imperiling of old and time-tried values and truths, and the efforts of reactionaries to stem the tide of changes that occur, are sufficient evidence, if evidence be needed to the contrary.

Of course the schools have mirrored the social changes that take place. The notion that the educational system has been static is too absurd for notice; it has been and still is in a state of flux.

The fact that it is possible to argue about the desirability of many of the changes that have occurred, and to give
valid reasons for deploring aspects of the flux, is not relevant to the main point. For the stronger the arguments
brought forth on these points, and the greater the amount
of evidence produced to show that the educational system
is in a state of disorder and confusion, the greater is the
proof that the schools have responded to, and have reflected, social conditions which are themselves in a state
of confusion and conflict.

Do those who hold the idea that the schools should not
attempt to give direction to social change accept compla-
cently the confusion that exists, because the schools *have*
followed in the track of one social change after another?
They certainly do not, although the logic of their position
demands it. For the most part they are severe critics of
the existing state of education. They are as a rule opposed
to the studies called modern and the methods called progressive. They tend to favor return to older types of
studies and to strenuous "disciplinary" methods. What
does this attitude mean? Does it not show that its advocates in reality adopt the position that the schools can do
something to affect positively and constructively social
conditions? For they hold in effect that the school should
discriminate with respect to the social forces that play
upon it; that instead of accepting the latter *in toto,* education should select and organize in a given direction. The
adherents of this view can hardly believe that the effect
of selection and organization will stop at the doors of
school rooms. They must expect some ordering and heal-
ing influence to be exerted sooner or later upon the structure and movement of life outside. What they are really
doing when they deny directive social effect to education
is to express their opposition to some of the directions

social change is actually taking, and their choice of other social forces as those with which education should throw in its lot so as to promote as far as may be their victory in the strife of forces. They are conservatives in education because they are socially conservative and vice-versa.

This is as it should be in the interest of clearness and consistency of thought and action. If these conservatives in education were more aware of what is involved in their position, and franker in stating its implications, they would help bring out the real issue. It is not whether the schools shall or shall not influence the course of future social life, but in what direction they shall do so and how. In some fashion or other, the schools will influence social life anyway. But they can exercise such influence in different ways and to different ends, and the important thing is to become conscious of these different ways and ends, so that an intelligent choice may be made, and so that if opposed choices are made, the further conflict may at least be carried on with understanding of what is at stake, and not in the dark.

There are three possible directions of choice. Educators may act so as to perpetuate the present confusion and possibly increase it. That will be the result of drift, and under present conditions to drift is in the end to make a choice. Or they may select the newer scientific, technological, and cultural forces that are producing change in the old order; may estimate the direction in which they are moving and their outcome if they are given freer play, and see what can be done to make the schools their ally. Or, educators may become intelligently conservative and strive to make the schools a force in maintaining the old order intact against the impact of new forces.

If the second course is chosen—as of course I believe it should be—the problem will be other than merely that of accelerating the rate of the change that is going on. The problem will be to develop the insight and understanding that will enable the youth who go forth from the schools to take part in the great work of construction and organization that will have to be done, and to equip them with the attitudes and habits of action that will make their understanding and insight practically effective.

There is much that can be said for an intelligent conservatism. I do not know anything that can be said for perpetuation of a wavering, uncertain, confused condition of social life and education. Nevertheless, the easiest thing is to refrain from fundamental thinking and let things go on drifting. Upon the basis of any other policy than drift —which after all is a policy, though a blind one—every special issue and problem, whether that of selection and organization of subject-matter of study, of methods of teaching, of school buildings and equipment, of school administration, is a special phase of the inclusive and fundamental problem: What movement of social forces, economic, political, religious, cultural, shall the school take to be controlling in its aims and methods, and with which forces shall the school align itself?

Failure to discuss educational problems from this point of view but intensifies the existing confusion. Apart from this background, and outside of this perspective, educational questions have to be settled *ad hoc* and are speedily unsettled. What is suggested does not mean that the schools shall throw themselves into the political and economic arena and take sides with some party there. I am not talking about parties; I am talking about social forces and their movement. In spite of absolute claims that are made for this party or that, it is altogether probable that existing parties and sects themselves suffer from existing confusions and conflicts, so that the understanding, the ideas, and attitudes that control their policies, need re-education and re-orientation. I know that there are some who think that the implications of what I have said point to abstinence and futility; that they negate the stand first taken. But I am surprised when educators adopt this position, for it shows a profound lack of faith in their own calling. It assumes that education as education has nothing or next to nothing to contribute; that formation of understanding and disposition counts for nothing; that only immediate overt action counts and that it can count equally whether or not it has been modified by education.

Before leaving this aspect of the subject, I wish to recur to the utopian nature of the idea that the schools can be completely neutral. This idea sets up an end incapable of accomplishment. So far as it is acted upon, it has a definite social effect, but that effect is, as I have said, perpetuation of disorder and increase of blind because unintelligent conflict. Practically, moreover, the weight of such action falls upon the reactionary side. Perhaps the most effective way of re-inforcing reaction under the name of neutrality, consists in keeping the oncoming generation ignorant of the conditions in which they live and the issues they have to face. This effect is the more pronounced because it is subtle and indirect; because neither teachers nor those taught are aware of what they are doing and what is being done to them. Clarity can develop only in the extent to which there is frank acknowledgment of the basic issue: Where shall the social emphasis of school life and work fall, and what are the educational policies which correspond to this emphasis?

III · Educators and the Class Struggle*

I find myself rather confused by the articles that have

* From *The Social Frontier*, May 1936.

appeared in *The Social Frontier* urging that educators adopt the class concept as their intellectual guide and practical dynamic. I do not know just what is meant by the class concept; what its implications are, intellectual and practical. The arguments, when boiled down, seem to amount to the following:

A radical reconstruction of the existing social order is demanded. The needed reconstruction is opposed by the powerful class now in control of social affairs, whose property, power, and prestige are threatened by the reconstruction that is required. On the other side are the workers who suffer in countless ways from the present social order and who will be the gainers in security, freedom, and opportunity, by basic change. Teachers are workers and their own class interest is with fellow-workers. Moreover, social consciousness and social conscience should lead them to side with the workers; they belong on that side of the struggle that is going on.

Now my confusion arises because I do not see the bearing of these considerations, even if they are admitted, upon the conclusion drawn; namely, that the *concept* of the class struggle is the one which will give educators the intellectual and practical direction they need. In fact, this conclusion seems to me to be of the nature of a *non sequitur*. At least it seems to be a *non-sequitur* except upon the basis of an unexpressed premise. This premise, made explicit, would be to the effect that recognition of certain facts, namely, those of class struggle, is sufficient to give direction to the thinking and activity that are to be brought to bear upon the facts. I can see that the empirical facts, as far as they are admitted to be facts, constitute a most serious problem. I do not see how the terms of a social problem are identical with the method of its solution, certainly not with a solution by any experimental method. I do not see how they constitute the leading ideas that will give direction to the efforts of educators. To know the empirical facts is one condition of experimental method; but the question of what to do about the facts and how to do it is another matter.

When the importance of the concept of class and class war is urged by those who have no use for the experimental point of view, I do not experience the confusion I have spoken of. For example, I do not find the gap I have mentioned in the position of communists of the current Marxist-Leninist type. For their premise is that class struggle is and always has been the source of social change; that class struggle by means of the forces of material productivity conditions the nature, the rise, and the fall of all social and cultural institutions; that at present the war is between the capitalist bourgeoisie and the proletariat; that the irrepressible conflict now going on will finally break out into overt civil war; that the end of the struggle will be the dictatorship of the proletariat as the means of final transition to a classless society. There is no ambiguity in this view. It is clear-cut and simple, for it rests upon the assumption that the class struggle determines of itself the course of events and their issue, either automatically or else because a sufficient number of persons become aware of the class struggle and become class conscious.

If this is the point of view of those who urge upon educators the importance of the class concept, it is free from the confusion to which I have referred. But such does not seem to be the case with some. I mention two points of serious difference. One of the articles points out that there is a subjective factor in every concept of class. This point of view is adequately stated in the article of Dr. Childs, who says: "All classifications are tools made for a purpose." From the standpoint of current Marxian orthodoxy, this position is thoroughly heterodox. For, according to the latter, the class concept is a strictly realistic apprehension of the *existing* social reality and of that which will exist.

The further difference that follows is of even greater significance. It concerns the nature of the educational process. If the essential facts are all in, and if these facts in and of themselves decide the nature of educational policy, then, when the essential facts are said to be those of class struggle, it follows that education becomes simply a matter of inculcation—in short, of agitation and propaganda. But some at least of those who urge the importance of the class concept do not seem to draw this conclusion. Yet what is the point of the class concept as a determining factor in educational procedure unless it is to have such a controlling influence on the latter that education becomes a special form of constant indoctrination? And in that case what becomes of the plea for freedom in teaching? Is it a plea merely for freedom to inculcate a certain view of society, logically entailing lack of freedom for presentation of other views?

The point may be made clearer by supposing that one adopts the position implied in the following question of Dr. Childs: "Is it not highly probable that they [a myriad of interest groups] will merge into large classes and that American society *ultimately* will be divided into .those who advocate and those who oppose this drastic reconstruction?" If one believes that this is likely to happen, what then? Shall the educator as an educator endeavor to hasten and intensify the division? And what attitude shall he take toward the problem of *how* drastic social reconstruction is to be affected? Does education have anything to do with development of the attitudes and convictions that influence the *manner* of the transition? Put-

ting the question in an extreme form, is it the task of educators, because of acceptance of the class concept, to intensify a consciousness of class division and class war, or
is it to help determine the kind of social awareness that is
to exist so that the transformation may be accomplished,
as far as possible, by educational means instead of by conflict? What kind of "classes" are we to have, as far as education has anything to say on that matter, whether its
influence be light or great? Is it enough, for the purpose of
effecting the needed social transformation, that the exploited class become conscious that it is an exploited group
and then try to gain the physical or even the political power to become the dominant class? From the standpoint of
those who put their faith in the idea that a violent revolution is the solution, and that subsequent dictatorship by
a class is the best or only means to effect the transformation, it is quite possible that this *is* enough, that anything
else would tend to hinder the day of reconstruction. But
I have difficulty in imagining any educator taking this
point of view unless he has abandoned in advance all faith
in education.

I hope the point of these questions is clear. What does
the acceptance of the class concept *mean* for the work of
the educators? I cannot but think that the acceptance of
a *social* point of view rather than that of a special class
has led those who have advocated the class concept to
adopt the convictions they hold about the place of education in social transformation. If this is so, it would seem as
if this broader and more inclusive point of view is the one
from which they should carry on their educational work.
The acceptance of this point of view does not mean that
they should close their minds to the injustices and inequi-
ties of the present order, to their effects—impoverishment
and insecurity—or to the disastrous effect of these tragic

evils upon the culture of all groups in society. But certainly those who believe that education in the schools has some part to play in bringing about social transformation have a greater responsibility than any others to consider the *means* by which the transformation is to be brought about and the especial place of educational means among the total means. Except as educators accept the current Marxian view of the means that are alone necessary, I can but conclude that my confusion in reading what has been said is a result of a confusion on the part of the writers. They seem to convert a just plea that educators should become aware of the existence of social injustice, oppression, and disorder into the idea that this recognition suffices of itself to determine educational policies and methods. I repeat that such recognition forms a significant part of the *problem* of education, but it does not provide a key to its solution.

For an American, at least, the acceptance of a social instead of an exclusive class point of view, means acceptance of the democratic idea as the frame of reference and the source of the directive ideas of educational action. I am most happy to associate myself with the position taken on this matter by Dr. Raup in his article in the January, 1936, number of this journal. The issue of whether educators shall stay out of the process of social transformation or shall participate in it is quite another question from that of whether their participation shall be controlled by the class concept. To see this point seems to me the beginning of clarity of thought upon the whole matter. And there need be no fear that honest adoption of the democratic idea and criterion will lead to apathy and complacency—save in the case of those so intellectually dishonest that they would find some evasion in any case. The democratic frame of reference is capable of energizing action as well as of directing critical reflection and educational thought.

As far as I can see, the ambiguity in the concept of class orientation arises from confusing orientation *toward* a class, the class of workers, with orientation *by* a class interest. One's sympathies and, as occasion presents itself, one's efforts may well be with workers as against an exploiting class. But one's frame of values and one's controlling framework of ideas may nevertheless be derived from a sense of a comprehensive social interest. As I read the articles to which reference has been made, this larger sense is in fact their animating spirit. The writers urge teachers to recognize that they too are workers and that their function and their success in performing their function are bound up with the struggle in which workers are engaged. I am not taking exception to this point of view nor am I urging that teachers should be "neutral"—an impossibility in any case. It is possible to be alert and active in the struggle for social reorganization and yet recognize that it is *social* reorganization that is required, and that it must be undertaken in the social, rather than a class interest. Because I am persuaded the writers recognize that educational means and methods, rather than those of brute force, should play as large a part as possible in bringing about the reorganization, I am concerned lest they urge their plea from the standpoint of a class rather than from that of our democratic tradition and its methods.

IV · The Schools and Religions*

It seems hard that a generation which has accumulated not only material wealth, but intellectual riches, to

* From *Characters and Events,* vol. II, pp. 504-516. (First published in *The Hibbert Journal,* July 1908 under title "Religion and Our Schools.")

the extent that it is compelled to pull down its barns—its systems of philosophy and doctrine—and build greater, should be lacking in just that grace and sanction of life which ignorant and poor people have possessed as matter of course. But our learnedly self-conscious generation is also mechanical. It has a tool for everything, and almost everything has become for it a tool. Why, then, should we longer suffer from deficiency of religion? We have discovered our lack: let us set the machinery in motion which will supply it. We have mastered the elements of physical well-being; we can make light and heat to order, and can command the means of transportation. Let us now put a similar energy, goodwill, and thoughtfulness into the control of the things of the spiritual life. Having got so far as to search for proper machinery, the next step is easy. Education is the modern universal purveyor, and upon the schools shall rest the responsibility for seeing to it that we recover our threatened religious heritage.

I cannot expect that those who are now especially concerned with the maintenance and the spread of conscious and explicit religious instruction (for the time being one must use this question-begging epithet) will recognise their attitude or intention in what I have just said. And it has no application to those who are already committed to special dogmas of religion which are the monopoly of special ecclesiastic institutions. With respect to them, the fight for special agencies and peculiar materials and methods of education in religion is a natural part of their business: just as, however, it is the business of those who do not believe that religion is a monopoly or a protected industry to contend, in the interest both of education and of religion, for keeping the schools free from what they must regard as a false bias. Those who believe that human nature without special divine assistance is lost, who believe that they have in their charge the special channels through which the needed assistance is conveyed, must, naturally, be strenuous in keeping open these channels to the minds of men. But when the arguments. for special religious education at special times and places by special means proceed from philosophic sources—from those whose primary premise is denial of any breach between man and the world and God, then a sense of unreality comes over me. The arguments perforce translate themselves ironically. They seem to say that, since religion is a universal function of life, we must particularly safeguard it lest it disappear; that since religion is the consciousness of the spiritual import of experience, we must find mechanical appliances for developing it.

Those who approach religion and education from the side of unconstrained reflection, not from the side of tradition, are of necessity aware of the tremendous transformation of intellectual attitude effected by the systematic denial of the supernatural; they are aware of the changes it imports not merely in special dogma and rites, but in the interpretation of the world, and in the projection of social, and, hence, moral life. It testifies to the current unreality of philosophy (itself probably a product of that forced idealism in which modern thought has taken refuge) that philosophers should seem to think that great intellectual generalizations may be, as it were, plastered over life to label its contents, and not imply profound practical alterations within life itself. In no other way is it easy to account for the attitude of those who are convinced of the final departure of the supernatural interpretation of the world and of man, and who yet think that agencies like the church and the school must not be thoroughly reconstructed before they can be fit organs for nurturing types of religious feeling and thought which are consistent with modern democracy and modern science.

That science has the same spiritual import as super-naturalism; that democracy translates into the same religious attitude as did feudalism; that it is only a matter of slight changes of phraseology, a development of old symbolisms into new shades of meaning—such beliefs testify to that torpor of imagination which is the uniform effect of dogmatic belief. The reconstruction of the Church is a matter which concerns, indeed, the whole community so far as its outcome is concerned; while the responsibility for its initiation belongs primarily to those within the churches. The burden of conducting the development, the reconstruction, of other educational agencies belongs, however, primarily to the community as a whole. With respect to its intellectual aspect, its philosophy, it belongs especially to those who, having become conscious in some degree of the modern ideas of nature, of man and society, are best able to forecast the direction which social changes are taking. It is lucidity, sincerity, and the sense of reality which demand that, until the non-supernatural view is more completely elaborated in all its implications and is more completely in possession of the machinery of education, the schools shall keep hands off and shall do as little as possible.

We need, however, to accept the responsibilities of living in an age marked by the greatest intellectual readjustment history records. There is undoubted loss of joy, of consolation, of some types of strength, and of some sources of inspiration in the change. There is a manifest increase of uncertainty; there is some paralysis of energy, and much excessive application of energy in materialistic directions. Yet nothing is gained by deliberate effort to return to ideas which have become incredible, and to symbols which have been emptied of their content of obvious meaning. Nothing can be gained by moves which will increase confusion and obscurity, which tend to an emotional hypocrisy and to a phrase-mongering or formulae which seem to mean one thing and really import the opposite. Bearing the losses and inconveniences of our time as best we may, it is the part of men to labor persistently and patiently for the clarification and development of the positive creed of life implicit in democracy and in science, and to work for the transformation of all practical instrumentalities of education till they are in harmony with these ideas. Till these ends are further along than we can honestly claim them to be at present, it is better that our schools should do nothing than that they should do wrong things. It is better for them to confine themselves to their obviously urgent tasks than that they should, under the name of spiritual culture, form habits of mind which are at war with the habits of mind congruous with democracy and with science. It is not laziness nor cynicism which calls for this policy; it is honesty, courage, sobriety, and faith.

If one inquires why the American tradition is so strong against any connection of State and Church, why it dreads even the rudiments of religious teaching in state-maintained schools, the immediate and superficial answer is not far to seek. The cause was not, mainly, religious indifference, much less hostility to Christianity, although the eighteenth century deism played an important role. The cause lay largely in the diversity and vitality of the various denominations, each fairly sure that, with a fair field and no favor, it could make its own way; and each animated by a jealous fear that, if any connection of State and Church were permitted, some rival denomination would get an unfair advantage. But there was a deeper and by no means wholly unconscious influence at work.

The United States became a nation late enough in the history of the world to profit by the growth of that modern (although Greek) thing—the state consciousness. This nation was born under conditions which enabled it to share in and to appropriate the idea that the state life, the vitality of the social whole, is of more importance than the flourishing of any segment or class. So far as church institutions were concerned, the doctrine of popular sovereignty was a reality, not a literary or legal fiction. Upon the economic side, the nation was born too soon to learn the full force of the state idea as against the class idea. Our fathers naïvely dreamed of the continuation of pioneer conditions and the free opportunity of every individual, and took none of the precautions to maintain the supremacy of the state over that of the class which newer commonwealths are taking. For that lack of foresight we are paying dearly, and are like to pay more dearly. But the lesson of the two and a half centuries lying between the Protestant revolt and the formation of the nation was well learned as respected the necessity of maintaining the integrity of the state as against all divisive ecclesiastical divisions. Doubtless many of our ancestors would have been somewhat shocked to realize the full logic of their own attitude with respect to the subordination of churches to the state (falsely termed the *separation* of Church and State); but the state idea was inherently of such vitality and constructive force as to carry the practical result; with or without conscious perception of its philosophy. And any general agitation in the United States of the question of religious instruction in the schools could have but one explanation. It would mean that, from economic segregation and unassimilated immigration, the state-consciousness of the country had been sapped by the growth of social factions.

As I recall, some of the Platonic dialogues discuss the question whether virtue can be taught, and all of them contain overtones or reminiscences of the topic. For the discussion led a long way. What is virtue? That is not an altogether easy question; and since to answer it we must know virtue and not merely have opinions about it, it will be well to find out what knowledge is. Moreover, teaching implies learning, and learning is coming to know, or knowledge in process of learning. What, then, is the connection of the becoming of knowledge with the being of knowledge? And since the teaching of virtue means, not getting knowledge "about" virtue, but the conversion of character to the good, what, after all, is the relation between becoming good and that becoming wise which is the result of learning?

Somehow, I am more aware that Plato discusses all these questions than I am certain of any final answer to the question whether virtue may be taught. Yet I seem to recall some hypothetical suggestions for an answer. If, as we have reason to believe, the soul of man is naturally akin to good—if, indeed, it truly *is* only through participation in the good—then may various objects, also in their measure expressions of good, serve to remind the soul of its own or original nature. If these various reminders may be organized into a comprehensive scheme, continuous and continual in operation—if, in other words, there may be found a state organized in righteousness—then may the soul be finally brought to the apprehension of its own being or good; and this coming to know and to be we may term learning. But, if I remember rightly, Plato always classed endeavors to teach virtue apart from an accompanying thorough reorganization of social life and of science as a piece of confused and self-contradictory thinking—as a case, that is, of sophistic.

Have we any reason for taking the present problem of teaching religion to be simpler in conception or easier in execution? The contemporary problem appears, indeed, to be more intricate and difficult. Varied and conflicting as were the views of Plato's Greek contemporaries as to what things should be included and taught under the head of virtues, the question of just what concretely comes under the caption of religion today is as much harder to decide as our social life is more heterogeneous in origin and composition than was the Athenian. We certainly cannot teach religion as an abstract essence. We have got to teach some·thing as religion, and that means practically some religion. Which? In America, at least, the answer cannot be summarily given even as Christianity in general. Our Jewish fellow citizens not only have the same "hands, organs, dimensions, senses, affections, passions" as the Christians, but, like them, they pay taxes, vote, and serve on school boards. But we should not be very much better off even if it were a question of Christianity alone. *Which* Christianity? Oriental in its origin, it has been since Latinized and Germanized, and there are even those who have dreamed of humanizing it.

The problem of today is more complex as respects also the process of learning, of coming to know. In the day of Plato, art and science, skilled practice and theory, were only beginning to be separated. Just as a man learned shoemaking in process of becoming a shoemaker, so might a man learn virtue in becoming a member of a good state —if such a thing could be found. Today knowledge is something specialised, and learning does not consist in intelligent mastery of an activity, but in acquiring a diversity of information about things, and control over technical methods for instituting symbolic references to things. Knowledge to Plato was the sort of thing that the forefathers of some of us called "getting religion." It was a personal experiencing and a vital realization. But what shall knowledge of religion as an outcome of instruction mean today? Shall it mean the conversion of character into spirituality? Shall it mean the accumulation of information *about* religion? Or are there those who still believe in some magic power resident in memorized words, phrases, and facts of transmuting themselves into personal insight, the development of fundamental mood and the formation of permanent attitudes towards experience?

When we consider knowledge from the side of its method and from the standpoint of what it takes to get something really worthy to be called knowledge, the problem increases in difficulty. As yet, the standpoint of science, its spirit, has not of course leavened very adequately our methods of teaching. From the standpoint of those methods of inquiry and testing which we call science, much, perhaps most, of what passes for knowledge is in reality what Plato called opinion. Our science is still an outward garb more or less awkwardly worn rather than a habit of mind. But none the less the scientific norm of mental activity presses daily closer upon life and upon the schools. We are getting daily further away from the conditions in which one subject more or less taught by dogmatic, catechetical and memoriter methods was of slight consequence. We are becoming aware of the absurdity implied in calling things which happen to be studied and learned in school "knowledge," when they have been acquired by methods frequently at odds with those necessary to give science. Can those who take the philosophic and historic view of religion as a flower and fruition of the human spirit in a congenial atmosphere tolerate the incongruity involved in "teaching" such an intimate and originally vital matter by external and formal methods?

And can those who hold that true religion is something externally imported tolerate any other methods? Is it not confusion to seek a reconciliation of two such disparate ideas?

Already the spirit of our schooling is permeated with the feeling that every subject, every topic, every fact, every professed truth must submit to a certain publicity and impartiality. All proffered samples of learning must go to the same assay-room and be subjected to common tests. It is the essence of all dogmatic faiths to hold that any such "show-down" is sacrilegious and perverse. The characteristic of religion, from their point of view, is that it is —intellectually—secret, not public; peculiarly revealed, not generally known; authoritatively declared, not communicated and tested in ordinary ways. What is to be done about this increasing antinomy between the standard for coming to know in other subjects of the school, and coming to know in religous matters? I am far from saying that the antinomy is an inherent one, or that the day may not come when religion will be so thoroughly naturalized in the hearts and minds of men that it can be considered publicly, openly, and by common tests, even among religious people. But it is pertinent to point out that, as long as religion is conceived as it now is conceived by the great majority of professed religionists, there is something self-contradictory in speaking of education in religion in the same sense in which we speak of education in topics where the method of free inquiry has made its way. The "religious" would be the last to be willing that either the history or the content of religion should be taught in this spirit; while those to whom the scientific standpoint is not a merely technical device, but is the embodiment of integrity of mind, must protest against its being taught in any other spirit.

As Plato brought out with reference to the teaching of virtue, there is one other factor in coming to know—the teachers. Plato was quite sure that, whether or no virtue might be taught, it might not be taught by its professed teachers—the sophists. I express my appreciation of Plato rather than my lack of appreciation of the professional teachers of our own day, when I say that if Plato were to return to take part in the current discussion, he would raise questions about those who were to teach religion analogous to those he brought up about the teachers of his own time. It is not that those into whose hands the giving of instruction would fall are so irreligious or so non-religious as to be unfitted for the task. The sophists were doubtless superior rather than inferior in personal virtues to their average neighbor. It is one thing to be fairly or even exceptionally virtuous; it is another thing to command the conditions and the qualifications for successful importation of virtue to others. Where are the experts in religion? and where are the authoritative teachers? There are theologians: do we want theology taught? There are historians, but I fear the day has not come when the history of religion can be taught as history. Here precisely is one of those fields of clarification and criticism where much labor needs to be done, and where the professional religionist is one of the most serious obstacles to reckon with, since a wider and deeper historic knowledge would overthrow his traditional basis.

There are preachers and catechists, but, unless we are committed to some peculiar faith or institution, it is not exhortation or discipline of this sort that constitutes religious instruction. There are psychologists: but is introspection our aim? There remains, indeed, the corps of faithful, more or less well-prepared, hard-working and hard-worked teachers. This brings us to the crux of the whole matter. Is religion a thing so specialized, so technical, so "informational" that, like geography or history or grammar, it may be taught at special hours, times, and places by those who have properly "got it up," and who have been approved as persons of fit character and adequate professional training?

This question of the mode, time, and stuff of specific instruction trenches indeed upon a question in which national temper and tradition count for much. We do not find it feasible or desirable to put upon the regular teachers the burden of teaching a subject which has the nature of religion. The alternative plan of parcelling out pupils among religious teachers drawn from their respective churches and denominations brings us up against exactly the matter which has done most to discredit the churches, and to discredit the cause, not perhaps of religion, but of organized and institutional religion: the multiplication of rival and competing religious bodies, each with its private inspiration and outlook. Our schools, in bringing together those of different nationalities, languages, traditions, and creeds, in assimilating them together upon the basis of what is common and public in endeavor and achievement, are performing an infinitely significant religious work. They are promoting the social unity out of which in the end genuine religious unity must grow. Shall we interfere with this work? Shall we run the risk of undoing it by introducing into education a subject which can be taught only by segregating pupils and turning them over at special hours to separate representatives of rival faiths? This would be deliberately to adopt a scheme which is predicated upon the maintenance of social divisions in just the matter, religion, which is empty and futile save as it expresses the basic unities of life.

We are far, indeed, from having attained an explicit

and articulated consciousness of the religious significance
of democracy in education, and of education in democracy.
But some underlying convictions get ingrained in unconscious habit and find expression in obscure intimation and
intense labor, long before they receive consistent theoretic formulation. In such dim, blind, but effective way
the American people is conscious that its schools serve best
the cause of religion in serving the cause of social unification; and that under certain conditions schools are more
religious in substance and in promise without any of the
conventional badges and machinery of religious instruction than they could be in cultivating these forms at the
expense of a state-consciousness.

We may indeed question whether it is true that in any
relative sense this is a peculiarly irreligious age. Absolutely speaking, it doubtless is so; but have superficiality,
flippancy, and externality of life been such uniformly absent traits of past ages? Our historic imagination is at best
slightly developed. We generalize and idealize the past
egregiously. We set up little toys to stand as symbols for
long centuries and the complicated lives of countless individuals. And we are still, even those who have nominally surrendered supernatural dogma, largely under the
dominion of the ideas of those who have succeeded in identifying religion with the rites, symbols, and emotions associated with these dogmatic beliefs. As we see the latter
disappearing, we think we are growing irreligious. For all
we know, the integrity of mind which is loosening the hold
of these things is potentially much more religious than
all that it is displacing. It is increased knowledge of nature
which has made supra-nature incredible, or at least difficult of belief. We measure the change from the standpoint of the supranatural and we call it irreligious. Possibly if we measured it from the standpoint of the natural

piety it is fostering, the sense of the permanent and inevitable implication of nature and man in a common career and destiny, it would appear as the growth of religion. We take note of the decay of cohesion and influence among the religiously organized bodies of the familiar historic type, and again we conventionally judge religion to be on the decrease. But it may be that their decadence is the fruit of a broader and more catholic principle of human intercourse and association which is too religious to tolerate these pretensions to monopolize truth and to make private possessions of spiritual insight and aspiration.

It may be so; it may be that the symptoms of religious ebb as conventionally interpreted are symptoms of the coming of a fuller and deeper religion. I do not claim to know. But of one thing I am quite sure: our ordinary opinions about the rise and falling off of religion are highly conventional, based mostly upon the acceptance of a standard of religion which is the product of just those things in historic religions which are ceasing to be credible. So far as education is concerned, those who believe in religion as a natural expression of human experience must devote themselves to the development of the ideas of life which lie implicit in our still new science and our still newer democracy. They must interest themselves in the transformation of those institutions which still bear the dogmatic and the feudal stamp (and which do not?) till they are in accord with these ideas. In performing this service, it is their business to do what they can to prevent all public educational agencies from being employed in ways which inevitably impede the recognition of the spiritual import of science and of democracy, and hence of that type of religion which will be the fine flower of the modern spirit's achievement.

V· Democracy in the Schools*

There is some kind of government, of control, wherever affairs that concern a number of persons who act together are engaged in. It is a superficial view that holds government is located in Washington or Albany. There is government in the family, in business, in the church, in every social group. There are regulations, due to custom if not to enactment, that settle how individuals in a group act in connection with one another.

It is a disputed question of theory and practice just how far a democratic political government should go in control of the conditions of action within special groups. At the present time, for example, there are those who think the federal and state governments leave too much freedom of independent action to industrial and financial groups, and there are others who think the government is going altogether too far at the present time. I do not need to discuss this phase of the problem, much less to try to settle it. But it must be pointed out that if the methods of regulation and administration in vogue in the conduct of secondary social groups are non-democratic, whether directly or indirectly or both, there is bound to be an unfavorable reaction back into the habits of feeling, thought and action of citizenship in the broadest sense of that word. The way in which any organized social interest is controlled necessarily plays an important part in forming the dispositions and tastes, the attitudes, interests, purposes and desires, of those engaged in carrying on the activities of the group. For illustration, I do not need to do more than point to the moral, emotional and intellectual effect upon both employers and laborers of the existing industrial system. Just what the effects specifically are is a matter about which we know very little. But I suppose

* From *School and Society*, April 3, 1937.

that every one who reflects upon the subject admits that it is impossible that the ways in which activities are carried on for the greater part of the waking hours of the day, and the way in which the share of individuals are involved in the management of affairs in such a matter as gaining a livelihood and attaining material and social security, can not but be a highly important factor in shaping personal dispositions; in short, forming character and intelligence.

In the broad and final sense all institutions are educational in the sense that they operate to form the attitudes, dispositions, abilities and disabilities that constitute a concrete personality. The principle applies with special force to the school. For it is the main business of the family and the school to influence directly the formation and growth of attitudes and dispositions, emotional, intellectual and moral. Whether this educative process is carried on in a predominantly democratic or non-democratic way becomes, therefore, a question of transcendent importance not only for education itself but for its final effect upon all the interests and activities of a society that is committed to the democratic way of life. Hence, if the general tenor of what I have said about the democratic ideal and method is anywhere near the truth, it must be said that the democratic principle requires that every teacher should have some regular and organic way in which he can, directly or through representatives democratically chosen, participate in the formation of the controlling aims, methods and materials of the school of which he is a part.

It is my impression that even up to the present democratic methods of dealing with pupils have made more progress than have similar methods of dealing with members of the teaching staff of the classroom. At all events, there has been an organized and vital movement in the first matter while that in the second is still in its early stage. All schools that pride themselves upon being up-to-date utilize methods of instruction that draw upon and utilize the life-experience of students and strive to individualize treatment of pupils. Whatever reasons hold for adopting this course with respect to the young certainly more strongly hold for teachers, since the latter are more mature and have more experience. Hence the question is in place: What are the ways by which can be secured more organic participation of teachers in the formation of the educational policies of the school?

Since it is the problem I wish to present rather than to lay down the express ways in which it is to be solved, I might stop at this point. But there are certain corollaries which clarify the meaning of the issue. Absence of participation tends to produce lack of interest and concern on the part of those shut out. The result is a corresponding lack of effective responsibility. Automatically and unconsciously, if not consciously, the feeling develops, "This is none of our affair; it is the business of those at the top; let that particular set of Georges do what needs to be done."

The countries in which autocratic government prevails are just those in which there is least public spirit and the greatest indifference to matters of general as distinct from personal concern. Can we expect a different kind of psychology to actuate teachers? Where there is little power, there is correspondingly little sense of positive responsibility. It is enough to do what one is told to do sufficiently well to escape flagrant unfavorable notice. About larger matters, a spirit of passivity is engendered. In some cases, indifference passes into evasion of duties when not directly under the eye of a supervisor; in other cases, a carping, rebellious spirit is engendered. A sort of game is instituted between teacher and supervisor like that which went on in the old-fashioned schools between teacher and pupil. Other teachers pass on, perhaps unconsciously, what they feel to be arbitrary treatment received by them to their pupils.

The argument that teachers are not prepared to assume the responsibility of participation deserves attention, with its accompanying belief that natural selection has operated to put those best prepared to carry the load in the positions of authority. Whatever the truth in this contention, it still is also true that incapacity to assume the responsibilities involved in having a voice in shaping policies is bred and increased by conditions in which that responsibility is denied. I suppose there has never been an autocrat, big or little, who did not justify his conduct on the ground of the unfitness of his subjects to take part in government. I would not compare administrators to political autocrats. Upon the whole, what exists in the schools is more a matter of habit and custom than it is of any deliberate autocracy.

But, as was said earlier, habitual exclusion has the effect of reducing a sense of responsibility for what is done and its consequences. What the argument for democracy implies is that the best way to produce initiative and constructive power is to exercise it. Power, as well as interest, comes by use and practice. Moreover, the argument from incapacity proves too much. If it is so great as to be a permanent bar, then teachers cannot be expected to have the intelligence and skill that are necessary to execute the directions given them. The delicate and difficult task of developing character and good judgment in the young needs every stimulus and inspiration possible. It is impossible that the work should not be better done when teachers have that understanding of what they are doing that comes from having shared in forming its guiding ideas.

Classroom teachers are those who are in continuous direct contact with those taught. The position of administrators is at best indirect by comparison. If there is any work in the world that requires the conservation of what is good in experience so that it may become an integral part of further experience, it is that of teaching. I often wonder how much waste there is in the traditional system. There is some loss even at the best of the potential capital acquired by successful teachers. It does not get freely transmitted to other teachers who might profit by it. Is not the waste very considerably increased when teachers are not called upon to communicate their successful methods and results in a form by which it would have organic effect upon general school policies? Add to this waste that which results when teachers are called upon to give effect in the classroom to courses of study they do not understand the reasons for, and the total loss mounts up so that it is a fair estimate that the absence of democratic methods is the greatest single cause of educational waste.

The present subject is one of peculiar importance at the present time. The fundamental beliefs and practices of democracy are now challenged as they never have been before. In some nations they are more than challenged. They are ruthlessly and systematically destroyed. Everywhere there are waves of criticism and doubt as to whether democracy can meet pressing problems of order and security. The causes for the destruction of political democracy in countries where it was nominally established are complex. But of one thing I think we may be sure. Wherever it has fallen it was too exclusively political in nature. It had not become part of the bone and blood of the people in daily conduct of its life. Democratic forms were limited to Parliament, elections and combats between parties. What is happening proves conclusively, I think, that unless democratic habits of thought and action are part of the fiber of a people, political democracy is insecure. It can not stand in isolation. It must be buttressed by the presence of democratic methods in all social relationships. The relations that exist in educational institutions are second only in importance in this respect to those which exist in industry and business, perhaps not even to them.

VI · Academic Freedom*

The old saying that "eternal vigilance is the price of liberty" has especial significance at the present time. Freedom from oppression was such a controlling purpose in the foundation of the American Republic, and the idea of freedom is so intimately connected with the very idea of democratic institutions, that it might seem as if in our own country it could be taken for granted as a social goal of education and, being taken for granted, be dismissed with a few words. But the lesson of history is that the forces which limit and restrict the life of individuals and thereby hinder freedom change with every great change in human relations. Consequently, freedom is an eternal goal and has to be forever struggled for and won anew. It does not automatically perpetuate itself and, unless it is continually rewon in new effort against new foes, it is lost.

The forces which work to undermine freedom appear in even subtler form as society grows more complex and operate more insidiously. They are more effective just because in their first appearance they do not seem to be oppressive of liberty. Indeed, in their first appearance and early stages of operation they are likely to be welcomed for

* From *Implications of Social-Economic Goals for Education,* pp. 99-105.

some obvious advantages they bring with them—possibly even as a promise of greater freedom. The freedom for which our forefathers fought was primarily freedom from a fairly gross and obvious form of oppression, that of arbitrary political power exercised from a distant center. In consequence, there developed among us the tradition that the chief enemy of liberty is governmental power. The maintenance of freedom came to be almost identified with jealous fear of and opposition to any and every extension of governmental action. It took generations to realize that a government of and by the people might be a positive and necessary organ for securing and extending the liberties of the individuals who both govern and are governed, instead of being an instrument of oppression. The lesson is still far from being completely learned.

There is, however, one domain in which fear of governmental action never became dominant in American life. That is the domain of education. In this field, the founding fathers proclaimed with well-nigh unanimous voice that government, local and state if not national, should act positively and constructively. This voice has been constantly re-echoed throughout the course of our history by political and educational statesmen alike. The voice has awakened a warmer response in the hearts of the American people than any other appeal made to them. Doubtless many parents have responded to the appeal because they felt that school education opened doors to material opportunity and success that were otherwise closed to their children. But the appeal and the response have not been merely material. The American faith in education has been grounded in the belief that without education the ideal of free and equal opportunity is an idle fantasy; that of all the guarantees of free development, education is the surest and the most effective.

This fact imposes a great responsibility upon the schools and upon the educators who conduct them. What have the schools done to bring the social-economic goal of freedom nearer to realization? What have they failed to do? What can and should they do to combat the threats which imperil freedom? The mere raising of these questions calls attention to one phase of freedom, a fundamental one—Intellectual Freedom. The Bill of Rights in the federal Constitution (unfortunately not found in all state constitutions) guarantees, as far as law can guarantee anything, freedom of belief, of speech, of the press, of assembly, and of petition. These are aspects of what I have called intellectual freedom, but which perhaps would better be called moral freedom. Eeternal vigilance is even more the price of liberty with respect to these liberties than in the case of liberty of external action. The enemies of liberty of thought and expression in fields where it is felt that this liberty might encroach upon privileges possessed and might disturb the existing order, are organized and determined. The ultimate stay and support of these liberties are the schools. For it is they which more than any other single agency, are concerned with development of free inquiry, discussion and expression.

Nor is it enough that the schools by example and precept should instill faith in the precious character of these forms of freedom, or even that they should themselves be living models of the practice of freedom of inquiry, experimentation, and communication. These things are indeed to be cultivated. But the schools have also the responsibility of seeing to it that those who leave its walls have ideas that are worth thinking and worth being expressed, as well as having the courage to express them against the opposition of reactionaries and standpatters. It is quite possible that in the long run the greatest friend of censorship, whether public and explicit or private and insidious, and the greatest foe to freedom of thought and expression, is not those who fear such freedom because of its possible effect upon their own standing and fortune, but is the triviality and irrelevancy of the ideas that are entertained, and the futile and perhaps corrupting way in which they are expressed.

It is indeed necessary to have freedom of thought and expression. But just because this is necessary for the health and progress of society, it is even more necessary that ideas should be genuine ideas, not sham ones, the fruit of inquiry, of observation and experimentation, the collection and weighing of evidence. The formation of the attitudes which move steadily in this direction is the work and responsibility of the school more than of any other single institution. Routine and formal instruction, undemocratic administration of schools, is perhaps the surest way of creating a human product that submits readily to external authority, whether that be imposed by force or by custom and tradition, or by the various forms of social pressure which the existing economic system produces. It is idle to expect the schools to send out young men and women who will stand actively and aggressively for the cause of free intelligence in meeting social problems and attaining the goal of freedom unless the spirit of free intelligence pervades the organization, administration, studies, and methods of the school itself.

Educators have a primary responsibility in this respect. The emphasis that is placed upon a greater measure of economic freedom for the mass of the people is not final. It does not stand alone. Ultimately, the economic freedom (which is dependent upon economic security) is a means to cultural freedom, to the release of the human spirit in all its capacities for development through science, art, and unconstrained human intercourse. The school is par excellence the potential social organ for promoting this liberation.

In ultimate analysis, freedom is important because it is a condition both of realization of the potentialities of an individual and of social progress. Without light, a people perishes. Without freedom, light grows dim and darkness comes to reign. Without freedom, old truths become so stale and worn that they cease to be truths and become mere dictates of external authority. Without freedom, search for new truth and the disclosure of new paths in which humanity may walk more securely and justly come to an end. Freedom which is liberation for the individual, is the ultimate assurance of the movement of society toward more humane and noble ends. He who would put the freedom of others in bond, especially freedom of inquiry and communication, creates conditions which finally imperil his own freedom and that of his offspring. Eternal vigilance is the price of the conservation and extension of freedom, and the schools should be the ceaseless guardians and creators of this vigilance.

VII · Education and American Culture*

I am one of those who think that the only test and justification of any form of political and economic society is its contribution to art and science—to what may roundly be called culture. That America has not yet so justified itself is too obvious for even lament. The explanation that the physical conquest of a continent had first to be completed is an inversion. To settle a continent is to put it in order, and this is a work which comes after, not before, great intelligence and great art. The accomplishment of the justification is then hugely difficult. For it means noth-

* From *Characters and Events,* vol. II, pp. 500-503.

ing less than the discovery and application of a method of subduing and settling nature in the interests of a democ-racy, that is to say of masses who shall form a community of directed thought and emotion in spite of being the masses. That this has not yet been effected goes without saying. It has never even been attempted before. Hence the puny irrelevancy that measures our strivings with yard sticks handed down from class cultures of the past.

That the achievement is immensely difficult means that it may fail. There is no inevitable predestined success. But the failure, if it comes, will be the theme of tragedy and not of complacent lamentation nor wilful satire. For while success is not predestined, there are forces at work which are like destiny in their independence of conscious choice or wish. Not conscious intent, either perverse or wise, is forcing the realistic, the practical, the industrial, into edu-cation. Not conscious deliberation causes college presi-dents who devote commencement day to singing the praises of pure culture to spend their working days in ar-ranging for technical and professional schools. It is not conscious preference which leads school superintendents who deliver orations at teachers' meetings upon the bless-ings of old-fashioned discipline and culture to demand from their boards new equipment, new courses and studies of a more "practical" and appealing kind. Political and economic forces quite beyond their control are compelling these things. And they will remain beyond the control of any of us save as men honestly face the actualities and busy themselves with inquiring what education they im-part and what culture may issue from *their* cultivation.

It is as elements in this heroic undertaking that cur-rent tendencies in American education can be appraised. Since we can neither beg nor borrow a culture without betraying both it and ourselves, nothing remains save to produce one. Those who are too feeble or too finicky to engage in the enterprise will continue their search for asylums and hospitals which they idealize into palaces. Others will either go their way still caught in the meshes of a mechanical industrialism, or will subdue the industrial machinery to human ends until the nation is endowed with soul.

Certain commonplaces must be reiterated till their import is acknowledged. The industrial revolution was born of the new science of nature. Any democracy which is more than an imitation of some archaic republican government must issue from the womb of our chaotic industrialism. Science makes democracy possible because it brings relief from depending upon massed human labor, because of the substitution it makes possible of inanimate forces for human muscular energy, and because of the resources for excess production and easy distribution which it effects. The old culture is doomed for us because it was built upon an alliance of political and spiritual powers, an equilibrium of governing and leisure classes, which no longer exists. Those who deplore the crudities and superficialities of thought and sensation which mark our day are rarely inhuman enough to wish the old régime back. They are merely unintelligent enough to want a result without the conditions which produced it, and in the face of conditions making the result no longer possible.

In short, our culture must be consonant with realistic science and with machine industry, instead of a refuge from them. And while there is no guaranty that an education which uses science and employs the controlled processes of industry as a regular part of its equipment will succeed, there is every assurance that an educational practice which sets science and industry in opposition to its ideal of culture will fail. Natural science has in its applications to economic production and exchange brought an industry and a society where quantity alone seems to count. It is for education to bring the light of science and the power of work to the aid of every soul that it may discover its quality. For in a spiritually democratic society every individual would realize distinction. Culture would then be for the first time in human history an individual achievement and not a class possession. An education fit for our ideal uses is a matter of actual forces not of opinions.

Our public education is the potential means for effecting the transfiguration of the mechanics of modern life into sentiment and imagination. We may, I repeat, never get beyond the mechanics. We may remain burly, merely vigorous, expending energy riotously in making money, seeking pleasure and winning temporary victories over one another. Even such an estate has a virility lacking to a culture whose method is reminiscence, and whose triumph is finding a place of refuge. But it is not enough to justify a democracy as against the best of past aristocracies even though return to them is forever impossible. To bring to the consciousness of the coming generation something of the potential significance of the life of today, to transmute it from outward fact into intelligent perception, is the first step in the creation of a culture. The teachers who are facing this fact and who are trying to use the vital unspiritualized agencies of today as means of effecting the perception of a human meaning yet to be realized are sharing in the act of creation. To perpetuate in the name of culture the tradition of aloofness from realistic science and compelling industry is to give them free course in their most unenlightened form. Not chiding but the sympathy and direction of understanding are what the harsh utilitarian and prosaic tendencies of present education require.

CHAPTER THIRTEEN

THE PSYCHOLOGY OF CONDUCT

I · Habits and Will*

HABITS may be profitably compared to physiological functions, like breathing, digesting. The latter are, to be sure, involuntary, while habits are acquired. But important as is this difference for many purposes it should not conceal the fact that habits are like functions in many respects, and especially in requiring the coöperation of organism and environment. Breathing is an affair of the air as truly as of the lungs; digesting an affair of food as truly as of tissues of stomach. Seeing involves light just as certainly as it does the eye and optic nerve. Walking implicates the ground as well as the legs; speech demands physical air and human companionship and audience as well as vocal organs. We may shift from the biological to the mathematical use of the word function, and say that natural operations like breathing and digesting, acquired ones like speech and honesty, are functions of the surroundings as truly as of a person. They are things done *by* the environment by means of organic structures or acquired dispositions. The same air that under certain conditions ruffles the pool or wrecks buildings, under other conditions purifies the blood and conveys thought. The outcome depends upon what air acts upon. The social environment acts through native impulses and speech and

* From *Human Nature and Conduct*, pp. 14-15; 24-27; 40-42; 70-71.

moral habitudes manifest themselves. There are specific good reasons for the usual attribution of acts to the person from whom they immediately proceed. But to convert this special reference into a belief of exclusive ownership is as misleading as to suppose that breathing and digesting are complete within the human body. To get a rational basis for moral discussion we must begin with recognizing that functions and habits are ways of using and incorporating the environment in which the latter has its say as surely as the former.

We may borrow words from a context less technical than that of biology, and convey the same idea by saying that habits are arts. They involve skill of sensory and motor organs, cunning or craft, and objective materials. They assimilate objective energies, and eventuate in command of environment. They require order, discipline, and manifest technique. They have a beginning, middle and end. Each stage marks progress in dealing with materials and tools, advance in converting material to active use. We should laugh at any one who said that he was master of stone working, but that the art was cooped up within himself and in no wise dependent upon support from objects and assistance from tools.

It is a significant fact that in order to appreciate the peculiar place of habit in activity we have to betake ourselves to bad habits, foolish idling, gambling, addiction to liquor and drugs. When we think of such habits, the union of habit with desire and with propulsive power is forced upon us. When we think of habits in terms of walking, playing a musical instrument, typewriting, we are much given to thinking of habits as technical abilities existing apart from our likings and as lacking in urgent impulsion. We think of them as passive tools waiting to be called into action from without. A bad habit suggests an inherent tendency to action and also a hold, command over us. It makes us do things we are ashamed of, things which we tell ourselves we prefer not to do. It overrides our formal resolutions, our conscious decisions. When we are honest with ourselves we acknowledge that a habit has this power because it is so intimately a part of ourselves. It has a hold upon us because we are the habit.

Our self-love, our refusal to face facts, combined perhaps with a sense of a possible better although unrealized self, lead us to eject the habit from the thought of ourselves and conceive it as an evil power which has somehow overcome us. We feed our conceit by recalling that the habit was not deliberately formed; we never intended to become idlers or gamblers or roués. And how can anything be deeply ourselves which developed accidentally, without set intention? These traits of a bad habit are precisely the things which are most instructive about all habits and about ourselves. They teach us that all habits are affections, that all have projectile power, and that a predisposition formed by a number of specific acts is an immensely more intimate and fundamental part of ourselves than are vague, general, conscious choices. All habits are demands for certain kinds of activity; and they constitute the self. In any intelligible sense of the word will, they *are* will. They form our effective desires and they furnish us with our working capacities. They rule our thoughts, determining which shall appear and be strong and which shall pass from light into obscurity.

We may think of habits as means, waiting, like tools in a box, to be used by conscious resolve. But they are something more than that. They are active means, means that project themselves, energetic and dominating ways of acting. We need to distinguish between materials, tools and means proper. Nails and boards are not strictly speaking means of a box. They are only materials for making it. Even the saw and hammer are means only when they are employed in some actual making. Otherwise they are tools, or potential means. They are actual means only when brought in conjunction with eye, arm and hand in some specific operation. And eye, arm and hand are, correspondingly, means proper only when they are in active operation. And whenever they are in action they are coöperating with external materials and energies. Without support from beyond themselves the eye stares blankly and the hand moves fumblingly. They are means only when they enter into organizations with things which independently accomplish definite results. These organizations are habits.

This fact cuts two ways. Except in a contingent sense, with an "if," neither external materials nor bodily and mental organs are in themselves means. They have to be employed in coördinated conjunction with one another to be actual means, or habits. This statement may seem like the formulation in technical language of a commonplace. But belief in magic has played a large part in human history. And the essence of all hocus-pocus is the supposition that results can be accomplished without the joint adaptation to each other of human powers and physical conditions. A desire for rain may induce men to wave willow branches and to sprinkle water. The reaction is natural and innocent. But men then go on to believe that their act has imediate power to bring rain without the coöperation of intermediate conditions of nature. This is magic; while it may be natural or spontaneous, it is not innocent. It obstructs intelligent study of operative conditions and wastes human desire and effort in futilities.

Belief in magic did not cease when the coarser forms of superstitious practice ceased. The principle of magic is found whenever it is hoped to get results without intelligent control of means; and also when it is supposed that means can exist and yet remain inert and inoperative. In morals and politics such expectations still prevail, and in so far the most important phases of human action are still affected by magic. We think that by feeling strongly enough about something, by wishing hard enough, we can get a desirable result, such as virtuous execution of a good resolve, or peace among nations, or good will in industry. We slur over the necessity of the coöperative action of objective conditions, and the fact that this cooperation is assured only by persistent and close study. Or, on the other hand, we fancy we can get these results by external machinery, by tools or potential means, without a corresponding functioning of human desires and capacities. Often times these two false and contradictory beliefs are combined in the same person. The man who feels that *his* virtues are his own personal accomplishments is likely to be also the one who thinks that by passing laws he can throw the fear of God into others and make them virtuous by edict and prohibitory mandate.

All habit involves mechanization. Habit is impossible without setting up a mechanism of action, physiologically engrained, which operates "spontaneously," automatically, whenever the cue is given. But mechanization is not of necessity *all* there is to habit. Consider the conditions under which the first serviceable abilities of life are formed. When a child begins to walk he acutely observes, he intently and intensely experiments. He looks to see what is going to happen and he keeps curious watch on every incident. What others do, the assistance they give, the models they set, operate not as limitations but as encouragements to his own acts, reinforcements of personal perception and endeavor. The first toddling is a romantic adventuring into the unknown; and every gained power is a delightful discovery of one's own powers and of the wonders of the world. We may not be able to retain in adult habits this zest of intelligence and this freshness of satisfaction in newly discovered powers. But there is surely a middle term between a normal exercise of power which includes some excursion into the unknown, and a mechanical activity hedged within a drab world. Even in dealing with inanimate machines we rank that invention higher which adapts its movements to varying conditions.

All life operates through a mechanism, and the higher the form of life the more complex, sure and flexible the mechanism. This fact alone should save us from opposing life and mechanism, thereby reducing the latter to unintelligent automatism and the former to an aimless splurge. How delicate, prompt, sure and varied are the movements of a violin player or an engraver! How unerringly they phrase every shade of emotion and every turn of idea! Mechanism is indispensable. If each act has to be consciously searched for at the moment and intentionally performed, execution is painful and the product is clumsy and halting. Nevertheless the difference between the artist and the mere technician is unmistakable. The artist is a masterful technician. The technique or mechanism is fused with thought and feeling. The "mechanical" performer permits the mechanism to dictate the performance. It is absurd to say that the latter exhibits habit and the former not. We are confronted with two kinds of habit, intelligent and routine. All life has its élan, but only the prevalence of dead habits deflects life into mere élan.

The word habit may seem twisted somewhat from its customary use when employed as we have been using it. But we need a word to express that kind of human activity which is influenced by prior activity and in that sense acquired; which contains within itself a certain ordering or

systematization of minor elements of action; which is pro,
jective, dynamic in quality, ready for overt manifestation;
and which is operative in some subdued subordinate form
even when not obviously dominating activity. Habit even
in its ordinary usage comes nearer to denoting these facts
than any other word. If the facts are recognized we may
also use the words attitude and disposition. But unless we
have first made clear to ourselves the facts which have
been set forth under the name of habit, these words are
more likely to be misleading than is the word habit. For
the latter conveys explicitly the sense of operativeness, actuality. Attitude and, as ordinarily used, disposition suggest something latent, potential, something which requires
a positive stimulus outside themselves to become active.
If we perceive that they denote positive forms of action
which are released merely through removal of some counteracting "inhibitory" tendency, and then become overt,
we may employ them instead of the word habit to denote
subdued, non-patent forms of the latter.

In this case, we must bear in mind that the word disposition means predisposition, readiness to act overtly in
a specific fashion whenever opportunity is presented, this
opportunity consisting in removal of the pressure due to
the dominance of some overt habit; and that attitude
means some special case of a predisposition, the disposition waiting as it were to spring through an opened door.
While it is admitted that the word habit has been used in
a somewhat broader sense than is usual, we must protest
against the tendency in psychological literature to limit
its meaning to repetition. This usage is much less in accord with popular usage than is the wider way in which we
have used the word. It assumes from the start the identity
of habit with routine. Repetition is in no sense the essence
of habit. Tendency to repeat acts is an incident of many

habits but not of all. A man with the habit of giving way to anger may show his habit by a murderous attack upon some one who has offended. His act is nonetheless due to habit because it occurs only once in his life. The essence of habit is an acquired predisposition to *ways* or modes of response, not to particular acts except as, under special conditions, these express a way of behaving. Habit means special sensitiveness or accessibility to certain classes of stimuli, standing predilections and aversions, rather than bare recurrence of specific acts. It means will.

II · Impulses and Instincts*

Habits as organized activities are secondary and acquired, not native and original. They are outgrowths of unlearned activities which are part of man's endowment at birth. The order of topics followed in our discussion may accordingly be questioned. Why should what is derived and therefore in some sense artificial in conduct be discussed before what is primitive, natural and inevitable? Why did we not set out with an examination of those instinctive activities upon which the acquisition of habits is conditioned?

The query is a natural one, yet it tempts to flinging forth a paradox. In conduct the acquired is the primitive. Impulses although first in time are never primary in fact; they are secondary and dependent. The seeming paradox in statement covers a familiar fact. In the life of the individual, instinctive activity comes first. But an individual begins life as a baby, and babies are dependent beings. Their activities could continue at most for only a few hours were it not for the presence and aid of adults with their formed habits. And babies owe to adults more than procreation, more than the continued food and protection

* From *Human Nature and Conduct*, pp. 89-101; 149-157; 164-166.

which preserve life. They owe to adults the opportunity to express their native activities in ways which have meaning. Even if by some miracle original activity could continue without assistance from the organized skill and art of adults, it would not amount to anything. It would be mere sound and fury.

In short, the *meaning* of native activities is not native; it is acquired. It depends upon interaction with a matured social medium. In the case of a tiger or eagle, anger may be identified with a serviceable life-activity, with attack and defense. With a human being it is as meaningless as a gust of wind on a mud puddle apart from a direction given it by the presence of other persons, apart from the responses they make to it. It is a physical spasm, a blind dispersive burst of wasteful energy. It gets quality, significance, when it becomes a smouldering sullenness, an annoying interruption, a peevish irritation, a murderous revenge, a blazing indignation. And although these phenomena which have a meaning spring from original native reactions to stimuli, yet they depend also upon the responsive behavior of others. They and all similar human displays of anger are not pure impulses; they are habits formed under the influence of association with others who have habits already and who show their habits in the treatment which converts a blind physical discharge into a significant anger.

After ignoring impulses for a long time in behalf of sensations, modern psychology now tends to start out with an inventory and description of instinctive activities. This is an undoubted improvement. But when it tries to explain complicated events in personal and social life by direct reference to these native powers, the explanation becomes hazy and forced. It is like saying the flea and the elephant, the lichen and the redwood, the timid hare and the ravening wolf, the plant with the most inconspicuous blossom and the plant with the most glaring color are alike products of natural selection. There may be a sense in which the statement is true; but till we know the specific environing conditions under which selection took place we really know nothing. And so we need to know about the social conditions which have educated original activities into definite and significant dispositions before we can discuss the psychological element in society. This is the true meaning of social psychology.

At some place on the globe, at some time, every kind of practice seems to have been tolerated or even praised. How is the tremendous diversity of institutions (including moral codes) to be accounted for? The native stock of instincts is practically the same everywhere. Exaggerate as much as we like the native differences of Patagonians and Greeks, Sioux Indians and Hindoos, Bushmen and Chinese, their original differences will bear no comparison to the amount of difference found in custom and culture. Since such a diversity cannot be attributed to an original identity, the development of native impulse must be stated in terms of acquired habits, not the growth of customs in terms of instincts.

Yet it goes without saying that original, unlearned activity has its distinctive place and that an important one in conduct. Impulses are the pivots upon which the reorganization of activities turn, they are agencies of deviation, for giving new directions to old habits and changing their quality. Consequently whenever we are concerned with understanding social transition and flux or with projects for reform, personal and collective, our study must go to analysis of native tendencies. Interest in progress and reform is, indeed, the reason for the present great development of scientific interest in primitive human nature. If we inquire why men were so long blind to the existence of powerful and varied instincts in human beings, the answer seems to be found in the lack of a conception of orderly progress. It is fast becoming incredible that psychologists disputed as to whether they should choose between innate ideas and an empty, passive, wax-like mind. For it seems as if a glance at a child would have revealed that the truth lay in neither doctrine, so obvious is the surging of specific native activities. But this obtuseness to facts was evidence of lack of interest in what could be done with impulses, due, in turn, to lack of interest in modifying existing institutions. It is no accident that men became interested in the psychology of savages and babies when they became interested in doing away with old institutions.

In the case of the young it is patent that impulses are highly flexible starting points for activities which are diversified according to the ways in which they are used. Any impulse may become organized into almost any disposition according to the way it interacts with surroundings. Fear may become abject cowardice, prudent caution, reverence for superiors or respect for equals; an agency for credulous swallowing of absurd superstitions or for wary scepticism. A man may be chiefly afraid of the spirits of his ancestors, of officials, of arousing the disapproval of his associates, of being deceived, of fresh air, or of Bolshevism. The actual outcome depends upon how the impulse of fear is interwoven with other impulses. This depends in turn upon the outlets and inhibitions supplied by the social environment.

In a definite sense, then, a human society is always starting afresh. It is always in process of renewing, and it endures only because of renewal. We speak of the peoples of southern Europe as Latin peoples. Their existing languages depart widely from one another and from the Latin mother tongue. Yet there never was a day when this alteration of speech was intentional or explicit. Persons always meant to reproduce the speech they heard from their elders and supposed they were succeeding. This fact may stand as a kind of symbol of the reconstruction wrought in habits because of the fact that they can be transmitted and be made to endure only through the medium of the crude activities of the young or through contact with persons having different habits.

Very early in life sets of mind are formed without attentive thought, and these sets persist and control the mature mind. The child learns to avoid the shock of unpleasant disagreement, to find the easy way out, to appear to conform to customs which are wholly mysterious to him in order to get his own way—that is to display some natural impulse without exciting the unfavorable notice of those in authority. Adults distrust the intelligence which a child has while making upon him demands for a kind of conduct that requires a high order of intelligence, if it is to be intelligent at all. The inconsistency is reconciled by instilling in him "moral" habits which have a maximum of emotional empressement and adamantine hold with a minimum of understanding. These habitudes, deeply engrained before thought is awake and even before the day of experiences which can later be recalled, govern conscious later thought. They are usually deepest and most unget-at-able just where critical thought is most needed—in morals, religion and politics. These "infantilisms" account for the mass of irrationalities that prevail among men of otherwise rational tastes. These personal "hang-overs" are the cause of what the student of culture calls survivals. But unfortunately these survivals are much more numerous and pervasive than the anthropologist and historian are wont to admit. To list them would perhaps oust one from "respectable" society.

And yet the intimation never wholly deserts us that there is in the unformed activities of childhood and youth the possibilities of a better life for the community as well as for individuals here and there. This dim sense is the ground of our abiding idealization of childhod. For with all its extravagancies and uncertainties, its effusions and reticences, it remains a standing proof of a life wherein growth is normal not an anomaly, activity a delight not a task, and where habit forming is an expansion of power not its shrinkage. Habit and impulse may war with each other, but it is a combat between the habits of adults and the impulses of the young, and not, as with the adult, a civil warfare whereby personality is rent asunder.

While childhood is the conspicuous proof of the renewing of habit rendered possible by impulse, the latter never wholly ceases to play its refreshing role in adult life. If it did, life would petrify, society stagnate. Instinctive reactions are sometimes too intense to be woven into a smooth pattern of habits. Under ordinary circumstances they appear to be tamed to obey their master, custom. But extraordinary crises release them and they show by wild violent energy how superficial is the control of routine. The saying that civilization is only skin deep, that a savage persists beneath the clothes of a civilized man, is the common acknowledgment of this fact. At critical moments of unusual stimuli the emotional outbreak and rush of instincts dominating all activity show how superficial is the modification which a rigid habit has been able to effect.

When we face this fact in its general significance, we confront one of the ominous aspects of the history of man. We realize how little the progress of man has been the product of intelligent guidance, how largely it has been a by-product of accidental upheavals, even though by an apologetic interest in behalf of some privileged institution we later transmute chance into providence. We have depended upon the clash of war, the stress of revolution, the emergence of heroic individuals, the impact of migrations generated by war and famine, the incoming of barbarians, to change established institutions. Instead of constantly utilizing unused impulse to effect continuous reconstruction, we have waited till an accumulation of stresses suddenly breaks through the dikes of custom.

In spite of what has been said, it will be asserted that there are definite, independent, original instincts which manifest themselves in specific acts in a one-to-one correspondence. Fear, it will be said, is a reality, and so is anger, and rivalry, and love of mastery of others, and self-abasement, maternal love, sexual desire, gregariousness and envy, and each has its own appropriate deed as a result. Of course they are realities. So are suction, rusting of metals, thunder and lightning and lighter-than-air flying machines. But science and invention did not get on as long as men indulged in the notion of special forces to account for such phenomena. Men tried that road, and it only led them into learned ignorance. They spoke of nature's abhorrence of a vacuum; of a force of combustion; of intrinsic nisus toward this and that; of heaviness and levity as forces. It turned out that these "forces" were only the phenomena over again, translated from a specific and concrete form (in which they were at least actual) into a generalized form in which they were verbal. They converted a problem into a solution which afforded a simulated satisfaction.

Advance in insight and control came only when the mind turned squarely around. After it had dawned upon inquirers that their alleged causal forces were only names which condensed into a duplicate form a variety of complex occurrences, they set about breaking up phenomena into minute detail and searching for correlations, that is, for elements in other gross phenomena which also varied. Correspondence of variations of elements took the place of large and imposing forces. The psychology of behavior is only beginning to undergo similar treatment. It is probable that the vogue of sensation-psychology was due to the fact that it seemed to promise a similar detailed treatment of personal phenomena. But as yet we tend to regard sex, hunger, fear, and even much more complex active interests as if they were lump forces, like the combustion or gravity of old-fashioned physical science.

It is not hard to see how the notion of a single and separate tendency grew up in the case of simpler acts like hunger and sex. The paths of motor outlet or discharge are comparatively few and are fairly well defined. Specific bodily organs are conspicuously involved. Hence there is suggested the notion of a correspondingly separate psychic force or impulse. There are two fallacies in this assumption. The first consists in ignoring the fact that no activity (even one that is limited by routine habit) is confined to the channel which is most flagrantly involved in its execution. The whole organism is concerned in every act to some extent and in some fashion, internal organs as well as muscular, those of circulation, secretion, etc. Since the total state of the organism is never exactly twice alike, in so far the phenomena of hunger and sex are never twice the same in fact. The difference may be negligible for some purposes, and yet give the key for the purposes of a psychological analysis which shall terminate in a correct judgment of value. Even physiologically the context of organic changes accompanying an act of hunger or sex makes the difference between a normal and a morbid phenomenon.

In the second place, the environment in which the act takes place is never twice alike. Even when the overt organic discharge is substantially the same, the acts impinge upon a different environment and thus have different consequences. It is impossible to regard these differences of objective result as indifferent to the quality of the acts. They are immediately sensed if not clearly perceived; and they are the only *components of the meaning* of the act. When feelings, dwelling antecedently in the soul, were supposed to be the causes of acts, it was natural to suppose that each psychic element had its own inherent quality which might be directly read off by introspection. But when we surrender this notion, it becomes evident that the only way of telling what an organic act is like is by the sensed or perceptible changes which it occasions. Some of these will be intra-organic, and (as just indicated) they will vary with every act. Others will be external to the organism, and these consequences are more important than the intra-organic ones for determining the quality of the act. For they are consequences in which others are concerned and which evoke reactions of favor and disfavor as well as coöperative and resisting activities of a more indirect sort.

A child gives way to what, grossly speaking, we call anger. Its felt or appreciated quality depends in the first place upon the condition of his organism at the time, and this is never twice alike. In the second place, the act is at once modified by the environment upon which it impinges so that different consequences are immediately reflected back to the doer. In one case, anger is directed say at older and stronger playmates who immediately avenge themselves upon the offender, perhaps cruelly. In another case, it takes effect upon weaker and impotent children, and the reflected appreciated consequence is one of achievement, victory, power and a knowledge of the means of having one's own way. The notion that anger still remains a single force is a lazy mythology. Even in the cases of hunger and sex, where the channels of action are fairly demarcated by antecedent conditions (or "nature"), the actual content and feel of hunger and sex, are indefinitely varied according to their social contexts. Only when a man is starving, is hunger an unqualified natural impulse; as it approaches this limit, it tends to lose, more-over, its psychological distinctiveness and to become a raven of the entire organism.

The treatment of sex by psychoanalysts is most instructive, for it flagrantly exhibits both the consequences of artificial simplification and the transformation of social results into psychic causes. Writers, usually male, hold forth on the psychology of woman, as if they were dealing with a Platonic universal entity, although they habitually treat men as individuals, varying with structure and environment. They treat phenomena which are peculiarly symptoms of the civilization of the West at the present time as if they were the necessary effects of fixed native impulses of human nature. Romantic love as it exists today, with all the varying perturbations it occasions, is as definitely a sign of specific historic conditions as are big battle ships with turbines, internal-combustion engines, and electrically driven machines. It would be as sensible to treat the latter as effects of a single psychic cause as to attribute the phenomena of disturbance and conflict which accompany present sexual relations as manifestations of an original single psychic force or *Libido*. Upon this point at least a Marxian simplification is nearer the truth than that of Jung.

Again it is customary to suppose that there is a single instinct of fear, or at most a few well-defined sub-species of it. In reality, when one is afraid the whole being reacts, and this entire responding organism is never twice the same. In fact, also, every reaction takes place in a different environment, and its meaning is never twice alike, since the difference in environment makes a difference in consequences. It is only mythology which sets up a single, identical psychic force which "causes" all the reactions of fear, a force beginning and ending in itself. It is true enough that in all cases we are able to identify certain more or less separable characteristic acts—muscular contractions, withdrawals, evasions, concealments. But in the latter words we have already brought in an environment. Such terms as withdrawal and concealment have no meaning except as attitudes toward objects. There is no such thing as an environment in general; there are specific changing objects and events. Hence the kind of evasion or running away or shrinking up which takes place is directly correlated with specific surrounding conditions. There is no one fear having diverse manifestations; there are as many qualitatively different fears as there are objects responded to and different consequences sensed and observed.

Fear of the dark is different from fear of publicity, fear of the dentist from fear of ghosts, fear of conspicuous success from fear of humiliation, fear of a bat from fear of a bear. Cowardice, embarrassment, caution and reverence may all be regarded as forms of fear. They all have certain physical organic acts in common—those of organic shrinkage, gestures of hesitation and retreat. But each is qualitatively unique. Each is what it is in virtue of its total interactions or correlations with other acts and with the environing medium, with consequences. High explosives and the aeroplane have brought into being something new in conduct. There is no error in calling it fear. But there is error, even from a limited clinical standpoint, in permitting the classifying name to blot from view the difference between fear of bombs dropped from the sky and the fears which previously existed. The new fear is just as much and just as little original and native as a child's fear of a stranger.

For any activity is original when it first occurs. As conditions are continually changing, new and *primitive* activities are continually occurring. The traditional psychology of instincts obscures recognition of this fact. It sets up a hard-and-fast preordained class under which specific acts are subsumed, so that their own quality and originality are lost from view. This is why the novelist and dramatist are so much more illuminating as well as more interesting commentators on conduct than the schematizing psychologist. The artist makes perceptible individual responses and thus displays a new phase of human nature evoked in new situations. In putting the case visibly and dramatically he reveals vital actualities. The scientific systematizer treats each act as merely another sample of some old principle, or as a mechanical combination of elements drawn from a ready-made inventory.

When we recognize the diversity of native activities and the varied ways in which they are modified through interactions with one another in response to different conditions, we are able to understand moral phenomena otherwise baffling. In the career of any impulse activity there are speaking generally three possibilities. It may find a surging, explosive discharge—blind, unintelligent. It may be sublimated—that is, become a factor coordinated intelligently with others in a continuing course of action. Thus a gust of anger may, because of its dynamic incorporation into disposition, be converted into an abiding conviction of social injustice to be remedied, and furnish the dynamic to carry the conviction into execution. Or an excitation of sexual attraction may reappear in art or in tranquil domestic attachments and services. Such an outcome represents the normal or desirable functioning of impulse; in which, to use our previous language, the impulse operates as a pivot, or reorganization of habit. Or again a released impulsive activity may be neither immediately expressed in isolated spasmodic action, nor indirectly employed in an enduring interest. It may be "suppressed."

Suppression is not annihilation. "Psychic" energy is no more capable of being abolished than the forms we recognize as physical. If it is neither exploded nor converted, it is turned inwards, to lead a surreptitious, subterranean life. An isolated or spasmodic manifestation is a sign of immaturity, crudity, savagery; a suppressed activity is the cause of all kinds of intellectual and moral pathology. One form of the resulting pathology constitutes "reaction" in the sense in which the historian speaks of reactions. A conventionally familiar instance is Stuart license after Puritan restraint. A striking modern instance is the orgy of extravagance following upon the enforced economies and hardships of war, the moral letdown after its highstrung exalted idealisms, the deliberate carelessness after an attention too intense and too narrow. Outward manifestation of many normal activities had been suppressed. But activities were not suppressed. They were merely dammed up awaiting their chance.

The development of mental pathologies to the point

where they need clinical attention has of late enforced a widespread consciousness of some of the evils of suppression of impulse. The studies of psychiatrists have made clear that impulses driven into pockets distill poison and produce festering sores. An organization of impulse into a working habit forms an interest. A surreptitious furtive organization which does not articulate in avowed expression forms a "complex." Current clinical psychology has undoubtedly overworked the influence of sexual impulse in this connection, refusing at the hands of some writers to recognize the operation of any other modes of disturbance. There are explanations of this onesidedness. The intensity of the sexual instinct and its organic ramifications produce many of the cases that are so noticeable as to demand the attention of physicians. And social tabus and the tradition of secrecy have put this impulse under greater strain than has been imposed upon others. If a society existed in which the existence of impulse toward food were socially disavowed until it was compelled to live an illicit, covert life, alienists would have plenty of cases of mental and moral disturbance to relate in connection with hunger.

The significant thing is that the pathology arising from the sex instinct affords a striking case of a universal principle. Every impulse is, as far as it goes, force, urgency. It must either be used in some function, direct or sublimated, or be driven into a concealed, hidden activity. It has long been asserted on empirical grounds that repression and enslavement result in corruption and perversion. We have at last discovered the reason for this fact. The wholesome and saving force of intellectual freedom, open confrontation, publicity, now has the stamp of scientific sanction. The evil of checking impulses is not that they are checked. Without inhibition there is no instigation of imagination, no redirection into more discriminated and comprehensive activities. The evil resides in a refusal of direct attention which forces the impulse into disguise and concealment, until it enacts its own unavowed uneasy private life subject to no inspection and no control.

A rebellious disposition is also a form of romanticism. At least rebels set out as romantics, or, in popular parlance, as idealists. There is no bitterness like that of conscious impotency, the sense of suffocatingly complete suppression. The world is hopeless to one without hope. The rage of total despair is a vain effort at blind destructiveness. Partial suppression induces in some natures a picture of complete freedom, while it arouses a destructive protest against existing institutions as enemies that stand in the way of freedom. Rebellion has at least one advantage over recourse to artificial stimulation and to subconscious nursings of festering sore spots. It engages in action and thereby comes in contact with realities. It contains the possibility of learning something. Yet learning by this method is immensely expensive. The costs are incalculable. As Napoleon said, every revolution moves in a vicious circle. It begins and ends in excess.

The use of the words instinct and impulse in the foregoing as practical equivalents is intentional, even though it may grieve critical readers. The word instinct taken alone is still too laden with the older notion that an instinct is always definitely organized and adapted—which for the most part is just what it is not in human beings. The word impulse suggests something primitive, yet loose, undirected, initial. Man can progress as beasts cannot, precisely because he has so many "instincts" that they cut across one another, so that most serviceable actions must be *learned*. In learning habits it is possible for man to learn the habit of learning. Then betterment becomes a conscious principle of life.

III · Intelligence*

In discussing habit and impulse we have repeatedly met topics where reference to the work of thought was imperative. Explicit consideration of the place and office of intelligence in conduct can hardly begin otherwise than by gathering together these incidental references and re-affirming their significance. The stimulation of reflective imagination by impulse, its dependence upon established habits, and its effect in transforming habit and regulating impulse forms, accordingly, our first theme.

Habits are conditions of intellectual efficiency. They operate in two ways upon intellect. Obviously, they restrict its reach, they fix its boundaries. They are blinders that confine the eyes of mind to the road ahead. They prevent thought from straying away from its imminent occupation to a landscape more varied and picturesque but irrelevant to practice. Outside the scope of habits, thought works gropingly, fumbling in confused uncertainty; and yet habit made complete in routine shuts in thought so effectually that it is no longer needed or possible. The routineer's road is a ditch out of which he cannot get, whose sides enclose him, directing his course so thoroughly that he no longer thinks of his path or his destination. All habit forming involves the beginning of an intellectual specialization which if unchecked ends in thoughtless action.

Significantly enough this fullblown result is called absentmindedness. Stimulus and response are mechanically linked together in an unbroken chain. Each successive act

* From *Human Nature and Conduct*, pp. 172-196; 254-255.

facilely evoked by its predecessor pushes us automatically into the next act of a predetermined series. Only a signal flag of distress recalls consciousness to the task of carrying on. Fortunately nature which beckons us to this path of least resistance also puts obstacles in the way of our complete acceptance of its invitation. Success in achieving a ruthless and dull efficiency of action is thwarted by untoward circumstance. The most skilful aptitude bumps at times into the unexpected, and so gets into trouble from which only observation and invention extricate it. Efficiency in following a beaten path has then to be converted into breaking a new road through strange lands.

Habit is however more than a restriction of thought. Habits become negative limits because they are first positive agencies. The more numerous our habits the wider the field of possible observation and foretelling. The more flexible they are, the more refined is perception in its discrimination and the more delicate the presentation evoked by imagination. The sailor is intellectually at home on the sea, the hunter in the forest, the painter in his studio, the man of science in his laboratory. These commonplaces are universally recognized in the concrete; but their significance is obscured and their truth denied in the current general theory of mind. For they mean nothing more or less than that habits formed in process of exercising biological aptitudes are the sole agents of observation, recollection, foresight and judgment: a mind or consciousness or soul in general which performs these operations is a myth.

Yet habit does not, of itself, know, for it does not of itself stop to think, observe or remember. Neither does impulse of itself engage in reflection or contemplation. It just lets go. Habits by themselves are too organized, too insistent and determinate to need to indulge in inquiry or imagination. And impulses are too chaotic, tumultuous and confused to be able to know even if they wanted to. Habit as such is too definitely adapted to an environ- ment to survey or analyze it, and impulse is too indeter- minately related to the environment to be capable of re porting anything about it. Habit incorporates, enacts oɪ overrides objects, but it doesn't know them. Impulse scat ters and obliterates them with its restless stir. A certaiɲ delicate combination of habit and impulse is requisite for observation, memory and judgment. Knowledge which is not projected against the black unknown lives in the muscles, not in consciousness.

We may, indeed, be said to *know how* by means of ouⱱ habits. And a sensible intimation of the practical function of knowledge has led men to identify all acquired practicaⅼ skill, or even the instinct of animals, with knowledge. We walk and read aloud, we get off and on street cars, we dress and undress, and do a thousand useful acts without thinking of them. We know something, namely, how to do them. Bergson's philosophy of intuition is hardly more than an elaborately documented commentary on the popu- lar conception that by instinct a bird knows how to build a nest and a spider to weave a web. But after all, this practical work done by habit and instinct in securing prompt and exact adjustment to the environment is not knowledge, except by courtesy. Or, if we choose to call it knowledge—and no one has the right to issue an ukase to the contrary—then other things also called knowledge, knowledge *of* and *about* things, knowledge *that* things are thus and so, knowledge that involves reflection and con- scious appreciation, remains of a different sort, unac- counted for and undescribed.

The problem of the place of knowledge and judgment in conduct depends upon getting the fundamental psychology of thought straightened out. We compare life to a traveler faring forth. We may consider him first at a moment when his activity is confident, straightforward, organized. He marches on giving no direct attention to his path, nor thinking of his destination. Abruptly he is pulled up, arrested. Something is going wrong in his activity. From the standpoint of an onlooker, he has met an obstacle which must be overcome before his behavior can be unified into a successful ongoing. From his own standpoint, there is shock, confusion, perturbation, uncertainty. For the moment he doesn't know what hit him, as we say, nor where he is going. But a new impulse is stirred which becomes the starting point of an investigation, a looking into things, a trying to see them, to find out what is going on. Habits which were interfered with begin to get a new direction as they cluster about the impulse to look and see. The blocked habits of locomotion give him a sense of where he *was* going, of what he had set out to do, and of the ground already traversed. As he looks, he sees definite things which are not just things at large but which are related to his course of action. The momentum of the activity entered upon persists as a sense of direction, of aim; it is an anticipatory project. In short, he recollects, observes and plans.

The trinity of these forecasts, perceptions and remembrances form a subject-matter of discriminated and identified objects. These objects represent habits turned inside out. They exhibit both the onward tendency of habit and the objective conditions which have been incorporated within it. Sensations in immediate consciousness are elements of action dislocated through the shock of interruption. They never, however, completely monopolize the scene; for there is a body of residual undisturbed habits which is reflected in remembered and perceived objects having a meaning. Thus out of shock and puzzlement there gradually emerges a figured framework of objects, past, present, future. These shade off variously into a vast penumbra of vague, unfigured things, a setting which is taken for granted and not at all explicitly presented. The complexity of the figured scene in its scope and refinement of contents depends wholly upon prior habits and their organization. The reason a baby can know little and an experienced adult know much when confronting the same things is not because the latter has a "mind" which the former has not, but because one has already formed habits which the other has still to acquire. The scientific man and the philosopher like the carpenter, the physician and politician know with their habits not with their "consciousness." The latter is eventual, not a source. Its occurrence marks a peculiarly delicate connection between highly organized habits and unorganized impulses. Its contents or objects, observed, recollected, projected and generalized into principles, represent the incorporated material of habits coming to the surface, because habits are disintegrating at the touch of conflicting impulses. But they also gather themselves together to comprehend impulse and make it effective.

Deliberation is a dramatic rehearsal (in imagination) of various competing possible lines of action. It starts from the blocking of efficient overt action, due to that conflict of prior habit and newly released impulse to which reference has been made. Then each habit, each impulse, involved in the temporary suspense of overt action takes its turn in being tried out. Deliberation is an experiment in finding out what the various lines of possible action are really like. It is an experiment in making various combinations of selected elements of habits and impulses, to see what the resultant action would be like if it were entered upon. But the trial is in imagination, not in overt fact. The experiment is carried on by tentative rehearsals in thought which do not affect physical facts outside the body. Thought runs ahead and foresees outcomes, and thereby avoids having to await the instruction of actual failure and disaster. An act overtly tried out is irrevocable, its consequences cannot be blotted out. An act tried out in imagination is not final or fatal. It is retrievable.

Each conflicting habit and impulse takes its turn in projecting itself upon the screen of imagination. It unrolls a picture of its future history, of the career it would have if it were given head. Although overt exhibition is checked by the pressure of contrary propulsive tendencies, this very inhibition gives habit a chance at manifestation in thought. Deliberation means precisely that activity is disintegrated, and that its various elements hold one another up. While none has force enough to become the center of a re-directed activity, or to dominate a course of action, each has enough power to check others from exercising mastery. Activity does not cease in order to give way to reflection; activity is turned from execution into intra-organic channels, resulting in dramatic rehearsal.

If activity were directly exhibited it would result in certain experiences, contacts with the environment. It would succeed by making environing objects, things and persons, co-partners in its forward movement; or else it would run against obstacles and be troubled, possibly defeated. These experiences of contact with objects and their qualities give meaning, character, to an otherwise fluid, unconscious activity. We find out what seeing means by the objects which are seen. They constitute the significance of visual activity which would otherwise remain a blank. "Pure" activity is for consciousness pure emptiness. It acquires a content or filling of meanings only in static termini, what it comes to rest in, or in the obstacles which check its onward movement and deflect it. As has been re-marked, the object is that which objects.

There is no difference in this respect between a visible course of conduct and one proposed in deliberation. We have no direct consciousness of what we purpose to do. We can judge its nature, assign its meaning, only by fol-lowing it into the situations whither it leads, noting the objects against which it runs and seeing how they rebuff or unexpectedly encourage it. In imagination as in fact we know a road only by what we see as we travel on it. Moreover the objects which prick out the course of a pro-posed act until we can see its design also serve to direct eventual overt activity. Every object hit upon as the habit traverses its imaginary path has a direct effect upon ex-isting activities. It reinforces, inhibits, redirects habits al-ready working or stirs up others which had not previously actively entered in. In thought as well as in overt action, the objects experienced in following out a course of action attract, repel, satisfy, annoy, promote and retard. Thus deliberation proceeds. To say that at last it ceases is to say that choice, decision, takes place.

What then is choice? Simply hitting in imagination upon an object which furnishes an adequate stimulus to the recovery of overt action. Choice is made as soon as some habit, or some combination of elements of habits and impulse, finds a way fully open. Then energy is re-leased. The mind is made up, composed, unified. As long as deliberation pictures shoals or rocks or troublesome gales as marking the route of a contemplated voyage, de-liberation goes on. But when the various factors in action fit harmoniously together, when imagination finds no an-noying hindrance, when there is a picture of open seas, filled sails and favoring winds, the voyage is definitely entered upon. This decisive direction of action constitutes choice. It is a great error to suppose that we have no preferences until there is a choice. We are always biased beings, tending in one direction rather than another. The occasion of deliberation is an *excess* of preferences, not natural apathy or an absence of likings. We want things that are incompatible with one another; therefore we have to make a choice of what we *really* want, of the course of action, that is, which most fully releases activities. Choice is not the emergence of preference out of indifference. It is the emergence of a unified preference out of competing preferences. Biases that had held one another in check now, temporarily at least, reinforce one another, and constitute a unified attitude. The moment arrives when imagination pictures an objective consequence of action which supplies an adequate stimulus and releases definitive action. All deliberation is a search for a *way* to act, not for a final terminus. Its office is to facilitate stimulation.

These facts give us the key to the old controversy as to the respective places of desire and reason in conduct. It is notorious that some moralists have deplored the influence of desire; they have found the heart of strife between good and evil in the conflict of desire with reason, in which the former has force on its side and the latter authority. But reasonableness is in fact a quality of an effective relationship among desires rather than a thing opposed to desire. It signifies the order, perspective, proportion which is achieved, during deliberation, out of a diversity of earlier incompatible preferences. Choice is reasonable when it induces us to act reasonably; that is, with regard to the claims of each of the competing habits and impulses. This implies, of course, the presence of a comprehensive object, one which coördinates, organizes and functions each factor of the situation which gave rise to conflict, suspense and deliberation. This is as true when some "bad" impulses and habits enter in as when approved ones require unification. We have already seen the effects of choking them off, of efforts at direct suppression. Bad habits can be subdued only by being utilized as elements in a new, more generous and comprehensive scheme of action, and good ones be preserved from rot only by similar use.

The conclusion is not that the emotional, passionate phase of action can be or should be eliminated in behalf of a bloodless reason. More "passions," not fewer, is the answer. To check the influence of hate there must be sympathy, while to rationalize sympathy there are needed emotions of curiosity, caution, respect for the freedom of others—dispositions which evoke objects which balance those called up by sympathy, and prevent its degeneration into maudlin sentiment and meddling interference. Rationality, once more, is not a force to evoke against impulse and habit. It is the attainment of a working harmony among diverse desires. "Reason" as a noun signifies the happy coöperation of a multitude of dispositions, such as sympathy, curiosity, exploration, experimentation, frankness, pursuit (to follow things through), circumspection (to look about at the context). The elaborate systems of science are born not of reason but of impulses at first slight and flickering; impulses to handle, move about, to hunt, to uncover, to mix things separated and divide things combined, to talk and to listen. Method is their effectual organization into continuous dispositions of inquiry, development and testing. It occurs after these acts and because of their consequences. Reason, the rational attitude, is the resulting disposition, not a ready-made antecedent which can be invoked at will and set into movement. The man who would intelligently cultivate intelligence will widen, not narrow, his life of strong impulses while aiming at their happy coincidence in operation.

Impulse is primary and intelligence is secondary and in some sense derivative. There should be no blinking of this fact. But recognition of it as a fact exalts intelligence. For thought is not the slave of impulse to do its bidding. Impulse does not know what it is after; it cannot give orders, not even if it wants to. It rushes blindly into any opening it chances to find. Anything that expends it, satisfies it. One outlet is like another to it. It is indiscriminate. Its vagaries and excesses are the stock theme of classical moralists; and while they point the wrong moral in urging the abdication of impulse in favor of reason, their characterization of impulse is not wholly wrong. What intelligence has to do in the service of impulse is to act not as its obedient servant but as its clarifier and liberator. And this can be accomplished only by a study of the conditions and causes, the workings and consequences of the greatest possible variety of desires and combinations of desire. Intelligence converts desire into plans, systematic plans based on assembling facts, reporting events as they happen, keeping tab on them and analyzing them.

CHAPTER FOURTEEN

INTELLIGENCE IN MORALS

I · Individual and Social Morality*

WHEN social life is stable, when custom rules, the problems of morals have to do with the adjustments which individuals make to the institutions in which they live, rather than with the moral quality of the institutions themselves. Men take their social relations for granted; they are what they are and, in being that, are what they *should* be. If anything is wrong it is due to the failure of individuals to do what social customs tell them to do. Only a few daring persons criticize ancestral habits, and then only guardedly. When social life is in a state of flux, moral issues cease to gather exclusively about personal conformity and deviation. They center in the value of social arrangements, of laws, of inherited traditions that have crystallized into institutions, in changes that are desirable. Institutions lose their quasi-sacredness and are the objects of moral questioning. We now live in such a period. Ever since the latter half of the eighteenth century the interesting and stirring human problems for intellectual inquiry as well as for practical application have arisen out of criticism of existing social arrangements and traditions, in State, government, law, church, family, industry, business, international relations. So far as moral theories have kept aloof from perplexities about social

* From *Ethics*, Dewey and Tufts (revised edition), pp. 347-353.

761

policies in these fields, so far as they have merely repeated commonplaces about personal conduct in isolation from social issues, they have become anemic and sterile.

Indeed, one of the chief values, from the standpoint of theory, of considering the moral bearing of social problems is that we are then confronted with live issues in which vital choices still have to be made, and with situations where principles are still in process of forming. We are thus saved from the "moralistic" narrowing down of morals; we appreciate that morals are as wide as the area of everything which affects the values of human living. These values are involved on the widest scale in social issues. Hence critical questioning of existing institutions and critical discussion of changes, proposed on the theory that they will produce social betterment, are the best means of enforcing the fact that moral theory is more than a remote exercise in conceptual analysis or than a mere mode of preaching and exhortation. When we take the social point of view we are compelled to realize the extent to which our moral beliefs are a product of the social environment and also the extent to which *thinking,* new ideas, can change this environment.

Study from this point of view also discloses in a concrete fashion the limitation of moral theory and the positive office which it can perform. It shows that it is *not* the business of moral theory to provide a ready-made solution to large moral perplexities. But it also makes it clear that while the solution has to be reached by *action* based on personal choice, theory can enlighten and guide choice and action by revealing alternatives, and by bringing to light what is entailed when we choose one alternative rather than another. It shows, in short, that the function of theory is not to furnish a substitute for personal reflective choice but to be an instrument for rendering deliberation more effective and hence choice more intelligent.

Again, conventionalized morals conceal from view the uncertainty which attends decision as to what is good in a concrete case, and covers up the problematic nature of what is right and obligatory. But consideration of social questions and conflicting proposals brings just these things home to us. It puts before us situations where the moral struggle is not just to be kept from departing from what we know already to be good and right, but where we need to *discover* what *is* good and right, and where reflection and experimentation are the sole means of discovery. There are still those who think they are in possession of codes and principles which settle finally and automatically the right and wrong of, say, divorce, the respective rights of capital and labor, the exact limits of private property, the extent to which legislation should go in deciding what individuals shall eat, drink, wear, etc. But there are also many other persons, an increasing number, who see that such questions as these cannot be settled by deduction from fixed premises, and that the attempt to decide them in that fashion is the road to the intolerant fanaticism, dogmatism, class strife, of the closed mind. Wars waged in the alleged interest of religion, or in defense of particular economic conceptions, prove the practical danger of carrying theoretical dogmatism into action. Since the right course is to bring the best intelligence we can command to bear upon such social problems, theory has a definite function in establishing the value of such intelligence and in promoting it by clarifying issues, proposing solutions, guiding the action which tests the worth of these proposals.

The foregoing remarks should make clear what is meant by that change from personal to social morality which has been referred to. It does *not* signify that morality becomes impersonal and collective; it remains and must remain personal in that social problems have to be faced by individuals, and decisions reached in the forum of individual minds have to be carried into effect by individual agents, who are in turn personally responsible for the consequences of their acts. Morals are personal because they spring from personal insight, judgment, and choice. Such facts as these, however, are wholly consistent with the fact that *what* men think and believe is affected by common factors, and that the thought and choice of one individual spread to others. They do not militate against the fact that men have to act together, and that their conjoint action is embodied in institutions and laws; that unified action creates government and legislative policies, forms the family, establishes schools and churches, manifests itself in business corporations of vast extent and power, in clubs and fraternities for enjoyment and recreation, and in armies which set nation against nation. In other words, it is a *fact* that a vast network of relations surrounds the individual: indeed, "surrounds" is too external a term, since every individual lives *in* the network as a part of it. The material of personal reflection and of choice comes to each of us from the customs, traditions, institutions, policies, and plans of these large collective wholes. They are the influences which form his character, evoke and confirm his attitudes, and affect at every turn the quality of his happiness and his aspirations. This statement is true not only of the associations of which he is a direct member but also of those which seem external to him; since through commerce, war, and intercommunication the action of one territorial nation affects the members of another, while the standards set by one social group, say that of wealth and prestige, affect the desires and the capabilities of individuals in other groups.

At the present time, almost all important ethical problems arise out of the conditions of associated life. As we have previously noted, in a stationary society, in one dominated by custom, the existing social order seems to be like the order of nature itself; as inevitable, and as necessary or as capricious as the case may be. Any suggestion for change is regarded as "unnatural." Even in present social life, any deep-seated change is opposed as contrary to nature; such was the case, for example, with "votes for women" a short time ago. Such is the case still with proposals for, say, doing away with war, or the elimination of the pecuniary profit motive from industry. Nevertheless, when inventions modify social conditions, when new wants and new satisfactions abound, when dislocations of elements of population through migration take place on a large scale, when cultures once separated mix and influence one another, when new modes of industry invade domestic life, when the emergence of increased leisure time coincides with new opportunities for amusement, when great combinations of capital arise which determine the opportunities of individuals for finding work, attention is forced to note the influence exerted upon individuals by collective conditions. Personal selves are forced, unless they are merely to drift, to consider their own action with respect to social changes. They are forced, if they engage in reflection at all, to determine what social tendencies they shall favor and which ones they shall oppose; which institutions they will strive to conserve and which they will endeavor to modify or abolish. That the present is a time of social changes is a commonplace; the mere existence alone of democratic government, for example, raises social issues for moral decision which did not exist for most men and women so long as government was autocratic and confined to a few.

The change from "personal" to "social" morality concerns then the kind of moral questions which are uppermost. For many individuals it is not now a question of whether they individually will appropriate property belonging to another, but whether existing large-scale economic arrangements operate to effect an equitable distribution of property; and if not, what they as individuals shall do about it. In one sense the change to social morality makes morals more acutely personal than they were when custom ruled. It forces the need of more personal reflection, more personal knowledge and insight, more deliberate and steadfast personal convictions, more resolute personal attitudes in action—more personal in the sense of being more *conscious* in choice and more voluntary in execution. It would then be absurd to suppose that "social morals" meant a swallowing up of individuality in an anonymous mass, or an abdication of personal responsibility in decision and action. It signifies that the social conditions and social consequences of personal action (which always exist in any case), are now brought to explicit consciousness so that they require searching thought and careful judgment in a way practically unprecedented formerly. It indicates that reflection is morally indispensable. It points out the material of reflection: the sort of things to which moral inquiry and judgment must go out.

II · Reflection in the Moral Situation*

There can, however, be no such thing as reflective morality except where men seriously ask by what purposes they should direct their conduct and why they should do

* From *Ethics*, Dewey and Tufts (revised edition), pp. 197-201; 223-230; 312-13.

so; what it is which makes their purposes good. This intellectual search for ends is bound to arise when customs fail to give required guidance. And this failure happens when old institutions break down; when invasions from without and inventions and innovations from within radically alter the course of life.

Every habit introduces continuity into activity; it furnishes a permanent thread or axis. When custom breaks down, the only thing which can link together the succession of various acts is a common purpose running through separate acts. An end-in-view gives unity and continuity, whether it be the securing of an education, the carrying on of a military campaign, or the building of a house. The more inclusive the aim in question the broader is the unification which is attained. Comprehensive ends may connect together acts performed during a long span of years. To the common soldier or even to the general in command, winning the campaign may be a sufficiently comprehensive aim to unify acts into conduct. But some one is bound to ask: What then? To what uses shall victory when achieved be put? At least that question is bound to be asked, provided men are intelligently interested in their behavior and are not governed by chance and the pressure of the passing moment. *The development of inclusive and enduring aims is the necessary condition of the application of reflection in conduct; indeed, they are two names for the same fact.* There can be no such thing as reflective morality where there is not solicitude for the ends to which action is directed.

An end-in-view differs on one side from a mere anticipation or prediction of an outcome, and on the other side from the propulsive force of mere habit and appetite. In distinction from the first, it involves a want, an impulsive urge and forward drive; in distinction from the second, it involves an intellectual factor, the thought of an object which gives meaning and direction to the urge. This connection between purpose and desire is the source of one whole class of moral problems. Attainment of learning, professional skill, wealth, power, would not be animating purposes unless the thought of some result were unified with some intense need of the self, for it takes *thought* to convert an impulse into a desire centered in an object. But on the other end, a strong craving tends to exclude thought. It is in haste for its own speedy realization. An intense appetite, say thirst, impels to immediate action without thought of its consequences, as a very thirsty man at sea tends to drink salt water without regard to objective results. Deliberation and inquiry, on the other hand, take time; they demand delay, the deferring of immediate action. Craving does not look beyond the moment, but it is of the very nature of thought to look toward a remote end.

There is accordingly a conflict brought about within the self. But while there is conflict, it is not between desire and reason, but between a desire which wants a nearby object and a desire which wants an object which is seen by thought to occur in consequence of an intervening series of conditions, or in the "long run"; it is a conflict between two objects presented in thought, one corresponding to a want or appetite just as it presents itself in isolation, the other corresponding to the want thought of in relation to other wants. Fear may suggest flight or lying to a man as ends to be sought; further thought may bring a man to a conviction that steadfastness and truthfulness will insure a much larger and more enduring good. There is an idea in each case; in the first case, an idea of personal safety; in the second instance, an idea of, say, the safety of others to be achieved by remaining at a post. In each case also there is desire; in the first instance a desire which lies close to natural impulse and instinct; in the second instance, a desire which would not be aroused were it not that *thought* brings into view remote consequences. *In one case, original impulse dictates the thought of the object; in the other case, this original impulse is transformed into a different desire because of objects which thought holds up to view.* But no matter how elaborate and how rational is the object of thought, it is impotent unless it arouses desire.

In its extreme and logical form the conception of ends has no great present vogue. Discussion of it is still important, however, because its underlying idea is perpetuated in the tendency to regard morals as a set of special and separate dispositions. Moral goodness is quite commonly divided off from interest in all the objects which make life fuller, and is confined to a narrow set of aims, which are prized too often merely because they involve inhibition and repression. Experience shows that the effect of this attitude is to keep attention fixed upon the things which are thought to be evil. The mind becomes obsessed with guilt and how to avoid it. In consequence, a sour and morose disposition is fostered. An individual affected in this way is given to condemnation of others and to looking for evil in them. The generosity of mind which is rooted in faith in human nature is stifled. Meanwhile, the positive interest in ends which is the source of abundant power grows weak. Normally, discipline comes about as a fruit of steady devotion to ends that are of positive value. The person thoroughly interested in an end—whether it be that of an art or a profession or calling—will endure hardship and repellent conditions because they are incidents of the pursuit of what is good. He will find in the course of his pursuit sufficient opportunity for exercise of the harder virtues. The man who can make a sport out of his endeavor to break a bad habit will succeed, while failure will await the person who concentrates his effort upon the negative idea of mere abstinence. There is a contrast between the natural goods—those which appeal to immediate desire—and the moral good, that which is approved after reflection. But the difference is not absolute and inherent. The moral good is some natural good which is sustained and developed through consideration of it in its relations; the natural enjoyment which conflicts with the moral good is that which accompanies some desire which persists because it is allowed to sway action by itself, apart from the connections which reflection would bring to light.

The idea of Ends and the Good is the counterpart of the *intellectual* aspect of character and conduct. The difficulty in the way of attaining and maintaining practical wisdom is the urgency of immediate impulse and desire which swell and swell until they crowd out all thought of remote and comprehensive goods. The conflict is a real one and is at the heart of many of our serious moral struggles and lapses. In the main, solution is found in utilizing all possible occasions, when we are not in the presence of conflicting desires, to cultivate interest in those goods which we do approve in our calm moments of reflection. John Stuart Mill remarked that "the cultivated mind . . . finds sources of inexhaustible interest in all that surrounds it; in the objects of nature, the achievements of art, the imaginations of poetry, the incidents of history, the ways of mankind, past, present and their prospects in the future." There are many times when the cultivation of these interests meets with no strong obstacle. The habits which are built up and reënforced under such conditions are the best bulwarks against weakness and surrender in the moments when the reflective or "true" good conflicts with that set up by temporary and intense desire. The proper course of action is, then, to multiply occasions for the enjoyment of these ends, to prolong and deepen the experiences connected with them. Morality then becomes positive instead of a struggle carried against the seductive force of lesser goods. This course of action gives no guarantee against occurrence of situations of conflict and of possible failure to maintain the greater good. But *reflective* attachment to the ends which reason presents is enormously increased when these ends have themselves been, on earlier occasions, *natural* goods enjoyed in the normal course of life. Ideal ends, those sustained by thought, do not lose their ideal character when they are directly appreciated; in the degree in which they become objects of positive interest their power to control and move conduct in times of stress is reënforced.

The truth hinted at in the hedonistic view of moral wisdom (that it consists in foresight and calculation of future enjoyments and sufferings) is that *present* enjoyment may accompany the thought of remote objects when they are held before the mind. Its error lies in supposing that in reflection our ideas go out to future pleasures instead of to future objects. A man in order to cultivate good health does not think of the pleasures it will bring to him: in thinking of the various objects and acts which will follow from good health he experiences a *present* enjoyment, and this enjoyment strengthens his effort to attain it. As Plato and Aristotle said over two thousand years ago, the aim of moral education is to develop a character which finds pleasure in right objects and pain in wrong ends.

Something similar is to be said of wisdom or prudence viewed as a judgment of ends which are expedient or that mark "good policy." As far as the maxim emphasizes means and conditions that are necessary to achievement,

thus taking morals out of the region of sentimental vapor-
ings and fantasies, miscalled idealism, the principle is
sound. Error lies in restriction of the domains of value in
which achievement is desirable. It is folly rather than wisdom to include in the concept of success only tangible
material goods and to exclude those of culture, art, science, sympathetic relations with others. Once a man has
experienced certain kinds of good in a concrete and intimate way, he would rather fail in external achievement
than forego striving for them. The zest of endeavor is itself an enjoyment to be fostered, and life is poor without
it. As John Stuart Mill said "some things called expedient
are not useful but in reality are one branch of the harmful." To due reflection, things sometimes regarded as
"practical" are in truth highly impolitic and shortsighted.
But the way to eliminate preference for narrow and short-
sighted expediencies is not to condemn the practical as low
and mercenary in comparison with spiritual ideals, but to
cultivate all possible opportunities for the actual enjoyment of the reflective values and to engage in the activity,
the practice, which extends their scope.

Finally, the underlying truth of what is called Epicure-
anism is this: the importance of nurturing the *present*
enjoyment of things worth while, instead of sacrificing
present value to an unknown and uncertain future. If this
course is popularly thought of as mere self-indulgence, as
selfish and destructive of consecutive striving for remote
ends, it is because emphasis is laid upon the bare fact of
enjoyment instead of upon the *values* enjoyed. Here as
with the other principles discussed, the conclusion is the
need of fostering at every opportunity direct enjoyment of
the kind of goods reflection approves. To deny direct satisfaction any place in morals is simply to weaken the moving force of the goods approved by thought.

In conclusion, we point out that the discussion enables us to give an empirically verifiable meaning to the conception of *ideal* values in contrast with *material* values. The distinction is one between goods which, when they present themselves to imagination, are approved by reflection after wide examination of their relations, and the goods which are such only because their wider connections are not looked into. We cannot draw up a catalogue and say that such and such goods are intrinsically and always ideal, and such and such other ones inherently base because material. There are circumstances under which enjoyment of a value called spiritual because it is associated with religion is mere indulgence; when its good, in other words, becomes one of mere sensuous emotion. There are occasions when attention to the material environment constitutes the ideal good because that is the act which thoroughgoing inquiry would approve. In a general way, of course, we can safely point out that certain goods are ideal in character: those of art, science, culture, interchange of knowledge and ideas, etc. But that is because past experience has shown that they are the *kind* of values which are likely to be approved upon searching reflection. Hence a *presumption* exists in their favor, but in concrete cases only a presumption. To suppose that the higher ideal value inheres in them *per se* would result in fostering the life of a dilettante and mere esthete, and would relegate all goods experienced in the natural course of life to a non-moral or anti-moral plane. There is in fact a place and time—that is, there are relationships—in which the satisfactions of the normal appetites, usually called physical and sensuous, have an ideal quality. Were it not so, some form of asceticism would be the only moral course. The business of reflection in determining the true good cannot be done once for all, as, for instance, by making out a table of values arranged in a hierarchical order of higher and lower. The business of reflection needs to be done, and done over and over and over again, in terms of the conditions of concrete situations as they arise. In short, the need for reflection and insight is perpetually recurring.

The need for constant revision and expansion of moral knowledge is one great reason why there is no gulf dividing non-moral knowledge from that which is truly moral. At any moment conceptions which once seemed to belong exclusively to the biological or physical realm may assume moral import. This will happen whenever they are discovered to have a bearing on the common good. When knowledge of bacteria and germs and their relation to the spread of disease was achieved, sanitation, public and private, took on a moral significance it did not have before. For they were seen to affect the health and well-being of the community. Psychiatrists and psychologists working within their own technical regions have brought to light facts and principles which profoundly affect old conceptions of, say, punishment and responsibility, especially as to their place in the formation of disposition. It has been discovered, for example, that "problem children" are created by conditions which exist in families and in the reaction of parents to the young. In a rough way, it may be asserted that most of the morbid conditions of mind and character which develop later have their origin in emotional arrests and maladjustments of early life. These facts have not as yet made their way very far into popular understanding and action, but their ultimate moral import is incalculable. Similarly, knowledge once technically confined to physics and chemistry is applied in industry and has an effect on the lives and happiness of individuals beyond all estimate. The list of examples might be extended indefinitely. The important point is that any restriction of

moral knowledge and judgments to a definite realm necessarily limits our perception of moral significance. A large
part of the difference between those who are stagnant and
reactionary and those who are genuinely progressive in social matters comes from the fact that the former think of
morals as confined, boxed, within a round of duties and
sphere of values which are fixed and final. Most of the
serious moral problems of the present time are dependent
for their solution upon a general realization that the contrary is the case. Probably the great need of the present
time is that the traditional barriers between scientific and
moral knowledge be broken down, so that there will be
organized and consecutive endeavor to use all available
scientific knowledge for humane and social ends.

III · Experimentalism in Moral Theory*

To assume the existence of final and unquestionable
knowledge upon which we can fall back in order to settle
automatically every moral problem involves commitment
to a dogmatic theory of morals. The alternative method
may be called experimental. It implies that reflective morality demands observation of particular situations, rather
than fixed adherence to *a priori* principles; that free inquiry and freedom of publication and discussion must be
encouraged and not merely grudgingly tolerated; that opportunity at different times and places must be given for
trying different measures so that their effects may be capable of observation and of comparison with one another.
It is, in short, the method of democracy, of a positive toleration which amounts to sympathetic regard for the intelligence and personality of others, even if they hold views
opposed to ours, and of scientific inquiry into facts and
testing of ideas.

* From *Ethics,* pp. 364-367.

The opposed method, even when we free it from the extreme traits of forcible suppression, censorship, and intolerant persecution which have often historically accompanied it, is the method of appeal to authority and to precedent. The will of divine beings, supernaturally revealed; of divinely ordained rulers; of so-called natural law, philosophically interpreted; of private conscience; of the commands of the state, or the constitution; of common consent; of a majority; of received conventions; of traditions coming from a hoary past; of the wisdom of ancestors; of precedents set up in the past, have at different times been the authority appealed to. The common feature of the appeal is that there is some voice so authoritative as to preclude the need of inquiry. The logic of the various positions is that while an open mind may be desirable in respect to physical truths, a completely settled and closed mind is needed in moral matters.

Adoption of the experimental method does not signify that there is no place for authority and precedent. On the contrary, precedent is a valuable *instrumentality*. But precedents are to be *used* rather than to be implicitly followed; they are to be used as tools of analysis of present situations, suggesting points to be looked into and hypotheses to be tried. They are of much the same worth as are personal memories in individual crises; a storehouse to be drawn upon for suggestion. There is also a place for the use of authorities. Even in free scientific inquiry, present investigators rely upon the findings of investigators of the past. They employ theories and principles which are identified with scientific inquirers of the past. They do so, however, only as long *as no evidence is presented calling for a reëxamination of their findings and theories*. They never assume that these findings are so final that under no circumstances can they be questioned and modified. Because of partisanship, love of certainty, and devotion to routine, accepted points of view gain a momentum which for long periods even in science may restrict observation and reflection. But this limitation is recognized to be a weakness of human nature and not a desirable use of the principle of authority.

In moral matters there is also a presumption in favor of principles that have had a long career in the past and that have been endorsed by men of insight; the presumption is especially strong when all that opposes them is the will of some individual seeking exemption because of an impulse or passion which is temporarily urgent. Such principles are no more to be lightly discarded than are scientific principles worked out in the past. But in one as in the other, newly discovered facts or newly instituted conditions may give rise to doubts and indicate the inapplicability of accepted doctrines. In questions of social morality, more fundamental than any particular principle held or decision reached is the attitude of *willingness to reëxamine and if necessary to revise current convictions, even if that course entails the effort to change by concerted effort existing institutions, and to direct existing tendencies to new ends.*

It is a caricature to suppose that emphasis upon the social character of morality leads to glorification of contemporary conditions just as they are. The position does insist that morals, to have vitality, must be related to these conditions or be up in the air. But there is nothing in the bare position which indicates whether the relation is to be one of favor or of opposition. A man walking in a bog must pay even more heed to his surroundings than a man walking on smooth pavement, but this fact does not mean that he is to surrender to these surroundings. The alternative is not between abdication and acquiescence on one side, and neglect and ignoring on the other; it is between a morals which is effective because related to what is, and a morality which is futile and empty because framed in disregard of actual conditions. Against the social consequences generated by existing conditions there always stands the idea of other and better social consequences which a change would bring into being.

IV · Endings in Nature and Ends for Man*

Empirically, the existence of objects of direct grasp, possession, use and enjoyment cannot be denied. Empirically, things are poignant, tragic, beautiful, humorous, settled, disturbed, comfortable, annoying, barren, harsh, consoling, splendid, fearful; are such immediately and in their own right and behalf. If we take advantage of the word esthetic in a wider sense than that of application to the beautiful and ugly, esthetic quality, immediate, final or self-inclosed, indubitably characterizes natural situations as they empirically occur. These traits stand in themselves on precisely the same level as colors, sounds, qualities of contact, taste and smell. Any criterion that finds the latter to be ultimate and "hard" data will, impartially applied, come to the same conclusion about the former. *Any* quality as such is final; it is at once initial and terminal; just what it is as it exists. It may be referred to other things, it may be treated as an effect or as a sign. But this involves an extraneous extension and use. It takes us beyond quality in its immediate qualitativeness. If experienced things are valid evidence, then nature in having qualities within itself has what in the literal sense must be called ends, terminals, arrests, enclosures.

It is dangerous to venture at all upon the use of the word "ends" in connection with existential processes. Apologetic and theological controversies cluster about it

* From *Experience and Nature,* pp. 96-112.

and affect its signification. Barring this connotation, the word has an almost inexpugnable honorific flavor, so that to assert that nature is characterized by ends, the most conspicuous of which is the life of mind, seems like engaging in a eulogistic, rather than an empirical account of nature. Something much more neutral than any such implication is, however, meant. We constantly talk about things coming or drawing to a close; getting ended, finished, done with, over with. It is a commonplace that no *thing* lasts forever. We may be glad or we may be sorry but that is wholly a matter of the kind of history which is being ended. We may conceive the end, the close, as due to fulfillment, perfect attainment, to satiety, or to exhaustion, to dissolution, to something having run down or given out. Being an end may be indifferently an ecstatic culmination, a matter-of-fact consummation, or a deplorable tragedy. Which of these things a closing or terminal object is, has nothing to do with the property of being an end.

The genuine implications of natural ends may be brought out by considering beginnings instead of endings. To insist that nature is an affair of beginnings is to assert that there is no one single and all-at-once beginning of everything. It is but another way of saying that nature is an affair *of* affairs, wherein each one, no matter how linked up it may be with others, has its *own* quality. It does not imply that every beginning marks an advance or improvement; as we sadly know, accidents, diseases, wars, lies and errors begin. Clearly the fact and idea of beginning is neutral, not eulogistic; temporal, not absolute. And since wherever one thing begins something else ends, what is true of beginnings is true of endings. Popular fiction and drama show the bias of human nature in favor of happy endings, but by being fiction and drama they show with even greater assurance that unhappy endings are natural events.

To minds inured to the eulogistic connotation of ends, such a neutral interpretation of the meaning of ends as has just been set forth may seem to make the doctrine of ends a matter of indifference. If ends are only endings or closings of temporal episodes, why bother to call attention to ends at all, to say nothing of framing a theory of ends and dignifying it with the name of natural teleology? In the degree, however, in which the mind is weaned from partisan and egocentric interest, acknowledgment of nature as a scene of incessant beginnings and endings, presents itself as the source of philosophic enlightenment. It enables thought to apprehend causal mechanisms and temporal finalities as phases of the same natural processes, instead of as competitors where the gain of one is the loss of the other. Mechanism is the order involved in an historic occurrence, capable of definition in terms of the order which various histories sustain to each other. Thus it is the instrumentality of control of any particular termination since a sequential order involves the last term.

The traditional conception of natural ends was to the effect that nature does nothing in vain; the accepted meaning of this phrase was that every change is for the sake of something which does not change, occurring in its behalf. Thus the mind started with a ready-made list of good things or perfections which it was the business of nature to accomplish. Such a view may verbally distinguish between something called efficient causation and something else called final causation. But in effect the distinction is only between the causality of the master who contents himself with uttering an order and the efficacy of the servant who actually engages in the physical work of execution. It is only a way of attributing ultimate causality to what is ideal and mental—the directive order of the master—while emancipating it from the supposed degradation of physical labor in carrying it out, as well as avoiding the difficulties of inserting an immaterial cause within the material realm. But in a legitimate account of ends as endings, all directional order resides in the sequential order. This no more occurs for the sake of the end than a mountain exists for the sake of the peak which is its end. A musical phrase has a certain close, but the earlier portion does not therefore exist for the sake of the close as if it were something which is done away with when the close is reached. And so a man is not an adult until after he has been a boy, but childhood does not exist for the sake of maturity.

Empirically, however, there is a history which is a succession of histories, and in which any event is at once both beginning of one course and close of another; is both transitive and static. The phrase constantly in our mouths, "state of affairs," is accurately descriptive, although it makes sheer nonsense of both the traditional spiritual and mechanistic theories.

There are no changes that do not enter into an affair, *Res,* and there is no affair that is not bounded and thereby marked off as a state or condition. When a state of affairs is perceived, the perceiving-of-a-state-of-affairs is a further state of affairs. Its subject-matter is a thing in the idiomatic sense of thing, *res,* whether a solar-system, a stellar constellation, an atom, or a diversified and more or less loose interconnection of events, falling within boundaries sufficiently definite to be capable of being approximately traced. Such is the unbiased evidence of experience in gross, and such in effect is the conclusion of recent physics as far as a layman can see. For this reason, and not because of any unique properties of a separate kind of existence, called psychic or mental, every situation or field of consciousness is marked by initiation, direction or intent, and consequence or import.

What is unique is not these traits, but the property of awareness or perception. Because of this property, the initial stage is capable of being judged in the light of its probable course and consequence. There is anticipation. Each successive event being a stage in a serial process is both expectant and commemorative. What is more precisely pertinent to our present theme, the terminal outcome when anticipated (as it is when a moving cause of affairs is perceived) becomes an end-in-view, an aim, purpose, a prediction usable as a plan in shaping the course of events.

In empirical fact, perceptions of ends are projections of possible consequences; they are ends-in-view. The inviewness of ends is as much conditioned by antecedent natural conditions as is perception of *contemporary* objects external to the organism, trees and stones or whatever. That is, natural processes must have actually terminated in specifiable consequences, which give those processes definition and character, before ends can be mentally entertained and be the objects of striving desire. But empirically ends-in-view are not objects of contemplative possession and use: they are intellectual and regulative means, degenerating into reminiscences or dreams unless they are employed as plans within the state of affairs.

It is not easy to distinguish between ends as *de facto* endings, and ends as fulfillments, and at the same time to bear in mind the connection of the latter with the former. We respond so directly to some objects in experience with intent to preserve and perpetuate them that it is difficult to keep the conception of a thing as terminus free from the element of deliberate choice and endeavor; when we think of it or discourse about it, we introduce connection. Since we turn away from trouble and suffering, since these things are not the objects of choice and effort save for avoidance, it seems forced to call them ends. To name them such appears an impropriety of language. I am quite willing to concede the linguistic point, provided its implications are acknowledged and adhered to. For in this case we are left, apart from a deliberately directed course of events, only with objects immediately used, enjoyed and suffered but having in themselves no claim to the title of ends. Health in this case is not in itself an end of any natural process; much less an end-in-itself. It is an enjoyed good when it happens, just as disease is a suffered ill. Similarly, truth of belief and statement is an affair that has the quality of good; but it is not an end just because it is good; it becomes an end only when, because of its goodness, it is actively sought for and reached as a conclusion. On this basis, all ends are ends-in-view; they are no longer ideal as characters of Being, as they were in Greek theory, but are the objects of conscious intent. When achieved in existence they are ends because they are then conclusions attained through antecedent endeavor, just as a post is not a goal in itself, but becomes a goal in relation to a runner and his race. Either we must consistently stick to the equivalence of ends with objectives of conscious endeavor, or admit that all things directly possessed of irreducible and self-sufficing quality, red and blue, pain, solidity, toughness, smoothness and so on through the list, are natural ends.

V · The Satisfying and the Valuable*

To say that something is enjoyed is to make a statement about a fact, something already in existence; it is

* From *The Quest for Certainty,* pp. 260-281.

not to judge the value of that fact. There is no difference between such a proposition and one which says that something is sweet or sour, red or black. It is just correct or incorrect and that is the end of the matter. But to call an object a value is to assert that it satisfies or fulfills certain conditions. Function and status in meeting conditions are a different matter from bare existence. The fact that something is desired only raises the *question* of its desirability; it does not settle it. Only a child in the degree of his immaturity thinks to settle the question of desirability by reiterated proclamation: "I want it, I want it, I want it." What is objected to in the current empirical theory of values is not connection of them with desire and enjoyment but failure to distinguish between enjoyments of radically different sorts. There are many common expressions in which the difference of the two kinds is clearly recognized. Take for example the difference between the ideas of "satisfying" and "satisfactory." To say that something satisfies is to report something as an isolated finality. To assert that it is satis*factory* is to define it in its connections and interactions. The fact that it pleases or is immediately congenial poses a problem to judgment. How shall the satisfaction be rated? Is it a value or is it not? Is it something to be prized and cherished, *to be* enjoyed? Not stern moralists alone but everyday experience informs us that finding satisfaction in a thing may be a warning, a summons to be on the lookout for consequences. To declare something satis*factory* is to assert that it meets specifiable conditions. It is, in effect, a judgment that the thing "will do." It involves a prediction; it contemplates a future in which the thing will continue to serve; it *will* do. It asserts a consequence the thing will actively institute; it will *do*. That it is satisfying is the content of a proposition of fact; that it is satisfactory is a judgment, an estimate, an appraisal. It denotes an attitude *to be* taken, that of striving to perpetuate and to make secure.

It is worth notice that besides the instances given, there are many other recognitions in ordinary speech of the distinction. The endings "able," "worthy" and "ful" are cases in point. Noted and notable, noteworthy; remarked and remarkable; advised and advisable; wondered at and wonderful; pleasing and beautiful; loved and lovable; blamed and blameable, blameworthy; objected to and objectionable; esteemed and estimable; admired and admirable; shamed and shameful; honored and honorable; approved and approvable, worthy of approbation. The multiplication of words adds nothing to the force of the distinction. But it aids in conveying a sense of the fundamental character of the distinction; of the difference between mere report of an already existent fact and judgment as to the importance and need of bringing a fact into existence; or, if it is already there, of sustaining it in existence. The latter is a genuine practical judgment, and marks the only type of judgment that has to do with the direction of action. Whether or no we reserve the term "value" for the latter (as seems to me proper) is a minor matter; that the distinction be acknowledged as the key to understanding the relation of values to the direction of conduct is the important thing.

Propositions about what is or has been liked are of instrumental value in reaching judgments of value, in as far as the conditions and consequences of the thing liked are thought about. In themselves they make no claims; they put forth no demand upon subsequent attitudes and acts; they profess no authority to direct. If one likes a thing he likes it; that *is* a point about which there can be no dispute—although it is not so easy to state just *what* is liked as is frequently assumed. A judgment about what is *to be* desired and enjoyed is, on the other hand, a claim on future action; it possesses *de jure* and not merely *de facto* quality. It is a matter of frequent experience that likings and enjoyments are of all kinds, and that many are such as reflective judgments condemn. By way of self-justification and "rationalization," an enjoyment creates a tendency to assert that the thing enjoyed is a value. This assertion of validity adds authority to the fact. It is a decision that the object has a right to exist and hence a claim upon action to further its existence.

Not even the most devoted adherents of the notion that enjoyment and value are equivalent facts would venture to assert that because we have once liked a thing we should go on liking it; they are compelled to introduce the idea that *some* tastes are to be cultivated. Logically, there is no ground for introducing the idea of cultivation; liking is liking, and one is as good as another. If enjoyments *are* values, the judgment of value cannot regulate the form which liking takes; it cannot regulate its own conditions. Desire and purpose, and hence action, are left without guidance, although the question of regulation of their formation is the supreme problem of practical life. Values (to sum up) may be connected inherently with liking, and yet not with *every* liking but only with those that judgment has approved, after examination of the relation upon which the object liked depends. A casual liking is one that happens without knowledge of how it occurs nor to what effect. The difference between it and one which is sought because of a judgment that it is worth having and is to be striven for, makes just the difference between enjoyments which are accidental and enjoyments that have value and hence a claim upon our attitude and conduct.

When theories of values do not afford intellectual assistance in framing ideas and beliefs about values that are adequate to direct action, the gap must be filled by other means. If intelligent method is lacking, prejudice, the pressure of immediate circumstance, self-interest and class-interest, traditional customs, institutions of accidental historic origin, are *not* lacking, and they tend to take the place of intelligence. Thus we are led to our main proposition: *Judgments about values are judgments about the conditions and the results of experienced objects; judgments about that which should regulate the formation of our desires, affections and enjoyments*. For whatever decides their formation will determine the main course of our conduct, personal and social.

If it sounds strange to hear that we should frame our judgments as to what has value by considering the connections in existence of what we like and enjoy, the reply is not far to seek. As long as we do not engage in this inquiry enjoyments (values if we choose to apply that term) are casual; they are given by "nature," not constructed by art. Like natural objects in their qualitative existence, they at most only supply material for elaboration in rational discourse. A *feeling* of good or excellence is as far removed from goodness in fact as a feeling that objects are intellectually thus and so is removed from their being actually so. To recognize that the truth of natural objects can be reached only by the greatest care in selecting and arranging directed operations, and then to suppose that values can be truly determined by the mere fact of liking seems to leave us in an incredible position. All the serious perplexities of life come back to the genuine difficulty of forming a judgment as to the values of the situation; they come back to a conflict of goods. Only dogmatism can suppose that serious moral conflict is between something clearly bad and something known to be good, and that uncertainty lies wholly in the will of the one choosing. Most conflicts of importance are conflicts between things which are or have been satisfying, not between good and evil. And to suppose that we can make a hierarchical table of values at large once for all, a kind of catalogue in which they are arranged in an order of ascending or descending worth, is to indulge in a gloss on our inability to frame intelligent judgments in the concrete. Or else it is to dignify customary choice and prejudice by a title of honor.

The alternative to definition, classification and systematization of satisfactions just as they happen to occur is judgment of them by means of the relations under which they occur. If we know the conditions under which the act of liking, of desire and enjoyment, takes place, we are in a position to know what are the consequences of that act. The difference between the desired and the desirable, admired and the admirable, becomes effective at just this point. Consider the difference between the proposition "That thing has been eaten," and the judgment "That thing is edible." The former statement involves no knowledge of any relation except the one stated; while we are able to judge of the edibility of anything only when we have a knowledge of its interactions with other things sufficient to enable us to foresee its probable effects when it is taken into the organism.

To assume that anything can be known in isolation from its connections with other things is to identify *knowing* with merely *having* some object before perception or in feeling, and is thus to lose the key to the traits that distinguish an object as known. It is futile, even silly, to suppose that some quality that is directly present constitutes the whole of the thing presenting the quality. It does not do so when the quality is that of being hot or fluid or heavy, and it does not when the quality is that of giving pleasure, or being enjoyed. Such qualities are, once more, effects, ends in the sense of closing termini of processes involving causal connections. They are something to be investigated, challenges to inquiry and judgment. The more connections and interactions we ascertain, the more we *know* the object in question. Thinking is search for these connections. Heat experienced as a consequence of directed operations has a meaning quite different from the heat that is casually experienced without knowledge of how it came about. The same is true of enjoyments. Enjoyments that issue from conduct directed by insight into relations have a meaning and a validity due to the way in which they are experienced. Such enjoyments are not repented of; they generate no after-taste of bitterness. Even in the midst of direct enjoyment, there is a sense of validity, of authorization, which intensifies the enjoyment. There is solicitude for perpetuation of the *object* having value which is radically different from mere anxiety to perpetuate the *feeling* of enjoyment.

Such statements as we have been making are, therefore, far from implying that there are values apart from things actually enjoyed as good. To find a thing enjoy*able* is, so to say, a *plus* enjoyment. We saw that it was foolish to treat the scientific object as a rival of or substitute for the perceived object, since the former is intermediate between uncertain and settled situations and those experienced under conditions of greater control. In the same way, judgment of the value of an object to be experienced is instrumental to appreciation of it when it is realized. But the notion that every object that happens to satisfy has an equal claim with every other to be a value is like supposing that every object of perception has the same cognitive force as every other. There is no knowledge without perception; but objects perceived are *known* only when they are determined as consequences of connective operations

There is no value except where there is satisfaction, but there have to be certain conditions fulfilled to transform a satisfaction into a value.

Change from forming ideas and judgments of value on the basis of conformity to antecedent objects, to constructing enjoyable objects directed by knowledge of consequences, is a change from looking to the past to looking to the future. I do not for a moment suppose that the experiences of the past, personal and social, are of no importance. For without them we should not be able to frame any ideas whatever of the conditions under which objects are enjoyed nor any estimate of the consequences of esteeming and liking them. But past experiences are significant in giving us intellectual instrumentalities of judging just these points. They are tools, not finalities. Reflection upon what we have liked and have enjoyed is a necessity. But it tells us nothing about the *value* of these things until enjoyments are themselves reflectively controlled, or, until, as they are recalled, we form the best judgment possible about what led us to like this sort of thing and what has issued from the fact that we liked it.

This is the significant meaning of transfer of experimental method from the technical field of physical experience to the wider field of human life. We trust the method in forming our beliefs about things not directly connected with human life. In effect, we distrust it in moral, political and economic affairs. In the fine arts, there are many signs of a change. In the past, such a change has often been an omen and precursor of changes in other human attitudes. But, generally speaking, the idea of actively adopting experimental method in social affairs, in the matters deemed of most enduring and ultimate worth, strikes most persons as a surrender of all standards and regulative authority. But in principle, experimental method does not signify random and aimless action; it implies direction by ideas and knowledge. The question at issue is a practical one. Are there in existence the ideas and the knowledge that permit experimental method to be effectively used in social interests and affairs?

Where will regulation come from if we surrender familiar and traditionally prized values as our directive standards? Very largely from the findings of the natural sciences. For one of the effects of the separation drawn between knowledge and action is to deprive scientific knowledge of its proper service as a guide of conduct—except once more in those technological fields which have been degraded to an inferior rank. Of course, the complexity of the conditions upon which objects of human and liberal value depend is a great obstacle, and it would be too optimistic to say that we have as yet enough knowledge of the scientific type to enable us to regulate our judgments of value very extensively. But we have more knowledge than we try to put to use, and until we try more systematically we shall not know what are the important gaps in our sciences judged from the point of view of their moral and humane use.

In fact, the most significant change that would issue from carrying over experimental method from physics to man concerns the status and import of standards, principles, rules. With the transfer, these, and all tenets and creeds about good and goods, would be recognized to be hypotheses. Instead of being rigidly fixed, they would be treated as intellectual instruments to be tested and confirmed—and altered—through consequences effected by acting upon them. They would lose all pretense of finality —the ulterior source of dogmatism. It is both astonishing and depressing that so much of the energy of mankind has gone into fighting for (with weapons of the flesh as well as

of the spirit) the truth of creeds, religious, moral and political, as distinct from what has gone into effort to try
creeds by putting them to the test of acting upon them.
The change would do away with the intolerance and fanaticism that attend the notion that beliefs and judgments
are capable of inherent truth and authority; inherent in
the sense of being independent of what they lead to when
used as directive principles. The transformation does not
imply merely that men are responsible for acting upon
what they profess to believe; that is an old doctrine. It
goes much further. Any belief as such is tentative, hypothetical; it is not just to be acted upon, but is to be *framed*
with reference to its office as a guide to action. Consequently, it should be the last thing in the world to be
picked up casually and then clung to rigidly. When it is apprehended as a tool and only a tool, as an instrumentality
of direction, then only will the same scrupulous care go to
its formation as now goes into the making of instruments
of precision in technical fields. Men, instead of being
proud of accepting and asserting beliefs and "principles"
on the ground of loyalty, will be as ashamed of that procedure as they would be to confess their assent to a scientific theory out of reverence for Newton or Helmholtz or
whomever, without regard to evidence.

The various modifications that would result from adoption in social and humane subjects of the experimental
way of thinking are perhaps summed up in saying that it
would place *method and means* upon the level of importance that has, in the past, been imputed exclusively to
ends. Means have been regarded as menial, and the useful
as the servile. Means have been treated as poor relations
to be endured, but not inherently welcome. The very
meaning of the word "ideals" is significant of the divorce
which has obtained between means and ends. "Ideals" are

thought to be remote and inaccessible of attainment; they
are too high and fine to be sullied by realization. They
serve vaguely to arouse "aspiration," but they do not
evoke and direct strivings for embodiment in actual existence. They hover in an indefinite way over the actual
scene; they are expiring ghosts of a once significant kingdom of divine reality whose rule penetrated to every detail
of life.

It is usual to condemn the amount of attention paid by
people in general to material ease, comfort, wealth, and
success gained by competition, on the ground that they
give to mere means the attention that ought to be given
to ends, or that they have taken for ends things which in
reality are only means. Criticisms of the place which economic interest and action occupy in present life are full of
complaints that men allow lower aims to usurp the place
that belongs to higher and ideal values. The final source
of the trouble is, however, that moral and spiritual "leaders" have propagated the notion that ideal ends may be
cultivated in isolation from "material" means, as if means
and material were not synonymous. While they condemn
men for giving to means the thought and energy that
ought to go to ends, the condemnation should go to them.
For they have not taught their followers to think of material and economic activities as *really* means. They have
been unwilling to frame their conception of the values that
should be regulative of human conduct on the basis of the
actual conditions and operations by which alone values
can be actualized.

CHAPTER FIFTEEN

PERCEPTION, LANGUAGE AND MIND

I · Theory of Perception*

RECENT theories have limited the signification of perception. In its older usage, it designated any awareness, any "seeing" whether of objects, ideas, principles, conclusions or whatever. In recent literature it is usually restricted to "sense-perception." There can be no quarrel about the meaning of words except a lexicographical quarrel. The issue at stake concerns then not the appropriate use of a word; it concerns certain matters of fact which are implied or usually associated with the present restricted usage. These implications are two: First, there exists a mode of consciousness or awareness which is original, primitive, simple, and which refers immediately and intrinsically to things in space external to the organism at the time of perception. Secondly, this reference is originally, and *ex proprio motu,* cognitive. Now as against these implications, the theory advanced asserts that awareness in the form of auditory and visual perception is, whenever it is *cognitive,* just as much a matter of inferential judgment, an instance of a way of taking and using meanings, as is any proposition found in the science of physics.

The current theory begins with a distinction between peripherally initiated and centrally initiated awareness.

* From *Experience and Nature,* pp. 332-339.

Peripheral initiation is the defining mark of such operations as are designated "perceptions." But awarenesses do not come to us labelled "I am caused by an event initiated on the surface of the body by other bodies"; and "I on the contrary originate in an intra-organic event only indirectly connected with surface-changes." The distinction is one made by analytic and classifying thought. This fact is enough to place in doubt the notion that some modes of consciousness are originally and intrinsically "sense-perception."

Moreover, there is no absolute separation between the skin and the interior of the body. No sooner is the distinction drawn than it has to be qualified. As a matter of fact there is no such *thing* as an *exclusively* peripherally initiated nervous event. Internal conditions, those of hunger, blood-circulation, endocrine functions, persistences of prior activities, pre-existent opened and blocked neuronic connections, together with a multitude of other intra-organic factors enter into the determination of a peripheral occurrence. And after the peripheral excitation has taken place, its subsequent career is not self-determined, but is affected by literally everything going on within the organism. It is pure fiction that a "sensation," or peripheral excitation, or stimulus, travels undisturbed in solitary state in its own coach-and-four to enter the brain or consciousness in its purity. A particular excitation is but one of an avalanche of contemporaneously occurring excitations, peripheral and from proprio-ceptors; each has to compete with others, to make terms with them; what happens is an integration of complex forces.

It requires therefore a highly technical apparatus of science to discriminate the exact place and nature of a peripheral stimulation, and to trace its normal course to just the junction point where it becomes effective for redirection of activity and thus capable of perception. "Peripheral origin" marks an interpretation of events, a discrimination scientifically valid and important, but no more an original datum than is the spectrum of Betelgeuse. The same thesis holds good, of course, of the "consciousness" corresponding to the centrally initiated processes. To suppose that there are inherently marked off different forms of awareness corresponding to the distinction arrived at by technical analysis is as flagrant a case of hypostatizing as can be found. The theory that certain kinds or forms of consciousness intrinsically have an intellectual or cognitive reference to things present in space is merely the traditional theory that knowledge is an immediate grasp of Being, clothed in the terminology of recent physiology. While it is offered as if it were established by physiological and psychological research, in reality it presents an intellectual hold-over, a notion picked up from early teachings which have not been subjected to any critical examination; physiology and psychology merely afford a vocabulary with which to deck out an unconscionable survival.

Reference to peripheral stimulation of eye or ear or skin or nose is, whether of the simpler and popular kind or of the more complex neurological kind, part of the technique of checking up the particular sort of extrinsic reference which *should* be given to an idea; discovery whether it is to be referred to a past, contemporary or future thing, or treated as due to wish and emotion. Even so, ascertainment of mode of stimulation and origin is always secondary and derived. We do not believe a thing to be "there" because we are directly cognizant of an external origin for our perception; we infer some external stimulation of our sensory apparatus because we are successfully engaged in motor response. Only when the latter fails, do we turn back and examine the matter of sensory stimulation. To say that I am now conscious of a typewriter as the source of sensory stimuli is to make a back-handed and sophisticated statement of the fact that I am engaged in active employment of the typewriter to produce certain consequences, so that what I am aware of is these consequences and the relation to them of parts of the typewriter as means of producing them. As a matter of fact, we *never* perceive the peripheral stimuli to which we are at *that* given time responding.

The notion that these stimuli are the appropriate and normal objects of simple original perceptions represents, as we have just said, an uncritical acceptance by psychologists of an old logical and metaphysical dogma, one having neither origin nor justification within scientific psychology. We are aware only of stimuli to other responses than those which we are now making; we become aware of them when we analyze some performed total act to discover the mechanism of its occurrence. To become aware of an optical or auditory stimulation involved in an act signifies that we now apprehend that an organic change is part of the means used in the act, so that soundness of its structure and working is requisite to efficient performance of the act. I do not usually, for example, hear the sounds made by the striking of the keys; hence I therefore bang at them or strike them unevenly. If I were better trained or more intelligent in the performance of this action, I should hear the sounds, for they would have ceased to be just stimuli and become means of direction of my behavior in securing consequences. Not having learned by the "touch-method," my awareness of contact-qualities as I hit the keys is intermittent and defective. Physiological stimulation of fingers is involved as a condition of my motor response; yet there is no consciousness of contact "sensations" or sensa. But if I used my sensory touch appreciation as means to the proper execution of the act of writing, I should be aware of these qualities. The wider and freer the employment of means, the larger the field of sensory perceptions.

It is usual in current psychology to assert or assume that qualities observed are those of the stimulus. This assumption puts the cart before the horse; qualities which are observed are those attendant upon response to stimuli. We are *observantly* aware (in distinction from inferentially aware) only of what *has* been done; we can perceive what is already there, what *has* happened. By description, a stimulus is not an object of perception, for stimulus is correlative to response, and is undetermined except as response occurs. I am not questioning as a fact of *knowledge* that certain things *are* the stimuli of visual and auditory perception. I am pointing out that we are aware of the stimuli only in terms of our response to them and of the consequences of this response.

Argument as to the impossibility of stimuli being the object of perception is of course dialectical; like all dialectic arguments it is not convincing if confronted with facts to the contrary. But facts agree. The whiteness of the paper upon which words are being written and the blackness of the letters have been constantly operative stimuli in what I have been doing. It is equally certain that they have not been constantly perceived objects. If I have perceived them from time to time, it is in virtue of prior responses of which they were consequences, and because of the need of employing these attained consequences as means in further action. In the laboratory, as in the painter's studio, colors are specific objects of perception. But as perceived, they are "stimuli" only proleptically and by a shift in the universe of discourse. The shift is evident in the fact that stimuli are stated as vibrations or electro-magnetic disturbance or in similar fashion; now vibrations are not observed while color, the consequence, the effected coordination, is in direct consciousness. The color now and here perceived, in consequence of an organic adjustment to other stimuli than color, is in subsequent situations a stimulus to other modes of behavior, unconscious in so far as just a stimulus; conscious as far as a deliberately utilized means.

While the word "perception" may be limited to designate awareness of objects contemporaneously affecting the bodily organs, there is no ground whatever for the assumption which has usually attended this narrowing of the older meaning of the word: namely, that sense-perception has *intrinsic* properties or qualities marking it off from other forms of consciousness. Much less is there justification for the assumption that such perceptions are the original form of elementary awareness from which other forms of cognitive consciousness develop. On the contrary, sensory-perceptual meanings are specifically discriminated objects of awareness; the discrimination takes place in the course of inquiry into causative conditions and consequences; the ultimate need for the inquiry is found in the necessity of discovering what is to be done, or of developing a response suitably adapted to the requirements of a situation.

When inquiry reveals that an object external to the organism is now operative and affecting the organism, the pertinency of overt action is established and the kind of overt adjustment that should be made is in evidence. Perceptual meanings (sensory-perceptual) contrast with other meanings in that either (a) the latter cannot be overtly acted upon *now* or immediately, but only at a deferred time, when specified conditions now absent have been brought into being—conceptual meanings; or (b) that the latter are such that action upon them at *any* time must be of a dramatic or literary or playful sort—non-cognitive meanings. The necessities of behavior en-force very early in life the difference between acts de-manded at once, and those pertinent only at a later time; yet making and refining the distinction are matters of con-stant search and discovery, not, as the traditional theory presumes, an original and ready-made affair.

II · Physical, Psychophysical and Mental*

Empirically speaking, the most obvious difference be-tween living and non-living things is that the activities of the former are characterized by needs, by efforts which are active demands to satisfy needs, and by satisfactions. In making this statement, the terms need, effort and sat-isfaction are primarily employed in a biological sense. By need is meant a condition of tensional distribution of energies such that the body is in a condition of uneasy or unstable equilibrium. By demand or effort is meant the fact that this state is manifested in movements which modify environing bodies in ways which react upon the body, so that its characteristic pattern of active equilib-rium is restored. By satisfaction is meant this recovery of equilibrium pattern, consequent upon the changes of en-vironment due to interactions with the active demands of the organism.

A plant needs water, carbon dioxide; upon occasion it needs to bear seeds. The need is neither an immaterial psychic force superimposed upon matter, nor is it merely a notional or conceptual distinction, introduced by thought after comparison of two different states of the organism, one of emptiness and one of repletion. It denotes a con-

* From *Experience and Nature*, pp. 252-261.

crete state of events: a condition of tension in the distribution of energies such as involves pressures from points of high potential to those of low potential which in turn effect distinctive changes such that the connection with the environment is altered, so that the organism acts differently upon the environment and is exposed to different influences from it. In this fact, taken by itself, there is nothing which marks off the plant from the physico-chemical activity of inanimate bodies. The latter also are subject to conditions of disturbed inner equilibrium, which lead to activity in relation to surrounding things, and which terminate after a cycle of changes—a terminus termed saturation, corresponding to satisfaction in organic bodies.

The difference between the animate plant and the inanimate iron molecule is not that the former has something in addition to physico-chemical energy; it lies in the *way* in which physico-chemical energies are interconnected and operate, whence different *consequences* mark inanimate and animate activity respectively. For with animate bodies, recovery or restoration of the equilibrium pattern applies to the complex integrated course or history. In inanimate bodies as such, "saturation" occurs indifferently, not in such a way as to tend to maintain a temporal pattern of activity. The interactions of the various constituent parts of a plant take place in such ways as to tend to continue a characteristically organized activity; they tend to utilize conserved consequences of past activities so as to adapt subsequent changes to the needs of the integral system to which they belong. Organization is a fact, though it is not an original organizing force. Iron as such exhibits characteristics of bias or selective reactions, but it shows no bias in favor of remaining simple iron; it had just as soon, so to speak, become iron-oxide. It shows no tendency in its interaction with water to modify the interaction so that consequences will perpetuate the characteristics of pure iron. If it did, it would have the marks of a living body, and would be called an organism. Iron as a genuine constituent of an *organized* body acts so as to tend to maintain the type of activity of the organism to which it belongs.

If we identify, as common speech does, the physical as such with the inanimate we need another word to denote the activity of organisms as such. Psycho-physical is an appropriate term. Thus employed, "psycho-physical" denotes the conjunctive presence in activity of need-demand-satisfaction, in the sense in which these terms have been defined. In the compound word, the prefix "psycho" denotes that physical activity has acquired additional properties, those of ability to procure a peculiar kind of interactive support of needs from surrounding media. Psycho-physical does not denote an abrogation of the physico-chemical; nor a peculiar mixture of something physical and something psychical (as a centaur is half man and half horse); it denotes the possession of certain qualities and efficacies not displayed by the inanimate.

Thus conceived there is no problem of the relation of physical *and* psychic. There are specifiable empirical events marked by distinctive qualities and efficacies. There is first of all, *organization* with all that is implied thereby. The problem involved is one of definite factual inquiry. Under exactly what conditions does organization occur, and just what are its various modes and their consequences? We may not be able to answer these questions satisfactorily; but the difficulties are not those of a philosophical mystery, but such as attend any inquiry into highly complex affairs. Organization is an empirical trait of some events, no matter how speculative and dubious theories about it may be; especially no matter how false are certain doctrines about it which have had great vogue —namely, those doctrines which have construed it as evidence of a special force or entity called life or soul. Organization is so characteristic of the nature of some events in their sequential linkages that no theory about it can be as speculative or absurd as those which ignore or deny its genuine existence. Denial is never based on empirical evidence, but is a dialectical conclusion from a preconception that whatever appears later in time must be metaphysically unreal as compared with what is found earlier, or from a preconception that since the complex is controlled by means of the simpler, the latter is more "real."

Differences in qualities (feelings) of acts when employed as indications of acts performed and to be performed, and as signs of their consequences, *mean* something. And they mean it directly; the meaning is *had* as their own character. Feelings make sense; as immediate meanings of events and objects, they are sensations, or, more properly, sensa. Without language, the qualities of organic action that are feelings are pains, pleasures, odors, colors, noises, tones, only potentially and proleptically. With language they are discriminated and identified. They are then "objectified"; they are immediate traits of things. This "objectification" is not a miraculous ejection from the organism or soul into external things, nor an illusory attribution of psychical entities to physical things. The qualities never were "in" the organism; they always were qualities of interactions in which both extra-organic things and organisms partake. When named, they enable identification and discrimination of things to take place as means in a further course of inclusive interaction. Hence they are as much qualities of the things engaged as of the organism. For purposes of control they may be referred specifically to either the thing or to the organism or to a specified structure of the organism. Thus color which turns out not to be a reliable sign of external events becomes a sign of, say, a defect in visual apparatus. The notion that sensory affections discriminate and identify themselves, apart from discourse, as being colors and sounds, etc., and thus *ipso facto* constitute certain elementary modes of knowledge, even though it be only knowledge of their own existence, is inherently so absurd that it would never have occurred to any one to entertain it, were it not for certain preconceptions about mind and knowledge. Sentiency in itself is anoetic; it exists as any immediate quality exists, but nevertheless it is an indispensable means of any noetic function.

For when, through language, sentience is taken up into a system of signs, when for example a certain quality of the active relationship of organism and environment is named hunger, it is seen as an organic demand for an extra-organic object. To term a quality "hunger," to name it, is to refer to an object, to food, to that which will satisfy it, toward which the active situation moves. Similarly, to name another quality "red," is to direct an interaction between an organism and a thing to some object which fulfills the demand or need of the situation. It requires but slight observation of mental growth of a child to note that organically conditioned qualities, including those of special sense-organs, are discriminated only as they are employed to designate objects; red, for instance, as the property of a dress or toy.

The difficulty in the way of identifying the qualities of acts conditioned by proprio-ceptor organs is notoriously enormous. They just merge in the general situation. If they entered into communication as shared means to social consequences they would acquire the same objective distinctiveness as do qualities conditioned by the extero-

ceptor organs. On the other hand, the qualities of the latter are just shades of the general tone of situations until
they are used, in language, as common or shared means to
common ends. Then they are identified as traits of objects. The child has to learn through social intercourse
that certain qualities of action mean greediness or anger
or fear or rudeness; the case is not otherwise with those
qualities which are identified as red, musical tone, a foul
odor. The latter may have instigated nausea, and "red"
may have excited uneasiness (as blood makes some persons faint); but discrimination of the nauseating object *as*
foul odor, and of the excitation *as* red occurs only when
they are designated as signs.

The qualities of situations in which organisms and surrounding conditions interact, when discriminated, make
sense. Sense is distinct from feeling, for it has a recognized reference; it is the qualitative characteristic of
something, not just a submerged unidentified quality or
tone. Sense is also different from signification. The latter
involves use of a quality as a sign or index of something
else, as when the red of a light signifies danger, and the
need of bringing a moving locomotive to a stop. The sense
of a thing, on the other hand, is an immediate and immanent meaning; it is meaning which is itself felt or directly
had. When we are baffled by perplexing conditions, and
finally hit upon a clew, and everything falls into place,
the whole thing suddenly, as we say, "makes sense." In
such a situation, the clew has signification in virtue of being an indication, a guide to interpretation. But the meaning of the *whole* situation as apprehended is sense. This
idiomatic usage of the word sense is much nearer the empirical facts than is the ordinary restriction of the word in
psychological literature to a single simple recognized quality, like sweet or red: the latter simply designates a case

of *minimum* sense, deliberately limited for purposes of intellectual safety-first. Whenever a situation has this double function of meaning, namely signification and sense, mind, intellect is definitely present.

The distinction between physical, psycho-physical, and mental is one of levels of increasing complexity and intimacy of interaction among natural events. Each one of these levels having its own characteristic empirical traits has its own categories. They are however categories of description, conceptions required to state the fact in question. They are not "explanatory" categories, as explanation is sometimes understood; they do not designate, that is, the operation of forces as "causes." They stick to empirical facts noting and denoting characteristic qualities and consequences peculiar to various levels of interaction. Viewed from this standpoint, the traditional "mechanical" and "teleological" theories both suffer from a common fallacy, which may be suggested by saying that they both purport to be explanatory in the old, non-historical sense of causality. One theory makes matter account for the existence of mind; the other regards happenings that precede the appearance of mind as preparations made for the sake of mind in a sense of preparation that is alleged to explain the occurrence of these antecedents.

III · Language and Mind*

Language is a natural function of human association; and its consequences react upon other events, physical and human, giving them meaning or significance. Events that are objects or significant exist in a context where they acquire new ways of operation and new properties. Words are spoken of as coins and money. Now gold, silver, and instrumentalities of credit are first of all, prior

* From *Experience and Nature*, pp. 173-180.

to being money, physical things with their own immediate and final qualities. But as money they are substitutes, representations, and surrogates, which embody relationships. As a substitute, money not merely facilitates exchange of such commodities as existed prior to its use, but it revolutionizes as well production and consumption of all commodities, because it brings into being new transactions, forming new histories and affairs. Exchange is not an event that can be isolated. It marks the emergence of production and consumption into a new medium and context wherein they acquire new properties.

Language is similarly not a mere agency for economizing energy in the interaction of human beings. It is a release and amplification of energies that enter into it, conferring upon them the added quality of meaning. The quality of meaning thus introduced is extended and transferred, actually and potentially, from sounds, gestures and marks, to all other things in nature. Natural events become messages to be enjoyed and administered, precisely as are song, fiction, oratory, the giving of advice and instruction. Thus events come to possess characters; they are demarcated, and noted. For character is general and distinguished.

When events have communicable meaning, they have marks, notations, and are capable of con-notation and denotation. They are more than mere occurrences; they have implications. Hence inference and reasoning are possible; these operations read the messages of things, which things utter because they are involved in human associations. When Aristotle drew a distinction between sensible things that are more noted—known—to us and rational things that are more noted—known—in themselves, he was actually drawing a distinction between things that operate in a local, restricted universe of discourse, and things whose marks are such that they readily enter into indefinitely extensive and varied discourse.

Gestures and cries are not primarily expressive and communicative. They are modes of organic behavior as much as are locomotion, seizing and crunching. Language, signs and significance, come into existence not by intent and mind but by over-flow, as by-products, in gestures and sound. The story of language is the story of the *use* made of these occurrences; a use that is eventual, as well as eventful. Those rival accounts of the origin of languages that go by the nicknames of bow-wow, pooh-pooh, and ding-dong theories are not in fact theories of the origin of *language*. They are accounts, of some plausibility, of how and why certain sounds rather than others were selected to signify objects, acts and situations. If the mere existence of sounds of these kinds constituted language, lower animals might well converse more subtly and fluently than man. But they became language only when used within a context of mutual assistance and direction. The latter are alone of prime importance in considering the transformation of organic gestures and cries into names, things with significance—the origin of language.

While signaling acts are a material condition of language they are not language nor yet are they its *sufficient* condition. Only from an external standpoint is the original action even a signal; the response of other animals to it is not to a sign, but, by some preformed mechanism, to a direct stimulus. By habit, by conditioned reflex, hens run to the farmer when he makes a clucking noise, or when they hear the rattle of grain in a pan. When the farmer raises his arms to throw the grain they scatter and fly, to return only when the movement ceases. They act as if alarmed; his movement is thus not a sign of food; it is a stimulus that evokes flight. But a human infant learns to discount such movements; to become interested in them as events preparatory to a desired consummation; he learns to treat them as signs of an ulterior event so that his response is to their meaning. He treats them as means to consequences. The hen's activity is egocentric; that of the human being is participative. The latter puts himself at the standpoint of a situation in which two parties share. This is the essential peculiarity of language, or signs.

The heart of language is not "expression" of something antecedent, much less expression of antecedent thought. It is communication; the establishment of coöperation in an activity in which there are partners, and in which the activity of each is modified and regulated by partnership. To fail to understand is to fail to come into agreement in action; to misunderstand is to set up action at cross purposes. Take speech as behavioristically as you will, including the elimination of all private mental states, and it remains true that it is markedly distinguished from the signaling acts of animals. Meaning is not indeed a psychic existence; it is primarily a property of behavior, and secondarily a property of objects. But the behavior of which it is a quality is a distinctive behavior; coöperative, in that response to another's act involves contemporaneous response to a thing as entering into the other's behavior, and this upon both sides. It is difficult to state the exact physiological mechanism which is involved. But about the fact there is no doubt. It constitutes the intelligibility of acts and things. Possession of the capacity to engage in such activity is intelligence. Intelligence and meaning are natural consequences of the peculiar form which interaction sometimes assumes in the case of human beings.

IV · Mind and Consciousness*

Popular psychology and much so-called scientific psychology have been pretty thoroughly infected by the idea of the separateness of mind and body. This notion of their separation inevitably results in creating a dualism between "mind" and "practice," since the latter must operate through the body. The idea of the separation perhaps arose, in part at least, from the fact that so much of mind at a given time is aloof from action. The separation, when it is once made, certainly confirms the theory that mind, soul, and spirit can exist and go through their operations without any interaction of the organism with its environment. The traditional notion of leisure is thoroughly infected by contrast with the character of onerous labor.

It seems to me, accordingly, that the idiomatic use of the word "mind" gives a much more truly scientific, and philosophic, approach to the actual facts of the case than does the technical one. For in its non-technical use, "mind" denotes every mode and variety of interest in, and concern for, things: practical, intellectual, and emotional. It never denotes anything self-contained, isolated from the world of persons and things, but is always used with respect to situations, events, objects, persons and groups. Consider its inclusiveness. It signifies memory. We are reminded of this and that. Mind also signifies attention. We not only keep things in mind, but we bring mind to bear on our problems and perplexities. Mind also signifies purpose; we have a mind to do this and that. Nor is mind in these operations something purely intellectual. The mother minds her baby; she cares for it with affection. Mind is care in the sense of solicitude, anxiety, as well as of active looking after things that need to be tended; we mind our

* From *Art as Experience*, pp. 262-266; *Experience and Nature*, pp. 305-08.

step, our course of action, emotionally as well as thoughtfully. From giving heed to acts and objects, mind comes also to signify, to obey—as children are told to mind their parents. In short "to mind" denotes an activity that is intellectual, to *note* something; affectional, as caring and liking, and volitional, practical, acting in a purposive way.

Mind is primarily a verb. It denotes all the ways in which we deal consciously and expressly with the situations in which we find ourselves. Unfortunately, an influential manner of thinking has changed modes of action into an underlying substance that performs the activities in question. It has treated mind as an independent entity *which* attends, purposes, cares, notices, and remembers. This change of ways of responding to the environment into an entity from which actions proceed is unfortunate, because it removes mind from necessary connection with the objects and events, past, present and future, of the environment with which responsive activities are inherently connected. Mind that bears only an accidental relation to the environment occupies a similar relation to the body. In making mind purely immaterial (isolated from the organ of doing and undergoing), the body ceases to be living and becomes a dead lump. This conception of mind as an isolated being underlies, for example, the conception that esthetic experience is merely something "in mind," and strengthens the conception which isolates the esthetic from those modes of experience in which the body is actively engaged with the things of nature and life. It takes art out of the province of the live creature.

In the idiomatic sense of the word "substantial," as distinct from the metaphysical sense of a substance, there is something substantial about mind. Whenever anything is undergone in consequence of a doing, the self is modified.

The modification extends beyond acquisition of greater facility and skill. Attitudes and interests are built up which embody in themselves some deposit of the meaning of things done and undergone. These funded and retained meanings become a part of the self. They constitute the capital with which the self notes, cares for, attends, and purposes. In this substantial sense, mind forms the background upon which every new contact with surroundings is projected; yet "background" is too passive a word, unless we remember that it is active and that, in the projection of the new upon it, there is assimilation and reconstruction both of background and of what is taken in and digested.

This active and eager background lies in wait and engages whatever comes its way so as to absorb it into its own being. Mind as background is formed out of modifications of the self that have occurred in the process of prior interactions with environment. Its animus is toward further interactions. Since it is formed out of commerce with the world and is set toward that world nothing can be further from the truth than the idea which treats it as something self-contained and self-enclosed. When its activity is turned upon itself, as in meditation and reflective speculation, its withdrawal is only from the immediate scene of the world during the time in which it turns over and reviews material gathered from that world.

Different kinds of minds are named from the different interests that actuate the gathering and assemblage of material from the encompassing world: the scientific, the executive, the artistic, the business mind. In each there is a preferential manner of selection, retention, and organization. These inherent impulses become mind when they fuse with a particular background of experience. Of this background, traditions form a large part. It is not enough to have direct contacts and observations, indispensable as these are. Even the work of an original individual may be relatively thin, as well as tending to the bizarre, when it is not informed with a wide and varied experience of the tradition in which he operates. For each great tradition is itself an organized habit of vision and of methods of ordering and conveying material. As this habit enters into native temperament and constitution it becomes an essential ingredient of the mind. Peculiar sensitiveness to certain aspects of nature is thereby developed into a power.

Mind is more than consciousness, because it is the abiding even though changing background of which consciousness is the foreground. Mind changes slowly through the joint tuition of interest and circumstance. Consciousness is always in rapid change, for it marks the place where the formed disposition and the immediate situation touch and interact. It is the continuous readjustment of self and the world in experience. "Consciousness" is the more acute and intense in the degree of the readjustments that are demanded, approaching the nil as the contact is frictionless and interaction fluid. It is turbid when meanings are undergoing reconstruction in an undetermined direction, and becomes clear as a decisive meaning emerges.

The relation between mind and consciousness may be indicated by a familiar happening. When we read a book, we are immediately conscious of meanings that present themselves, and vanish. These meanings existentially occurring are *ideas*. But we are capable of getting ideas from what is read because of an organized system of meanings of which we are not at any one time completely aware. Our mathematical or political "mind" is the system of such meanings as possess and determine our particular apprehensions or ideas. There is, however, a continuum or spectrum between this containing system and the meanings which, being focal and urgent, are the ideas of the moment. There is a contextual field between the latter and those meanings which determine the habitual direction of our conscious thoughts and supply the organs for their formation. One great mistake in the orthodox psychological tradition is its exclusive preoccupation with sharp focalization to the neglect of the vague shading off from the foci into a field of increasing dimness.

Discrimination in favor of the clearly distinguished has a certain practical justification, for the vague and extensive background is present in every conscious experience and therefore does not define the character of any one in particular. It represents that which is being used and taken for granted, while the focal phase is that which is imminent and critical. But this fact affords no justification for neglect and denial in theory of the dim and total background of consciousness of every distinct thought. If there were a sharp division between the ideas that are focal as we read a certain section of a book and what we have already read, if there were not carried along a sense of the latter, what we now read could not take the form of an idea. Indeed, the use of such words as context and background, fringe, etc., suggests something too external to meet the facts of the case. The larger system of meaning suffuses, interpenetrates, colors what is now and here uppermost; it gives them sense, feeling, as distinct from signification.

Change the illustration from reading a book to seeing and hearing a drama. The emotional as well as intellectual meaning of each presented phase of a play depends upon the operative presence of a continuum of meanings.

If we have to remember what has been said and done at any particular point, we are not aware of what is now said and done; while without its suffusive presence in what is now said and done we lack clew to its meaning. Thus the purport of past affairs is present in the momentary cross-sectional idea in a way which is more intimate, direct and pervasive than the way of recall. It is positively and integrally carried in and by the incidents now happening; these incidents are, in the degree of genuine dramatic quality, fulfillments of the meanings constituted by past events; they also give this system of meanings an unexpected turn, and constitute a suspended and still indeterminate meaning, which induces alertness, expectancy. It is this double relationship of continuation, promotion, carrying forward, and of arrest, deviation, need of supplementation, which defines that focalization of meanings which is consciousness, awareness, perception. Every case of consciousness is dramatic; drama is an enhancement of the conditions of consciousness.

These considerations enable us to give a formal definition of consciousness in relation to mind or meanings. Consciousness, an idea, is that phase of a system of meanings which at a given time is undergoing re-direction, transitive transformation. The current idealistic conception of consciousness as a power which modifies events is an inverted statement of this fact. To treat consciousness as a power accomplishing the change, is but another instance of the common philosophic fallacy of converting an eventual function into an antecedent force or cause. Consciousness *is* the meaning of events in course of remaking; its "cause" is only the fact that this is one of the ways in which nature goes on. In a proximate sense of causality, namely as place in a series history, its causation is the need and demand for filling out what is indeterminate.

V · The Unity of the Human Being*

I make no apology for starting out by saying that we have no words that are prepared in advance to be fit for framing and expressing sound and tested ideas about the unity of the human being, the wholeness of the self. If we ask an economist "What is money?" the proper official reply is that it is a medium of exchange. The answer does not stand in the way of a great deal of money being accumulated by using it to obstruct the processes of exchange. Similarly, we say that words are a means of communicating ideas. But upon some subjects—and the present one falls in this class—the words at our disposal are largely such as to *prevent* the communication of ideas. The words are so loaded with associations derived from a long past that instead of being tools for thought, our thoughts become subservient tools of words.

The meanings of such words as soul, mind, self, unity, even body, are hardly more than condensed epitomes of mankind's agelong efforts at interpretation of its experience. These efforts began when man first emerged from the state of the anthropoid ape. The interpretations which are embodied in the words that have come down to us are the products of desire and hope, of chance circumstance and ignorance, of the authority exercised by medicine men and priests as well as of acute observation and sound judgment.

Physicists had in the beginning a like problem. They are solving it by the invention of technical terms and a technical language. Symbols have, in principle, only the meanings that are put upon them because of special inquiries engaged in. It will be a long time before anything of this sort will be accomplished for human beings. To expel tra-

* An address delivered before the College of Physicians in St. Louis, April 21, 1937. First time published.

ditional meanings and replace them by ideas that are products of controlled inquiries is a slow and painful process.

Doubtless advance is possible, and will be made, by invention of words that are not charged with the debris of man's past experience. But it is also possible that this process cannot be carried with safety as far as it can be with physical things. Our technical terms might easily represent such artificial constructions that they would fail to help us in dealings with human beings—with the John Smiths and Susan Joneses with whom we rub elbows in daily life.

The words in which I try to communicate ideas to you are, then, at best, but means of stimulating personal observation and reflection. This statement holds even of the phrase "the unity of the human being." At first, the words have only a meaning derived from a contrast effect. The idea of man as an integral whole is projected against a background of beliefs about man which are chiefly of emotional origin and force; against belief in a dualism that was the expression of religious and moral institutions and traditions.

The phrase "unity of man" has at first, accordingly, a negative meaning. It expresses a way of *not* talking about soul *and* body, body *and* mind. The word "unity" is a protest against the canonized dualism expressed in the presence of the word "and." Nevertheless, the split expressed in this word is so engrained in our emotional and intellectual habits that no sooner have we consciously rejected it in one form than it recurs in another. The dualism is found today even among those who have abandoned its earlier manifestations. It is shown in separations made between the structural and the functional; between the brain and the rest of the body; between the central nervous system and the vegetative nervous system and viscera; and most fundamentally, between the organism and the environment. For the first of each of these pairs of terms —structure, brain, organism—retains something of the isolation and alleged independence that used to belong to the "soul" and the "mind" and later to "consciousness."

While it is necessary to advance from the negative meaning of the phrase "the unity of man" the idea of unity also has its perils. For it has taken on associations during centuries of philosophic discussion that make it a dangerous word. It has become almost an invitation to set an abstraction in place of concrete phenomena. You and I can easily think of comprehensive systems—psychiatric, therapeutic, philosophical and psychological—suggested in the first place by undoubted facts, which under the protecting shield of the idea of unity, have been built up so as to force the facts, disguising and distorting them. At the present time there is a revulsion against the endless splitting up of human beings into bits. It is going on with respect to cells, structures and organs, sensations, ideas, reflexes; and with respect to atoms and electrons. The phrase "unity of man" is a protest against analysis of man into separate ultimate elements, as well as against the traditional split into body and soul. But it is easier, much easier, to set up the idea of unity in a vague way, than it is to translate it into definite facts.

"Unity of the human being" only indicates, at best, a point of view, and the point of view has no meaning save as it is used as a vantage point from which to observe and interpret actual phenomena.

We often hear such phrases as the unity of a family, the unity of a nation. These phrases stand for something Yet in the history of social and political speculation, men have allowed the words to take the bit in their teeth and run away from inquiry into the actual facts to which they refer. These instances of the use of "unity" may, however, provide a suggestion from which it is safe to set out. Whatever else the unity is or is not, it at least means the way in which a number of different persons and things work together toward a common end. This *working together* exists in action, operation, not as a static object or collection of objects. It is this kind of unity that seems to me to give the clew to understanding the unity of the human being.

We can recognize and identify a man as a single object, a numerical unit, by observation which marks out boundaries, as we note that the bounded object moves as a whole. In that way you recognize me as a single object standing here on the stage before you. That is the way in which we recognize a rock, tree or house as a single object, as a unity and whole. But that which makes a rock a single whole is the interaction of swarms of molecules, atoms, and electrons; its unity is an affair of the way elements work together. The boundaries by which we mark off a human being as a unit are very different from the energies and organization of energies that make *him* a *unified human being*. We can observe the boundaries at a single moment. We can grasp the unity only, so to speak, longitudinally—only as something that goes on in a stretch of time. It is not found in any number of cross-sectional views.

Nevertheless, if we could look into the minds of our neighbors, I think we should not be much surprised to find in them quite frequently the notion that a man exists within the boundaries which are visible, tangible, and observable. In a word, the man is identified with what is underneath his skin. We incline to suppose that we would know all about him if we could find out everything that is happening in his brain and other parts of his nervous system: in his glands, muscles, viscera, heart and lungs and so on.

Now up to a certain point we are on the right track, provided we emphasize sufficiently the interaction, the working together, of all these diverse processes. We can get a better idea of the unity of the human being as we know more about all these processes and the way they work together, as they check, and stimulate one another and bring about a balance. But the one positive point I wish to present is that while this is necessary it is not enough. We must observe and understand these internal processes and their interactions from the standpoint of their interaction with what is going on outside the skin—with that which is called the *environment*—if we are to obtain a genuine conception of the unity of the human being.

Our attitude with respect to this matter is a strange mixture. In special points we take for granted the inclusion of the conditions and energies that are outside the boundaries set by the skin. No one supposes for a moment that there can be respiration without the surrounding air; or that the lungs are anything more than organs of interaction with what is outside the body. No one thinks of separating the processes of digestion from connection with foodstuffs derived by means of other organs from the environment. We know that eye, ear and hand, and somatic musculature, are concerned with objects and events outside the boundaries of the body. These things we take for granted so regularly and unconsciously that it seems foolish to mention them. Physiologists at least recognize that what is true of breathing and digestion holds also of the circulation of fluids that goes on entirely within the body, although the connection of these processes with environing conditions is a stage more indirect. The structure and processes of the central nervous system do not have that immediate connection with the outside world that the peripheral neural structures have.

Yet an authority upon the anatomy and physiology of the nervous system recently used these words: "Every movement is the result of the messages which pass from the central mass of nerve cells to the muscles, and the outgoing messages are varied according to the reports submitted by the sense organs. These show what is happening in the world outside, and the nervous system must evolve a plan of action appropriate to the occasion."*

That movements affected by the muscles have to do, directly and indirectly, with activities of seeking, defense, and taking possession of energies of the outside world is obvious. The central nervous system has the function of evolving the plans and procedures that take effect in dealing with outside conditions as they are reported through sense organs—and I suppose it would be admitted that these reports vary, depending upon what the body was doing previously in connection with outside conditions.

In other words, with respect to every special set of organic structures and processes, we take it for granted that things beyond the body are involved in interaction with those inside the body, and that we cannot understand the latter in isolation. I did not give the quotation from Dr. Adrian because it presented a novel revelation. Actually, it states a fact so generally recognized as to be a commonplace. The strangeness of the mixture of which I spoke consists in the fact that while we recognize the involvement of conditions external to the body in all organic processes, when they are taken one by one, we often fail to recognize and act upon the idea as an inclusive principle

* N. Adrian, *Harvard Tercentenary Publications*, vol. I, p. 4.

by which to understand the unity of man and the disorders which result from disruption of this unity.

Whole philosophical systems have been built up, for
example, by treating thinking, especially in so-called abstract ideas, as having no connection with the activities
the body executes in the environment in use and enjoyment of the conditions it presents. There is many a mathematician who would be shocked if he were told that his
constructions had anything to do with activities carried
on in the environment. Yet we know that neural structures
and processes developed in control and use of the environment are the organs of all thinking. Even some who call
themselves behaviorists, who pride themselves on their
strictly scientific attitude, have identified the behavior
about which they talk with the behavior of the nervous
system in and by itself. Having, for example, identified
thought with language—a position for which much may be
said—they go on to locate language in the vocal cords,
ignoring the transaction of communication in which, directly and indirectly, other human beings take part. It
may even be that on occasion physicians think of diseases,
and even psychical disorders, as something that goes on
wholly inside the body, so that they treat what goes on
outside as, at most, an external cause rather than a constituent and interacting factor in the disease.

At all events, there is a good deal of description and
interpretation in many fields in which the structural and
static lord it over the active and functioning. Whenever
we find this to be the case we may be sure that some structure of the body has been described and interpreted in
isolation from its connection with an activity in which an
environment plays an integral part.

On the other hand, when physicians proceed to regulate
the diet, sleep and exercise of patients, when they inquire

into and give advice about their habits, they are dealing with the "use of the self" in its active functional connection with the outside world. What, then, I am urging is simply the systematic and constant projection of what is here involved into all our observations, judgments and generalizations about the unity and the breakdowns of unity of human beings. For its implications are that all beliefs and practices which gratuitously split up the unity of man have their final root in the separation of what goes on inside the body from integrated interaction with what goes on outside.

This abstract principle becomes concrete as soon as one thinks not of environment in general, but of the human environment—that which is formed by contacts and relations with our human fellows. Psychiatrists have made us familiar with disturbances labeled "withdrawal from reality." They have pointed out the role of this withdrawal in many pathological occurrences. What are these withdrawals but cases of the interruption or cessation of "the active operative presence of environing conditions in the activities of a human being"? What are the resulting pathological phenomena but evidences that the self loses its integrity *within itself* when it loses integration with the medium in which it lives?

It is only necessary to think of those mild instances of withdrawal, forming ordinary day-dreaming and fantasy building, to appreciate that the environment which is involved is human or social. When a person builds up not only a systematized delusion of wealth but engages in a day-dream in which he has come into possession of a large sum of money, it is not the physical money he is thinking of, but the prestige and power it gives him over his fellows. If a fantasy becomes habitual and controlling, it brings about, sooner or later, retraction from even the physical

environment. But these withdrawals from physical surroundings originate in disturbances of relationship with
the human environment. They go back to such things as
pettings and coddlings, personal rejections, failure to win
recognition and approvals, fear of those in authority, frustration of hope and desire by social conditions.

We may then anticipate a time when our entire traditional psychology will be looked upon as extraordinarily
one-sided in its exclusive concern with actions and reactions of human beings with their physical surroundings to
the neglect of interpersonal relationships. We have, to be
sure, reached a point where we have chapters and books
entitled "social psychology." But we are far from having
reached the point in which it is seen that the whole difference between animal and human psychology is constituted
by the transforming effect exercised upon the former by
intercourse and association with other persons and groups
of persons. For, apart from unconditioned reflexes, like the
knee-jerk, it may be questioned whether there is a single
human activity or experience which is not profoundly affected by the social and cultural environment. Would we
have any intellectual operations without the language
which is a social product? As for our emotional life, permit me to cite two passages written by a physician: "Contact with human beings is the stimulus that elicits emotional and visceral reactions. It is not the clatter of railways and motors, this 'fast hurrying age in which we live'
so often spoken of; it is rather the pride, the envy, the
ambition, the rage, the disappointment, the defeat that develop in purely human relations that stir the viscera"; and
again: "There is an immense amount of hokum uttered
about the psychological tensions caused by our swiftly
moving era, as though the telephone, the radio, and the
electric refrigerator were instruments that could swerve

the viscera. The emotional life does not actually hinge on machinery but on the type of response to living situations, situations that for the most part are created by human contacts."*

I do not believe I am going beyond the implications of these passages when I say that the operation of "living situations created by human contacts" is the only intelligible ground upon which we can distinguish between what we call the *higher* and the *lower* (the physical on one side and the ideal and "spiritual" on the other) in human experience. The occurrence of a sensation, for example, may be described as an interaction between certain neural processes and certain vibrations. The principle involved here is the same in animals and in man. But the *significance* of a quality of red depends upon the part it plays in the customary uses and enjoyments of the social group of which a person is a member. To a bull, its presence is a purely physiological stimulus. For a child, it may be that a dress, worn perhaps only on a festal occasion or a ribbon worn for adornment in the presence of others, is that which fixes the significance of red. When we wait in an automobile for a traffic light to turn, red is still a physiological stimulus. But it has its *significance* in terms of adaptation of the behavior of individuals to one another. The emotional import of red in a red, white and blue flag to a patriotic American citizen is surely not native in physiological structure.

Examples do not *prove* the principle laid down. But I do believe that reflection upon these and similar cases will show that the only verifiable basis we have for marking off the experiences that have practical, emotional and intellectual significance from those which do not is the in-

* Houston, *The Art of Treatment,* pp. 348-349; p. 450.

fluence of cultural and social forces upon internal physio.
logical processes.

At least, what I have said is a challenge to produce any
instance of an experience having so-called ideal or even
"spiritual" meaning that cannot be accounted for on this
ground. Otherwise we must have recourse to the old division between soul and body. Take the case of those who revolt against the old dualism, and who because of their revolt imagine they must throw away and deny the existence
of all phenomena that go by the names of "higher," intellectual and moral. Such persons exist. They suppose they
are not scientific unless they reduce everything to the exclusively somatic and physiological. This procedure is a
conspicuous instance of what must happen when observation, description and interpretation of human events are
confined to what goes on under the skin to the exclusion
of their integrated interaction with environmental conditions, particularly the environment formed by other human beings. Knowledge of strictly somatic organs and
processes is certainly necessary for scientific understanding of "higher" phenomena. But only half-way science
neglects and rules out the other factor.

We may reject the traditional dualism. In my conviction
we should reject it. We cannot be scientific save as we
seek for the physiological, the physical factor in every
emotional, intellectual and volitional experience. As more
is known of this factor, more intellectual capital and more
resources of control are at our command. In the case of the
physician especially is it so true as to be a truism, that the
more anatomical, chemical and immunological information
he has, the better prepared is he for his work. And it is
also true that our knowledge of social relations and their
effects upon native and original physiological processes is

scanty and unorganized in comparison with the physical knowledge at command.

But in view of the role played by human contacts and relations in developing and sustaining the emotional and intellectual quality of human experience on one side, and in bringing disturbance and disorder into it on the other, this fact is all the more reason for devoting constant attention to the as yet relatively unknown factor in the case of every human being who comes under observation. This need cannot be met by knowledge of even the most up-to-date scientific psychology which now exists. For, unfortunately, this psychology suffers for the most part from exactly the one-sided concern in question: the failure to take into account the operations and effects of relationships between human beings.

To me, a layman, it appears that physicians have a unique opportunity for building up just the kind of knowledge that is now so largely lacking. Physicians are the persons who have the most direct, intimate and continued contact with the living situations in which the problem is most acutely present. Since the decline of the influence of priest and pastor, no other professional body is in a position to make such a contribution and render such a service—though it should be acknowledged that the group of teachers also has an opportunity of which it fails to take adequate advantage. I am impressed, as every one else naturally is, with the now oft-made statement that at least one-half of those who consult physicians are suffering from ailments having a strictly neural basis and that show psychopathological traits. Indeed, this statement seems to me to be actually a great under-statement of the seriousness of the situation.

For the conception of good health is so vague that most persons do not go to see a physician until their ailments have become rather extreme. No one knows how many who do not come suffer loss of energy, efficiency and happiness because of difficulties that have a psychic aspect. A fair guess would be, I take it, that this group includes, in some degree, everybody. If the factor of human relationships is as fundamental in production of these disorders, slight and intense, as we now have reason to believe is the case, it is impossible to over-state the extent or the importance of the concrete body of knowledge physicians can build up.

At this point, I must invite your attention again to the dubious and controversial state in which the whole matter of so-called higher mental states finds itself, and the disastrous consequences that ensue. In saying this, I am not referring to controversies between philosophers and psychologists about the relations of the mental and physical—controversies that pass under the names of interactionism, parallelism, materialism, etc. I think these are of no great practical importance save as they reflect certain divisions of a more practical kind that are rife. There are some who are so impressed with the influence of mind upon body, and with opportunities for exploiting those whose troubles have a marked psychic phase, that they form special cults, while there are others who react to the opposite extreme. They will have as little to do with anything that cannot be located and described in some specific lesion or specific somatic process. The respective views and practices of the two groups supply ammunition the one to the other. It is this situation which gives practical point to the search for the unity of the human being, and that justifies presentation of the view that unity and its breakdowns must be sought for in the interactions between individual organisms and their environment, especially that of human associations.

In this connection may be cited some rather simple facts which indicate that there is nothing mystical or meta-physical in acknowledgment of the "higher" functions when they are interpreted by the view that has been set forth. When one of us steps on the toes of his neighbor in a crowded place, we offer regrets—since otherwise we are likely to subject ourselves to sour looks, irritation and re-sentment. A strictly physical event has taken place, but even from an ordinary common-sense point of view, the physical is not the whole of the matter. The presence of a personal relation introduces a qualifying factor.

If I stub my toe on an object left lying on a public street my response is quite different from that which hap-pens if I stub it on the root of a tree in climbing a moun-tain. In the first case, I feel the object has no business there, that somebody has been careless, that something ought to be done about such things. A personal element has modified an otherwise purely physical reaction. In the second case, I may suffer equal or greater pain, but if the pain should be partly that of irritation, the irritation is directed at my own awkwardness. Again, I can hardly imagine anyone thinking that the pain a child suffers from colic is of the same quality as the agony of torture a sen-sitive child suffers from an act of injustice or unkindness at the hands of some one from whom he expects different treatment.

Sentimentalists put the pain a dog suffers in undergoing an act of vivisection on the same level with what a parent suffers who has lost a child. To other people, this attitude seems to display rather extraordinary callousness towards distinctively human pain—a pain that is what it is because the processes of the human organism have been pro-foundly affected by relations with another human being.

The point illustrated by these simple instances is that

the whole ground for the difference between a sensation and an emotion seems to lie in the absence or presence of a response coming from another human being. Persons acquire likes and dislikes for physical objects and physical scenes. But upon the strictly physical level—meaning by that, one in which a human relation plays no part—a dislike is expressed by simple rejection, as, say, one "doesn't like olives or castor oil." When the rejection is accompanied by emotion, even a layman suspects there is something back of it. When such cases are studied it is found, practically without exception, that the object rejected is of a kind that has been socially "conditioned," as the term goes. The strong stirring of emotional interest that most people experience when revisiting, after a lapse of years, the scenes of their childhood is called out by the fact that these scenes were not merely the theatrical stage and properties of early activities, but have entered so intimately into personal relations with father and mother, brother and sisters and playmates, that it is impossible to draw a line and say the influence of the physical ends *here* and that of the social begins *there*.

It may be assumed, I suppose, that all students of biology and physiology now take it for granted that there is no recollection apart from a modification of neural structure undergone in consequence of an earlier experience. But would any one attempt to read off from even the most minute and thorough study of the structure of the modified neural cells and the chemical processes going on in them, what the nature of the earlier experience was? I imagine not; I also imagine that there are few indeed who think any possible future development of knowledge will enable this result to come to pass, making it possible to reconstitute a past experience on the basis of what can be observed about an organic structure. What is relied upon is personal contact and communication; while personal attitudes, going deeper than the mere asking of questions, are needed in order to establish the confidence which is a condition for the patient's telling the story of his past. The organic modification is there—it is indispensable. Without it the patient would not be able to recall past incidents. But this is not enough. The physical fact has to be taken up into the context of personal relations between human being and human being before it becomes a fact of the living present.

Intellectual operations are discriminative. They bring things to a focus, to a point, down, as we say, to brass tacks. But when we are angry or depressed, we are mad or sad all over. A *physical* pain may be more or less definitely and accurately localized. But while we may feel severe local burnings and constrictions in the case of severe grief, there is also a *total* experienced response which occurs. It operates through organic structures, especially the viscera. But if it were referred exclusively to them, to the exclusion of a relation to another human being, it would not *be* grief.

I remember as a child trying to reinstate on a hot summer's day, the experience of a day in winter—not just to recall intellectually that it was cold, but to recover the actual feeling. Naturally, I never succeeded, and I was not aware that if I had succeeded it would have been an hallucination. What I was attempting, was, however, hardly more difficult than it is, when we are experiencing an intense emotion, to procure or permit the introduction of ideas associated with another mood. Elation and strong hope take such possession of us that we cannot entertain ideas that suggest the possibility of failure as long as the emotions last. The person depressed with melancholy has no room for any idea connected with success or vital hope.

Now it may be doubted whether there is any idea, no matter how intellectual and abstract, that is not tinged, if not dyed, with the emotion that arises from the total response of the whole organism to its surroundings. The cases, then, of the influence of emotions upon somatic conditions, even to the extent of producing neuroses in some cases and creating astonishing recoveries in other cases, have nothing mystical or metaphysical about them. They are expressions of the regulative force exercised over partial organic processes by the whole of which they are part.

I have given a number of illustrations which by themselves are commonplace rather than weighty. The principle they are intended to illustrate is, however, of the utmost importance. For, as I have suggested, disruption of the unity of the self is not limited to the cases that come to physicians and institutions for treatment. They accompany every disturbance of normal relations of husband and wife, parent and child, group and group, class and class, nation and nation. Emotional responses are so total as compared with the partial nature of intellectual responses, of ideas and abstract conceptions, that their consequences are more pervasive and more enduring. I can, accordingly, think of nothing of greater practical importance than that the psychic effects of human relationships, normal and abnormal, should be the object of continued study, including among the consequences the indirect somatic effects.

We cannot understand the conditions that produce unity in the human being and conditions that generate disruptions of this unity until the study of the relations of human beings to one another is as alert, as unremitting and as systematic as the study of strictly physiological and anatomical processes and structures has been in the past. The plea is not for any remission on the side of the latter. But we need to recover from the impression, now widespread, that the essential problem is solved when chemical, immunological, physiological and anatomical knowledge is sufficiently obtained. We cannot understand and employ this knowledge until it is placed integrally in the context of what human beings do to one another in the vast variety of their contacts and associations. Until the study is undertaken in this spirit, neglect will continue to breed and so support belief in the soul, and in mental processes supposed to be wholly independent of the organism and of somatic conditions. The consequences produced by this belief will not be confined to errors of theory. The practical outcome is division and conflict in action where unity and coöperation of social effort are urgently required.

I may rephrase what I have said by saying that the fine old saying "A sound mind in a sound body" can and should be extended to read "A sound human being in a sound human environment." The mere change in wording is nothing. A change in aims and methods of working in that direction would mean more than any of us can estimate. Is there anything in the whole business of politics, economics, morals, education—indeed in any profession —save the construction of a proper human environment that will serve, by its very existence, to produce sound and whole human beings, who in turn will maintain a sound and healthy human environment?

This is the universal and all-embracing human task. Its first phase cannot be turned over to politicians alone, and the second phase cannot be turned over to parents, preachers and teachers alone. It is not the peculiar business of any special calling. Yet perhaps there is none who is more intimately concerned with aiding production of sound individual human beings than the physician. There is none who has as much opportunity as he has to observe the effects of disturbed and disordered human relations in production of warped and divided personalities. The situations with which physicians deal are not artificially produced in laboratories. They are nevertheless sufficiently extensive and varied to provide conditions of control like those of the laboratory.

I cannot help thinking that the idea of preventive medicine and of public health policies have bearing and application upon the point made. Because of the unity of the human being, because of the inextricable intertwining of the physical and psychical in his make-up, the work of preventing disease and disorders is not completely done when the physical conditions of sanitation, pure water, and milk supply, sewage disposal, and healthy homes have been attended to. The social conditions that make for the production of unified, effective, reasonably happy human beings and their opposites, come into the picture also. We may solve the problems of dualism and monism satisfactorily in theory, and yet not have touched the sore spots in society and in individuals, and this is the place where they have to be resolved practically.

The one way out of the division that has disclosed itself to my vision is continued and persistent study of the concrete effect of social situations upon individual human beings, and the effect, in return, of human beings upon social relations. I believe that the honor of addressing this College of Physicians has not unduly influenced me and I hope you will not believe otherwise if I close by saying that in this study the physician has a position of unique opportunity and responsibility.

CHAPTER SIXTEEN

THINKING AND MEANING

I · The Natural History of Thinking*

·THE man in the street, when asked what he thinks
about a certain matter, often replies that he does not think
at all; he knows. The suggestion is that thinking is a case
of active uncertainty set over against conviction or unquestioning assurance. When he adds that he does not
have to think, but knows, the further implication is that
thinking, when needed, leads to knowledge; that its purpose or object is to secure stable equilibrium. It is my
purpose to show some of the main stages through which
thinking, understood in this way, actually passes in its attempt to reach its most effective working; that is, the
maximum of reasonable certainty.

I wish to show how a variety of modes of thinking,
easily recognizable in the progress of both the race and the
individual, may be identified and arranged as successive
species of the relationship which doubting bears to assurance; as various ratios, so to speak, which the vigor of
doubting bears to mere acquiescence. The presumption is
that the function of questioning is one which has continually grown in intensity and range, that doubt is continually chased back, and, being cornered, fights more
desperately, and thus clears the ground more thoroughly.
Its successive stations or arrests constitute stages of think·

* From *Essays in Experimental Logic*, pp. 183-216.

ing. Or to change the metaphor, just in the degree that what has been accepted as fact—the object of assurance—loses stable equilibrium, the tension involved in the questioning attitude increases, until a readjustment gives a new and less easily shaken equilibrium.

The natural tendency of man is not to press home a doubt, but to cut inquiry as short as possible. The practical man's impatience with theory has become a proverb; it expresses just the feeling that, since the thinking process is of use only in substituting certainty for doubt, any apparent prolongation of it is useless speculation, wasting time and diverting the mind from important issues. To follow the line of least resistance is to cut short the stay in the sphere of doubts and suggestions, and to make the speediest return into the world where one can act. The result, of course, is that difficulties are evaded or surmounted rather than really disposed of. Hence, in spite of the opposition of the would-be practical man, the needs of practice, of economy, and of efficiency have themselves compelled a continual deepening of doubt and widening of the area of investigation.

It is within this evolution that we have to find our stages of thinking. The initial stage is where the doubt is hardly endured but not entertained; it is no welcome guest but an intruder, to be got rid of as speedily as possible. Development of alternative and competitive suggestions, the forming of suppositions (of ideas), goes but a little way. The mind seizes upon the nearest or most convenient instrument of dismissing doubt and reattaining security. At the other end is the definitive and conscious search for problems, and the development of elaborate and systematized methods of investigation—the industry and technique of science. Between these limits come processes which have started out upon the path of doubt and inquiry, and then halted by the way.

In the first stage of the journey, beliefs are treated as something fixed and static. To those who are using them they are simply another kind of fact. They are used to settle doubts, but the doubts are treated as arising quite outside the ideas themselves. Nothing is further from recognition than that ideas themselves are open to doubt, or need criticism and revision. Indeed, the one who uses static meanings is not even aware that they originated and have been elaborated for the sake of dealing with conflicts and problems. The ideas are just "there," and they may be used like any providential dispensation to help men out of the troubles into which they have fallen.

Words are generally held responsible for this fixation of the idea, for this substantiation of it into a kind of thing. A long line of critics has made us familiar with the invincible habit "of supposing that wherever there is a name there is some reality corresponding to it"; of supposing that general and abstract words have their equivalent objects somewhere *in rerum natura,* as have also singular and proper names. We know with what simplicity of self-confidence the English empirical school has accounted for the ontological speculation of Plato. Words tend to fix intellectual contents, and give them a certain air of independence and individuality. That some truth is here expressed there can be no question.

But this petrifying influence of words is after all only a superficial explanation. There must be some meaning present or the word could not fix it; there must be something which accounts for the disposition to use names as a medium of fossilization. There is, in truth, a certain real fact—an existent reality—behind both the word and the meaning it stands for. This reality is social usage. The person who consults a dictionary *is* getting an established fact when he turns there for the definition of a term. He finds the sense in which the word is currently used.

Ideas, or meanings fixed in terms, show the scheme of values which the community uses in appraising matters that need consideration and which are indeterminate or unassured. They are held up as standards for all its members to follow. The fixed or static idea is a fact expressing an established social attitude, a custom. It is not merely verbal, because it denotes a force which operates, as all customs do, in controlling particular cases. But since it marks a mode of interpretation, a scheme for assigning values, a way of dealing with doubtful cases, it falls within the sphere of ideas. Or, coming to the life of the individual, the fixed meaning represents, not a state of consciousness fixed by a name, but a recognition of a habitual way of belief: a habit of understanding.

With advance in the complexity of life, however, rules accumulate, and discrimination—that is, a certain degree of inquiring and critical attitude—enters in. Inquiry takes effect, however, in seeking among a collection of fixed ideas just the one to be used, rather than in directing suspicion against any rule or idea as such, or in an attempt to discover or constitute a new one. It is hardly necessary to refer to the development of casuistry, or to the multiplication of distinctions within dogmas, or to the growth of ceremonial law in cumbrous detail, to indicate what the outcome of this logical stage is likely to be. The essential thing is that doubt and inquiry are directed neither at the nature of the intrinsic fact itself, nor at the value of the idea as such, but simply at the manner in which one is attached to the other. Thinking falls outside both fact and idea, and into the sphere of their external connection. It is still a fiction of judicial procedure that there is already in existence some custom or law under which every possible dispute—that is, every doubtful or unassured case—falls, and that the judge only declares which law is applicable in the particular case. This point of view has tremendously affected the theory of logic in its historic development.

In this form ideas become the chief instruments of social conservation. Judicial decision and penal correction are restricted and ineffective methods of maintaining social institutions unchanged, compared with instilling in advance uniform ideas—fixed modes of appraising all social questions and issues. These set ideas thus become the embodiment of the values which any group has realized and intends to perpetuate. The fixation supports them against dissipation through attrition of circumstance, and against destruction through hostile attack.

When we substitute for ideas as uniform rules by which to decide doubtful cases that making over of ideas which is requisite to make them fit, the quality of thought alters. We may fairly say that we have come into another stage. The idea is now regarded as essentially subject to change, as a manufactured article needing to be made ready for use. As the scheduled stock of fixed ideas grows larger, their application to specific questions becomes more difficult, prolonged, and roundabout. There has to be a definite hunting for the specific idea which is appropriate; there has to be comparison of it with other ideas. This comes to involve a certain amount of mutual compromise and modification before selection is possible. The idea thus gets somewhat shaken. It has to be made over so that it may harmonize with other ideas possessing equal worth. Often the very accumulation of fixed ideas commands this reconstruction. The dead weight of the material becomes so great that it cannot sustain itself without a readjustment of the center of gravity. Simplification and systematization are required, and these call for reflection. Critical cases come up in which the fiction of an idea or rule already in existence cannot be maintained. It is impossible to conceal that old ideas have to be radically modified before the situation can be dealt with. The friction of circumstance melts away their congealed fixity. Judgment becomes legislative.

Discussion is an apt name for this attitude of thought. It is bringing various beliefs together; shaking one against another and tearing down their rigidity. It is conversation of thoughts; it is dialogue—the mother of dialectic in more than the etymological sense. No process is more recurrent in history than the transfer of operations carried on between different persons into the arena of the individual's own consciousness. The discussion which at first took place by bringing ideas from different persons into contact, by introducing them into the forum of competition, and by subjecting them to critical comparison and selective decision, finally became a habit of the individual with himself. He became a miniature social assemblage, in which pros and cons were brought into play struggling for the mastery—for final conclusion. In some such way we conceive reflection to be born.

It is evident that discussion, the agitation of ideas, if judged from the standpoint of the older fixed ideas, is a destructive process. Ideas are not only shaken together and apart, they are so shaken in themselves that their whole validity becomes doubtful. Mind, and not merely beliefs, becomes uncertain. The attempt to harmonize different ideas means that in themselves they are discrepant. The search for a conclusion means that accepted ideas are only points of view, and hence personal affairs. Needless to say it was the Sophists who emphasized and generalized this negative aspect—this presupposition of loss of assurance, of inconsistency, of "subjectivity." They took it as applying not only to this, that, and the other idea, but to ideas as ideas. Since ideas are no longer fixed contents, they are just expressions of an individual's way of thinking. Lacking inherent value, they merely express the interests that induce the individual to look this way rather than that. They are made by the individual's point of view, and hence will be unmade if he can be led to change his point of view. Where all was fixity, now all is instability: where all was certitude, nothing now exists save opinion based on prejudice, interest, or arbitrary choice.

The modern point of view, while condemning sophistry, yet often agrees with it in limiting the reflective attitude as such to self-involution and self-conceit. Such wholesale depreciation ignores the value inherent even in the most subjective reflection, for it takes the settled estate which is proof that thought is not needed, or that it has done its work, as if it supplied the standard for the occasions in which problems are hard upon us, and doubt is rife. It takes the conditions which come about after and because we have thought to measure the conditions which call out thinking. Whenever we really need to reflect, we cannot appeal directly to the "fact," for the adequate reason that the stimulus to thinking arises just because "facts" have slipped away from us.

Reflection involves running over various ideas, sorting them out, comparing one with another, trying to get one which will unite in itself the strength of two, searching for new points of view, developing new suggestions; guessing, suggesting, selecting, and rejecting. The greater the problem, and the greater the shock of doubt and resultant confusion and uncertainty, the more prolonged and more necessary is the process of "mere thinking." It is a more obvious phase of biology than of physics, of sociology than of chemistry; but it persists in established sciences.

What makes the essential difference between modern research and the reflection of, say, the Greeks, is not the absence of "mere thinking," but the presence of conditions for testing its results; the elaborate system of checks and balances found in the technique of modern experimentation. The thinking process does not now go on endlessly in terms of itself, but seeks outlet through reference to particular experiences. It is tested by this reference; not, however, as if a theory could be tested by directly comparing it with facts—an obvious impossibility—but through use in facilitating commerce with facts. It is tested as glasses are tested; things are looked at through the medium of specific meanings to see if thereby they assume a more orderly and clearer aspect, if they are less blurred and obscure.

Discussion, whether with ourselves or others, goes on by suggestion of clews, as the uppermost object of interest opens a way here or there. It is discursive and haphazard. This gives it the devious tendency indicated in Plato's remark that it needs to be tied to the post of reason. It needs, that is, to have the ground or basis of its various component statements brought to consciousness in such a way as to define the exact value of each. The Socratic contention is the need of compelling the common denominator, the common subject, underlying the diversity of views to exhibit itself. It alone gives a sure standard by which the claims of all assertions may be measured. Until this need is met, discussion is a self-deceiving play with unjudged, unexamined matters, which, confused and shifting, impose themselves upon us.

By Aristotle's time the interest was not so much in the existence of standards of decision in cases of doubt and dispute as in the technique of their use. The judge was firmly seated on the bench. The parties in controversy recognized his jurisdiction, and their respective claims were submitted for adjudicature. The need was for rules of procedure by which the judge might, in an obvious and impartial way, bring the recognized universal or decisive law to bear upon particular matters. Hence the elaboration of those rules of evidence, those canons of demonstrative force, which are the backbone of the Aristotelian logic. There was a code by which to decide upon the admissibility and value of proffered testimony—the rules of the syllogism. The judge knew what testimony to permit, when and how it should be introduced, how it could be impeached or have its competence lessened, and how the evidence was to be arranged so that a summary would also be an exhibit of its value in establishing a conclusion.

This means that there now is a distinctive type of thinking marked off from mere discussion and reflection. It may be called either reasoning or proof. It is reasoning when we think of the regularity of the method for getting at and employing the unquestioned grounds which give validity to other statements. It is proof as regards the degree of logical desert thereby measured out to such propositions. Proof is the acceptance or rejection justified through the reasoning.

Reasoning is marshaling a series of terms and propositions until we can bind some doubtful fact firmly to an unquestioned, although remote, truth; it is the regular way in which a certain proposition is brought to bear on a precarious one, clothing the latter with something of the peremptory quality of the former. So far as we reach this result, and so far as we can exhibit each step in the nexus and be sure it has been rightly performed, we have proof.

Hence the Aristotelian logic necessarily assumes certain

first or fundamental truths unquestioned and unquestionable, self-evident and self-evidencing, neither established nor modified by thought, but standing firm in their own right. This assumption was not, as modern dealers in formal logic would sometimes have it, an external psychological or metaphysical attachment to the theory of reasoning, to be omitted at will from logic as such. It was an essential factor of knowledge that there should be necessary propositions directly apprehended by reason and particular ones directly apprehended by sense. Reasoning could then join them. Without the truths we have only the play of subjective, arbitrary, futile opinion. *Judgment* has not taken place, and assertion is without warrant. Hence the scheduling of first truths is an organic part of any reasoning which is occupied with securing demonstration, surety of assent, or valid conviction. To deny the necessary place of ultimate truths in the logical system of Aristotle and his followers is to make them players in a game of social convention. It is to overlook, to invert, the fact that they were sincerely concerned with the question of attaining the grounds and process of assurance. Hence they were obliged to assume primary intuitions, metaphysical, physical, moral, and mathematical axioms, in order to get the pegs of certainty to which to tie the bundles of otherwise contingent propositions.

It is not enough, however, to account for the ultimate major premises, for the unconditioned grounds upon which credibility is assigned. We have also to report where the other side comes from: matters so uncertain in themselves as to require that they have their grounds supplied from outside. The answer in the Aristotelian scheme is an obvious one. It is the very nature of sense, of ordinary experience, to supply us with matters which in themselves are only contingent. There is a certain portion of the intellectual sphere, that derived from experience, which is infected throughout by its unworthy origin. It stands forever condemned to be merely empirical—particular, more or less accidental, inherently irrational. You cannot make gold from dross, and the best that can be done for and with material of this sort is to bring it under the protection of truth which has warrant and weight in itself.

We may now characterize this stage of thinking with reference to our original remark that different stages denote various degrees in the evolution of the doubt-inquiry function. As compared with the period of fixed ideas, doubt is awake, and inquiry is active, but in itself it is rigidly limited. On one side it is bounded by fixed ultimate truths, whose very nature is that they cannot be doubted, which are not products or functions in inquiry, but bases that investigation fortunately rests upon. In the other direction all "matters of fact," all "empirical truths" belong to a particular sphere or kind of existence, and one intrinsically open to suspicion. The region is condemned in a wholesale way. In itself it exhales doubt; it cannot be reformed; it is to be shunned, or, if this is not possible, to be escaped from by climbing up a ladder of intermediate terms until we lay hold on the universal. The very way in which doubt is objectified, taken all in a piece, marks its lack of vitality. It is arrested and cooped up in a particular place. As with any doubtful character, the less of its company the better. Uncertainty is not realized as a necessary instrument in compelling experienced matters to reveal their meaning and inherent order.

This limitation upon inquiry settles the interpretation to be given thought at this stage. Thought has only a formal value. It is of service in exhibiting and arranging grounds upon which any particular proposition may be acquitted or condemned, upon which anything already current may be assented to, or upon which belief may reasonably be withheld.

The metaphor of the law court is apt. There is assumed some matter to be either proved or disproved. As matter, as content, it is furnished. It is not to be found out. In the law court it is not a question of discovering what a man specifically is, but simply of finding reasons for regarding him as guilty or innocent. There is no all-around play of thought directed to the institution of something as fact, but a question of whether grounds can be adduced justifying acceptance of some proposition already set forth. The significance of such an attitude comes into relief when we contrast it with what is done in the laboratory. In the laboratory there is no question of proving that things are just thus and so, or that we must accept or reject a given statement; there is simply an interest in finding out what sort of things we are dealing with. Any quality or change that presents itself may be an object of investigation, or may suggest a conclusion; for it is judged, not by reference to pre-existent truths, but by its suggestiveness, by what it may lead to. The mind is open to inquiry in any direction.

Hence the fourth stage—covering what is popularly known as inductive and empirical science. Thought takes the form of inference instead of proof. Proof, as we have already seen, is accepting or rejecting a given proposition on the ground of its connection or lack of connection with some other proposition conceded or established. But inference does not terminate in any given proposition; it is after precisely those not given. It wants more facts, different facts. Thinking in the mode of inference insists upon terminating in an intellectual advance, in a consciousness of truths hitherto escaping us. Our thinking must not now "pass" certain propositions after challenging them, must not admit them because they exhibit certain credentials, showing a right to be received into the upper circle of intellectual society. Thinking endeavors to compel things as they present themselves, to yield up something hitherto obscure or concealed. This advance and extension of knowledge through thinking seems to be well designated by the term "inference." It does not certify what is otherwise doubtful, but "goes from the known to the unknown." It aims at pushing out the frontiers of knowledge, not at marking those already attained with signposts. Its technique is not a scheme for assigning status to beliefs already possessed, but is a method for making friends with facts and ideas hitherto alien. Inference reaches out, fills in gaps. Its work is measured not by the patents of standing it issues, but by the material increments of knowledge it yields. *Inventio* is more important than *judicium*, discovery than "proof."

With the development of empirical research, uncertainty or contingency is no longer regarded as infecting in a wholesale way an entire region, discrediting it save as it can be brought under the protecting aegis of universal truths as major premises. Uncertainty is now a matter of detail. It is the question whether the particular fact is really what it has been taken to be. It involves contrast, not of a fact as a fixed particular over against some fixed universal, but of the existing mode of apprehension with another possible better apprehension.

The emphasis of modern science upon control flows from the same source. Interest is in the new, in extension, in discovery. Inference is the advance into the unknown, the use of the established to win new worlds from the void. This requires and employs regulation—that is, method—

in procedure. There cannot be a blind attack. A plan of campaign is needed. Hence the so-called practical applications of science, the Baconian "knowledge is power," the Comteian "science is prevision," are not extralogical addenda or supererogatory benefits. They are intrinsic to the logical method itself, which is just the orderly way of approaching new experiences so as to grasp and hold them.

The attitude of research is necessarily toward the future. The application of science to the practical affairs of life, as in the stationary engine, or telephone, does not differ in principle from the determination of wave-lengths of light through the experimental control of the laboratory. Science lives only in arranging for new contacts, new insights. The school of Kant agrees with that of Mill in asserting that judgment must, in order to be judgment, be synthetic or instructive; it must extend, inform, and purvey. When we recognize that this service of judgment in effecting growth of experience is not accidental, but that judgment means exactly the devising and using of suitable instrumentalities for this end, we remark that the so-called practical uses of science are only the further and freer play of the intrinsic movement of discovery itself.

We began with the assumption that thought is to be interpreted as a doubt-inquiry function, conducted for the purpose of arriving at that mental equilibrium known as assurance or knowledge. We assumed that various stages of thinking could be marked out according to the amount of play which they give to doubt, and the consequent sincerity with which thinking is identified with free inquiry. Modern scientific procedure, as just set forth, seems to define the ideal or limit of this process. It is inquiry emancipated, universalized, whose sole aim and criterion is discovery, and hence it marks the terminus of our description.

II · The Pattern of Reflective Thinking*

Persons do not just think at large, nor do ideas arise out of nothing. Go through your own experience and you will not find a case where thinking started up out of nothing. Sometimes the train of thoughts will have taken you so far away from the starting point that you will have diffi- culty in getting back to that prior something out of which the thinking arose, but follow the thread far enough and you will find some situation that is directly experienced, something undergone, done, enjoyed, or suffered, and not just thought of. Reflection is occasioned by the character of this primary situation. It does not merely *grow out* of it, but it *refers back* to it. Its aim and outcome are de- cided by the situation out of which it arose.

The function of reflection is to bring about a new situa- tion in which the difficulty is resolved, the confusion cleared away, the trouble smoothed out, the question it puts answered. Any particular process of thinking natu- rally comes to its close when the situation before the mind is settled, decided, orderly, clear, for then there is nothing to call out reflection until a new bothersome or doubtful situation arises.

The function of reflective thought is, therefore, to trans- form a situation in which there is experienced obscurity, doubt, conflict, disturbance of some sort, into a situation that is clear, coherent, settled, harmonious.

When a situation arises containing a difficulty or per- plexity, the person who finds himself in it may take one of a number of courses. He may dodge it, dropping the ac- tivity that brought it about, turning to something else. He may indulge in a flight of fancy, imagining himself power- ful or wealthy, or in some other way in possession of the

* From *How We Think* (revised edition), pp. 99-116.

means that would enable him to deal with the difficulty. Or, finally, he may face the situation. In this case, he begins to reflect.

The moment he begins to reflect, he begins of necessity to observe in order to take stock of conditions. Some of these observations are made by direct use of the senses; others by recollecting observations previously made either by himself or by others. The person who had the engagement to keep, notes with his eyes his present location, recalls the place where he should arrive at one o'clock, and brings back to mind the means of transportation with which he is acquainted and their respective locations. In this way he gets as clear and distinct a recognition as possible of the nature of the situation with which he has to deal. Some of the conditions are obstacles and others are aids, resources. No matter whether these conditions come to him by direct perception or by memory, they form the "*facts* of the case." They are the things that are *there,* that have to be reckoned with. Like all facts, they are stubborn. They cannot be got out of the way by magic just because they are disagreeable. It is no use to *wish* they did not exist or were different. They must be taken for just what they are. Hence observation and recollection must be used to the full so as not to glide over or to mistake important features. Until the habit of thinking is well formed, facing the situation to discover the facts requires an effort. For the mind tends to dislike what is unpleasant and so to sheer off from an adequate notice of that which is especially annoying.

Along with noting the conditions that constitute the facts to be dealt with, suggestions arise of possible courses of action. These alternative suggestions compete with one another. By comparison he judges which alternative is best, which one is the more likely to give a satisfactory solution. The comparison takes place indirectly. The moment one thinks of a possible solution and holds it in suspense, he turns back to the facts. He has now a point of view that leads him to new observations and recollections and to a reconsideration of observations already made in order to test the worth of the suggested way out. Unless he uses the suggestion so as to guide to new observations instead of exercising suspended judgment, he accepts it as soon as it presents itself. Then he falls short of truly reflective thought. The newly noted facts may (and in any complex situation surely will) cause new suggestions to spring up. These become clews to further investigation of conditions. The results of this survey test and correct the proposed inference or suggest a new one. This continuous interaction of the facts disclosed by observation and of the suggested proposals of solution and the suggested methods of dealing with conditions goes on till some suggested solution meets all the conditions of the case and does not run counter to any discoverable feature of it.

A technical term for the observed facts is data. The data form the material that has to be interpreted, accounted for, explained; or, in the case of deliberation as to what to do or how to do it, to be managed and utilized. The suggested solutions for the difficulties disclosed by observation form *ideas*. Data (facts) and ideas (suggestions, possible solutions) thus form the two indispensable and correlative factors of all reflective activity. The two factors are carried on by means respectively of *observation* (in which for convenience is included memory of prior observations of similar cases) and *inference*. The latter runs beyond what is actually noted, beyond what is found, upon careful examination, to be actually present. It relates, therefore, to what is *possible*, rather than to what is actual. It proceeds by anticipation, supposition, conjecture, imagination. All foresight, prediction, planning, as well as theorizing and speculation, are characterized by excursion from the actual into the possible. Hence what is inferred demands a double test: first, the process of form-ing the idea or supposed solution is checked by constant cross reference to the conditions observed to be actually present; secondly, the idea *after* it is formed is tested by *acting* upon it, overtly if possible, otherwise in imagina-tion. The consequences of this action confirm, modify, or refute the idea.

We shall illustrate what has been said by a simple case. Suppose you are walking where there is no regular path. As long as everything goes smoothly, you do not have to think about your walking; your already formed habit takes care of it. Suddenly you find a ditch in your way. You think you will jump it (supposition, plan); but to make sure, you survey it with your eyes (observation), and you find that it is pretty wide and that the bank on the other side is slippery (facts, data). You then wonder if the ditch may not be narrower somewhere else (idea), and you look up and down the stream (observation) to see how matters stand (test of idea by observation). You do not find any good place and so are thrown back upon forming a new plan. As you are casting about, you dis-cover a log (fact again). You ask yourself whether you could not haul that to the ditch and get it across the ditch to use as a bridge (idea again). You judge that idea is worth trying, and so you get the log and manage to put it in place and walk across (test and confirmation by overt action).

If the situation were more complicated, thinking would of course be more elaborate. You can imagine a case in which making a raft, constructing a pontoon bridge, or making a dugout would be the ideas that would finally come to mind and have to be checked by reference to conditions of action (facts). Simple or complicated, relating to what to do in a practical predicament or what to infer in a scientific or philosophic problem, there will always be the two sides: the conditions to be accounted for, dealt with, and the ideas that are plans for dealing with them or are suppositions for interpreting and explaining the phenomena.

The two limits of every unit of thinking are a perplexed, troubled, or confused situation at the beginning and a cleared-up, unified, resolved situation at the close. The first of these situations may be called *pre*-reflective. It sets the problem to be solved; out of it grows the question that reflection has to answer. In the final situation the doubt has been dispelled; the situation is *post*-reflective; there results a direct experience of mastery, satisfaction, enjoyment. Here, then, are the limits within which reflection falls.

In between, as states of thinking, are (1) *suggestions*, in which the mind leaps forward to a possible solution; (2) an intellectualization of the difficulty or perplexity that has been *felt* (directly experienced) into a *problem* to be solved, a question for which the answer must be sought; (3) the use of one suggestion after another as a leading idea, or *hypothesis*, to initiate and guide observation and other operations in collection of factual material; (4) the mental elaboration of the idea or supposition as an idea or supposition (*reasoning*, in the sense in which reasoning is a part, not the whole, of inference); and (5) testing the hypothesis by overt or imaginative action.

The five phases, terminals, or functions of thought that we have noted do not follow one another in a set order. On the contrary, each step in genuine thinking does something to perfect the formation of a suggestion and promote its change into a leading idea or directive hypothesis. It does something to promote the location and definition of the problem. Each improvement in the idea leads to new observations that yield new facts or data and help the mind judge more accurately the relevancy of facts already at hand. The elaboration of the hypothesis does not wait until the problem has been defined and adequate hypothesis has been arrived at; it may come in at any intermediate time. And as we have just seen, any particular overt test need not be final; it may be introductory to new observations and new suggestions, according to what happens in consequence of it.

There is, however, an important difference between test by overt action in practical deliberations and in scientific investigations. In the former the practical commitment involved in overt action is much more serious than in the latter. An astronomer or a chemist performs overt actions, but they are for the sake of knowledge; they serve to test and develop his conceptions and theories. In practical matters, the main result desired lies outside of knowledge. One of the great values of thinking, accordingly, is that it defers the commitment to action that is irretrievable, that, once made, cannot be revoked. Even in moral and other practical matters, therefore, a thoughtful person treats his overt deeds as experimental so far as possible; that is to say, while he cannot call them back and must stand their consequences, he gives alert attention to what they teach him about his conduct as well as to the non-intellectual consequences. He makes a problem out of consequences of conduct, looking into the causes from which they probably resulted, especially the causes that lie in his own habits and desires.

In complicated cases some of the five phases are so extensive that they include definite subphases within themselves. In this case it is arbitrary whether the minor functions are regarded as parts or are listed as distinct phases. There is nothing especially sacred about the number five.

In conclusion, we point out that the five phases of reflection that have been described represent only in outline the indispensable traits of reflective thinking. In practice, two of them may telescope, some of them may be passed over hurriedly, and the burden of reaching a conclusion may fall mainly on a single phase, which will then require a seemingly disproportionate development. No set rules can be laid down on such matters. The way they are managed depends upon the intellectual tact and sensitiveness of the individual. When things have come out wrong, it is, however, a wise practice to review the methods by which the unwise decision was reached, and see where the misstep was made.

III · The Development of Meanings*

The idea put forth about the connection of meaning with language is not to be confused with traditional nominalism. It does not imply that meaning and essence are adventitious and arbitrary. The defect of nominalism lies in its virtual denial of interaction and association. It regarded the word not as a mode of social action with which to realize the ends of association, but as an expression of a ready-made, exclusively individual, mental state; sensation, image or feeling, which, being an existence, is necessarily particular. For the sound, gesture, or written mark which is involved in language is a particular existence. But as such it is not a *word*, and it does not become a word by declaring a mental existence; it becomes a word by gaining meaning; and it gains meaning when its use establishes a genuine community of action. Interaction, op-

* From *Experience and Nature*, pp. 182-196; 317-326.

erative relationship, is as much a fact about events as are particularity and immediacy. Language and its consequences are characters taken on by natural interaction and natural conjunction in specified conditions of organization. Nominalism ignores organization, and thus makes nonsense of meanings.

Language is specifically a mode of interaction of at least two beings, a speaker and a hearer; it presupposes an organized group to which these creatures belong, and from whom they have acquired their habits of speech. It is therefore a relationship, not a particularity. This consideration alone condemns traditional nominalism. The meaning of signs moreover always includes something common as between persons and an object. When we attribute meaning to the speaker as *his* intent, we take for granted another person who is to share in the execution of the intent, and also something, independent of the persons concerned, through which the intent is to be realized. Persons and things must alike serve as means in a common, shared consequence. This community of partaking is meaning.

The discussion has explicitly gone on the basis that *what* is perceived are meanings, rather than just events or existences. In this respect, the view presented agrees with classic teaching, according to which perception, apprehension, lays hold of form, not of matter. I believe this view properly understood is inherently sound; the error in the classic theory lies in its accompanying assumption that all perceptions are intrinsically cognitive.

When it is denied that we are conscious of *events* as such it is not meant that we are not aware of *objects*. Objects are precisely what we are aware of. For objects are events *with* meanings; tables, the milky way, chairs, stars, cats, dogs, electrons, ghosts, centaurs, historic epochs and all the infinitely multifarious subject-matter of discourse designatable by common nouns, verbs and their qualifiers. So intimate is the connection of meanings with consciousness that there is no great difficulty in resolving "consciousness," as a recent original and ingenious thinker has done, into knots, intersections or complexes of universals.

Serious difficulty sets in however when *events* are resolved into such combinations. The matter is referred to here not to be argued; but to indicate that a "realist" has gone even further than the theory now presented goes in identifying the subject-matter of which there is awareness with meanings, or at least with universals which, as simple subject-matter, colors, sounds, etc., and as complex subject-matter, plants, animals, atoms, etc., are precisely the same as meanings. To cause existences in their particularity to disappear into combinations of universals is at least an extreme measure. And the present thesis sticks to the common-sense belief that universals, relations, meanings, are of and about existences, not their exhaustive ingredients.

Common sense has no great occasion to distinguish between bare events and objects; objects being events-with-meanings. Events are present and operative *anyway;* what concerns us is their meanings expressed in expectations, beliefs, inferences, regarding their potentialities. The nearest approach that occurs in ordinary life to making the distinction is when there occurs some brute, dumb shock, which we are constrained to interpret, to assign meaning to, that is, to convert into an object. Such situations supply direct empirical evidence of the difference between events and objects; but common-sense does not need to formulate the difference as a distinction. Events have effects or consequences anyway; and since meaning is awareness of these consequences before they actually occur, reflective inquiry which converts an event into an object is the same thing as finding out a meaning which the event already possesses by imputation. It is the essence of common sense, one might say, to treat potentialities as given actualities; since its interest is universally practical, bent upon fruitage, there is no need to note its bent in any particular case. The eventual outcome is for it the "reality" of the present situation.

But not so with philosophic discourse. Philosophy must explicitly note that the business of reflection is to take events which brutely occur and brutely affect us, to convert them into objects by means of inference as to their probable consequences. These are the meanings imputed to the events under consideration. Otherwise philosophy finds itself in a hopeless impasse. For, apart from making a distinction between events and objects, it has no way of differentiating cognitive from esthetic and literary meanings, and within cognitive meanings it has no way of distinguishing the valid from the invalid. The outcome of failure in this respect is exemplified in those discussions which find an inherent and generic cognitive problem in the occurrence of dreams, reveries and hallucinations, a problem other than the scientific one of ascertaining their antecedents and effects. For if intrinsic cognitive intent is ascribed to all perceptions, or forms of awareness, which are alleged to pick out a "reality" to which they refer as an image or sign, dreams, etc., have to be squared to this assumption. Draw the distinction between events and objects, and dream-objects are just what they are, events with one kind of meaning, while scientific-objects are just what they are, events with another kind of meaning, a kind that involves an extrinsic and additive function not contained in dream-objects.

The same existential events are capable of an infinite number of meanings. Thus an existence identified as "paper," because the meaning uppermost at the moment is "something to be written upon," has as many other explicit meanings as it has important consequences recognized in the various connective interactions into which it enters. Since possibilities of conjunction are endless, and since the consequences of any of them may at some time be significant, its potential meanings are endless. It signifies something to start a fire with; something like snow; made of wood-pulp; manufactured for profit; property in the legal sense; a definite combination illustrative of certain principles of chemical science; an article the invention of which has made a tremendous difference in human history, and so on indefinitely. There is no conceivable universe of discourse in which the thing may not figure, having in each its own characteristic meaning. And if we say that after all it is "paper" which has all these different meanings, we are at bottom but asserting that all the different meanings have a common existential reference, converging to the same vent. We are virtually asserting that the *existence* whose usual, standardized meaning in discourse is paper, also has a multitude of other meanings; we are saying in effect that its existence is not exhausted in its being paper, although paper is its ordinary meaning for human intercourse.

Essence is but a pronounced instance of meaning; to be partial, and to assign *a* meaning to a thing as *the* meaning is but to evince human subjection to bias. Since consequences differ also in their consequence and hence importance, practical good sense may attach to this one-sided partiality, for the meaning seized upon as essence may designate extensive and recurrent consequences. Thus is explained the seeming paradox of the distinction and connection of essence and existence. Essence is never existence, and yet it is the essence, the distilled import, of existence; the significant thing about it, its intellectual voucher, the means of inference and extensive transfer, and object of esthetic intuition. In it, feeling and understanding are one; the meaning of a thing is the sense it makes.

Since the consequences which are liked have an emphatic quality, it is not surprising that many consequences, even though recognized to be inevitable, are regarded as if they were accidental and alien. Thus the very essence of a thing is identified with those consummatory consequences which the thing has when conditions are felicitous. Thus *the* essence, one, immutable and constitutive, which *makes* the thing *what* it is, emerges from the various meanings which vary with varying conditions and transitory intents. When essence is then thought to contain existence as the perfect includes the imperfect, it is because a legitimate, practical measure of reality in terms of importance is illegitimately altered into a theoretical measure.

Every meaning is generic or universal. It is something common between speaker, hearer and the thing to which speech refers. It is universal also as a means of generalization. For a meaning is a method of action, a way of using things as means to a shared consummation, and method is general, though the things to which it is applied are particular. The meaning, for example, of portability is something in which two persons and an object share. But portability after it is once apprehended becomes a way of treating other things; it is extended widely. Whenever there is a chance, it is applied; application ceases only when a thing refuses to be treated in this way. And even then refusal may be only a challenge to develop the meaning of portability until the thing can be transported. Meanings are rules for using and interpreting things; interpretation being always an imputation of potentiality for some consequence.

It would be difficult to imagine any doctrine more absurd than the theory that general ideas or meanings arise by the comparison of a number of particulars, eventuating in the recognition of something common to them all. Such a comparison may be employed to check a suggested widened application of a rule. But generalization is carried spontaneously as far as it will plausibly go; usually much further than it will actually go. A newly acquired meaning is forced upon everything that does not obviously resist its application, as a child uses a new word whenever he gets a chance or as he plays with a new toy. Meanings are self-moving to new cases. In the end, conditions force a chastening of this spontaneous tendency. The scope and limits of application are ascertained experimentally in the process of application. The history of science, to say nothing of popular beliefs, is sufficient indication of the difficulty found in submitting this irrational generalizing tendency to the discipline of experience. To call it *a priori* is to express a fact; but to impute the *a priori* character of the generalizing force of meanings to *reason* is to invert the facts. Rationality is acquired when the tendency becomes circumspect, based upon observation and tested by deliberate experiment.

Meaning is objective as well as universal. Originating as a concerted or combined method of using or enjoying things, it indicates a possible interaction, not a thing in separate singleness. A meaning may not of course have the particular objectivity which is imputed to it, as whistling does not actually portend wind, nor the ceremonial sprinkling of water indicate rain. But such magical imputations of external reference testify to the objectivity of meaning as such. Meanings are naturally the meaning of something or other; difficulty lies in discriminating the right thing. It requires the discipline of ordered and deliberate experimentation to teach us that some meanings delightful or horrendous as they are, are meanings communally developed in the process of communal festivity and control, and do not represent the polities, and ways and means of nature apart from social arts. Scientific meanings were superadded to esthetic and affectional meanings when objects instead of being defined in terms of their consequences in social interactions and discussion were defined in terms of their consequences with respect to one another. This discrimination permitted esthetic and affective objects to be freed from magical imputations, which were due to attributing to them *in rerum natura* the consequences they had in the transmitted culture of the group.

Meanings are objective because they are modes of natural interaction; such an interaction—although primarily between organic beings—as includes things and energies external to living creatures. The regulative force of legal meanings affords a convenient illustration. A traffic policeman holds up his hand or blows a whistle. His act operates as a signal to direct movements. But it is more than an episodic stimulus. It embodies a rule of social action. Its proximate meaning is its near-by consequences in coördination of movements of persons and vehicles; its ulterior and permanent meaning—essence—is its consequence in the way of security of social movements. Failure to observe the signal subjects a person to arrest, fine or imprisonment. The essence embodied in the policeman's whistle is not an occult reality superimposed upon a sensuous or physical flux and imparting form to it; a mysterious subsistence somehow housed within a psychical event. Its essence is the rule, comprehensive and persisting, the standardized habit, of social interaction, and for the sake of which the whistle is used. The pattern, archetype, that forms the essence of the whistle as a particular noise, is an orderly arrangement of the movements of persons and vehicles established by social agreement as its consequence. This meaning is independent of the psychical landscape, the sensations and imagery, of the policeman and others concerned. But it is not on that account a timeless spiritual ghost nor pale logical subsistence divorced from events.

The case is the same with the essence of any non-human event, like gravity, or virtue, or vertebrate. Some consequences of the interaction of things concern us; the consequences are not *merely* physical; they enter finally into human action and destiny. Fire burns and the burning is of moment. It enters experience; it is fascinating to watch swirling flames; it is important to avoid its dangers and to utilize its beneficial potencies. When we name an event, calling it fire, we speak proleptically; we do not name an immediate event; that is impossible. We employ a term of discourse; we invoke a meaning, namely, the potential consequences of the existence. The ultimate meaning of the noise made by the traffic officer is the total consequent system of social behavior, in which individuals are subjected, by means of noise, to social coördination; its proximate meaning is a coördination of the movements of persons and vehicles in the neighborhood and directly affected. Similarly the ultimate meaning, or essence, denominated fire, is the consequences of certain natural events within the scheme of human activities, in the experience of social intercourse, the hearth and domestic altar, shared comfort, working of metals, rapid transit, and other such affairs. "Scientifically," we ignore these ulterior meanings.

And quite properly; for when a sequential order of changes is determined, the final meaning in immediate enjoyments and appreciations is capable of control.

The capacity of essences to enter readily into any number of new combinations, and thereby generate further meanings more profound and far reaching than those from which they sprang, gives them a semblance of independent life and career, a semblance which is responsible for their elevation by some thinkers into a realm separate from that of existence and superior to it. Consider the interpretations that have been based upon such essences as four, plus, the square root of minus one. These are at once so manipulable and so fertile in consequences when conjoined with others that thinkers who are primarily interested in their performances treat them not as significant terms of discourse, but as an order of entities independent of human invention and use. The fact that we can watch them and register what happens when they come together, and that the things that happen are as independent of our volition and expectation as are the discoveries of a geographic exploration, is taken as evidence that they constitute entities having subsistent Being independently not only of us but of all natural events whatever.

Alternatives are too narrowly conceived. Because meanings and essences are not states of mind, because they are as independent of immediate sensation and imagery as are physical things, and because nevertheless they are not physical things, it is assumed that they are a peculiar kind of thing, termed metaphysical, or "logical" in a style which separates logic from nature. But there are many other things which are neither physical nor psychical existences, and which are demonstrably dependent upon human association and interaction. Such things function moreover in liberating and regulating subsequent human intercourse; their essence is their contribution to making that intercourse more significant and more immediately rewarding. Take the sort of thing exemplified in the regulation of traffic. The sound of a whistle is a particular existential event numerically separate, with its own peculiar spatial temporal position. This may not be said of the rule or method of social coöperative interaction which it manifests and makes effective. A continuous way of organized action is not a particular, and hence is not a physical or psychical existence. Yet the consequences of using the method of adjusting movements, so that they do not interfere with one another, have both a physical and a mental phase. Physically, there is modification of the changes in space which would otherwise occur. Mentally, there are enjoyments and annoyances which would not otherwise happen. But no one of these incidents nor all of them put together form the essence or ulterior meaning of the sound of the whistle; they are qualifications of a more secure concert of human activity which, as a consequence of a legal order incarnate in the whistling, forms its significance.

IV · Systems of Meanings and Symbols*

Does the doctrine of the operational and experimentally empirical nature of conceptions break down when applied to "pure" mathematical objects? The key to the answer is to be found in a distinction between operations overtly performed (or imagined to be performed) and operations *symbolically* executed. When we act overtly, consequences ensue; if we do not like them, they are nevertheless there in existence. We are entangled in the outcome of what we do; we have to stand its consequences. We shall put a question that is so elementary that it may seem silly. How

* From *The Quest for Certainty,* pp. 150-166.

can we have an end *in view* without having an end, an existential result, in fact? With the answer to this question is bound up the whole problem of intentional regulation of what occurs. For unless we can have ends-in-view without experiencing them in concrete fact, no regulation of action is possible. The question might be put thus: How can we act without acting, without doing something?

If, by a contradiction in terms, it had been possible for men to think of this question before they had found how to answer it, it would have been given up as insoluble. How can man make an anticipatory projection of the outcome of an activity in such a way as to direct the performance of an act which shall secure or avert that outcome? The solution must have been hit upon accidentally as a by-product, and then employed intentionally. It is natural to suppose that it came as a product of social life by way of communication; say, of cries that having once directed activities usefully without intent were afterwards used expressly for that purpose. But whatever the origin, a solution was found when *symbols* came into existence. By means of symbols, whether gestures, words or more elaborate constructions, we act without acting. That is, we perform experiments by means of symbols which have results which are themselves only symbolized, and which do not therefore commit us to actual or existential consequences. If a man starts a fire or insults a rival, effects follow; the die is cast. But if he rehearses the act in symbols in privacy, he can anticipate and appreciate its results. Then he can act or not act overtly on the basis of what is anticipated and is not there in fact. The invention or discovery of symbols is doubtless by far the single greatest event in the history of man. Without them, no intellectual advance is possible; with them, there is no limit set to intellectual development except inherent stupidity.

For long ages, symbols were doubtless used to regulate activity only *ad hoc;* they were employed incidentally and for some fairly immediate end. Moreover, the symbols used at first were not examined nor settled upon with respect to the office they performed. They were picked up in a casual manner from what was conveniently at hand. They carried all sorts of irrelevant associations that hampered their efficacy in their own special work. They were neither whittled down to accomplish a single function nor were they of a character to direct acts to meet a variety of situations—they were neither definite nor comprehensive. Definition and generalization are incompetent without invention of proper symbols. The loose and restricted character of popular thinking has its origin in these facts; its progress is encumbered by the vague and vacillating nature of ordinary words. Thus the second great step forward was made when special symbols were devised that were emancipated from the load of irrelevancy carried by words developed for social rather than for intellectual purposes, their meaning being helped out by their immediate local context. This liberation from accidental accretions changed clumsy and ambiguous instruments of thought into sharp and precise tools. Even more important was the fact that instead of being adapted to local and directly present situations, they were framed in detachment from direct overt use and *with respect to one another.* One has only to look at mathematical symbols to note that the operations they designate are others of the same kind as themselves, that is, symbolic not actual. The invention of technical symbols marked the possibility of an advance of thinking from the common-sense level to the scientific.

The formation of geometry by the Greeks is probably that which historically best illustrates the transition. Be-

fore this episode, counting and measuring had been employed for "practical" ends, that is, for uses directly involved in near-by situations. They were restricted to particular purposes. Yet having been invented and having
found expression in definite symbols, they formed, as far
as they went, a subject-matter capable of independent
examination. New operations could be performed upon
them. They could, and in no disrespectful sense, be played
with; they could be treated from the standpoint of a fine
art rather than from that of an immediately useful economic craft. The Greeks with their dominant esthetic interest were the ones who took this step. Of the creation of
geometry by the Greeks it has been said that it was stimulated "by the art of designing, guided by an esthetic application of symmetrical figures. The study of such figures, and the experimental construction of tile figures,
decorative borders, conventional sculptures, moldings and
the like had made the early Greeks acquainted not only
with a great variety of regular geometrical forms, but
with techniques by which they could be constructed, compounded and divided exactly, in various ways. Unlike
their predecessors, the Greeks made an intellectual diversion of all they undertook." Having discovered by trial
and error a large number of interrelated properties of figures, they proceeded to correlate these with one another
and with new ones. They effected this work "in ways which
gradually eliminated from their thought about them all
guesswork, all accidental experiences such as errors of actual drawing and measurement, and all ideas except those
which were absolutely essential. Their science thus became a science of ideas exclusively." *

The importance of the intellectual transition from con-

* Barry, *The Scientific Habit of Thought,* New York, 1927, pp.
212-213.

crete to abstract is generally recognized. But it is often misconceived. It is not infrequently regarded as if it signified simply the selection by discriminative attention of some one quality or relation from a total object already sensibly present or present in memory. In fact it marks a change in dimensions. Things are concrete to us in the degree in which they are either means directly used or are ends directly appropriated and enjoyed. Mathematical ideas were "concrete" when they were employed exclusively for building bins for grain or measuring land, selling goods, or aiding a pilot in guiding his ship. They became abstract when they were freed from connection with any particular existential application and use. This happened when operations made possible by symbols were performed exclusively with reference to facilitating and directing other operations *also symbolic in nature*. It is one kind of thing, a concrete one, to measure the area of a triangle so as to measure a piece of land, and another kind—an abstract one—to measure it simply as a means of measuring other areas symbolically designated. The latter type of operation makes possible a system of conceptions related together *as* conceptions; it thus prepares the way for formal logic.

Abstraction from use in special and direct situations was coincident with the formation of a science of ideas, of meanings, whose relations to one another rather than to things was the goal of thought. It is a process, however, which is subject to interpretation by a fallacy. Independence from any specified application is readily taken to be equivalent to independence from application as such; it is as if specialists, engaged in perfecting tools and having no concern with their use and so interested in the operation of perfecting that they carry results beyond any existing possibilities of use, were to argue that therefore they are dealing with an independent realm having no connection with tools or utilities. This fallacy is especially easy to fall into on the part of intellectual specialists. It played its part in the generation of *a priori* rationalism. It is the origin of that idolatrous attitude toward universals so often recurring in the history of thought. Those who handle ideas through symbols as if they were things —for ideas *are* objects of thought—and trace their mutual relations in all kinds of intricate and unexpected relationships, are ready victims to thinking of these objects as if they had no sort of reference to things, to existence.

In fact, the distinction is one between operations to be actually performed and possible operations as such, as merely possible. Shift of reflection to development of possible operations in their logical relations *to one another* opens up opportunities for operations that would never be directly suggested. But its origin and eventual meaning lie in acts that deal with concrete situations. As to origin in overt operations there can be no doubt. Operations of keeping tally and scoring are found in both work and games. No complex development of the latter is possible without such acts and their appropriate symbols. These acts are the originals of number and of all developments of number. There are many arts in which the operations of enumeration characteristic of keeping tally are explicitly used for measuring. Carpentry and masonry for example cannot go far without some device, however rude, for estimating size and bulk. If we generalize what happens in such instances, we see that the indispensable need is that of *adjusting things as means, as resources, to other things as ends.*

The origin of counting and measuring is in economy and efficiency of such adjustments. Their results are expressed by physical means, at first notches, scratches, tying knots; later by figures and diagrams. It is easy to find at least three types of situations in which adjustments of means to ends are practical necessities. There is the case of allotment or distribution of materials; of accumulation of stores against anticipated days of need; of exchange of things in which there is a surplus for things in which there is a deficit. The fundamental mathematical conceptions of equivalence, serial order, sum and unitary parts, of correspondence and substitution, are all implicit in the operations that deal with such situations, although they become explicit and generalized only when operations are conducted symbolically in reference to one another.

The failure of empiricism to account for mathematical ideas is due to its failure to connect them with acts performed. In accord with its sensationalistic character, traditional empiricism sought their origin in sensory impressions, or at most in supposed abstraction from properties antecedently characterizing physical things. Experimental empiricism has none of the difficulties of Hume and Mill in explaining the origin of mathematical truths. It recognizes that experience, the actual experience of men, is one of doing acts, performing operations, cutting, marking off, dividing up, extending, piecing together, joining, assembling and mixing, hoarding and dealing out; in general, selecting and adjusting things as means for reaching consequences. Only the peculiar hypnotic effect exercised by exclusive preoccupation with knowledge could have led thinkers to identify experience with reception of sensations, when five minutes' observation of a child would have disclosed that sensations count only as stimuli and registers of motor activity expended in doing things.

All that was required for the development of mathematics as a science and for the growth of a logic of ideas that is, of implications of operations with respect one to another, was that some men should appear upon the scene who were interested in the operations on their own account, as operations, and not as means to specified particular uses. When symbols were devised for operations cut off from concrete application, as happened under the influence of the esthetic interest of the Greeks, the rest followed naturally. Physical means, the straight edge, the compass and the marker remained, and so did physical diagrams. But the latter were only "figures," images in the Platonic sense. Intellectual force was carried by the operations they symbolized, ruler and compass were only means for linking up with one another a series of operations represented by symbols. Diagrams, etc., were particular and variable, but the operations were uniform and general in their intellectual force—that is, in their relation to other operations.

When once the way was opened to thinking in terms of possible operations irrespective of actual performance, there was no limit to development save human ingenuity. In general, it proceeded along two lines. On the one hand, for the execution of tasks of physical inquiry, special intellectual instrumentalities were needed, and this need led to the invention of new operations and symbolic systems. The Cartesian analytics and the calculuses of Leibniz and Newton are cases in point. Such developments have created a definite body of subject-matter that, historically, is as empirical as is the historic sequence of, say, spinning-machines. Such a body of material arouses need for examination on its own account. It is subjected to careful inspection with reference to the relations found within its own content. Indications of superfluous operations are eliminated; ambiguities are detected and analyzed; massed operations are broken up into definite constituents; gaps and unexplained jumps are made good by insertion of connecting operations. In short, certain canons of rigorous interrelation of operations are developed and the old material is correspondingly revised and extended.

Nor is the work merely one of analytic revision. The detection, for example, of the logical looseness of the Euclidean postulate regarding parallels suggested operations previously unthought of, and opened up new fields—those of the hyper-geometries. Moreover, the possibility of combining various existing branches of geometry as special cases of more comprehensive operations (illustrated by the same instance) led to creation of mathematics of a higher order of generality.

I am not interested in tracing the history of mathematics. What is wanted is to indicate that once the idea of possible operations, indicated by symbols and performed *only* by means of symbols, is discovered, the road is opened to operations of ever-increasing definiteness and comprehensiveness. Any group of symbolic operations suggests further operations that may be performed. *Technical* symbols are framed with precisely this end in view. They have three traits that distinguish them from casual terms and ideas. They are selected with a view to designating unambiguously one mode of interaction and one only. They are linked up with symbols of other operations forming a system such that transition is possible with the utmost economy of energy from one to another. And the aim is that these transitions may occur as far as possible in *any* direction. (1) "Water" for example suggests an indefinite number of acts; seeing, tasting, drinking, washing, without specification of one in preference to another. It also marks off water from other colorless liquids only in a vague way. (2) At the same time, it is restricted; it does not connect the liquid with solid and gaseous forms, and still less does it indicate operations which link the production of water to other things into which its constituents, oxygen and hydrogen, enter. It is isolated instead of being a transitive concept. (3) The chemical conception, symbolized by H_2O, not only meets these two requirements which "water" fails to meet, but oxygen and hydrogen are in turn connected with the whole system of chemical elements and specified combinations among them in a systematic way. Starting from the elements and the relation defined in H_2O, one can, so to speak, travel through all the whole scope and range of complex and varied phenomena. Thus the scientific conception carries thought and action away from qualities which are finalities as they are found in direct perception and use, to the mode of production of these qualities, and it performs this task in a way which links this mode of generation to a multitude of other "efficient" causal conditions in the most economical and effective manner.

Mathematical conceptions, by means of symbols of operations that are irrespective of actual performance, carry abstraction much further; one has only to contrast "2" as attached physically to H, to "2" as pure number. The latter designates an operative relation applic*able* to anything whatsoever, though not actually applied to any specified object. And, of course, it stands in defined relations to all other numbers, and by a system of correspondences with continuous quantities as well. That numbers disregard all qualitative distinctions is a familiar fact. This disregard is the consequence of construction of symbols dealing with possible operations in abstraction from the actuality of performance. If time and knowledge permitted, it could be shown that the difficulties and paradoxes which have been found to attend the logic of number disappear when instead of their being treated as either essences or as properties of things in existence, they are viewed as designations of potential operations. Mathematical space is not a kind of space distinct from so-called physical and empirical space, but is a name given to operations ideally or formally possible with respect to things having spacious qualities: it is not a mode of Being, but a way of thinking things so that connections among them are liberated from fixity in experience and implication from one to another is made possible.

The distinction between physical and mathematical conception may be brought out by noting an ambiguity in the term "possible" operations. Its primary meaning is actually, existentially, possible. Any idea as such designates an operation that *may* be performed, not something in actual existence. The *idea* of the sweetness of, say, sugar, is an indication of the consequences of a possible operation of tasting as distinct from a directly experienced quality. Mathematical ideas are designations of possible operations in another and secondary sense, previously expressed in speaking of the possibility of symbolic operations with respect *to one another*. This sense of possibility is *com*possibility of operations, not possibility of performance with respect to existence. Its test is non-incompatibility. The statement of this test as consistency hardly carries the full meaning. For consistency is readily interpreted to signify the conformity of one meaning with others already had, and is in so far restrictive. "Non-incompatibility" indicates that all developments are welcome as long as they do not conflict with one another, or as long as restatement of an operation prevents actual conflict. It is a canon of liberation rather than of restriction. It may be compared with natural selection, which is a principle of elimination but not one controlling positive development.

Mathematics and formal logic thus mark highly specialized branches of intellectual industry, whose working principles are very similar to those of works of fine art. The trait that strikingly characterizes them is combination of freedom with rigor—freedom with respect to development of new operations and ideas; rigor with respect to formal compossibilities. The combination of these qualities, characteristic also of works of great art, gives the subject great fascination for some minds. But the belief that these qualifications remove mathematical objects from all connection with existence expresses a religious mood rather than a scientific discovery.

The significant difference is that of two types of possibility of operation, material and symbolic. This distinction when frozen into the dogma of two orders of Being, existence and essence, gives rise to the notion that there are two types of logic and two criteria of truth, the formal and the material, of which the formal is higher and more fundamental. In truth, the formal development is a specialized offshoot of material thinking. It is derived ultimately from acts performed, and constitutes an extension of such acts, made possible by symbols, on the basis of congruity with one another. Consequently formal logic represents an analysis of exclusively symbolic operations; it is, in a pregnant and not external sense, symbolic logic. This interpretation of mathematical and (formal) logical ideas is not a disparagement of them except from a mystical point of view. Symbols, as has already been noted, afford the only way of escape from submergence in existence. The liberation afforded by the free symbolism of mathematics is often a means of ulterior return to existential operations that have a scope and penetrating power not otherwise attainable. The history of science is full of illustrations of cases in which mathematical ideas for which no physical application was known suggested in time new existential relations.

The theory which has been advanced of the nature of essences (universals, invariants) may be tested by comparing the conditions which symbolic operations fulfill with the attributes traditionally imputed to the former. These attributes are ideality, universality, immutability, formality, and the subsistence of relations of implication that make deduction possible. There is a one-to-one correspondence between these characters and those of objects of thought which are defined in terms of operations that are compossible with respect to one another.

The correspondence will be approached by pointing out the traits of a machine which marks its structure in view of the function it fulfills. It is obvious that this structure can be understood not by sense but only by *thought* of the relations which the parts of the machine sustain to one another, in connection with the work the machine as a whole performs (the consequences it effects). Sensibly, one is merely overwhelmed in the presence of a machine by noises and forms. Clarity and order of perceived objects are introduced when forms are judged in relation to operations, and these in turn in relation to work done. Movements may be seen in isolation, and products, goods turned out, may be perceived in isolation. The machine is *known* only when these are *thought* in connection with one another. In this thought, motions and parts are judged as *means;* they are referred intellectually to something else; to think of anything as means is to apprehend an object in *relation.* Correlatively, the physical effect is judged as *consequence*—something related. The relation of means-consequence may thus justifiably be termed ideal in the sense of ideational.

Operations as such, that is, as connective interactions,

are uniform. Physically and sensibly, a machine changes through friction, exposure to weather, etc., while products vary in quality. Processes are local and temporal, particular. But the relation of means and consequence which defines an operation remains one and the same in spite of these variations. It is a universal. A machine turns out a succession of steel spheres, like ball-bearings. These closely resemble one another, because they are products of like process. But there is no absolute exactitude among them. Each process is individual and not exactly identical with others. But the *function* for which the machine is designed does not alter with these changes; an operation, being a relation, is not a process. An operation determines any number of processes and products all differing from one another; but *being* a telephone or a cutting tool is a self-identical universal, irrespective of the multiplicity of special objects which manifest the function.

The relation is thus invariant. It is eternal, not in the sense of enduring throughout all time, or being everlasting like an Aristotelian species or a Newtonian substance, but in the sense that an operation as a relation which is grasped in thought is independent of the instances in which it is overtly exemplified, although its meaning is found only in the *possibility* of these actualizations.

The relation, between things as means and things as consequences, which defines a machine is ideal in another sense. It is the standard by which the value of existential processes are estimated. The deterioration or improvement in use of a concrete machine and the worth of an invention are judged by reference to efficiency in accomplishment of a function. The more adequately the functional relation can be apprehended in the abstract, the better can the engineer detect defects in an existent machine and proper improvements in it. Thus the thought of it operates as a model; it has an archetypal character with respect to particular machines.

Thought of an object as an ideal therefore determines a characteristic internal structure or form. This formal structure is only approximated by existing things. One may conceive of a steam engine which has a one hundred per cent efficiency, although no such ideal is even remotely approached in actuality. Or, one may like Helmholtz conceive an ideal optical apparatus in which the defects of the existing human eye are not found. The ideal relationship of means to ends exists as a formal possibility determined by the nature of the case even though it be not thought of, much less realized in fact. It subsists as a possibility, and as a possibility it is in its formal structure necessary. That is to say, the conditions which have to be met and fulfilled in the idea of a machine having an efficiency of one hundred per cent are set by the necessities of the case; they do not alter with defects in our apprehension of them. Hence essences may be regarded as having Being independent of and logically prior to our thought of them. There is, however, in this fact nothing of the mystery or transcendental character which is often associated with it. It signifies that *if* one is to attain a specified result one must conform to the conditions which are means of securing this result; *if* one is to get the result with the maximum of efficiency, there are conditions having a necessary relationship to that intent.

This necessity of a structure marked by formal relationships which fulfill the conditions of serving as means for an end, accounts for the relations of implication which make deduction possible. One goes into a factory and finds that the operation of reaching an end, say, making in quantity shoes of a uniform standard, is subdivided into a number of processes, each of which is adapted to the one which precedes, and, until the final one, to that which follows. One does not make a miracle or mystery of the fact that while each machine and each process is physically separate, nevertheless all are adapted to one another. For he knows that they have been designed, through a "rationalization" of the undertaking, to effect this end.

The act of knowing is also highly complex. Experience shows that it also may be best effected by analysis into a number of distinct processes, which bear a serial relation to one another. Terms and propositions which symbolize the possible operations that are to control these processes are designed so that they will lead one to another with the maximum of definiteness, flexibility and fertility: In other words, they are constructed with reference to the function of implication. Deduction or dialectic is the operation of developing these implications, which may be novel and unexpected just as a tool often gives unexpected results when working under new conditions. One is entitled to marvel at the constructive power with which symbols have been devised having far-reaching and fruitful implications. But the wonder is misdirected when it is made the ground for hypostatizing the objects of thought into a realm of transcendent Being.

This phase of the discussion is not complete till it has been explicitly noted that all general conceptions (ideas, theories, thought) are hypothetical. Ability to frame hypotheses is the means by which man is liberated from submergence in the existences that surround him and that play upon him physically and sensibly. It is the positive phase of abstraction. But hypotheses are conditional; they have to be tested by the consequences of the operations they define and direct. The discovery of the value of hypothetical ideas when employed to suggest and direct concrete processes, and the vast extension of this operation in the modern history of science, mark a great emancipation and correspondent increase of intellectual control. But their final value is not determined by their internal elaboration and consistency, but by the consequences they effect in existence as that is perceptibly experienced. Scientific conceptions are not a revelation of prior and independent reality. They are a system of hypotheses, worked out under conditions of definite test, by means of which our intellectual and practical traffic with nature is rendered freer, more secure and more significant.

Our discussion has been one-sided in that it has dealt with the matter of conceptions mainly in reference to the "rationalistic" tradition of interpretation. The reasons for this emphasis are too patent to need exposition. But before leaving the topic, it should be noted that traditional empiricism has also misread the significance of conceptions or general ideas. It has steadily opposed the doctrine of their *a priori* character; it has connected them with experience of the actual world. But even more obviously than the rationalism it has opposed, empiricism has connected the origin, content and measure of validity of general ideas with *antecedent* existence. According to it, concepts are formed by comparing particular objects, already perceived, with one another, and then eliminating the elements in which they disagree and retaining that which they have in common. Concepts are thus simply memoranda of identical features in objects already perceived; they are conveniences, bunching together a variety of things scattered about in concrete experience. But they have to be *proved* by agreement with the material of particular *antecedent* experiences; their value and function are essentially retrospective. Such ideas are dead, incapable of performing a regulative office in new situations. They are "empirical" in the sense in which the term is opposed to scientific—that is, they are mere summaries of results obtained under more or less accidental circumstances.

CHAPTER SEVENTEEN

PRINCIPLES OF LOGIC*

I · The Genesis of Logical Forms†

INQUIRY, in spite of the diverse subjects to which it applies, and the consequent diversity of its special techniques, has a common structure or pattern. This common structure is applied both in common sense and science, although because of the nature of the problems with which they are respectively concerned, the emphasis upon the factors involved varies widely in the two modes.

Logical forms accrue to subject-matter when the latter is subjected to controlled inquiry. The fact that new formal properties accrue to subject-matter in virtue of its subjection to certain types of operation is familiar to us in certain fields, even though the idea corresponding to this fact is unfamiliar in logic. Two outstanding instances are provided by art and law. In music, the dance, painting, sculpture, literature, and the other fine arts, subject-matters of every-day experience are *transformed* by the development of forms which render certain products of doing and making objects of fine art. The materials of legal regulations are transactions occurring in the ordinary activities of human beings and groups of human beings;

---

* All selections in this Chapter are from *Logic: The Theory of Inquiry*, shortly to be published by Henry Holt and Company. The selections were taken from the manuscript, hence only references to chapters are here given.

† From *Logic: The Theory of Inquiry,* Ch. VI—"The Common Pattern of Inquiry."

transactions of a sort that are engaged in quite apart from law. As certain aspects and phases of these transactions are legally formalized, conceptions such as misdemeanor, crime, torts, contracts and so on arise. These formal conceptions arise out of the ordinary transactions; they are not imposed upon them from on high or from any external and *a priori* source. But when they are formed, they are also *formative;* they regulate the proper conduct of the activities out of which they develop.

All of these formal logical conceptions are operational in nature. They formulate and define *ways* of operation on the part of those engaged in transactions into which a number of persons or groups enter as "parties" and they defined the ways of operation of those who have jurisdiction in deciding whether established forms have been complied with together with the existential consequences of failure of compliance. The forms in question are not fixed-and-eternal. They change, though as a rule too slowly, with changes in the habitual transactions in which individuals and groups engage, and the changes that occur in the consequences of these transactions. However hypothetical may be the conception that *logical* forms accrue to existential materials in virtue of the control exercised over inquiries in order that they may fulfill their end, the conception is descriptive of something that verifiably exists. The development of forms in consequence of operations is an established fact in some fields; it is not invented *ad hoc* in relation to logical forms.

The existence of inquiries is not a matter of doubt. They enter into every area of life and into every aspect of every area. In every day living, men examine; they turn things over intellectually; they infer and judge as "naturally" as they reap and sow, produce and exchange commodities. As a mode of conduct, inquiry is as acces-

sible to objective study as are these other modes of behavior. Because of the intimate and decisive way in which inquiry and its conclusions enter into the management of all
affairs of life, no study of the latter is adequate save as it
is noted how they are affected by the methods and instruments of inquiry that currently obtain.

Quite apart then from the particular hypothesis about
logical forms that is here put forth, study of the objective
facts of inquiry is a matter of tremendous import, practically and intellectually. These materials provide the
theory of logical forms with a subject-matter that is not
only objective, but is objective in a fashion that enables
logic to avoid the three mistakes most characteristic of its
history.

(1) In virtue of its concern with objectively observable
subject-matter by reference to which reflective conclusions
can be tried and tested, dependence upon subjective and
"mentalistic" states and processes is eliminated. (2) The
distinctive existence and nature of forms is acknowledged.
Logic is not compelled, as historic "empirical" logic felt
compelled to do, to reduce logical forms to mere trans-
cripts of the empirical materials that antecede the existence of the former. Just as art-forms and legal forms are
capable of independent discussion and development, so are
logical forms, even though the "independence" in question
is intermediate, not final and complete. As in the case of
the other forms, they originate *out of* experiential material, and when constituted introduce new ways of operating
with prior materials, which ways modify the material out
of which they develop. (3) Logical theory is liberated
from the unobservable, transcendental, and "intuitional."

When methods and results of inquiry are studied as
objective data, the distinction that has often been drawn
between noting and reporting the ways in which men *do*

think, and prescribing the ways in which they *ought* to think, takes on a very different interpretation from that usually given. The usual interpretation is in terms of the difference between the psychological and the logical, the latter consisting of "norms" provided from some source wholly outside of and independent of "experience." The way in which men *do* "think" denotes, as it is *here* interpreted, simply the ways in which men at a given time carry on their inquiries. So far as it is used to register a distinction from the ways in which they *ought* to think, it denotes a difference like that between good and bad farming or good and bad medical practice. Men think in ways they should not when they follow methods of inquiry that experience of past inquiries shows are not competent to reach the intended end of the inquiries in question.

Everybody knows that today there are in vogue methods of farming generally followed in the past, which compare very unfavorably in their results with those obtained by practices that have already been introduced and tested. When an expert tells a farmer he *should* do thus and so, he is not setting up for a bad farmer an ideal drawn from the blue. He is instructing him in methods that have been tried and that have proved successful in procuring results. In a similar way we are able to contrast various kinds of inquiry that are in use or that have been used in respect to their economy and efficiency in reaching warranted conclusions. We know that some methods of inquiry are better than others in just the same way in which we know that some methods of surgery, farming, road-making, navigating or what-not are better than others. It does not follow in any of these cases that the "better" methods are ideally perfect, or that they are regulative or "normative" because of conformity to some absolute forms. They are the methods which experience up to the present time shows to be the best methods available for achieving certain results, while abstraction of these methods does supply a (relative) norm or standard for further undertakings.

Observed facts of the case and the ideational contents expressed in ideas are related to each other as, respectively, a clarification of the problem involved and the proposal of some possible solution; they are, accordingly, functional divisions in the work of inquiry. Observed facts in their office of locating and describing the problem are existential; ideational subject-matter is non-existential. How then do they coöperate with each other in the resolution of an existential situation? The problem is insoluble save as it is recognized that both observed facts and entertained ideas are operational. Ideas are operational in that they instigate and direct further operations of observation; they are proposals and plans for acting upon existing conditions to bring new facts to light and to organize all the selected facts into a coherent whole.

What is meant by calling facts operational? Upon the negative side what is meant is that they are not self-sufficient and complete in themselves. They are selected and described for a purpose, namely statement of the problem involved in such a way that its material both indicates a meaning relevant to resolution of the difficulty and serves to test its worth and validity. In regulated inquiry facts are selected and arranged with the express intent of fulfilling this office. They are not merely *results* of operations of observation which are executed with the aid of bodily organs and auxiliary instruments of art, but they are the particular facts and kinds of facts that will link up with one another in the definite ways that are required to produce a definite end. Those not found to connect with others in furtherance of this end are dropped and others are sought for. Being functional, they are necessarily operational. Their function is to serve as evidence and their evidential quality is judged on the basis of their capacity to form an ordered whole in response to operations prescribed by the ideas they occasion and support. If "the facts of the case" were final and complete in themselves, if they did not have a special operative force in resolution of the problematic situation, they could not serve as evidence.

The operative force of facts is apparent when we consider that no fact in isolation has evidential potency. Facts are evidential and are tests of an idea in so far as they are capable of being organized with one another. The organization can be achieved only as they *interact* with one another. When the problematic situation is such as to require extensive inquiries to effect its resolution, a series of interactions intervenes. Some observed facts point to an idea that stands for a *possible* solution. This idea evokes more observations. Some of the newly observed facts link up with those previously observed and are such as to rule out other observed things with respect to *their* evidential function. The new order of facts suggests a modified idea (or hypothesis) which occasions new observations which result again determines a new order of facts, and so on until the existing order is both unified and complete. In the course of this serial process, the ideas that represent *possible* solutions are tested or "proved".

Meantime, the orders of fact, which present themselves in consequence of the experimental observations the ideas call out and direct, are *trial* facts. They are provisional. They are "facts" if they are observed by sound organs and techniques. But they are not on that account the *facts of the case*. They are tested or "proved" with respect to their evidential function just as much as ideas (hypotheses) are tested with reference to their power to exercise the function of resolution. The operative force of both ideas and facts is thus practically recognized in the degree in which they are connected with *experiment*. Naming them "operational" is but a theoretical recognition of what is involved whenever inquiry satisfies the conditions imposed by the necessity for experimentation.

It is obvious, on the face of matters, that a *possible* mode of solution must be carried in symbolic form since it is a possibility, not an assured present existence. It might seem, therefore, that symbols are not required for referring to them. But if they are not carried and treated by means of symbols, they lose their provisional character, and in losing this character they are categorically asserted and inquiry comes to an end. The carrying on of inquiry requires that the facts be taken as *representative* and not just as *pre*-sented. This demand is met by formulating them in propositions—that is, by means of symbols. Unless they are so represented they relapse into the total qualitative situation.

II · Explanation of *Situation**

What is the denotative force of the word *situation?* Its import may perhaps be most readily indicated by means of a preliminary negative statement. What is designated by the word "situation" is *not* a single object or event or set of objects and events. For we never experience nor form judgments about objects and events in isolation, but only in connection with a contextual whole. This latter is what is called a "situation." I have mentioned the extent in which modern philosophy had been concerned with the problem of existence as perceptually and conceptually de-

* From *Logic: The Theory of Inquiry*, Ch. IV—"Common Sense and Scientific Inquiry."

termined. The confusions and fallacies that attend the discussion of this problem have a direct and close connection with the difference between an object and a situation. Psychology has paid much attention to the question of the *process* of perception, and has for its purpose described the perceived object in terms of the results of the analysis of the process.

I pass over the fact that, no matter how legitimate the virtual identification of process and product may be, for the special purpose of *psychological* theory, the identification is thoroughly dubious as a generalized ground of philosophical discussion and theory. I do so in order to call attention to the fact that by the very nature of the case the psychological treatment takes a *singular* object or event for the subject-matter of its analysis. In actual experience, there is never any such isolated singular object or event; *an* object or event is always a special part, phase or aspect of an environing experienced world—a situation. The singular object stands out conspicuously because of its especially focal and crucial position at a given time in determination of some problem of use or enjoyment which the *total* complex environment presents. There is always a *field* in which observation of *this* or *that* object or event occurs. Observation of the latter is made for the sake of finding out what that *field* is with reference to some active adaptive response to be made in carrying forward a *course* of behavior. One has only to recur to animal perception, occurring by means of sense organs, to note that isolation of what is perceived from the course of life-behavior would be not only futile, but obstructive, in many cases fatally so.

A further conclusion follows: When the act and object of perception are isolated from their place and function in promoting and directing a successful course of activities in behalf of use-enjoyment, they are taken to be exclusively *cognitive*. The perceived object, orange, rock, piece of gold or whatever, is taken to be an object of *knowledge per se*. In the sense of being discriminatingly noticed, it *is* an object of knowledge, but not of knowledge as ultimate and self-sufficient. It is noted or "known" only so far as guidance is thereby given to direction of behavior —so that the situation in which it is found can be appropriately enjoyed or some of its conditions be so used that enjoyment will result or suffering be obviated. It is only when an object of focal observation is regarded as an object of knowledge in isolation that there arises the notion that there are two kinds of knowledge, and two kinds of objects of knowledge, so opposed to each other that philosophy must either choose which is "real" or find some way of reconciling their respective "realities." When it is seen that in common-sense inquiry there is no attempt made to know the object or event as such but only to determine what it signifies with respect to the way in which the entire situation should be dealt with, the opposition and conflict do not arise. The object or event in question is perceived as part of the environing world, not in and by itself; it is rightly (validly) perceived if and when it acts as clew and guide in use-enjoyment. We live and act in connection with the existing environment, not in connection with isolated objects, even though a singular thing may be crucially significant in deciding how to respond to a total environment.

Recurring to the main topic, it is to be remarked that a situation is a whole in virtue of its immediately pervasive quality. When we describe it from the psychological side, we have to say that the situation as a qualitative whole is sensed or *felt*. Such an expression, is, however, valuable only as it is taken negatively to indicate that it is *not,* as such, an object in *discourse.* Stating that it is *felt* is wholly misleading if it gives the impression that the situation *is* a feeling or an emotion or anything mentalistic. On the contrary, feeling, sensation and emotion have themselves to be identified and described in terms of the immediate presence of a total qualitative situation.

The pervasive qualitative is not only that which binds all constituents into a whole but it is also unique; it constitutes each situation an *individual* situation, indivisible and unduplicable. Distinctions and relations are instituted *within* a situation; *they* are recurrent and repeatable in different situations. Discourse that is not controlled in reference to a situation is not discourse, but a meaningless jumble, just as a mass of pied type is not a font, much less a sentence. A universe of experience is the precondition of a universe of discourse. Without its controlling presence, there is no way to determine the relevancy, weight or coherence of any designated distinction or relation. The universe of experience surrounds and regulates the universe of discourse but never appears as such within the latter. It may be objected that what was previously said contradicts this statement. For we have been discoursing about universes of experience and situations, so that the latter have been brought within the domain of symbols. The objection, when examined, serves to elicit an important consideration. It is a commonplace that a universe of discourse cannot be a term or element within itself. One universe of discourse may, however, be a term of discourse within *another* universe. The same principle applies in the case of universes of experience.

The reader, whether he agrees or not with what has been said, even whether he understands it or not, has, as he reads the above passages, a uniquely qualified experienced situation, and his reflective understanding of what is said is controlled by the nature of that immediate situation. One cannot decline to *have* a situation, for that is equivalent to having no experience, not even one of disagreement. The most that can be refused or declined is the having of that *specific* situation in which there is reflective recognition (discourse) of the presence of former situations of the kind stated. This very declination is, nevertheless, identical with initiation of another encompassing qualitative experience as a unique whole.

In other words, it *would* be a contradiction if I attempted to demonstrate by means of discourse, the existence of universes of experience. It is not a contradiction, by means of discourse, to *invite* the reader to have for himself that kind of an immediately experienced situation in which the presence of a situation as a universe of discourse is seen to be the encompassing and regulating condition of all discourse.

There is another difficulty in grasping the meaning of what has been said. It concerns the use of the word "quality." The word is usually associated with something specific, like *red, hard, sweet;* that is, with distinctions made within a total experience. The contrasting meaning intended, may be suggested, although not adequately exemplified, by considering such qualities as are designated by the terms distressing, perplexing, cheerful, disconsolate. For these words do not designate specific qualities in the way in which *hard*, say, designates a particular quality of a rock. For such qualities permeate and color *all* the objects and events that are involved in an experience. The phrase "tertiary qualities" happily introduced by Santayana, does not refer to a third quality like in kind to the "primary" and "secondary" qualities of Locke and merely happening to differ in content. For a tertiary quality qualifies *all* the constituents to which it applies in thoroughgoing fashion.

Probably the meaning *quality,* in the sense in which quality is said to pervade all elements and relations that are or can be instituted in discourse and thereby to constitute them an individual whole, can be most readily apprehended by referring to the esthetic use of the word. A painting is said to have quality, or a particular painting to have a Titian or Rembrandt quality. The word thus used most certainly does not refer to any particular line, color or part of the painting. It is something that affects and modifies all the constituents of the picture and all of their relations. It is not anything that can be expressed in words for it is something that must be *had.* Discourse may, however, point out the qualities, lines and relations by means of which pervasive and unifying quality is achieved. But so far as this is separated from *having* the immediate total experience, a reflective object takes the place of an esthetic one. Esthetic experience, in its emphatic sense, is mentioned as a way of calling attention to situations and universes of experience. The intended force of the illustration would be lost if esthetic experience as such were supposed to exhaust the scope and significance of a "situation." As has been said, a qualitative and qualifying situation is present as the background and the control of *every* experience. It was for a similar reason that it was earlier stated that reference to tertiary qualities was not adequately exemplary. For such qualities as are designated by "distressing," "cheerful," etc. are *general,* while the quality of distress and cheer that marks an existent situation is not general but is unique and inexpressible in words.

I give one further illustration from a different angle of

approach. It is more or less a commonplace that it is possible to carry on observations that amass facts tirelessly and yet the observed "facts" lead nowhere. On the other hand, it is possible to have the work of observation so controlled by a conceptual framework fixed in advance that the very things which are genuinely decisive in the problem in hand and its solution are completely overlooked. Everything is forced into the predetermined conceptual and theoretical scheme. The way, and the only way, to escape these two evils, is sensitivity to the quality of the situation as a whole. In ordinary language, a problem must be felt before it can be stated. If the unique quality of the situation is *had* immediately, then there is something which regulates the selection and the weighing of observed facts and their conceptual ordering.

III · Judgment and Proposition*

Judgment may be identified as the settled outcome of inquiry. It is concerned with the concluding objects that emerge from inquiry in their status of being conclusive. Judgment in this sense is distinguished from *propositions*. The content of the latter is intermediate and representative, and is carried by symbols; while judgment as finally made has direct existential import. The terms *affirmation* and *assertion* are employed in current speech interchangeably. But there is a difference which should have linguistic recognition, between the logical status of intermediate subject-matters that are taken for use, in conrection with what they may lead to as means, and subject-matter which has been prepared to be final. I shall use *assertion* to designate the latter logical status and *affirmation* to name the former. Even from the standpoint of or-

* From *Logic: The Theory of Inquiry,* Ch. VII—"The Construction of Judgment."

dinary speech, "assertion" has a quality of insistence that is lacking in the connotation of the word "affirmation". We can usually substitute the phrase "it is *held*" or "it is said" for "*it is affirmed*". However, the important matter is not the words, but the logical properties characteristic of different subject-matters.

A literal instance of judgment in the sense defined is provided by the judgments of a court of law in settling some issue which, up to that point, has been in controversy.

(1) The occurrence of a trial-at-law is equivalent to the occurrence of a problematic situation which requires settlement. There is uncertainty and dispute about what shall be done because there is conflict about the *significance* of what has taken place, even if there is agreement about what has taken place as a matter of fact, which of course is not always the case. The judicial settlement is a settlement of an *issue* because it decides existential conditions in their bearing upon further activities: the essence of the significance of any state of facts.

(2) This settlement or judgment is the outcome of inquiry conducted in the court-hearings. On the one hand, propositions are advanced about the state of facts involved. Witnesses testify to what they have heard and seen; written records are offered, etc. This subject-matter is capable of direct observation and has existential reference. As each party to the discussion produces its evidential material, the latter is intended to point to a determinate decision as a resolution of the as yet undetermined situation. The decision takes effect in a definite existential reconstruction. On the other hand, there are propositions about conceptual subject-matter; rules of law are adduced to determine the admissibility (relevancy) and the weight of facts offered as evidence. The *significance* of factual ma-

terial is fixed by the rules of the existing juridical system; it is not carried by the facts independent of the conceptual structure which interprets them. And yet, the quality of the problematic situation determines which rules of the total system are selected. They are different in civil and criminal cases; in cases of trespass and of breach of contract. Conceptions have been organized in the past under definite rubrics which summarize the *kinds* of interpreting principles which past experience has shown to be applicable in the variety of special cases that normally arise. The theoretical ideal sought to guide judicial deliberation is a network of relations and procedures which express the closest possible correspondence between facts and the legal meanings which give them their significance: that is, settle the consequences which, in the existing social system, flow from them.

(3) The final judgment arrived at is a settlement. The case is disposed of; the disposition takes effect in existential consequences. The sentence or proposition is not an end in itself but a decisive directive of future activities. The consequences of these activities bring about an existential determination of the prior situation which was indeterminate as to its issue. A man is set free, sent to prison, pays a fine, or has to execute an agreement or pay damages to an injured party. It is this resulting state of actual affairs—this changed situation—that is the matter of the final settlement or judgment. The sentence itself is a proposition, differing, however, from the propositions formed during the trial, whether they concern matters of fact or legal conceptions, in that it takes overt effect in operations which construct a new qualitative situation. While prior propositions are means of instituting the sentence, the sentence is terminal as a means of instituting a definite existential situation.

Judgment figures, however, in determination of the intermediate propositions. When it is ruled that certain evidence is admissible and that certain rules of law (conceptual material) are applicable rather than others, *something* is settled. It is through a series of such intervening settlements that the final settlement is constructed. Judgment as final settlement is dependent upon a series of partial settlements. The judgments by which propositions are determined are recognized and marked off linguistically by such words as *estimates, appraisals, evaluations*. In resolution of problems that are of a looser quality than legal cases we call them *opinions* to distinguish them from warranted judgment or assertion. But if the opinion held is grounded it is itself the product of inquiry and *in so far* is a judgment.* Estimates and appraisals are provisional; they are means, not ends. Even a judgment of appraisal by judges on the bench may be reversed in a higher court while in freer conduct of scientific inquiry such judgments are expressly made subject to modification. The consequences they produce in the conduct of further inquiry are the criteria of their value. The judgments which intervene are ad-judgments.

Final judgment is individual. This statement is elliptical. It means that the subject-matter (object, situation) of final judgment is explained; it is a qualitative existential whole, which is unique. "Individual" as here used has nothing to do with simplicity of constituents. On the contrary, every situation, when it is analyzed, is extensive containing within itself diverse distinctions and relations which, in spite of their diversity, form a unified qualitative whole. What is designated by the word *individual* has,

---

* Opinion in common speech often means a belief entertained without examination, being generated by custom, tradition, or desire.

accordingly, to be distinguished from that which is designated by the word *singular*. Singulars are named by de-
monstratives, such as *this, that, here, now,* or in some
cases by proper nouns. The difference between a singular
and an individual is the same as that previously pointed
out between *an* object (or set of objects in their severalty)
and a situation. Singular objects exist and singular events
occur within a field or situation. *This* or *that* star, man,
rock or whatever is always a discrimination or selection
made for a purpose, or for the sake of some objective consequence within an inclusive field. The singular has no import save as term of differentiation and a contrast. If its
object is taken to be complete in itself, loss of differential
force destroys all power of reference on the part of the
demonstrative act. The very existence of differentiation, on
the other hand, shows that the singular exists within an
extensive field.

It follows that determination of a singular is also instrumental in the determination of a situation which is itself
not complete and self-sufficient. It is a means of identifying a situation in reference to the problem set to inquiry.
It represents, at a given stage of inquiry, what is crucial,
critical, differentiatingly significant. An artisan in carrying
on his work at any given time takes note of certain aspects
and phases of the situation in which his activities are involved. He notes *just that* object or occurrence which is
decisive in the stage of development arrived at in the
whole situation which is determinative of what is to be
next. The objects which are *this* and *that,* to which his
inquiry and activity are immediately directed, are, therefore, constantly changing. As one phase of the problem offered by his work is resolved, another phase, presented by
a new object or occurrence, takes its place. Were not the
sequence determined by an inclusive situation, whose qual-

itative nature pervades and holds together each successive step, activity would be a meaningless hop-skip-jump affair. Objects observed and dealt with would be a shifting panorama of sudden disconnected appearances and disappearances. Exactly the same account may be given of the succession of observations which deal with singular objects and occurrences in scientific inquiry. The singular is that upon which inquiry into an individual situation pivots under the special conditions which at a given time fix the problem with respect to the conditions to be dealt with forthwith.

The discriminative or differential aspect of the demonstrative act and its singular object is suggested in ordinary speech by the expression "pointing *out*." It is impossible merely to point *at* something. For anything or everything in the *line* of vision or gesture may be equally pointed *at*. The act of pointing is wholly indeterminate as to its object. It is not selective within a situation, because it is not controlled by the problem which the situation sets and the necessity for determining the conditions which then and there point to the way in which it shall be resolved.

IV · Interpretation of the Syllogism*

(1) *The Subject of Judgment.* What was said concerning the pattern of inquiry† enables us to identify the structure of judgment as conjugate distinction and relation of subject-predicate. Observed facts of the case in their dual function of bringing the problem to light and of providing evidential material with respect to its solution constitute what has traditionally been called the *subject*. The conceptual contents which anticipate a possible solution and which direct observational operations constitute

* From *Logic: The Theory of Inquiry,* Ch. VII—"The Construction of Judgment."
† See also *supra,* Ch. XIV, Section II.—Ed.

what has traditionally been called the *predicate*. Their functional and operative correspondence with each other constitutes the *copula*.

Suppose that in a given case, *this* is characterized "Washington Monument". The act of pointing does not determine any one "this" rather than another since everything in the line of pointing is pointed *at*. In the second place, even when we suppose that the act of pointing happens to land, so to speak, upon one singular rather than another, it is only a group of sensible qualities that is indicated. There is nothing in these qualities, apart from control exercised upon their interpretation by an inclusive situation, to justify characterizing them as the Washington Monument—or as a memorial of any kind. The most that could be said is that the qualities observed in consequence of the demonstrative act are just the qualities they are. The nub of any existential identification or characterization of a thing as such-and-such lies in the ground it offers for giving the object a description in terms of what is *not* then and there observed. Apart from an inclusive situation which determines in *correspondence with each other* the material that constitutes the observed singular this and the kind of characterizing predicate applicable to it, predication is totally arbitrary or ungrounded. There must be some one *question* to which both the subject "this" and the predicate (say, *Washington Monument*) are relevant. That question grows out of and is controlled by some total situation. Otherwise propositions made are pointless.

Any proposition in which "this" appears is, then, instituted by a judgment of appraisal in which "this" is determined in order to provide evidential grounds for the qualification attached to it by the predicate. This fact is inconsistent with "this" being a *mere* this. There is, however, no incompatibility between the fact that *it* is just what it is existentially and the estimate that it is the needed evidential ground of a definite characterization. Stating the matter positively, the operations that institute a "this" as subject are always selective-restrictive of something from out of a larger field. What is selected and what is rejected flow from an estimate of their probable evidential significance.

The subject is existential, either a singular *this,* or a set of singulars. But there are conditions of inquiry which must be satisfied by anything taken to be a subject. It must delimit and describe the problem in such a way as to indicate a possible solution. It must be such that new data, instituted by observational operations directed by the provisional predicate (representing a possible solution) will unite with its subject-matter to form a coherent whole. The latter constitutes a substantial object in the logical sense of that term, or is on its way to becoming such an object. For it is union of connected distinctions held together that it may be acted upon, or with, as a whole; or it is capable of incorporating into itself other predicated qualifications until it becomes, as such, a unity of inter-connected distinctions, or "properties."

Take, for an example, such an elementary proposition as "this is sweet". *This,* as has been shown, marks a selective-restriction, made for a definite purpose, within an inclusive qualitative problematic situation. The purpose is the final consequence of a resolved situation. The purpose is the final consequence of a resolved situation in attainment of which *"this"* has a special function to perform. If the predicate *"is sweet"* is an *anticipation* of the resolved situation, it means "this" *will sweeten* something if that operation is performed which is required to generate a definite perceptible consequence. Or, it may record the achieved result of the execution of the operation: "This *has* sweetened something." When the operation is completed, *this* is definitely qualified as sweet. This fact is manifest not in a proposition (although a proposition may report it for purposes of record or communication of information) nor in symbols, but in a directly experienced existence. Henceforth, "this" is a sweet *somewhat*. The quality *sweet* does not stand alone but is definitely connected with other observed qualities. As thus characterized, it enters into further situations in which it incorporates into itself additional qualifications. It is a sweet, white, granular, more or less gritty thing or substance, say, *sugar*.

"Substance" represents a logical, not an ontological determination. Sugar, for example, is a substance because through a number of partial judgments completed in operations which have existential consequences, a variety of qualifications so cohere as to form an object that may be used and enjoyed as a unified whole. Its substantial character is quite independent of its physical duration, to say nothing of its immutability. The object, *sugar,* may disappear in solution. It is then further qualified; it is a soluble object. In a chemical interaction its constitution may be so changed that it is no longer sugar. Capacity for undergoing this change is henceforth an additional qualification or property of anything that is sugar. The condition—and the sole condition that has to be satisfied in order that there may be substantiality—is that certain qualifications hang together as dependable signs that certain consequences will follow when certain interactions take place. This is what is meant when it is said that substantiality is a logical, not a primary ontological determination.

It is a form that accrues to original existence when the latter operates in a specified functional way as a consequence of operations of inquiry. It is not postulated that certain qualities always cohere in existence. It is postulated that they cohere as dependable evidential signs. The conjoining properties that mark off and identify a chair, a piece of granite, a meteor, are not sets of qualities given existentially as such and such. They are certain qualities which constitute in their ordered conjunction with one another valid signs of what will ensue when certain operations are performed. An object, in other words, is a set of qualities regarded as *potentialities* for specified existential consequences. Powder is what will explode under certain conditions; water as a substantial object is that group of connected qualities which will quench thirst, and so on. The greater the number of interactions, of operations, and of consequences, the more complex is the constitution of a given substantial object.

(2) *The Predicate of Judgment.* The logical meaning of *predicate* has been anticipated in the discussion of the logical subject, because of the strict correlativity of respective existential and ideational contents. The meanings which are suggested as possible solutions of a problem, which are then used to direct further operations of experimental observation, form the predicational content of judgments. The latter is related to the factual content, that is, the subject, as the possible to the actual. For example, in the illustration considered above, when *"this"* is estimated (before the act of tasting) to be *sweet,* a certain consequence is anticipated to which is assigned a definite connection in the total situation. If, however, it is at once asserted "this is sweet", the assertion is logically premature and ungrounded. The anticipation functions logically to instigate and direct an operation of experimental observation. When the consequences of the latter combine with

facts already ascertained so as to constitute a unified total situation, inquiry comes to an end. But there is always danger that the congeniality or plausibility of the content of the predicate-meaning will lead directly to its acceptance. In that case, it is not operationally checked. It possesses *logical* status only as it is taken for what it is *qua* predicate: namely, a *method* of solution not itself a solution. There is also danger that pains will not be taken, even when an operation is performed, to scrutinize its results in order to ascertain whether the existential conditions actually cohere in a unified way. These two failures are the common source of premature, hasty, and therefore, ungrounded assertion.

The essential error of the "rationalistic" tradition in logical theory consists in taking the consistency of the constituents of the conceptual contents (which form the predicate) as a final criterion of truth or assertibility. Subject-matter which in its logical form is a means for performing experimental activities to modify prior existences is mistaken to be final and complete in itself. Thereby an inherent ontological status is imputed to it. As has been pointed out, in classic logic, subject-matter endowed with "rational" form was treated as constituting a superior realm of "Reality", in comparison with which material capable of sensible observation was by nature metaphysically inferior. The latter was "known" only in so far as it could be directly subsumed under the conceptual material. A more recent tendency is to regard the conceptual subject-matter as constituting a realm of abstract possibility also taken as complete in itself, not as indicating possibilities of operations to be performed. While the resulting metaphysical status assigned is very different from that of classic ontology, there is nevertheless the same hypostatization of a logical function into a supra-empirical entity. Meantime, the practice of scientific inquiry has provided the foundations for a correct logical interpretation.

The conceptual and "rational" contents are *hypotheses*. In their more comprehensive forms they are theories. As such they may be and usually are abstracted from application to this and that immediate existential situation. But on that very account, they are instruments of a wide, indefinite scope of operational applications, actual application being made as special conditions present themselves.

(3) *The Copula.* The logical import of copulation is involved in the prior account of subject and predicate. It is neither a separate and independent element nor yet does it affect the predicate alone, attaching the latter to an independently and externally given singular subject, whether the latter be taken to be an object, a quality, or a sense-datum. It does express the act of predication. But it also expresses the act or operation of "subjecting"; that is, of constituting the subject. It is a name for the complex of operations by means of which (a) certain existences are restrictively-selected to delimit a problem and provide evidential testing material, and by which (b) certain conceptual meanings, ideas, hypotheses, are used as characterizing predicates. It is a name for the functional correspondence between subject and predicate in their relation to each other. The operations which it expresses distinguish and relate at the same time.

(4) *The Judgment.* Inquiry demands, as we have seen, operations of both observation and ideation. There would be no control of the process of inquiry if each of these operations were not expressly formed each with reference to the other. It is easy to see what would happen if observation were directed to material which had no connection with entertained ideas and hypotheses, and if the latter

went off on a track of their own, having no connection with the material obtained by observation. In the process of reasoning, especially in scientific inquiry, there is often a considerable period in which conceptual material is developed on its own account, leaving observed material temporarily in abeyance. But nonetheless in *controlled* inquiry, the entire object of this seemingly independent development is to obtain *that* meaning or conceptual structure which is best adapted to instigate and direct just those operations of observation which will secure as their consequence just those existential facts that are needed to solve the problem in hand.

Final judgment is attained through a series of partial judgments—those to which the name *estimates* or *appraisals* has been given. Judgment is not something occurring all at once. Since it is a manifestation of inquiry, it cannot be instantaneous and yet be inquiry. Short of attainment of a finally resolved situation (the result of final judgment and assertion) respective subject-and-predicate contents are *provisionally* instituted in distinction from and correlation with each other. Were subject-and-predicate contents final, rather than provisional, distinction and relation *would* constitute a state of irreconcilable opposition. Since they are functional and operative, there is no more conflict than there is in the fact that in the course of every complex productive activity, industrial or social divisions of labor are instituted which nevertheless are functionally connected with one another. For they are instituted as coördinating means of a common unified outcome. Were a complex undertaking in which extensive division of labor prevailed arrested short of its temporal issue, and were the various activities and their respective partial products taken at the moment of arrest to provide a final interpretation of what was going on, the conclusion might not be that there was inherent contradiction among them—but the idea that irrelevancy and disorganization existed would be justified. The result of the discussion is, then, to show how indispensable it is to acknowledge that judgment, like inquiry, is temporal. It is temporal not in the external sense that the act of judging takes time, but in the sense that its subject-matter undergoes reconstitution in attaining the final state of determinate resolution and unification which is the objective which governs judgment.

It is necessarily involved in what has been said that the linguistic form which expresses, or is the symbol of, judgment is a true verb; that is, one expressing action and change.

When *is* appears in *judgment* it has temporal force, distinct from *was* or *will be,* and distinct from the "is" of a proposition where "is" designates a non-temporal or strictly logical relation between meanings. When it is stated that "the boy is running" the reference to change, time and place lies on the surface. When one says "this is red" the temporal reference is linguistically disguised. But the statement certainly does not mean that *this* is inherently red or is always red. Color quality changes to some extent with every change in light. It is red *now,* under a specifiable set of consequences, and a completely grounded judgment would demand that the conditions be stated. "Is red" sets forth what in ordinary language is called an effect or change brought about, or else a capacity to produce change, a power to redden other things.

Etymologically, the word *is* derives from a root meaning to stand or to stay. To remain and endure is a mode of action. At least, it indicates a temporal equilibrium of interactions. Now a spatio-temporal change is existential. Consequently the copula in judgment, whether as a transitive or intransitive verb, or in the ambiguous form "is," has inherent existential reference. In such a proposition as "Justice is a virtue" *is*, on the other hand, stands for a relation between two abstractions or meanings, and accordingly is non-temporal. It is a mark of a logical relation such that in any proposition in which "justice" appears there is an implicatory relation to some proposition in which "virtue" appears. The *situation* to which the sentence refers determines unambiguously whether "is" has an active force, expressing a change going on actually or potentially, or whether it stands for a relation between meanings or ideas. In a sentence having no contextual situation, its logical force is indeterminate. For any sentence isolated from place and function in inquiry is logically indeterminate.

The copula in a judgment, in distinction from the formal term of relation expresses, accordingly, the actual transformation of the subject-matter of an indeterminate situation into a determinate one. So far is the copula from being an isolable constituent that it might be regarded as what sets the subject-and-predicate contents at work executing their functions in relation to one another. In complex undertakings a plan for division of functions is usually laid out on paper. But this plan is not the actual division of labor. The latter consists in the actual distribution of the active factors of what is doing in their coöperation with one another. The distribution, as well as the coöperation, is arranged with reference to an end or objective consequence.

The plan may be set forth and explained in propositions; its propositional exposition may be a means of criticism and of re-arrangement of the plan of distribution. But the *actual* division can only be enacted. As just indicated, it may be stated in symbols, and symbolic representation of the division may be an indispensable means of actual enactment. But it no more *is* a functioning division of labor than a blueprint is a house in process of building or a map is a journey. Blueprints and maps are propositions and they exemplify what it is to *be* propositional. Moreover, a map is no less a means of directing journeys because it is not constantly in use. Similarly, general propositions are no less a means of constructing judgments because they are not always operative in the existential work of reconstituting existential material.

Like a chart, indeed, like any physical tool or physiological organ, a proposition must be defined by its function. Furthermore, there is the same sort of advantage in having conceptual frameworks manufactured and on hand in advance of actual occasions for their use, as there is in having tools ready instead of improvising them when need arises. Just as a complex undertaking in any field demands prepared *materials* as well as prepared instrumentalities, so propositions which describe conjunctions of existential materials—ultimately reducible to space-time connections —are required in effective inquiry. At the outset, substantial objects-events serve this purpose as more or less secondary by-products or deposits from prior inquiries. But finally, they are deliberately constituted by critical inquiry intended to produce objects that will operate as effective and economical means when they are needed: a differentia of commonsense and scientific objects. Propositions about subject-contents, about spatial-temporal conjunctions of properties of existence, thus undergo independent development just as do propositions about meanings and their relations. The former I call *material means* and the latter *procedural means,* it being remembered that both are operational since they are means of determining the final situation and judgment.

V · Induction and Deduction*

Whatever else scientific method is or is not, it is concerned with ascertaining the conjunctions of characteristic traits which descriptively determine kinds in relation to one another, and with the interrelations of characters constituting abstract conceptions of wide applicability. The propositions which result are generalizations of two forms, generic and universal; one existential in content, the other non-existential. The methods by which generalizations are arrived at have received the name "induction"; the methods by which already existing generalizations are employed have received the name "deduction.' These considerations at least delimit the field of discussion Any account of scientific method must be capable of offering a coherent doctrine of the nature of induction and deduction and of their relations to one another and the doctrine must accord with what takes place in actual scientific practice.

With respect to both induction and deduction, the logical terrain is still occupied with remnants, some more or less coherent and some more or less of the nature of debris, of logical conceptions that were formed prior to the development of scientific method. There is, accordingly, no field of logical subject-matter in which the need of thoroughgoing reform of theory is as urgent as in the case of induction and deduction. It has become traditional to repeat the statements that induction goes from particulars to the general and deduction from the general to the particulars. The extent to which these conceptions are valid, i.e., in harmony with scientific practice, is not critically examined. The result too frequently is that actual scientific procedure is forced into the strait-jacket of irrelevant pre-

* From *Logic: The Theory of Inquiry,* Ch. XXI—"Scientific Method: Induction and Deduction."

conceptions. Escape from this procedure depends upon analyses of induction and deduction from the point of view of method as exhibited in actual methods of inquiry.

The traditional and still current conceptions of induction and deduction are derived from Aristotelian logic, which, as has been shown, was a systematization of logical forms on the basis of certain cosmological beliefs.* Since the actual progress of scientific inquiry has led to an abandonment of these underlying beliefs concerning the structure of Nature, it might be antecedently expected that the doctrines about induction and deduction which are found in the Aristotelian logic, will be so irrelevant to existing scientific practice as to be the source of confusion and uncertainty when they are employed as rubrics of interpretation.

A. *Induction and Deduction in Aristotelian Logic.* The conception of induction as a procedure that goes from particulars to the general, and of deduction as the reverse movement, has its origin in the Aristotelian formulation. More important than the mere question of its historical derivation is the fact that the Aristotelian conceptions were relevant to, and grounded in, the subject-matter of natural science *as that subject-matter, the structure of nature, was then understood.* There is no need at this point to expound at length the characteristic features of the conception of nature entertained by Aristotle. The distinction between immutable Being, existing at all times in identical form, and the mutable, which in its mutability is convincing proof of partial and incomplete Being provided the ground of the distinction made between induction and rationally complete, scientific demonstration or deduction. Since the immutable was constituted by

* See Ch. Two, Ch. Three, Section II, and Ch. Sixteen, Section I.
—Ed.

fixed species, each of which was defined by an essence, it followed that strictly scientific or demonstrative knowledge consisted in a classificatory ordering of fixed species, in which inclusive species hierarchically determined included species of a more limited range. This ordering is effected in the demonstrative syllogism. Scientific knowledge of changing things is, on the contrary, possible only when and as these things are caught and placed within the fixed limits constituted by essences that define species. The result here was also expressed in the syllogism, but in a contingent syllogism as distinct from the rational necessity of the demonstrative syllogism.*

In each of these forms, the deductive is identified with the syllogistic. Given the underlying cosmological assumptions, there is genuine meaning in the conception of going from the general to the more particular. In the case of the demonstrative syllogism, the movement is from the more to the less inclusive. Where "particular" is to be understood in a strictly logical sense—as equivalent to the more specific in its distinction from the universal inclusive species. In the case of the contingent syllogism, "particular" has a different meaning. Anything which is mutable is particular in the sense of being partial, incomplete. Now the objects of sense perception are observed things in their severalty in distinction from the species to which they belong. They are, as just noted, truly known only when and as they are subsumed under universal propositions, which state the inherent nature of species. As thus subsumed, they "follow" as particulars from the general.

At this point, I shall briefly indicate the difference be-

---

* To express the contingent nature of this form of syllogism, Aristotle frequently uses the expression "dialectic syllogisms." Their conclusions are true as a rule, "upon the whole," usually, but not always, since they are not derived from subject-matters which are themselves necessary.

tween this conception of rational demonstration and that which is in accord with present scientific practice. Mathematical discourse is now the outstanding exemplar of deductive demonstration; but (i) no mathematician would regard it as logically important to reduce a chain of related mathematical propositions to the syllogistic form, nor would he suppose that such reduction added anything to the force of his demonstration*; and (ii) such deductions *do not* necessarily proceed from the more general to the less general even with respect to conceptions: while (iii) (as is generally acknowledged), it is impossible to proceed directly from a universal proposition to one about an existential particular or singular. It is true (with regard to the second point) that sometimes in mathematical reasoning the final proposition has less scope or "comprehension," a narrower range of applicability, than do the preceding propositions from which it "follows." When, for example, an ellipse is defined as a curve so moving that its distance from a fixed line bears a constant ratio to its distance from a fixed point, the logical movement is from a conception of wider applicability to one restricted by introduction of a special limiting condition. But when the properties of an ellipse are defined by reasoning from the properties of a conic section, the logical movement is from the narrower to the wider range of applicability. When the equilateral is derived from the equiangular, there is neither gain nor loss in comprehension or scope. The fact is that about mathematical reasoning, as an example of deduction, no general statement whatever can be made as to the breadth of the premises in relation to that of the conclusion. Such differences as

---

* This statement should not, of course, be taken as implying that mathematical propositions can be reduced to the syllogistic form. They cannot.—Ed.

may be present depend upon the special methods used and the nature of the problem dealt with. So much, in general, for the irrelevancy of the Aristotelian conception of deduction to modern scientific practice.

With respect to the formulation of the inductive pro. cedures of ancient and modern science respectively, there exists a verbal similarity. Both start from scattered data (or particulars) and move toward institution of generalizations. But the similarity does not extend beyond the vague formula of "going from particulars to generals." For (a) particulars are conceived in radically different ways and (b) the process of "going," or the way in which generals are arrived at from particulars, is very different. A survey of the Aristotelian conception of induction suffices to show its intrinsic unfitness to serve the logical conditions of present science. The cosmological theory of Aristotle postulates that every knowable thing is of some kind or species. Even sense-perception is a mode of low-grade knowledge in so far as what is seen, heard and touched is apprehended as being of a kind. The very lowest grade of knowledge, mere sensation, directly apprehends qualities determined by "sensible forms," such as, in touch, hard soft. Sensation and sense-perception are modes of knowledge in which "matter," the principle of change and hence of lack of Being, predominates, as, *e.g.*, when the dry changes to the wet. In general, the "particular" which is "known" in sense perception is subject to generation and dissolution, to "birth" and "death," as a tree grows from seed, decays and vanishes. *Recurrent* perceptions then constitute experience. In persons who are happily constituted by natural endowment, who have the scientific and philosophic *nisus* or potentiality, the form is gradually apprehended *as such,* first as subduing matter, and then finally as completely free from any connection with matter.

Definition and classification are thus instituted and there is scientific knowledge on the basis of rational apprehension or notation. In short, the universal is grasped in its own inherent nature. This process constitutes in the classic scheme the "going" from particulars to the universal which is induction. "Forms" which are immutable, necessary and universal, are present from the first in qualities and objects of sensation and sense perception. Induction is but the process by which these forms are so *elicited* from entanglement in "matter" that they are perceived by reason in their own essential nature, "reason" being defined precisely as this actualization in knowledge of pure forms of Being.

"Induction" on this basis is a psychological process, although not in the subjective sense of psychological which has controlled so much of modern speculation. The process in question is rather biological, and the biological is an actualization of the cosmological. It is, accordingly, perhaps better to think of it as a *pedagogical* process in which certain select persons in whom the potentiality of reason is brought to actuality by means of the forms that are implicit in objects of experience, are *led up to* or *induced* to apprehend universals which have been necessarily involved, all the time, in sense qualities and objects of empirical perception. *Epagoge,* the word translated by our word "induction," is then precisely the process of being *led or brought up to* apprehension of fixed and essential forms in and of themselves.

B. *The Nature of Induction on the Ground of Prior Analyses*. I shall give a brief *formal* statement of its nature in the light of previous discussion. (i) Particulars are *selectively* discriminated so as to determine a *problem* whose nature is such as to indicate possible modes of solution. This selective redetermination of perceived objects

and their qualities necessarily involves experimental transformation of objects and qualities in their given "natural"
state, whereas in the classic logic they were taken "as is."
(ii) The particulars of observations which are experimentally instituted not only form the subject-matter of
a *problem* so as to indicate an appropriate mode of solution, but are also such as to have *evidential and testing*
value with respect to indicated modes of solution. Operations are deliberately performed that experimentally modify given antecedent objects of perception, so as to produce *new* data in new ordered arrangement. Institution
of new data which are relevant and effective with respect
to any conclusion that is hypothetically entertained, forms
the most indispensable and difficult part of inquiry in
the natural sciences. Objects and qualities as they naturally present themselves or as they are "given," are not
only *not* the data of science, but they constitute the most
direct and important obstacle to formation of those ideas
and hypotheses that are genuinely relevant and effective.

The primary meanings and associations of ideas and
hypotheses are derived from their position and force in
common sense situations of use-enjoyment. They are expressed in symbols developed originally for the sake of
social communication rather than to serve the conditions
of controlled inquiry. The symbols are therefore loaded
with meanings that are irrelevant to inquiry conducted for
the sake of attaining knowledge as such. These meanings
are familiar and influentially persuasive because of their
established associations. The result is that the historic advance of science is marked and accompanied by deliberate elimination of such terms and institution in their
stead of a new set of symbols constituting a new technical
language. The progress of every science—physics, chemistry, biology, and even mathematics—in general and in

particular, is evidence both of the difficulty and the necessity of instituting data of a new order.

What is the analysis of those scientific procedures to which the name induction may be applied if the word has any application at all? For the question is not about the meaning of a word, even of a word that has been sanctioned by long usage, but of the actual procedures by which generalizations are established in the natural sciences. Moreover, generalizations are of two forms. There are those which institute a relation of including and included kinds, and there are those which institute universal *if-then* propositions as hypotheses and theories. Any adequate account of scientific methods as the means by which warranted generalizations are achieved must, therefore, be applicable to both of these two forms. This consideration is, in effect, a warning in advance of the impossibility of making a sharp division between "induction" as the operation by which *existential* generalizations are established, and "deduction" as the operation concerned with the relations of universal propositions in discourse. As far as physical inquiry, at least, is concerned, induction and deduction must be so interpreted that they will be seen to be coöperative phases of the same ultimate set of operations.

This is a summary statement of conclusions regarding the distinctively inductive and deductive phases of inquiry, and their interrelation, or functional correspondence, with each other. (a) The inductive phase consists of the complex of experimental operations by which antecedently existing conditions are so modified that data are obtained which indicate and test proposed modes of solution. (b) Any suggested or indicated mode of solution must be formulated as a *possibility*. Such formulation constitutes a hypothesis. The *if-then* proposition which results must be developed in ordered relation to other propositions of like form (or in discourse), until related contents are obtained forming the special *if-then* proposition that directs experimental observations yielding new data. The criterion for the validity of such hypotheses is the capacity of the new data they produce to combine with earlier data (describing the problem) so that they institute a whole of unified significance. (c) The nature of the interrelation or functional correspondence of these two phases of inquiry directly follows. The propositions which formulate data must, to satisfy the conditions of inquiry, be such as to determine a problem in the form that indicates a possible solution, while the hypothesis in which the latter is formulated must be such as operationally to provide the new data that fill out and order those previously obtained. There is a continued to-and fro movement between the set of existential propositions about data and the non-existential propositions about related conceptions.

This formulation agrees up to a certain point with current statements about scientific inquiry as *hypothetical-deductive* in nature. But it emphasizes two necessary conditions which are usually slurred in statement of that position: (a) The necessity of observational determinations in order to indicate a relevant hypothesis, and (b) the necessity of *existential* operational application of the hypothesis in order to institute existential material capable of testing the hypothesis. These conditions place the hypothetical-deductive stage of inquiry as intermediate. When this stage is taken in isolation from the initial and terminal stages of inquiry (concerned with existential observations), it is disconnected from its occasion in problems, and from its application in their solution. It is probable that in the current formulation of the position, these stages are taken for granted or are "understood." But it is necessary to state them explicitly in order that the hypothetical-deductive stage may be relevant and controlled in its contents and their order of relation. Otherwise it is assumed (a) that existential propositions are "implied" by universal propositions, and (b) that affirming the antecedent when and because the consequent is affirmed, is valid.

The conjugate relation of the inductive and deductive is exemplified in the correlative nature of inference and proof, where "proof" means ostensive demonstration. That it is highly uneconomical from the practical point of view to separate the two functions of inference and test is clear without extensive argument. Economy makes it important that the material *from* which an inference is drawn should also be such as far as is possible to test the inference that is made. For it is important that the inference drawn should be such as to indicate *what* new kinds of data are required and give some suggestion as to *how* they are to be obtained. But the importance of including within one and the same set of methodic procedures, operations that produce material which is both evidentially indicative, testing and testable, is much more than a matter of practical economy. It is logically necessary. For an "inference" that is not *grounded* in the evidential nature of the material from which it is drawn is *not* an inference. It is a more or less wild guess. To say that an inference is *grounded* in any degree whatever is equivalent to saying that the material upon which it is based is such as to be a factor in warranting its validity: not in its isolation, but in connection with the new data obtained as consequences of the operations to which the inference, as a hypothesis, led. The progress made by inquiry in any branch may, then, be measured by the extent to which it has succeeded in developing methods of inquiry that, at one and the same time, provide material data having conjunct inferential and testing force. *Satisfaction of this condition provides the definition of inductive procedures.*

Uncritical adherence to Aristotelian conceptions has combined with the prestige of physics, especially of mathematical physics, to generate the conception that physics is not only the *most* advanced form of scientific inquiry (which it undeniably is), but that it is *alone* scientific in nature. From a popular standpoint, application of physical generalizations, as in the technologies of the electric and chemical engineer and in the methods used by "medical science" (if the term be allowed) appeal chiefly because of their practical consequences. But from a logical standpoint the applications are integral parts of the verification of the generalizations themselves. The drainage of swamps where anopheles mosquitoes breed is prized because it helps to eliminate malaria. But from the scientific standpoint it is an experiment which confirms a theory. In general, wide social application of the results of physics and chemistry provides added test and security for conclusions reached.

The issue involved is a far-reaching one. Dogmatic restriction of science to generalizations compels denial of scientific traits and value to every form of practice. It obliterates, logically, the enormous difference that exists between activities that are routine and those that are intelligent; between action dictated by caprice and the conduct of arts that embody technologies and techniques expressing systematically tested ideas. Even more to the point is the fact that it involves logical suicide of the sciences with respect even to generalizations. For there is no ground whatever upon which a logical line can be drawn between the operations and techniques of experimentation in the natural sciences and the same operations and techniques employed for distinctively practical ends. Nothing so fatal to science can be imagined as elimination of experimentation, and experimentation is a form of doing and making. Application of conceptions and hypotheses to existential matters through the medium of doing and making is an intrinsic constituent of scientific method. No hard and fast line can be drawn between such forms of "practical" activity and those which apply *their* conclusions to human social ends without involving disastrous consequences to science in its narrower sense.

CHAPTER EIGHTEEN

KNOWLEDGE SCIENCE AND TRUTH

I · Meanings: Valid and Invalid*

GHOSTS, centaurs, tribal gods, Helen of Troy and Ophelia of Denmark are as much the meanings of events as are flesh and blood, horses, Florence Nightingale and Madam Curie. This statement does not mark a discovery; it enunciates a tautology. It seems questionable only when its significance is altered; when it is taken to denote that, because they are all meanings of events, they all are the same kind of meaning with respect to validity of reference. Because perception of a ghost does not signify a subtle, intangible form, filling space as it moves about, it does not follow that it may not signify some other existential happening like disordered nerves, a religious animistic tradition; or, as in the play of Hamlet, that it may not signify an enhancement of the meaning of a moving state of affairs. The existential events that form a drama have their own characteristic meanings, which are not the less meanings of those events because their import is dramatic, not authentically cognitive. So when men gather in secret to plot a conspiracy, their plans are not the less meanings of certain events because they have not been already carried out; and they remain meanings of events even if the conspiracy comes to naught.

The proposition that the perception of a horse is ob-

* From *Experience and Nature,* pp. 320-324.

jectively valid and that of a centaur fanciful and mythical does not denote that one is a meaning of natural events and the other is not. It denotes that they are meanings referable to *different* natural events, and that confused and harmful consequences result from attributing them to the same events. The idea that the consciousness of a horse as now present and of a centaur differ *as* perceptions, or states of awareness, is an illustration of the harm wrought by introspective psychology, which, here as elsewhere, treats *relationships of objects* as if they were inherent qualities of an immediate subject-matter, ignoring the fact that causal relationships to unperceived things are involved. The matter of the cognitive validity of the horse-perception and the cognitive invalidity of the centaur-perception is not an affair of intrinsic difference in the two perceptions, which inspection of the two states of awareness as such can ever bring to light; it is a causal matter, brought to light as we investigate the causal antecedents and consequents of the events having the meanings.

In other words, the difference between assertion of a perception, belief in it, and merely having it is an extrinsic difference; the belief, assertion, cognitive reference is something additive, never merely immediate. Genuinely to believe the centaur-meaning is to assert that events characterized by it interact in certain ways with other now unperceived events. Since belief that centaur has the same kind of objective meaning as has horse denotes expectation of like efficacies and consequences, the difference of validity between them is extrinsic. It is capable of being revealed only by the results of acting upon them. The awareness of centaur meaning is fanciful not simply because part of its conditions lie within the organism; part of the conditions of *any* perception, valid as well as invalid, scientific as well as esthetic, lie within the organism. Nor is it fanciful, simply because it is supposed not to have adequate existential antecedents. Natural conditions, physiological, physical and social, may be specified in one case as in the other. But since the conditions in the two cases are different, consequences are bound to be different. Knowing, believing, involves something additive and extrinsic to having a meaning.

No knowledge is ever merely immediate. The proposition that the perception of a horse is valid and that a centaur is fanciful or hallucinatory, does not denote that there are two modes of awareness, differing intrinsically from each other. It denotes something with respect to causation, namely, that while both have their adequate antecedent conditions, the specific causal conditions are ascertained to be different in the two cases. Hence it denotes something with respect to consequences, namely, that action upon the respective meanings will bring to light (to apparency or awareness) such different kinds of consequences that we should use the two meanings in very different ways. Both acts and consequences lie outside the primary perceptions; both have to be diligently sought for and tested. Since conditions in the two cases *are* different, they operate differently. That is, they belong to different histories, and the matter of the history to which a given thing belongs is just the matter with which knowledge is concerned.

The conscious or perceived affair is itself a consequence of antecedent conditions. But were this conscious or apparent (evident, focal) consequence the *only* consequence of the conditions, if there were not other as yet unapparent consequences, we should have absolutely no way to tell in what sequence of events a perception belongs, and hence absolutely no way of determining its validity or cognitive standing. It is because conditions which generate the perception of a horse have other and different consequences than the perception (and similarly of those which generate the idea of the centaur), that it is possible to make a distinction between the value in knowledge of the two ideas. By discovering the different sequential affairs to which they respectively belong we can differentiate their import for knowledge. Failure to recognize this fact is the ultimate condemnation, it may be remarked in passing, of idealistic theories of knowledge, which identify knowledge with immediate consciousness. If an all-inclusive consciousness were to exist, it would be a piece of esthetic scenery, interesting or tedious as the case might be, but having no conceivable cognitive standing.

That a perception is cognitive means, accordingly, that it is used; it is treated as a sign of conditions that implicate other as yet unperceived consequences in addition to the perception itself. That a perception is *truly* cognitive means that its active use or treatment is followed by consequences which fit appropriately into the other consequences which follow independently of its being perceived. To discover that a perception or an idea is cognitively invalid is to find that the consequences which follow from acting upon it entangle and confuse the other consequences which follow from the causes of the perception, instead of integrating or coördinating harmoniously with them. The special technique of scientific inquiry may be defined as consisting of procedures which make it possible to perceive the eventual agreement or disagreement of the two sets of consequences. For experience proves that it is possible for great disparity between them to exist, and yet the conflict not be perceived or else be explained away as of no importance.

II · Knowledge as Instrumental and Hypothetical*

There is no miracle in the fact that tool and material are adapted to each other in the process of reaching a valid conclusion. Were they external in origin to each other and to the result, the whole affair would, indeed, present an insoluble problem—so insoluble that, if this were the true condition of affairs, we never should even know that there was a problem. But, in truth, both material and tool have been secured and determined with reference to economy and efficiency in effecting the end desired—the maintenance of a harmonious experience. The builder has discovered that his building means building tools, and also building material. Each has been slowly evolved with reference to its fit employ in the entire function; and this evolution has been checked at every point by reference to its own correspondent. The carpenter has not thought at large on his building and then constructed tools at large, but has thought of his building in terms of the material which enters into it, and through that medium has come to the consideration of the tools which are helpful.

Thinking is adaptation *to* an end *through* the adjustment of particular objective contents. The thinker, like the carpenter, is at once stimulated and checked in every stage of his procedure by the particular situation which confronts him. A person is at the stage of wanting a new house: well, then, his materials are available resources, the price of labor, the cost of building, the state and needs of his family, profession, etc.; his tools are paper and pencil and compass, or possibly the bank as a credit instrumentality, etc. Again, the work is beginning. The

* From *Essays in Experimental Logic,* pp. 13-18; 94-95; 176-178 242-244.

foundations are laid. This in turn determines its own specific materials and tools. Again, the building is almost ready for occupancy. The concrete process is that of taking away the scaffolding, clearing up the grounds, furnishing and decorating rooms, etc. This specific operation again determines its own fit or relevant materials and tools. It defines the time and mode and manner of beginning and ceasing to use them. Logical theory will get along as well as does the practice of knowing when it sticks close by and observes the directions and checks inherent in each successive phase of the evolution of the cycle of experience. The problem in general of validity of the thinking process as distinct from the validity of this or that process arises only when thinking is isolated from its historic position and its material context.

In the course of changing experience we keep our balance in moving from situations of an affectional quality to those which are practical or appreciative or reflective, because we bear constantly in mind the context in which any particular distinction presents itself. As we submit each characteristic function and situation of experience to our gaze, we find it has a dual aspect. Wherever there is striving there are obstacles; wherever there is affection there are persons who are attached; wherever there is doing there is accomplishment; wherever there is appreciation there is value; wherever there is thinking there is material-in-question. We keep our footing as we move from one attitude to another, from one characteristic quality to another, because of the position occupied in the whole movement by the particular function in which we are engaged.

The distinction *between* each attitude and function and its predecessor and successor is serial, dynamic, operative. The distinctions *within* any given operation or function are structural, contemporaneous, and distributive. Thinking follows striving, and doing follows thinking. Each in the fulfilment of its own function inevitably calls out its successor. But coincident, simultaneous, and correspondent *within* doing is the distinction of doer and of deed; *within* the function of thought, of thinking and material thought upon; within the function of striving, of obstacle and aim, of means and end. We keep our paths straight because we do not confuse the sequential and functional relationship of types of experience with the contemporaneous and structural distinctions of elements within a given function. In the seeming maze of endless confusion and unlimited shiftings, we find our way by the means of the stimulations and checks occurring within the process in which we are actually engaged. Operating within empirical situations we do not contrast or confuse a condition which is an element in the formation of one operation with the status which is one of the distributive terms of another function. When we ignore these specific empirical clews and limitations, we have at once an insoluble, because meaningless, problem upon our hands.

All knowledge, as issuing from reflection, is experimental in the literal physical sense of experimental. Thinking, or knowledge-getting, is far from being the armchair thing it is often supposed to be. The reason it is not an armchair thing is that it is not an event going on exclusively within the cortex or the cortex and vocal organs. It involves the explorations by which relevant data are procured and the physical analyses by which they are refined and made precise; it comprises the readings by which information is got hold of, the words which are experimented with, and the calculations by which the significance of entertained conceptions or hypotheses is elaborated. Hands and feet, apparatus and appliances of all kinds are as much a part of it as changes in the brain. Since these physical operations (including the cerebral events) and equipments are a part of thinking, thinking is mental, not because of a peculiar stuff which enters into 't or of peculiar non-natural activities which constitute it, but because of what physical acts and appliances *do:* the distinctive purpose for which they are employed and the distinctive results which they accomplish.

That reflection terminates, through a definitive overt act,* in another non-reflectional situation, within which incompatible responses may again in time be aroused, and so another problem in reflection be set, goes without saying. Certain things about this situation, however, do not at the present time speak for themselves and need to be set forth. Let me in the first place call attention to an ambiguity in the term "knowledge." The statement that all knowledge involves reflection—or, more concretely, that it denotes an inference from evidence—gives offense to many; it seems a departure from fact as well as a wilful limitation of the word "knowledge."

(1) It may well be admitted that there is a real sense in which knowledge (as distinct from thinking or inquiring with a guess attached) does not come into existence till thinking has terminated in the experimental act which fulfils the specifications set forth in thinking. But what is also true is that the object thus determined is an object of *knowledge* only because of the thinking which has preceded it and to which it sets a happy term. To run against a hard and painful stone is not of itself, I should say, an act of knowing; but if running into a hard and painful thing is an outcome predicted after inspection of data and

---

* For emphasis I am here exaggerating by condensing into a single decisive act an operation which is continuously going on.

elaboration of a hypothesis, then the hardness and the painful bruise which define the thing as a stone also constitute it emphatically an object of knowledge. In short, the object of knowledge in the strict sense is its objective; and this objective is not constituted till it is reached. Now this conclusion—as the word denotes—is thinking brought to a close, done with.

If the reader does not find this statement satisfactory, he may at least recognize that the doctrine set forth has no difficulty in connecting knowledge with inference, and at the same time admitting that knowledge in the emphatic sense does not exist till inference has ceased. Seen from this point of view, so-called immediate knowledge or simple apprehension or acquaintance knowledge represents a critical skill, a certainty of response which has accrued in consequence of reflection. A like sureness of footing apart from prior investigations and testings is found in instinct and habit. I do not deny that these may be better than knowing, but I see no reason for complicating an already too confused situation by giving them the name "knowledge" with its usual intellectual implications. From this point of view, the subject-matter of knowledge is precisely that which we do *not* think of, or mentally refer to in any way, being that which is taken as matter of course, but it is nevertheless knowledge in virtue of the inquiry which has led up to it.

(2) Definiteness, depth, and variety of meaning attach to the objects of an experience just in the degree in which they have been previously thought about, even when present in an experience in which they do not evoke inferential procedures at all. Such terms as "meaning," "significance," "value," have a double sense. Sometimes they mean a function: the office of one thing representing another, or pointing to it as implied; the operation, in short,

of serving as sign. In the word "symbol" this meaning is practically exhaustive. But the terms also sometimes mean an inherent quality, a quality intrinsically characterizing the thing experienced and making it worth while. The word "sense," as in the phrase "sense of a thing" (and non-sense) is devoted to this use as definitely as are the words "sign" and "symbol" to the other. In such a pair as "import" and "importance," the first tends to select the reference to another thing while the second names an intrinsic content.

In reflection, the extrinsic reference is always primary. The height of the mercury means rain; the color of the flame means sodium; the form of the curve means factors distributed accidentally. In the situation which follows upon reflection, meanings are intrinsic; they have no instrumental or subservient office, because they have no office at all. They are as much qualities of the objects in the situation as are red and black, hard and soft, square and round. And every reflective experience adds new shades of such intrinsic qualifications. In other words, while reflective knowing is instrumental to gaining control in a troubled situation (and thus has a practical or utilitarian force), it is also instrumental to the enrichment of the immediate significance of subsequent experiences. And it may well be that this by-product, this gift of the gods, is incomparably more valuable for living a life than is the primary and intended result of control, essential as is that control to having a life to live.

Words are treacherous in this field; there are no accepted criteria for assigning or measuring their meanings; but if one use the term "consciousness" to denote immediate values of objects, then it is certainly true that "consciousness is a lyric cry even in the midst of business." But it is equally true that if someone else understands by consciousness the function of effective reflection, then consciousness is a business—even in the midst of writing or singing lyrics. But the statement remains inadequate until we add that knowing as a business, inquiry and invention as enterprises, as practical acts, become themselves charged with the meaning of what they accomplish as *their* own immediate quality. There exists no disjunction between esthetic qualities which are final yet idle, and acts which are practical or instrumental. The latter have their own delights and sorrows.

The intellectual definition or delimitation assigned to the "given" is as tentative and experimental as that ascribed to the idea. In form both are categorical, and in content both are hypothetical. Facts really exist just as facts, and meanings exist as meanings. One is no more superfluous, more subjective, or less necessitated than the other. In and of themselves as existences both are equally realistic and compulsive. But on the basis of existence, there is no element in either which may be strictly described as intellectual or cognitional. There is only a practical situation in its brute and unrationalized form.

What is uncertain about the facts as given at any moment is whether the right exclusions and selections have been made. Since that is a question which can be decided finally only by the experimental issue, this ascription of character is itself tentative and experimental. If it works, the characterization and delineation are found to be proper ones; but every admission prior to inquiry, of unquestioned, categorical, rigid objectivity, compromises the probability that it will work. The character assigned to the datum must be taken as hypothetically as possible in order to preserve the elasticity needed for easy and prompt consideration. Any other procedure virtually insists that all facts and details anywhere happening to exist and happening to present themselves (all being equally real) must all be given equal status and equal weight, and that their outer ramifications and internal complexities must be indefinitely followed up. The worthlessness of this sheer accumulation of realities, its total irrelevancy, the lack of any way of judging the significance of the accumulations are good proofs of the fallacy of any theory which ascribes objective logical content to facts wholly apart from the needs and possibilities of a situation.

The more stubbornly one maintains the *full* reality of either his facts or his ideas, just as they stand, the more accidental is the discovery of relevantly significant facts and of valid ideas—the more accidental, the less rational, is the issue of the knowledge situation. Due progress is reasonably probable in just the degree in which the meaning, categorical in its existing imperativeness, and the fact, equally categorical in its brute coerciveness, are assigned only a provisional and tentative nature with reference to control of the situation. That this surrender of a rigid and final character for the content of knowledge on the sides both of fact and of meaning, in favor of experimental and functioning estimations, is precisely the change which has marked the development of modern from medieval and Greek science, seems undoubted.

To learn the lesson one has only to contrast the rigidity of phenomena and conceptions in Greek thought (Platonic ideas, Aristotelian forms) with the modern experimental selection and determining of facts and experimental employment of hypotheses. The former have ceased to be ultimate realities of a nondescript sort and have become provisional data; the latter have ceased to be eternal meanings and have become working theories. The fruitful application of mathematics and the evolution of a technique of experimental inquiry have coincided with this change. That realities exist independently of their use as intellectual data, and that meanings exist apart from their utilization as hypotheses, are the permanent truths of Greek realism as against the exaggerated subjectivism of modern philosophy; but the conception that this existence is to be defined in the same way as are contents of knowledge, so that perfect being is object of perfect knowledge and imperfect being object of imperfect knowledge, is the fallacy which Greek thought projected into modern. Science has advanced in its methods in just the degree in which it has ceased to assume that prior realities and prior meanings retain fixedly and finally, when entering into reflective situations, the characters they had prior to this entrance; and in which it has realized that their very presence within the knowledge situation signifies that they have to be redefined and revalued from the standpoint of the new situation.

III · Experimental Verification and Truth*

That fruitful thinking—thought that terminates in valid knowledge—goes on in terms of the distinction of facts and judgment, and that valid knowledge is precisely genuine correspondence or agreement, *of some sort,* of fact and judgment, is the common and undeniable assumption. But the discussions are largely carried on in terms of an epistemological dualism, rendering the solution of the problem impossible in virtue of the very terms in which it is stated. The distinction is at once identified with that between mind and matter, consciousness and objects, the psychical and the physical, where each of these terms is supposed to refer to some fixed order of existence, a world in itself. Then, of course, there comes up the question of the nature of the agreement, and of the recognition of it·

* From *Essays in Experimental Logic,* pp. 231-241.

What is the experience in which the survey of both idea and existence is made and their agreement recognized? Is it an idea? Is the agreement ultimately a matter of self-consistency of ideas? Then what has become of the postulate that truth is agreement of idea with existence beyond idea? Is it an absolute which transcends and absorbs the difference? Then, once more, what is the test of any specific judgment? What has become of the correspondence of fact and thought? Or, more urgently, since the pressing problem of life, of practice and of science, is the discrimination of the *relative,* or *superior,* validity of this or that theory, plan, or interpretation, what is the criterion of truth within present non-absolutistic experience, where the distinction between factual conditions and thoughts and the necessity of some working adjustment persists?

Putting the problem in yet another way, either both fact and idea are present all the time or else only one of them is present. But if the former, why should there be an idea at all, and why should it have to be tested by the fact? When we already have what we want, namely, existence, reality, why should we take up the wholly supernumerary task of forming more or less imperfect ideas of those facts, and then engage in the idle performance of testing them by what we already know to be? But if only ideas are present, it is idle to speak of comparing an idea with facts and testing its validity by its agreement. The elaboration and refinement of ideas to the uttermost still leaves us with an idea, and while a self-consistent idea stands a show of being true in a way in which an incoherent one does not, a self-consistent idea is still but a hypothesis, a candidate for truth. Ideas are not made true by getting bigger. But if only "facts" are present, the whole conception of agreement is once more given up—not to mention that such a situation is one in which there is by definition no thinking or reflective factor at all.

This suggests that a strictly monistic epistemology, whether idealistic or realistic, does not get rid of the problem. Suppose for example we take a sensationalistic idealism. It does away with the ontological gulf between ideas and facts, and by reducing both terms to a common denominator seems to facilitate fruitful discussion of the problem. But the problem of the distinction and reference (agreement, correspondence) of two types or sorts of sensations still persists. If I say the box there is square, and call "box" one of a group of ideas or sensations and "square" another sensation or "idea," the old question comes up: Is "square" already a part of the "facts" of the box, or is it not? If it is, it is a supernumerary, an idle thing, both as an idea and as an assertion of fact; if it is not, how can we compare the two ideas, and what on earth or in heaven does their agreement or correspondence mean? If it means simply that we experience the two "sensations" in juxtaposition, then the same is true, of course, of any casual association or hallucination. On the sensational basis, accordingly, there is still a distinction of something "given," "there," brutally factual, the box, and something else which stands on a different level, ideal, absent, intended, demanded, the "square," which is asserted to hold good or be true of the thing "box." The fact that both are sensations throws no light on the logical validity of any proposition or belief, because by theory a like statement holds of every possible proposition.

The same problem recurs on a realistic basis. For example, there has recently been propounded the doctrine of the distinction between relations of space and time and relations of meaning or significance, as a key to the problem of knowledge. Things exist in their own characters, in their temporal and spatial relations. When knowledge intervenes, there is nothing new of a subjective or psychical sort, but simply a new relation of the things—the suggesting or signifying of one thing by another. Now this seems to be an excellent way of stating the logical problem, but, I take it, it states and does not solve. For the characteristic of such situations, claiming to terminate in knowledge, is precisely that the meaning-relation is predicated *of* the other relations; it is referred to them; it is not simply a supervention existing side by side with them, like casual suggestions or the play of fantasy. It is something which the facts, the qualitative space and time things, must bear the burden of, must accept and take unto themselves as part of themselves. Until this happens, we have only "thinking," not accomplished knowledge. Hence, logically, the existential relations play the role of fact, and the relation of signification that of idea, distinguished from fact and yet, if valid, to hold *of* fact. In other words, "ideas" is a term capable of assuming any definition which is logically appropriate—say, meaning. It need not have anything to do with the conception of little subjective entities or psychical stuffs.

This appears quite clearly in the following quotation: "It is the ice which means that it will cool the water, just as much as it is the ice which does cool the water when put into it." There is, however, a possible ambiguity in the statement. That the "ice" (the thing regarded as ice) *suggests* cooling is as real as is a case of actual cooling. But, of course, not every suggestion is valid. The "ice" may be a crystal, and it will not cool water at all. So far as it is already certain that this *is* ice, and also certain that ice, under all circumstances, cools water, the meaning-relation stands on the same level as the physical, being not merely suggested, but part of the facts ascertained. It is not a meaning-relation as such at all. We already have truth; the entire work of knowing as logical is done; we have no longer the relation characteristic of reflective situations Here again the implication of the thinking situation is of some "correspondence" or "agreement" between two sets of distinguished relations; the problem of valid determination remains the central question of any theory of knowing in its relation to facts and truth.

I hope the above statement of the difficulty, however inadequate, will serve at least to indicate that a functional logic inherits the problem in question and does not create it; that it has never for a moment denied the *prima facie* working distinction between "ideas," "thoughts," and "facts," "existences," "the environment," or the necessity of a control of meaning by facts. It is concerned not with denying, but with understanding. What is denied is not the genuineness of the problem of the terms in which it is stated, but the reality and value of the orthodox interpretation. What is insisted upon is the relative, instrumental, or working character of the distinction—that it *is a logical* distinction, instituted and maintained in the interests of intelligence, with all that intelligence imports in the exercise of the life functions.

It may prove convenient to take an illustration of a man lost in the woods, taking this case as typical of any reflective situation in so far as it involves perplexity—a problem to be solved. The problem is to find a correct idea of the way home—a practical idea or plan of action which will lead to success, or the realization of the purpose to get home. Now the critics of the experimental theory of logic make the point that this practical idea, the truth of which is evidenced in the successful meeting of a need, is dependent for its success upon a purely presentative idea, that of the existent environment, whose validity has nothing to do with success but depends on agreement with the given state of affairs. It is said that what makes a man's idea of his environment true is its agreement with the actual environment, and "generally a true idea in any situation consists in its agreement with reality." I have already indicated my acceptance of this formula. But it was long my misfortune not to be possessed offhand of those perfectly clear notions of just what is meant in this formula by the terms "idea," "existence," and "agreement" which are possessed by other writers on epistemology; and when I analyzed these notions I found the distinction between the practical idea and the theoretical not fixed nor final, and I found a somewhat startling similarity between the notions of "success" and "agreement."

Just what is the environment of which an idea is to be formed: *i.e.*, what is the intellectual content or objective detail to be assigned to the term "environment"? It can hardly mean the actual visible environment—the trees, rocks, etc., which a man is actually looking at. These things are there and it seems superfluous to form an idea of them; moreover, the wayfaring man, though lost, would have to be an unusually perverse fool if under such circumstances he were unable to form an idea (supposing he chose to engage in this luxury) in agreement with these facts. The environment must be a larger environment than the visible facts; it must include things not within the direct ken of the lost man; it must, for instance, extend from where he is now to his home, or to the point from which he started. It must include unperceived elements in their contrast with the perceived. Otherwise the man would not be lost. Now we are at once struck with the facts that the lost man has no alternative except either to wander aimlessly or else to *conceive* this inclusive environment; and that this conception is just what is meant by

idea. It is not some little psychical entity or piece of con-
sciousness-stuff, but is *the interpretation of the locally
present environment in reference to its absent portion,*
that part to which it is referred as another part so as to
give a view of a whole. Just how such an idea would differ
from one's plan of action in finding one's way, I do not
know. For one's plan (if it be really a plan, a method) is a
conception of what is given in its hypothetical relations to
what is not given, employed as a guide to that act which
results in the absent being also given. It is a map constructed with one's self lost and one's self found, whether
at starting or at home again, as its two limits. If this map
in its specific character is not also the only guide to the
way home, one's only plan of action, then I hope I may
never be lost. It is the *practical* facts of being lost and desiring to be found which constitute the limits and the
content of the "environment."

Then comes the test of *agreement* of the idea and the
environment. Supposing the individual stands still and attempts to compare his idea with the reality, with what
reality is he to compare it? Not with the presented reality,
for *that* reality is the reality of himself lost; not with the
complete reality, for at this stage of proceedings he has
only the idea to stand for the complete theory. What kind
of comparison is possible or desirable then, save to treat
the mental layout of the whole situation as a working hypothesis, as a plan of action, and proceed to *act* upon it,
to use it as a director and controller of one's divagations
instead of stumbling blindly around until one is either exhausted or accidentally gets out? Now suppose one uses
the idea—that is to say, the present facts projected into a
whole in the light of absent facts—as a guide of action.
Suppose, by means of its specifications, one works one's
way along until one comes upon familiar ground—finds

one's self. *Now,* one may say, my idea was right, it was in accord with facts; it agrees with reality. That is, acted upon sincerely, it has led to the desired conclusion; it has, *through action,* worked out the state of things which it contemplated or intended. The agreement, correspondence, is between purpose, plan, and its own execution, fulfillment; between a map of a course constructed for the sake of guiding behavior and the result attained in acting upon the indications of the map. Just how does such agreement differ from success?

If we exclude acting upon the idea, no conceivable amount or kind of intellectualistic procedure can confirm or refute an idea, or throw any light upon its validity. How does the non-pragmatic view consider that verification takes place? Does it suppose that we first look a long while at the facts and then a long time at the idea, until by some magical process the degree and kind of their agreement become visible? Unless there is some such conception as this, what conception of agreement is possible except the experimental or practical one? And if it be admitted that verification involves action, how can that action be relevant to the truth of an idea, unless the idea is itself already relevant to action? If by acting in accordance with the experimental definition of facts (viz., as obstacles and conditions), and the experimental definition of the end or intent (viz., as plan and method of action) a harmonized situation effectually presents itself, we have the adequate and the only conceivable verification of the intellectual factors. If the action indicated be carried out and the disordered or disturbed situation persists, then we have not merely confuted the tentative positions of intelligence, but we have in the very process of acting introduced new data and eliminated some of the old ones, and thus afforded an opportunity for the resurvey of the facts and the revision of the plan of action. By acting faithfully upon an inadequate reflective presentation, we have at least secured the elements for its improvement. This, of course, gives no absolute guaranty that the reflection will at any time be so performed as to prove its validity in fact. But the self-rectification of intellectual content through acting upon it in good faith is the "absolute" of knowledge, loyalty to which is the religion of intellect.

IV · Pure and Applied Science*

Knowledge is a word of various meanings. Etymologically, "science" may signify tested and authentic instance of knowledge. But knowledge has also a meaning more liberal and more humane. It signifies events understood, events so discriminately penetrated by thought that mind is literally at home in them. It means comprehension, or inclusive reasonable agreement. What is sometimes termed "applied" science, may then be more truly science than is what is conventionally called pure science. For it is directly concerned with not just instrumentalities, but instrumentalities at work in effecting modifications of existence in behalf of conclusions that are reflectively preferred. Thus conceived the characteristic subject-matter of knowledge consists of fulfilling objects, which as fulfillments are connected with a history to which they give character. Thus conceived, knowledge exists in engineering, medicine and the social arts more adequately than it does in mathematics, and physics. Thus conceived, history and anthropology are scientific in a sense in which bodies of information that stop short with general formulae are not.

"Application" is a hard word for many to accept. It suggests some extraneous tool ready-made and complete

* From *Experience and Nature*, pp. 161-165.

which is then put to uses that are external to its nature. To call the arts applications of science is then to introduce something foreign to the sciences which the latter irrelevantly and accidentally serve. Since the application is in human use, convenience, enjoyment and improvement, this view of application as something external and arbitrary reflects and strengthens the theories which detach man from nature, which, in the language of philosophy, oppose subject and object. But if we free ourselves from preconceptions, application of "science" means application *in*, not application *to*. Application *in* something signifies a more extensive interaction of natural events with one another, an elimination of distance and obstacles; provision of opportunities for interactions that reveal potentialities previously hidden and that bring into existence new histories with new initiations and endings. Engineering, medicine, social arts realize relationships that were unrealized in actual existences. Surely in their new context the latter are understood or known as they are not in isolation. Prejudice against the abstract, as something remote and technical, is often irrational; but there is sense in the conviction that in the abstract there is something lacking which should be recovered. The serious objection to "applied" science lies in limitation of the application, as to private profit and class advantage.

"Pure" science is of necessity relational and abstract: it fulfills its meaning and gains full truth when included within a course of concrete events. The proposition that "pure" science is non-existential is a tacit admission that only "applied" science is existential. Therefore, more than history and anthropology lose all scientific standing when standards of "purity" are set up as ultimate—all sciences of existential events lose standing. There is superstitious awe reflected in the current estimate of science. If we could free ourselves from a somewhat abject emotion, it would be clear enough that what makes any proposition scientific is its power to yield understanding, insight, intellectual at-homeness, in connection with any existential state of affairs, by filling events with coherent and tested meanings. The case of history is typical and basic. Upon the current view, it is a waste of time to discuss whether there can be such a thing as a science of history. History and science are by definition at opposite poles. And yet if all natural existences *are* histories, divorce between history and the logical mathematical schemes which are the appropriate objects of pure science, terminates in the conclusion that of existences there is no science, no adequate knowledge.

Aside from mathematics, all knowledge is historic; chemistry, geology, physiology, as well as anthropology and those human events to which, arrogantly, we usually restrict the title of history. Only as science is seen to be fulfilled and brought to itself in intelligent management of historical processes in their continuity can man be envisaged as within nature, and not as a supernatural extrapolation. Just because nature is what it is, history is capable of being more truly known—understood, intellectually realized—than are mathematical and physical objects. Do what we can, there always remains something recondite and remote in the latter, until they are restored in the course of affairs from which they have been sequestrated. While the humanizing of science contributes to the life of humanity, it is even more required in behalf of science, in order that it may be intelligible, simple and clear; in order that it may have that correspondence with reality which true knowledge claims for itself.

One can understand the sentiment that animates the bias of scientific inquirers against the idea that all science is ultimately applied. It is justified in the sense in which it is intended; for it is directed against two conceptions which are harmful, but which, also, are irrelevant to the position here taken. One of these conceptions is that the concern or personal motive of the inquirer should be in each particular inquiry some specific practical application. This is just as it happens to be. Doubtless many important scientific discoveries have been thus instigated, but that is an incident of human history rather than of scientific inquiry as such. And upon the whole, or if this animating interest were to become general, the undoubted effect is limitation of inquiry and thereby in the end of the field of application. It marks a recurrence to the dogma of fixed predetermined ends, while emancipation from the influence of this dogma has been the chief service rendered modern scientific methods.

The evil thus effected is increased by the second notion, namely, that application is identical with "commercialized" use. It is an incident of human history, and a rather appalling incident, that applied science has been so largely made an equivalent of use for private and economic class purposes and privileges. When inquiry is narrowed by such motivation or interest, the consequence is in so far disastrous both to science and to human life. But this limitation does not spring from nor attach to the conception of "application" which has been just presented. It springs from defects and perversions of morality as that is embodied in institutions and their effects upon personal disposition. It may be questioned whether the notion that science is pure in the sense of being concerned exclusively with a realm of objects detached from human concerns has not conspired to reinforce this moral deficiency. For in effect it has established another class interest, that of intellectualists and aloof specialists. And it is of the nature of any class interest to generate and confirm other class interests, since division and isolation in a world of continuities are always reciprocal. The institution of an interest labelled ideal and idealistic in isolation tends of necessity to evoke and strengthen other interests lacking ideal quality. The genuine interests of "pure" science are served only by broadening the idea of application to include all phases of liberation and enrichment of human experience.

V · Social Science and Social Control*

It would require a technical survey, which would be out of place here, to prove that the existing limitations of "social science" are due mainly to unreasoning devotion to physical science as a model, and to a misconception of physical science at that. Without making any such survey, attention may be directly called to one outstanding difference between physical and social facts. The ideal of the knowledge dealing with the former is the elimination of all factors dependent upon distinctively human response. "Fact," physically speaking, is the ultimate residue after human purposes, desires, emotions, ideas and ideals have been systematically excluded. A social "fact," on the other hand, is a concretion in external form of precisely these human factors.

An occurrence is a physical fact only when its constituents and their relations remain the same, irrespective of the human attitude toward them. A species of mosquitoes is the carrier of the germs of malaria, whether we like or dislike malaria. Drainage and oil-spraying to destroy mosquitoes are a social fact because their use depends upon human purpose and desire. A steam locomotive or a dynamo is a physical fact in its structure; it is a social fact when its existence depends upon the desire for rapid and

* From *The New Republic,* July 29, 1931.

cheap transportation and communication. The machine itself may be understood physically without reference to human aim and motive. But the railway or public-utility system cannot be understood without reference to human purposes and human consequences.

I may illustrate the present practice of slavishly following the technique of physical science and the uselessness of its results by the present zeal for "fact finding." Of course, one cannot think, understand and plan without a basis of fact, and since facts do not lie around in plain view, they have to be discovered. But for the most part, the data which now are so carefully sought and so elaborately scheduled are not social facts at all. For their connection with any system of human purposes and consequences, their bearing as means and as results upon human action, are left out of the picture. At best they are mere physical and external facts. They are unlike the facts of physical science, because the latter are found by methods which make their interrelations and their laws apparent, while the facts of social "fact finding" remain a miscellaneous pile of meaningless items. Since their connections with human wants and their effect on human values are neglected, there is nothing which binds them together into an intelligible whole.

It may be retorted that to connect facts with human desires and their effect upon human values is subjective and moral, and to an extent that makes it impossible to establish any conclusions upon an objective basis: that to attempt inference on this point would land us in a morass of speculative opinion. Suppose, for example, all the facts about the working of the prohibition law and its enforcement were much more completely known than they are; even so, to establish a connection between these facts and the human attitudes lying back of them would be a matter of guesswork. As things stand, there is much force in the objection. But if made universal, it would overlook the possibility of another kind of situation.

Wherever purposes are employed deliberately and systematically for the sake of certain desired social results, there it is possible, within limits, to determine the connection between the human factor and the actual occurrence, and thus to get a complete social fact, namely, the actual external occurrence in its human relationships. Prohibition, whether noble or not, is not an experiment in any intelligent scientific sense of the term. For it was undertaken without the effort to obtain the conditions of control which are essential to any experimental determination of fact. The Five Year Plan of Russia, on the other hand, whether noble or the reverse, has many of the traits of a social experiment, for it is an attempt to obtain certain specified social results by the use of specified definite measures, exercised under conditions of considerable, if not complete, control.

The point I am making may be summed up by saying that it is a complete error to suppose that efforts at social control depend upon the prior existence of a social science. The reverse is the case. The building up of social science, that is, of a body of knowledge in which facts are ascertained in their significant relations, is dependent upon putting social planning into effect. It is at this point that the misconception about physical science, when it is taken as a model for social knowledge, is important. Physical science did not develop because inquirers piled up a mass of facts about observed phenomena. It came into being when men intentionally experimented, on the basis of ideas and hypotheses, with observed phenomena to modify them and disclose new observations. This process is self-corrective and self-developing. Imperfect and even wrong hypotheses, when *acted upon,* brought to light significant phenomena which made improved ideas and improved experimentations possible. The change from a passive and accumulative attitude into an active and productive one is the secret revealed by the progress of physical inquiry. Men obtained knowledge of natural energies by trying deliberately to control the conditions of their operation. The result was knowledge, and then control on a larger scale by the application of what was learned.

It is a commonplace of logical theory that laws are of the "if-then" type. *If* something occurs, *then* something else happens; if certain conditions exist, they are accompanied by certain other conditions. Such knowledge alone is knowledge of a fact in any intelligible sense of the word. Although we have to act in order to discover the conditions underlying the "if" in physical matters, yet the material constituting the "if" is there apart from our action; like the movements of sun and earth in an eclipse. But in social phenomena the relation is: "If we *do* something, something else will happen." The objective material constituting the "if" belongs to us, not to something wholly independent of us. We are concerned, not with a bare relation of cause and effect, but with one of means and consequences, that is, of causes deliberately used for the sake of producing certain effects. As far as we intentionally do and make, we shall know; as far as we "know" without making, our so-called knowledge is a miscellany, or at most antiquarian, and hence without relevance to future planning. Only the knowledge which is itself the fruit of a technology can breed further technology.

I want to make the same point with reference to social prediction. Here, too, the assumption is generally made that we must be able to predict before we can plan and control. Here again the reverse is the case. We can predict the occurrence of an eclipse precisely because we cannot control it. If we could control it, we could not predict, except contingently; just as we can predict a collision when we see two trains approaching on the same track—provided that a human being does not foresee the possibility and take measures to avert its happening. The other day I ran across a remark of Alexander Hamilton's to the effect that instead of awaiting an event to know what measures to take, we should take measures to bring the event to pass. And I would add that only then can we genuinely forecast the future in the world of social matters.

Empirical, rule-of-thumb practices were the mothers of the arts. But the practices of the arts were in turn the source of science, when once the empirical methods were freed in imagination and used with some degree of freedom of experimentation. There cannot be a science of an art until the art has itself made some advance, and the significant development occurs when men intentionally try to use such art as they have already achieved in order to obtain results which they conceive to be desirable. If we have no social technique at all, it is impossible to bring planning and control into being. If we do have at hand a reasonable amount of technique, then it is by deliberately using what we have that we shall in the end develop a dependable body of social knowledge. If we want foresight, we shall not obtain it by any amount of fact finding so long as we disregard the human aims and desires producing the facts which we find. But if we decide upon what we want socially, what sort of social consequences we wish to occur, and then use whatever means we possess to effect these intended consequences, we shall find the road that leads to foresight. Forethought and planning must come before foresight.

I am not arguing here for the desirability of social planning and control. That is another question. Those who are satisfied with present conditions and who are hopeful of turning them to account for personal profit and power will answer it in the negative. What I am saying is that if we want something to which the name "social science" may be given, there is only one way to go about it, namely, by entering upon the path of social planning and control. Observing, collecting, recording and filing tomes of social phenomena without deliberately trying to do something to bring a desired state of society into existence only encourages a conflict of opinion and dogma in their interpretation. If the social situation out of which these facts emerge is itself confused and chaotic because it expresses socially unregulated purpose and haphazard private intent, the facts themselves will be confused, and we shall add only intellectual confusion to practical disorder. When we deliberately employ whatever skill we possess in order to serve the ends which we desire, we shall begin to attain a measure of at least intellectual order and understanding. And if past history teaches anything, it is that with intellectual order we have the surest possible promise of advancement to practical order.

CHAPTER NINETEEN

THE ARTISTIC-ESTHETIC IN EXPERIENCE

I · The Roots of Esthetic Experience*

WHY is the attempt to connect the higher and ideal things of experience with basic vital roots so often regarded as betrayal of their nature and denial of their value? Why is there repulsion when the high achievements of fine art are brought into connection with common life, the life that we share with all living creatures? Why is life thought of as an affair of low appetite, or at its best a thing of gross sensation, and ready to sink from its best to the level of lust and harsh cruelty? A complete answer to the question would involve the writing of a history of morals that would set forth the conditions that have brought about contempt for the body, fear of the senses, and the opposition of flesh to spirit.

One aspect of this history is so relevant to our problem that it must receive at least passing notice. The institutional life of mankind is marked by disorganization. This disorder is often disguised by the fact that it takes the form of static division into classes, and this static separation is accepted as the very essence of order as long as it is so fixed and so accepted as not to generate open conflict. Life is compartmentalized and the institutionalized compartments are classified as high and as low; their

* From *Art as Experience*, pp. 13-23.

values as profane and spiritual, as material and ideal. Interests are related to one another externally and mechanically, through a system of checks and balances. Since religion, morals, politics, business has each its own compartment, within which it is fitting each should remain, art, too, must have its peculiar and private realm. Compartmentalization of occupations and interests brings about separation of that mode of activity commonly called "practice" from insight, of imagination from executive doing, of significant purpose from work, of emotion from thought and doing. Each of these has, too, its own place in which it must abide. Those who write the anatomy of experience then suppose that these divisions inhere in the very constitution of human nature.

Of much of our experience as it is actually lived under present economic and legal institutional conditions, it is only too true that these separations hold. Only occasionally in the lives of many are the senses fraught with the sentiment that comes from deep realization of intrinsic meanings. We undergo sensations as mechanical stimuli or as irritated stimulations, without having a sense of the reality that is in them and behind them: in much of our experience our different senses do not unite to tell a common and enlarged story. We see without feeling; we hear, but only a second-hand report, second-hand because not reenforced by vision. We touch, but the contact remains tangential because it does not fuse with qualities of senses that go below the surface. We use the senses to arouse passion but not to fulfill the interest of insight, not because that interest is not potentially present in the exercise of sense but because we yield to conditions of living that force sense to remain an excitation on the surface. Prestige goes to those who use their minds without participation of the body and who act vicariously through control of the bodies and labor of others.

Under such conditions, sense and flesh get a bad name. The moralist, however, has a truer sense of the intimate connections of sense with the rest of our being than has the professional psychologist and philosopher, although his sense of these connections takes a direction that reverses the potential facts of our living in relation to the environment. Psychologist and philosopher have in recent times been so obsessed with the problem of knowledge that they have treated "sensations" as mere elements of knowledge. The moralist knows that sense is allied with emotion, impulse and appetition. So he denounces the lust of the eye as part of the surrender of spirit to flesh. He identifies the sensuous with the sensual and the sensual with the lewd. His moral theory is askew, but at least he is aware that the eye is not an imperfect telescope designed for intellectual reception of material to bring about knowledge of distant objects.

"Sense" covers a wide range of contents: the sensory, the sensational, the sensitive, the sensible, and the sentimental, along with the sensuous. It includes almost everything from bare physical and emotional shock to sense itself—that is, the meaning of things present in immediate experience. Each term refers to some real phase and aspect of the life of an organic creature as life occurs through sense organs. But sense, as meaning so directly embodied in experience as to be its own illuminated meaning, is the only signification that expresses the function of sense organs when they are carried to full realization. The senses are the organs through which the live creature participates directly in the ongoings of the world about him. In this participation the varied wonder and splendor of this world are made actual for him in the qualities he experiences. This material cannot be opposed to action, for motor apparatus and "will" itself are the means by which this participation is carried on and directed. It cannot be opposed to "intellect," for mind is the means by which participation is rendered fruitful through sense; by which meanings and values are extracted, retained, and put to further service in the intercourse of the live creature with his surroundings.

Experience is the result, the sign, and the reward of that interaction of organism and environment which, when it is carried to the full, is a transformation of interaction into participation and communication. Since sense-organs with their connected motor apparatus are the means of this participation, any and every derogation of them, whether practical or theoretical, is at once effect and cause of a narrowed and dulled life-experience. Oppositions of mind and body, soul and matter, spirit and flesh all have their origin, fundamentally, in fear of what life may bring forth. They are marks of contraction and withdrawal. Full recognition, therefore, of the continuity of the organs, needs and basic impulses of the human creature with his animal forbears, implies no necessary reduction of man to the level of the brutes. On the contrary, it makes possible the drawing of a ground-plan of human experience upon which is erected the superstructure of man's marvelous and distinguishing experience. What is distinctive in man makes it possible for him to sink below the level of the beasts. It also makes it possible for him to carry to new and unprecedented heights that unity of sense and impulse, of brain and eye and ear, that is exemplified in animal life, saturating it with the conscious meanings derived from communication and deliberate expression.

While man is other than bird and beast, he shares basic vital functions with them and has to make the same basal adjustments if he is to continue the process of living. Having the same vital needs, man derives the means by which he breathes, moves, looks and listens, the very brain with which he coördinates his senses and his movements, from his animal forbears. The organs with which he maintains himself in being are not of himself alone, but by the grace of struggles and achievements of a long line of animal ancestry.

Fortunately a theory of the place of the esthetic in experience does not have to lose itself in minute details when it starts with experience in its elemental form. Broad outlines suffice. The first great consideration is that life goes on in an environment; not merely *in* it but because of it, through interaction with it. No creature lives merely under its skin; its subcutaneous organs are means of connection with what lies beyond its bodily frame, and to which, in order to live, it must adjust itself, by accommodation and defense but also by conquest. At every moment, the living creature is exposed to dangers from its surroundings, and at every moment, it must draw upon something in its surroundings to satisfy its needs. The career and destiny of a living being are bound up with its interchanges with its environment, not externally but in the most intimate way.

The growl of a dog crouching over his food, his howl in time of loss and loneliness, the wagging of his tail at the return of his human friend are expressions of the implication of a living creature in a natural medium which includes man along with the animal he has domesticated. Every need, say hunger for fresh air or food, is a lack that denotes at least a temporary absence of adequate adjustment with surroundings. But it is also a demand, a reaching out into the environment to make good the lack and to restore adjustment by building at least a temporary equilibrium. Life itself consists of phases in which the organism falls out of step with the march of surrounding things and then recovers unison with it—either through effort or by some happy chance. And, in a growing life, the recovery is never mere return to a prior state, for it is enriched by the state of disparity and resistance through which it has successfully passed. If the gap between organism and environment is too wide, the creature dies. If its activity is not enhanced by the temporary alienation, it merely subsists. Life grows when a temporary falling out is a transition to a more extensive balance of the energies of the organism with those of the conditions under which it lives.

These biological commonplaces are something more than that; they reach to the roots of the esthetic in experience. The world is full of things that are indifferent and even hostile to life; the very processes by which life is maintained tend to throw it out of gear with its surroundings. Nevertheless, if life continues and if in continuing it expands, there is an overcoming of factors of opposition and conflict; there is a transformation of them into differentiated aspects of a higher powered and more significant life. The marvel of organic, of vital, adaptation through expansion (instead of by contraction and passive accommodation) actually takes place. Here in germ are balance and harmony attained through rhythm. Equilibrium comes about not mechanically and inertly but out of, and because of, tension.

There is in nature, even below the level of life, something more than mere flux and change. Form is arrived at whenever a stable, even though moving, equilibrium is reached. Changes interlock and sustain one another. Wherever there is this coherence there is endurance. Order is not imposed from without but is made out of the relations of harmonious interactions that energies bear to one another. Because it is active (not anything static because foreign to what goes on) order itself develops. It comes to include within its balanced movement a greater variety of changes.

Order cannot but be admirable in a world constantly threatened with disorder—in a world where living creatures can go on living only by taking advantage of whatever order exists about them, incorporating it into themselves. In a world like ours, every living creature that attains sensibility welcomes order with a response of harmonious feeling whenever it finds a congruous order about it.

For only when an organism shares in the ordered relations of its environment does it secure the stability essential to living. And when the participation comes after a phase of disruption and conflict, it bears within itself the germs of a consummation akin to the esthetic.

There are two sorts of possible worlds in which esthetic experience would not occur. In a world of mere flux, change would not be cumulative; it would not move toward a close. Stability and rest would have no being. Equally is it true, however, that a world that is finished, ended, would have no traits of suspense and crisis, and would offer no opportunity for resolution. Where everything is already complete, there is no fulfillment. We envisage with pleasure Nirvana and a uniform heavenly bliss only because they are projected upon the background of our present world of stress and conflict. Because the actual world, that in which we live, is a combination of movement and culmination, of breaks and re-unions, the experience of a living creature is capable of esthetic quality. The live being recurrently loses and reëstablishes equilibrium with his surroundings. The moment of passage from disturbance into harmony is that of intensest life. In a finished world, sleep and waking could not be distinguished. In one wholly perturbed, conditions could not even be struggled with. In a world made after the pattern of ours, moments of fulfillment punctuate experience with rhythmically enjoyed intervals.

It is mere ignorance that leads to the supposition that connection of art and esthetic perception with experience signifies a lowering of their significance and dignity. Experience in the degree in which it *is* experience is heightened vitality. Instead of signifying being shut up within one's own private feelings and sensations, it signifies active and alert commerce with the world; at its height it signifies complete interpenetration of self and the world of objects and events. Instead of signifying surrender to caprice and disorder, it affords our sole demonstration of a stability that is not stagnation but is rhythmic and developing. Because experience is the fulfillment of an organism in its struggles and achievements in a world of things, it is art in germ. Even in its rudimentary forms, it contains the promise of that delightful perception which is esthetic experience.

II · The Experience of Esthetic Quality*

Experience occurs continuously, because the interaction of live creature and environing conditions is involved in the very process of living. Under conditions of resistance and conflict, aspects and elements of the self and the world that are implicated in this interaction qualify experience with emotions and ideas so that conscious intent emerges. Oftentimes, however, the experience had is inchoate. Things are experienced but not in such a way that they are composed into *an* experience. There are distraction and dispersion; what we observe and what we think, what

* From *Art as Experience*, pp. 35-43.

we desire and what we get, are at odds with each other. We put our hands to the plow and turn back; we start and then we stop, not because the experience has reached the end for the sake of which it was initiated but because of extraneous interruptions or of inner lethargy.

In contrast with such experience, we have *an* experience when the material experienced runs its course to fulfillment. Then and then only is it integrated within and demarcated in the general stream of experience from other experiences. A piece of work is finished in a way that is satisfactory; a problem receives its solution; a game is played through; a situation, whether that of eating a meal, playing a game of chess, carrying on a conversation, writing a book, or taking part in a political campaign, is so rounded out that its close is a consummation and not a cessation. Such an experience is a whole and carries with it its own individualizing quality and self-sufficiency. It is *an* experience.

Philosophers, even empirical philosophers, have spoken for the most part of experience at large. Idiomatic speech, however, refers to experiences each of which is singular, having its own beginning and end. For life is no uniform uninterrupted march or flow. It is a thing of histories, each with its own plot, its own inception and movement toward its close, each having its own particular rhythmic movement; each with its own unrepeated quality pervading it throughout. A flight of stairs, mechanical as it is, proceeds by individualized steps, not by undifferentiated progression, and an inclined plane is at least marked off from other things by abrupt discreteness.

Experience in this vital sense is defined by those situations and episodes that we spontaneously refer to as being "real experiences"; those things of which we say in recalling them, "that *was* an experience." It may have been something of tremendous importance—a quarrel with one who was once an intimate, a catastrophe finally averted by a hair's breadth. Or it may have been something that in comparison was slight—and which perhaps because of its very slightness illustrates all the better what is to be an experience. There is that meal in a Paris restaurant of which one says "that *was* an experience." It stands out as an enduring memorial of what food may be. Then there is that storm one went through in crossing the Atlantic—the storm that seemed in its fury, as it was experienced, to sum up in itself all that a storm can be, complete in itself, standing out because marked out from what went before and what came after.

In such experiences, every successive part flows freely, without seam and without unfilled blanks, into what ensues. At the same time there is no sacrifice of the self-identity of the parts. A river, as distinct from a pond, flows. But its flow gives a definiteness and interest to its successive portions greater than exist in the homogenous portions of a pond. In an experience, flow is from something to something. As one part leads into another and as one part carries on what went before, each gains distinctness in itself. The enduring whole is diversified by successive phases that are emphases of its varied colors.

Because of continuous merging, there are no holes, mechanical junctions, and dead centers when we have *an* experience. There are pauses, places of rest, but they punctuate and define the quality of movement. They sum up what has been undergone and prevent its dissipation and idle evaporation. Continued acceleration is breathless and prevents parts from gaining distinction. In a work of art, different acts, episodes, occurrences melt and fuse into unity, and yet do not disappear and lose their own character as they do so—just as in a genial conversation there is a continuous interchange and blending, and yet each speaker not only retains his own character but manifests it more clearly than is his wont.

An experience has a unity that gives it its name, that meal, that storm, that rupture of friendship. The existence of this unity is constituted by a single *quality* that pervades the entire experience in spite of the variation of its constituent parts. This unity is neither emotional, practical, nor intellectual, for these terms name distinctions that reflection can make within it. In discourse *about* an experience, we must make use of these adjectives of interpretation. In going over an experience in mind *after* its occurrence, we may find that one property rather than another was sufficiently dominant so that it characterizes the experience as a whole. There are absorbing inquiries and speculations which a scientific man and philosopher will recall as "experiences" in the emphatic sense. In final import they are intellectual. But in their actual occurrence they were emotional as well; they were purposive and volitional. Yet the experience was not a sum of these different characters; they were lost in it as distinctive traits. No thinker can ply his occupation save as he is lured and rewarded by total integral experiences that are intrinsically worth while. Without them he would never know what it is really to think and would be completely at a loss in distinguishing real thought from the spurious article. Thinking goes on in trains of ideas, but the ideas form a train only because they are much more than what an analytic psychology calls ideas. They are phases, emotionally and practically distinguished, of a developing underlying quality; they are its moving variations, not separate and independent like Locke's and Hume's so-called ideas and impressions, but are subtle shadings of a pervading and developing hue.

Hence *an* experience of thinking has its own esthetic quality. It differs from those experiences that are acknowledged to be esthetic, but only in its materials. The material of the fine arts consists of qualities; that of experience having intellectual conclusion are signs or symbols having no intrinsic quality of their own, but standing for things that may in another experience be qualitatively experienced. The difference is enormous. It is one reason why the strictly intellectual art will never be popular as music is popular. Nevertheless, the experience itself has a satisfying emotional quality because it possesses internal integration and fulfillment reached through ordered and organized movement. This artistic structure may be immediately felt. In so far, it is esthetic. What is even more important is that not only is this quality a significant motive in undertaking intellectual inquiry and in keeping it honest, but that no intellectual activity is an integral event (is *an* experience) unless it is rounded out with this quality. Without it, thinking is inconclusive. In short, esthetic cannot be sharply marked off from intellectual experience since the latter must bear an esthetic stamp to be itself complete.

The same statement holds good of a course of action that is dominantly practical, that is, one that consists of overt doings. It is possible to be efficient in action and yet not have a conscious experience. The activity is too automatic to permit of a sense of what it is about and where it is going. It comes to an end but not to a close or consummation in consciousness. Obstacles are overcome by shrewd skill, but they do not feed experience. There are also those who are wavering in action, uncertain, and inconclusive like the shades in classic literature. Between the poles of aimlessness and mechanical efficiency, there lie those courses of action in which through successive deeds there runs a sense of growing meaning conserved and accumulating toward an end that is felt as accomplishment of a process. There is interest in completing an experience. The experience may be one that is harmful to the world and its consummation undesirable. But it has esthetic quality.

The Greek identification of good conduct with conduct having proportion, grace, and harmony, the *kalon-agathon,* is a more obvious example of distinctive esthetic quality in moral action. One great defect in what passes as morality is its anesthetic quality. Instead of exemplifying wholehearted action, it takes the form of grudging piecemeal concessions to the demands of duty. But illustrations may only obscure the fact that any practical activity will, provided that it is integrated and moves by its own urge to fulfillment, have esthetic quality.

In much of our experience we are not concerned with the connection of one incident with what went before and what comes after. There is no interest that controls attentive rejection or selection of what shall be organized into the developing experience. Things happen, but they are neither definitely included nor decisively excluded; we drift. We yield according to external pressure, or evade and compromise. There are beginnings and cessations, but no genuine initiations and concludings. One thing replaces another, but does not absorb it and carry it on. There is experience, but so slack and discursive that it is not *an* experience. Needless to say, such experiences are anesthetic.

Thus the non-esthetic lies within two limits. At one pole is the loose succession that does not begin at any particular place and that ends—in the sense of ceasing—at no particular place. At the other pole is arrest, constriction, proceeding from parts having only a mechanical connection with one another. There exists so much of one and the other of these two kinds of experience that unconsciously they come to be taken as norms of all experience. Then, when the esthetic appears, it so sharply contrasts with the picture that has been formed of experience, that it is impossible to combine its special qualities with the features of the picture and the esthetic is given an outside place and status. The account that has been given of experience dominantly intellectual and practical is intended to show that there is no such contrast involved in having an experience; that, on the contrary, no experience of whatever sort is a unity unless it has esthetic quality.

The enemies of the esthetic are neither the practical nor the intellectual. They are the humdrum; slackness of loose ends; submission to convention in practice and intellectual procedure. Rigid abstinence, coerced submission, tightness on one side and dissipation, incoherence and aimless indulgence on the other, are deviations in opposite directions from the unity of an experience. Some such considerations perhaps induced Aristotle to invoke the "mean proportional" as the proper designation of what is distinctive of both virtue and the esthetic. He was formally correct. "Mean" and "proportion" are, however, not self-explanatory, nor to be taken over in a prior mathematical sense, but are properties belonging to an experience that has a developing movement toward its own consummation.

I have spoken of the esthetic quality that rounds out an experience into completeness and unity as emotional. The reference may cause difficulty. We are given to thinking of emotions as things as simple and compact as are the words by which we name them. Joy, sorrow, hope, fear, anger, curiosity, are treated as if each in itself were a sort of entity that enters full-made upon the scene, an entity that may last a long time or a short time, but whose duration, whose growth and career, is irrelevant to its nature. In fact emotions are qualities, when they are significant, of a complex experience that moves and changes. I say, when they are *significant,* for otherwise they are but the outbreaks and eruptions of a disturbed infant. All emotions are qualifications of a drama and they change as the drama develops. Persons are sometimes said to fall in love at first sight. But what they fall into is not a thing of that instant. What would love be were it compressed into a moment in which there is no room for cherishing and for solicitude? The intimate nature of emotion is manifested in the experience of one watching a play on the stage or reading a novel. It attends the development of a plot; and a plot requires a stage, a space, wherein to develop and time in which to unfold. Experience is emotional but there are no separate things called emotions in it.

By the same token, emotions are attached to events and objects in their movement. They are not, save in pathological instances, private. And even an "objectless" emotion demands something beyond itself to which to attach itself, and thus it soon generates a delusion in lack of something real. Emotion belongs of a certainty to the self. But it belongs to the self that is concerned in the movement of events toward an issue that is desired or disliked. We jump instantaneously when we are scared, as we blush on the instant when we are ashamed. But fright and shamed modesty are not in this case emotional states. Of themselves they are but automatic reflexes. In order to become emotional they must become parts of an inclusive and enduring situation that involves concern for objects and their issues. The jump of fright becomes emotional fear when there is found or thought to exist a threatening object that must be dealt with or escaped from. The blush becomes the emotion of shame when a person connects, in thought, an action he has performed with an unfavorable reaction to himself of some other person.

There are, therefore, common patterns in various experiences, no matter how unlike they are to one another in the details of their subject-matter. There are conditions to be met without which an experience cannot come to be. The outline of the common pattern is set by the fact that every experience is the result of interaction between a live creature and some aspect of the world in which he lives. A man does something; he lifts, let us say, a stone. In consequence he undergoes, suffers, something: the weight, strain, texture of the surface of the thing lifted. The properties thus undergone determine further doing. The stone is too heavy or too angular, not solid enough; or else the properties undergone show it is fit for the use for which it is intended. The process continues until a mutual adaptation of the self and the object emerges and that particular experience comes to a close. What is true of this simple instance is true, as to form, of every experience. The creature operating may be a thinker in his study and the environment with which he interacts may consist of ideas instead of a stone. But interaction of the two constitutes the total experience that is had, and the close which completes it is the institution of a felt harmony.

An experience has pattern and structure, because it is not just doing and undergoing in alternation, but consists of them in relationship. To put one's hand in the fire that consumes it is not necessarily to have an experience. The action and its consequence must be joined in perception. This relationship is what gives meaning; to grasp it is the objective of all intelligence. The scope and content of the relations measure the significant content of an experience.

III · The Work of Art and Esthetic Perception*

We have no word in the English language that unambiguously includes what is signified by the two words "artistic" and "esthetic." Since "artistic" refers primarily to the act of production and "esthetic" to that of perception and enjoyment, the absence of a term designating the two processes taken together is unfortunate. Sometimes, the effect is to separate the two from each other, to regard art as something superimposed upon esthetic material, or, upon the other side, to an assumption that, since art is a process of creation, perception and enjoyment of it have nothing in common with the creative act. In any case, there is a certain verbal awkwardness in that we are compelled sometimes to use the term "esthetic" to cover the entire field and sometimes to limit it to the receiving perceptual aspect of the whole operation. I refer to these obvious facts as preliminary to an attempt to show how the conception of conscious experience as a perceived relation between doing and undergoing enables us to understand the connection that art as production and perception and appreciation as enjoyment sustain to each other.

Art denotes a process of doing or making. This is as true of fine as of technological art. Art involves molding of clay, chipping of marble, casting of bronze, laying on of pigments, construction of buildings, singing of songs, playing of instruments, enacting roles on the stage, going through rhythmic movements in the dance. Every art does something with some physical material, the body or something outside the body, with or without the use of intervening tools, and with a view to production of something visible, audible, or tangible. So marked is the active or "doing" phase of art, that the dictionaries usually de-

* From *Art as Experience,* pp. 46-57.

fine it in terms of skilled action, ability in execution. The Oxford Dictionary illustrates by a quotation from John Stuart Mill: "Art is an endeavor after perfection in execution" while Matthew Arnold calls it "pure and flawless workmanship."

The word "esthetic" refers, as we have already noted, to experience as appreciative, perceiving, and enjoying. It denotes the consumer's rather than the producer's standpoint. It is gusto, taste; and, as with cooking, overt skillful action is on the side of the cook who prepares, while taste is on the side of the consumer, as in gardening there is a distinction between the gardener who plants and tills and the householder who enjoys the finished product.

These very illustrations, however, as well as the relation that exists in having an experience between doing and undergoing, indicate that the distinction between esthetic and artistic cannot be pressed so far as to become a separation. Perfection in execution cannot be measured or defined in terms of execution; it implies those who perceive and enjoy the product that is executed. The cook prepares food for the consumer and the measure of the value of what is prepared is found in consumption. Mere perfection in execution, judged in its own terms in isolation, can probably be attained better by a machine than by human art. By itself, it is at most technique, and there are great artists who are not in the first ranks as technicians (witness Cezanne), just as there are great performers on the piano who are not great esthetically, and as Sargent is not a great painter.

Craftsmanship to be artistic in the final sense must be "loving"; it must care deeply for the subject-matter upon which skill is exercised. To be truly artistic, a work must also be esthetic—that is, framed for enjoyed receptive perception. Constant observation is, of course, necessary for the maker while he is producing. But if his perception is not also esthetic in nature, it is a colorless and cold recognition of what has been done, used as a stimulus to the next step in a process that is essentially mechanical.

In short, art, in its form, unites the very same relation of doing and undergoing, outgoing and incoming energy, that makes an experience to be an experience. Because of elimination of all that does not contribute to mutual organization of the factors of both action and reception into one another, and because of selection of just the aspects and traits that contribute to their interpenetration of each other, the product is a work of esthetic art. Man whittles, carves, sings, dances, gestures, molds, draws and paints. The doing or making is artistic when the perceived result is of such a nature that *its* qualities *as perceived* have controlled the question of production. The act of producing that is directed by intent to produce something that is enjoyed in the immediate experience of perceiving has qualities that a spontaneous or uncontrolled activity does not have. The artist embodies in himself the attitude of the perceiver while he works.

Suppose, for the sake of illustration, that a finely wrought object, one whose texture and proportions are highly pleasing in perception, has been believed to be a product of some primitive people. Then there is discovered evidence that proves it to be an accidental natural product. As an external thing, it is now precisely what it was before. Yet at once it ceases to be a work of art and becomes a natural "curiosity." It now belongs in a museum of natural history, not in a museum of art. And the extraordinary thing is that the difference that is thus made is not one of just intellectual classification. A difference is made in appreciative perception and in a direct way. The esthetic experience—in its limited sense—is thus seen to be inherently connected with the experience of making.

The sensory satisfaction of eye and ear, when esthetic, is so because it does not stand by itself but is linked to the activity of which it is the consequence. Even the pleasures of the palate are different in quality to an epicure than in one who merely "likes" his food as he eats it. The difference is not of mere intensity. The epicure is conscious of much more than the taste of the food. Rather, there enter into the taste, as directly experienced, qualities that depend upon reference to its source and its manner of production in connection with criteria of excellence. As production must absorb into itself qualities of the product as perceived and be regulated by them, so, on the other side, seeing, hearing, tasting, become esthetic when relation to a distinct manner of activity qualifies what is perceived.

There is an element of passion in all esthetic perception. Yet when we are overwhelmed by passion, as in extreme rage, fear, jealousy, the experience is definitely non-esthetic. There is no relationship felt to the qualities of the activity that has generated the passion. Consequently, the material of the experience lacks elements of balance and proportion. For these can be present only when, as in the conduct that has grace or dignity, the act is controlled by an exquisite sense of the relations which the act sustains— its fitness to the occasion and to the situation.

The process of art in production is related to the esthetic in perception organically—as the Lord God in creation surveyed his work and found it good. Until the artist is satisfied in perception with what he is doing, he continues shaping and reshaping. The making comes to an end when its result is experienced as good—and that experience comes not by mere intellectual and outside judgment but in direct perception. An artist, in comparison with his fellows, is one who is not only especially gifted in powers of execution but in unusual sensitivity to the qualities of things. This sensitivity also directs his doings and makings.

As we manipulate, we touch and feel, as we look, we see; as we listen, we hear. The hand moves with etching needle or with brush. The eye attends and reports the consequence of what is done. Because of this intimate connection, subsequent doing is cumulative and not a matter of caprice nor yet of routine. In an emphatic artistic-esthetic experience, the relation is so close that it controls simultaneously both the doing and the perception. Such vital intimacy of connection cannot be had if only hand and eye are engaged. When they do not, both of them, act as organs of the whole being, there is but a mechanical sequence of sense and movement, as in walking that is automatic. Hand and eye, when the experience is esthetic, are but instruments through which the entire live creature, moved and active throughout, operates. Hence the expression is emotional and guided by purpose.

Because of the relation between what is done and what is undergone, there is an immediate sense of things in perception as belonging together or as jarring; as reënforcing or as interfering. The consequences of the act of making as reported in sense show whether what is done carries forward the idea being executed or marks a deviation and break. In as far as the development of an experience is *controlled* through reference to these immediately felt relations of order and fulfillment, that experience becomes dominantly esthetic in nature. The urge to action becomes an urge to that kind of action which will result in an object satisfying in direct perception. The potter shapes his clay to make a bowl useful for holding grain; but he makes it in a way so regulated by the series of perceptions that sum up the serial acts of making, that the bowl is marked by enduring grace and charm. The general situation remains the same in painting a picture or molding a bust. Moreover, at each stage there is anticipation of what is to come. This anticipation is the connecting link between the next doing and its outcome for sense. What is done and what is undergone are thus reciprocally, cumulatively, and continuously instrumental to each other.

It is not so easy in the case of the perceiver and appreciator to understand the intimate union of doing and undergoing as it is in the case of the maker. We are given to supposing that the former merely takes in what is there in finished form, instead of realizing that this taking in involves activities that are comparable to those of the creator. But receptivity is not passivity. It, too, is a process consisting of a series of responsive acts that accumulate toward objective fulfillment. Otherwise, there is not perception but recognition. The difference between the two is immense. Recognition is perception arrested before it has a chance to develop freely. In recognition there is a beginning of an act of perception. But this beginning is not allowed to serve the development of a full perception of the thing recognized. It is arrested at the point where it will serve some *other* purpose, as we recognize a man on the street in order to greet or to avoid him, not so as to see him for the sake of seeing what is there.

The esthetic or undergoing phase of experience is receptive. It involves surrender. But adequate yielding of the self is possible only through a controlled activity that may well be intense. In much of our intercourse with our surroundings we withdraw; sometimes from fear, if only of expending unduly our store of energy; sometimes from preoccupation with other matters, as in the case of recognition. Perception is an act of the going-out of energy in order to receive, not a withholding of energy. To steep ourselves in a subject-matter we have first to plunge into it. When we are only passive to a scene, it overwhelms us and, for lack of answering activity, we do not perceive that which bears us down. We must summon energy and pitch it at a responsive key in order to *take* in.

Every one knows that it requires apprenticeship to see through a microscope or telescope, and to see a landscape as the geologist sees it. The idea that esthetic perception is an affair for odd moments is one reason for the backwardness of the arts among us. For to perceive, a beholder must *create* his own experience. And his creation must include relations comparable to those which the original producer underwent. They are not the same in any literal sense. But with the perceiver, as with the artist, there must be an ordering of the elements of the whole that is in form, although not in details, the same as the process of organization the creator of the work consciously experienced. Without an act of recreation the object is not perceived as a work of art. The artist selected, simplified, clarified, abridged and condensed according to his interest. The beholder must go through these operations according to his point of view and interest. In both, an act of abstraction, that is of extraction of what is significant, takes place. In both, there is comprehension in its literal signification—that is, a gathering together of details and particulars physically scattered into an experienced whole. There is work done on the part of the percipient as there is on the part of the artist. The one who is too lazy, idle, or indurated in convention to perform this work will not see or hear. His "appreciation" will be a mixture of scraps of learning with conformity to norms of conventional admiration and with a confused, even if genuine, emotional excitation.

The considerations that have been presented imply both the community and the unlikeness, because of specific emphasis, of *an* experience, in its pregnant sense, and esthetic experience. The former has esthetic quality; otherwise its materials would not be rounded out into a single coherent experience. It is not possible to divide in a vital experience the practical, emotional, and intellectual from one another and to set the properties of one over against the characteristics of the others. The emotional phase binds parts together into a single whole; "intellectual" simply names the fact that the experience has meaning; "practical" indicates that the organism is interacting with events and objects which surround it. The most elaborate philosophic or scientific inquiry and the most ambitious industrial or political enterprise has, when its different ingredients constitute an integral experience, esthetic quality. For then its varied parts are linked to one another, and do not merely succeed one another. And the parts through their experienced linkage move toward a consummation and close, not merely to cessation in time. This consummation, moreover, does not wait in consciousness for the whole undertaking to be finished. It is anticipated throughout and is recurrently savored with special intensity.

Nevertheless, the experiences in question are dominantly intellectual or practical, rather than *distinctively* esthetic, because of the interest and purpose that initiate and control them. In an intellectual experience, the conclusion has value on its own account. It can be extracted as a formula or as a "truth," and can be used in its independent entirety as factor and guide in other inquiries. In a work of art there is no such single self-sufficient deposit. The end, the terminus, is significant not by itself but as the integration of the parts. It has no other existence. A drama or novel is not the final sentence, even if the characters are disposed of as living happily ever after. In a distinctively esthetic experience, characteristics that are subdued in other experiences are dominant; those that are subordinate are controlling—namely, the characteristics in virtue of which the experience is an integrated complete experience on its own account.

In every integral experience there is form because there is dynamic organization. I call it the organization dynamic because it takes time to complete it, because it is a growth. There is inception, development, fulfillment. Material is ingested and digested through interaction with that vital organization of the results of prior experience that constitutes the mind of the worker. Incubation goes on until what is conceived is brought forth and is rendered perceptible as part of the common world. An esthetic experience can be crowded into a moment only in the sense that a climax of prior long-enduring processes may arrive in an outstanding movement which so sweeps everything else into it that all else is forgotten. That which distinguishes an experience as esthetic is conversion of resistance and tensions, of excitations that in themselves are temptations to diversion, into a movement toward an inclusive and fulfilling close.

Experiencing like breathing is a rhythm of intakings and outgivings. Their succession is punctuated and made a rhythm by the existence of intervals, periods in which one phase is ceasing and the other is inchoate and preparing. William James aptly compared the course of a conscious experience to the alternate flights and perchings of a bird. The flights and perchings are intimately connected with one another; they are not so many unrelated lightings succeeded by a number of equally unrelated hoppings. Each resting place in experience is an undergoing in which is absorbed and taken home the consequences of prior doing, and, unless the doing is that of utter caprice or sheer routine, each doing carries in itself meaning that has been extracted and conserved. As with the advance of an army, all gains from what has been already effected are periodically consolidated, and always with a view to what is to be done next. If we move too rapidly, we get away from the base of supplies—of accrued meanings—and the experience is flustered, thin, and confused. If we dawdle too long after having extracted a net value, experience perishes of inanition.

The *form* of the whole is therefore present in every member. Fulfilling, consummating, are continuous functions, not mere ends, located at one place only. An engraver, painter, or writer is in process of completing at every stage of his work. He must at each point retain and sum up what has gone before as a whole and with reference to a whole to come. Otherwise there is no consistency and no security in his successive acts. The series of doings in the rhythm of experience give variety and movement; they save the work from monotony and useless repetitions. The undergoings are the corresponding elements in the rhythm, and they supply unity; they save the work from the aimlessness of a mere succession of excitations. An object is peculiarly and dominantly esthetic, yielding the enjoyment characteristic of esthetic perception, when the factors that determine anything which can be called *an* experience are lifted high above the threshold of perception and are made manifest for their own sake.

IV · Substance and Form*

Because objects of art are expressive, they are a language. Rather they are many languages. For each art has

* From *Art as Experience*, pp. 106-133.

its own medium and that medium is especially fitted for one kind of communication. Each medium says something that cannot be uttered as well or as completely in any other tongue. The needs of daily life have given superior practical importance to one mode of communication, that of speech. This fact has unfortunately given rise to a popular impression that the meanings expressed in architecture, sculpture, painting, and music can be translated into words with little if any loss. In fact, each art speaks an idiom that conveys what cannot be said in another language and yet remain the same.

Language exists only when it is listened to as well as spoken. The hearer is an indispensable partner. The work of art is complete only as it works in the experience of others than the one who created it. Thus language involves what logicians call a triadic relation. There is the speaker, the thing said, and the one spoken to. The external object, the product of art, is the connecting link between artist and audience. Even when the artist works in solitude all three terms are present. The work is there in progress, and the artist has to become vicariously the receiving audience. He can speak only as his work appeals to him as one spoken to through what he perceives. He observes and understands as a third person might note and interpret. Matisse is reported to have said: "When a painting is finished, it is like a new-born child. The artist himself must have time for understanding it." It must be lived with as a child is lived with, if we are to grasp the meaning of his being.

All language, whatever its medium, involves *what* is said and *how* it is said, or substance and form. The great question concerning substance and form is: Does matter come first ready-made, and search for a discovery of form in which to embody it come afterwards? Or is the whole creative effort of the artist an endeavor to form material so that it will be in actuality the authentic substance of a work of art? The question goes far and deep. The answer given it determines the issue of many other controverted points in esthetic criticism. Is there one esthetic value belonging to sense materials and another to a form that renders them expressive? Are all subjects fit for esthetic treatment or only a few which are set aside for that end by their intrinsically superior character? Is "beauty" another name for form descending from without, as a transcendent essence, upon material, or is it a name for the esthetic quality that appears whenever *material is formed* in a way that renders it adequately expressive? Is form, in its esthetic sense, something that uniquely marks off as esthetic from the beginning a certain realm of objects, or is it the abstract name for what emerges whenever an experience attains complete development?

If an art product is taken to be one of *self*-expression and the self is regarded as something complete and self-contained in isolation, then of course substance and form fall apart. That in which a self-revelation is clothed, is, by the underlying assumption, external to the things expressed. The externality persists no matter which of the two is regarded as form and which as substance. It is also clear that if there be *no* self-expression, no free play of individuality, the product will of necessity be but an instance of a species; it will lack the freshness and originality found only in things that are individual on their own account. Here is a point from which the relation of form and substance may be approached.

The *material* out of which a work of art is composed belongs to the common world rather than to the self, and yet there is self-expression in art because the self assimilates that material in a distinctive way to reissue it into the public world in a form that builds a new object. This new object may have as its consequence similar reconstructions, recreations, of old and common material on the part of those who perceive it, and thus in time come to be established as part of the acknowledged world—as "universal." The material expressed cannot be private; that is the state of the madhouse. But the *manner* of saying it is individual, and, if the product is to be a work of art, induplicable. Identity of mode of production defines the work of a machine, the esthetic counterpart of which is the academic. The quality of a work of *art* is *sui generis* because the manner in which general material is rendered transforms it into a substance that is fresh and vital.

What is true of the producer is true of the perceiver. He may perceive academically, looking for identities with which he already is familiar; or learnedly, pedantically, looking for material to fit into a history or article he wishes to write, or sentimentally for illustrations of some theme emotionally dear. But if he perceives esthetically, he will create an experience of which the intrinsic subject-matter, the substance, is new.

A work of art no matter how old and classic is actually, not just potentially, a work of art only when it lives in some individualized experience. As a piece of parchment, of marble, of canvas, it remains (subject to the ravages of time) self-identical throughout the ages. But as a work of art it is recreated every time it is esthetically experienced. No one doubts this fact in the rendering of a musical score; no one supposes that the lines and dots on paper are more than the recorded means of evoking the work of art. But what is true of it is equally true of the Parthenon as a building. It is absurd to ask what an artist "really" meant by his product; he himself would find different meanings in it at different days and hours and in different stages of his own development. If he could be articulate, he would say "I meant just *that,* and *that* means whatever you or any one can honestly, that is in virtue of your own vital experience, get out of it." Any other idea makes the boasted "universality" of the work of art a synonym for monotonous identity. The Parthenon, or whatever, is universal because it can continuously inspire new personal realizations in experience.

It is simply an impossibility that any one today should experience the Parthenon as the devout Athenian contemporary citizen experienced it, any more than the religious statuary of the twelfth century can mean, esthetically, even to a good Catholic today just what it meant to the worshipers of the old period. The "works" that fail to become *new* are not those which are universal but those which are "dated." The enduring art-product may have been, and probably was, called forth by something occasional, something having its own date and place. But *what* was evoked is a substance so formed that it can enter into the experiences of others and enable them to have more intense and more fully rounded out experiences of their own.

This is what it is to have form. It marks a way of envisaging, of feeling, and of presenting experienced matter so that it most readily and effectively becomes material for the construction of adequate experience on the part of those less gifted than the original creator. Hence there can be no distinction drawn, save in reflection, between form and substance. The work itself *is* matter formed into esthetic substance. The critic, the theorist, as a reflective student of the art product, however, not only may but must draw a distinction between them. Any skilled observer of a pugilist or a golf-player will, I suppose, institute distinctions between *what* is done and *how* it is done

—between the knockout and the manner of the delivery of a blow; between the ball driven so many yards to such and such a line and the way the drive was executed. The artist, the one engaged in doing, will effect a similar distinction when he is interested in correcting an habitual error, or learning how better to secure a given effect. Yet the act itself is exactly *what* it is because of *how* it is done. In the act there is no distinction, but perfect integration of manner and content, form and substance.

Mr. Bradley, in an essay on *Poetry for Poetry's Sake,* draws a distinction between subject and substance. The distinction may, I think, be paraphrased as that between matter *for* and matter *in* artistic production. The subject, as Bradley says, is outside the poem; the substance is within *it;* rather, *it is* the poem. "Subject," however, itself varies over a wide range. It may be hardly more than a label; it may be the occasion that called out the work; or it may be the subject-matter which as raw material entered into the new experience of the artist and found transformation. The poems of Keats and Shelley on the sky-lark and nightingale probably did not have the songs of these birds alone for an occasioning stimulus. It is well, then, for the sake of clarity to discriminate not only substance from theme or topic, but both of them from antecedent subject-matter. The "subject" of the "Ancient Mariner" is the killing of an albatross by a sailor and what happened in consequence thereof. Its matter is the poem itself. Its subject-matter is all the experiences a reader brings with him of cruelty and pity in connection with a living creature. The artist himself can hardly begin with a subject alone. If he did, his work would almost surely suffer from artificiality. First comes subject-matter, then the substance or matter of the work; finally the determination of topic or theme.

Antecedent subject-matter is not instantaneously changed into the matter of a work of art in the mind of an artist. It is a developing process. As we have already seen, the artist finds where he is going because of what he has previously done; that is, the original excitation and stir of some contact with the world undergo successive transformation. That state of the matter he has arrived at sets up demands to be fulfilled and it institutes a framework that limits further operations. As the experience of transforming subject-matter into the very substance of the work of art proceeds, incidents and scenes that figured at first may drop out and others take their place, being drawn in by the suction of the qualitative material that aroused the original excitement.

The distinctions made are elementary; but they are basic in esthetic theory. When there is an end of confusion of subject and substance, there will also be an end, for example, of the ambiguities regarding representation. Mr. Bradley calls attention to the common tendency to treat a work of art as a mere reminder of something, by the illustration of the sight-seer in a picture-gallery who remarks as he moves along, "This picture is so like my cousin," or that picture "the image of my birthplace," and who, after satisfying himself that one painting is about Elijah, passes on rejoicing to discover the subject and nothing but the subject of the next one. Unless the radical difference between subject and substance is appreciated, not only does the casual visitor go wrong, but critics and theorists judge objects of art in terms of their preconceptions as to what the subject-matter of art ought to be. The critics who drag in extraneous subject-matter—historical, moral, sentimental, or in the guise of established canons that prescribe proper themes—may be vastly superior in learning to the guide in the gallery who says nothing about paintings as pictures and a great deal about the occasions which produced them and the sentimental associations they arouse, the majesty of Mount Blanc or the tragedy of Anne Boleyn; but esthetically they stand on the same level.

The fact that form and matter are connected in a work of art does not mean they are identical. It signifies that in the work of art they do not offer themselves as two distinct things: the work is formed matter. But they are legitimately distinguished when reflection sets in, as it does in criticism and in theory. We are then compelled to inquire as to the formal structure of the work, and in order to carry on this inquiry intelligently, we must have a conception of what form is generically. We may get a key to this idea by starting from the fact that one idiomatic use of the word makes it equivalent with shape or figure. Especially in connection with pictures is form frequently identified simply with the patterns defined by linear outlines of shapes. Now shape is only an element in esthetic form; it does not constitute it. In ordinary perception we recognize and identify things by their shapes; even words and sentences have shapes, when heard as well as when seen. Consider how a misplaced accent disturbs recognition more than does any other kind of mispronunciation.

For shape in relation to recognition is not limited to geometric or spatial properties. The latter play a part only as they are subordinated to *adaptation to an end*. Shapes that are not in our minds associated with any function are hard to grasp and retain. The shapes of spoons, knives, forks, household articles, pieces of furniture, are means of identification because of their association with purpose. Up to a certain point, then, shape is allied with form in its artistic sense. In both there is organization of constituent parts. In some sense the typical shape of even a utensil and tool indicates that the meaning of the whole has entered into the parts to qualify them. This is the fact that has led some theorists, like Herbert Spencer, to identify the source of "beauty" with efficient and economical adaptation of parts to the function of a whole. In some cases fitness is indeed so exquisite as to constitute visible grace independent of the thought of any utility. But this special case indicates the way in which shape and form differ generically. For there is more to grace than just lack of clumsiness, in the sense in which "clumsy" means inefficiency of adaptation to an end. In shape as such adaptation is intrinsically limited to a particular end—like that of a spoon for carrying liquids to the mouth. The spoon that in addition has that esthetic form called grace bears no such limitation.

A good deal of intellectual effort has been expended in trying to identify efficiency for a particular end with "beauty" or esthetic quality. But these attempts are bound to fail, fortunate as it is that in some cases the two coincide and humanly desirable as it is that they should always meet. For adaptation to a particular end is often (always in the case of complicated affairs) something perceived by thought, while esthetic effect is found directly in sense-perception. A chair may serve the purpose of affording a comfortable and hygienically efficient seat, without serving at the same time the needs of the eye. If, on the contrary, it blocks rather than promotes the role of vision in an experience, it will be ugly no matter how well adapted to use as a seat. There is no preëstablished harmony that guarantees that what satisfies the need of one set of organs will fulfill that of all the other structures and needs that have a part in the experience, so as to bring it to completion as a complex of all elements. All we can say is that in the absence of disturbing contexts, such as production of objects for a maximum of private profit, a balance tends to be struck so that objects will be satisfactory—"useful" in the strict sense—to the self as a whole, even though some specific efficiency be sacrificed in the process. In so far there is a tendency for dynamic shape (as distinguished from bare geometric figure) to blend with artistic form.

Objects of industrial arts have form—that adapted to their special uses. These objects take on esthetic form, whether they are rugs, urns, or baskets, when the material is so arranged and adapted that it serves immediately the enrichment of the immediate experience of the one whose attentive perception is directed to it. No material can be adapted to an end, be it that of use as spoon or carpet, until raw material has undergone a change that shapes the parts and that arranges these parts with reference to one another with a view to the purpose of the whole. Hence the object has form in a definitive sense. When this form is liberated from limitation to a specialized end and serves also the purposes of an immediate and vital experience, the form is esthetic and not merely useful.

Only when the constituent parts of a whole have the unique end of contributing to the consummation of a conscious experience, do design and shape lose superimposed character and become form. They cannot do this so long as they serve a specialized purpose; while they can serve the inclusive purpose of having *an* experience only when they do not stand out by themselves but are fused with all other properties of the work of art. This interfusion of all properties of the medium is necessary if the object in question is to serve the whole creature in his unified vitality. It therefore defines the nature of form in all the arts. With respect to a specialized utility, we can characterize design as being related to this and that end. One chair has a design fitted to give comfort; another, to hygiene; a third, to regal splendor. Only when all means are diffused through one another does the whole suffuse the parts so as to constitute an experience that is unified through inclusion instead of by exclusion.

Beauty, conventionally assumed to be the especial theme of esthetics, has hardly been mentioned in what precedes. It is properly an emotional term, though one denoting a characteristic emotion. In the presence of a landscape, a poem or a picture that lays hold of us with immediate poignancy, we are moved to murmur or to exclaim "How beautiful." The ejaculation is a just tribute to the capacity of the object to arouse admiration that approaches worship. Beauty is at the furthest remove from an analytic term, and hence from a conception that can figure in theory as a means of explanation or classification. Unfortunately, it has been hardened into a peculiar object; emotional rapture has been subjected to what philosophy calls hypostatization, and the concept of beauty as an essence of intuition has resulted. For purposes of theory, it then becomes an obstructive term. In case the term is used in theory to designate the total esthetic quality of an experience, it is surely better to deal with the experience itself and show whence and how the quality proceeds. In that case, beauty is the response to that which to reflection is the consummated movement of matter integrated through its inner relations into a single qualitative whole.

There is another and more limited use of the term in which beauty is set off against other modes of esthetic quality—against the sublime, the comic, grotesque. Judging from results, the distinction is not a happy one. It tends to involve those who engage in it in dialectical manipulation of concepts and a compartmental pigeon-holing that obstructs rather than aids direct perception. Instead of favoring surrender to the object, ready-made divisions lead one to approach an esthetic object with an intent to compare and thus to restrict the experience to a partial grasp of the unified whole. An examination of the cases in which the word is commonly used, apart from its immediate emotional sense mentioned above, reveals that one significance of the term is the striking presence of decorative quality, of immediate charm for sense. The other meaning indicates the marked presence of relations of fitness and reciprocal adaptation among the members of the whole, whether it be object, situation, or deed.

Demonstrations in mathematics, operations in surgery, are thus said to be beautiful—even a case of disease may be so typical in its exhibition of characteristic relations as to be called beautiful. Both meanings, that of sensuous charm and of manifestation of a harmonious proportion of parts, mark the human form in its best exemplars. The efforts that have been made by theorists to reduce one meaning to the other illustrate the futility of approaching the subject-matter through fixed concepts. The facts throw light upon the immediate fusion of form and matter, and upon the relativity of what is taken as form or as substance in a particular case to the purpose animating reflective analysis.

The sum of the whole discussion is that theories which separate matter and form, theories that strive to find a special locus in experience for each, are, in spite of their oppositions to one another, cases of the same fundamental fallacy. They rest upon separation of the live creature from the environment in which it lives. One school, one which becomes the "idealistic" school in philosophy when its implications are formulated, makes the separation in the interest of meanings or relations. The other school, the sensational-empiricist, makes the separation in behalf of the primacy of sense qualities. Esthetic experience has not been trusted to generate its own concepts for interpretation of art. These have been superimposed through being carried over, ready-made, from systems of thought framed without reference to art.

Since the ultimate cause of the union of form and matter in experience is the intimate relation of undergoing and doing in interaction of a live creature with the world of nature and man, the theories, which separate matter and form, have their ultimate source in neglect of this relation. Qualities are then treated as impressions made by things, and relations that supply meaning as either associations among impressions, or as something introduced by thought. There *are* enemies of the union of form and matter. But they proceed from our own limitations; they are not intrinsic. They spring from apathy, conceit, self-pity, tepidity, fear, convention, routine, from the factors that obstruct, deflect and prevent vital interaction of the life creature with the environment in which he exists. Only the being who is ordinarily apathetic finds merely transient excitement in a work of art; only one who is depressed, unable to face the situations about him, goes to it merely for medicinal solace through values he cannot find in his world. But art itself is more than a stir of energy in the doldrums of the dispirited, or a calm in the storms of the troubled.

Through art, meanings of objects that are otherwise dumb, inchoate, restricted, and resisted are clarified and concentrated, and not by thought working laboriously upon them, nor by escape into a world of mere sense, but by creation of a new experience. Whatever path the work of art pursues, it, just because it is a full and intense experience, keeps alive the power to experience the common

world in its fullness. It does so by reducing the raw materials of that experience to matter ordered through form.

V · Art, Philosophy and Morals*

Esthetic experience is imaginative. This fact, in connection with a false idea of the nature of imagination, has
obscured the larger fact that all *conscious* experience has
of necessity some degree of imaginative quality. For while
the roots of every experience are found in the interaction
of a live creature with its environment, that experience
becomes conscious, a matter of perception, only when
meanings enter it that are derived from prior experiences.
Imagination is the only gateway through which these
meanings can find their way into a present interaction; or
rather, as we have just seen, the conscious adjustment of
the new and the old *is* imagination. Interaction of a living
being with an environment is found in vegetative and animal life. But the experience enacted is human and conscious only as that which is given here and now is extended by meanings and values drawn from what is absent in
fact and present only imaginatively.

There is always a gap between the here and now of direct interaction and the past interactions whose funded result constitutes the meanings with which we grasp and understand what is now occurring. Because of this gap, all
conscious perception involves a risk; it is a venture into
the unknown, for as it assimilates the present to the past
it also brings about some reconstruction of that past.
When past and present fit exactly into one another, when
there is only recurrence, complete uniformity, the resulting experience is routine and mechanical; it does not come
to consciousness in perception. The inertia of habit overrides adaptation of the meaning of the here and now with

* From *Art as Experience*, pp. 272-274; 344-349.

that of experiences, without which there is no consciousness, the imaginative phase of experience.

Mind, that is the body of organized meanings by means
of which events of the present have significance for us,
does not always enter into the activities and undergoings
that are going on here and now. Sometimes it is baffled
and arrested. Then the stream of meanings aroused into
activity by the present contact remains aloof. Then it
forms the matter of reverie, of dream; ideas are floating,
not anchored to any existence as its property, its possession of meanings. Emotions that are equally loose and
floating cling to these ideas. The pleasure they afford is
the reason why they are entertained and are allowed to occupy the scene; they are attached to existence only in a
way that, as long as sanity abides, is felt to be only fanciful and unreal.

In every work of art, however, these meanings are actually embodied in a material which thereby becomes the
medium for their expression. This fact constitutes the peculiarity of all experience that is definitely esthetic. Its
imaginative quality dominates, because meanings and values that are wider and deeper than the particular here
and now in which they are anchored are realized by way
of *expressions* although not by way of an object that is
physically efficacious in relation to other objects. Not
even a useful object is produced except by the intervention of imagination. Some existent material was perceived
in the light of relations and possibilities not hitherto realized when the steam engine was invented. But when the
imagined possibilities were embodied in a new assemblage
of natural materials, the steam engine took its place in nature as an object that has the same physical effects as
those belonging to any other physical object. Steam did
the physical work and produced the consequences that

attend any expanding gas under definite physical conditions. The sole difference is that the conditions under which it operates have been arranged by human contrivance.

The work of art, however, unlike the machine, is not only the outcome of imagination, but operates imaginatively rather than in the realm of physical existences. What it does is to concentrate and enlarge an immediate experience. The formed matter of esthetic experience directly *expresses,* in other words, the meanings that are imaginatively evoked; it does not, like the material brought into new relations in a machine, merely provide *means* by which purposes over and beyond the existence of the object may be executed. And yet the meanings imaginatively summoned, assembled, and integrated are embodied in material existence that here and now interacts with the self. The work of art is thus a challenge to the performance of a like act of evocation and organization, through imagination, on the part of the one who experiences it. It is not just a stimulus to and means of an overt course of action.

This fact constitutes the uniqueness of esthetic experience, and this uniqueness is in turn a challenge to thought. It is particularly a challenge to that systematic thought called philosophy. For esthetic experience is experience in its integrity. Had not the term "pure" been so often abused in philosophic literature, had it not been so often employed to suggest that there is something alloyed, impure, in the very nature of experience and to denote something beyond experience, we might say that esthetic experience is pure experience. For it is experience freed from the forces that impede and confuse its development as experience; freed, that is, from factors that subordinate an experience as it is directly had to something beyond it.

self. To esthetic experience, then, the philosopher must go to understand what experience is. For philosophy like art moves in the medium of imaginative mind, and, since art is the most direct and complete manifestation there is of experience *as* experience, it provides a unique control for the imaginative ventures of philosophy.

For this reason, while the theory of esthetics put forth by a philosopher is incidentally a test of the capacity of its author to have the experience that is the subject-matter of his analysis, it is also much more than that. It is a test of the capacity of the system he puts forth to grasp the nature of experience itself. There is no test that so surely reveals the one-sidedness of a philosophy as its treatment of art and esthetic experience. Imaginative vision is the power that unifies all the constituents of the matter of a work of art, making a whole out of them in all their variety. Yet all the elements of our being that are displayed in special emphases and partial realizations in other experiences are merged in esthetic experience. And they are so completely merged in the immediate wholeness of the experience that each is submerged: it does not present itself in consciousness as a distinct element.

In art as an experience, actuality and possibility or ideality, the new and the old, objective material and personal response, the individual and the universal, surface and depth, sense and meaning, are integrated in an experience in which they are all transfigured from the significance that belongs to them when isolated in reflection. "Nature," said Goethe, "has neither kernel nor shell." Only in esthetic experience is this statement completely true. Of art as experience it is also true that nature has neither subjective nor objective being; is neither individual nor universal, sensuous nor rational. The significance of art as experience is, therefore, incomparable for the adventure of philosophic thought.

The moral office and human function of art can be intelligently discussed only in the context of culture. A particular work of art may have a definite effect upon a particular person or upon a number of persons. The social effect of the novels of Dickens or of Sinclair Lewis is far from negligible. But a less conscious and more massed constant adjustment of experience proceeds from the total environment that is created by the collective art of a time. Just as physical life cannot exist without the support of a physical environment, so moral life cannot go on without the support of a moral environment. Even technological arts, in their sum total, do something more than provide a number of separate conveniences and facilities. They shape collective occupations and thus determine direction of interest and attention, and hence affect desire and purpose.

Shelley did not exaggerate when he said that moral science only "arranges the elements that poetry has created," if we extend "poetry" to include all products of imaginative experience. The sum total of the effect of all reflective treatises on morals is insignificant in comparison with the influence of architecture, novel, drama, on life, becoming important when "intellectual" products formulate the tendencies of these arts and provide them with an intellectual base. An "inner" rational check is a sign of withdrawal from reality unless it is a reflection of substantial environing forces. The political and economic arts that may furnish security and competency are no warrants of a rich and abundant human life as they are attended by the flourishing of the arts that determine culture.

Words furnish a record of what has happened and give

direction by request and command to particular future actions. Literature conveys the meaning of the past that is significant in present experience and is prophetic of the larger movement of the future. Only imaginative vision elicits the possibilities that are interwoven within the texture of the actual. The first stirrings of dissatisfaction and the first intimations of a better future are always found in works of art. The impregnation of the characteristically new art of a period with a sense of different values from those that prevail is the reason why the conservative finds such art to be immoral and sordid, and is the reason why he resorts to the products of the past for esthetic satisfaction. Factual science may collect statistics and make charts. But its predictions are, as has been well said, but past history reversed. Change in the climate of the imagination is the precursor of the changes that affect more than the details of life.

The theories that attribute direct moral effect and intent to art fail because they do not take account of the collective civilization that is the context in which works of art are produced and enjoyed. I would not say that they tend to treat works of art as a kind of sublimated Aesop's fables. But they all tend to extract particular works, regarded as especially edifying, from their milieu and to think of the moral function of art in terms of a strictly personal relation between the selected works and a particular individual. Their whole conception of morals is so individualistic that they miss a sense of the *way* in which art exercises its humane function.

Matthew Arnold's dictum that "poetry is criticism of life" is a case in point. It suggests to the reader a moral intent on the part of the poet and a moral judgment on the part of the reader. It fails to see or at all events to state *how* poetry is a criticism of life; namely, not di-

rectly, but by disclosure, through imaginative vision addressed to imaginative experience (not to set judgment)
of possibilities that contrast with actual conditions. A
sense of possibilities that are unrealized and that might
be realized are when they are put in contrast with actual
conditions, the most penetrating "criticism" of the latter
that can be made. It is by a sense of possibilities opening
before us that we become aware of constrictions that hem
us in and of burdens that oppress.

It is by way of communication that art becomes the incomparable organ of instruction, but the way is so remote
from that usually associated with the idea of education, it
is a way that lifts art so far above what we are accustomed to think of as instruction, that we are repelled by
any suggestion of teaching and learning in connection
with art. But our revolt is in fact a reflection upon education that proceeds by methods so literal as to exclude the
imagination and one not touching the desires and emotions of men. Shelley said, "The imagination is the great
instrument of moral good, and poetry administers to the
effect by acting upon the causes." Hence it is, he goes on
to say, "a poet would do ill to embody his own conceptions of right and wrong, which are usually those of his
own time and place, in his poetical creations. . . . By the
assumption of this inferior office . . . he would resign participation in the cause"—the imagination. It is the lesser
poets who "have frequently affected a moral aim, and the
effect of their poetry is diminished in exact proportion as
they compel us to advert to this purpose." But the power
of imaginative projection is so great that he calls poets
"the founders of civil society."

The problem of the relation of art and morals is too
often treated as if the problem existed only on the side of
art. It is virtually assumed that morals are satisfactory in

idea if not in fact, and that the only question is whether and in what ways art should conform to a moral system already developed. But Shelley's statement goes to the heart of the matter. Imagination is the chief instrument of the good. It is more or less a commonplace to say that a person's ideas and treatment of his fellows are dependent upon his power to put himself imaginatively in their place. But the primacy of the imagination extends far beyond the scope of direct personal relationships. Except where "ideal" is used in conventional deference or as a name for a sentimental reverie, the ideal factors in every moral outlook and human loyalty are imaginative. The historic alliance of religion and art has its roots in this common quality. Hence it is that art is more moral than moralities. For the latter either are, or tend to become, consecrations of the *status quo,* reflections of custom, reënforcements of the established order. The moral prophets of humanity have always been poets even though they spoke in free verse or by parable. Uniformly, however, their vision of possibilities has soon been converted into a proclamation of facts that already exist and hardened into semi-political institutions. Their imaginative presentation of ideals that should command thought and desire have been treated as rules of policy. Art has been the means of keeping alive the sense of purposes that outrun evidence and of meanings that transcend indurated habit.

Morals are assigned a special compartment in theory and practice because they reflect the divisions embodied in economic and political institutions. Wherever social divisions and barriers exist, practices and ideas that correspond to them fix metes and bounds, so that liberal action is placed under restraint. Creative intelligence is looked upon with distrust; the innovations that are the essence of individuality are feared, and generous impulse is put un-

der bonds not to disturb the peace. Were art an acknowledged power in human association and not treated as the
pleasuring of an idle moment or as a means of ostentatious
display, and were morals understood to be identical with
every aspect of value that is shared in experience, the
"problem" of the relation of art and morals would not
exist.

CHAPTER TWENTY

THE RELIGIOUS IN EXPERIENCE*

NEVER before in history has mankind been so much of two minds, so divided into two camps, as it is today. Religions have traditionally been allied with ideas of the supernatural, and often have been based upon explicit beliefs about it. Today there are many who hold that nothing worthy of being called religious is possible apart from the supernatural. Those who hold this belief differ in many respects. They range from those who accept the dogmas and sacraments of the Greek and Roman Catholic Church as the only sure means of access to the supernatural to the theist or mild deist. Between them are the many Protestant denominations who think the Scriptures, aided by a pure conscience, are adequate avenues to supernatural truth and power. But they agree in one point: the necessity for a Supernatural Being and for an immortality that is beyond the power of nature.

The opposed group consists of those who think the advance of culture and science has completely discredited the supernatural and with it all religions that were allied with belief in it. But they go beyond this point. The extremists in this group believe that with elimination of the supernatural not only must historic religions be dismissed but with them everything of a religious nature. When historical knowledge has discredited the claims made for the

* From *A Common Faith*. The selections are from all parts of the book.

supernatural character of the persons said to have founded historic religions; when the supernatural inspiration attributed to literatures held sacred has been riddled, and when anthropological and psychological knowledge has disclosed the all-too-human source from which religious beliefs and practices have sprung, everything religious must, they say, also go.

There is one idea held in common by these two opposite groups: identification of the religious with the supernatural. The question I shall raise [in these chapters] concerns the ground for and the consequences of this identification: its reasons and its value. In the discussion I shall develop another conception of the nature of the religious phase of experience, one that separates it from the supernatural and the things that have grown up about it. I shall try to show that these derivations are encumbrances and that what is genuinely religious will undergo an emancipation when it is relieved from them; that then, for the first time, the religious aspect of experience will be enabled to develop freely on its own account.

This view is exposed to attack from both the other camps. It goes contrary to traditional religions, including those that have the greatest hold upon the religiously minded today. The view announced will seem to them to cut the vital nerve of the religious element itself in taking away the basis upon which traditional religions and institutions have been founded. From the other side, the position I am taking seems like a timid halfway position, a concession and compromise unworthy of thought that is thoroughgoing. It is regarded as a view entertained from mere tendermindedness, as an emotional hangover from childhood indoctrination, or even as a manifestation of a desire to avoid disapproval and curry favor.

The heart of my point is that there is a difference between religion, *a* religion, and the religious; between anything that may be denoted by a noun substantive and the quality of experience that is designated by an adjective. It is not easy to find a definition of religion in the substantive sense that wins general acceptance. However, in the *Oxford Dictionary* I find the following: "Recognition on the part of man of some unseen higher power as having control of his destiny and as being entitled to obedience, reverence and worship."

This particular definition is less explicit in assertion of the supernatural character of the higher unseen power than are others that might be cited. It is, however, surcharged with implications having their source in ideas connected with the belief in the supernatural, characteristic of historic religions. Let us suppose that one familiar with the history of religions, including those called primitive, compares the definition with the variety of known facts and by means of the comparison sets out to determine just what the definition means. I think he will be struck by three facts that reduce the terms of the definition to such a low common denominator that little meaning is left.

He will note that the "unseen powers" referred to have been conceived in a multitude of incompatible ways. Eliminating the differences, nothing is left beyond the bare reference to something unseen and powerful. This has been conceived as the vague and undefined Mana of the Melanesians; the Kami of primitive Shintoism; the fetish of the Africans; spirits, having some human properties, that pervade natural places and animate natural forces; the ultimate and impersonal principle of Buddhism; the unmoved mover of Greek thought; the gods and semidivine heroes of the Greek and Roman Pantheons; the personal and loving Providence of Christianity, omnipotent, and limited by a corresponding evil power; the arbitrary Will of Moslemism; the supreme legislator and judge of deism. And these are but a few of the outstanding varieties of ways in which the invisible power has been conceived.

There is no greater similarity in the ways in which obedience and reverence have been expressed. There has been worship of animals, of ghosts, of ancestors, phallic worship, as well as of a Being of dread power and of love and wisdom. Reverence has been expressed in the human sacrifices of the Peruvians and Aztecs; the sexual orgies of some Oriental religions; exorcisms and ablutions; the offering of the humble and contrite mind of the Hebrew prophet, the elaborate rituals of the Greek and Roman Churches. not even sacrifice has been uniform; it is highly sublimated in Protestant denominations and in Moslemism. Where it has existed it has taken all kinds of forms and been directed to a great variety of powers and spirits. It has been used for expiation, for propitiation and for buying special favors. There is no conceivable purpose for which rites have not been employed.

Finally, there is no discernible unity in the moral motivations appealed to and utilized. They have been as far apart as fear of lasting torture, hope of enduring bliss in which sexual enjoyment has sometimes been a conspicuous element; mortification of the flesh and extreme asceticism; prostitution and chastity; wars to extirpate the unbeliever; persecution to convert or punish the unbeliever, and philanthropic zeal; servile acceptance of imposed dogma, along with brotherly love and aspiration for a reign of justice among men.

I have, of course, mentioned only a sparse number of the facts which fill volumes in any well-stocked library. It may be asked by those who do not like to look upon the darker side of the history of religions why the darker facts should be brought up. We all know that civilized man has a background of bestiality and superstition and that these elements are still with us. Indeed, have not some religions, including the most influential forms of Christianity, taught that the heart of man is totally corrupt? How could the course of religion in its entire sweep not be marked by practices that are shameful in their cruelty and lustfulness, and by beliefs that are degraded and intellectually incredible? What else than what we find could be expected, in the case of people having little knowledge and no secure method of knowing; with primitive institutions, and with so little control of natural forces that they lived in a constant state of fear?

I gladly admit that historic religions have been relative to the conditions of social culture in which peoples lived. Indeed, what I am concerned with is to press home the logic of this method of disposal of outgrown traits of past religions. Beliefs and practices in a religion that now prevails are by this logic relative to the present state of culture. If so much flexibility has obtained in the past regarding an unseen power, the way it affects human destiny, and the attitudes we are to take toward it, why should it be assumed that change in conception and action has now come to an end? The logic involved in getting rid of inconvenient aspects of past religions compels us to inquire how much in religions now accepted are survivals from outgrown cultures. It compels us to ask what conception of unseen powers and our relations to them would be consonant with the best achievements and aspirations of the present. It demands that in imagination we wipe the slate clean and start afresh by asking what would be the idea of the unseen, of the manner of its control over us and the ways in which reverence and obedience would be manifested, if whatever is basically religious in experience had the opportunity to express itself free from all historic encumbrances.

So we return to the elements of the definition that has been given. What boots it to accept, in defense of the universality of religion, a definition that applies equally to the most savage and degraded beliefs and practices that have related to unseen powers and to noble ideals of a religion having the greatest share of moral content? There are two points involved. One of them is that there is nothing left worth preserving in the notions of unseen powers, controlling human destiny to which obedience, reverence and worship are due, if we glide silently over the nature that has been attributed to the powers, the radically diverse ways in which they have been supposed to control human destiny, and in which submission and awe have been manifested. The other point is that when we begin to select, to choose, and say that some present ways of thinking about the unseen powers are better than others; that the reverence shown by a free and self-respecting human being is better than the servile obedience rendered to an arbitrary power by frightened men; that we should believe that control of human destiny is exercised by a wise and loving spirit rather than by madcap ghosts or sheer force—when, I say, we begin to choose, we have entered upon a road that has not yet come to an end. We have reached a point that invites us to proceed farther.

For we are forced to acknowledge that concretely there is no such thing as religion in the singular. There is only a multitude of religions. "Religion" is a strictly collective term and the collection it stands for is not even of the kind illustrated in textbooks of logic. It has not the unity of a regiment or assembly but that of any miscellaneous aggregate. Attempts to prove the universality prove too much or too little. It is probable that religions have been universal in the sense that all the peoples we know anything about have had *a* religion. But the differences among them are so great and so shocking that any common element that can be extracted is meaningless. The idea that religion is universal proves too little in that the older apologists for Christianity seem to have been better advised than some modern ones in condemning every religion but one as an impostor, as at bottom some kind of demon worship or at any rate a superstitious figment. Choice among religions is imperative, and the necessity for choice leaves nothing of any force in the argument from universality. Moreover, when once we enter upon the road of choice, there is at once presented a possibility not yet generally realized.

For the historic increase of the ethical and ideal content of religions suggests that the process of purification may be carried further. It indicates that further choice is imminent in which certain values and functions in experience may be selected. This possibility is what I had in mind in speaking of the difference between the religious and a religion. I am not proposing a religion, but rather the emancipation of elements and outlooks that may be called religious. For the moment we have a religion, whether that of the Sioux Indian or of Judaism or of Christianity, that moment the ideal factors in experience that may be called religious take on a load that is not inherent in them, a load of current beliefs and of institutional practices that are irrelevant to them.

I can illustrate what I mean by a common phenomenon in contemporary life. It is widely supposed that a person who does not accept any religion is thereby shown to be a non-religious person. Yet it is conceivable that the present depression in religion is closely connected with the fact that religions now prevent, because of their weight of historic encumbrances, the religious quality of experience from coming to consciousness and finding the expression that is appropriate to present conditions, intellectual and moral. I believe that such is the case. I believe that many persons are so repelled from what exists as a religion by its intellectual and moral implications, that they are not even aware of attitudes in themselves that if they came to fruition would be genuinely religious. I hope that this remark may help make clear what I mean by the distinction between "religion" as a noun substantive and "religious" as adjectival.

To be somewhat more explicit, a religion (and as I have just said there is no such thing as religion in general) always signifies a special body of beliefs and practices having some kind of institutional organization, loose or tight. In contrast, the adjective "religious" denotes nothing in the way of a specifiable entity, either institutional or as a system of beliefs. It does not denote anything to which one can specifically point as one can point to this and that historic religion or existing church. For it does not denote anything that can exist by itself or that can be organized into a particular and distinctive form of existence. It denotes attitudes that may be taken toward every object and every proposed end or ideal.

Before, however, I develop my suggestion that realization of the distinction just made would operate to emancipate the religious quality from encumbrances that now smother or limit it, I must refer to a position that in some respects is similar in words to the position I have taken, but that in fact is a whole world removed from it. I have several times used the phrase "religious elements of experience." Now at present there is much talk, especially in liberal circles, of religious experience as vouching for the

authenticity of certain beliefs and the desirability of certain practices, such as particular forms of prayer and
worship. It is even asserted that religious experience is
the ultimate basis of religion itself. The gulf between this
position and that which I have taken is what I am now
concerned to point out.

Those who hold to the notion that there is a definite
kind of experience which is itself religious, by that very
fact make out of it something specific, as a kind of experience that is marked off from experience as esthetic, scientific, moral, political; from experience as companionship and friendship. But "religious" as a quality of experience signifies something that may belong to all these experiences. It is the polar opposite of some type of experience that can exist by itself. The distinction comes out
clearly when it is noted that the concept of this distinct
kind of experience is used to validate a belief in some special kind of object and also to justify some special kind of
practice.

The discussion may be made more definite by introducing, at this point, a particular illustration of this type of
reasoning. A writer says: "I broke down from overwork
and soon came to the verge of nervous prostration. One
morning after a long and sleepless night. . . I resolved
to stop drawing upon myself so continuously and begin
drawing upon God. I determined to set apart a quiet
time every day in which I could relate my life to its ultimate source, regain the consciousness that in God I live,
move and have my being. That was thirty years ago.
Since then I have had literally not one hour of darkness
or despair."

This is an impressive record. I do not doubt its authenticity nor that of the experience related. It illustrates a
religious aspect of experience. But it illustrates also the

use of that quality to carry a superimposed load of a particular religion. For having been brought up in the Christian religion, its subject interprets it in the terms of the personal God characteristic of that religion. Taoists, Buddhists, Moslems, persons of no religion including those who reject all supernatural influence and power, have had experiences similar in their effect. Yet another author commenting upon the passage says: "The religious expert can be more sure that this God exists than he can of either the cosmological God of speculative surmise or the Christlike God involved in the validity of moral optimism," and goes on to add that such experiences "mean that God the savior, the power that gives victory over sin on certain conditions that man can fulfill, is an existent, accessible and scientifically knowable reality." It should be clear that this inference is sound only if the conditions, of whatever sort, that produce the effect are called "God." But most readers will take the inference to mean that the existence of a particular Being, of the type called "God" in the Christian religion, is proved by a method akin to that of experimental science.

In reality, the only thing that can be said to be "proved" is the existence of some complex of conditions that have operated to effect an adjustment in life, an orientation, that brings with it a sense of security and peace. The particular interpretation given to this complex of conditions is not inherent in the experience itself. It is derived from the culture with which a particular person has been imbued.

The intent of this discussion is not to deny the genuineness of the result nor its importance in life. It is not, save incidentally, to point out the possibility of a purely naturalistic explanation of the event. My purpose is to indicate what happens when religious experience is already set aside as something *sui generis*. The actual religious quality in the experience described is the *effect* produced, the better adjustment in life and its conditions, not the manner and cause of its production. The way in which the experience operated, its function, determines its religious value. If the reorientation actually occurs, it, and the sense of security and stability accompanying it, are forces on their own account. It takes place in different persons in a multitude of ways. It is sometimes brought about by devotion to a cause; sometimes by a passage of poetry that opens a new perspective; sometimes as was the case with Spinoza —deemed an atheist in his day—through philosophical reflection.

The difference between an experience having a religious force because of what it does in and to the processes of living and religious experience as a separate kind of thing gives me occasion to refer to a previous remark. If this function were rescued through emancipation from dependence upon specific types of beliefs and practices, from those elements that constitute a religion, many individuals would find that experiences having the force of bringing about a better, deeper and enduring adjustment in life are not so rare and infrequent as they are commonly supposed to be. They occur frequently in connection with many significant moments of living. The idea of invisible powers would take on the meaning of all the conditions of nature and human association that support and deepen the sense of values which carry one through periods of darkness and despair to such an extent that they lose their usual depressive character.

I do not suppose for many minds the dislocation of the religious from a religion is easy to effect. Tradition and custom, especially when emotionally charged, are a part of the habits that have become one with our very being.

But the possibility of the transfer is demonstrated by its actuality. Let us then for the moment drop the term "religious," and ask what are the attitudes that lend deep and enduring support to the processes of living. I have, for example, used the words "adjustment" and "orientation." What do they signify?

While the words "accommodation," "adaptation," and "adjustment" are frequently employed as synonyms, attitudes exist that are so different that for the sake of clear thought they should be discriminated. There are conditions we meet that cannot be changed. If they are particular and limited, we modify our own particular attitudes in accordance with them. Thus we accommodate ourselves to changes in weather, to alterations in income when we have no other recourse. When the external conditions are lasting we become inured, habituated, or, as the process is now often called, conditioned. The two main traits of this attitude, which I should like to call accommodation, are that it affects *particular* modes of conduct, not the entire self, and that the process is mainly *passive*. It may, however, become general and then it becomes fatalistic resignation or submission. There are other attitudes toward the environment that are also particular but that are more active. We react against conditions and endeavor to change them to meet our wants and demands. Plays in a foreign language are "adapted" to meet the needs of an American audience. A house is rebuilt to suit changed conditions of the household; the telephone is invented to serve the demand for speedy communication at a distance; dry soils are irrigated so that they may bear abundant crops. Instead of accommodating ourselves to conditions, we modify conditions so that they will be accommodated to our wants and purposes. This process may be called adaptation.

Now both of these processes are often called by the more general name of adjustment. But there are also changes in ourselves in relation to the world in which we live that are much more inclusive and deep seated. They relate not to this and that want in relation to this and that condition of our surroundings, but pertain to our being in its entirety. Because of their scope, this modification of ourselves is enduring. It lasts through any amount of vicissitude of circumstances, internal and external. There is a composing and harmonizing of the various elements of our being such that, in spite of changes in the special conditions that surround us, these conditions are also arranged, settled, in relation to us. This attitude includes a note of submission. But it is voluntary, not externally imposed; and as voluntary it is something more than a mere Stoical resolution to endure unperturbed throughout the buffetings of fortune. It is more outgoing, more ready and glad, than the latter attitude, and it is more active than the former. And in calling it voluntary, it is not meant that it depends upon a particular resolve or volition. It is a change *of* will conceived as the organic plenitude of our being, rather than any special change *in* will.

It is the claim of religions that they effect this generic and enduring change in attitude. I should like to turn the statement around and say that whenever this change takes place there is a definitely religious attitude. It is not *a* religion that brings it about, but when it occurs, from whatever cause and by whatever means, there is a religious outlook and function. As I have said before, the doctrinal or intellectual apparatus and the institutional accretions that grow up are, in a strict sense, adventitious to the intrinsic quality of such experiences. For they are affairs of the traditions of the culture with which individuals are inoculated.

The connection between imagination and the harmonizing of the self is closer than is usually thought. The idea of a whole, whether of the whole personal being or of the world, is an imaginative, not a literal, idea. The limited world of our observation and reflection becomes the Universe only through imaginative extension. It cannot be apprehended in knowledge or realized in reflection. Neither observation, thought, nor practical activity can attain that complete unification of the self which is called a whole. The *whole* self is an ideal, an imaginative projection. Hence the idea of a thoroughgoing and deepseated harmonizing of the self with the Universe (as a name for the totality of conditions with which the self is connected) operates only through imagination—which is one reason why this composing of the self is not voluntary in the sense of an act of special volition or resolution. An "adjustment" possesses the will rather than is its express product. Religionists have been right in thinking of it as an influx from sources beyond conscious deliberation and purpose—a fact that helps explain, psychologically, why it has so generally been attributed to a supernatural source and that, perhaps, throws some light upon the reference of it by William James to unconscious factors. And it is pertinent to note that the unification of the self throughout the ceaseless flux of what it does, suffers, and achieves, cannot be attained in terms of itself. The self is always directed toward something beyond itself and so its own unification depends upon the idea of the integration of the shifting scenes of the world into that imaginative totality we call the Universe.

The intimate connection of imagination with ideal elements in experience is generally recognized. Such is not the case with respect to its connection with faith. The latter has been regarded as a substitute for knowledge, for sight. It is defined, in the Christian religion, as *evidence* of things not seen. The implication is that faith is a kind of anticipatory vision of things that are now invisible because of the limitations of our finite and erring nature. Because it is a substitute for knowledge, its material and object are intellectual in quality. As John Locke summed up the matter, faith is "assent to a proposition . . . on the credit of its proposer." Religious faith is then given to a body of propositions as true on the credit of their supernatural author, reason coming in to demonstrate the reasonableness of giving such credit. Of necessity there results the development of theologies, or bodies of systematic propositions, to make explicit in organized form the content of the propositions to which belief is attached and assent given. Given the point of view, those who hold that religion necessarily implies a theology are correct.

But belief or faith has also a moral and practical import. Even devils, according to the older theologians, believe—and tremble. A distinction was made, therefore, between "speculative" or intellectual belief and an act called "justifying" faith. Apart from any theological context, there is a difference between belief that is a conviction that some end should be supreme over conduct, and belief that some object or being exists as a truth for the intellect. Conviction in the moral sense signifies being conquered, vanquished, in our active nature by an ideal end; it signifies acknowledgment of its rightful claim over our desires and purposes. Such acknowledgment is practical, not primarily intellectual. It goes beyond evidence that can be presented to *any* possible observer. Reflection, often long and arduous, may be involved in arriving at the conviction, but the import of thought is not exhausted in discovery of evidence that can justify intellectual assent. The authority of an ideal over choice and conduct is the authority of an ideal, not of a fact, of a truth guaranteed to intellect, not of the status of the one who propounds the truth.

Such moral faith is not easy. It was questioned of old whether the Son of Man should find faith on the earth in his coming. Moral faith has been bolstered by all sorts of arguments intended to prove that its object is not ideal and that its claim upon us is not primarily moral or practical, since the ideal in question is already embedded in the existent frame of things. It is argued that the ideal is already the final reality at the heart of things that exist, and that only our senses or the corruption of our natures prevent us from apprehending its prior existential being. Starting, say, from such an idea as that justice is more than a moral ideal because it is embedded in the very make-up of the actually existent world, men have gone on to build up vast intellectual schemes, philosophies, and theologies, to prove that ideals are real not as ideals but as antecedently existing actualities. They have failed to see that in converting moral realities into matters of intellectual assent they have evinced lack of *moral* faith. Faith that something should be in existence as far as lies in our power is changed into the intellectual belief that it is already in existence. When physical existence does not bear out the assertion, the physical is subtly changed into the metaphysical. In this way, moral faith has been inextricably tied up with intellectual beliefs about the supernatural.

What has been said does not imply that all moral faith in ideal ends is by virtue of that fact religious in quality. The religious is "morality touched by emotion" only when the ends of moral conviction arouse emotions that are not only intense but are actuated and supported by ends so inclusive that they unify the self. The inclusiveness of the end in relation to both self and the "universe" to which an inclusive self is related is indispensable. According to the best authorities, "religion" comes from a root that means being bound or tied. Originally, it meant being bound by vows to a particular way of life—as *les religieux* were monks and nuns who had assumed certain vows. The religious attitude signifies something that is bound through imagination to a *general* attitude. This comprehensive attitude, moreover, is much broader than anything indicated by "moral" in its usual sense. The quality of attitude is displayed in art, science and good citizenship.

If we apply the conception set forth to the terms of the definition earlier quoted, these terms take on a new significance. An unseen power controlling our destiny becomes the power of an ideal. All possibilities, as possibilities, are ideal in character. The artist, scientist, citizen, parent, as far as they are actuated by the spirit of their callings, are controlled by the unseen. For all endeavor for the better is moved by faith in what is possible, not by adherence to the actual. Nor does this faith depend for its moving power upon intellectual assurance or belief that the things worked for must surely prevail and come into embodied existence. For the authority of the object to determine our attitude and conduct, the right that is given it to claim our allegiance and devotion is based on the intrinsic nature of the ideal. The outcome, given our best endeavor, is not with us. The inherent vice of all intellectual schemes of idealism is that they convert the idealism of action into a system of beliefs about antecedent reality. The character assigned this reality is so different from that which observation and reflection lead to and support that these schemes inevitably glide into alliance with the supernatural.

All religions, marked by elevated ideal quality, have dwelt upon the power of religion to introduce perspective into the piecemeal and shifting episodes of existence. Here too we need to reverse the ordinary statement and say that whatever introduces genuine perspective is religious, not that religion is something that introduces it. There can be no doubt (referring to the second element of the definition) of our dependence upon forces beyond our control. Primitive man was so impotent in the face of these forces that, especially in an unfavorable natural environment, fear became a dominant attitude, and, as the old saying goes, fear created the gods.

With increase of mechanisms of control, the element of fear has, relatively speaking, subsided. Some optimistic souls have even concluded that the forces about us are on the whole essentially benign. But every crisis, whether of the individual or of the community, reminds man of the precarious and partial nature of the control he exercises. When man, individually and collectively, has done his uttermost, conditions that at different times and places have given rise to the ideas of Fate and Fortune, of Chance and Providence, remain. It is the part of manliness to insist upon the capacity of mankind to strive to direct natural and social forces to humane ends. But unqualified absolutistic statements about the omnipotence of such endeavors reflect egoism rather than intelligent courage.

The fact that human destiny is so interwoven with forces beyond human control renders it unnecessary to suppose that dependence and the humility that accompanies it have to find the particular channel that is prescribed by traditional doctrines. What is especially significant is rather the form which the sense of dependence takes. Fear never gave stable perspective in the life of anyone. It is dispersive and withdrawing. Most religions have in fact added rites of communion to those of expiation and propitiation. For our dependence is manifested in those relations to the environment that support our undertakings and aspirations as much as it is in the defeats inflicted upon us. The essentially unreligious attitude is that which attributes human achievement and purpose to man in isolation from the world of physical nature and his fellows. Our successes are dependent upon the coöperation of nature. The sense of the dignity of human nature is as religious as is the sense of awe and reverence when it rests upon a sense of human nature as a coöperating part of a larger whole. Natural piety is not of necessity either a fatalistic acquiescence in natural happenings or a romantic idealization of the world. It may rest upon a just sense of nature as the whole of which we are parts, while it also recognizes that we are parts that are marked by intelligence and purpose, having the capacity to strive by their aid to bring conditions into greater consonance with what is humanly desirable. Such piety is an inherent constituent of a just perspective in life.

Understanding and knowledge also enter into a perspective that is religious in quality. Faith in the continued disclosing of truth through directed coöperative human endeavor is more religious in quality than is any faith in a completed revelation. It is of course now usual to hold that revelation is not completed in the sense of being ended. But religions hold that the essential framework is settled in its significant moral features at least, and that new elements that are offered must be judged by conformity to this framework. Some fixed doctrinal apparatus is necessary for *a* religion. But faith in the possibilities of continued and rigorous inquiry does not limit access to truth to any channel or scheme of things. It does not first say that truth is universal and then add there is but one road to it. It does not depend for assurance upon subjection to any dogma or item of doctrine. It trusts that the natural interactions between man and his environment will breed more intelligence and generate more knowledge provided the scientific methods that define intelligence in operation are pushed further into the mysteries of the world, being themselves promoted and improved in the operation. There is such a thing as faith in intelligence becoming religious in quality—a fact that perhaps explains the efforts of some religionists to disparage the possibilities of intelligence as a force. They properly feel such faith to be a dangerous rival.

ii

The view I have advanced is sometimes treated as if the identification of the divine with ideal ends left the ideal wholly without roots in existence and without support from existence. The objection implies that my view commits one to such a separation of the ideal and the existent that the ideal has no chance to find lodgment even as a seed that might grow and bear fruit. On the contrary, what I have been criticizing is the *identification* of the ideal with a particular Being, especially when that identification makes necessary the conclusion that this Being is outside of nature, and what I have tried to show is that the ideal itself has its roots in natural conditions; it emerges when the imagination idealizes existence by laying hold of the possibilities offered to thought and action. There are values, goods, actually realized upon a natural basis—the goods of human association, of art and knowledge. The idealizing imagination seizes upon the most pre-

cious things found in the climacteric moments of experience and projects them. We need no external criterion and
guarantee for their goodness. They are had, they exist as
good, and out of them we frame our ideal ends.

Moreover, the ends that result from our projection of
experienced goods into objects of thought, desire and effort exist only they exist *as* ends. Ends, purposes, exercise
determining power in human conduct. The aims of philanthropists, of Florence Nightingale, of Howard, of Wilber-
force, of Peabody, have not been idle dreams. They have
modified institutions. Aims, ideals, do not exist simply in
"mind"; they exist in character, in personality and action. One might call the roll of artists, intellectual inquirers, parents, friends, citizens who are neighbors, to
show that purposes exist in an *operative* way. What I have
been objecting to, I repeat, is not the idea that ideals are
linked with existence and that they themselves exist,
through human embodiment, as forces, but the idea that
their authority and value depend upon some prior complete
embodiment—as if the efforts of human beings in behalf
of justice, or knowledge or beauty, depended for their
effectiveness and validity upon assurance that there already existed in some supernal region a place where
criminals are humanely treated, where there is no serfdom
or slavery, where all facts and truths are already discovered and possessed, and all beauty is eternally displayed in actualized form.

The aims and ideals that move us are generated through
imagination. But they are not made out of imaginary stuff.
They are made out of the hard stuff of the world of physical and social experience. The locomotive did not exist
before Stevenson, nor the telegraph before the time of
Morse. But the conditions for their existence were there in
physical material and energies and in human capacity.

Imagination seized hold upon the idea of a rearrangement of existing things that would evolve new objects. The same thing is true of a painter, a musician, a poet, a philanthropist, a moral prophet. The new vision does not arise out of nothing, but emerges through seeing, in terms of possibilities, that is, of imagination, old things in new relations serving a new end which the new end aids in creating.

Moreover the process of creation is experimental and continuous. The artist, scientific man, or good citizen, depends upon what others have done before him and are doing around him. The sense of new values that become ends to be realized arises first in dim and uncertain form. As the values are dwelt upon and carried forward in action they grow in definiteness and coherence. Interaction between aim and existent conditions improves and tests the ideal; and conditions are at the same time modified. Ideals change as they are applied in existent conditions. The process endures and advances with the life of humanity. What one person and one group accomplish becomes the standing ground and starting point of those who succeed them. When the vital factors in this natural process are generally acknowledged in emotion, thought and action, the process will be both accelerated and purified through elimination of that irrelevant element that culminates in the idea of the supernatural. When the vital factors attain the religious force that has been drafted into supernatural religions, the resulting reinforcement will be incalculable.

These considerations may be applied to the idea of God, or, to avoid misleading conceptions, to the idea of the divine. This idea is, as I have said, one of ideal possibilities unified through imaginative realization and projection. But this idea of God, or of the divine, is also connected with all the natural forces and conditions—including man and human association—that promote the growth of the ideal and that further its realization. We are in the presence neither of ideals completely embodied in existence nor yet of ideals that are mere rootless ideals, fantasies, utopias. For there are forces in nature and society that generate and support the ideals. They are further unified by the action that gives them coherence and solidity. It is this *active* relation between ideal and actual to which I would give the name "God." I would not insist that the name *must* be given. There are those who hold that the associations of the term with the supernatural are so numerous and close that any use of the word "God" is sure to give rise to misconception and be taken as a concession to traditional ideas.

They may be correct in this view. But the facts to which I have referred are there, and they need to be brought out with all possible clearness and force. There exist concretely and experimentally goods—the values of art in all its forms, of knowledge, of effort and of rest after striving, of education and fellowship, of friendship and love, of growth in mind and body. These goods are there and yet they are relatively embryonic. Many persons are shut out from generous participation in them; there are forces at work that threaten and sap existent goods as well as prevent their expansion. A clear and intense conception of a union of ideal ends with actual conditions is capable of arousing steady emotion. It may be fed by every experience, no matter what its material.

In a distracted age, the need for such an idea is urgent. It can unify interests and energies now dispersed; it can direct action and generate the heat of emotion and the light of intelligence. Whether one gives the name "God" to this union, operative in thought and action, is a matter for individual decision. But the *function* of such a working union of the ideal and actual seems to me to be identical with the force that has in fact been attached to the conception of God in all the religions that have a spiritual content; and a clear idea of that function seems to me urgently needed at the present time.

The sense of this union may, with some persons, be furthered by mystical experiences, using the term "mystical" in its broadest sense. That result depends largely upon temperament. But there is a marked difference between the union associated with mysticism and the union which I had in mind. There is nothing mystical about the latter; it is natural and moral. Nor is there anything mystical about the perception or consciousness of such union. Imagination of ideal ends pertinent to actual conditions represents the fruition of a disciplined mind. There is, indeed, even danger that resort to mystical experiences will be an escape, and that its result will be the passive feeling that the union of actual and ideal is already accomplished. But in fact this union is active and practical; it is a *uniting,* not something given.

One reason why personally I think it fitting to use the word "God" to denote that uniting of the ideal and actual which has been spoken of, lies in the fact that aggressive atheism seems to me to have something in common with traditional supernaturalism. I do not mean merely that the former is mainly so negative that it fails to give positive direction to thought, though that fact is pertinent. What I have in mind especially is the exclusive preoccupation of both militant atheism and supernaturalism with man in isolation. For in spite of supernaturalism's reference to something beyond nature, it conceives of this earth as the moral center of the universe and of man as the apex of the whole scheme of things. It regards the drama of sin and redemption enacted within the isolated and lonely soul of man as the one thing of ultimate importance. Apart from man, nature is held either accursed or negligible. Militant atheism is also affected by lack of natural piety. The ties binding man to nature that poets have always celebrated are passed over lightly. The attitude taken is often that of man living in an indifferent and hostile world and issuing blasts of defiance. A religious attitude, however, needs the sense of a connection of man, in the way of both dependence and support, with the enveloping world that the imagination feels is a universe. Use of the words "God" or "divine" to convey the union of actual with ideal may protect man from a sense of isolation and from consequent despair or defiance.

In any case, whatever the name, the meaning is selective. For it involves no miscellaneous worship of everything in general. It selects those factors in existence that generate and support our idea of good as an end to be striven for. It excludes a multitude of forces that at any given time are irrelevant to this function. Nature produces whatever gives reinforcement and direction but also what occasions discord and confusion. The "divine" is thus a term of human choice and aspiration. A humanistic religion, if it excludes our relation to nature, is pale and thin, as it is presumptuous, when it takes humanity as an object of worship. Matthew Arnold's conception of a "power not ourselves" is too narrow in its reference to operative and sustaining conditions. While it is selective, it is too narrow in its basis of selection—righteousness. The conception thus needs to be widened in two ways. The powers that generate and support the good as experienced and as ideal, work *within* as well as without. There seems to be a reminiscence of an external Jehovah in Arnold's statement. And the powers work to enforce other values and ideals than righteousness. Arnold's sense of an opposition between Hellenism and Hebraism resulted in exclusion of beauty, truth, and friendship from the list of the consequences toward which powers work within and without.

What would be the consequences upon the values of human association if intrinsic and immanent satisfactions and opportunities were clearly held to and cultivated with the ardor and the devotion that have at times marked historic religions? The contention of an increasing number of persons is that depreciation of natural social values has resulted, both in principle and in actual fact, from reference of their origin and significance to supernatural sources. Natural relations, of husband and wife, of parent and child, friend and friend, neighbor and neighbor, of fellow workers in industry, science, and art, are neglected, passed over, not developed for all that is in them. They are, moreover, not merely depreciated. They have been regarded as dangerous rivals of higher values; as offering temptations to be resisted; as usurpations by flesh of the authority of the spirit; as revolts of the human against the divine.

History seems to exhibit three stages of growth. In the first stage, human relationships were thought to be so infected with the evils of corrupt human nature as to require redemption from external and supernatural sources. In the next stage, what is significant in these relations is found to be akin to values esteemed distinctively religious. This is the point now reached by liberal theologians. The third stage would realize that in fact the values prized in those religions that have ideal elements are idealizations of things characteristic of natural association, which have then been projected into a supernatural realm for safe-keeping and sanction. Note the role of such terms as Father, Son, Bride, Fellowship and Communion in the vocabulary of Christianity, and note also the tendency, even if a somewhat inchoate one, of terms that express the more intimate phases of association to displace those of legal, political origin: King, Judge, and Lord of Hosts.

Unless there is a movement into what I have called the third stage, fundamental dualism and a division in life continue. The idea of a double and parallel manifestation of the divine, in which the latter has superior status and authority, brings about a condition of unstable equilibrium. It operates to distract energy, through dividing the objects to which it is directed. It also imperatively raises the question as to why having gone far in recognition of religious values in normal community life, we should not go further. The values of natural human intercourse and mutual dependence are open and public, capable of verification by the methods through which all natural facts are established. By means of the same experimental method, they are capable of expansion. Why not concentrate upon nurturing and extending them? Unless we take this step, the idea of two realms of spiritual values is only a softened version of the old dualism between the secular and the spiritual, the profane and the religious.

iii

The core of religions has generally been found in rites and ceremonies. Legends and myths grow up in part as decorative dressings, in response to the irrepressible human tendency toward story-telling, and in part as attempts to explain ritual practices. Then as culture advances, stories are consolidated, and theogonies and cosmogonies are formed—as with the Babylonians, Egyptians, Hebrews and Greeks. Legends along with rites and ceremonies came under the guardianship of a special body, the priesthood, and were subject to the special arts which it possessed. A special group was set aside as the responsible owners, protectors, and promulgators of the corpus of beliefs.

But the formation of a special social group having a peculiar relation to both the practices and the beliefs of religion is but part of the story. In the widest perspective, it is the less important part. The more significant point as regards the social import of religion is that the priesthoods were official representatives of some community, tribe, city-state or empire. Whether there was a priesthood or not, individuals who were members of a community were born into a religious community as they were into social and political organization. Each social group had its own divine beings who were its founders and protectors. Its rites of sacrifice, purification, and communion were manifestations of organized civic life. The temple was a public institution, the focus of the worship of the community; the influence of its practices extended to all the customs of the community, domestic, economic, and political. Even wars between groups were usually conflicts of their respective deities.

An individual did not join a church. He was born and reared in a community whose social unity, organization and traditions were symbolized and celebrated in the rites, cults and beliefs of a collective religion. Education was the induction of the young into community activities that were interwoven at every point with customs, legends and ceremonies intimately connected with and sanctioned by a religion. There are a few persons, especially those brought up in Jewish communities in Russia, who can understand without the use of imagination what a religion means socially when it permeates all the customs and activities of group life. To most of us in the United States such a situation is only a remote historic episode.

The change that has taken place in conditions once universal and now infrequent is in my opinion the greatest change that has occurred in religion in all history. The intellectual conflict of scientific and theological beliefs has attracted much more attention. It is still near the focus of attention. But the change in the social center of gravity of religion has gone on so steadily and is now so generally accomplished that it has faded from the thought of most persons, save perhaps the historians, and even they are especially aware of it only in its political aspect. For the conflict between state and church still continues in some countries.

There are even now persons who are born into a particular church, that of their parents, and who take membership in it almost as a matter of course; indeed, the fact of such membership may be an important, even a determining, factor in an individual's whole career. But the thing new in history, the thing once unheard of, is that the organization in question is a *special* institution within a secular community. Even where there are established churches, they are constituted by the state and may be unmade by the state. Not only the national state but other forms of organization among groups have grown in power and influence at the expense of organizations built upon and about a religion. The correlate of this fact is that membership in associations of the latter type is more and more a matter of the voluntary choice of individuals, who may tend to accept responsibilities imposed by the church but who accept them of their own volition. If they do accept them, the organization they join is, in many nations, chartered under a general corporation law of the political and secular entity.

The shift in what I have called the social center of gravity accompanies the enormous expansion of associa-

tions formed for educational, political, economic, philanthropic and scientific purposes, which has occurred independently of any religion. These social modes have grown
so much that they exercise the greater hold upon the
thought and interest of most persons, even of those holding membership in churches. This positive extension of interests which, from the standpoint of a religion, are non-
religious, is so great that in comparison with it the direct
effect of science upon the creeds of religion seems to me
of secondary importance.

I say, the *direct* effect; for the indirect effect of science
in stimulating the growth of competing organizations is
enormous. Changes that are purely intellectual affect at
most but a small number of specialists. They are secondary to consequences brought about through impact upon
the *conditions* under which human beings associate with
one another. Invention and technology, in alliance with industry and commerce, have, needless to say, profoundly
affected these underlying conditions of association. Every
political and social problem of the present day reflects
this indirect influence, from unemployment to banking,
from municipal administration to the great migration of
peoples made possible by new modes of transportation,
from birth control to foreign commerce and war. The social changes that have come about through application of
the new knowledge affect everyone, whether he is aware or
not of the source of the forces that play upon him. The
effect is the deeper, indeed, because so largely unconscious.
For, to repeat what I have said, the *conditions* under
which people meet and act together have been modified.

These movements and others not mentioned are the intellectual reflex of the greatest revolution that has taken
place in religions during the thousands of years that man
has been upon earth. For, as I have said, this change has

to do with the *social* place and function of religion. Even the hold of the supernatural upon the general mind has become more and more disassociated from the power of ecclesiastic organization—that is, of any particular form of communal organization. Thus the very idea that was central in religions has more and more oozed away, so to speak, from the guardianship and care of any particular social institution. Even more important is the fact that a steady encroachment upon ecclesiastic institutions of forms of association once regarded as secular has altered the way in which men spend their time in work, recreation, citizenship, and political action. The essential point is not just that secular organizations and actions are legally or externally severed from the control of the church, but that interests and values unrelated to the offices of any church now so largely sway the desires and aims of even believers.

The individual believer may indeed carry the disposition and motivation he has acquired through affiliation with a religious organization into his political action, into his connection with schools, even into his business and amusements. But there remain two facts that constitute a revolution. In the first place, conditions are such that this action is a matter of personal choice and resolution on the part of individuals, not of the very nature of social organization. In the second place, the very fact that an individual imports or carries his personal attitude into affairs that are innerently secular, that are outside the scope of religion, constitutes an enormous change, in spite of the belief that secular matters *should* be permeated by the spirit of religion. Even if it be asserted, as it is by some religionists, that all the new movements and interests of any value grew up under the auspices of a church and received their impetus from the same source, it must be admitted that once the vessels have been launched, they are sailing on strange seas to far lands.

Criticism of the commitment of religion to the supernatural is thus positive in import. All modes of human association are "affected with a public interest," and full realization of this interest is equivalent to a sense of a significance that is religious in its function. The objection to supernaturalism is that it stands in the way of an effective realization of the sweep and depth of the implications of natural human relations. It stands in the way of using the means that are in our power to make radical changes in these relations. It is certainly true that great material changes might be made with no corresponding improvement of a spiritual or ideal nature. But development in the latter direction cannot be introduced from without; it cannot be brought about by dressing up material and economic changes with decorations derived from the supernatural. It can come only from more intense realization of values that inhere in the actual connections of human beings with one another. The attempt to segregate the implicit public interest and social value of all institutions and social arrangements in a particular organization is a fatal diversion.

Were men and women actuated throughout the length and breadth of human relations with the faith and ardor that have at times marked historic religions the consequences would be incalculable. To achieve this faith and *élan* is no easy task. But religions have attempted something similar, directed moreover toward a less promising object—the supernatural. It does not become those who hold that faith may move mountains to deny in advance the possibility of its manifestation on the basis of verifiable realities. There already exists, though in a rudimentary form, the capacity to relate social conditions and events to their causes, and the ability will grow with exercise. There is the technical skill with which to initiate a campaign for social health and sanity analogous to that made in behalf of physical public health. Human beings have impulses toward affection, compassion and justice, equality and freedom. It remains to weld all these things together. It is of no use merely to assert that the intrenched foes of class interest and power in high places are hostile to the realization of such a union. As I have already said, if this enemy did not exist, there would be little sense in urging *any* policy of change. The point to be grasped is that, unless one gives up the whole struggle as hopeless, one has to choose between alternatives. One alternative is dependence upon the supernatural; the other, the use of natural agencies.

The coincidence of the realm of social interests and activities with a tribal or civic community has vanished. Secular interests and activities have grown up outside of organized religions and are independent of their authority. The hold of these interests upon the thoughts and desires of men has crowded the social importance of organized religions into a corner and the area of this corner is decreasing. This change either marks a terrible decline in everything that can justly be termed religious in value, in traditional religions, or it provides the opportunity for expansion of these qualities on a new basis and with a new outlook. It is impossible to ignore the fact that historic Christianity has been committed to a separation of sheep and goats; the saved and the lost; the elect and the mass. Spiritual aristocracy as well as *laissez faire* with respect to natural and human intervention, is deeply embedded in its traditions. Lip service—often more than lip service—has been given to the idea of the common brotherhood of all men. But those outside the fold of the church and those who do not rely upon belief in the supernatural have been regarded as only potential brothers, still requiring adoption into the family. I cannot understand how any realization of the democratic ideal as a vital moral and spiritual ideal in human affairs is possible without surrender of the conception of the basic division to which supernatural Christianity is committed. Whether or no we are, save in some metaphorical sense, all brothers, we are at least all in the same boat traversing the same turbulent ocean. The potential religious significance of this fact is infinite.

Lives that are consciously inspired by loyalty to such ideals as have been mentioned are still comparatively infrequent to the extent of that comprehensiveness and intensity which arouse an ardor religious in function. But before we infer the incompetency of such ideals and of the actions they inspire, we should at least ask ourselves how much of the existing situation is due to the fact that the religious factors of experience have been drafted into supernatural channels and thereby loaded with irrelevant encumbrances. A body of beliefs and practices that are apart from the common and natural relations of mankind must, in the degree in which it is influential, weaken and sap the force of the possibilities inherent in such relations. Here lies one aspect of the emancipation of the religious from religion.

Any activity pursued in behalf of an ideal end against obstacles and in spite of threats of personal loss because of conviction of its general and enduring value is religious in quality. Many a person, inquirer, artist, philanthropist, citizen, men and women in the humblest walks of life, have achieved, without presumption and without display, such unification of themselves and of their relations to the conditions of existence. It remains to extend their spirit and inspiration to ever wider numbers. If I have said anything about religions and religion that seems harsh, I have said those things because of a firm belief that the claim on the part of religions to possess a monopoly of ideals and of the supernatural means by which alone, it is alleged, they can be furthered, stands in the way of the realization of distinctively religious values inherent in natural experience. For that reason, if for no other, I should be sorry if any were misled by the frequency with which I have employed the adjective "religious" to conceive of what I have said as a disguised apology for what have passed as religions. The opposition between religious values as I conceive them and religions is not to be bridged. Just because the release of these values is so important, their identification with the creeds and cults of religions must be dissolved.

CHAPTER TWENTY-ONE

COMPREHENSIVE WORKING IDEAS *

I · Continuities in Nature†

THE philosophy here presented may be termed either empirical naturalism or naturalistic empiricism or, taking "experience" in its usual signification, naturalistic humanism.

To many the associating of the two words will seem like talking of a round square, so engrained is the notion of the separation of man and experience from nature. Experience, they say, is important for those beings who have it, but is too casual and sporadic in its occurrence to carry with it any important implications regarding the nature of Nature. Nature, on the other hand, is said to be complete apart from experience. Indeed, according to some thinkers

---

* Perhaps no reader would erroneously infer from the title of this chapter that *all* the comprehensive working ideas of John Dewey's philosophy are here gathered together, but to avoid any possible misunderstanding let it be explicitly stated that this chapter does *not* perform such an impossible feat—impossible because a chapter cannot have the size of a book. Special note needs to be made of the fact that the discussion of the interrelation of the two comprehensive working ideas—"continuity" and "interaction"—is to be found in Ch. Eleven, Section 4. To have included these pages here would have added more formal virtue to this chapter; but to have taken them out of their clarifying context would have materially detracted from the actual virtue of this book. It may be said that it required no protracted and involved deliberation to decide upon what to do when faced with the *Either-Or* choice: *either* pay exaggerated homage to the formal demands of systematic presentation, *or* pay attention to the real demands of the meaning and spirit of John Dewey's philosophy.—Ed.

† From *Experience and Nature* (second edition), Ch. I.

the case is even in worse plight: Experience to them is not only something extraneous which is occasionally superimposed upon nature, but it forms a veil or screen which shuts us off from nature, unless in some way it can be "transcended." So something non-natural by way of reason or intuition is introduced, something supra-empirical. According to an opposite school experience fares as badly, nature being thought to signify something wholly material and mechanistic; to frame a theory of experience in naturalistic terms is, accordingly, to degrade and deny the noble and ideal values that characterize experience.

In the natural sciences, however, there is a union of experience and nature which is not greeted as a monstrosity; on the contrary, the inquirer must use empirical method if his findings are to be treated as genuinely scientific. The investigator assumes as a matter of course that experience, controlled in specifiable ways, is the avenue that leads to the facts and laws of nature. He uses reason and calculation freely; he could not get along without them. But he sees to it that ventures of this theoretical sort start from and terminate in directly experienced subject-matter. Theory may intervene in a long course of reasoning, many portions of which are remote from what is directly experienced. But the vine of pendant theory is attached at both ends to the pillars of observed subject-matter. And this experienced material is the same for the scientific man and the man in the street. The latter cannot follow the intervening reasoning without special preparation. But stars, rocks, trees, and creeping things are the same material of experience for both.

These commonplaces take on significance when the relation of experience to the formation of a philosophic theory of nature is in question. They indicate that experience, if scientific inquiry is justified, is no infinitesimally thin layer or foreground of nature, but that it penetrates into it, reaching down into its depths, and in such a way that its grasp is capable of expansion; it tunnels in all directions and in so doing brings to the surface things at first hidden—as miners pile high on the surface of the earth treasures brought from below.

Experience is *of* as well as *in* nature. It is not experience which is experienced, but nature—stones, plants, animals, diseases, health, temperature, electricity and so on. Things interacting in certain ways *are* experience; they are what is experienced. Linked in certain other ways with another natural object—the human organism— they are *how* things are experienced as well.

The same considerations apply to the other objection that was suggested, namely, that to view experience naturalistically is to reduce it to something materialistic, depriving it of all ideal significance. If experience actually presents esthetic and moral traits, then these traits may also be supposed to reach down into nature, and to testify to something that belongs to nature as truly as does the mechanical structure attributed to it in physical science. To rule out that possibility by some general reasoning is to forget that the very meaning and purport of empirical method is that things are to be studied on their own account, so as to find out what is revealed when they are experienced. The traits possessed by the subject-matters of experience are as genuine as the characteristics of sun and electron. They are *found,* experienced, and are not to be shoved out of being by some trick of logic. When found, their ideal qualities are as relevant to the philosophic theory of nature as are the traits found by physical inquiry.

Philosophy, like all forms of reflective analysis, takes us away, for the time being, from the things had in primary experience as they directly act and are acted upon, used and enjoyed. Now the standing temptation of philosophy, as its course abundantly demonstrates, is to regard the results of reflection as having, in and of themselves, a reality superior to that of the material of any other mode of experience. The commonest assumption of philosophies, common even to philosophies very different from one another, is the assumption of the identity of objects of knowledge and ultimately real objects. The assumption is so deep that it is usually not expressed; it is taken for granted as something so fundamental that it does not need to be stated. That esthetic and moral experience reveal traits of real things as truly as does intellectual experience, that poetry may have a metaphysical import as well as science, is rarely affirmed, and when it is asserted, the statement is likely to be meant in some mystical or esoteric sense rather than in a straightforward everyday sense.

Suppose, however, that we start with no presuppositions save that what is experienced, since it is a manifestation of nature, may, and indeed, must be used as testimony of the characteristics of natural events. Upon this basis, reverie and desire are pertinent for a philosophic theory of the true nature of things: the possibilities present in imagination that are not found in observation, are something to be taken into account. The features of objects reached by scientific or reflective experiencing are important, but so are all the phenomena of magic, myth, politics, painting and penitentiaries. The phenomena of social life are as relevant to the problem of the relation of the individual and universal as are those of logic; the existence in political organization of boundaries and barriers, of expansion and absorption, will be quite as important for metaphysical theories of the discrete and the continuous as is anything derived from chemical analysis. The existence of ignorance as well as of wisdom, of error and even insanity as well as of truth will be taken into account.

That is to say, nature is construed in such a way that all these things, since they are actual, are naturally possible; they are not explained away into mere "appearance" in contrast with reality. Illusions are illusions, but the occurrence of illusions is not an illusion, but a genuine reality. What is really "in" experience extends much further than that which at any time is *known*. From the standpoint of knowledge, objects must be distinct; their traits must be explicit; the vague and unrevealed is a limitation. Hence whenever the habit of identifying reality with the object of knowledge as such prevails, the obscure and vague are explained away. It is important for philosophic theory to be aware that the distinct and evident are prized and why they are. But it is equally important to note that the dark and twilight abound. For in any object of primary experience there are always potentialities which are not explicit; any object that is overt is charged with possible consequences that are hidden; the most overt act has factors which are not explicit. Strain thought as far as we may and not all consequences can be foreseen or made an express or known part of reflection and decision. In the face of such empirical facts, the assumption that nature in itself is all of the same kind, all distinct, explicit and evident, having no hidden possibilities, no novelties or obscurities, is possible only on the basis of a philosophy which at some point draws an arbitrary line between nature and experience. An empirical philosophy must replace the traditional separation of nature and experience with the idea of continuity.

II · The Methods of Philosophy*

If the empirical method were universally or even generally adopted in philosophizing, there would be no need of referring to experience. The scientific inquirer talks and writes about particular observed events and qualities, about specific calculations and reasonings. He makes no allusion to experience; one would probably have to search a long time through reports of special researches in order to find the word. The reason is that everything designated by the word "experience" is so adequately incorporated into scientific procedures and subject-matter that to mention experience would be only to duplicate in a general term what is already covered in definite terms. Of course, this was not always so. And we may, if sufficiently hopeful, anticipate a similar outcome in philosophy. But the date does not appear to be close at hand; we are, in philosophic theory, nearer to the time of Roger Bacon than to that of Newton.

It is the contrast of empirical method with other methods employed in philosophizing, together with the striking dissimilarity of results yielded by an empirical method and professed non-empirical methods that make the discussion of the methodological import of "experience" for philosophy pertinent and indeed indispensable.

The consideration of method may suitably begin with the contrast between gross macroscopic, crude subject-matters in primary experience and the refined, derived objects of reflection. The distinction is one between what is experienced as the result of a minimum of incidental reflection and what is experienced in consequence of continued and regulated reflective inquiry. For derived and refined products are experienced only because of the inter-

* From *Experience and Nature* (second edition), Ch. I.

vention of systematic thinking. The objects of both science and philosophy obviously belong chiefly to the secondary and refined system. But at this point we come to a marked divergence between science and (non-empirical) philosophy. For the natural sciences not only draw their material from primary experience, but they refer it back again for test.

That the subject-matter of primary experience sets the problems of science and furnishes the first data of the reflection which constructs the secondary objects is evident; it is also obvious that test and verification of the latter are secured only by return to things of crude or macroscopic experience—the sun, earth, plants and animals of common everyday life. But when the secondary objects, the refined objects, are employed as a method or road for coming at them, they get the meaning contained in a whole system of related objects; they are rendered continuous with the rest of nature and take on the import of the things they are now seen to be continuous with. The phenomena observed in the eclipse tested and, as far as they went, confirmed Einstein's theory of deflection of light by mass. But that is far from being the whole story. The phenomena themselves got a far-reaching significance they did not previously have.

That philosophy is a mode of reflection, often of a subtle and penetrating sort, goes without saying. The charge that is brought against the non-empirical method of philosophizing is not that it depends upon theorizing, but that it fails to use refined, secondary products as a path pointing and leading back to something in primary experience. The resulting failure is threefold.

First, there is no verification, no effort even to test and check. What is even worse, secondly, is that the things of ordinary experience do not get enlargement and enrichment of meaning as they do when approached through the medium of scientific principles and reasonings: This lack of function reacts, in the third place, back upon the philosophic subject-matter in itself. Not tested by being employed to see what it leads to in ordinary experience and what new meanings it contributes, this subject-matter becomes arbitrary and aloof—what is called "abstract" when that word is used in a bad sense to designate something which exclusively occupies a realm of its own without contact with the things of ordinary experience.

A first-rate test of the value of any philosophy which is offered us is this: Does it end in conclusions which, when they are referred back to ordinary life-experiences and their predicaments, render them more significant, more luminous to us, and make our dealings with them more fruitful? Or does it terminate in rendering the things of ordinary experience more opaque than they were before, and in depriving them of having in "reality" even the significance they had previously seemed to have? Does it yield the enrichment and increase of power of ordinary things which the results of physical science afford when applied in every-day affairs? Or does it become a mystery that these ordinary things should be what they are, or indeed that they should be at all, while philosophic concepts are left to dwell in separation in some technical realm of their own? It is the fact that so many philosophies terminate in conclusions that make it necessary to disparage and condemn primary experience, leading those who hold them to measure the sublimity of their "realities" as philosophically defined by remoteness from the concerns of daily life, which leads cultivated common sense to look askance at philosophy.

What empirical method exacts of philosophy is two things: First, that refined methods and products be traced back to their origin in primary experience, in all its heterogeneity and fullness; so that the needs and problems out of which they arise and which they have to satisfy be acknowledged. Secondly, that the secondary methods and conclusions be brought back to the things of ordinary experience, in all their coarseness and crudity, for verification. In this way, the methods of analytic reflection yield materials which form the ingredients of a method of designation, denotation, in philosophy. A scientific work in physics or astronomy gives a record of calculations and deductions that were derived from past observations and experiments. But it is more than a record; it is also an indication, an assignment, of further observations and experiments to be performed. No scientific report would get a hearing if it did not describe the apparatus by means of which experiments were carried on and results obtained; not that apparatus is worshipped, but because this procedure tells other inquirers how they are to go to work to get results which will agree or disagree in their experience with those previously arrived at, and thus confirm, modify and rectify the latter. The recorded scientific result is in effect a *designation* of a method to be followed and a *prediction* of what will be found when specified observations are set on foot. That is all a philosophy can be or do.

III · Precarious and Stable Events*

i

Upon their surface, the reports of the world which form our different philosophies are various to the point of stark contrariness. They range from spiritualism to materialism, from absolutism to relativistic phenomenalism, from transcendentalism to positivism, from rationalism to sensation-

* From *Experience and Nature,* pp. 28-30; 46-48; 70-71.

alism, from idealism to realism, from subjectivism to bald
objectivism, from Platonic realism to nominalism. The ar-
ray of contradictions is so imposing as to suggest to scep-
tics that the mind of man has tackled an impossible job,
or that philosophers have abandoned themselves to va-
gary. These radical oppositions in philosophers suggest
however another consideration. They suggest that all their
different philosophies have a common premise, and that
their diversity is due to *acceptance* of a common premise.
Variant philosophies may be looked at as different ways of
supplying recipes for denying to the universe the character
of contingency which it possesses so integrally that its denial leaves the reflecting mind without a clew, and puts
subsequent philosophising at the mercy of temperament,
interest and local surroundings.

Quarrels among conflicting types of philosophy are thus
family quarrels. They go on within the limits of a too
domestic circle, and can be settled only by venturing
further afield, and out of doors. Concerned with imputing
complete, finished and sure character to the world of real
existence, even if things have to be broken into two disconnected pieces in order to accomplish the result, the
character desiderated can plausibly be found in reason or
in mechanism; in rational conceptions like those of mathematics, or brute things like sensory data; in atoms or in
essences; in consciousness or in a physical externality
which forces and overrides consciousness.

As against this common identification of reality with
what is sure, regular and finished, experience in unsophisticated forms gives evidence of a different world and
points to a different metaphysics. We live in a world
which is an impressive and irresistible mixture of sufficien-
cies, tight completenesses, order, recurrences which make
possible prediction and control, and singularities, ambigui-

ties, uncertain possibilities, processes going on to consequences as yet indeterminate. They are mixed not mechanically but vitally like the wheat and tares of the parable. We may recognize them separately but we cannot
divide them, for unlike wheat and tares they grow from
the same root. Qualities have defects as necessary conditions of their excellencies; the instrumentalities of truth
are the causes of error; change gives meaning to permanence and recurrence makes novelty possible. A world that
was wholly risky would be a world in which adventure is
impossible, and only a living world can include death.
Such facts have been celebrated by thinkers like Heraclei-
tus and Laotze; they have been greeted by theologians as
furnishing occasions for exercise of divine grace; they
have been elaborately formulated by various schools under
a principle of relativity, so defined as to become itself final and absolute. But they have rarely been frankly recognized as fundamentally significant for the formation of a
naturalistic metaphysics.

ii

The value of the notion of experience for philosophic
reflection is that it denotes both the field, the sun and
clouds and rain, seeds and harvest, and the man who
labors, who plans, invents, uses, suffers, and enjoys. Experience denotes what is experienced, the world of events
and persons; and it denotes that world caught up into experiencing, the career and destiny of mankind.

The denotations that constitute experience point to history, to temporal process. The technically expert are
aware how much ingenuity has been spent upon discovering something which shall be wholly present, so completely present as to exclude movement and change.
There are *phases* of things to which this search is perti-

nent. There are moments of consummation when before and after are legitimately forgotten, and the sole stake of man is in the present. But even such objects are discovered to arise as culminations of processes, and to be in turn transitive and effective, while they may be also predictive or cognitively significant. The legitimacy of timeless absorption is no argument in behalf of the legitimacy of timeless objects. Experience is history; and the *taking* of some objects as final is itself an episode in history. The testimony of an absorbed consciousness that at last it rests upon something superior to the vicissitudes of time is of no more cognitive worth than the testimony of any other purely immediate consciousness. That is, it is not testimony at all, it is a having, not a knowing. And hence when treated as cognition, it is never natural and naïve; it is suborned in the interest of a sophisticated metaphysics. There is no testimony in such moments just because of absorption in the immediate qualities of the object. There are enjoyment and possession, with no need of thought as to how the object came or whither it is going, what evidence it gives. And when it turns evidence, it always testifies to an existence which is partial or particular, and local.

The assumption that the ultimate and the immediate object is timeless is responsible for one of the insoluble problems of certain types of philosophy. The past and future are rendered purely inferential, speculative, something to be reached by pure faith. But in fact anything denoted is found to have temporal quality and reference; it has movement from and toward *within* it; it is marked by waxings and wanings. The translation of temporal quality into an *order* of time is an intellectual arrangement, and is subject to doubt and error. Although pastness and futurity are qualities of everything present, such presence does not guarantee the date at which Columbus discovered America nor when the next eclipse of the moon will occur. For these things are matters that require measurements, comparisons, connection with remote occurrences. But objects of present experience have the actuality of a temporal procession, and accordingly reflection may assign things an order of succession within something which non-reflectively exists and is had.

The conjunction of problematic and determinate characters in nature renders every existence, as well as every idea and human act, an experiment in fact, even though not in design. To be intelligently experimental is but to be conscious of this intersection of natural conditions so as to profit by it instead of being at its mercy. The Christian idea of this world and this life as a probation is a kind of distorted recognition of the situation; distorted because it applied wholesale to one stretch of existence in contrast with another, regarded as original and final. But in truth anything which can exist at any place and at any time occurs subject to tests imposed upon it by surroundings, which are only in part compatible and reënforcing. These surroundings test its strength and measure its endurance. As we can discourse of change only in terms of velocity and acceleration which involve relations to other things, so assertion of the permanent and enduring is comparative. The stablest thing we can speak of is not free from conditions set to it by other things. That even the solid earth, mountains, the emblems of constancy, appear and disappear like the clouds is an old theme of moralists and poets. The fixed and unchanged being of the Democritean atom is now reported by inquirers to possess some of the traits of his non-being, and to embody a temporary equilibrium in the economy of nature's compromises and adjustments. A thing may endure *secula seculorum* and

yet not be everlasting; it will crumble before the gnawing tooth of time, as it exceeds a certain measure. Every
existence is an event.

IV · Process and Structure*

This fact—that every existence is an event—is nothing
at which to repine and nothing to gloat over. It is something to be noted and used. If it is discomfiting when applied to good things, to our friends, possessions and precious selves, it is consoling also to know that no evil endures forever; that the longest lane turns sometime, and
that the memory of loss of nearest and dearest grows dim
in time. The eventful character of all existences is no reason for consigning them to the realm of mere appearance
any more than it is a reason for idealizing flux into a
deity. The important thing is measure, relation, ratio,
knowledge of the comparative tempos of change. In mathematics some variables are constants in some problems;
so it is in nature and life. The rate of change of some
things is so slow, or is so rhythmic, that these changes
have all the advantages of stability in dealing with more
transitory and irregular happenings—if we know enough.
Indeed, if any one thing that concerns us is subject to
change, it is fortunate that all other things change. A
thing "absolutely" stable and unchangeable would be out
of the range of the principle of action and reaction, of resistance and leverage as well as of friction. Here it would
have no applicability, no potentiality of use as measure
and control of other events. To designate the slower and
the regular rhythmic events structure, and more rapid and
irregular ones process, is sound practical sense. It expresses the function of one in respect to the other.

But spiritualistic idealism and materialism alike treat

* From *Experience and Nature*, pp. 71-74.

this relational and functional distinction as something fixed and absolute. One doctrine finds structure in a framework of ideal forms, the other finds it in matter. They agree in supposing that structure has some superlative reality. This supposition is another form taken by preference for the stable over the precarious and uncompleted. The fact is that all structure is structure of something; anything defined as structure is a character of *events*, not something intrinsic and *per se*. A set of traits is called structure, because of its limiting function in relation to other traits of events. A house has a structure; in comparison with the disintegration and collapse that would occur without its presence, this structure is fixed. Yet it is not something external to which the changes involved in building and using the house have to submit. It is rather an arrangement of changing events such that properties which change slowly, limit and direct a series of quick changes and give them an order which they do not otherwise possess. Structure is constancy of means, of things used for consequences, not of things taken by themselves or absolutely. Structure is what makes construction possible and cannot be discovered or defined except in some realized construction, construction being, of course, an evident order of changes. The isolation of structure from the changes whose stable ordering it is, renders it mysterious—something that is metaphysical in the popular sense of the word, a kind of ghostly queerness.

The "matter" of materialists and the "spirit" of idealists is a creature similar to the constitution of the United States in the minds of unimaginative persons. Obviously the real constitution is certain basic relationships among the activities of the citizens of the country; it is a property or phase of these processes, so connected with them as to influence their rate and direction of change. But by literalists it is often conceived of as something external to them; in itself fixed, a rigid framework to which *all* changes must accommodate themselves. Similarly what we call matter is that character of natural events which is so tied up with changes that are sufficiently rapid to be perceptible as to give the latter a characteristic rhythmic order, the causal sequence. It is no cause or source of events or processes; no absolute monarch; no principle of explanation; no substance behind or underlying changes—save in that sense of substance in which a man well fortified with this world's goods, and hence able to maintain himself through vicissitudes of surroundings, is a man of substance. The name designates a character in operation, not an entity.

That structure, whether of the kind called material or of the kind summed up in the word mental, is stable or permanent relationally and in its office, may be shown in another way. There is no action without reaction; there is no exclusively one-way exercise of conditioning power, no mode of regulation that operates wholly from above to below or from within outwards or from without inwards. Whatever influences the changes of other things is itself changed. The idea of an activity proceeding only in one direction, of an unmoved mover, is a survival of Greek physics. It has been banished from science, but remains to haunt philosophy. The vague and mysterious properties assigned to mind and matter, the very conceptions of mind and matter in traditional thought, are ghosts walking underground. The notion of matter actually found in the practice of science has nothing in common with the matter of materialists—and almost everybody is still a materialist as to matter, to which he merely adds a second rigid structure which he calls mind. The matter of science is a character of natural events and changes as they change; *their* character of regular and stable order.

V · Causes and Effects (Means and Ends)*

By the nature of the case, causality, however it be defined, consists in the sequential order itself, and not in a last term which as such is irrelevant to causality, although it may, of course, be, in addition, an initial term in another sequential order. The view held—or implied—by some "mechanists," which treats an initial term as if it had an inherent generative force which it somehow emits and bestows upon its successors, is all of a piece with the view held by teleologists which implies that an end brings about its own antecedents. Both isolate an event from the history in which it belongs and in which it has its character. Both make a factitiously isolated position in a temporal order a mark of true reality, one theory selecting initial place and the other final place. But in fact causality is another name for the sequential order itself; and since this is an order of a history having a beginning and end, there is nothing more absurd than setting causality over against either initiation or finality.

From the standpoint of control and utilization, the tendency to assign superior reality to causes is explicable. A "cause" is not merely an antecedent; it is that antecedent which if manipulated regulates the occurrence of the consequent. This is why the sun rather than night is the causal condition of day. Knowing that consequences will take care of themselves if conditions can be had and managed, an ineradicable natural pragmatism indulges in a cheap and short conversion, and conceives the cause as intrinsically more primary and necessary. This practical

* From *Experience and Nature,* pp. 109-111; 114-116.

tendency is increased by the fact that time is a softener and dignifier; present troubles lose their acuteness when they are no longer present. Old times are proverbially the good old times, and history begins with a Garden of Paradise or a Golden Age. Good, being congenial, is held to be normal; and what is suffered is a deviation, creating the problem of evil. Thus the earlier gets moral dignity as well as practical superiority. But in existence, or metaphysically, cause and effect are on the same level; they are portions of one and the same historic process, each having immediate or esthetic quality and each having efficacy, or serial connection. Since existence is historic it can be known or understood only as each portion is distinguished and related. For knowledge "cause" and "effect" alike have a partial and truncated being. It is as much a part of the real being of atoms that they give rise in time, under increasing complication of relationships, to qualities of blue and sweet, pain and beauty, as that they have at a cross-section of time extension, mass, or weight.

The problem is neither psychological nor epistemological. It is metaphysical or existential. It is whether existence consists of events, or is possessed of temporal quality, characterized by beginning, process and ending. If so, the affair of later and earlier, however important it is for particular practical matters, is indifferent to a theory of valuation of existence. It is as arbitrary to assign complete reality to atoms at the expense of mind and conscious experience as it is to make a rigid separation between here and there in space. Distinction is genuine and for some purposes necessary. But it is not a distinction of kinds or degrees of reality. Space here is joined to space there, and events then are joined to events now; the reality is as much in the joining as in the distinction. In order to control the course of events it is indispensable to know their conditions. But to characterize the conditions, it is necessary to have followed them to some term, which is not fully followed till we arrive at something enjoyed or suffered, had and used, in conscious experience. Vital and conscious events exhibit actualization of properties that are not fully displayed in the simpler relationships that are by definition termed physical.

If we discount practical bias toward the regular and repeated, and hence toward "causes" as opposed to consequences, all that is indicated by the transiency of immediate qualitative affairs is that immediacy is immediacy. By the nature of the case the occurrence of the immediate is at the mercy of the sequential order. In the case of the things which appeal to common-sense as substances, properties like mass and inertia, unchanged solidity and extension, count most. Rate of change is slow; and presents itself as a matter of attrition and accumulation; spatial qualities which are static chiefly figure. Time is of comparative indifference to the change of solid substances; a million years is a day. But whatever depends for its existence upon the interaction of a large number of independent variables is in unstable equilibrium; its rate of change is rapid; successive qualities have no obvious connection with one another; any shift of any part may alter the whole pattern. Thus, while light and water are "substances," a rainbow, depending upon a highly specialized conjunction of light and vapor, and being transient, is only a "phenomenon." Such immediate qualities as red and blue, sweet and sour, tone, the pleasant and unpleasant, depend upon an extraordinary variety and complexity of conditioning events; hence they are evanescent. They are never exactly reduplicated, because the exact combination of events of which they are termini does not precisely recur. Hence they are even more "phenomenal" than a rainbow; they must be hitched to substance as its "modes" to get standing in "reality."

Thus the things that are most precious, that are final, being just the things that are unstable and most easily changing, seem to be different in kind from good, solid, old-fashioned substance. Matter has turned out to be nothing like as lumpy and chunky as unimaginative prejudice conceived it to be. But as compared with the changes of immediate qualities it seems in any case solid and substantial; a fact which accounts, I suppose, for the insertion of an immaterial sort of substance, after the analogy of matter-substance, underneath mental affairs. But when it is recognized that the latter are eventual and consummatory to highly complicated interactions of natural events, their transiency becomes itself intelligible; it is no ground of argument for a radical difference from the physical, the latter being also resolvable into a character of the course of events. While "consciousness" as the conspicuous and vivid presence of immediate qualities and of meanings, is alone of direct worth, things not immediately present, whose intrinsic qualities are not directly had, are primary from the standpoint of control. For just because the things that are directly had are both precious and evanescent, the only thing that can be thought of is the conditions under which they are had. The common, pervasive and repeated *is* of superior rank from the standpoint of safeguarding and buttressing the having of terminal qualities. Directly we can do nothing with the latter save have, enjoy and suffer them. So reflection is concerned with the order which conditions, prevents and secures their occurrence. The irony of many historic systems of philosophy is that they have so inverted the actualities of the case. The general, recurrent and extensive has been treated as the worthy and superior kind of Be-

ing; the immediate, intensive, transitory, and qualitatively
individualized has been taken to be of importance only
when it is imputed to something ordinary, which is all the
universal can denotatively mean. In truth, the universal
and stable are important because they are the instrumentalities, the efficacious conditions, of the occurrence of the
unique, unstable and passing.

To point out something as a fact is not the same thing
as to commend or eulogize the fact. I am not saying that
it is a fine and noble thing that whatever is immediately
consummatory and precious should be also evanescent and
unique, never completely subject to principle and rule. A
reporter is not necessarily to blame for the state of things
that he reports. The fact hereby reported is so unescap-
able and so obvious to a candid empiricist that there is
no occasion for either eulogy or condemnation.

VI · The Social*

There are at the present time a considerable number of
persons who habitually employ the social as a principle of
philosophic reflection and who assign it a force equal and
even superior to that ascribed the physical, vital and mental. There are others, probably a greater number, who decline to take "social" seriously as a category of description and interpretation for purposes of philosophy, and
who conceive any attempt so to take it as involving a
confusion of anthropology and sociology with metaphysics.
The most they would concede is that cultural material
may throw light on the genesis and history of human beliefs about ultimate subject-matter. Then it is asserted that
it is but a case of the familiar genetic fallacy, the confusion of the history of belief with the nature of that believed, to assign to such an account a place anywhere ex-

* From *Philosophy and Civilization*, pp. 77-92.

cept within the history of human culture. Such a situation solicits attention; and I desire to state as far as time permits what is the intent of those who attribute genuine philosophic import to the idea of the social.

A start may be conveniently made by noting that associated or conjoint behavior is a universal characteristic of all existences. Knowledge is in terms of related objects and unless it is supposed that relations are a subjective intrusion, or that, *á la* Hume, only *ideas* are associated, relation as the nerve of science correlates with association among things. This fact being noted, we observe that the qualities of associated things are displayed only in association, since in interactions alone are potentialities released and actualized. Furthermore, the manifestation of potentialities varies with the manner and range of association. This statement is only a formal way of calling attention to the fact that we characterize an element, say hydrogen, not only, as the name implies, in terms of its water-forming potentiality but ultimately in terms of consequences effected in a whole range of modes of conjoint behavior.*

These considerations being premised, attention fastens upon the fact that the more numerous and varied the forms of association into which anything enters, the better basis we have for describing and understanding it, for the more complex is an association the more fully are potentialities released for observation. Since things present themselves to us in such fashion that narrower and wider ranges, simpler and more complex ones, are readily distin-

---

* In case there is objection to the use of the conceptions of potentiality and actualization, it may be pointed out that the same facts may be stated, though as it seems to me more awkwardly, by saying that things in different modes of association occasion different effects and that our knowledge of them is adequate in the degree in which it includes a broad range of effects due to a variety of associated operations.

guished, it would appear that metaphysical description and understanding is demarcated as that which has to do with the widest and fullest range of associated activity. And I remark that if the phrase "degrees of reality" can be given an empirically intelligible meaning, that meaning would seem to depend upon following out the line of thought thus suggested.* In short, there appears to be a fairly straight road to the conclusion that a just gauge of the adequacy of any philosophic account of things is found in the extent to which that account is based upon taking things in the widest and most complex scale of associations open to observation.

In making this statement I am not unaware that the opposite method has been pursued and is still recommended by philosophers in good repute: namely, a method based on predilection for ultimate and unattached simples, called by various writers essences, data, etc. The question of whether we should begin with the simple or the complex appears to me the most important problem in philosophic method at the present time, cutting under, for example, the traditional distinctions of real and ideal. Or, if it be said that while perforce we are compelled psychologically and practically to begin with the complex, *philosophy* begins only when we have come upon simples, the problem of method still remains. Are these simples isolated and self-sufficient, or are they the results of intellectual analysis, themselves intellectual rather than existential in quality, and therefore of value only in the degree in which they afford us means of arriving at a better understanding of the complex wholes with which we began? Time forbids consideration of this fundamental

* It is perhaps worth while in passing to note also that such concepts as "levels" and "emergence" seem to be most readily definable upon the basis of this consideration.

question. I content myself with observing that the hypothesis that ultimate and detached simples are the only reals for philosophy seems to be the sole logical alternative to the position that the wider and more complex the range of associated interaction with which we deal, the more fully is the nature of the object of philosophic thought revealed to us. Hence, the issue as to method reduces itself to the question whether isolated simples can be asserted without self-contradiction to be ultimate and self-sufficient on their own account. Those who do not accept them as the real, appear committed to the position herein stated.

While the fact of association and of range of associations as determining "degrees of reality" gives us our starting point, it gives *only* a starting point for discussing the value of "social" as a philosophic category. For by the social as a distinctive mode of association is denoted specifically human forms of grouping, and these, according to the findings of science, appear only late in time. Hence, the objection which readily occurs to mind. The view that "social" in its characteristically human sense is an important category is met with the retort that, on the contrary, it is but a highly special case of association and as such is restricted in significance, humanly interesting of course, but a matter of detail rather than of an important principle. My introductory remarks were intended as an anticipatory reply to such an objection. The bare concept of association is a wholly formal category. It acquires content only by considering the different forms of association which constitute the material of experience. Thus, while it is admitted that society, in the human sense, is a form of association that is restricted in its space-time manifestation, it cannot be placed in contrast with association in general. Its import can be determined not by comparing it with association in its generic formal sense, but only by comparing and contrasting it with other special types of association.

This fact gives what has been said regarding the importance of range and complexity of association as a philosophic measure its special import. If reference to association is to be anything more than a ceremonial and barren act of deference, if it is to be used in an enterprise of philosophic description and understanding, it indicates the necessity of study and analysis of the different modes of association that present themselves in experience. And the implication of our argument is that in such a comparison of definite types of association, the social, in its human sense, is the richest, fullest and most delicately subtle of any mode actually experienced. There is no need to go through the form of discovering, as if for the first time, the different typical modes which are to be compared and contrasted. They have been made familiar enough in the course of thought. Aside from social, whose thoroughgoing admission still awaits adequate acknowledgment, they are the physical, the vital or organic, and the mental. The gist of our problem consists in deciding which of these forms presents the broadest and fullest range of associations. Association in general is but a matrix; its fillings are the facts of association actually displayed in nature. Indeed, the category of association is but a highly abstract notation of what is formally common to the special modes.

Denial of opposition between the social and natural is an important element of the *meaning* of "social" as a category; and if anyone is interested in finding out the intent of those who would employ "social" as a philosophic category, that one should begin by asking himself what are the implications of the current separation of natural and social sciences, and whether upon reflection he is willing to stand by them. A denial of the separation is not only possible to a sane mind, but is demanded by any methodological adoption of the principle of continuity, and also, as will be indicated later, by social phenomena themselves. Upon the hypothesis of continuity—if that is to be termed a hypothesis which cannot be denied without self-contradiction—the social, in spite of whatever may be said regarding the temporal and spatial limitation of its manifestations, furnishes philosophically the inclusive category.

A twofold harm is wrought by the current separation of social and natural science and by accepting the meaning which attaches to social after it has been thus divorced. The chief point at which philosophy may be of aid in the pursuits of the social sciences lies precisely here. In the degree in which what passes for social science is built upon the notion of a gap between natural and social phenomena, that science is truncated, arbitrary and insecure. An analytic survey of the present status of the social sciences would be needed to justify this remark. But there are only a few sociologists who have ventured as yet to assert that there is something distinctive or unique in social phenomena: so we are met with a paradoxical situation in which social phenomena are isolated from physical and organic considerations and yet are explained in physical, organic or psychological terms instead of in characteristically social terms. In psychology the persisting tradition of a purely individualistic and private subject-matter is to be attributed directly to neglect of the social conditions of mental phenomena, while indirectly this neglect goes back to a separation of social from natural; since only acknowledgment of the continuity of the social and the natural provides the intermediary terms which link psychological phenomena with others.

These are but too casual and abbreviated hints of the meaning of the assertion that the performance of the service which philosophy might theoretically render to the social sciences waits upon the frank acknowledgment of the social as a category continuous with and inclusive of the categories of the physical, vital and mental.

This reference to the sciences is not to be regarded, however, as implying an adoption of that conception of philosophy which identifies it exclusively with either an analysis or a synthesis of the premises or results of the special sciences. On the contrary, the sciences themselves are outgrowths of some phase of social culture, from which they derive their instruments, physical and intellectual, and by which their problems and aims are set. The only philosophy which can "criticize" the premises of the special sciences, without running the danger of being itself a pseudo-science, is that which takes into account the anthropological (in its broadest sense) basis of the sciences, just as the only one that can synthesize their conclusions, without running a like danger, is the one which steps outside these conclusions to place them in the broader context of social life.

In now turning to the main point, the social as a ranking philosophic category, on the ground that it is indicative of the widest and richest range of association empirically accessible (and no apology is offered for basing philosophy upon the empirically manifest rather than upon the occult), it is necessary to point out a certain ambiguity of language which because of brevity of exposition, necessarily attaches to our statement. Social *phenomena* are not of themselves, of course, equivalent to social as a *category*. The latter is derived from the former by means of an intellectual analysis which determines what is their distinctive character. Now I am not here dealing with the important and eventually imperative problem of the category *of* the social, or the determination of the characteristics which constitute the distinguishing nature of the social, but rather with social phenomena *en gross* as comprehending, for philosophic analysis, physical, organic and mental phenomena in a mode of association in which the latter take on new properties and exercise new functions. In other words, I am here implying that social phenomena do as a matter of fact manifest *something* distinctive, and that that something affords the key to a naturalistic account of phenomena baffling philosophic interpretation when it is left out of account. To those who accept this view, the burden of proof as to the value of "social" as a metaphysical category lies upon those who habitually treat its worth as trivial. For what do *they* mean by social phenomena? If social phenomena are not an exemplification upon the widest and most intricate scale of the generic trait of associated behavior or interaction, what do they signify? I see but one kind of answer open to them, covering two alternatives: Either social phenomena are anomalous, an excrescence or intrusion, supervening in an accidental and meaningless way upon other phenomena, or else they have no distinctive import, being in reality *nothing but* physical, vital or psychological phenomena. Does not each of these views contradict the observable traits of social phenomena?

Upon a *prima facie* view, social phenomena take up and incorporate within themselves things associated in the narrower way which we term the physical. It gives a ludicrous result to think of social phenomena merely as lying on top of physical phenomena; such a notion is negated by the most casual observation of the facts. What would social phenomena be without the physical factor of land, including all the natural resources (and obstacles) and forms of energy for which the word "land" stands? What would social phenomena be without the tools and machines by which physical energies are utilized? Or what would they be without physical appliances and apparatus, from clothes and houses to railways, temples and printing-presses? No, it is not the social which is a superficial category. The view of those is superficial who fail to see that in the social the physical is taken up into a wider and more complex and delicate system of interactions so that it takes on new properties by release of potentialities previously confined because of absence of full interaction.

The same consideration applies to the inclusion within the social of the vital or organic. The members of society are living human beings with the characteristics of living creatures; but as they enter into distinctively human associations their strictly organic properties are modified and even transformed. Certain physiological factors of sex, of procreation, immaturity and need of care, are assuredly implicated in the functions expressed in family life. But however great the role of animal lust, there is something more in any family association than bare physiological factors. The fact of transformation of the purely organic by inclusion within the scope of human association is so obvious—note the significant case of change of cries into speech—that it has indeed led to belief in the intrusive intervention of unnatural and supernatural factors in order to account for the differences between the animal and the human. The disjunction between the assertion that the human is the merely animal and the assertion that an extraneous force is obtruded is not, however, exhaustive. There remains an alternative which is most fully confirmed by empirical fact, namely that the difference is made when new potentialities are actualized, when the range of interactions that delimits the organic is taken up into the wider and more subtly complex association which forms human society.

Since traits derived from the physical mode have been admitted into philosophy (materialism in other words is at least grudgingly admitted into philosophic companionship); and since organic philosophies, framed on the pattern of vital phenomena, upon conceptions of species, development and purpose, are freely admitted, it seems arbitrary, to say the least, to exclude the social from the role of a legitimate category.

That the mental has a recognized claim to serve as a category of description and interpretation of natural existence is evident in the very existence of idealistic philosophies. There are those who deny the ability of these theories to execute their claim, just as there are those who deny the capacity of the physical and vital to make good. But thought, as well as matter and life, is at least admitted to rank as a respectable figure in the gallery of categories. Now of the mental as of the physical and organic it may be said that it operates as an included factor within social phenomena, since the mental is empirically discernible only where association is manifested in the form of participation and communication. It would therefore appear legitimate to adopt as a hypothesis worthy of being tried out, the idea that the ulterior meaning of the mental as well as of the physical and vital is revealed in this form of associational interaction. The implication is not that they have no describable *existence* outside the social, but that in as far as they appear and operate outside of that large interaction which forms the social they do not reveal that full force and import with which it is the traditional business of philosophy to occupy itself.

It is the historic claim of philosophy that it occupies it-

self with the ideal of wholes and the whole. It is submitted
that either the whole is manifested in concretely empirical
ways, and in ways consonant with infinite variety, or else
wholeness is but a dialectical speculation. I do not say
that the social as we know it *is* the whole, but I do emphatically suggest that it is the widest and richest manifestation of the whole accessible to our observation. As
such it is at least the proper point of departure for any
more imaginative construings of the whole one may wish
to undertake. And in any case it furnishes the terms in
which any consistent *empirical* philosophy must speak.
Only by whole-hearted adoption of it as a ranking fact
and idea can empirical philosophy come into its own.

INDEX